742 Fast-to-Fix Foods At Your Fingertips!

SINCE the first issue of *Quick Cooking* magazine was published in 1998, nearly 3 million subscribers have come to enjoy its speedy recipes full of "from scratch" flavor.

In keeping with *QC*'s time-saving appeal, this *2000 Quick Cooking Annual Recipes* conveniently gathers every rapid recipe published in *QC* during 1999—*742 recipes in all*—into one timeless treasury. Here's what you'll find inside:

Chapters to Fit Any Lifestyle. This classic collection's 21 handy chapters correspond to favorite features in *Quick Cooking* magazine. It's easy to find just the right recipe for your taste *and* time.

For example, if you're too rushed and tired at the end of the day to prepare an elaborate dinner, the 12 complete meals in "30 Minutes to Mealtime" will halt your family's hunger in a hurry.

Or, wouldn't it be great to walk in the door to a delicious dish that's been simmering all day and is ready to eat *right now*? Turn to "Timeless Recipes with Kitchen Tools" for 37 switch-and-go slow cooker creations that do the work while you're away. (A complete list of chapters can be found on page 5.)

Easy-to-Use Indexes. To make all 742 recipes fast to find, we've listed them in three simple-to-use indexes. (See page 338.) The general index lists every recipe by food category and/or major ingredient. The alphabetical listing of recipes is perfect for folks who are looking for a specific family favorite. The third index designates all recipes that use less fat, sugar or salt and include Nutritional Analysis and Diabetic Exchanges.

Large Print and Color Photos. For easier reading while cooking, we've used large print throughout the book (even the index!). What's more, hundreds of full-color photos let you easily see what the finished foods will look like *before* you begin cooking.

What's on the Menu? To make meal planning even more simple, our food editors "grouped" several recipes from various chapters to create a host of around-the-clock suggested menus. (This time-saving tool appears on page 6.)

Every rapid recipe and helpful tip in this *2000 Quick Cooking Annual Recipes* cookbook was specifically selected with the busy cook in mind. We hope you enjoy this recipe treasury for years to come...and treat your loved ones to comforting, wholesome home cooking without spending all your precious time in the kitchen.

2000 Quick Cooking Annual Recipes

Editor: Julie Schnittka

Art Director: Maribeth Greinke

Food Editor: Janaan Cunningham

Associate Editor: Jean Steiner

Assistant Art Directors: Linda Dzik, Claudia Wardius, Bonnie Ziolecki

Production: Ellen Lloyd

Cover Food Photography: Scott Anderson

Cover Food Photography Artist: Stephanie Marchese

Taste of Home Books
©1999 Reiman Publications, LLC
5400 S. 60th St., Greendale WI 53129

International Standard Book Number:
0-89821-282-0
International Standard Serial Number:
1522-6603

PICTURED ON THE COVER: Mushroom Salisbury Steak (p. 292), Colorful Corn (p. 25), Garlic Mashed Potatoes (p. 313) and Chocolate Raspberry Torte (p. 313).

To order additional copies of this book or any other Reiman Publications books, write: *Taste of Home* Books, P.O. Box 990, Greendale WI 53129; call toll-free 1-800/558-1013 to order with a credit card or visit our Web site at **www.reimanpub.com**.

Taste of Home's QUICK COOKING

Editor: Julie Kastello

Executive Editor: Kathy Pohl

Food Editor: Janaan Cunningham

Associate Food Editors: Coleen Martin, Diane Werner

Senior Recipe Editor: Sue A. Jurack

Recipe Editor: Janet Briggs

Associate Editors: Kristine Krueger, Ann Kaiser, Faithann Stoner

Test Kitchen Director: Karen Johnson

Test Kitchen Home Economists: Karen Wright, Julie Herzfeldt, Sue Draheim, Pat Schmeling, Wendy Stenman

Test Kitchen Assistants: Suzanne Hampton, Sue Hampton

Editorial Assistant: Ursula Maurer

Design Director: Jim Sibilski

Art Director: Julie Wagner

Food Photography: Scott Anderson

Food Photography Artist: Stephanie Marchese

Photo Studio Manager: Anne Schimmel

Production: Ellen Lloyd, Claudia Wardius

Publisher: Roy Reiman

⏱ Contents

What's on The Menu?

GRAB A MENU from the best "fast food" place in town—your kitchen! The price is right, the atmosphere is relaxing, and the service couldn't be friendlier nor the guests more appreciative. And with the *2000 Quick Cooking Annual Recipes* book in your hands, you've already given yourself a generous tip!

Here's how to use the menu ideas featured here: Our food editors screened all the recipes that appear in this book, then "grouped" several from various chapters to make up menus for everyday and special-occasion family meals. Plus, you can mix and match recipes to make up menus of your own.

For even more complete meals, turn to the following chapters: The Busiest Cooks in the Country (p. 8), 30 Minutes to Mealtime (p. 22), Thinking Up a Theme (p. 36) and Company's Coming! (p. 306).

Six Breakfast Choices

Eighteen Lunch Choices

Thirty-Two Dinner Choices

IF YOU'RE like most busy cooks across the country, you probably pack your typical days with work, school and a host of other family activities.

So you likely think there's little extra time to prepare a wholesome, hearty dinner for your hungry brood. But this chapter deliciously proves that memorable family meals are possible.

Six fellow frenzied cooks share their favorite tried-and-true recipes, time-saving kitchen tips and menu-planning pointers that are guaranteed to put you on the meal-making fast track in a flash.

MEAL IN MINUTES. Clockwise from lower left: Spinach Alfredo Lasagna, Angel Food Delight, Bread Machine Garlic Bread and Icy Lemonade (all recipes on pp. 12 and 13).

Rustle Up Swift, Satisfying Suppers

SERVING up hearty meals is nothing new for Kathie Morris. The only daughter in a ranching family, she was not yet a teenager when she took over meal preparation.

"Mom was needed out in the fields," Kathie explains. "So, at age 12, I became responsible for family meals. After a few weeks of 'burnt offerings', I was able to make most of the meat-and-potatoes meals our family was accustomed to."

These days, the Redmond, Oregon cook still serves stick-to-your-ribs suppers for her husband, Kevin, and children, Logan and Devon Kay. But now she relies on shortcuts that fit her busy lifestyle.

In addition to working outside the home, Kathie often attends the kids' sports, school and church activities. To keep her taxing schedule in check, Kathie has plenty of strategies for simplifying mealtime.

"I use my slow cooker whenever I can," she shares. "Getting up 15 minutes early in the morning gives me enough time to start a main dish in the slow cooker that'll be ready when I get home from work.

"This gives me time to spend with the kids at night and hear about their days," she says.

"Also, while cleaning up after dinner, I sometimes do some of the prep work for the next day's meal, such as cleaning and chopping vegetables, or make the kids' school lunches to ease the morning rush."

Filling Fare

One family-favorite menu starts with Slow-Cooked Swiss Steak. "I modified Mom's recipe as I became a more experienced cook," Kathie comments. "Everyone raves about how tender and rich this dish is. I make it about every 2 weeks during the winter."

Doubling this recipe leaves leftovers for Stroganoff the next night. "I crumble the meat, add Worcestershire sauce and sour cream to the gravy and serve it over egg noodles with a salad and biscuits. The kids love it!" she promises.

The Swiss steak with its savory gravy is wonderful served over pretty Parsley Potatoes. "A neighbor who always had a large garden showed me how to make these easy, buttery potatoes," Kathie remarks. "For a flavor twist, sometimes I substitute fresh or dried dill for the parsley."

Kathie has no trouble getting her kids to eat their veggies—even brussels sprouts! "Exposing them to a variety of vegetables at an early age helped," she admits. "They love tender Almond Brussels Sprouts, which have just the right amount of nutty crunch.

"I often serve this fresh-tasting side dish when I'm planning a nice company dinner," she adds.

For a comforting ending to her old-fashioned meal, Kathie simmers up Spiced Apple Sundaes. "This dessert was inspired by Logan, who commented one day that it was too bad it took so long to make apple pie," she explains.

"Cinnamon and allspice add warm, spicy flavor to the tender apples and golden raisins in this dessert—it tastes like an apple pie without the crust.

"I usually start the apples at the same time I start my potatoes for dinner," Kathie says. "Right before serving dinner, I set the apples aside to cool a bit. When we're ready for dessert, our No. 1 favorite dessert is ready, too!"

Slow-Cooked Swiss Steak

3/4 cup all-purpose flour
1 teaspoon pepper
1/4 teaspoon salt
2 to 2-1/2 pounds boneless round steak
1 to 2 tablespoons butter *or* margarine
1 can (10-3/4 ounces) condensed cream of mushroom soup, undiluted
1-1/3 cups water
1 cup sliced celery, optional
1/2 cup chopped onion
1 garlic clove, minced
1 to 3 teaspoons beef bouillon granules

Quick Keys to Kitchen

- In the morning, I fill the bread machine with ingredients and set its timer so I can come home to fresh bread or just-kneaded dough ready for calzones, rolls or pizza.

- When making double batches of lasagna, soup, chili and other entrees, I use disposable casserole dishes to cook and freeze the second portion. This makes storage and cleanup a real breeze—without monopolizing my daily cookware.

- Before freezing these meals, I double-wrap the containers in foil. Using freezer tape, I identify the contents, the date and the cooking instructions. This makes it easy for my husband to heat up dinner.

- I love this idea my mother-in-law shared: To keep the freezer organized, buy inexpensive multicolored plastic baskets. Store beef in the red basket, pork in the pink one, chicken in the yellow one, vegetables in the green one, etc. The baskets stack nicely, and you can see at a glance what you have on hand and what needs restocking. —*Kathie Morris*

In a shallow bowl, combine flour, pepper and salt. Cut steak into six serving-size pieces; dredge in flour mixture. In a skillet, brown steak in butter. Transfer to a slow cooker. Combine the remaining ingredients; pour over steak. Cover and cook on low for 8-9 hours or until the meat is tender. **Yield:** 6 servings.

Parsley Potatoes

    6 medium red potatoes, cut into cubes
1/4 cup butter *or* margarine
    1 to 2 tablespoons minced fresh parsley
Salt and pepper to taste

Place potatoes in a large saucepan and cover with water. Bring to a boil over medium heat. Reduce heat; cover and simmer for 20 minutes or until tender. Drain. Add butter, parsley, salt and pepper; stir until combined. **Yield:** 6 servings.

Almond Brussels Sprouts

    1 pound fresh brussels sprouts, halved
1/2 cup chicken broth

1/2 cup sliced almonds, toasted
    1 teaspoon butter *or* margarine

Place brussels sprouts and broth in a saucepan; bring to a boil. Reduce heat; cover and simmer for 6-8 minutes or until tender. Add almonds and butter; stir until combined. **Yield:** 6 servings.

Spiced Apple Sundaes

    6 large tart apples, peeled and cut into chunks
    1 cup golden raisins
2/3 cup apple juice
    2 tablespoons sugar
    2 teaspoons ground cinnamon
1/8 teaspoon ground allspice
Vanilla ice cream
Granola *or* wheat germ, optional

In a saucepan, combine the first six ingredients. Cover and cook over medium heat until the apples are tender. Remove from the heat; mash apples slightly. Let stand for 20 minutes. Serve over ice cream. Sprinkle with granola if desired. **Yield:** 6-8 servings.

Cook Sings Praises of Fast Freezer Fare

THERE'S no doubt that made-in-minutes meals strike a chord with Beth Stephas. The wife and mother of four from Eagle Grove, Iowa appreciates rapid recipes that are in perfect harmony with her family's up-tempo lifestyle.

Any given week you might find Beth playing piano for her church's Sunday worship services, singing with the local chorale or rehearsing for a community theater production.

After a full day as a guidance counselor, she chauffeurs Grant, Amanda, Rebekah and Noah to 4-H meetings, church activities, and music, dance and tae kwan do lessons.

"Despite our busy schedules, we sit down together every night for dinner," Beth relates. Husband Ed works long hours but makes a point of returning in time for supper.

"This is an important time as we share our day's happenings, discuss plans for the next day and spend a few minutes with a daily devotion," she explains.

Make-Ahead Meals

"After a long day, I don't feel like spending hours in the kitchen," she says. "So I set aside time every month or so to prepare big batches of our favorite one-dish meals, such as sweet-and-sour chicken, creamy chicken and macaroni casserole or beef and rice bake topped with chow mein noodles.

"In 3 or 4 hours, I can have 15 to 20 dishes labeled with baking instructions and ready for the freezer."

When she knows time will be tight, Beth puts a frozen casserole in the fridge overnight to thaw, then pops it in the oven when she gets home from work. "With fresh bread, a vegetable side dish and a green salad or sliced fresh fruit, it makes a terrific, time-easing meal," she promises.

When Beth invites company over for Sunday dinner, she often falls back on the special menu she shares here.

"The dishes use several convenience foods, so they're easy to fix," she reports. "Served with a crisp lettuce salad, this meal is a crowd favorite."

The hearty Spinach Alfredo Lasagna relies on a jar of store-bought Alfredo sauce to make it different from traditional tomato-based lasagnas.

"While I'm browning the sausage, I soak the noodles in hot water rather than boiling them. It really saves time, and the dish turns out great!"

A blender speeds preparation of refreshing Icy Lemonade. Lemon-lime soda adds the sparkle to this light, lemony beverage.

With the help of her bread machine, Beth bakes a pretty parsley-flecked loaf of Bread Machine Garlic Bread. Soft slices make a flavorful accompaniment to the lasagna or most any main dish.

"This recipe is perfect for delayed baking," she comments. "On weekdays, I put all the ingredients in the bread machine pan before going to work in the morning and set the timer. It's wonderful to come home after a busy day to the aroma of fresh bread."

For a show-stopping ending to the meal, Beth needs just four ingredients to assemble Angel Food Delight. "It's so simple to make ahead of time, but it looks like I spent hours fussing," she remarks.

Spinach Alfredo Lasagna

12 ounces lasagna noodles
1 pound bulk pork sausage
1 package (10 ounces) frozen chopped spinach, thawed and well drained
1 jar (17 ounces) Alfredo sauce
1/2 teaspoon salt
1/4 teaspoon pepper
1 egg
2 cups (8 ounces) shredded cheddar cheese
1 carton (15 ounces) ricotta cheese
1/2 cup grated Parmesan cheese
1 cup (4 ounces) shredded mozzarella cheese

Soak the noodles in hot water for 15 minutes. Meanwhile, in a skillet, brown the sausage. Drain noodles; set aside. Drain sausage; add spinach, Alfredo sauce, salt and pepper. In a bowl, combine the egg and cheddar, ricotta and Parmesan cheeses; mix well. In an ungreased 13-in. x 9-in. x 2-in. baking dish, layer a third of the sausage mixture, noodles and cheese mixture. Repeat layers twice. Sprinkle with mozzarella cheese. Cover and bake at 350° for 45 minutes. Let stand for 15 minutes before cutting. **Yield:** 8-10 servings.

Icy Lemonade

✓ Uses less fat, sugar or salt. Includes Nutritional Analysis and Diabetic Exchanges.

1 can (12 ounces) frozen lemonade concentrate
30 ice cubes
4 cups lemon-lime soda, chilled

Place half of the lemonade concentrate and 12-15 ice cubes in a blender; add 2 cups soda. Cover and process on high until ice is crushed. Repeat. Serve immediately. **Yield:** 10 servings. **Nutritional Analysis:** One 1-cup serving (prepared with diet soda) equals 62 calories, 11 mg sodium, 0 cholesterol, 16 gm carbohydrate, trace protein, trace fat. **Diabetic Exchange:** 1 fruit.

Bread Machine Garlic Bread

✓ Uses less fat, sugar or salt. Includes Nutritional Analysis and Diabetic Exchanges.

  1 cup warm water (70° to 80°)
  1 tablespoon butter *or* margarine, softened
  1 tablespoon instant nonfat dry milk powder
  1 tablespoon sugar
1-1/2 teaspoons salt
4-1/2 teaspoons dried parsley flakes
  2 teaspoons garlic powder
  3 cups bread flour
  2 teaspoons active dry yeast

In bread machine pan, place all ingredients in order suggested by manufacturer. Select basic bread setting. Choose crust color and loaf size if available. Bake according to bread machine directions (check the dough after 5 minutes of mixing; add 1 to 2 tablespoons of water or flour if needed). **Yield:** 1 loaf, 16 slices (about 1-1/2 pounds). **Nutritional Analysis:** One slice (prepared with margarine) equals 108 calories, 229 mg sodium, trace cholesterol, 21 gm carbohydrate, 4 gm protein, 1 gm fat. **Diabetic Exchange:** 1-1/2 starch.

Angel Food Delight

  1 carton (8 ounces) frozen whipped topping, thawed
  1 jar (16 ounces) chocolate fudge sauce
  1 prepared angel food cake (8 inches)
3/4 cup English toffee bits

Fold whipped topping into chocolate sauce just until blended. Split cake horizontally into three layers; place one layer on a serving plate. Spread with a fourth of the topping mixture and a fourth of the toffee bits. Repeat layers. Top with remaining cake layer. Frost the top and sides with remaining topping mixture; sprinkle with remaining toffee bits. Cover and refrigerate for 4 hours. Store in the refrigerator. **Yield:** 8-10 servings.

Basics for Stocking Up

- Our family eats plenty of fresh fruits and vegetables, so I prefer to make one quick trip to the store each week rather than a big monthly shopping trip. Because the trips are short, I can finish them while the girls are at dance lessons.
- To make these weekly shopping trips even quicker, we keep our freezer stocked with a variety of meats.
- I always have pasta in the pantry and ground beef in the freezer for fixing fast meals. I also keep a convenient brownie mix or cake mix on hand for times I need a speedy dessert or the kids need to take treats to school or other activities.
                 —*Beth Stephas*

Fabulous Meals with Casual Style

HAIRDRESSER Linda Hartsell does not need scissors to cut the time it takes to make dinner. Instead, she plans meals that can be assembled during a short break at work. That's because, for Linda, the kitchen is just a few steps away.

"My husband, Bob, and I added a beauty shop on to our house years ago so I could be at home while raising our daughters," explains the Apple Creek, Ohio mother of three. (Daughter Heather is now married to Erich and has a young son, Brevin. Holly and Heidi still live at home.)

"I work into the evening to accommodate customers who are on the day shift," Linda notes. "So I've come to rely on suppers I can throw into the slow cooker during dryer time or oven meals I can start while a perm processes."

Besides her full-time duties at the beauty shop, Linda's appointment calendar is booked with plenty of other activities. She teaches Sunday school, gives haircuts to shut-in friends and provides day care for Brevin on her day off so Heather can take college courses.

Despite this harried schedule, Linda finds time to enjoy flower gardening, working in the yard, taking walks, doing crafts and, of course, cooking.

Fuss-Free Family Time

"Working around my evening appointments, Heidi's cheerleading and show choir practices and Holly's college schedule, we manage to have sit-down family meals most evenings," Linda informs.

"Friday evenings, I work up until dinnertime. Then it's off to football or basketball games!

"Enjoying our family and our grandson is a priority, so we have 'Family Night' almost every Sunday evening," shares Linda. "We invite Heather's family and our other two daughters' boyfriends, which makes nine of us.

"The idea is to relax and enjoy each other's company, so I try to keep the menu stress-free and simple." It might include pizza, sloppy joes or the hearty ham sandwiches she shares here.

"The recipe for Hot Ham 'n' Cheese came from a dear aunt," Linda relates. A fast four-ingredient spread makes them a cut above the ordinary.

"They can be made ahead of time, so they're a great snack after games," she reports. "I wrap them individually in foil and keep them in the fridge. Then I just pop them in the oven when needed."

Seasoned Potato Wedges are a tasty accompaniment to the satisfying sandwiches or most any entree.

"After many years of working in a beauty shop, I have quite a collection of delicious recipes from many wonderful cooks...and this is one of our favorites," Linda notes. "It's easy because you don't peel the potatoes—and you can sprinkle different seasonings on for variety."

Flavorful bacon and a sweet sauce spark the flavor of Barbecue Butter Beans. "It takes only minutes to stir together this speedy side dish, making it perfect for potlucks," she assures.

Linda uses a convenient boxed cake mix to shave minutes off the prep time of Cream-Filled Chocolate Cake. It gets a homemade touch from a yummy vanilla layer and from-scratch frosting.

"When in a rush, I use a can of prepared frosting rather than making my own," she comments. "Depending on the brand, I sometimes thin it with a tablespoon or two of milk to get the right consistency."

Linda says the cake serves plenty, so it's handy to take to family gatherings or carry-in dinners.

Hot Ham 'n' Cheese

1/4 cup butter *or* margarine, softened
2 tablespoons horseradish mustard*
2 tablespoons finely chopped onion
2 teaspoons poppy seeds
4 hamburger buns, split
8 thin slices fully cooked ham
4 slices Swiss cheese

In a bowl, combine the butter, mustard, onion and poppy seeds. Spread over cut sides of buns. Layer ham and cheese on bottom halves; replace tops. Wrap each sandwich in foil; place on a baking sheet. Bake at 350° for 25-30 minutes or until cheese is melted. **Yield:** 4 servings.

Meal-Planning Pointers

- We keep a grocery list in the kitchen for all family members to help complete. When someone uses the last of an item, he or she adds it to the list. Any special requests, such as ingredients needed for bake sale treats, also are included.

- I've learned to plan the week's menus ahead of time, often using foods that are on sale. With one weekly shopping trip, we have all the groceries we need in the house. A well-stocked freezer and pantry also prevents panic when we have extra dinner guests.

- Getting your family involved helps a lot. Although I plan the weekly menu and compile most of the grocery list, Bob and the girls do the shopping. Bob often finishes making dinner or barbecues a meal if he's home from his sales job before I'm done for the day. Plus, the girls are very helpful around the house.
  —*Linda Hartsell*

*Editor's Note: As a substitute for horseradish mustard, combine 1 tablespoon spicy brown mustard with 1 tablespoon prepared horseradish.

Seasoned Potato Wedges

    4 medium russet potatoes
    2 to 3 tablespoons mayonnaise
    1 to 2 teaspoons seasoned salt

Cut the potatoes in half lengthwise; cut each half lengthwise into three wedges. Place in a single layer on a greased baking sheet. Spread mayonnaise over cut sides of potatoes; sprinkle with seasoned salt. Bake at 350° for 50-60 minutes or until tender. **Yield:** 4 servings.

Barbecue Butter Beans

    2 cans (15 ounces *each*) butter beans, rinsed
      and drained
    3/4 cup packed brown sugar
    1/2 cup ketchup
    1/2 cup chopped onion
    3 bacon strips, diced

In a bowl, combine the beans, brown sugar, ketchup and onion. Transfer to a greased 1-1/2-qt. baking dish. Sprinkle with bacon. Bake, uncovered, at 350° for 1-1/2 hours. **Yield:** 4-6 servings.

Cream-Filled Chocolate Cake

    1 package (18-1/4 ounces) chocolate cake mix
    5 tablespoons all-purpose flour
  1-1/4 cups milk
    1/2 cup butter *or* margarine, softened
    1/2 cup shortening
    1 cup sugar
Pinch salt
FROSTING:
    1/2 cup butter *or* margarine, softened
    1/4 cup baking cocoa
    1 teaspoon vanilla extract
    3 cups confectioners' sugar
    4 to 5 tablespoons hot water

Prepare cake batter according to package directions; pour into a greased 15-in. x 10-in. x 1-in. baking pan. Bake at 350° for 20-25 minutes or until a toothpick inserted near the center comes out clean. Cool on a wire rack. Meanwhile, for filling, combine flour and milk in a saucepan until smooth. Bring to a boil over medium heat, stirring frequently. Cook and stir for 2 minutes; remove from the heat and cool completely. In a mixing bowl, cream butter, shortening, sugar and salt until fluffy. Add flour mixture; beat until fluffy, about 4 minutes. Spread over cake. Freeze for 15 minutes. For frosting, beat butter, cocoa and vanilla in a mixing bowl until fluffy. Beat in sugar and water. Spread over filling. Store in the refrigerator. **Yield:** 16-20 servings.

Rapid Rural Recipes Get Top Votes

FOR Rhonda Knight, being involved in small-town politics in Hecker, Illinois means more than getting out to vote. The stay-at-home mother of son Remington and daughter Madison recently campaigned to get a new school built.

"I put up signs and made calls to voters and news agencies to get them involved," she shares. "I was even interviewed on the local news."

Her efforts helped make the project a success, and the new school is now under construction. But Rhonda's community participation doesn't stop there.

"I'm also involved in our church, which is very rewarding for me," she says. Rhonda handles the church's public relations work, is a member of its women's leadership team, and plans and teaches at retreats, women's meetings and other functions.

Yet she still finds time to carpool Remington and his teammates to soccer, baseball and basketball games, use her computer to do the billing for her brother's lawn-care business, exercise at the YMCA three or four times a week and prepare sit-down meals almost every night.

Homemade TV Dinners

When planning menus, Rhonda selects dishes that can easily be reheated for husband Richard, who works two full-time jobs as a Ford auto technician and a federal security officer.

"There are days when he works 8 hours at one job, then goes immediately to another 8-hour job. So I pack meals for him accordingly," she explains.

Like many busy cooks, Rhonda finds that spending a day cooking several meals to store in the freezer means fuss-free dinners in the future.

She also creates her own frozen TV dinners for nights the family's running to ball games or other activities, and she uses time-saving appliances to streamline meal preparation.

"I make a lot of meals in the slow cooker," she relates. "And my family loves the taste of homemade bread, so I'm always taking a fresh loaf out of the bread machine."

When Rhonda's schedule is tight, she relies on meals that go together in a jiffy.

"A few years ago, I ran a day care in our home," she recalls. "Sometimes, the children wouldn't be picked up until 6 p.m. By then, our family would be famished, so I needed a meal I could put on the table in no time."

A favorite menu then—and now—starts with Breaded Turkey Breasts. A tasty crumb coating seasoned with Parmesan cheese and Italian herbs gives them delicious flavor.

"I saw a celebrity demonstrate this recipe on TV, but I modified it to reduce fat," Rhonda notes.

"The thin turkey slices take just a few minutes on the stovetop, so be careful not to overcook them," she advises.

Fresh produce (shared from neighbors' gardens or picked up at the local farmer's market) is showcased in the Garden Pasta Salad that Rhonda makes to accompany her main dish.

"Richard is not too crazy about plain vegetables, so I came up with this colorful salad," she shares. "He loves it, and so does our son."

Convenient bottled dressing, with added spark from Dijon mustard, gives fast flavor to the cool combination that's a perfect side dish. Rhonda sometimes uses already chopped vegetables from the store.

Folks who love chocolate chip cookies will enjoy that same great flavor in Chocolate Chip Blondies.

"These golden bars can be mixed up in a jiffy and taste wonderful," Rhonda promises. They're perfect for occasions when company drops by unexpectedly or you need a treat in a hurry.

Breaded Turkey Breasts

1 cup dry bread crumbs
1/4 cup grated Parmesan cheese
2 teaspoons Italian seasoning
1 cup milk
1 pound boneless skinless turkey breast slices
1/4 cup olive *or* vegetable oil

In a shallow bowl, combine the bread crumbs, Parmesan cheese and Italian seasoning. Pour milk into another shallow bowl. Dip turkey in milk, then in the crumb mixture. In a large skillet over medium heat, cook turkey in oil for 8-10 minutes or until juices run clear. Drain on paper towels. **Yield:** 4 servings.

Garden Pasta Salad

✓ Uses less fat, sugar or salt. Includes Nutritional Analysis and Diabetic Exchanges.

2 cups uncooked spiral pasta
1 cup broccoli florets
1/4 cup sliced carrots
1/4 cup chopped green pepper
1/4 cup chopped sweet red pepper
1/4 cup sliced zucchini
1/2 cup ranch salad dressing
1 tablespoon Dijon mustard

Cook pasta according to package directions. Meanwhile, combine broccoli, carrots, peppers and zucchini in a large bowl. Rinse pasta in cold water; drain and add to vegetables. Combine salad dressing and mustard; add to pasta mixture and toss to coat. Refrigerate until serving. **Yield:** 4 servings. **Nutritional Analysis:** One 1-cup serving (prepared with fat-free ranch dressing) equals 239 calories, 414 mg sodium, 0 cholesterol, 49 gm carbohydrate, 7 gm protein, 1 gm fat. **Diabetic Exchanges:** 3 starch, 1 vegetable.

Chocolate Chip Blondies

1-1/2 cups packed brown sugar
1/2 cup butter (no substitutes), melted
2 eggs, beaten
1 teaspoon vanilla extract
1-1/2 cups all-purpose flour
1/2 teaspoon baking powder
1/2 teaspoon salt
1 cup (6 ounces) semisweet chocolate chips

In a large bowl, combine brown sugar, butter, eggs and vanilla just until blended. Combine flour, baking powder and salt; add to brown sugar mixture. Stir in chocolate chips. Spread into a greased 13-in. x 9-in. x 2-in. baking pan. Bake at 350° for 18-20 minutes or until a toothpick inserted near the center comes out clean. Cool on a wire rack. Cut into bars. **Yield:** 3 dozen.

Fast Freezer Tips

- Before going to the hospital to deliver our daughter, I prepared 15 main dishes and stored them in the freezer. I labeled all the dishes with thawing and cooking directions, so all my husband needed to do was pop them in the oven. When I came home, I didn't have to cook a thing. It was wonderful!

- When I make my own frozen dinners, I use a square aluminum pan for the main portion. Then I cut apart foil muffin tins to hold side dishes. The individual foil cups work great for vegetables and mashed potatoes with gravy. This way, the food doesn't run together before it's frozen.

—Rhonda Knight

Meal Plan Includes Pantry Items

YOU DON'T have to read between the lines to figure out Robin Stevens of Cadiz, Kentucky is one busy lady. This wife and mother could write the book on preparing dinners in a dash.

As a free-lance writer and media consultant, Robin works out of her and husband Ralph's home in the country, which allows her to spend time with their children, Aaron and Brooklyn.

"I do consulting work for a few local companies," she notes. "I also cover events and write press releases and newsletters for the Kentucky Soybean Association."

When the former newspaper editor isn't penning an article or finishing a book project, you might find her crafting, painting or gardening.

She also enjoys photography and volunteers at her church and the community food pantry.

"Our family is always on the go, running home to grab a bite, then running off again," Robin reports.

Ralph works for the local school system and attends college full-time.

"His schedule often includes night classes," Robin shares. "So quick-and-easy meals—including those he can eat on the run—are a must."

Quick Fixes

With all these activities to juggle, mealtime at the Stevens household can be hectic.

"The less time that we spend fixing meals, the more time we have to enjoy them," Robin remarks.

"So I have a golden rule of cooking that I stick to when I'm in a hurry—which is almost always: I don't attempt anything with more than five ingredients unless I'm really good at fixing it, in the mood or have lots of time."

A popular menu at Robin's dinner table was inspired by her family's love of Italian food.

"Chicken Parmigiana is a favorite dish at our house," Robin shares. "Since most of the recipes I found were time-consuming, I came up with this version that bakes in about a half hour.

"When I serve it to company, my guests are always amazed that I've gone to such trouble, but it's so easy," she assures. "I just throw a few ingredients together, pop the dish in the oven and forget it!"

When time is really tight, Robin relies on convenience foods to save seconds in the kitchen.

"To make preparation time for this tender baked chicken even shorter, I sometimes substitute store-bought spaghetti sauce," she notes.

Robin also uses a shortcut to speed cleanup. "I line my baking pan with aluminum foil," she relates. "This keeps me from having to scrub away any baked-on sauce and cheese."

As a pretty complement to the flavorful chicken, Robin serves Broccoli Fettuccine Alfredo.

"This versatile side dish is a variation of a recipe I've had for years," she notes. "Instead of broccoli, you can use green beans, carrots or your family's favorite vegetable. You can even add cubed cooked chicken and turn it into a main dish," she suggests.

To top off the meal, Robin uses refrigerated biscuits to assemble Apple Cinnamon Turnovers in a jiffy.

An easy filling made with chopped apple and applesauce tastes delicious, especially when the craving for apple pie hits.

"Sprinkled with cinnamon and sugar, these golden treats get rave reviews at church potlucks," Robin adds.

Chicken Parmigiana

    4 boneless skinless chicken breast halves
    1 can (6 ounces) tomato paste
  3/4 cup water
    2 garlic cloves, minced
    1 tablespoon dried parsley flakes
    1 teaspoon salt
  1/4 teaspoon pepper
  1/2 teaspoon Italian seasoning
  1/2 teaspoon dried oregano
  1/4 teaspoon crushed red pepper flakes, optional
    2 cups (8 ounces) shredded mozzarella cheese
  1/4 cup grated Parmesan cheese

Place the chicken in a greased 8-in. square baking dish. In a saucepan, combine tomato paste, water, garlic and seasonings; bring to a boil. Pour over chicken. Bake, uncovered, at 400° for 15-20 minutes or until chicken juices run clear. Sprinkle with cheeses; bake 10 minutes longer or until the cheese is melted. **Yield:** 4 servings.

Tried-and-True Tips

- My pantry's always stocked with canned soups, including cream of chicken and cream of mushroom. I love to use them in casserole dishes for lots of flavor with little fuss.

- I also keep flour tortillas, rice and potatoes on hand and boneless skinless chicken breasts and frozen veggies in the freezer. They're the main ingredients in many speedy suppers.

- I cook as much as possible on our gas grill. It's fast, easy to clean up and a lot of fun.

- Because we have two preschoolers, I don't worry much about meal presentation. To keep little fingers out of the dishes, we often eat buffet-style.
  —*Robin Stevens*

Broccoli Fettuccine Alfredo

1 package (12 ounces) fettuccine
1 cup chopped fresh *or* frozen broccoli
3 tablespoons butter *or* margarine
1 tablespoon all-purpose flour
2/3 cup milk
1/4 cup grated Parmesan cheese

Cook fettuccine according to package directions. Meanwhile, in a saucepan over medium heat, cook broccoli in a small amount of water until crisp-tender, about 5 minutes; drain. In a saucepan over medium heat, melt butter. Stir in flour until smooth. Gradually whisk in milk. Bring to a boil; cook and stir for 2 minutes or until thickened. Remove from the heat; stir in Parmesan cheese and broccoli. Drain fettuccine; top with the broccoli mixture. **Yield:** 4 servings.

Apple Cinnamon Turnovers

1 medium tart apple, peeled and chopped
1/2 cup applesauce
3/4 teaspoon ground cinnamon, *divided*
Dash ground nutmeg
1 tube (7-1/2 ounces) refrigerated biscuits
1 tablespoon butter *or* margarine, melted
2 tablespoons sugar

In a bowl, combine the apple, applesauce, 1/4 teaspoon cinnamon and nutmeg. Separate biscuits; roll out each into a 6-in. circle. Place on greased baking sheets. Place a heaping tablespoonful of apple mixture in the center of each. Fold in half and pinch edges to seal. Brush with butter. Combine sugar and remaining cinnamon; sprinkle over tops. Bake at 400° for 8-10 minutes or until edges are golden brown. Serve warm. **Yield:** 10 servings.

Busy Student's Recipes Earn High Marks

A MOTHER who prepared delicious Thanksgiving dinners, special orange rolls Christmas morning and hearty suppers throughout the year instilled in Annette Self a love of cooking that flourishes to this day.

"Mom was a great influence on me as a cook," says the Junction City, Ohio wife and mother. "She taught me to plan menus, fix well-balanced meals and be creative when trying new recipes."

Annette uses these skills daily preparing meals for her husband, Eric, and their active son, Philip.

"No matter how busy I am, I like to do most of the cooking in our house," she informs. "We usually have sit-down meals three or four times a week, including our Sunday dinner, which I try to make special."

In their small town of 700, Eric is a substitute teacher in the local school district and minister of a church where Annette sings, teaches Sunday school and is assistant pianist.

"All my life, I've collected new recipes," she adds. "In fact, I have three cooking programs for my computer and I use them all."

Cupboards Are Full

To save time and money, Annette plans menus ahead of time and grocery shops accordingly, often incorporating items that are on sale that week.

"I buy some convenience foods, but I doctor them up to give them my own touch," she notes. "I also cook large batches of soups and baked goods when I have time, then freeze the extras to enjoy on rushed days."

Basil adds Italian flair to Flavorful Frittata, a cheesy egg dish that cooks on the stovetop. Canned mushrooms and store-bought spaghetti sauce cut seconds off the prep time.

"Spicy pork sausage adds to the appeal, but it's tasty when made with ham, too," Annette promises.

To complement the frittata, Annette serves slices of Golden Garlic Bread. "This is a quick way to dress up French bread—just top halves with the four-ingredient spread and broil," she relates.

Canned fruit and packaged gelatin are the convenient keys to her delicious Cottage Cheese Fluff.

"It's not your ordinary salad," assures Annette. "You can vary the flavor of gelatin or the type of fruits to suit your family's tastes," she suggests.

For a short, sweet ending to brunch, Annette fixes Microwave Oatmeal Bars.

"My mother shared this speedy recipe with me," she notes. "There are not a lot of ingredients, so these chewy treats are easy to fix in the microwave."

Flavorful Frittata

1 small onion, chopped
1 jar (4-1/2 ounces) sliced mushrooms, drained
1 cup cooked bulk pork sausage*
1 to 2 tablespoons vegetable oil, butter *or* margarine
12 eggs
1/4 cup half-and-half cream
1 teaspoon dried basil
1/2 teaspoon salt
1 cup (4 ounces) shredded mozzarella cheese
2 cups meatless spaghetti sauce, warmed

In a large nonstick skillet, saute the onion, mushrooms and sausage in oil until onion is tender. In a mixing bowl, beat eggs, cream, basil and salt; pour over sausage mixture. As eggs set, lift edges, allowing uncooked portion to flow underneath. When eggs are nearly set, sprinkle with cheese. Cook until the cheese is melted. Cut into wedges; serve with spaghetti sauce. **Yield:** 8 servings. ***Editor's Note:** 1 cup cubed fully cooked ham can be substituted for the pork sausage.

Golden Garlic Bread

1/3 cup butter *or* margarine, softened
1/4 cup grated Parmesan cheese
1 to 2 garlic cloves, minced
1 teaspoon dried basil
1 loaf (1 pound) French bread, halved lengthwise

In a bowl, combine the butter, Parmesan cheese, garlic and basil; mix well. Spread over cut sides of bread. Place on an ungreased baking sheet. Broil 4 in. from the heat until golden brown, about 3 minutes. Cut into 3-in. pieces. **Yield:** 6-8 servings.

Cottage Cheese Fluff

✓ Uses less fat, sugar or salt. Includes Nutritional Analysis and Diabetic Exchanges.

1 cup (8 ounces) small-curd cottage cheese
1 package (3 ounces) gelatin flavor of your choice
1 can (11 ounces) mandarin oranges, drained
1 cup unsweetened crushed pineapple, drained
1/2 cup chopped pecans, optional
1 carton (8 ounces) frozen whipped topping, thawed

In a bowl, combine the cottage cheese and gelatin powder; mix well. Stir in oranges, pineapple and pecans if desired. Just before serving, fold in the whipped topping. **Yield:** 8 servings. **Nutritional Analysis:** One 3/4-cup serving (prepared with fat-free cottage cheese, sugar-free gelatin and light frozen whipped topping and without pecans) equals 120 calories, 124 mg sodium, 2 mg cholesterol, 16 gm carbohydrate, 5 gm protein, 4 gm fat. **Diabetic Exchanges:** 1 lean meat, 1 fruit.

Microwave Oatmeal Bars

    2 cups quick-cooking oats
    1/2 cup packed brown sugar
    1/2 cup butter *or* margarine, melted
    1/4 cup corn syrup
      1 cup (6 ounces) semisweet chocolate chips

In a bowl, combine oats and brown sugar. Stir in butter and corn syrup. Press into a greased 9-in. square microwave-safe dish. Microwave, uncovered, on high for 2 minutes. Rotate a half turn; microwave 2 minutes longer. Sprinkle with chocolate chips. Microwave at 30% power for 6 minutes or until chips are glossy; spread chocolate evenly over top. Refrigerate for 15-20 minutes before cutting. **Yield:** 8-10 servings. **Editor's Note:** This recipe was tested in an 850-watt microwave.

Chapter 2

⏱ 30 Minutes to Mealtime

AS THE KITCHEN CLOCK ticks closer to dinnertime, do you scratch your head trying to figure out what to feed your famished family? There's no need to pop in a frozen pizza or pick up fast food.

Just turn to these 12 complete meals that you can put together in 30 minutes or less.

Hurried cooks share all the fixin's—including timeless preparation tips—for their family-favorite meal. Each tried-and-true dish is sure to earn you rave reviews in your kitchen as well.

So the next time your family is eyeing the table while you're eyeing the clock, turn to this lifesaving section.

HALF-AN-HOUR WONDER. Clockwise from upper right: Herbed French Bread, Scrumptious Spaghetti, Raspberry Cream Croissants and Cauliflower Spinach Salad (all recipes on p. 30).

Shredded cheese and chopped green onions sprinkled on top make this filling meat-and-potatoes main dish even more appealing. Or add whatever toppings your family prefers.

Beef Soup Spuds

4 medium baking potatoes
1 can (19 ounces) ready-to-serve chunky vegetable beef soup
2 cups cooked broccoli florets
1/8 teaspoon pepper
1 cup (4 ounces) shredded cheddar cheese
Chopped green onions, optional

Scrub and pierce the potatoes; place on a microwave-safe plate. Microwave, uncovered, on high for 12-14 minutes or until tender, turning once. Meanwhile, in a saucepan, combine soup, broccoli and pepper; heat through. With a sharp knife, cut an X in the top of each potato; fluff pulp with a fork. Top with soup mixture, cheese and onions if desired. **Yield:** 4 servings.

Cool-as-a-Cucumber Salad

1/2 cup mayonnaise
1/4 cup half-and-half cream
1/4 cup sugar
1/2 teaspoon celery seed
1/2 teaspoon dill weed
3 medium cucumbers, sliced

In a bowl, combine the first five ingredients; mix well. Add cucumbers and stir to coat. Refrigerate until serving. **Yield:** 4-6 servings.

Rosy Rhubarb Crisp

1 cup all-purpose flour
1 cup packed brown sugar
3/4 cup quick-cooking oats
1 teaspoon ground cinnamon
1/2 cup cold butter *or* margarine
3 cups finely chopped fresh *or* frozen rhubarb, thawed and drained
1 cup sugar
2 tablespoons cornstarch
1 cup water
1 teaspoon vanilla extract
Whipped cream, fresh mint and additional cinnamon, optional

In a bowl, combine the first four ingredients; cut in butter until crumbly. Press half of the mixture into a greased 8-in. square baking dish. Sprinkle rhubarb over the crust; set aside. In a saucepan, combine sugar, cornstarch, water and vanilla until smooth. Bring to a boil; cook and stir for 2 minutes or until thickened. Pour over rhubarb. Sprinkle with the remaining crumb mixture. Bake at 350° for 17-22 minutes or until golden brown. Garnish with whipped cream, mint and cinnamon if desired. **Yield:** 4-6 servings.

Hurry-Up Meal Is Hearty

IT'S NOT unusual for Joleen Jackson from Zumbrota, Minnesota to be up before the sun rises. Her workday (at an organization that tests cows' milk) starts at 6 a.m. and ends when all the milk is tested. Afterward, she pursues other interests including cooking and baking.

Joleen often looks for a meal that's short on time and long on flavor, like the menu she shares here.

"My boyfriend, Tony, is a farmer, and he eats big," Joleen reports. "This hearty meal satisfies even his appetite, so I make it often."

The Rosy Rhubarb Crisp needs time to bake, so she works backward and assembles the dessert first.

"My grandmother shared the recipe for this tasty crisp that showcases fresh or frozen rhubarb," she says. "It's yummy served warm with whipped cream or ice cream."

With dessert in the oven, Joleen whisks together the fast five-ingredient dressing for Cool-as-a-Cucumber Salad. The lightly sweet blend adds a refreshing touch to sliced cukes right out of the garden.

Then she puts the salad in the fridge to chill while she stirs up Beef Soup Spuds.

"Canned soup is the convenient base for this colorful tater topper," Joleen notes. As the potatoes are baked in the microwave, the chunky soup—along with bright broccoli for color and flavor—is heated in a snap on the stovetop.

Easy Meal Is Pretty *and* Pleasing

TASTY SURPRISES are common at Donna Gonda's home in North Canton, Ohio. Each week, she prepares several new recipes for her husband, Ken.

"Cooking has been my hobby for more than 50 years," Donna explains.

"I found the recipe for Ham-It-Up Spaghetti in a church cookbook I bought while touring the New England states," she relates.

"Using common ingredients, it's easy to assemble, especially when you cook the spaghetti while mixing up the remaining ingredients," she continues.

After popping the casserole in the oven, Donna skips to dessert, stirring up a batch of Chocolate Oatmeal Bars, which bake at the same temperature.

To round out dinner, Donna dishes up Colorful Corn. It starts with frozen corn and gets garden-fresh taste from green pepper, tomato and onion.

Ham-It-Up Spaghetti

    1 package (16 ounces) spaghetti, broken into 2-inch pieces
    2 cans (10-3/4 ounces *each*) condensed cream of mushroom soup, undiluted
1-3/4 cups milk
    1 tablespoon dried minced onion
    2 teaspoons dried parsley flakes
    1 teaspoon Worcestershire sauce
    2 cups cubed fully cooked ham (about 1 pound)
    2 cups (8 ounces) shredded cheddar cheese

Cook spaghetti according to package directions. Meanwhile, in a large bowl, combine soup, milk, onion, parsley and Worcestershire sauce. Drain spaghetti; add to soup mixture with ham. Transfer to a lightly greased 2-1/2-qt. baking dish. Sprinkle with cheese. Cover and bake at 375° for 15 minutes. Uncover and bake 5 minutes longer or until lightly browned and heated through. **Yield:** 6-8 servings.

Colorful Corn

(Also pictured on front cover)

✓ Uses less fat, sugar or salt. Includes Nutritional Analysis and Diabetic Exchanges.

    1 package (20 ounces) frozen corn
1/4 cup butter *or* margarine, melted
    1 small onion, thinly sliced
1/2 cup julienned green pepper
1/2 to 1 teaspoon salt, optional
1/4 cup milk
    2 medium tomatoes, chopped

In a saucepan, cook corn according to package directions; drain. Add butter, onion, green pepper and salt if desired. Cook over low heat for 3-5 minutes or until vegetables are heated through. Add milk; bring to a boil. Reduce heat; simmer for 2 minutes or until heated through. Remove from the heat; stir in tomatoes. **Yield:** 6-8 servings. **Nutritional Analysis:** One 3/4-cup serving (prepared with margarine and skim milk and without salt) equals 171 calories, 101 mg sodium, trace cholesterol, 24 gm carbohydrate, 4 gm protein, 8 gm fat. **Diabetic Exchanges:** 1-1/2 fat, 1 starch, 1 vegetable.

Chocolate Oatmeal Bars

1/2 cup butter *or* margarine, softened
1/2 cup packed brown sugar
    1 egg
    1 teaspoon vanilla extract
1/2 cup all-purpose flour
1/2 cup quick-cooking oats
    1 cup (6 ounces) semisweet chocolate chips
1/2 cup chopped pecans

In a mixing bowl, cream butter and sugar. Beat in egg and vanilla. Add the flour and oats; mix well. Pour into a lightly greased 11-in. x 7-in. x 2-in. baking pan. Bake at 375° for 15-20 minutes or until lightly browned. Cool on a wire rack for 3-5 minutes. Sprinkle with chips; when melted, spread chocolate over bars. Top with nuts. **Yield:** about 1-1/2 dozen.

Swift, Sunny Morning Meal

FAST-TO-FIX dishes provide Phyllis and Millard Carlson of Gardner, Kansas with more time to pursue their favorite pastimes. The couple shares a passion for Kansas City Chiefs football and get-togethers with their family.

The simple menu here is handy for a Saturday breakfast or Sunday brunch.

Picante Omelet Pie has been in Phyllis' recipe collection for more than 25 years.

"This zippy egg bake is a favorite of one of my daughters," she reports. "She comes for brunch every week before church, so I serve it often."

With the omelet pie in the oven, Phyllis stirs up the batter for Strawberry Muffins, which can be popped alongside since both bake at the same temperature.

"I sometimes make these moist, fruity muffins a day early to cut down on last-minute preparation," she notes. They get a special touch from a quick-to-fix cinnamon-honey spread.

Phyllis rounds out breakfast with refreshing Fruit with Yogurt Dip. The three-ingredient dip is creamy and has a nice brown sugar flavor.

Picante Omelet Pie

    1/2 cup picante sauce
      1 cup (4 ounces) shredded Monterey Jack cheese
      1 cup (4 ounces) shredded cheddar cheese
      6 eggs
      1 cup (8 ounces) sour cream
    Tomato slices and chopped fresh cilantro or parsley, optional

Pour the picante sauce into a lightly greased 10-in. pie plate or quiche dish. Sprinkle with cheeses; set aside. In a blender or food processor, process eggs and sour cream until smooth. Pour over cheese. Bake at 375° for 20-25 minutes or until a knife inserted near the center comes out clean. Let stand 5 minutes before cutting. Garnish with tomato and cilantro if desired. **Yield:** 6 servings.

Strawberry Muffins

      3 cups all-purpose flour
      2 cups sugar
      1 tablespoon ground cinnamon
      1 teaspoon baking soda
      1 teaspoon salt
      2 cups frozen sweetened strawberries, thawed, undrained
      1 cup vegetable oil
      3 eggs, beaten
    1/4 to 1/2 teaspoon red food coloring, optional
  1-1/2 cups chopped pecans, optional
  CINNAMON-HONEY SPREAD:
    1/2 cup butter or margarine, softened
      1 cup confectioners' sugar
    1/4 cup honey
    1/4 teaspoon ground cinnamon

In a large bowl, combine flour, sugar, cinnamon, baking soda and salt. In another bowl, mix strawberries, oil, eggs and food coloring if desired; stir into dry ingredients just until moistened. Fold in pecans if desired. Fill greased muffin cups three-fourths full. Bake at 375° for 15-18 minutes or until muffins test done. Meanwhile, combine spread ingredients in a small mixing bowl; beat until blended. Serve with the muffins. Store spread in the refrigerator. **Yield:** 2-1/2 dozen (3/4 cup spread).

Fruit with Yogurt Dip

✓ Uses less fat, sugar or salt. Includes Nutritional Analysis and Diabetic Exchanges.

      1 carton (8 ounces) vanilla yogurt
      2 tablespoons brown sugar
    1/4 teaspoon lemon juice
    Strawberries, bananas and apples or other fresh fruit

In a small bowl, combine yogurt, brown sugar and lemon juice. Serve with fruit. **Yield:** 1 cup. **Nutritional Analysis:** 3 tablespoons of dip (prepared with nonfat yogurt) equals 58 calories, 31 mg sodium, 1 mg cholesterol, 12 gm carbohydrate, 2 gm protein, trace fat.

Variety Spices Up Supper

THERE'S little chance that Gaylene Anderson's family will get bored with the meals she puts on the table. The busy Sandy, Utah cook loves to try new recipes and rarely makes the same dish twice.

"Despite my hurried, hectic schedule, I love preparing a variety of menus and cooking daily sit-down dinners for husband Russell and our four children, Paul, Carli, Jeff and Janalyn," she notes.

"This meal tastes like you've been slaving all afternoon. But it is as easy as can be!" she assures.

Gaylene relies on pantry staples to create crowd-pleasing Beef-Topped Bean Enchiladas. "The recipe for this spicy main dish came from my collection of Relief Society cookbooks compiled by the women's organization of our church," she relates.

"With the oven busy, I stir up a big batch of easy Peanut Cookie Bars on the stovetop," she shares. "These chewy no-bake goodies have big peanut taste.

"We're chocolate fans, so I sometimes add a bag of chips to make the bars an even bigger hit," she notes.

While they cool, Gaylene completes the meal with Ready-to-Serve Salad. "A good friend and neighbor brought over this colorful blend after I returned from a hospital stay," she recalls.

A fast dressing adds refreshing flavor to a unique combination of ingredients that gets a head start from packaged salad and canned mandarin oranges.

Beef-Topped Bean Enchiladas

1-1/2 pounds ground beef
    1 medium onion, chopped
    1 jar (16 ounces) salsa
    1 can (8 ounces) tomato sauce
    1 to 2 teaspoons ground cumin
  1/8 teaspoon garlic salt
    1 can (16 ounces) refried beans
  12 flour tortillas (7 inches)
1-1/2 cups (6 ounces) shredded cheddar cheese, *divided*
1-1/2 cups (6 ounces) shredded Monterey Jack cheese, *divided*
    2 cans (2-1/4 ounces *each*) sliced ripe olives, drained, *divided*

In a skillet, cook beef and onion until meat is no longer pink; drain. Stir in the salsa, tomato sauce, cumin and garlic salt; cook for 3 minutes or until heated through. Meanwhile, spread 2-3 tablespoons refried beans over each tortilla. Sprinkle each with 1 tablespoon cheddar cheese, 1 tablespoon of Monterey Jack cheese and 1 tablespoon olives. Roll up. Place seam side down in a greased 13-in. x 9-in. x 2-in. baking dish. Top with beef mixture. Sprinkle with remaining cheeses and olives. Bake, uncovered, at 350° for 20 minutes or until heated through. **Yield:** 6 servings.

Ready-to-Serve Salad

    1 package (16 ounces) ready-to-serve salad
    8 bacon strips, cooked and crumbled
    1 can (11 ounces) mandarin oranges, drained
  1/2 cup chopped red onion
  1/4 cup sliced almonds
    1 cup (4 ounces) shredded mozzarella cheese, optional
  1/2 cup vegetable oil
    2 tablespoons sugar
    2 tablespoons vinegar
  1/4 to 1/2 teaspoon salt

In a large salad bowl, toss the first six ingredients. Combine the remaining ingredients in a jar with a tight-fitting lid; shake well. Pour over salad and toss to coat. **Yield:** 6 servings.

Peanut Cookie Bars

  12 cups cornflakes, crushed
    1 jar (16 ounces) dry roasted peanuts
1-1/2 cups corn syrup
    1 cup sugar
    1 cup packed brown sugar
    1 cup peanut butter

In a large bowl, combine cornflakes and peanuts; mix well. In a saucepan, combine corn syrup and sugars; bring to a boil. Boil for 1 minute. Remove from the heat; stir in peanut butter. Pour over cornflake mixture and mix gently. Press into a greased 15-in. x 10-in. x 1-in. baking pan. Cool slightly; cut into bars. **Yield:** 2 dozen.

Savor Super Summertime Menu

COOKING is truly a passion for Stephanie Moon. You will often find the Green Bay, Wisconsin homemaker baking her family's favorite muffins, experimenting with new recipes or collecting cookbooks.

"Although I love to cook, I appreciate recipes that have me in and out of the kitchen with little fuss, so I can spend time with my family," she says.

Stephanie and husband Don, who's in the Navy, have three children: Tyler, Joshua and Kylie.

"I often rely on quick recipes," she says. A popular menu at her house during summer starts with Pineapple Chicken Salad.

"Our kids love this filling salad's sweet dressing," Stephanie shares. "While the chicken's grilling, I prepare the dressing and vegetables.

"A must-have accompaniment is Basil Garlic Bread," she adds. "Everyone loves it."

To top off the meal, Stephanie makes the best of fresh berries with Strawberry Biscuit Shortcake.

Pineapple Chicken Salad

        4 boneless skinless chicken breast halves
    1/4 teaspoon lemon-pepper seasoning
        1 can (8 ounces) unsweetened sliced pineapple
        3 tablespoons vegetable oil
        2 tablespoons soy sauce
        1 tablespoon vinegar
        1 tablespoon honey
    1/4 teaspoon ground ginger
        8 cups assorted vegetables (lettuce, red onion, carrots, sweet red pepper and broccoli)
Salted peanuts, optional

Sprinkle chicken with lemon-pepper. Grill over medium-hot heat or broil 4-6 in. from the heat for 15-18 minutes or until juices run clear, turning once. Set aside and keep warm. Drain pineapple, reserving 2 tablespoons juice (discard remaining juice or save for another use); set pineapple aside. In a jar with a tight-fitting lid, combine oil, soy sauce, vinegar, honey, ginger and reserved pineapple juice; shake well. Brush some of the dressing over pineapple; grill or broil for 2 minutes. Cut chicken into strips. Arrange vegetables on serving plates; top with pineapple and chicken. Sprinkle with peanuts if desired. Serve with remaining dressing. **Yield:** 4 servings.

Basil Garlic Bread

    1/4 cup butter or margarine
        2 tablespoons minced fresh parsley
    1-1/2 teaspoons minced fresh basil or 1/2 teaspoon dried basil
        1 garlic clove, minced
    1/4 cup grated Parmesan cheese
        1 loaf (8 ounces) French bread

In a microwave-safe bowl, combine butter, parsley, basil and garlic. Cover and microwave until butter melts. Stir in Parmesan cheese. Cut bread in half lengthwise; place cut side down on an uncovered grill over medium heat for 2 minutes, or broil cut side up for 2 minutes until lightly toasted. Brush cut side with butter mixture. Grill or broil 1-2 minutes more. **Yield:** 4 servings.

Strawberry Biscuit Shortcake

        2 cups all-purpose flour
        3 tablespoons sugar, *divided*
        1 tablespoon baking powder
    1/2 teaspoon salt
    1/4 cup cold butter or margarine
        1 cup milk
        2 pints strawberries, sliced
        1 tablespoon orange juice
    1-1/2 cups whipped topping

In a large bowl, combine flour, 2 tablespoons sugar, baking powder and salt. Cut in butter until mixture resembles coarse crumbs. Gradually stir in milk until a soft dough forms. Drop the dough by heaping tablespoonfuls into eight mounds on a lightly greased baking sheet. Bake at 425° for 12-15 minutes or until lightly browned. Cool on a wire rack. Meanwhile, place strawberries, orange juice and remaining sugar in a bowl; toss gently. Split shortcakes in half horizontally. Place bottom halves on serving plates; top with whipped topping and strawberries. Replace tops. **Yield:** 8 servings.

Harvest Fresh Garden Flavor

TRAVEL was a big part of Fran Shaffer's life when her husband, Dave, now a retired Army colonel, took assignments in Germany, England and all over the U.S.

She still enjoys traveling, but now Fran, Dave and son Darryl are happily settled in Coatesville, Pennsylvania among sprawling farms in a predominantly Amish area.

Dave's an engineer, while Fran has a challenging full-time job as an assistant to a busy banking executive. She also attends college part-time in pursuit of a business degree.

Besides belonging to many social and volunteer organizations, Fran loves to quilt, play tennis and go fishing with her husband and son.

But on most weeknights, she still manages to prepare a sit-down dinner like the one she shares here.

"When our garden was overflowing with squash, Mom and I experimented with recipes and came up with Ham-Stuffed Squash Boats," Fran explains.

Pretty yellow summer squash are mounded with a flavorful filling featuring ham and two kinds of cheese.

While the squash shells simmer, Fran needs just three ingredients to stir together Buttered Cornsticks.

She then pops both the entree and quick bread in the oven; they conveniently bake at the same temperature for the same length of time.

This gives her the opportunity to fix Raspberry Pudding Parfaits, a fresh, flavorful dessert that has been in Fran's family for ages.

"It's so easy to prepare, and you can substitute strawberries or blueberries with equally tempting results," she notes.

Ham-Stuffed Squash Boats

      4 medium yellow summer squash *or* zucchini
        (about 6 inches)
      1 small onion, finely chopped
      2 tablespoons butter *or* margarine
      1 cup diced fully cooked ham
  1/2 cup dry bread crumbs
  1/2 cup shredded cheddar cheese
  1/2 cup shredded Parmesan cheese, *divided*
      1 egg, beaten
      1 teaspoon paprika
  1/4 teaspoon pepper

Cut squash in half lengthwise; scoop out pulp, leaving a 3/8-in. shell. Chop pulp and set aside. In a large saucepan, cook shells in boiling water for 4-5 minutes.

Drain and set aside. In another saucepan, saute onion in butter until tender; remove from the heat. Add ham, bread crumbs, cheddar cheese, 1/4 cup of Parmesan cheese, egg, paprika, pepper and squash pulp; mix well. Spoon into shells. Place on a lightly greased baking sheet. Sprinkle with remaining Parmesan cheese. Bake at 425° for 12-15 minutes or until heated through. **Yield:** 4 servings.

Buttered Cornsticks

  2-2/3 cups biscuit/baking mix
      1 can (8-1/2 ounces) cream-style corn
  1/4 cup butter *or* margarine, melted

In a bowl, combine biscuit mix and corn. Stir until a soft dough forms. Knead on a lightly floured surface for 3 minutes. Roll into a 10-in. x 6-in. rectangle. Cut into 3-in. x 1-in. strips. Dip in butter. Place in an ungreased 15-in. x 10-in. x 1-in. baking pan. Bake at 425° for 12-15 minutes or until golden brown. **Yield:** about 20 breadsticks.

Raspberry Pudding Parfaits

  1-1/2 cups cold milk
      1 package (5.1 ounces) instant vanilla pudding
        mix
      1 package (12 ounces) unsweetened frozen
        raspberries, thawed
  Whipped topping, optional

In a mixing bowl, combine milk and pudding mix; beat for 2 minutes or until thickened. Spoon half into four parfait glasses. Top with half of the raspberries. Repeat layers. Garnish with whipped topping if desired. **Yield:** 4 servings.

1 garlic clove, minced
1 tablespoon olive *or* vegetable oil
1 can (15 ounces) tomato sauce
2 tablespoons sugar
1/2 to 1 teaspoon dried oregano
1 package (16 ounces) spaghetti
1/4 cup grated Parmesan cheese, optional

In a skillet, saute green pepper, onion and garlic in oil until tender. Add tomato sauce, sugar and oregano. Simmer for 20 minutes, stirring occasionally. Meanwhile, cook spaghetti according to package directions. Drain; top with sauce. Sprinkle with Parmesan cheese if desired. **Yield:** 4-6 servings.

Herbed French Bread

1/2 cup butter *or* margarine, softened
1/2 teaspoon paprika
1/2 teaspoon dried rosemary, crushed
1/4 teaspoon dried thyme
1/4 teaspoon dried marjoram
1 loaf (1/2 pound) French bread, cut into 1/2-inch slices

In a bowl, combine butter and seasonings. Spread on cut sides of each slice of bread. Reassemble the loaf; wrap in heavy-duty foil. Bake at 400° for 15-20 minutes or until heated through. **Yield:** 4-6 servings.

Cauliflower Spinach Salad

1 cup mayonnaise *or* salad dressing
1/4 cup grated Parmesan cheese
2 tablespoons sugar
1 tablespoon finely chopped onion
1 tablespoon minced fresh parsley
1 small head cauliflower, broken into florets
1 package (10 ounces) fresh spinach, torn
1 cup sliced fresh mushrooms
1/2 to 3/4 pound bacon, cooked and crumbled

In a small bowl, combine the first five ingredients. In a large salad bowl, combine cauliflower, spinach, mushrooms and bacon. Add dressing and toss to coat; serve immediately. **Yield:** 6-8 servings.

Raspberry Cream Croissants

4 to 6 croissants
1/2 cup seedless raspberry jam
Whipped cream in a can *or* whipped topping
1-1/4 cups fresh *or* frozen unsweetened raspberries, thawed
Confectioners' sugar, optional

Cut the croissants in half horizontally; spread cut halves with jam. Spread whipped cream over bottom halves; top with raspberries. Replace tops. Dust with confectioners' sugar if desired. Serve immediately. **Yield:** 4-6 servings.

Enjoy Fuss-Free Food

DURING the day, Sherry Horton of Sioux Falls, South Dakota works full-time. But on summer evenings and weekends, you'll find her planting flowers, weeding rows of vegetables and harvesting herbs.

"At the end of a long day, I'd much rather be outside than spend hours in the kitchen. That's why this quick menu is one of my favorites.

"I start the chunky sauce for the Scrumptious Spaghetti first so it can simmer while I ready the rest of the meal," she says.

Sherry uses dried homegrown herbs to season buttery Herbed French Bread.

Once that's in the oven warming, she prepares crisp Cauliflower Spinach Salad. "When I have fresh lettuce from the garden, I'll use that in place of spinach...and occasionally, I toss in broccoli instead of cauliflower," she notes.

A heavenly dessert of Raspberry Cream Croissants takes seconds to assemble because it begins with bakery croissants, whipped topping and store-bought jam.

Scrumptious Spaghetti

1 medium green pepper, chopped
1 medium onion, chopped

Count on Foiled Feast

COOKING a trio of meals a day has added up to lots of experience in the kitchen for Edna Shaffer of Beulah, Michigan.

"I've been married to my husband, Howard, for more than 56 years, and I estimate I've cooked at least 61,320 meals in that time!" she exclaims.

Besides sharing their table with four daughters, 14 grandchildren and three great-grandchildren, the couple's made room for plenty of guests over the years.

"Howard was a Methodist pastor until he retired, so we always had people coming and going," Edna relates. "We're still blessed with visits from many of those wonderful church families.

"I think having company should be fun—not cause for concern. So I keep my cupboards and freezer well-stocked for these occasions," she explains.

"People think I fussed when I serve Chicken Veggie Packets. Individual aluminum foil pouches hold the juices in during baking to keep the herbed chicken moist and tender.

"Instead of foil, you can seal each serving in baking parchment, which can be found in rolls next to the foil and waxed paper in the grocery store," Edna notes. "Either way saves time because it makes cleanup a breeze."

A can of cheese soup gives Edna a head start on Cheesy Cauliflower. "This beautiful side dish takes less than 10 minutes to fix and disappears as soon as I serve it," she says.

To complete this meal, Edna blends convenient canned lemon pie filling with whipped topping to make Mousse in a Minute.

"It's light, tangy and a snap to whip up," she adds.

Chicken Veggie Packets

✓ Uses less fat, sugar or salt. Includes Nutritional Analysis and Diabetic Exchanges.

- 4 boneless skinless chicken breast halves (1 pound)
- 1/2 pound fresh mushrooms, sliced
- 1-1/2 cups baby carrots, halved lengthwise
- 1 cup frozen pearl onions, thawed
- 1/2 cup julienned sweet red pepper
- 1/4 teaspoon pepper
- 1 teaspoon dried thyme, optional
- 1/2 teaspoon salt, optional

Flatten chicken breasts to 1/2-in. thickness; place each on a piece of heavy-duty foil (about 12 in. x 12 in.). Layer mushrooms, carrots, onions and red pepper over chicken; sprinkle with pepper, thyme and salt if desired. Fold foil around chicken and vegetables and seal tightly. Place on a baking sheet. Bake at 375° for 20 minutes or until chicken juices run clear. **Yield:** 4 servings. **Nutritional Analysis:** One serving (prepared without salt) equals 220 calories, 92 mg sodium, 80 mg cholesterol, 17 gm carbohydrate, 30 gm protein, 4 gm fat. **Diabetic Exchanges:** 3 very lean meat, 1 starch.

Cheesy Cauliflower

- 1 medium head cauliflower (1-1/2 pounds)
- 1 can (10-3/4 ounces) condensed cheddar cheese soup, undiluted
- 1/8 teaspoon salt
- 1/4 teaspoon paprika

Break cauliflower into florets or leave whole; place in Dutch oven or large saucepan. Add 1 in. of water. Cover and steam until tender, 7-10 minutes for florets or 15-20 minutes for the whole head. Meanwhile, heat soup and salt; serve over cauliflower. Sprinkle with paprika. **Yield:** 4-6 servings.

Mousse in a Minute

- 1-1/2 cups whipped topping
- 1 can (15-3/4 ounces) lemon pie filling
- 4 individual graham cracker tart shells *or*
- 1 graham cracker crust (9 inches), optional
- Shredded lemon peel, optional

In a bowl, fold the whipped topping into the pie filling. Spoon into dessert dishes, tart shells or crust. Refrigerate until serving. Garnish with lemon peel if desired. **Yield:** 4 servings.

Quick Meal Has Family Appeal

FAMILY-PLEASING meals are a must at Sherry Lee's home in rural Shelby, Alabama. When dinnertime rolls around, she and husband Tom have nine mouths to feed: Tiffiny, Jordan, Emily, Bethany, Abigail, Joshua, Jacob, Johnathon and Hannah Joy.

"I keep busy by home-schooling our children, cooking three meals a day and reading," Sherry says.

"Tom's a project manager for a construction company, so he usually leaves by 5 a.m. and returns about 5:30 p.m.

"Because our day begins so early, we like to have supper ready as soon as he gets home from work," Sherry relates. "This gives us time for a sit-down dinner, family time and devotions."

Quick recipes, like the ones she shares here, help keep the Lees on schedule. Sherry starts by assembling hearty Pinto Bean Casserole.

Next, Sherry stirs together Banana Split Pudding. "Our kids love banana splits, so I came up with this simple dessert," Sherry explains.

To round out the menu, Sherry prepares Salsa Tossed Salad. Salsa and ranch dressing give Mexican flair to a mixture of greens and vegetables.

Pinto Bean Casserole

- 1 package (9 ounces) tortilla chips
- 2 cans (30 ounces *each*) pinto beans, rinsed and drained
- 1 can (15 ounces) whole kernel corn, drained
- 1 can (14-1/2 ounces) diced tomatoes, drained
- 1 can (8 ounces) tomato sauce
- 1 envelope taco seasoning
- 2 cups (8 ounces) shredded cheddar cheese
- Shredded lettuce, sour cream and salsa, optional

Crush tortilla chips and sprinkle into a greased 13-in. x 9-in. x 2-in. baking dish. In a large bowl, combine beans, corn, tomatoes, tomato sauce and taco seasoning; mix well. Pour over chips. Sprinkle with cheese. Bake, uncovered, at 350° for 18-25 minutes or until heated through. Serve with lettuce, sour cream and salsa if desired. **Yield:** 6-8 servings.

Salsa Tossed Salad

✓ Uses less fat, sugar or salt. Includes Nutritional Analysis and Diabetic Exchanges.

- 8 cups torn mixed salad greens
- 1 medium tomato, cut into wedges
- 1 cup sliced sweet yellow pepper
- 1/3 cup sliced red onion
- 1/3 cup salsa
- 1/3 cup ranch salad dressing *or* dressing of your choice
- 1/2 cup corn chips, coarsely crushed, optional
- 1/2 cup shredded cheddar cheese

In a large bowl, toss greens, tomato, pepper and onion. Combine salsa and salad dressing; mix well. Pour over salad and toss to coat. Sprinkle with chips if desired and cheese. Serve immediately. **Yield:** 6 servings. **Nutritional Analysis:** One 1-cup serving (prepared with fat-free ranch dressing and reduced-fat cheddar cheese and without corn chips) equals 84 calories, 301 mg sodium, 7 mg cholesterol, 11 gm carbohydrate, 5 gm protein, 2 gm fat. **Diabetic Exchanges:** 2 vegetable, 1/2 meat.

Banana Split Pudding

- 3 cups cold milk
- 1 package (5.1 ounces) instant vanilla pudding mix
- 1 medium firm banana, sliced
- 1 cup sliced fresh strawberries
- 1 can (8 ounces) crushed pineapple, drained
- 1 carton (8 ounces) frozen whipped topping, thawed
- 1/4 cup chocolate syrup
- 1/4 cup chopped pecans
- Additional sliced strawberries and bananas, optional

In a bowl, whisk milk and pudding mix for 2 minutes. Add banana, strawberries and pineapple; transfer to a serving bowl. Dollop with whipped topping. Drizzle with chocolate syrup; sprinkle with pecans. Top with strawberries and bananas if desired. **Yield:** 6-8 servings.

“When I was a girl growing up on the farm, my mom often fixed these when we were late in the field,” she recalls. “They're also tasty with chopped green peppers added to the mixture.”

Speedy Salmon Patties

- 1 can (12 *or* 14-3/4 ounces) salmon,* drained
- 1/3 cup finely chopped onion
- 1 egg
- 5 saltines, crushed
- 1/2 teaspoon Worcestershire sauce
- 1/4 teaspoon salt
- 1/8 teaspoon pepper
- 2 teaspoons butter *or* margarine

In a bowl, combine the first seven ingredients; mix well. Shape into six patties. In a skillet, fry patties in butter over medium heat for 3-4 minutes on each side or until heated through. **Yield:** 3 servings. ***Editor's Note:** Salmon in 12-ounce cans has already been boned and skinned. If using a 14-3/4-ounce can, remove the bones and skin after draining.

Potato Green Bean Medley

- 4 bacon strips, diced
- 4 to 6 medium red potatoes, cut into small wedges
- 1-1/2 cups cut fresh green beans (1-inch pieces)
- 3/4 cup water
- 1/4 teaspoon salt
- 1/8 teaspoon pepper

In a large saucepan, cook bacon until crisp. Remove bacon to paper towels. Drain, reserving 1 tablespoon drippings. To reserved drippings, add potatoes, green beans, water, salt and pepper. Bring to a boil; reduce heat. Cover and cook for 15-20 minutes or until the vegetables are tender. Drain if necessary. Sprinkle with bacon. **Yield:** 3 servings.

Fruit Cocktail Delight

✓ Uses less fat, sugar or salt. Includes Nutritional Analysis and Diabetic Exchanges.

- 1 can (15 ounces) fruit cocktail, undrained
- 1 package (3.4 ounces) instant vanilla pudding mix
- 1/2 cup miniature marshmallows
Chopped nuts, optional

In a bowl, combine fruit cocktail and pudding mix; mix well. Fold in marshmallows just before serving. Garnish with nuts if desired. Refrigerate leftovers. **Yield:** 6 servings. **Nutritional Analysis:** One serving (prepared with light fruit cocktail and sugar-free pudding mix and without nuts) equals 95 calories, 667 mg sodium, 0 cholesterol, 24 gm carbohydrate, trace protein, trace fat. **Diabetic Exchange:** 1-1/2 fruit.

Stovetop Supper Is a Time-Saver

FOR Bonnie Evans of Cameron, North Carolina, mealtime is an important part of the day. “It's our sharing time, and at night, it's devotion time,” she relates.

Bonnie and husband Chris have four children: Chrissy and Dulcie, both married, and Cynthia and Crystal at home.

Bonnie owns and manages a trailer park, while Chris works as a range control maintenance worker at Fort Bragg, North Carolina. Both are members of the U.S. Air Force Reserve at Charleston, South Carolina. “We travel there once a month to load and unload cargo onto planes as part of the 81st Aerial Port squadron,” she explains.

Bonnie also volunteers at school, attends church and youth activities and enjoys gardening.

“With sports, music, church and work, I often need quick meals like this speedy supper,” she reports.

“I start the Potato Green Bean Medley first, often with fresh beans from our big backyard vegetable garden,” she notes.

“While the veggies cook, I use convenient canned fruit cocktail and instant pudding to prepare Fruit Cocktail Delight,” Bonnie says.

“It makes a refreshing and pretty finale to any meal, especially when it's served in glass dishes. I sometimes garnish each serving with whipped cream and a cherry,” she adds.

Then Bonnie combines seven easy ingredients to make nicely seasoned Speedy Salmon Patties.

Fast Fare Has Seasonal Flair

MEAL-PLANNING took a different turn for Carole Martin when her husband, Jimmy, a minister, accepted a new job. "We moved to Tallahassee, Florida to become houseparents to 18 children at the Florida Baptist Children's Home," she writes.

"I enjoy getting the kids involved in planning and preparing sit-down family meals every day of the week," she says. "Together we select menus, go shopping for ingredients, then cook and serve the meals."

Carole says the young cooks often refer to a notebook of favorite recipes she compiled before moving. It includes this made-in-minutes meal that's special enough for the holidays.

"I suggest that you prepare the Sweet Spinach Salad first," Carole recommends. "The dressing is my own concoction and is delicious over fresh fruit, too," she adds.

"Quick Carbonara is an adaptation of a dish originally made by my Sunday school teacher, who brought it to church dinners," Carole recalls.

"Be sure to prepare plenty, because seconds are always requested," she assures. "It's also good with cubed cooked turkey instead of ham.

"Festive Mint Sundaes are reminiscent of the special desserts served at ladies' club meetings I attended when we lived in Mississippi," Carole says.

Her version gets its holiday look from chopped green cherries and its tempting taste from chocolate mint candies that are melted and drizzled on top.

Quick Carbonara

1 package (12 ounces) spaghetti
3 tablespoons butter *or* margarine
3 tablespoons vegetable oil
2 garlic cloves, minced
3 cups cubed fully cooked ham
8 bacon strips, cooked and crumbled
2 tablespoons minced fresh parsley
3/4 teaspoon salt
3/4 cup sliced ripe *or* stuffed olives
1/2 cup grated Parmesan cheese

Cook spaghetti according to package directions. Meanwhile, in a large skillet, heat butter, oil and garlic; mix well. Drain spaghetti; add to skillet with ham, bacon, parsley and salt. Cook and stir until heated through, about 3 minutes. Remove from the heat. Gently stir in olives and Parmesan cheese. **Yield:** 6 servings.

Sweet Spinach Salad

1 package (10 ounces) fresh spinach, torn
1 can (11 ounces) mandarin oranges, drained
10 cherry tomatoes, halved
1 cup sliced fresh mushrooms
DRESSING:
1/3 cup sugar
3 tablespoons cider vinegar
1 tablespoon honey
1/2 teaspoon dried minced onion
1/2 teaspoon celery seed
1/2 teaspoon ground mustard
1/2 teaspoon paprika
1/2 teaspoon lemon juice
1/2 cup vegetable oil
1 can (2.8 ounces) french-fried onions

In a large salad bowl, toss spinach, oranges, tomatoes and mushrooms; set aside. In a microwave-safe bowl, combine first eight dressing ingredients. Microwave on high for 1 to 1-1/2 minutes. Stir until sugar is dissolved. Whisk in oil. Drizzle over salad and toss to coat. Sprinkle with onions. Serve immediately. **Yield:** 6-8 servings.

Festive Mint Sundaes

1 jar (8 ounces) green maraschino cherries, undrained
Vanilla ice cream
18 mint Andes candies

Place cherries with juice in a blender or food processor; cover and chop. Spoon ice cream into bowls; top with cherries. Place six mints in a small heavy-duty resealable plastic bag; microwave just until melted. Snip a small opening in one corner of bag; squeeze melted chocolate over sundaes. Garnish with remaining mints; serve. **Yield:** 6 servings.

Dinner Shines with Sunny Flavor

RETIREMENT provides Janice and Clyde Mitchell of Aurora, Colorado with plenty of time to visit their four grown children and seven grandchildren.

When she's not trying recipes, Janice falls back on this family-favorite menu.

"I get the Orange Rice started first," she says. "We prefer long grain rice, but you can use instant to save time.

"I make colorful Sunshine Chicken at least once a month—our grandkids love it," she informs. "The original recipe called for a cut-up fryer, but boneless chicken breasts cook more quickly."

For an elegant ending to the meal, Janice prepares Simple Bananas Foster.

Sunshine Chicken

✓ Uses less fat, sugar or salt. Includes Nutritional Analysis and Diabetic Exchanges.

    1 pound boneless skinless chicken breasts, cut
      into 1/2-inch strips
    2 tablespoons butter *or* margarine
    1 teaspoon salt, optional
  1/8 teaspoon pepper
  1/8 teaspoon ground ginger
    2 cups sliced carrots
    1 small onion, sliced into rings
    1 tablespoon cornstarch
  2/3 cup orange juice
  1/3 cup orange marmalade
    3 to 4 tablespoons brown sugar
    1 tablespoon lemon juice

In a skillet, saute chicken in butter for 4-5 minutes or until lightly browned. Sprinkle with salt if desired, pepper and ginger. Stir in carrots and onion. In a small bowl, combine cornstarch and orange juice until smooth. Stir in marmalade, brown sugar and lemon juice; add to skillet. Bring to a boil. Reduce heat; cover and simmer for 10-15 minutes or until vegetables are tender. **Yield:** 4 servings. **Nutritional Analysis:** One serving (prepared with reduced-fat margarine, spreadable fruit orange marmalade and artificial sweetener equivalent to 4 tablespoons sugar and without salt) equals 280 calories, 151 mg sodium, 73 mg cholesterol, 32 gm carbohydrate, 28 gm protein, 7 gm fat. **Diabetic Exchanges:** 4 very lean meat, 1-1/2 fruit, 1 vegetable.

Orange Rice

  2/3 cup diced celery
  1/4 cup butter *or* margarine
1-1/2 cups orange juice
    1 cup uncooked long grain rice

  3/4 cup water
    2 tablespoons grated orange peel
    1 tablespoon dried minced onion
    1 teaspoon salt
  1/8 teaspoon dried thyme

In a saucepan, saute celery in butter until tender. Add the remaining ingredients; mix well. Bring to a boil. Reduce heat; cover and simmer for 20 minutes or until the rice is tender. **Yield:** 4-6 servings.

Simple Bananas Foster

✓ Uses less fat, sugar or salt. Includes Nutritional Analysis and Diabetic Exchanges.

    1 can (5-1/2 ounces) unsweetened apple juice
  1/8 teaspoon apple pie spice
1-1/2 teaspoons cornstarch
    1 tablespoon cold water
  1/4 teaspoon rum extract
  1/8 teaspoon maple flavoring
  1/8 teaspoon butter flavoring *or* vanilla extract
    2 medium firm bananas, sliced
Vanilla ice cream *or* frozen yogurt

In a saucepan, combine the apple juice and pie spice; mix well. In a small bowl, combine cornstarch, water and flavorings; stir into apple juice mixture. Bring to a boil. Reduce heat; cook and stir for 2 minutes or until slightly thickened. Add bananas and heat through. Serve warm over ice cream. **Yield:** 4 servings. **Nutritional Analysis:** One serving (calculated without ice cream) equals 79 calories, 2 mg sodium, 0 cholesterol, 20 gm carbohydrate, 1 gm protein, trace fat. **Diabetic Exchange:** 1-1/2 fruit.

Chapter 3

◉ *Thinking Up a Theme*

THE NEXT time you're looking to host a fun and festive get-together, don't panic! Our talented *Quick Cooking* kitchen staff has taken the guesswork out of party planning by creating six easy theme-related menus.

From a heartfelt Valentine's Day dinner, a bird-themed bash and a playful zoo-inspired party to a St. Patrick's Day celebration, a colorful fall feast and a tree-trimming gala, you can easily create long-remembered occasions for your family and friends with just a short time spent in the kitchen.

FUN FESTIVITIES. Clockwise from upper right: Swift Strawberry Salad, Bird's Nest Egg Salad and Feathered Friend Cookies (all recipes on p. 43).

Demonstrate Your Devotion

SURPRISING the sweethearts in your life with a special Valentine's dinner doesn't have to be a heart-breaking affair. Even if you don't have a passion for parties, you'll fall head over heels for these heart-warming ideas dreamed up by the home economists in our test kitchen.

Irresistible individual pizzas require little prep time because guests make their own with convenient refrigerated biscuits and prepared sauce.

The fun fruit kabobs are simple to assemble, while the lip-smacking dip that accompanies them takes just minutes to stir up.

Top off the meal with the home-baked goodness of cupcakes and cookies.

Heart's Desire Pizzas

Valentines of all ages will have a delightful time sprinkling these fun heart-shaped personal pizzas with whatever tasty toppings their hearts desire.

   1 tube (17.3 ounces) large refrigerated biscuits
   1 jar (14 ounces) pizza sauce
   1-1/2 to 2 cups toppings—sliced ripe olives, sliced and quartered pepperoni, chopped fresh mushrooms, chopped green *and/or* sweet yellow pepper
   1-1/2 cups (6 ounces) shredded mozzarella cheese
   1-1/2 cups (6 ounces) shredded cheddar cheese

Cut eight 6-in.-square pieces of aluminum foil; place on baking sheets. Lightly coat foil with nonstick cooking spray; set aside. On a lightly floured surface, roll each biscuit to a 5-in. square. Cut a 1-in. triangle from center top and place on the center bottom, forming a heart. Press edges to seal. Transfer to foil squares. Spoon pizza sauce over dough to within 1/4 in. of edges. Sprinkle with desired toppings and cheeses. Bake at 425° for 10-15 minutes or until golden brown. **Yield:** 8 pizzas.

Cupid's Kabobs

Who wouldn't fall in love with these colorful skewered snacks that resemble the winged fellow's well-aimed arrows? The pretty selection of fresh fruit is dreamy when served with a light and wonderfully smooth cherry dip.

1-1/2 cups cold milk
   1 package (3.4 ounces) instant vanilla pudding mix
   1 cup (8 ounces) cherry vanilla yogurt
   1 carton (8 ounces) frozen whipped topping, thawed

Create Heart-Shaped Cupcakes

To make heart-shaped cupcakes, fill paper- or foil-lined muffin cups half full of batter. Then tuck a 1/2-inch foil ball or a marble between the liner and the cup to form a heart shape. Bake cupcakes as directed.

Assorted fruit—seedless grapes, apple chunks, strawberry halves *and/or* pineapple chunks
Fresh mint sprigs

In a bowl, combine the milk and pudding mix; mix well. Let stand 2-3 minutes. Add yogurt; mix well. Fold in whipped topping. Refrigerate. Thread fruit onto bamboo skewers; add a mint sprig on the end to resemble feathers on an arrow. Serve with dip. **Yield:** 4 cups dip.

Conversation Cupcakes

It's a snap to spell out sweet sentiments on these quaint cupcakes when you bake a batch ahead of time using a convenient cake mix. You don't even need a heart-shaped muffin tin to make them.

   1 package (18-1/4 ounces) white cake mix
1/2 cup butter *or* margarine, softened
1/2 cup shortening
   1 teaspoon vanilla extract
1/8 teaspoon butter flavoring, optional
   4 cups confectioners' sugar
   2 tablespoons milk
   1 to 2 drops red food coloring
   1 to 2 drops yellow food coloring
   1 to 2 drops blue food coloring

Prepare cake mix according to package directions. Place paper or foil liners in a heart-shaped or standard muffin tin. Fill cups half full of batter. (If using a standard tin, see the tip below left to create heart-shaped cupcakes.) Bake according to package directions for cupcakes. Cool for 10 minutes; remove from pans to wire racks to cool completely. For frosting, cream butter and shortening in a small mixing bowl. Add vanilla and butter flavoring if desired. Add sugar, 1 cup at a time, beating well after each addition. Beat in milk until light and fluffy. Divide frosting into fourths; place in four separate bowls. Leave one bowl untinted. Add food coloring to the other three bowls; stir until well blended. Frost cupcakes. Pipe untinted frosting around edges of cupcakes and decorate tops with Valentine phrases. **Yield:** 28 cupcakes.

Hugs 'n' Kisses Cookies

Refrigerated cookie dough takes the work out of these adorable treats that are sure to X-press your O-verwhelming affection for your guests.

   1 package (18 ounces) refrigerated sugar cookie dough
Red colored sugar, optional

Cut cookie dough into 1/4-in. slices. On a floured surface, roll each slice into a 6-in. rope. Cut half of the ropes in half widthwise. Form into X's on ungreased baking sheets; seal edges and flatten slightly. Shape remaining ropes into O's on ungreased baking sheets; seal the edges and flatten slightly. Sprinkle with sugar if desired. Bake at 350° for 8-10 minutes or until the edges are lightly browned. Cool for 3 minutes; remove from pans to wire racks to cool completely. **Yield:** about 5 dozen.

Celebrate
St. Pat's Day

IRISH EYES will be smiling when you serve this mouth-watering menu to mark St. Patrick's Day.

Shamrock Sandwiches

Substitute horseradish for the mustard and garlic powder for the dill for a fun variation of these sandwiches.

    1 package (8 ounces) cream cheese, softened
1/4 cup mayonnaise
    2 tablespoons Dijon mustard
    1 package (2-1/2 ounces) thinly sliced cooked corned beef, chopped
    2 tablespoons grated red onion
    2 teaspoons snipped fresh dill *or* 3/4 teaspoon dill weed
1/4 teaspoon salt
    1 pound thinly sliced seedless rye bread
Fresh dill sprigs, optional

In a mixing bowl, beat cream cheese, mayonnaise and mustard. Add corned beef, onion, dill and salt; mix well. Using a 2-in. shamrock cookie cutter, cut out two shamrocks from each slice of bread. Spread table-spoonfuls of filling over half of the bread; top with remaining bread. Garnish with dill if desired. **Yield:** about 16 sandwiches.

Pot o' Gold Potato Soup

This golden soup may not be what you expect to find at the end of the rainbow, but you'll treasure its rich flavor.

    3/4 cup chopped celery
    3/4 cup chopped onion
    1/4 cup butter *or* margarine
        2 cans (14-1/2 ounces *each*) chicken broth
    2-1/3 cups mashed potato flakes
    1-1/2 cups milk
    1/2 cup cubed process American cheese
    3/4 teaspoon garlic salt
    1/8 to 1/4 teaspoon chili powder
    1/2 cup sour cream

In a 3-qt. saucepan, saute celery and onion in butter for 2-3 minutes. Stir in broth; bring to boil. Reduce heat. Add potato flakes; cook and stir for 5-7 minutes. Add milk, cheese, garlic salt and chili powder. Cook and stir until cheese is melted. Just before serving, add sour cream and heat through (do not boil). **Yield:** 6 servings.

Blarney Stone Bars

A lip-smacking layer of tinted frosting is the crowning touch to these butterscotch bars laden with pecans.

    1/2 cup butter *or* margarine, softened
    3/4 cup packed brown sugar
        2 eggs
        1 tablespoon milk
        1 teaspoon vanilla extract
    3/4 cup all-purpose flour
    3/4 cup quick-cooking oats
    1/2 teaspoon baking powder
    1/4 teaspoon salt
    3/4 cup English toffee bits
    1/3 cup chopped pecans
        4 drops green food coloring
    3/4 cup vanilla frosting

In a mixing bowl, cream butter and sugar. Beat in eggs, milk and vanilla. Combine flour, oats, baking powder and salt; add to the creamed mixture. Fold in the toffee bits and pecans. Spread into a greased 9-in. square baking pan. Bake at 350° for 20-24 minutes or until a tooth-pick comes out clean. Cool on a wire rack. Add food coloring to frosting; spread over the bars. Cut into dia-mond shapes. **Yield:** about 3-1/2 dozen.

Leprechaun Lime Drink

Cheery garnishes can be fixed in a wink to dress up each guest's glass of this refreshing beverage.

✓ Uses less fat, sugar or salt. Includes Nutritional Analysis and Diabetic Exchanges.

        1 quart lime sherbet, softened
    1/2 cup limeade concentrate
        2 tablespoons sugar
        2 cans (12 ounces *each*) lemon-lime soda, chilled
        1 to 2 cups crushed ice

In a mixing bowl, blend sherbet, limeade and sugar. Stir in soda and ice. Pour into glasses. Garnish if desired (see the box below). **Yield:** 7 cups. **Nutritional Analysis:** One 1-cup serving (prepared with sugar-free sherbet and diet soda) equals 209 calories, 62 mg sodium, 6 mg cholesterol, 49 gm carbohydrate, 1 gm protein, 2 gm fat. **Diabetic Exchanges:** 3 fruit, 1/2 fat.

Slice Sunny Citrus Garnishes

- To make lemon wheels, use a citrus stripper, large zester or sharp paring knife to make evenly spaced vertical matches around a lemon. Cut the lemon into 1/8-inch slices. Make one cut from the center of each slice through the peel to place over rim of glass.

- To make lime spirals, use a vegetable peeler to remove the peel of a lime in one continuous spiral motion, working from end to end. Us-ing a sharp knife or scissors, trim the edges of the peel so it's uni-form in width. Cut in-to 1/8-inch strips; wind strips tightly around a skew-er, securing with a stick pin. Drape over rim of glass.

Backyard Banquet
Is for the Birds

FEELING cooped up? Don't let spring fever get the best of you. Celebrate the season with these delightful dishes. They are sure to become fast favorites at a lively ladies' luncheon, a backyard garden party or a bird-themed bash.

Bird's Nest Egg Salad

Create these cute chow mein noodle nests with just three ingredients, then fill them with mounds of a nicely seasoned egg salad for tasty results.

   1 egg
   3 cups chow mein noodles
1/4 teaspoon garlic salt
EGG SALAD:
   6 hard-cooked eggs, chopped
1/3 cup mayonnaise
1/3 cup finely chopped celery
   2 tablespoons finely chopped onion
   2 tablespoons minced fresh parsley
1-1/2 teaspoons ground mustard
1/2 teaspoon lemon juice
1/4 teaspoon seasoned salt
Lettuce leaves, optional

In a small bowl, beat egg. Add chow mein noodles and garlic salt; stir to coat. Drop by 1/3 cupfuls onto a greased baking sheet. Using fingers, shape each into a nest; make an indentation in the center of each. Bake at 350° for 11-13 minutes or until set. Cool for 2 minutes; remove to a wire rack to cool completely. In a bowl, combine the first eight egg salad ingredients; mix well. Just before serving, spoon 1/4 cupful into each nest. Serve on a lettuce-lined plate if desired. **Yield:** 6 servings.

Birdhouse Bread

Dried rosemary and thyme give a tasty herb flavor and a rustic outdoor appearance to this buttery snack bread.

   2 tablespoons butter *or* margarine
   1 teaspoon beef bouillon granules
1/4 teaspoon garlic powder
   1 tube (11 ounces) refrigerated breadsticks
   1 to 2 tablespoons dried rosemary
1/2 teaspoon dried thyme

In a small saucepan over low heat, melt butter. Stir in bouillon and garlic powder. Remove from the heat; let stand until bouillon is dissolved. Meanwhile, unroll breadsticks and separate into 12 sticks. Place eight sticks lengthwise side by side on a greased baking sheet.

"Painting" with Egg Yolks

Before baking the cookies, decorate them with a glaze made of food coloring, egg yolk and water, using a small new paintbrush to apply the glaze. If glaze thickens, stir in a few drops of water.

Place another breadstick along the bottom of the house, stretching dough as needed. To create the entrance, move two center sticks so they extend 2 in. above the other sticks. To form the roof, place two of the remaining sticks on top of the house so they extend about 1 in. beyond the sides. Cut remaining breadstick as needed to fill spaces beneath the roof. Gently pinch edges of breadsticks together to seal seams. Brush with the butter mixture; sprinkle with rosemary and thyme. Bake at 375° for 11-13 minutes or until lightly browned. Cool for 2 minutes before carefully transferring to a serving platter. **Yield:** 6 servings.

Swift Strawberry Salad

A simple blend of syrup, orange juice and caramel topping forms the light dressing for the fresh berries and the crunchy cashews found in this sensational salad.

   4 cups sliced fresh strawberries
   2 tablespoons caramel ice cream topping
   2 tablespoons maple syrup
   1 tablespoon orange juice
1/3 cup cashew halves

Place strawberries in a serving bowl. Combine caramel topping, syrup and orange juice; mix well. Drizzle over strawberries. Sprinkle with cashews. **Yield:** 4-6 servings.

Feathered Friend Cookies

Let your imagination soar as egg yolk glaze transforms plain sugar cookies into fanciful winged wonders.

1/2 cup butter *or* margarine, softened
1/4 cup shortening
   1 cup sugar
   2 eggs
   2 tablespoons sour cream
   1 teaspoon vanilla extract
1/4 teaspoon almond extract
2-3/4 cups all-purpose flour
1-1/2 teaspoons baking powder
   1 teaspoon salt
GLAZE:
   4 to 6 egg yolks
   1 to 1-1/2 teaspoons water
Paste food coloring

In a mixing bowl, cream butter, shortening and sugar. Beat in eggs, sour cream and extracts. Combine flour, baking powder and salt; add to the creamed mixture and mix well. Chill for about 1 hour or until easy to handle. On a floured surface, roll out dough to 1/4-in. thickness. Cut with a 4-in. bird cookie cutter. Place 1 in. apart on ungreased baking sheets. For each color of glaze, beat 1 egg yolk and 1/4 teaspoon water in a custard cup; tint with paste food coloring. Decorate cookies as desired (see tip box at left). Bake at 375° for 7-9 minutes or until edges are lightly browned. Cool for 1-2 minutes before removing to wire racks. **Yield:** 3-1/2 dozen. **Editor's Note:** Any sugar cookie dough can be used to make these cookies.

Walk on the
Wild Side

EXPLORING ideas for a birthday bash, preteen party, club meeting or other special event? Animal lovers of all ages will go wild over this zoo-inspired menu.

Lazy Lion Melt

We're not lyin' when we say youngsters will love these open-face turkey and cheese sandwiches. If you don't think your guests will each eat a whole sandwich, place the turkey slices on the lion's head, omitting the rest of the body and creating the face as directed.

    1 to 2 tablespoons mayonnaise
    1 to 2 tablespoons prepared mustard
    2 carrot slices (1/8 inch thick)
    3 hamburger buns, split
    6 slices process Swiss cheese
    12 ripe olive slices
    12 pimiento slices
    6 hot dog buns, split
    6 thin slices cooked turkey *or* other deli meat
    12 slices process American cheese
    1 cup (4 ounces) shredded cheddar cheese
    18 potato sticks
Shredded lettuce, optional

Combine mayonnaise and mustard; set aside. Cut each carrot slice into three triangles; set aside. For each lion, place half of a hamburger bun, cut side up, on an ungreased baking sheet (three lions per sheet). Spread with a small amount of the mayonnaise mixture. Top with a slice of Swiss cheese. Add two olives for eyes, a carrot triangle for nose and two pimientos for mouth. Position the top half of a hot dog bun, cut side up, below head for body. Spread with mayonnaise mixture. Top with turkey and American cheese, cutting to fit the bun. For the tail, slice 1/2 in. from one end of the hot dog bun bottom (see Fig. 1). Cut remaining portion into four 2-1/4-in. strips for legs. Position the legs and tail with cut side up; spread with mayonnaise mixture. Cut one slice of American cheese into strips to fit over legs and tail. Place over the mayonnaise mixture, tucking under cheese on the body. Broil 6 in. from the heat until cheese is slightly melted and the lion holds its shape, about 2 minutes. Sprinkle shredded cheese on the end of the tail and around head. Broil 30 seconds longer or until cheese is melted. Transfer to a serving plate. Add potato sticks for whiskers. If desired, add lettuce under legs for grass. **Yield:** 6 servings.

Fig. 1
Cutting bun

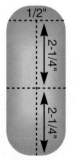

Perky Olive Penguins

These tuxedo-clad tidbits are actually ripe olives stuffed with a subtly seasoned cream cheese filling.

    1 can (5-3/4 ounces) jumbo pitted ripe olives, drained
    1 package (3 ounces) cream cheese, softened
    1/2 teaspoon dried minced onion
    1/4 teaspoon prepared horseradish

    1/8 teaspoon salt
Dash pepper
Dash garlic powder
    1 medium carrot, cut into 1/4-inch slices
    12 small pitted ripe olives
    12 toothpicks with cellophane frilled tops
    1 jar (2 ounces) sliced pimientos

Cut a slit from the top to bottom of 12 jumbo olives; set aside. In a mixing bowl, combine the next six ingredients; mix well. Fill a small heavy-duty plastic bag with cream cheese mixture. Cut a small hole in the corner of the bag; carefully pipe mixture into jumbo olives. Set aside. Cut a small triangle out of each carrot slice; press triangles into small olives for a beak. On each notched carrot slice, position a jumbo olive so the white chest is lined up with the notch. Place the small olive, hole side down, over the jumbo olive so the beak, chest and feet are aligned. Carefully insert a toothpick through the top of head into body and carrot base. Wrap a pimiento around neck for a scarf. **Yield:** 1 dozen.

Zebra Sweets

A horse-shaped cookie cutter is the key to these tasty treats made with marshmallows and crisp rice cereal. Melted vanilla and chocolate chips create the eye-catching stripes.

    8 cups miniature marshmallows
    6 tablespoons butter *or* margarine
    12 cups crisp rice cereal
    1 cup vanilla chips
    1 teaspoon shortening, *divided*
    1 cup semisweet chocolate chips

In a Dutch oven or large saucepan, heat marshmallows and butter until almost melted. Remove from the heat; stir in cereal and mix well. Press firmly into a greased 15-in. x 10-in. x 1-in. baking pan. Cut with a horse-shaped cookie cutter. Remove cutouts to waxed paper; set aside. In a microwave or double boiler, melt vanilla chips and 1/2 teaspoon shortening. Spread over cutouts. Let dry on waxed paper. Melt chocolate chips and remaining shortening; place in a heavy-duty plastic bag. Cut a small hole in the corner of the bag; pipe mane, stripes, hooves, etc. on zebras. **Yield:** about 1 dozen.

Monkey Lover's Shakes

This cool beverage is smooth, creamy and gets its tropical taste from bananas and orange juice concentrate.

1-1/4 cups milk
    2 medium ripe bananas, sliced 1/4 inch thick and frozen
    2 cups vanilla ice cream
    1/3 cup orange juice concentrate
    2 to 3 tablespoons sugar
    2 to 3 drops yellow food coloring, optional

In a blender, combine all ingredients. Cover and process for 45 seconds or until smooth. Stir if necessary. Pour into glasses and serve. **Yield:** 4 servings.

Hearty Harvest Supper

AUTUMN is an excellent time to gather family and friends around the warmth of your table to celebrate the season. To make your get-together special, try this crop of crowd-pleasing ideas that capture the rich flavors and colors of fall.

Harvest Stew

This warming stew features tasty golden squash, moist tender pork and sweet apples for an interesting change of pace from traditional beef stew.

1-1/2 pounds boneless pork, cut into 1-inch cubes
   1 medium onion, chopped
   2 garlic cloves, minced
   2 tablespoons butter *or* margarine
   3 cups chicken broth
  3/4 teaspoon salt
  1/4 teaspoon dried rosemary, crushed
  1/4 teaspoon rubbed sage
   1 bay leaf
   1 medium butternut squash, peeled and cubed
    (3 cups)
   2 medium apples, peeled and cubed

In a large saucepan, cook the pork, onion and garlic in the butter until meat is no longer pink; drain. Add the broth, salt, rosemary, sage and bay leaf. Cover and simmer for 20 minutes. Add squash and apples; simmer, uncovered, for 20 minutes or until squash and apples are tender. Discard bay leaf. **Yield:** 6 servings.

Bacon Bean Stalks

You'll need just three ingredients to assemble this fun fall side dish. Wax beans are bundled with bacon strips to look like shocks of cornstalks.

   1 pound fresh wax *or* green beans
   6 bacon strips
  1/4 teaspoon onion powder

Place beans in a saucepan and cover with water; bring to a boil. Cook, uncovered, for 8 minutes or until crisp-tender. Meanwhile, in a skillet or microwave, cook bacon until partially cooked, about 3 minutes; drain on paper towels. Drain beans; place about 12 beans on each bacon strip. Position one end of beans so they are nearly even; cut about 1/4 in. from that end so stalks will stand when served. Wrap bacon strip around beans; secure with a toothpick. Lay stalks flat on an ungreased baking sheet. Sprinkle with onion powder. Bake, uncovered, at 400° for 10-15 minutes or until bacon is crisp. **Yield:** 6 servings.

Maple Leaf Biscuits

These corn bread biscuits not only have a pretty maple leaf shape, but a mild maple flavor and glossy sheen from a syrup and butter mixture brushed on top.

1-1/2 cups all-purpose flour
  1/2 cup cornmeal
   1 tablespoon baking powder
   1 teaspoon sugar
  1/2 teaspoon salt
  1/2 teaspoon cream of tartar
  1/3 cup shortening
  2/3 cup milk
   1 tablespoon butter *or* margarine, melted
   1 tablespoon maple syrup

In a bowl, combine flour, cornmeal, baking powder, sugar, salt and cream of tartar. Cut in shortening until mixture resembles coarse crumbs. Stir in milk just until moistened. Turn onto a floured surface; lightly knead 10-12 times. Roll or pat to 1/2-in. thickness. Cut with a 2-1/2-in. maple leaf cookie cutter or a biscuit cutter. Place on a lightly greased baking sheet. Combine butter and syrup; lightly brush over tops of biscuits. Bake at 425° for 10-12 minutes or until golden brown. Brush with remaining syrup mixture. **Yield:** about 1-1/2 dozen.

Truffle Acorns

Neighborhood squirrels will be envious when you serve these darling acorn-shaped chocolates. The nuts are a nice finishing touch that complements the almond extract in the rich truffles.

   2 cups (12 ounces) semisweet chocolate chips
   1 package (3 ounces) cream cheese, softened
   1 teaspoon water
  1/2 teaspoon almond extract
  1/4 cup dark chocolate candy coating* (about
    1/8 pound)
  1/3 cup finely chopped almonds, toasted
Slivered almonds

Melt chocolate chips in a microwave or double boiler. Stir in cream cheese, water and extract until well blended. Chill for 1 hour or until easy to handle. Shape teaspoonfuls into slightly oblong balls with one flatter end; place on a waxed paper-lined baking sheet. Refrigerate for 1-2 hours or until firm. In microwave or double boiler, melt candy coating. Dip the flat end of each acorn about 1/8 in. into the chocolate, then dip in chopped almonds (see box below). Insert a slivered almond into the top for a stem. Return to waxed paper to harden. **Yield:** about 3 dozen. ***Editor's Note:** Candy coating, the product used for dipping chocolate, is found in the baking section of most grocery stores. It is often sold in bulk packages of 1 to 1-1/2 pounds.

Creating Truffle Acorns

Once the acorn-shaped chocolates have chilled and are firm, dip the flat end into melted candy coating, then into the chopped almonds to form an acorn cap. Insert a slivered almond into each for a stem.

Merry Christmas Menu

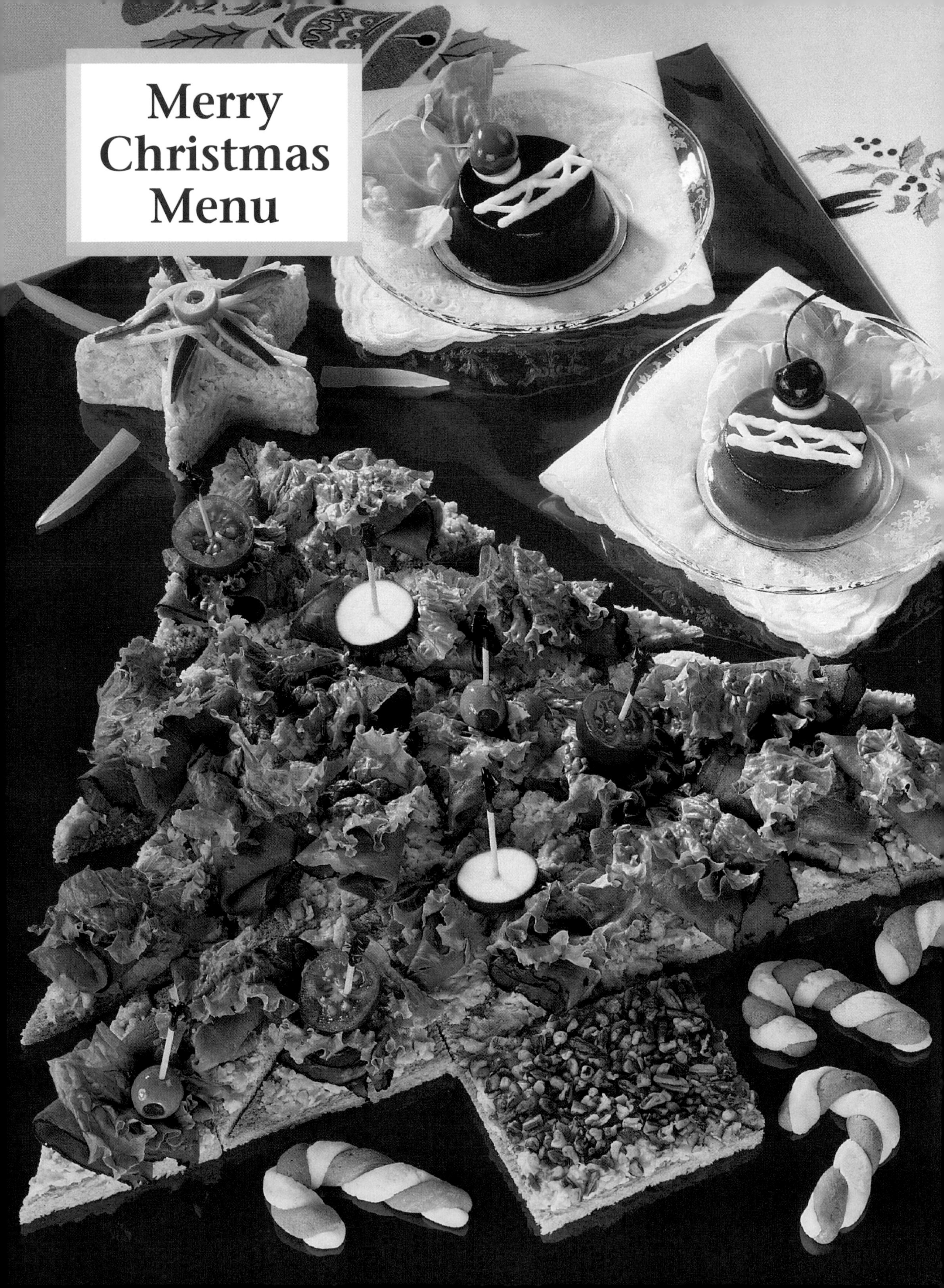

DECORATING the Christmas tree is a special holiday tradition for many families. Why not share the joy by inviting friends to join in on the fun?

"Yule" love these dishes that give you and your guests the freedom to snack while decorating.

Starry Cheese Spread

This creamy mixture is terrific served with crackers, raw veggies or on the appetizers that make up the tempting Party Sandwich Tree.

        6 cups (24 ounces) shredded sharp cheddar
           cheese
        1 package (3 ounces) cream cheese, softened
    1/4 cup butter *or* margarine, softened
        2 tablespoons prepared horseradish
    2/3 cup apple juice
        2 tablespoons chopped stuffed olives
Sliced pimientos, yellow pepper strips and one
    stuffed olive slice

In a mixing bowl, beat cheeses, butter, horseradish, apple juice and olives on low speed for 1 minute. Beat on high until almost smooth. Press 3/4 cup into a 4-in. star-shaped mold coated with nonstick cooking spray. Cover and chill for 3 hours or until set. Refrigerate remaining cheese mixture for another use or for the Party Sandwich Tree. Run a sharp knife around mold to loosen cheese spread and unmold. Garnish with pimientos, peppers and olive. **Yield:** about 3-3/4 cups.

Party Sandwich Tree

Cherry tomatoes, radish slices and green olives decorate this festive fir formed by arranging open-face sandwich triangles. An assortment of meats and cheese spreads can be used to suit varying tastes.

       11 slices thin rye bread
        3 cups Starry Cheese Spread (recipe above)
           or cheese spread of your choice
Chopped pecans
       10 slices deli roast beef, halved
Leaf lettuce
Stuffed olives, halved cherry tomatoes and sliced
    radishes

Cut each slice of bread into a 3-1/2-in. x 3-in. rectangle, removing crusts. Spread with cheese spread. Cut each rectangle in half diagonally, forming triangles. On a 24-in. x 18-in. serving tray or covered board, form the tree (see diagram below). Near the top, place two bread triangles 1/2 in. apart with 3-in. sides facing. (Leave room at the top of the tray for the Starry Cheese Spread mold if desired.) For the second, third and fourth rows, place two triangles with long sides together to form six rectangles as shown at left. Place a triangle on either side of rectangles. Center two remaining triangles

Forming the tree

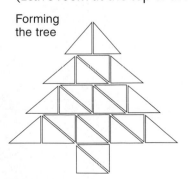

under last row for trunk; sprinkle with pecans. Top the rest of the triangles with beef and lettuce. Add olive, tomato and radish "ornaments" with toothpicks. **Yield:** 22 appetizers.

Candy Cane Cookies

These mild mint cookies are easy to form once you color the dough—just roll into ropes and twist together.

    1/2 cup butter (no substitutes), softened
    1/2 cup shortening
        1 cup sugar
    1/4 cup confectioners' sugar
    1/2 cup milk
        1 egg
        1 teaspoon peppermint extract
        1 teaspoon vanilla extract
    3-1/2 cups all-purpose flour
    1/4 teaspoon salt
Green and red food coloring

In a bowl, cream butter, shortening and sugars. Beat in milk, egg and extracts. Gradually add flour and salt. Set aside half of the dough. Divide remaining dough in half; add green food coloring to one portion and red food coloring to the other. Wrap dough separately in plastic wrap. Refrigerate for 1 hour or until easy to handle. Roll 1/2 teaspoonfuls of each color of dough into 3-in. ropes. Place each green rope next to a white rope; press together gently and twist. Repeat with red ropes and remaining white ropes. Place 2 in. apart on ungreased baking sheets. Curve one end, forming a cane. Bake at 350° for 11-13 minutes or until set. Cool for 2 minutes; carefully remove to wire racks. **Yield:** about 6 dozen.

Gelatin Christmas Ornaments

Muffin tins are the key to making these individual gelatin salads. Once chilled, they're easy to embellish with mayonnaise, sour cream or whipped cream. Maraschino cherries with stems give the look of wire hangers.

    3-1/4 cups white grape juice
        1 package (6 ounces) lime gelatin
        1 package (6 ounces) raspberry gelatin
        6 *each* red and green maraschino cherries with
           stems
Mayonnaise, sour cream *or* whipped cream in a can

In a saucepan, bring grape juice to a boil. Place lime gelatin in a bowl; add half of the juice and stir until completely dissolved. Repeat with raspberry gelatin. Pour lime gelatin into six muffin cups (about 1/3 cup in each) coated with nonstick cooking spray. Repeat, filling six more cups with raspberry gelatin. Refrigerate for 4 hours or until firm. Loosen gelatin around the edges with a sharp knife; invert muffin tin onto waxed paper. Use a metal spatula to transfer to serving plates. Fill a small plastic bag with mayonnaise; cut a small hole in corner of bag. Pipe a small circle near one edge of each ornament; place cherry in center. Decorate ornaments with additional mayonnaise if desired. **Yield:** 1 dozen.

Chapter 4

TODAY'S cooks are pressed for time in the kitchen. So they're always searching for ways to make wholesome foods for their families in a hurry.

They know that fewer ingredients means faster meals (and less mess to clean up!).

But you don't need to sacrifice flavor when you steer clear of long lists of ingredients.

This chapter's delicious entrccs, salads, snacks, beverages, side dishes and desserts feature just five ingredients—or fewer. So they're a snap to prepare.

But while they're short on ingredients, each and every one is long on flavor!

LESS IS MORE. Clockwise from upper right: Honey-Dijon Ham, Creamy Sweet Corn and Macaroon Bars (all recipes on p. 54).

Home-Style Potatoes

This is a deliciously different way to prepare potatoes, and it's so easy. If there happen to be any leftovers, they're just as good the next day.
—June Formanek
Belle Plaine, Iowa

- 6 medium potatoes, sliced 1/4 inch thick
- 3/4 cup water
- 1/2 cup butter *or* margarine
- 1 envelope onion soup mix
- 1/2 teaspoon dried rosemary, crushed

Place potatoes in a greased 2-qt. baking dish. In a saucepan, combine water, butter, soup mix and rosemary; heat until butter is melted. Pour over potatoes. Cover and bake at 350° for 40 minutes. Uncover; bake 20 minutes longer or until the potatoes are tender. **Yield:** 6-8 servings.

Quick Crab Mornay

This recipe blends together a rich, cheesy sauce that showcases canned crab meat. The creamy mixture can be served with toast points for a special lunch or over chicken, rice or potatoes for a distinctive dinner. —Geneva Schmidtka
Canandaigua, New York

- 1 can (10-3/4 ounces) condensed cream of chicken soup, undiluted
- 1/3 cup white wine *or* chicken broth
- 1 egg, lightly beaten
- 1 can (6 ounces) crabmeat, drained, flaked and cartilage removed
- 1/2 cup shredded cheddar cheese

In a small saucepan, combine soup and wine or broth. Cook and stir over medium heat until blended and heated through. Stir 1/2 cupful into the egg; return all to the pan. Place the crab in a greased shallow 1-qt. baking dish; top with soup mixture. Sprinkle with cheese. Bake, uncovered, at 350° for 20 minutes or until the top is lightly browned and cheese is melted. **Yield:** 4-6 servings.

Butterscotch Snack Cake

Handy pantry ingredients, including cake and pudding mixes, are the key to this moist, golden cake. It has a chewy, nutty topping and big butterscotch flavor.
—Joanie Ward, Brownsburg, Indiana

- 1 package (3.5 ounces) cook-and-serve butterscotch pudding
- 2 cups milk
- 1 package (18-1/4 ounces) yellow cake mix
- 1 package (11 ounces) butterscotch baking chips
- 1/2 cup chopped pecans *or* walnuts

In a large saucepan, combine pudding mix and milk. Bring to a boil over medium heat, stirring constantly. Remove from the heat; stir in dry cake mix. Pour into a greased 13-in. x 9-in. x 2-in. baking pan. Sprinkle with butterscotch chips and nuts. Bake at 350° for 35-40 minutes or until a toothpick inserted near the center comes out clean. Cool on a wire rack. **Yield:** 12-16 servings.

Apricot Cashew Clusters

Guests will enjoy the fruity surprise they find in these scrumptious nut candies. I make them often because they can be whipped up in no time. Everyone will love the unusual combination.
—Pamela Wagner
Madison, Wisconsin

- 1 package (11-1/2 ounces) milk chocolate chips
- 1 cup chopped dried apricots
- 1 cup chopped salted cashews

In a microwave or double boiler, melt the chocolate chips; stir until smooth. Stir in apricots and cashews. Drop by rounded tablespoonfuls onto waxed paper-lined baking sheets. Chill until set, about 15 minutes. Store in an airtight container. **Yield:** 2-1/2 dozen.

Sausage Green Bean Bake

You can make and bake this saucy dish in less than an hour. The Italian sausage really makes it a treat. I sometimes serve it over noodles for a complete meal.
—Mary Detweiler, West Farmington, Ohio

- 1 jar (28 ounces) spaghetti sauce
- 1-1/2 pounds Italian sausage links, cooked and cut into 1/2-inch pieces
- 1 package (16 ounces) frozen cut green beans
- 2 jars (4-1/2 ounces *each*) sliced mushrooms, drained
- 2 cups (8 ounces) shredded mozzarella cheese

In a large bowl, combine the spaghetti sauce, sausage, beans and mushrooms; mix well. Transfer to a greased 13-in. x 9-in. x 2-in. baking dish; sprinkle with mozzarella cheese. Bake, uncovered, at 350° for 40-45 minutes or until cheese is melted. **Yield:** 6 servings.

Chocolate Peanut Treats
(Pictured above right)

When I was in high school, I took these sweet and crunchy squares to bake sales—they were the first to go. I still make them for family and friends who love the classic combination of chocolate and peanut butter.
—Christy Asher, Colorado Springs, Colorado

- 3/4 cup graham cracker crumbs (about 12 squares)
- 1/2 cup butter *or* margarine, melted
- 2 cups confectioners' sugar
- 1/2 cup chunky peanut butter
- 1 cup (6 ounces) semisweet chocolate chips

In a bowl, combine cracker crumbs and butter; mix well. Stir in sugar and peanut butter. Press into a greased 8-in. square pan. In a microwave or double boiler, melt the chocolate chips and stir until smooth. Spread over

Chocolate Peanut Treats
Beefy Biscuit Cups
Baked Hash Browns

peanut butter layer. Chill for 30 minutes; cut into squares. Chill until firm, about 30 minutes longer. Store in the refrigerator. **Yield:** about 2 dozen.

for 15-17 minutes or until golden brown. Sprinkle with cheese; bake 3 minutes longer or until the cheese is melted. **Yield:** 8 servings.

Beefy Biscuit Cups

(Pictured above)

On-the-go families will love these hand-held pizzas. They're made in a wink with convenient refrigerated biscuits and a jar of prepared spaghetti sauce.
—*Kimberly Leddon, St. Marys, Georgia*

- 1 pound ground beef
- 1 jar (14 ounces) spaghetti sauce
- 2 tubes (8 ounces *each*) large refrigerated biscuits
- 1 cup (4 ounces) shredded cheddar cheese

In a skillet, brown beef; drain. Stir in the spaghetti sauce; cook over medium heat for 5-10 minutes or until heated through. Press biscuits onto the bottom and up the sides of greased muffin cups. Spoon 2 tablespoonfuls meat mixture into the center of each cup. Bake at 375°

Baked Hash Browns

(Pictured above)

Mother always served this creamy, satisfying potato dish to company, and now I do, too. It tastes especially good with roast beef.   —*Julie Driskel, Magnolia, Arkansas*

- 8 frozen hash brown patties
- 1 teaspoon salt
- 1/2 teaspoon garlic powder
- 1 cup whipping cream
- 1 cup (4 ounces) shredded cheddar cheese

Place the patties in a greased 13-in. x 9-in. x 2-in. baking dish. Sprinkle with salt and garlic powder. Pour cream over patties. Bake, uncovered, at 350° for 50 minutes. Sprinkle with the cheese. Bake 5-10 minutes longer or until the potatoes are tender and cheese is melted. **Yield:** 8 servings.

Macaroon Bars
Honey-Dijon Ham
Creamy Sweet Corn

Creamy Sweet Corn

(Pictured above and on page 50)

I use cream to dress up fresh or frozen corn. The simple side dish tastes rich and takes just minutes to simmer together. —Florence Jacoby, Granite Falls, Minnesota

    2 cups fresh or frozen corn
  1/4 cup half-and-half cream
    2 tablespoons butter or margarine
    1 tablespoon sugar
  1/2 teaspoon salt

In a saucepan, combine all ingredients. Bring to a boil over medium heat; reduce heat. Simmer, uncovered, for 6-8 minutes or until heated through. **Yield:** 4 servings.

Honey-Dijon Ham

(Pictured above and on page 51)

Your family will think you took hours to prepare this delicious ham. The tasty glaze combines honey, brown sugar and mustard. —Karin Young, Carlsbad, California

    1 boneless fully cooked ham (about 3 pounds)
  1/3 cup honey
    2 tablespoons Dijon mustard
    2 tablespoons brown sugar
    1 tablespoon water

Place ham on a greased rack in a shallow roasting pan. Bake, uncovered, at 325° for 50-60 minutes. Combine honey, mustard and sugar; brush about 3 tablespoonfuls over ham. Bake 10-15 minutes longer or until a meat thermometer reads 140° and ham is heated through. Stir water into remaining glaze; heat through and serve with the ham. **Yield:** 8-10 servings.

Macaroon Bars

(Pictured above and on page 50)

Guests will never recognize the refrigerated crescent roll dough in these bars. —Carolyn Kyzer, Alexander, Arkansas

3-1/4 cups flaked coconut, *divided*
    1 can (14 ounces) sweetened condensed milk

1 teaspoon almond extract
1 tube (8 ounces) refrigerated crescent rolls

Sprinkle 1-1/2 cups coconut into a well-greased 13-in. x 9-in. x 2-in. baking pan. Combine milk and extract; drizzle half over the coconut. Unroll crescent dough; arrange in a single layer over coconut. Drizzle with remaining milk mixture; sprinkle with remaining coconut. Bake at 350° for 30-35 minutes or until golden brown. Cool completely before cutting. Store in the refrigerator. **Yield:** 3 dozen.

Salmon Cheese Spread

Pickle relish livens up canned salmon in this deliciously different sandwich filling. The fast-to-fix spread is good on crackers, too.   —Mrs. Dale Cocklin, Kasilof, Alaska

1 package (3 ounces) cream cheese, softened
1 can (7-1/2 ounces) salmon, drained, bones and skin removed
1/3 cup shredded cheddar cheese
1/4 cup sweet pickle relish
Bread *or* crackers

In a bowl, combine the first four ingredients. Use as a sandwich spread or serve on crackers. **Yield:** 1 cup.

Sunday Chicken and Stuffing

This hearty entree is a surefire family pleaser. It's easy to prepare because you don't have to brown the chicken. Plus it looks so nice you can serve it to company.
—Charlotte Kidd, Lagrange, Ohio

1 package (6 ounces) instant chicken stuffing mix
6 boneless skinless chicken breast halves
1 can (10-3/4 ounces) condensed cream of chicken soup, undiluted
1/3 cup milk
1 tablespoon dried parsley flakes

Prepare stuffing according to package directions; spoon down the center of a greased 13-in. x 9-in. x 2-in. baking dish. Place chicken around stuffing. Combine soup, milk and parsley; pour over chicken. Cover and bake at 400° for 20 minutes. Uncover and bake 10-15 minutes longer or until chicken juices run clear. **Yield:** 6 servings.

Stewed Tomato Pasta

I'm the mother of two very active boys, and this flavorful dish is one they'll always eat. Another reason I love it is I usually have the ingredients on hand.   —Tracey Jones Chesapeake, Virginia

✓ Uses less fat, sugar or salt. Includes Nutritional Analysis and Diabetic Exchanges.

2 cans (14-1/2 ounces *each*) Italian stewed tomatoes, undrained
1 can (14-1/2 ounces) chicken broth
2 tablespoons vegetable oil

1 teaspoon Italian seasoning
1 package (12 ounces) spiral pasta

In a large saucepan or Dutch oven, combine the tomatoes, broth, oil and Italian seasoning; bring to a boil. Add pasta. Reduce heat; cover and simmer for 16-18 minutes or until pasta is tender, stirring occasionally. **Yield:** 8-10 servings. **Nutritional Analysis:** One 3/4-cup serving (prepared with low-sodium broth) equals 217 calories, 243 mg sodium, 1 mg cholesterol, 37 gm carbohydrate, 6 gm protein, 5 gm fat. **Diabetic Exchanges:** 2 starch, 1 vegetable, 1 fat.

Warm Fruit Compote

Orange marmalade is the secret to the easy sauce that I spoon over canned pineapple and fresh grapes. I then sprinkle the combination with coconut and broil it to create a warm, fruity surprise.
—Doris Heath Franklin, North Carolina

✓ Uses less fat, sugar or salt. Includes Nutritional Analysis and Diabetic Exchanges.

1 can (20 ounces) unsweetened pineapple chunks
2 cups seedless grapes
3 tablespoons orange marmalade
4 teaspoons flaked coconut

Drain pineapple, reserving 2/3 cup juice. Combine the pineapple and grapes in a shallow 1-qt. broiler-proof dish. In a saucepan, combine marmalade and reserved pineapple juice; cook over medium heat until the marmalade is melted. Pour over fruit. Sprinkle with coconut. Broil 5-6 in. from the heat for 3 minutes or until coconut is toasted. **Yield:** 4 servings. **Nutritional Analysis:** One 1-cup serving (prepared with reduced-sugar marmalade) equals 168 calories, 7 mg sodium, 0 cholesterol, 43 gm carbohydrate, 1 gm protein, 1 gm fat. **Diabetic Exchange:** 3 fruit.

Cookie Brittle

This recipe originally called for chocolate chips, but my family and friends like it better when I use peanut butter chips.   —Betty Byrnes Consbruck, Gainesville, Florida

1 cup butter (no substitutes), softened
1 cup sugar
2 cups all-purpose flour
1-1/4 cups peanut butter chips
1/2 cup coarsely chopped pecans

In a mixing bowl, cream the butter and sugar. Gradually add flour; mix well. Stir in peanut butter chips. Line a 15-in. x 10-in. x 1-in. baking pan with foil; coat with non-stick cooking spray. Gently press dough into the pan; sprinkle with pecans and press into dough. Bake at 350° for 20-25 minutes or until golden brown. Cool in pan on a wire rack. Invert pan and remove foil. Break brittle into pieces; store in an airtight container. **Yield:** about 4 dozen.

Lemon-Berry Pitcher Punch

(Pictured below right)

If you need to satisfy a large group, you can double or triple the recipe for this refreshing beverage. The tangy combination of lemonade and cranberry juice is a real thirst-quencher on a warm day.
—*Margaret O'Bryon, Bel Air, Maryland*

- 1/2 cup sweetened lemonade drink mix
- 4 cups cold water
- 2/3 cup cranberry juice, chilled
- 1-1/2 cups lemon-lime soda, chilled

In a pitcher, combine drink mix, water and cranberry juice. Stir in soda. Serve immediately. **Yield:** about 6 cups.

Dressed-Up Broccoli

Only four ingredients turn ordinary broccoli into a dressed-up side dish. The garlic in the broiled crumb topping really comes through. —*Bryan Forster, Clayton, Ontario*

✓ Uses less fat, sugar or salt. Includes Nutritional Analysis and Diabetic Exchanges.

- 3-1/2 cups broccoli florets
- 3 tablespoons dry bread crumbs
- 2 tablespoons grated Parmesan cheese
- 1 tablespoon butter *or* margarine, melted
- 2 to 3 garlic cloves, minced

Place broccoli and a small amount of water in a microwave- and broiler-safe 1-1/2-qt. dish. Cover and microwave on high until crisp-tender, about 6 minutes; drain. Combine remaining ingredients; sprinkle over broccoli. Broil for 4-5 minutes or until lightly browned. **Yield:** 7 servings. **Nutritional Analysis:** One 1/2-cup serving (prepared with margarine) equals 45 calories, 89 mg sodium, 1 mg cholesterol, 4 gm carbohydrate, 2 gm protein, 2 gm fat. **Diabetic Exchanges:** 1 vegetable, 1/2 fat. **Editor's Note:** This recipe was tested in an 850-watt microwave.

Noodle Pepperoni Pizza

My family would eat wedges of this great-tasting skillet dinner without any complaint several nights a week. I love it because it's inexpensive and can be made in a snap.
—*Gayle Lizotte, Merrimack, New Hampshire*

- 4 packages (3 ounces *each*) ramen noodles
- 1 tablespoon olive *or* vegetable oil
- 1 cup spaghetti *or* pizza sauce
- 1 cup (4 ounces) shredded mozzarella cheese
- 1 package (3 ounces) sliced pepperoni, cut into strips

Discard seasoning packets from noodles or save for another use. Cook noodles according to package directions; drain. Heat oil in a 10-in. ovenproof skillet. Press noodles into skillet, evenly covering the bottom of pan.

Cook until bottom of crust is lightly browned, about 5 minutes. Pour spaghetti sauce over the crust. Sprinkle with cheese and pepperoni. Broil 4 to 6 in. from the heat for 3-4 minutes or until heated through and cheese is melted. **Yield:** 4-6 servings.

Malted Milk Pie

Malted milk balls provide the delightful flavor you'll find in each cool bite of this light dessert. It's easy to assemble and a longtime favorite of my family.
—*Jann Marie Foster, Minneapolis, Minnesota*

- 1 package (7 ounces) malted milk balls, chopped
- 1 pint vanilla ice cream, softened
- 1 carton (8 ounces) frozen whipped topping, thawed
- 2 chocolate crumb crusts (9 inches)
- Additional whipped topping, optional

Set aside 1/4 cup malted milk balls for topping. Place ice cream in a large bowl; fold in whipped topping and remaining malted milk balls. Spoon into crusts. Cover and freeze. Garnish with additional whipped topping if desired and reserved malted milk balls. Remove from the freezer 20 minutes before serving. **Yield:** 2 pies (6-8 servings each).

Cheddar Cheese Puffs

These cheesy appetizers are so easy to make and so quick to bake. A warm batch makes a savory snack or an appealing addition to a soup lunch.
—*Tonya Farmer Iowa City, Iowa*

- 1 cup (4 ounces) shredded cheddar cheese
- 1/2 cup all-purpose flour
- 1/4 cup butter *or* margarine, softened
- 1/2 teaspoon ground mustard

In a bowl, combine all ingredients; mix well. Roll into 1-in. balls. Place at least 1 in. apart on an ungreased baking sheet. Bake at 400° for 12-15 minutes or until lightly browned. Serve warm. **Yield:** 2 dozen.

Reuben Party Spread

This speedy sandwich spread makes an appearance at almost all of our family gatherings. It tastes like a traditional Reuben sandwich, but it's easier to assemble.
—*Connie Thompson, Racine, Wisconsin*

- 1 pound fully cooked ham, chopped
- 4 cups (1 pound) shredded Swiss cheese
- 1 can (8 ounces) sauerkraut, drained
- 1/2 cup Thousand Island salad dressing
- Rye bread

In a microwave-safe bowl, combine the ham, cheese, sauerkraut and salad dressing. Cover and microwave on high for 1 to 1-1/2 minutes or until cheese is melted, stirring once. Serve on rye bread. **Yield:** 6 cups. **Ed-**

Tropical Fruit Cream Pie

Crunchy toasted coconut adds a special touch to this sweet and fruity pie. It can be stirred up in a jiffy with handy pantry staples. —Carolyn Dixon, Monticello, Arkansas

- 2 cups cold milk
- 1 package (3.4 ounces) instant coconut cream pudding mix
- 1 can (15-1/4 ounces) tropical fruit salad, drained
- 1/2 cup flaked coconut, toasted
- 1 graham cracker crust (9 inches)

In a bowl, beat milk and pudding mix for 2 minutes or until smooth. Let stand until slightly thickened, about 2 minutes. Add fruit and coconut; mix well. Pour into crust. Refrigerate until serving. **Yield:** 6-8 servings.

Bacon Cheese Fries

(Pictured below)

These tempting potatoes are one finger food I can make a meal of. Quick to fix, they're a hit at parties and as a snack. Ranch dressing is a tasty alternative to sour cream. —Marilyn Dutkus, Laguna Beach, California

- 1 package (32 ounces) frozen French fries
- 1 cup (4 ounces) shredded cheddar cheese
- 1/2 cup thinly sliced green onions
- 1/4 cup cooked crumbled bacon

Ranch salad dressing

Cook French fries according to package directions. Place fries on a broiler-safe dish or platter. Sprinkle with cheese, onions and bacon. Broil for 1-2 minutes or until cheese is melted. Serve with ranch dressing. **Yield:** 8-10 servings.

Cherry S'mores

(Pictured below)

If you like s'mores, you'll enjoy this dressed-up variation. Each open-face treat gets a boost of sweetness from cherry pie filling. —Margery Bryan, Royal City, Washington

- 1 plain milk chocolate candy bar (7 ounces)
- 8 graham cracker squares
- 8 large marshmallows
- 1 cup cherry pie filling

Divide chocolate into eight pieces; place a piece on each graham cracker. Top with a marshmallow. Place two crackers at a time on a microwave-safe plate. Microwave on high for 15-35 seconds or until chocolate is melted and marshmallow is puffed. Top each with 1 tablespoon pie filling. **Yield:** 8 servings. **Editor's Note:** This recipe was tested in an 850-watt microwave.

Bacon Cheese Fries
Lemon-Berry Pitcher Punch
Cherry S'mores

Crab and Pea Salad

(Pictured below)

From picnics to potlucks, this fast-to-fix combination receives rave reviews. I often garnish it with paprika, sliced hard-cooked eggs, tomatoes or croutons. —Janine Gillespie
Milwaukie, Oregon

    1 package (10 ounces) frozen peas, thawed
    1 package (8 ounces) imitation crabmeat, flaked
    6 to 8 bacon strips, cooked and crumbled
    1/2 cup mayonnaise
    1/4 teaspoon onion powder

In a bowl, combine peas, crab and bacon. Combine mayonnaise and onion powder; fold into the crab mixture. Cover and refrigerate until serving. **Yield:** 4-6 servings.

Pimiento Potato Salad

(Pictured below)

A neighbor shared the recipe for this easy overnight salad. Tender potatoes and crunchy celery get refreshing flavor from a bottle of Italian dressing. —Dora Ledford
Rockwall, Texas

✓ Uses less fat, sugar or salt. Includes Nutritional Analysis and Diabetic Exchanges.

    2 pounds small red potatoes (about 12), cooked
    4 green onions, thinly sliced
    3 celery ribs, thinly sliced
    1 jar (2 ounces) diced pimientos, drained
    1 bottle (8 ounces) Italian salad dressing

Cut potatoes into 1/4-in. slices. In an ungreased 13-in.

Catalina Tomato Salad
Crab and Pea Salad
Pimiento Potato Salad

x 9-in. x 2-in. dish, layer half of the potatoes, onions, celery and pimientos. Repeat layers. Pour dressing over all. Cover and refrigerate overnight. Stir before serving. **Yield:** 12 servings. **Nutritional Analysis:** One 3/4-cup serving (prepared with fat-free salad dressing) equals 65 calories, 202 mg sodium, 0 cholesterol, 13 gm carbohydrate, 2 gm protein, trace fat. **Diabetic Exchange:** 1 starch.

Catalina Tomato Salad

(Pictured below right)

I'm a tomato lover, and this is my favorite summertime salad. With its sweet dressing and tangy olives, the unique blend disappears almost immediately at picnics and barbecues. —*Lora Billmire, Spokane, Washington*

>   6 cups chopped plum tomatoes
>   1 jar (5-1/4 ounces) stuffed olives, drained and halved
>   3/4 cup Catalina salad dressing
>   1 small onion, chopped
>   1/4 to 1/2 teaspoon pepper

In a bowl, combine all ingredients; mix well. Cover and refrigerate for at least 2 hours. **Yield:** 8 servings.

Easy Strawberry Napoleon

This rich pudding-like dessert is one of my family's absolute favorites. Fresh strawberries make a pretty topping while convenient saltine crackers form a no-fuss crust. —*Karen Sawatsky, Vineland, Ontario*

>   2 cups cold milk
>   1 package (3.4 ounces) instant vanilla pudding mix
>   1 cup whipping cream, whipped
> 36 saltines
>   1 pint fresh strawberries, sliced

In a mixing bowl, beat milk and pudding mix on low speed for 2 minutes. Fold in the whipped cream. Place a third of the crackers in an ungreased 8-in. square dish (break crackers to completely cover bottom of dish). Top with a third of the pudding mixture. Repeat the layers twice. Cover and refrigerate for at least 6 hours. Top with strawberries just before serving. **Yield:** 9-12 servings.

Chicken Spaghetti

My family loves this meal of tender chicken and noodles tossed with zippy tomatoes and a creamy cheese sauce. I like it because it doesn't heat up the kitchen on hot days. —*Regina Clack, Booneville, Arkansas*

>   1 package (7 ounces) thin spaghetti
>   1 pound process American cheese, cubed
>   1 can (10 ounces) diced tomatoes and green chilies, undrained
>   4 cups cubed cooked chicken

Cook the spaghetti according to package directions. Meanwhile, in a saucepan, combine the cheese and tomatoes; cook and stir until cheese is melted. Add chicken; heat through. Drain spaghetti; toss with cheese sauce. **Yield:** 4-6 servings.

Sour Cream Tarts

This last-minute dessert is delicious, especially with cherry pie filling on top. For even quicker assembly, use a prepared 9-inch graham cracker crust. —*Crystal Fogelsanger, Newville, Pennsylvania*

> 1-1/2 cups cold milk
>   1 package (5.1 ounces) instant vanilla pudding mix
>   2 cups (16 ounces) sour cream
>   2 packages (6 count *each*) individual graham cracker tart shells
>   1 can (21 ounces) fruit pie filling

In a mixing bowl, beat milk and pudding mix on low speed for 2 minutes. Fold in sour cream. Spoon about 1/3 cup into each tart shell; top with pie filling. Serve immediately. **Yield:** 12 servings.

Zesty Vegetable Salad

This fresh-tasting medley is a terrific way to use your garden bounty. When people rave about it, I'm almost embarrassed to tell them how easy it is to make. —*Dana Nemecek, Skiatook, Oklahoma*

✓ Uses less fat, sugar or salt. Includes Nutritional Analysis and Diabetic Exchanges.

> 10 fresh mushrooms, sliced
>   2 medium tomatoes, chopped
>   2 medium cucumbers, peeled and chopped
>   1 small onion, chopped
>   1 bottle (8 ounces) zesty Italian salad dressing

In a bowl, combine mushrooms, tomatoes, cucumbers and onion. Add dressing; toss to coat. Cover and chill at least 2 hours. Serve with a slotted spoon. **Yield:** 12 servings. **Nutritional Analysis:** One 1/2-cup serving (prepared with fat-free salad dressing) equals 29 calories, 137 mg sodium, 0 cholesterol, 5 gm carbohydrate, 1 gm protein, trace fat. **Diabetic Exchange:** 1 vegetable.

Peppy Pork 'n' Beans

I like to serve this saucy baked bean dish at cookouts. Pepperoni adds a fun twist to canned baked beans. With grilled meat and potato salad, I have a great summer meal. —*Lee Deneau, Lansing, Michigan*

> 20 pepperoni slices, quartered
>   1 small onion, chopped
>   2 cans (16 ounces *each*) pork and beans
> 1/2 cup barbecue sauce
>   1 teaspoon prepared mustard

In a saucepan, cook the pepperoni and onion until the onion is tender. Stir in the remaining ingredients; bring to a boil. Reduce heat; simmer, uncovered, for 10-15 minutes, stirring occasionally. **Yield:** 6-8 servings.

Salsa Sausage Quiche

A prepared pastry crust hurries along the assembly of this hearty appetizer. Served with sour cream and additional salsa, it's a party favorite in our retirement community. If you're feeding a crowd, bring two—they disappear fast! —Dorothy Sorensen, Naples, Florida

        3/4 pound bulk pork sausage
          1 unbaked pastry shell (9 inches)
          2 cups (8 ounces) shredded cheddar cheese,
            divided
          3 eggs
          1 cup salsa

In a skillet over medium heat, cook the sausage until no longer pink; drain. Transfer to the pastry shell. Sprinkle with half of the cheese. In a small bowl, lightly beat the eggs; stir in salsa. Pour over cheese. Bake at 375° for 30-35 minutes or until a knife inserted near the center comes out clean. Sprinkle with the remaining cheese. Bake 5 minutes longer or until the cheese is melted. **Yield:** 6-8 servings.

Two-Bean Salad

Bottled dressing adds flavor in a flash to this salad. The recipe can be doubled or even tripled for potlucks, picnics or barbecues. —Sue Ross, Casa Grande, Arizona

✓ Uses less fat, sugar or salt. Includes Nutritional Analysis and Diabetic Exchanges.

          1 package (10 ounces) frozen cut green beans,
            cooked and drained
          1 cup canned garbanzo beans, rinsed and
            drained
        1/3 cup julienned red onion
        1/4 cup Italian salad dressing
        1/8 teaspoon salt *or* salt-free seasoning blend

In a bowl, combine beans and onion. Add dressing and salt; toss to coat. Cover and chill until serving. **Yield:** 4 servings. **Nutritional Analysis:** One 1/2-cup serving (prepared with fat-free dressing and salt-free seasoning) equals 83 calories, 374 mg sodium, 0 cholesterol, 16 gm carbohydrate, 3 gm protein, 1 gm fat. **Diabetic Exchange:** 1 starch.

Chow Mein Chicken

This basic recipe can be expanded many ways, but it's quite a success by itself. Sometimes I add sliced water chestnuts for extra crunch or a green vegetable for a burst of color. —Roberta Fall, Paw Paw, Michigan

          1 can (10-3/4 ounces) condensed cream of
            chicken soup, undiluted
          1 can (10-1/2 ounces) condensed chicken with
            rice soup, undiluted
          1 can (5 ounces) evaporated milk
          2 cups cubed cooked chicken
          1 can (3 ounces) chow mein noodles

In a bowl, combine soups and milk. Stir in chicken. Transfer to a greased 8-in. square baking dish. Bake, uncovered, at 350° for 40 minutes; stir. Sprinkle with chow mein noodles. Bake 5-10 minutes longer or until bubbly and noodles are crisp. **Yield:** 4 servings.

Oatmeal Shortbread

These rich buttery cookies are great with a steaming cup of coffee or hot chocolate. My family enjoys these chewy treats very much. I like them because they're so quick to prepare. —Marion Hall, Etobicoke, Ontario

          1 cup butter (no substitutes), softened
        3/4 cup sugar
      1-1/2 cups all-purpose flour
      1-1/2 cups quick-cooking oats
        3/4 teaspoon salt

In a mixing bowl, cream butter and sugar until light and fluffy. Gradually add the flour, oats and salt. Press into a greased 13-in. x 9-in. x 2-in. baking pan. Prick with a fork if desired. Bake at 325° for 30-35 minutes or until lightly browned. Cool for 10 minutes before cutting. **Yield:** about 5 dozen.

Cider Cranberry Salad

(Pictured at right)

The area we live in grows lots of cranberries, and we really like them. This tasty gelatin salad has lovely orange and apple flavors that accent the tart cranberry sauce. —Barbara Taylor, Ocean Park, Washington

          1 package (3 ounces) orange gelatin
        3/4 cup boiling apple cider
        3/4 cup cold apple cider
          1 can (16 ounces) whole-berry cranberry sauce

In a bowl, dissolve gelatin in boiling cider. Stir in cold cider and cranberry sauce. Pour into individual dishes. Chill until firm. **Yield:** 6-8 servings.

Zesty Red Potatoes

(Pictured at right)

The crushed red pepper comes through in these zippy potatoes. This dish is good with or without the onion. Either way, you're not likely to have leftovers. —Marilyn Weaver, Sparks, Maryland

          6 medium red potatoes, halved and thinly
            sliced
          1 small onion, halved and thinly sliced
        1/2 cup butter *or* margarine, melted
        1/2 teaspoon crushed red pepper flakes
Salt to taste

Arrange potatoes and onion in an ungreased 9-in. square baking dish. Combine butter, pepper flakes and salt; drizzle over potatoes and onion. Cover and bake at 400° for 25 minutes. Uncover; bake 15-20 minutes longer or until potatoes are tender. **Yield:** 6-8 servings.

Zesty Red Potatoes
Cider Cranberry Salad
Turkey Tenderloin Supreme

Turkey Tenderloin Supreme

(Pictured above)

We're a busy hockey and figure skating family, so we're always on the go. Served over rice, this fast skillet supper makes a good home-cooked meal when there's little time.
—Nancy Levin, Chesterfield, Missouri

✓ Uses less fat, sugar or salt. Includes Nutritional Analysis and Diabetic Exchanges.

6 turkey breast tenderloin slices (3/4 inch thick and 4 ounces *each*)
1 tablespoon butter *or* margarine
3 green onions, thinly sliced
1 can (10-3/4 ounces) condensed cream of chicken soup, undiluted
1/4 cup water

In a large skillet, brown turkey in butter. Add onions; cook for 1-2 minutes. Combine soup and water; pour over turkey. Bring to a boil. Reduce heat; cover and simmer for 8-10 minutes or until meat juices run clear. **Yield:** 6 servings. **Nutritional Analysis:** One serving (prepared with reduced-fat margarine and low-fat soup) equals 175 calories, 264 mg sodium, 81 mg cholesterol, 5 gm carbohydrate, 26 gm protein, 5 gm fat. **Diabetic Exchanges:** 3 very lean meat, 1 vegetable, 1 fruit.

Fruity Sherbet Punch
Ham Roll-Ups
Turkey Meatballs
Sausage Biscuit Bites

Sausage Biscuit Bites

(Pictured above)

I sometimes bake these delightful little morsels the night before, refrigerate them, then put them in the slow cooker in the morning so my husband can share them with his co-workers. They're always gone in a hurry.
—Audrey Marler, Kokomo, Indiana

1 tube (7-1/2 ounces) refrigerated buttermilk biscuits
1 tablespoon butter *or* margarine, melted
4-1/2 teaspoons grated Parmesan cheese
1 teaspoon dried oregano
1 package (8 ounces) brown-and-serve sausage links

On a lightly floured surface, roll out each biscuit into a 4-in. circle; brush with butter. Combine Parmesan cheese and oregano; sprinkle over butter. Place a sausage link in the center of each; roll up. Cut each widthwise into four pieces; insert a toothpick into each. Place on an ungreased baking sheet. Bake at 375° for 8-10 minutes or until golden brown. **Yield:** 40 appetizers.

Fruity Sherbet Punch

(Pictured above)

Everybody loves glasses of this sweet fruit punch. When entertaining, I start with a quart of sherbet, then add more later so it all doesn't melt right away. —Betty Eberly
Palmyra, Pennsylvania

4 cups *each* apple, pineapple and orange juice, chilled
2 liters ginger ale, chilled
1 to 2 quarts orange *or* pineapple sherbet

Combine juices in a punch bowl. Stir in ginger ale. Top with sherbet. Serve immediately. **Yield:** 15-20 servings (about 5 quarts).

Turkey Meatballs

(Pictured at left)

I hate to cook, so I'm always looking for fast and easy recipes like this one. A sweet sauce coats these firm meatballs that are made with ground turkey for a nice change of pace. —Hazel Bates, Clinton, Oklahoma

✓ Uses less fat, sugar or salt. Includes Nutritional Analysis and Diabetic Exchanges.

1 pound ground turkey
1/4 cup oat bran cereal
1 bottle (14 ounces) ketchup
1 cup grape jelly
3 to 4 tablespoons lemon juice

In a bowl, combine turkey and cereal; mix well. Shape into 1-in. balls. In a Dutch oven, combine ketchup, jelly and lemon juice; bring to a boil. Add meatballs. Reduce heat; simmer, uncovered, for 30-35 minutes or until meat is no longer pink, stirring several times. **Yield:** 4-1/2 dozen. **Nutritional Analysis:** One serving of 5 meatballs (prepared with ground turkey breast, no-salt-added ketchup and low-sugar grape jelly) equals 137 calories, 36 mg sodium, 20 mg cholesterol, 24 gm carbohydrate, 11 gm protein, 1 gm fat. **Diabetic Exchanges:** 1 very lean meat, 1 starch, 1/2 fruit.

Cheesy Beef Buns

These satisfying sandwiches would be great to put together ahead of time and wrap in foil until ready to bake. Warm from the oven, the crispy buns are piled with cheesy slices of roast beef. —Marlene Harguth, Maynard, Minnesota

1 medium onion, chopped
2 tablespoons butter *or* margarine
1 jar (8 ounces) process cheese sauce
1 pound thinly sliced cooked roast beef
6 French *or* Italian sandwich buns, split

In a skillet, saute onion in butter until tender. Stir in cheese sauce until melted. Cook and stir until heated through. Stir in beef until evenly coated. Spoon onto buns; wrap each in aluminum foil. Bake at 350° for 8-10 minutes or until bread is crispy. **Yield:** 6 servings.

Ham Roll-Ups

(Pictured above left)

Green onions and ripe olives give lively flavor to these bite-size appetizers. They're quick to assemble and can be made the day before they're needed. They're very popular with my friends and family. —Kathleen Green, Republic, Missouri

✓ Uses less fat, sugar or salt. Includes Nutritional Analysis and Diabetic Exchanges.

1 package (8 ounces) cream cheese, softened
1 can (2-1/4 ounces) chopped ripe olives, drained
1/3 cup thinly sliced green onions
8 to 10 thin slices fully cooked ham

In a mixing bowl, beat cream cheese until smooth; stir in the olives and onions. Spread over ham slices. Roll up, jelly-roll style, starting with a short side. Chill for at least 1 hour. Just before serving, cut into 1-in. pieces. **Yield:** 40 appetizers. **Nutritional Analysis:** One serving of 2 roll-ups (prepared with fat-free cream cheese and low-fat ham) equals 27 calories, 259 mg sodium, 7 mg cholesterol, 1 gm carbohydrate, 4 gm protein, 1 gm fat. **Diabetic Exchange:** 1/2 meat.

Pea and Broccoli Bake

When I'm pressed for time, I find this take-along casserole is easy to fix. The crouton-topped combination is not only attractive but tasty, too. —Pat Waymire, Yellow Springs, Ohio

1 package (16 ounces) frozen peas, thawed
1 package (16 ounces) frozen chopped broccoli, thawed and drained
1 can (10-3/4 ounces) condensed cream of mushroom soup, undiluted
1 jar (8 ounces) process cheese sauce
1 cup seasoned salad croutons

In a bowl, combine the peas, broccoli, soup and cheese sauce. Transfer to a greased 2-qt. baking dish. Sprinkle with croutons. Bake, uncovered, at 350° for 12-17 minutes or until bubbly. **Yield:** 4-6 servings.

Pecan Peach Cobbler

The nutmeg comes through in this effortless version of peach cobbler. For faster preparation, this recipe relies on convenient canned pie filling and refrigerated biscuits. It is very good served warm. —Phyllis Schmalz, Kansas City, Kansas

1 can (21 ounces) peach pie filling
2/3 cup water
1/8 to 1/4 teaspoon ground nutmeg
1/3 cup chopped pecans
1 tube (7-1/2 ounces) refrigerated buttermilk biscuits

In a bowl, combine the pie filling, water and nutmeg. Transfer to a greased 9-in. x 5-in. x 3-in. loaf pan. Sprinkle with pecans. Separate the biscuits and arrange over the pecans. Bake, uncovered, at 375° for 30-35 minutes or until biscuits are golden brown. Serve warm. **Yield:** 5 servings.

Chapter 5

SOMETIMES when you're hungry, hurried and truly "down to the wire" on feeding your family, you can only afford a few minutes in the kitchen.

So the next time you're running behind schedule and need to put a homemade-tasting meal on the table, take a deep breath and count to 10.

Then turn to these mouthwatering dishes that can be table-ready in just 10 minutes. With such fantastic flavor, these reliable recipes give folks the impression that you were in the kitchen all day long!

MEALS IN MINUTES. Clockwise from upper right: Onion Vinaigrette Salad (p. 68), Chicken Salsa Pizza (p. 68) and Crunchy Chocolate Sauce (p. 69).

Simple Salad Dressing
Salmon Quesadillas

Salmon Quesadillas

(Pictured above)

I like simple recipes that get me out of the kitchen fast, so my husband and I can spend more time with our two boys. These super-quick wedges are always a hit...and a tasty change of pace from salmon patties.
—Heidi Main, Anchorage, Alaska

    2 garlic cloves, minced
    1 teaspoon vegetable oil
    1 can (14-3/4 ounces) salmon, drained, bones and skin removed
    1 to 2 teaspoons dried basil
    1/2 teaspoon pepper
    1 tablespoon butter *or* margarine, softened
    4 flour tortillas (8 inches)
    2 cups (8 ounces) shredded mozzarella cheese
Guacamole *or* salsa

In a skillet, saute garlic in oil until tender. Stir in salmon, basil and pepper. Cook over medium heat until heated through. Meanwhile, spread butter over one side of each tortilla. Place tortillas, buttered side down, on a griddle. Sprinkle each with 1/2 cup cheese. Spread 1/2 cup of salmon mixture over half of each tortilla. Fold over and cook on low for 1-2 minutes on each side. Cut into wedges; serve with guacamole or salsa. **Yield:** 4 servings.

Three-Step Stir-Fry

I based this flavorful stir-fry on a fabulous dish I sampled in a San Francisco restaurant. It truly is a 10-minute main dish that looks and tastes like it took a lot longer. —Amy Masson, Cypress, California

    1 envelope stir-fry seasoning mix
    1 package (16 ounces) broccoli coleslaw
    2 tablespoons vegetable oil
    8 ounces thinly sliced roast beef *or* other deli meat, cut into 1/2-inch strips
    1 can (8 ounces) sliced water chestnuts, drained
    3 plum tomatoes, quartered
    2 teaspoons sesame seeds

Prepare seasoning mix according to package directions; set aside. In a skillet, stir-fry coleslaw in oil for 3 minutes or until crisp-tender. Add beef, water chestnuts, tomatoes, sesame seeds and seasoning sauce. Cook 4 minutes longer or until heated through. **Yield:** 7 servings.

Ham 'n' Noodle Toss

My family likes ramen noodles, so I'm always looking for new ways to use them. This satisfying supper is a much-requested favorite. —Margaret Pache, Mesa, Arizona

    2 cups broccoli florets
1-3/4 cups water
1-1/4 cups cubed fully cooked ham
    1 tablespoon soy sauce
    2 packages (3 ounces *each*) oriental-flavored ramen noodles
Sliced ripe olives, optional

In a large saucepan, combine broccoli, water, ham, soy sauce and one flavoring packet from the noodles (discard second packet or save for another use). Break noodles into small pieces; add to pan. Simmer, uncovered, for 6-8 minutes or until noodles are tender, stirring frequently. Top with olives if desired. **Yield:** 4 servings.

Simple Salad Dressing

(Pictured at left)

A friend created this mild and light dressing that's a snap to whip up with on-hand ingredients. Whenever I serve it, someone asks for the recipe.
—Joan Rose
Langley, British Columbia

1/2 cup olive *or* vegetable oil
1/4 cup sugar
  3 tablespoons cider vinegar
  1 tablespoon minced fresh parsley
1/2 teaspoon salt
1/4 teaspoon pepper
Salad greens and vegetables of your choice

Combine the first six ingredients in a jar with a tight-fitting lid; shake until blended. Store in the refrigerator. Shake before serving; drizzle over salad. **Yield:** about 1 cup.

Zippy Beans and Corn

Onion and hot pepper sauce spark up the flavor of this unique side dish.
—Marsha Ransom
South Haven, Michigan

  1 medium onion, cut into 1/4-inch wedges
  1 tablespoon vegetable oil
  1 can (16 ounces) baked beans
  1 package (10 ounces) frozen corn
  2 teaspoons vinegar
1/2 teaspoon hot pepper sauce

In a saucepan, saute onion in oil until tender. Add beans and corn; bring to a boil. Reduce heat; cover and simmer for 5 minutes or until heated through. Stir in vinegar and hot pepper sauce. **Yield:** 4 servings.

10-Minute Taco Salad

(Pictured at right)

Mom often made this hearty main-dish salad for my three brothers and me when we were growing up. Now it's one of my husband's favorite meals—and one we frequently fix for weekend guests.
—Cindy Stephan
Owosso, Michigan

  2 cans (16 ounces *each*) chili beans, undrained
  1 package (10-1/2 ounces) corn chips
  2 cups (8 ounces) shredded cheddar cheese
  4 cups chopped lettuce
  2 small tomatoes, chopped
  1 small onion, chopped
  1 can (2-1/4 ounces) sliced ripe olives, drained
1-1/4 cups salsa
1/2 cup sour cream

In a saucepan or microwave-safe bowl, heat the beans. Place corn chips on a large platter. Top with beans, cheese, lettuce, tomatoes, onion, olives, salsa and sour cream. Serve immediately. **Yield:** 8 servings.

Vegetarian Pasta

I add a can of beans to noodles to create this fast, flavorful lunch fare. You can use any type of pasta you have on hand to make this filling dish.
—Mary Feichtel
Binghamton, New York

✓ Uses less fat, sugar or salt. Includes Nutritional Analysis and Diabetic Exchanges.

  1 can (15-1/2 ounces) great northern beans, rinsed and drained
  2 cups hot cooked angel hair pasta
  3 tablespoons butter *or* margarine
1/4 teaspoon garlic salt, optional
1/4 cup shredded Parmesan *or* Romano cheese
Minced fresh parsley

Place beans in a microwave-safe dish; cover and microwave on high for 2 minutes or until heated through. Place pasta in a serving bowl. Add butter and garlic salt if desired; toss until the butter is melted. Add beans and cheese; toss to coat. Sprinkle with parsley. Serve immediately. **Yield:** 4 servings. **Nutritional Analysis:** One 1-cup serving (prepared with margarine and non-fat Parmesan cheese topping and without garlic salt) equals 311 calories, 202 mg sodium, 1 mg cholesterol, 44 gm carbohydrate, 14 gm protein, 9 gm fat. **Diabetic Exchanges:** 3 starch, 1 fat, 1/2 meat.

10-Minute Taco Salad

Fruit Crumble

Fruit is a good dessert for most any meal, but it seems to be even more special when it's dressed up like this. Convenient canned pie filling makes this crumble a snap to prepare.
—Jackie Heyer, Cushing, Iowa

  1/3 cup butter *or* margarine
1-1/3 cups graham cracker crumbs (about 22
      squares)
    3 tablespoons sugar
    1 can (21 ounces) raspberry *or* cherry pie
      filling
  1/4 teaspoon almond extract
Whipped cream

In a skillet, melt the butter. Add cracker crumbs and sugar; cook and stir until crumbs are lightly browned. Meanwhile, combine the pie filling and extract in a microwave-safe bowl. Cover and microwave on high for 2-3 minutes or until heated through. Spoon into individual dishes; sprinkle with crumbs. Top with whipped cream. **Yield:** 4-6 servings. **Editor's Note:** This recipe was tested in an 850-watt microwave.

Chicken Salsa Pizza

(Pictured below and on page 64)

This zippy chicken pizza is sure to become the most-requested version in the house. The cooked chicken and a prebaked crust make it quick, easy and oh-so-good.
—Mrs. Guy Turnbull, Arlington, Massachusetts

    1 prebaked Italian bread shell crust
    2 cups (8 ounces) shredded cheddar cheese,
      divided
    1 jar (11 ounces) salsa
    1 cup cubed cooked chicken

Place bread shell on an ungreased 12-in. pizza pan. Sprinkle with 3/4 cup of cheese. Top with salsa, chicken and remaining cheese. Bake at 450° for 8-10 minutes or until cheese is bubbly. **Yield:** 4 servings.

Onion Vinaigrette Salad

(Pictured below and on page 64)

The recipe for this pretty salad dressing was given to me a long time ago by my sister-in-law. We like the mixture's onion flavor so much we keep some in our refrigerator year-round.
—Harriet Stichter, Milford, Indiana

    1 cup sugar
    1 cup vinegar
  1/2 cup vegetable oil
  1/4 cup chopped onion
1-1/2 teaspoons salt
  1/4 teaspoon paprika
  1/4 teaspoon ground mustard
Dash pepper
Torn salad greens
Cherry tomatoes, sliced cucumber and grated
    carrots *or* vegetables of your choice

In a jar with a tight-fitting lid, combine the first eight ingredients; shake well. In a salad bowl, combine greens

Onion Vinaigrette Salad
Chicken Salsa Pizza
Crunchy Chocolate Sauce

and vegetables. Drizzle with dressing and toss to coat. Store any leftover dressing in the refrigerator. **Yield:** 2-1/2 cups dressing.

Crunchy Chocolate Sauce

(Pictured below left and on page 64)

I use this easy three-ingredient topping that's full of nuts to liven up ordinary ice cream. As this rich chocolate sauce cools over the ice cream, it forms a hard shell that kids (and adults) love.
—Dolores Kastello, Waukesha, Wisconsin

> **1 cup chopped walnuts *or* pecans**
> **1/2 cup butter (no substitutes)**
> **1 cup (6 ounces) semisweet chocolate chips**
> **Ice cream**

In a skillet, saute nuts in butter until golden. Remove from the heat; stir in chocolate chips until melted. Serve warm over ice cream (sauce will harden). Store in the refrigerator. This sauce can be reheated in the microwave. **Yield:** about 1-1/2 cups.

Peach Pudding

(Pictured at right)

This light peach dessert is so fresh it tastes just like summertime. With sliced fresh peaches and whipped topping, it's a quick way to dress up instant vanilla pudding. —Shelby Nicodemus
New Carlisle, Ohio

> **1/4 cup peach gelatin powder**
> **1/2 cup hot milk**
> **1-1/2 cups cold milk**
> **1 package (3.4 ounces) instant vanilla pudding mix**
> **Sliced fresh peaches and whipped topping, optional**

In a bowl, dissolve gelatin in hot milk; set aside. Meanwhile, in a mixing bowl, beat cold milk and pudding mix on low speed for 2 minutes. Add gelatin mixture; mix well. Let stand for 5 minutes. Spoon into individual dishes. Garnish with peaches and whipped topping if desired. **Yield:** 4 servings.

Creamy Corn Salad

My daughter-in-law shared this fast five-ingredient recipe. It sounds too simple to be so good. You can easily double the recipe if you're serving several. —June Mullins
Livonia, Missouri

✓ Uses less fat, sugar or salt. Includes Nutritional Analysis and Diabetic Exchanges.

> **1 can (15-1/4 ounces) whole kernel corn, drained**

Peach Pudding
Red, White and Blue Refresher

> **1 medium tomato, seeded and diced**
> **2 tablespoons chopped onion**
> **1/3 cup mayonnaise**
> **1/4 teaspoon dill weed, optional**

In a small bowl, combine all ingredients; mix well. Cover and refrigerate until serving. **Yield:** 4 servings. **Nutritional Analysis:** One 1/2-cup serving (prepared with fat-free mayonnaise) equals 109 calories, 374 mg sodium, 0 cholesterol, 25 gm carbohydrate, 3 gm protein, 1 gm fat. **Diabetic Exchanges:** 1 starch, 1 vegetable.

Red, White and Blue Refresher

(Pictured above)

This colorful combination of pineapple sherbet, berries and grape juice makes a refreshing dessert on a hot day. Serve it at your Fourth of July party! —Carol Gillespie
Chambersburg, Pennsylvania

> **1 quart pineapple *or* lemon sherbet**
> **1 cup sliced strawberries**
> **1/2 cup blueberries**
> **1/2 cup white grape juice**

Divide the sherbet between four dessert cups or bowls. Top with the berries and grape juice. **Yield:** 4 servings.

Peppy Parmesan Pasta

(Pictured at right)

When my husband and I needed dinner in a hurry, we came up with this dish that gets spicy flavor from pepperoni. We like to use angel hair pasta because it cooks faster than other noodles. —Debbie Horst, Phoenix, Arizona

Peppy Parmesan Pasta

- **8 ounces angel hair pasta**
- **1 large tomato, chopped**
- **1 package (3 ounces) sliced pepperoni**
- **1 can (2-1/4 ounces) sliced ripe olives, drained**
- **1/4 cup grated Parmesan cheese**
- **3 tablespoons olive *or* vegetable oil**
- **1/2 teaspoon salt *or* salt-free seasoning blend, optional**
- **1/4 teaspoon garlic powder**

Cook pasta according to package directions. Meanwhile, in a serving bowl, combine the tomato, pepperoni, olives, Parmesan cheese, oil, salt if desired and garlic powder. Drain pasta; add to the tomato mixture and toss to coat. **Yield:** 4 servings.

Lemon Pineapple Dessert

I need just four ingredients to prepare this refreshing lemon fluff. It's sweet, creamy and special enough for company. This cool treat is a fitting finale to many meals.
—Patricia Aurand, Arcadia, Ohio

- **1 can (20 ounces) crushed pineapple, drained**
- **1 can (15-3/4 ounces) lemon pie filling**
- **1 can (14 ounces) sweetened condensed milk**
- **1 carton (8 ounces) frozen whipped topping, thawed**

Lemon slices, optional

In a bowl, combine the pineapple, pie filling and condensed milk. Fold in whipped topping. Spoon into bowls; garnish with lemon if desired. **Yield:** 12-14 servings.

Creamy Cucumber Salad

When cousins visited from Russia, they made us a meal that included this wonderful vegetable salad. Its refreshing flavor goes over well at family get-togethers.
—Rhonda Egler, Mooresville, Indiana

✓ Uses less fat, sugar or salt. Includes Nutritional Analysis and Diabetic Exchanges.

- **1 medium cucumber, diced**
- **2 plum tomatoes, diced**
- **4 green onions with tops, sliced**
- **1/2 cup sour cream**
- **1/4 teaspoon celery salt *or* salt-free seasoning blend**
- **1/8 teaspoon pepper**

Combine all ingredients in a bowl. Refrigerate until serving. **Yield:** 4 servings. **Nutritional Analysis:** One 3/4-cup serving (prepared with nonfat sour cream and salt-free seasoning) equals 55 calories, 31 mg sodium, 3 mg cholesterol, 10 gm carbohydrate, 3 gm protein, trace fat. **Diabetic Exchange:** 2 vegetable.

Caramel Fruit Dip

I love this smooth and creamy dip as a party appetizer or anytime snack. The sweet four-ingredient blend is good with any fruit, but especially tasty with tart apples.
—Polly Lynam-Bloom, Mequon, Wisconsin

- **1 package (8 ounces) cream cheese, softened**
- **1/2 cup caramel ice cream topping**
- **1/4 cup honey**
- **1/4 teaspoon ground cinnamon**

Fresh fruit

In a small mixing bowl, beat the cream cheese until smooth. Beat in caramel topping, honey and cinnamon. Serve with fruit. Store in the refrigerator. **Yield:** 2 cups.

Black Bean Burritos

My neighbor and I discovered these delicious low-fat burritos a few years ago. On nights my husband or I have a meeting, we can have a satisfying supper on the table in minutes. —Angela Studebaker, Goshen, Indiana

✓ Uses less fat, sugar or salt. Includes Nutritional Analysis and Diabetic Exchanges.

- **3 tablespoons chopped onion**
- **3 tablespoons chopped green pepper**

1 can (15 ounces) black beans, rinsed and drained
4 flour tortillas (7 inches), warmed
1 cup (4 ounces) shredded Mexican cheese blend *or* cheddar cheese
1 medium tomato, chopped
1 cup shredded lettuce
Salsa, optional

In a nonstick skillet coated with nonstick cooking spray, saute onion and green pepper until tender. Add beans; heat through. Spoon about 1/2 cupful off center on each tortilla. Sprinkle with cheese, tomato and lettuce. Fold sides and ends over filling and roll up. Serve with salsa if desired. **Yield:** 4 servings. **Nutritional Analysis:** One serving (prepared with fat-free tortillas and reduced-fat cheddar cheese; calculated without salsa) equals 288 calories, 672 mg sodium, 19 mg cholesterol, 41 gm carbohydrate, 18 gm protein, 6 gm fat. **Diabetic Exchanges:** 2-1/2 starch, 1 meat, 1 vegetable.

Cran-Apple Sauce

I often fix this sweet-tart combination as a side dish with a turkey dinner. It's also delicious as a last-minute dessert topped with whipped cream. —Romaine Wetzel
Lancaster, Pennsylvania

1 can (8 ounces) jellied cranberry sauce
1 jar (24 ounces) applesauce
Whipped topping, optional

In a bowl, break apart cranberry sauce with a fork. Stir in applesauce. Refrigerate until serving. Garnish with whipped topping if desired. **Yield:** 4-6 servings.

Sunshine Salad

This summery salad combines cucumbers, oranges and a tangy dressing with fresh-tasting results. Sometimes I sprinkle sunflower kernels over the top before serving for extra crunch. —Edna Shaffer
Beulah, Michigan

☑ Uses less fat, sugar or salt. Includes Nutritional Analysis and Diabetic Exchanges.

2 small cucumbers, thinly sliced
1 large navel orange, peeled and sliced
1 carton (8 ounces) sweetened plain yogurt
1/2 teaspoon orange juice
Dash salt, optional

In a bowl, combine cucumbers and orange slices. Combine yogurt and orange juice; pour over salad and toss to coat. Cover and refrigerate until serving. Just before serving, season with salt if desired. **Yield:** 4 servings. **Nutritional Analysis:** One 3/4-cup serving (prepared without salt) equals 71 calories, 46 mg sodium, 1 mg cholesterol, 13 gm carbohydrate, 5 gm protein, trace fat. **Diabetic Exchanges:** 1-1/2 vegetable, 1/2 fruit.

Deluxe Chocolate Pudding

(Pictured below)

Make instant pudding special in no time with this rapid recipe. Creamy servings get a little zip from almond or rum extract, richness from sour cream and a pleasant crunch from pecans. —Audrey Thibodeau
Mesa, Arizona

☑ Uses less fat, sugar or salt. Includes Nutritional Analysis and Diabetic Exchanges.

1-3/4 cups cold milk
1 package (3.9 ounces) instant chocolate pudding mix
1/4 cup sour cream
1/2 teaspoon almond *or* rum extract
1/4 cup chopped pecans, optional
4 pecan halves, optional

In a bowl, combine milk, pudding mix, sour cream and extract. Whisk until slightly thickened, about 2-3 minutes. Stir in pecans if desired. Spoon into four bowls. Top with pecan halves if desired. **Yield:** 4 servings. **Nutritional Analysis:** One serving (prepared with skim milk, instant sugar-free pudding and light sour cream and without pecans) equals 140 calories, 369 mg sodium, 7 mg cholesterol, 27 gm carbohydrate, 7 gm protein, 1 gm fat. **Diabetic Exchanges:** 1-1/2 starch, 1/2 skim milk.

Deluxe Chocolate Pudding

Chapter 6

Handy Mix Tricks

IT'S HANDY to have recipes that take advantage of ingredients you likely keep in your pantry or freezer.

By relying on canned goods, boxed mixes, prepared sauces and other convenience foods, you can come up with fast fixes to your dining dilemmas.

This chapter also offers an appealing assortment of homemade mix recipes that are quick to assemble in advance. They save you shopping time and money, too.

With these handy mix tricks, good eating doesn't require a lot of extra effort!

PRONTO PANTRY ITEMS. Clockwise from upper right: Spicy Ravioli Salad (p. 83), Caramel-Fudge Chocolate Cake (p. 85), Chunky Seafood Chowder (p. 78) and Sloppy Joe Under a Bun (p. 82).

Fast Fixes With Mixes

WHEN the clock starts ticking closer to dinnertime and you're at a loss for what you ought to make, just peek into your pantry! You can have a tasty home-prepared meal ready in minutes by simply dressing up a boxed mix or combining canned soups.

Great Pumpkin Dessert

(Pictured below)

I rely on canned pumpkin and a yellow cake mix to fix this effortless alternative to pumpkin pie. It's a tried-and-true dessert that always elicits compliments and requests for the recipe. —Linda Guyot, Fountain Valley, California

        1 can (15 ounces) solid-pack pumpkin
        1 can (12 ounces) evaporated milk
        3 eggs
        1 cup sugar
        4 teaspoons pumpkin pie spice
        1 package (18-1/4 ounces) yellow cake mix
      3/4 cup butter *or* margarine, melted
  1-1/2 cups chopped walnuts
Vanilla ice cream *or* whipped cream

In a mixing bowl, combine the first five ingredients. Transfer to a greased 13-in. x 9-in. x 2-in. baking pan. Sprinkle with dry cake mix and drizzle with butter. Top with walnuts. Bake at 350° for 1 hour or until a knife inserted near the center comes out clean. Serve with ice cream or whipped cream. **Yield:** 12-16 servings.

Great Pumpkin Dessert

Vegetable Beef Soup

This quick and colorful soup goes together in minutes. Even my husband—who admits he's no cook—makes it on occasion. —Agnes Bierbaum, Gainesville, Florida

      1/2 pound ground beef
        2 cups water
        1 can (14-1/2 ounces) stewed tomatoes
        1 package (10 ounces) frozen mixed vegetables
        1 can (8 ounces) tomato sauce
        1 envelope onion soup mix
      1/2 teaspoon sugar

In a saucepan over medium heat, cook beef until no longer pink; drain. Add the remaining ingredients; bring to a boil. Reduce heat; cover and simmer for 10-15 minutes or until the vegetables are tender. **Yield:** 6 servings.

Cheese-Swirl Chocolate Cake

I recently made this moist chocolate cake for my sister and her husband. I've never seen cake disappear so quickly! It's great with or without the pretty strawberry sauce. —Jennifer Bangerter, Warrensburg, Missouri

        1 package (8 ounces) cream cheese, softened
        4 eggs
      1/4 cup sugar
      1/2 teaspoon vanilla extract
        1 package (18-1/4 ounces) devil's food cake mix
  1-1/4 cups water
      1/2 cup vegetable oil
        1 package (10 ounces) frozen sweetened sliced strawberries, thawed

In a small mixing bowl, combine cream cheese, 1 egg, sugar and vanilla; mix well. Set aside. In a large mixing bowl, combine dry cake mix, water, oil and remaining eggs. Beat on low speed until moistened; beat on high for 2 minutes. Pour half of the batter into a greased 13-in. x 9-in. x 2-in. baking pan. Drop half of the cream cheese mixture by tablespoonfuls over the batter. Repeat layers. Cut through batter with a knife to swirl the cream cheese mixture. Bake at 350° for 35-40 minutes or until a toothpick inserted near the center comes out clean (cake may crack). Cool on a wire rack. Meanwhile, process strawberries in a blender or food processor until smooth. Serve over cake. **Yield:** 12 servings.

Honey Bubble Ring

(Pictured above right)

When our daughters were little, they enjoyed helping me make this sweet pull-apart bread. We still enjoy it around the holidays. —Jane Waters, Lincoln, Missouri

      1/2 cup honey
      1/3 cup sugar
      1/4 cup chopped pecans
        1 tablespoon orange juice

Honey Bubble Ring
Rippled Coffee Cake

1 teaspoon ground cinnamon
1/2 teaspoon grated orange peel
3 tubes (12 ounces *each*) refrigerated
  buttermilk biscuits

In a bowl, combine the first six ingredients. Cut each biscuit into four pieces; dip each piece halfway into honey mixture. Layer in a greased 10-in. tube pan. Bake at 375° for 30-35 minutes or until golden brown. Cool for 10 minutes; invert pan onto a serving platter. **Yield:** 12-15 servings. **Editor's Note:** Only a one-piece tube pan should be used for this recipe.

Rippled Coffee Cake

(Pictured above)

I add a fun layer of brown sugar and cinnamon to a yellow cake mix. This delicious glazed treat is good for breakfast or dessert.　　　—Jane Lear, Portland, Tennessee

1 package (18-1/4 ounces) yellow cake mix
1 cup (8 ounces) sour cream
4 eggs
2/3 cup vegetable oil
1 cup packed brown sugar
1 tablespoon ground cinnamon
ICING:
  2 cups confectioners' sugar
1/4 cup milk
  2 teaspoons vanilla extract

In a mixing bowl, combine dry cake mix, sour cream, eggs and oil; beat well. Spread half of the batter into a greased 13-in. x 9-in. x 2-in. baking pan. Combine brown sugar and cinnamon; sprinkle over batter. Carefully spread remaining batter on top. Bake at 350° for 30-35 minutes or until a toothpick inserted near the center comes out clean. Combine confectioners' sugar, milk and extract and drizzle over warm cake. **Yield:** 16-20 servings.

Coconut Poppy Seed Cake
Fruity Brownie Pizza

Fruity Brownie Pizza

(Pictured above)

I start with a basic brownie mix to create this luscious treat that's sure to impress company. Sometimes I add mandarin oranges for even more color. —Nancy Johnson
Laverne, Oklahoma

> 1 package brownie mix (8-inch pan size)
> 1 package (8 ounces) cream cheese, softened
> 1/3 cup sugar
> 1 can (8 ounces) pineapple tidbits
> 1 small firm banana, sliced
> 1 medium kiwifruit, peeled and sliced
> 1 cup sliced fresh strawberries
> 1/4 cup chopped pecans
> 1 square (1 ounce) semisweet chocolate
> 1 tablespoon butter (no substitutes)

Prepare brownie mix according to package directions. Spread the batter into a greased 12-in. pizza pan. Bake at 375° for 15-20 minutes or until a toothpick inserted near the center comes out clean. Cool completely. In a mixing bowl, beat cream cheese and sugar until smooth. Spread over crust. Drain pineapple, reserving juice. Toss banana slices with juice; drain well. Arrange banana, kiwi, strawberries and pineapple over cream cheese lay-er; sprinkle with pecans. In a microwave, melt choco-late and butter; stir until smooth. Drizzle over fruit. Re-frigerate for 1 hour. **Yield:** 12-14 servings.

Coconut Poppy Seed Cake

(Pictured above)

This moist coconut cake is definitely one of my most-re-quested desserts. Use different cake mixes and pudding fla-vors for variety. —Gail Cayce, Wautoma, Wisconsin

> 1 package (18-1/4 ounces) white cake mix
> 1/4 cup poppy seeds
> 1/4 teaspoon coconut extract, optional
> 3-1/2 cups cold milk
> 2 packages (3.4 ounces *each*) instant coconut cream pudding mix
> 1 carton (8 ounces) frozen whipped topping, thawed
> 1/3 cup flaked coconut, toasted, optional

Prepare cake according to package directions, adding poppy seeds and coconut extract if desired to batter. Pour into a greased 13-in. x 9-in. x 2-in. baking pan. Bake at 350° for 20-25 minutes or until a toothpick inserted near the center comes out clean. Cool completely. In a mixing bowl, beat milk and pudding mix on low speed for 2 minutes. Spread over the cake. Spread with whipped topping. Sprinkle with coconut if desired. **Yield:** 20-24 servings.

Rice Mix Meatballs

Mom prepared these easy meatballs with a thick gravy often when I was growing up. Now I make them for my family as a nice change of pace from hamburgers. With a boxed rice mix and five other ingredients, they're a snap to whip up. —Marcy Paden, Louisville, Nebraska

> 1 package (6.8 ounces) beef-flavored rice mix
> 1 egg, beaten
> 1 pound ground beef
> 2-1/2 cups boiling water
> 2 tablespoons cornstarch
> 3 tablespoons cold water

Set contents of rice seasoning packet aside. In a bowl, combine the rice and egg. Add beef and mix well. Shape into 1-in. balls. In a large skillet over medium heat, brown the meatballs on all sides. Meanwhile, in a small bowl, combine reserved seasoning packet and boiling water. Add to skillet; cover and simmer for 30 minutes or until the rice is tender. Combine cornstarch and cold water until smooth; add to skillet. Bring to a boil. Cook and stir for 2 minutes or until thickened. **Yield:** 8-10 servings.

Bavarian Sausage Supper

(Pictured at right)

My mom, who's a great cook, shared the recipe for this easy skillet meal. Spicy kielbasa makes a flavored noodle and sauce mix truly delicious.
—Pat Frankovich
North Olmsted, Ohio

> 2 cups coleslaw mix
> 1 cup thinly sliced carrots
> 2 tablespoons butter *or* margarine
> 2-1/4 cups water
> 3/4 pound fully cooked kielbasa *or* Polish sausage, sliced
> 1 package (4-1/2 ounces) quick-cooking noodles and sour cream chive sauce mix
> 1/2 teaspoon caraway seeds, optional

In a skillet, saute coleslaw mix and carrots in butter until crisp-tender. Add water; bring to a boil. Stir in remaining ingredients. Return to a boil; cook for 8 minutes or until noodles are tender, stirring occasionally. **Yield:** 5 servings.

Bavarian Sausage Supper

- Dab a few teaspoons of maple syrup onto ham slices when they're almost done frying. Turn the slices several times so the syrup glazes the meat. It gives it a candied flavor. —*Alfred Seltz Jr. Fergus Falls, Minnesota*

- My sister-in-law shared this tip with me. For a flavorful beef stew, add a diced dill pickle and a tablespoon of pickle juice 15-20 minutes before serving. This also works with vegetable beef soup. —*Len Klonicki, Rockford, Illinois*

- Give your sloppy joes a sweet-and-sour twist by adding a can of crushed pineapple, juice and all. —*Lana Cook, Bend, Oregon*

- Crush butter-flavored crackers very finely and use them to coat chicken or fish fillets before frying. The coating is delicious and eliminates the need for salt. To spark up the taste, on occasion I add a little seafood seasoning or some salt-free seasoning blend to the crumbs. —*Anne Ralph, Roselle, New Jersey*

- I add a can of chili with beans to homemade vegetable soup instead of shredded or ground beef. It's a quick, inexpensive way to add spice (and protein) to the soup. It slightly thickens it, too. —*Kay Martin, Greenville, South Carolina*

- To make an excellent glaze for chicken, turkey or pork, I combine a half cup of whatever jelly or jam I have on hand with a tablespoon of Dijon mustard. Apricot jam and red currant jelly work well. If the spread is on the tart side (like orange marmalade), I add some brown sugar. Then I just brush this glaze on the meat before it goes in the oven. —*Isabel Karon, Longville, Minnesota*

Zesty Macaroni Soup

(Pictured below)

The recipe for this thick, zippy soup first caught my attention for two reasons—it calls for ingredients that are found in my pantry, and it can be prepared in a jiffy. A chili macaroni mix provides this dish with a little spice, but sometimes I jazz it up with a can of chopped green chilies. It's a family favorite. —*Joan Hallford*
North Richland Hills, Texas

1 pound ground beef
1 medium onion, chopped
5 cups water
1 can (15 ounces) pinto beans, rinsed and drained
1 can (14-1/2 ounces) diced tomatoes, undrained
1 can (7 ounces) whole kernel corn, drained
1 can (4 ounces) chopped green chilies, optional
1/2 teaspoon ground mustard
1/2 teaspoon salt
1/8 teaspoon pepper
1 package (7-1/2 ounces) chili macaroni dinner mix*
Salsa con queso dip*

In a saucepan, cook beef and onion until meat is no longer pink; drain. Stir in water, beans, tomatoes, corn and chilies if desired. Stir in mustard, salt, pepper and contents of macaroni sauce mix. Bring to a boil. Reduce heat; cover and simmer for 10 minutes. Stir in contents of macaroni packet. Cover and simmer 10-14 minutes longer or until macaroni is tender, stirring once. Serve with salsa con queso dip. **Yield:** 8-10 servings (about 2-1/2 quarts). ***Editor's Note:** This recipe was tested with Hamburger Helper brand chili macaroni. Salsa con queso dip can be found in the international food section or snack aisle of most grocery stores.

Chunky Seafood Chowder

(Pictured on page 72)

This creamy chowder brimming with tender potato and crab tastes so good guests will never guess it starts with canned soup. Half-and-half cream makes it rich enough for special occasions. I often serve it with crackers or French bread after a sporting event or outing.
—*Irene Craigue, Claremont, New Hampshire*

1 medium onion, chopped
2 tablespoons butter *or* margarine
2 pints half-and-half cream
1 can (10-3/4 ounces) condensed New England clam chowder, undiluted
3 medium potatoes, peeled and cubed
1 teaspoon salt
1/4 teaspoon white pepper
1 package (8 ounces) imitation crabmeat, flaked

In a saucepan, saute onion in butter until tender. Add cream and canned chowder; bring to a boil. Stir in the potatoes, salt and pepper. Reduce heat; simmer, un-

Zesty Macaroni Soup

Better Breakfasts

- When making French toast, I give it a boost by using a flavored nondairy coffee creamer instead of milk in the egg-milk mixture. French vanilla is especially yummy. —*Cathy Bodell, Frankfort, Michigan*

- Give homemade taste to pancakes from a mix. Simply add one of the following to the batter: ground cinnamon, ginger or nutmeg, orange extract or chocolate chips. —*Kathleen Stratten*
Narvon, Pennsylvania

- Stir 1 to 2 tablespoons of orange marmalade into a cup of warm maple syrup to perk up an ordinary pancake breakfast. —*Helen Gagne*
Dover, New Hampshire

- When making muffins from a mix, I top each muffin with a teaspoon of brown sugar and a few slivered almonds before baking. They taste like they came from a bakery. —*Elaine Cianciolo*
Warren, Michigan

- I sometimes substitute equal amounts of apple juice for the milk called for in store-bought coffee cake mixes, then I add 1-1/2 teaspoons of ground cinnamon to the batter. When friends ask for the recipe, they're always amazed at this easy twist of ingredients. —*Joanne Hoschette*
Warminster, Pennsylvania

Chili Nacho Supper

1 pound ground beef
1/4 cup chopped onion
1-1/2 cups salsa
1/2 cup fresh *or* frozen corn
1 can (2-1/4 ounces) sliced ripe olives, drained
3 tablespoons diced pimientos
Shredded cheddar cheese
Chopped tomato

Set aside cheese sauce mix from macaroni and cheese; cook macaroni according to package directions. Meanwhile, in a large saucepan, cook beef and onion until meat is no longer pink; drain. Add the salsa, corn, olives and pimientos; heat through. Drain macaroni; add to beef mixture with contents of cheese sauce mix. Mix well; heat through. Garnish with cheese and tomato. **Yield:** 4-6 servings. ***Editor's Note:** The milk and butter listed on the macaroni and cheese package are not used in this recipe.

covered, for 15-20 minutes or until the potatoes are tender. Stir in crab and heat through. **Yield:** 8 servings (about 2 quarts).

Chili Nacho Supper

(Pictured above)

The recipe for this creamy, chili-like dish was passed down through our church years ago. It's so warm and filling that we often prepare it when we take skiing trips to Colorado. It can be served over corn chips and eaten with a fork...or kept warm in a slow cooker and served as a hearty dip at parties. —Laurie Withers, Wildomar, California

2-1/2 pounds ground beef
3 cans (15 ounces *each*) tomato sauce
2 cans (16 ounces *each*) pinto beans, rinsed and drained
1 can (10 ounces) diced tomatoes and green chilies, undrained
2 envelopes chili mix
2 pounds process American cheese, cubed
1 cup whipping cream
2 packages (16 ounces *each*) corn chips
Sour cream

In a Dutch oven, cook the beef until no longer pink; drain. Add tomato sauce, beans, tomatoes and chili mix; heat through. Add cheese and cream; cook until the cheese is melted. Serve over chips. Top with sour cream. **Yield:** 14-16 servings.

Meaty Mac 'n' Cheese

(Pictured at right)

My husband is disabled and requires constant care. This doesn't leave me a lot of time to cook, so I came up with this tasty way to beef up a box of macaroni and cheese. Corn, ripe olives and zippy salsa give extra flavor. —Charlotte Kremer, Pahrump, Nevada

1 package (7-1/4 ounces) macaroni and cheese*

Hearty Hamburger Casserole

I love to invent my own recipes. I used convenient stuffing mix and canned vegetable soup to come up with this tasty and satisfying supper. —Regan Delp Independence, Virginia

1 pound ground beef
1 can (19 ounces) ready-to-serve chunky vegetable soup
1 package (6 ounces) instant stuffing mix
1/2 cup shredded cheddar cheese

In a skillet, cook beef until no longer pink; drain. Stir in soup and set aside. Prepare stuffing mix according to package directions; spoon half into a greased 2-qt. baking dish. Top with beef mixture, cheese and remaining stuffing. Bake, uncovered, at 350° for 30-35 minutes or until heated through. **Yield:** 4 servings.

Meaty Mac 'n' Cheese

Buttermilk Fruit Topping

(Pictured at right)

Instant vanilla pudding mix is the key to this creamy, low-fat fruit topping. It's delicious served over slices of angel food cake, too.
                              —*Cathy Adams*
                              Parkersburg, West Virginia

✓ Uses less fat, sugar or salt. Includes Nutritional Analysis and Diabetic Exchanges.

1-1/2 cups cold buttermilk
   1 package (3.4 ounces) instant vanilla
     pudding mix
   1 carton (8 ounces) frozen whipped
     topping, thawed
Fresh fruit

In a mixing bowl, combine buttermilk and pudding mix. Beat on low speed for 2 minutes. Fold in whipped topping. Chill for 1 hour. Serve over fruit. **Yield:** about 4-1/2 cups. **Nutritional Analysis:** 2 tablespoons of topping (prepared with sugar-free pudding and light whipped topping) equals 22 calories, 43 mg sodium, trace cholesterol, 3 gm carbohydrate, trace protein, 1 gm fat. **Diabetic Exchange:** Free food.

Buttermilk Fruit Topping

Jalapeno Appetizer Pancakes

Jalapeno peppers and mozzarella cheese give a tasty twist to these bite-size pancakes made from a mix. My grandchildren love them as a side dish or appetizer.
                              —*Lorraine Watson, Malta, Montana*

   2 cups pancake mix
1-1/2 cups water
   2 cups (8 ounces) shredded mozzarella cheese
   1 can (4 ounces) diced jalapeno peppers,
     drained
Ranch salad dressing *or* salsa

In a bowl, combine pancake mix and water; mix well. Stir in cheese and peppers. Pour the batter by heaping tablespoonfuls onto a greased hot griddle; turn when bubbles form on top of pancakes. Cook until second side is golden brown. Serve warm with dressing or salsa. **Yield:** about 2-1/2 dozen.

Tex-Mex Biscuits

(Pictured below left)

I love cooking with green chilies because they add so much flavor to ordinary dishes. Once while making a pot of chili, I had some green chilies left over and mixed them into my biscuit dough, creating this recipe. The fresh-from-the-oven treats are a wonderful accompaniment to soup or chili.   —*Angie Trolz, Jackson, Michigan*

   2 cups biscuit/baking mix
2/3 cup milk
   1 cup (4 ounces) finely shredded cheddar
     cheese
   1 can (4 ounces) chopped green chilies,
     drained

In a bowl, combine biscuit mix and milk until a soft dough forms. Stir in cheese and chilies. Turn onto a floured surface; knead 10 times. Roll out to 1/2-in. thickness; cut with a 2-1/2-in. biscuit cutter. Place on an ungreased baking sheet. Bake at 450° for 8-10 minutes or until golden brown. Serve warm. **Yield:** about 1 dozen.

Nacho Rice Dip

Spanish rice mix adds an interesting twist to this effortless appetizer. Every time I serve this dip at get-togethers, my guests gobble it up.   —*Audra Hungate, Holt, Missouri*

   1 package (6.8 ounces) Spanish rice and
     vermicelli mix
   2 tablespoons butter *or* margarine
   2 cups water
   1 can (14-1/2 ounces) diced tomatoes,
     undrained

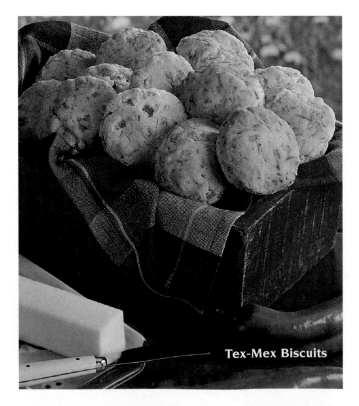
Tex-Mex Biscuits

1 pound ground beef
1 pound (16 ounces) process American cheese,
   cubed
1 can (14-1/2 ounces) stewed tomatoes
1 jar (8 ounces) process cheese sauce
Tortilla chips

In a large saucepan, cook rice mix in butter until golden. Stir in water and diced tomatoes; bring to a boil. Reduce heat; cover and simmer for 15-20 minutes or until rice is tender. Meanwhile, in a skillet, cook beef until no longer pink. Drain and add to the rice. Stir in cheese, stewed tomatoes and cheese sauce; cook and stir until cheese is melted. Transfer to a slow cooker; cover and keep warm on low. Serve with tortilla chips. **Yield:** about 8 cups.

Corny Green Bean Casserole

Crushed crackers and french-fried onions create the fast and flavorful topping for this home-style corn and green bean casserole. It's terrific to take to potluck dinners.
                      —*Dorothy Bahlmann, Clarksville, Iowa*

1 package (16 ounces) frozen french-style
   green beans, thawed and drained
2 cups frozen corn, thawed and drained
1 can (10-3/4 ounces) condensed cream of
   celery soup, undiluted
1 cup chopped onion
1 cup (8 ounces) sour cream
1 cup (4 ounces) shredded cheddar cheese
Salt and pepper to taste
1-1/2 cups crushed butter-flavored crackers (about
   36 crackers)
1/2 cup french-fried onions

In a bowl, combine beans, corn, soup, onion, sour cream, cheese, salt and pepper. Transfer to a greased 13-in. x 9-in. x 2-in. baking dish. Sprinkle with crackers and french-fried onions. Bake, uncovered, at 350° for 25-35 minutes or until heated through. **Yield:** 8 servings.

Simple Herb Rice

I revised a traditional time-consuming stuffing recipe several times to come up with this simple savory side dish. It's a breeze to prepare using instant rice. Everyone agrees its wonderful herb flavor pairs well with many dishes.   —*Lisa Mathew, Buffalo, Missouri*

✓ Uses less fat, sugar or salt. Includes Nutritional Analysis and Diabetic Exchanges.

1/4 cup chopped onion
2 tablespoons butter *or* margarine
3 chicken bouillon cubes
2 cups boiling water
2 cups instant rice
2 tablespoons dried parsley flakes
1/2 teaspoon rubbed sage
1/4 teaspoon celery salt, optional

In a skillet, saute onion in butter until tender. Dissolve bouillon in boiling water; add to the skillet. Stir in the rice, parsley, sage and celery salt if desired. Bring to a boil. Reduce heat; cover and simmer for 5-8 minutes or until the rice is tender. **Yield:** 4 servings. **Nutritional Analysis:** One 3/4-cup serving (prepared with reduced-fat margarine and low-sodium bouillon and without celery salt) equals 202 calories, 76 mg sodium, 0 cholesterol, 37 gm carbohydrate, 4 gm protein, 4 gm fat. **Diabetic Exchanges:** 2 starch, 1 fat.

Snappy Salads and Side Dishes

- Everyone loves it when I make instant rice with a can of beef consomme instead of water. Since you use equal amounts of liquid and rice, I use the soup can to measure the rice...no water is needed.
                      —*Marsha Grady, Cass City, Michigan*
- I sprinkle fresh or canned fruit with confectioners' sugar and a teaspoon of orange drink mix. It adds some zest and keeps the fruit from turning brown.
                      —*Jan Thompson, Vancouver, Washington*
- Sprinkle your chicken salad with a little cinnamon to make it really special. I learned this easy trick from a small local restaurant.   —*Myrtle Scott*
                      Franklin, North Carolina
- For a deliciously different side dish, I stir a can of peach pie filling into 2 pounds of cooked sliced carrots. It's a nice change of pace.   —*Gladys Gierl*
                      Pittsburgh, Pennsylvania
- Instead of topping salads with regular croutons, I use the instant stuffing mix for chicken that you can buy in a canister. The seasonings are already mixed in, and the croutons are smaller so you can enjoy their crunch in just about every bite.   —*Terry Bray*
                      Haines City, Florida
- For a quick, easy gelatin salad our children have always enjoyed, I dissolve a small package of berry-flavored gelatin in 1 cup of boiling water, then add 1/2 cup cold water and 3/4 cup of applesauce.
                      —*Becky Karam, Mansfield, Ohio*
- For my potato salad, I stir a teaspoon of horseradish into the dressing before tossing with the potatoes. It gives it a little more zing.   —*Luella Parry*
                      St. Edward, Nebraska
- When I make ham salad, I throw a few chunks of pineapple in the food processor along with the other ingredients. It adds a hint of sweetness.
                      —*Lois Bishop, Indianola, Iowa*
- For a tasty topping on everyday baked beans, sprinkle finely crushed gingersnaps over the top after the beans are heated through.   —*Renee Zimmer*
                      Tacoma, Washington
- My secret to a great gelatin salad is to substitute canned fruit juices for water. For example, I use apricot nectar and the reserved juice from mandarin oranges in a salad made with apricot gelatin, mandarin oranges and shredded carrots.
                      —*Laura McCormick, Kerrville, Texas*

Coconut Gingerbread Cake

Coconut Gingerbread Cake

(Pictured above)

This unusual dessert came from a little book I bought at a flea market many years ago. The broiled orange-coconut topping really dresses up a boxed gingerbread mix. When I bring it to potlucks and family get-togethers, it never lasts long! —Paula Hartlett, Mineola, New York

   1 package (14-1/2 ounces) gingerbread mix
   1 large navel orange
1-1/3 cups flaked coconut
  1/2 cup packed brown sugar
   2 tablespoons orange juice

Prepare and bake cake according to package directions, using a greased 8-in. square baking pan. Meanwhile, grate 1 tablespoon of peel from the orange; set aside. Peel and section the orange, removing white pith; dice the orange. When cake tests done, remove from the oven and cool slightly. Combine coconut, brown sugar, orange juice, diced orange and reserved peel; spread over warm cake. Broil 4 in. from the heat for 2-3 minutes or until the top is lightly browned. Cool on a wire rack. **Yield:** 9 servings.

Sloppy Joe Under a Bun

(Pictured on page 72)

I usually keep a can of sloppy joe sauce in the pantry, because our kids love sloppy joes. But sometimes I don't have buns on hand. With this fun casserole, we can still enjoy the flavor that they love in a flash. The bun-like top crust is made with biscuit mix, sprinkled with sesame seeds and baked until golden. —Trish Bloom, Romeo, Michigan

1-1/2 pounds ground beef
   1 can (15-1/2 ounces) sloppy joe sauce
   2 cups (8 ounces) shredded cheddar cheese
   2 cups biscuit/baking mix
   2 eggs, beaten

   1 cup milk
   1 tablespoon sesame seeds

In a skillet, cook beef until no longer pink; drain. Stir in sloppy joe sauce; mix well. Transfer to a lightly greased 13-in. x 9-in. x 2-in. baking dish; sprinkle with cheese. In a bowl, combine biscuit mix, eggs and milk just until blended. Pour over cheese; sprinkle with sesame seeds. Bake, uncovered, at 400° for 25 minutes or until golden brown. **Yield:** 8 servings.

Au Gratin Sausage Skillet

(Pictured below)

Using frozen vegetables and a package of au gratin potatoes, I can get this satisfying stovetop supper on the table in no time. Even our oldest daughter, who can be a picky eater, loves it—and it is an excellent way of getting her to eat her vegetables. —Penny Greene, Lancaster, Ohio

   1 pound fully cooked kielbasa *or* Polish sausage, halved and sliced 1/2 inch thick
   2 tablespoons vegetable oil
   1 package (5-1/4 ounces) au gratin potatoes*
2-1/2 cups water
   1 package (8 ounces) frozen California blend vegetables
   1 to 2 cups (4 to 8 ounces) shredded cheddar cheese

In a skillet, cook sausage in oil until lightly browned; drain. Add potatoes with contents of sauce mix and water. Cover and cook over medium heat for 18-20 minutes or until the potatoes are almost tender, stirring occasionally. Add vegetables; cover and cook for 8-10 minutes or until potatoes and vegetables are tender. Sprin-

Au Gratin Sausage Skillet

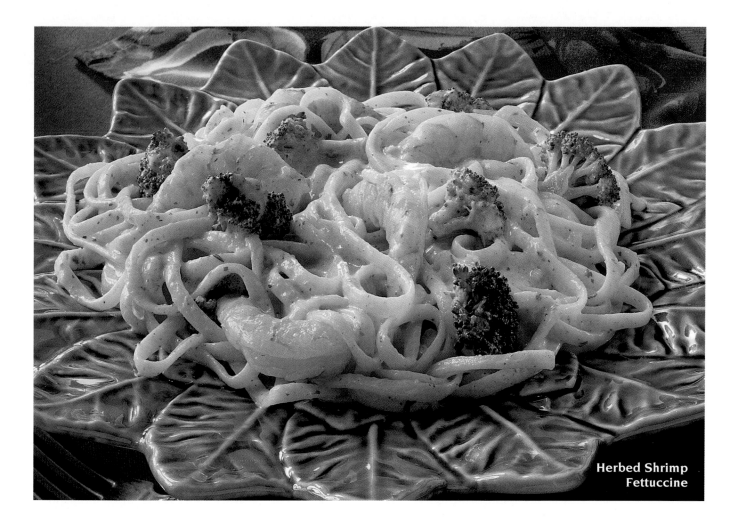

Herbed Shrimp Fettuccine

kle with cheese. Remove from the heat; cover and let stand for 2 minutes or until the cheese is melted. **Yield:** 4 servings. ***Editor's Note:** The milk and butter listed on the potato package are not used in this recipe.

Spicy Ravioli Salad

(Pictured on page 73)

A convenient combination of frozen ravioli and pantry staples (including canned tomatoes, corn and olives) is dressed with easy taco sauce for tangy, fresh-tasting results. —*Paula Marchesi, Lenhartsville, Pennsylvania*

　1 **package (25 ounces) frozen beef, sausage *or* cheese ravioli**
　1 **can (10 ounces) diced tomatoes and green chilies, undrained**
　1 **can (8-3/4 ounces) whole kernel corn, drained**
　1 **bottle (8 ounces) taco sauce**
　1 **can (2-1/4 ounces) sliced ripe olives, drained**
　1 **small cucumber, peeled, seeded and chopped**
　1 **small red onion, sliced**
　2 **garlic cloves, minced**
1/4 **teaspoon ground cumin**
1/4 **teaspoon salt**
1/4 **teaspoon pepper**

Cook ravioli according to package directions. Meanwhile, combine remaining ingredients in a large bowl. Drain ravioli; stir into tomato mixture. Cover and refrigerate for at least 2 hours. **Yield:** 8-10 servings.

Herbed Shrimp Fettuccine

(Pictured above)

Everyone will think you went all out when you serve this impressive seafood entree. You'll be amazed, though, at how easy and quick it is to fix. —*Marilyn Weaver Sparks, Maryland*

　　6 **ounces fettuccine *or* medium egg noodles**
　　1 **envelope herb and garlic soup mix**
1-3/4 **cups milk**
　　1 **pound uncooked shrimp, peeled and deveined**
　　2 **cups broccoli florets**
　1/4 **cup grated Parmesan cheese**

Cook fettuccine according to package directions. Meanwhile, combine soup mix and milk in a saucepan. Cook and stir over medium heat until smooth. Add shrimp and broccoli; simmer, uncovered, for 3-5 minutes or until shrimp are pink (do not boil). Drain pasta; toss with the shrimp mixture. Sprinkle with Parmesan cheese. **Yield:** 4 servings.

Special Wild Rice Salad

(Pictured below)

A friend fixed this for a company outing a few years ago, and it has since become my favorite picnic salad. Jars of marinated mushrooms and artichoke hearts, along with fresh vegetables, turn prepared rice mix into something special. —Suzanne Strocsher, Bothell, Washington

    2 packages (6 ounces *each*) long grain and
      wild rice mix
    2 to 3 ripe avocados, peeled and chopped
    1 jar (8 ounces) marinated whole mushrooms,
      undrained
    1 jar (6-1/2 ounces) marinated artichoke
      hearts, undrained
    1 to 2 medium tomatoes, diced
    2 celery ribs, chopped
    2 to 3 green onions, chopped
    1/2 cup Italian salad dressing

Prepare the rice according to package directions. Cool; transfer to a large bowl. Add remaining ingredients and toss to coat. Cover and refrigerate overnight. **Yield:** 10-12 servings.

Zucchini Carrot Muffins

(Pictured below)

I use carrot cake mix to stir up these moist muffins chock-full of zucchini, nuts and raisins. They make great snacks and are wonderful for dessert when spread with cream cheese frosting. —Anita Sterrett Anchorage, Alaska

      1 package (18 ounces) carrot cake mix
      1 egg
    1/2 cup applesauce
    1/4 cup vegetable oil
  1-1/2 cups shredded zucchini
    1/2 cup raisins
    1/2 cup chopped pecans

In a mixing bowl, combine the cake mix, egg, applesauce and oil; mix well. Stir in the zucchini, raisins and

Zucchini Carrot Muffins
Special Wild Rice Salad

pecans. Fill greased or paper-lined muffin cups three-fourths full. Bake at 350° for 25-30 minutes or until muffins test done. **Yield:** about 16 muffins.

Artichoke Heart Salad

(Pictured at right)

I put together this fast five-ingredient salad after sampling a similar mixture from a salad bar. Bottled Italian dressing gives robust flavor to this simple treatment for canned artichoke hearts. It is a snap to make as a last-minute side dish.
—Elizabeth Birkenmaier, Gladstone, Missouri

    1 can (14 ounces) artichoke hearts,
        quartered and drained
    1 can (2-1/4 ounces) sliced ripe olives,
        drained, optional
1/3 cup chopped green pepper
1/3 cup thinly sliced green onions
3/4 cup Italian salad dressing

In a bowl, combine artichokes, olives if desired, green pepper and onions. Add dressing and toss to coat. Cover and refrigerate for at least 30 minutes. Serve with a slotted spoon. **Yield:** 3-4 servings.

Artichoke Heart Salad

Caramel-Fudge Chocolate Cake

(Pictured on page 73)

To satisfy the chocolate lovers in our family, I added hot fudge topping and chocolate chips to a caramel-covered dessert that's quite popular in our area. The moist cake layer is a breeze to prepare using a boxed mix…and the rich toppings make it especially decadent.
—Karen Stucky, Freeman, South Dakota

    1 package (18-1/4 ounces) chocolate cake mix
    1 cup miniature semisweet chocolate chips,
        divided
    1 jar (12-1/4 ounces) caramel ice cream
        topping, warmed
    1 jar (11-3/4 ounces) hot fudge ice cream
        topping, warmed
    1 carton (8 ounces) frozen whipped topping,
        thawed
1/2 cup English toffee bits *or* almond brickle
        chips

Prepare cake batter according to package directions. Stir in 3/4 cup chocolate chips. Pour into a greased 13-in. x 9-in. x 2-in. baking pan. Bake at 350° for 35-40 min-

utes or until a toothpick inserted near the center comes out clean. Immediately poke holes in the cake with a meat fork or skewer. Spread caramel and fudge toppings over cake. Cool on a wire rack. Frost with whipped topping. Sprinkle with toffee bits and remaining chocolate chips. Store in the refrigerator. **Yield:** 12-15 servings.

Spicy Pumpkin Spread

I love pumpkin pie and bread, but as a diabetic, I can't have the sugar. This spread has the same spicy pumpkin flavor, so it's a good alternative.
—Rita Barnes
Fort Dodge, Iowa

> ✓ Uses less fat, sugar or salt. Includes Nutritional Analysis and Diabetic Exchanges.

1-1/4 cups cold apple juice
    1 package (3.4 ounces) instant vanilla pudding
        mix
    1 cup cooked *or* canned pumpkin
1/2 to 1 teaspoon pumpkin pie spice
Bagels *or* toast

In a mixing bowl, combine apple juice and dry pudding mix. Beat on low speed for 2 minutes. Stir in pumpkin and pie spice. Let stand for 5 minutes. Serve on bagels or toast. Store in the refrigerator up to 3 days. **Yield:** about 3 cups. **Nutritional Analysis:** One 2-tablespoon serving (prepared with sugar-free pudding mix and unsweetened apple juice; calculated without bread) equals 22 calories, 167 mg sodium, 0 cholesterol, 5 gm carbohydrate, trace protein, trace fat. **Diabetic Exchange:** Free food.

Spice Substitute

If a recipe calls for pumpkin pie spice and you find you don't have any, use this handy alternative. Mix 1/2 teaspoon ground cinnamon, 1/4 teaspoon ground nutmeg, 1/8 teaspoon ground ginger and 1/8 teaspoon ground cloves. This combination provides the same flavor as 1 teaspoon of pumpkin pie spice.
—Sue Mackey, Galesburg, Illinois

Reuben Chowder
Lasagna Soup

Lasagna Soup

(Pictured above)

This recipe is excellent for working mothers because it's fast to make and very flavorful. Fresh zucchini and corn add color and crunch to a boxed lasagna dinner mix.
—*Gladys Shaffer, Elma, Washington*

- 1 pound ground beef
- 1/2 cup chopped onion
- 1 package (7-3/4 ounces) lasagna dinner mix
- 5 cups water
- 1 can (14-1/2 ounces) diced tomatoes, undrained
- 1 can (7 ounces) whole kernel corn, undrained
- 2 tablespoons grated Parmesan cheese
- 1 small zucchini, chopped

In a Dutch oven or soup kettle, cook beef and onion over medium heat until meat is no longer pink; drain. Add contents of lasagna dinner sauce mix, water, tomatoes, corn and Parmesan cheese; bring to a boil. Reduce heat; cover and simmer for 10 minutes, stirring occasionally. Add the lasagna noodles and zucchini. Cover and simmer for 10 minutes or until noodles are tender. Serve immediately. **Yield:** 10 servings (2-1/2 quarts).

Pork Chops in Gravy

A good friend made me these tender chops in a flavorful gravy for my birthday. I immediately asked for the recipe and have served them many times since. There are never leftovers. —*Meg Griesdorn, Murraysville, West Virginia*

- 1 egg
- 2 tablespoons water
- 8 pork loin chops (1/2 inch thick)
- 3/4 cup seasoned bread crumbs
- 2 tablespoons vegetable oil

1 can (10-3/4 ounces) condensed cream of
   mushroom soup, undiluted
1 can (10-1/2 ounces) condensed
   French onion soup, undiluted
1/4 cup grated Parmesan cheese
Hot mashed potatoes

In a shallow bowl, beat egg and water. Dip pork chops in egg mixture, then coat with bread crumbs. In a large skillet, brown chops in oil. Transfer to a greased 13-in. x 9-in. x 2-in. baking dish. Combine the soups; pour over chops. Sprinkle with cheese. Cover and bake at 325° for 1-1/2 hours or until meat is tender. Serve with mashed potatoes. **Yield:** 8 servings.

Reuben Chowder

(Pictured at left)

If you like Reuben sandwiches, you'll be delighted with the flavor of this unusual soup. Crunchy rye bread croutons top a hearty blend of convenient canned soups, sauerkraut, corned beef and mozzarella cheese. —Iola Egle
McCook, Nebraska

1 tablespoon butter *or* margarine, softened
3 slices rye bread
1 can (11 ounces) condensed nacho cheese
   soup, undiluted
1 can (10-3/4 ounces) condensed cream of
   mushroom soup, undiluted
3 cups milk
1 can (14 ounces) sauerkraut, rinsed and
   drained
12 ounces deli corned beef, diced
1 cup (4 ounces) shredded mozzarella
   cheese

Butter bread on both sides; cube. Place on an ungreased baking sheet. Bake at 375° for 6-8 minutes or until browned. Meanwhile, in a large saucepan, combine the soups, milk, sauerkraut and corned beef; cook and stir over medium heat for 8-10 minutes or until heated through. Add cheese; stir until melted. Top with croutons. **Yield:** 8 servings (2 quarts).

Lattice-Top Chicken Stew

(Pictured at right)

Convenient crescent roll dough turns into the pretty topping on this creamy casserole filled with chicken and vegetables. While it's baking, I prepare a simple salad and dessert. It's a nice meal for company, too. —Janet Aselage, Sidney, Ohio

1 package (16 ounces) frozen California-
   blend vegetables, thawed and drained
2 cups cubed cooked chicken
1 cup milk
1 can (10-3/4 ounces) condensed cream of
   potato soup, undiluted
1/2 cup shredded cheddar cheese
1/2 cup french-fried onions

1/2 teaspoon seasoned salt
1 tube (8 ounces) refrigerated crescent rolls

In a bowl, combine the vegetables, chicken, milk, soup, cheese, onions and seasoned salt. Transfer to a greased 13-in. x 9-in. x 2-in. baking dish. Bake, uncovered, at 350° for 20 minutes. Meanwhile, separate crescent dough into two rectangles. Seal perforations; cut each rectangle lengthwise into four strips. Working quickly, weave strips over warm filling, forming a lattice crust. Bake 15 minutes longer or until crust is golden brown. **Yield:** 6-8 servings.

Swiss Chicken

Your guests will be impressed with this palate-pleasing chicken topped with stuffing and Swiss cheese. I usually serve it with corn and a salad, since the stuffing is a side dish in itself. —Elizabeth Montgomery
Taylorville, Illinois

6 boneless skinless chicken breast halves
1 cup (4 ounces) shredded Swiss cheese
5 cups seasoned stuffing mix
1 can (10-3/4 ounces) condensed cream of
   mushroom soup, undiluted
1 cup (8 ounces) sour cream

Place chicken in a greased 13-in. x 9-in. x 2-in. baking dish; sprinkle with the cheese and stuffing mix. Combine soup and sour cream; spread over stuffing. Bake, uncovered, at 375° for 1 hour or until the meat juices run clear. **Yield:** 6 servings.

Lattice-Top Chicken Stew

Pumpkin Bundt Cake
Brownie Delight

Pumpkin Bundt Cake

(Pictured above)

Our family grows lots of pumpkins, but I have to put dibs on some or the children will carve every one! I like to use them—or convenient canned pumpkin—in this moist cake.
—Margaret Slocum, Ridgefield, Washington

    1/4 cup butter *or* margarine, softened
      1 cup sugar
      1 cup packed brown sugar
      4 eggs
      1 can (15 ounces) solid-pack pumpkin *or* 1-3/4
        cups cooked pumpkin
      3 cups biscuit/baking mix
GLAZE:
      1 cup confectioners' sugar
      1 tablespoon milk
    1/2 teaspoon vanilla extract

In a mixing bowl, cream butter and sugars. Add the eggs, one at a time, beating well after each addition. Beat in pumpkin; mix well. Gradually add baking mix until combined. Pour into a greased and floured 10-in.
fluted tube pan. Bake at 350° for 55-60 minutes or until a toothpick inserted near the center comes out clean. Cool for 10 minutes before removing from pan to a wire rack. Combine glaze ingredients; drizzle over cooled cake. **Yield:** 12-16 servings.

Cranberry Upside-Down Cake

When I'm rushed for a dessert for a Christmas potluck, I grab the recipe for this old-fashioned cake. A cake mix gets special treatment from walnuts, pineapple and cranberries.
—Ruth Marie Lyons, Boulder, Colorado

      1 can (20 ounces) pineapple tidbits
    1/2 cup butter *or* margarine, melted
      1 cup packed brown sugar
      1 cup fresh *or* frozen cranberries
    1/2 cup walnut halves
      1 package (18-1/4 ounces) yellow cake mix
      3 eggs
    1/4 cup vegetable oil

Drain pineapple, reserving juice. Add water to juice to measure 1-1/4 cups; set aside. Pour butter into a greased 13-in. x 9-in. x 2-in. baking dish. Sprinkle with brown sugar, cranberries and walnuts. Top with pineapple. In a mixing bowl, combine dry cake mix, eggs, oil and reserved pineapple juice. Beat on medium speed for 2 minutes. Pour into prepared pan. Bake at 350° for 25-35 minutes or until a toothpick inserted near the center comes out clean. Cool for 10 minutes before inverting onto a large serving platter (top will have an uneven appearance). **Yield:** 12-16 servings.

Brownie Delight

(Pictured at left)

Brownie mix and instant pudding hurry along the preparation of this scrumptious layered dessert. My family asks for this rich treat for birthdays instead of a cake.

—Opal Erickson, Branson, Missouri

- 1 package brownie mix (13-inch x 9-inch pan size)
- 2 packages (one 8 ounces, one 3 ounces) cream cheese, softened
- 2 cups confectioners' sugar
- 1 carton (16 ounces) frozen whipped topping, thawed, *divided*
- 2 cups cold milk
- 1 package (3.9 ounces) instant chocolate pudding mix
- 1/2 cup chopped pecans

Prepare and bake brownies according to package directions, using a greased 13-in. x 9-in. x 2-in. baking pan. Cool completely. In a mixing bowl, beat cream cheese and sugar for 2 minutes. Fold in 2 cups whipped topping. Spread over brownies. In another bowl, combine the milk and pudding mix; beat until smooth. Refrigerate for 5 minutes; spread over the cream cheese layer. Spread with remaining whipped topping; sprinkle with pecans. Refrigerate until serving. **Yield:** 12-15 servings.

No-Bake Cherry Cheesecake

(Pictured above right)

My husband and I both work full-time, and taxiing our two teenagers around town leaves me little time in the kitchen. Using a prepared graham cracker crust and canned pie filling, I can extend a no-bake mix to make two light, fancy-looking pies in less than 15 minutes.

—Pam Noffke, Tyler, Texas

- 1 package (11.1 ounces) no-bake cheesecake mix
- 1/3 cup butter *or* margarine, melted
- 2 tablespoons sugar
- 1-1/2 cups cold milk
- 1 package (8 ounces) cream cheese, softened
- 1 cup confectioners' sugar
- 2 cups whipped topping
- 1 graham cracker crust (9 inches)
- 2 cans (21 ounces *each*) cherry pie filling

In an ungreased 9-in. pie plate, combine cheesecake crust mix, butter and sugar; mix until the crumbs are moistened. Press onto the bottom and up the sides of

No-Bake Cherry Cheesecake

the plate. Refrigerate. In a mixing bowl, combine cheesecake filling mix and milk; beat on medium speed for 3 minutes. In another mixing bowl, beat cream cheese and confectioners' sugar. Add to cheesecake mixture; beat well. Fold in whipped topping. Spoon into chilled crust and purchased crust. Refrigerate for at least 1 hour. Top with pie filling. **Yield:** 2 pies (6-8 servings each).

No-Fuss Desserts

- Before baking chocolate cake from a mix, I add 1/2 cup of boysenberry jam to the batter. I also dot jam over the white frosting for a pretty effect. Everyone raves over this yummy dessert. *—Isabella Castro Gustine, California*
- For special ice cream sundaes, I blend 1/4 teaspoon each of ground cloves and ground cinnamon into a 12-ounce jar of hot fudge topping. *—Sharon Muldoon, Lockport, New York*
- To make a terrific dessert, pour a thin layer of GrapeNuts cereal into dessert bowls and slowly add your favorite prepared pudding. In 2 hours, the cereal forms a crunchy crust. In 6 hours or overnight, it's a softer crust. Top with whipped topping. *—Diana Dube, Rockland, Maine*
- When baking a pie using canned cherries, stir in a couple teaspoons of unsweetened cherry soft drink mix to perk up the color and flavor. *—Lela Josephson, Peoria, Illinois*
- For from-scratch flavor, add 1 teaspoon of vanilla extract and one whole egg to a white cake mix in place of an egg white. *—Marcia Castro, Toledo, Ohio*
- When preparing brownies, I add mint extract and chocolate chips to the batter before baking. *—Colleen Wuethrich, Francesville, Indiana*
- I stir a small box of dry vanilla pudding mix into my oatmeal cookie dough. It makes the cookies moist and chewy. *—Nancy Hilburn, Blue Eye, Missouri*
- When I didn't have pecans to add to my chocolate chip cookie dough, I added a cup of toffee bits instead. The cookies were so rich and buttery that now I make them this way all the time. *—Brenda Sanders Hampstead, North Carolina*

Homemade Mixes

HANDY homemade mixes deliver all the great taste of the popular specialty products offered today but for far less cost. You'll find they're convenient to have on hand as a head start to any fast meal.

Crisp Sugar Cookie Mix

(Pictured below)

I have relied on the mix for these light sugar cookies for years, even selling it at bazaars. I package it in a plastic bag tied with pretty ribbon and attach a cookie cutter and copy of the recipe. —Eneatha Attig Secrest
Mattoon, Illinois

        5 cups all-purpose flour
        3 cups confectioners' sugar
        2 teaspoons baking soda
        2 teaspoons cream of tartar
ADDITIONAL INGREDIENTS:
        1 cup butter (no substitutes), softened
        1 egg
        1 teaspoon vanilla extract
    1/2 teaspoon almond extract
Colored sugar, optional*

In a bowl, combine the first four ingredients; mix well. Store in an airtight container in a cool dry place for up to 6 months. **Yield:** 2 batches (8 cups total). **To prepare cookies:** In a mixing bowl, cream the butter. Beat in egg and extracts. Gradually add 4 cups cookie mix; mix well. Cover and chill for 2-3 hours or overnight. On a lightly floured surface, roll out dough to 1/8-in. thickness. Cut with a 2-1/2-in. cookie cutter dipped in flour. Place 1

Crisp Sugar Cookie Mix

in. apart on ungreased baking sheets. Sprinkle with colored sugar if desired. Bake at 375° for 7-9 minutes or until the edges are lightly browned. Cool on wire racks. **Yield:** about 4 dozen per batch. ***Editor's Note:** Omit colored sugar if you want to frost the cookies.

Poppy Seed Bread Mix

This simple seeded loaf is delicious alone or spread with cream cheese or jam. It freezes well, too.
—Laurie Marini, Newport, North Carolina

    10 cups all-purpose flour
     4 cups sugar
     1 cup poppy seeds
    1/4 cup plus 2 teaspoons baking powder
     4 teaspoons salt
ADDITIONAL INGREDIENTS:
     1 egg
    1-1/4 cups milk
    1/3 cup vegetable oil
     1 teaspoon vanilla extract

In a large bowl, combine the first five ingredients; mix well. Store in an airtight container in a cool dry place for up to 6 months. **Yield:** 4 batches (16 cups total). **To prepare one loaf:** In a mixing bowl, combine the egg, milk, oil and vanilla. Add 4 cups bread mix; stir just until moistened. Pour into a greased 9-in. x 5-in. x 3-in. loaf pan. Bake at 350° for 55-60 minutes or until a toothpick inserted near the center comes out clean. Cool for 10 minutes; remove from pan to a wire rack. **Yield:** 1 loaf per batch.

Versatile Pudding Mix

Stir the dry mixture well before using—if the cornstarch settles to the bottom, the pudding won't thicken properly.
—Renee Schwebach, Dumont, Minnesota

        5 quarts instant nonfat dry milk powder (not reconstituted)
    3-1/2 cups sugar
    1-3/4 cups cornstarch
    2-1/4 teaspoons salt
ADDITIONAL INGREDIENTS FOR VANILLA PUDDING:
        2 cups water
        1 egg yolk, lightly beaten
        2 teaspoons vanilla extract
ADDITIONAL INGREDIENTS FOR CHOCOLATE PUDDING:
    1/4 cup baking cocoa
        2 cups water
        1 egg yolk, lightly beaten
        2 teaspoons vanilla extract

In a large bowl, whisk together the dry milk powder, sugar, cornstarch and salt. Store in an airtight container or resealable plastic bag for up to 1 year. **Yield:** about 10 batches (21 cups total). **To prepare vanilla pudding:** In a saucepan, combine 2 cups pudding mix and water. Bring to a boil over medium heat, stirring constantly. Remove from the heat. Gradually stir about 1 cup hot

Salad Crunchers

(Pictured at left)

This crunchy seasoned oat mixture dresses up salads, soups, casseroles and other dishes in a dash. We especially like these sprinkled on top of scalloped potatoes.
— *Tami Hermesch, Nineveh, Indiana*

- 2 cups old-fashioned oats
- 1/2 cup butter *or* margarine, melted
- 1/3 cup grated Parmesan cheese
- 1/3 cup wheat germ
- 1 teaspoon dried oregano
- 1/2 teaspoon dried thyme
- 1/4 teaspoon seasoned salt

In a mixing bowl, combine all ingredients; mix well. Spread into an ungreased 15-in. x 10-in. x 1-in. baking pan. Bake at 350° for 15-18 minutes or until lightly browned. Cool in pan on a wire rack. Store in an airtight container in the refrigerator for up to 3 months. **Yield:** 2-1/2 cups.

Three-Grain Muffins
Salad Crunchers
Ranch Dressing Mix Plus

mixture into egg yolk; return all to the pan. Bring to a gentle boil; cook and stir for 2 minutes. Remove from the heat; stir in vanilla. Pour into dessert dishes. Refrigerate. **Yield:** 6 servings per batch. **To prepare chocolate pudding:** Add the cocoa to 2 cups pudding mix. Prepare according to directions for vanilla pudding. **Yield:** 6 servings per batch.

Three-Grain Muffins

(Pictured above)

A new neighbor brought me a batch of this muffin mix. I was pleasantly surprised at how well it kept in the fridge and what delicious, moist muffins it created.
— *Dorothy Collins, Winnsboro, Texas*

- 2 cups quick-cooking oats
- 2 cups crushed Shredded Wheat (about 4 large)
- 2 cups All-Bran
- 1 quart buttermilk
- 1 cup boiling water
- 1 cup vegetable oil
- 4 eggs, beaten
- 2-1/4 cups packed brown sugar
- 5 cups all-purpose flour
- 5 teaspoons baking soda
- 1 teaspoon salt

In a large bowl, combine oats, Shredded Wheat and bran. Add buttermilk, water, oil and eggs; stir for 1 minute. Stir in the brown sugar. Combine flour, baking soda and salt; add to the cereal mixture and stir well. Fill greased or paper-lined muffin cups two-thirds full. Bake at 400° for 18-20 minutes. Cool for 10 minutes; remove from pans to wire racks. **Yield:** 4 dozen. **Editor's Note:** Muffin batter can be stored in the refrigerator for up to 1 week.

Ranch Dressing Mix Plus

(Pictured above left)

Dry mixes like the one for this versatile dressing are great because they're so quick to prepare and save money. Simple ingredients added to the basic ranch blend produce two tasty options.
— *Iola Egle, McCook, Nebraska*

- 1 cup dried parsley flakes
- 1/2 cup finely crushed saltines (about 15 crackers)
- 1/2 cup dried minced onion
- 1/2 cup garlic salt
- 1/2 cup onion salt
- 1/4 cup garlic powder
- 1/4 cup onion powder
- 2 tablespoons dill weed

ADDITIONAL INGREDIENTS:
- 2 cups mayonnaise
- 2 cups buttermilk

FOR THOUSAND ISLAND DRESSING:
- 1/4 cup chili sauce
- 2 tablespoons sweet pickle relish

FOR CUCUMBER DRESSING:
- 1 medium cucumber, peeled, seeded and pureed
- 1 teaspoon celery seed

In a large bowl, combine the first eight ingredients; mix well. Store in an airtight container in a cool dry place. **Yield:** 3 cups mix (enough to make 24 batches of ranch salad dressing). **For ranch dressing:** In a bowl, whisk together 2 tablespoons of mix with mayonnaise and buttermilk. Refrigerate until serving. **Yield:** 4 cups. **For Thousand Island dressing:** Add chili sauce and pickle relish to 1 cup prepared ranch dressing. **For cucumber dressing:** Add cucumber and celery seed to 1 cup prepared ranch dressing.

Cinnamon Nut Loaf
Homemade Pizza

minutes. Bake at 350° for 30 minutes or until loaf sounds hollow when lightly tapped. Remove from pan and cool on a wire rack. **Yield:** 1 loaf.

Homemade Pizza

(Pictured at left)

By varying a few of the ingredients required for the basic loaf, I can create a delicious thick pizza crust in a jiffy. —Lois Fleming

> 2 cups Shortcut Bread Mix (recipe on this page)
> 1 teaspoon quick-rise yeast
> 2/3 cup warm water (120° to 130°)
> 1 tablespoon butter *or* margarine, melted
> 1 tablespoon cornmeal
> Pizza sauce, sausage and cheese *or* toppings of your choice

In a mixing bowl, combine 1 cup bread mix and yeast. Add water and butter; beat until smooth. Stir in the remaining bread mix to form a soft dough. Turn onto a floured surface; knead until smooth and elastic, about 4-6 minutes. Cover and let rest for 10 minutes. On a floured surface, roll dough into a 14-in. circle. Sprinkle cornmeal on an ungreased 14-in. pizza pan; transfer dough to pan. Bake at 450° for 10 minutes. Top with pizza sauce, sausage and cheese. Bake 10-15 minutes longer or until golden brown. **Yield:** 1 pizza.

Shortcut Bread Mix

Versatile is the word for this terrific time-saving mix. It's the basis for a dough that can be baked into a tender loaf of lightly sweet bread or shaped into 18 delicious dinner rolls. It's also used to make the other two tasty recipes on this page. —Lois Fleming, Monroeville, Pennsylvania

BREAD MIX:
> 5 pounds all-purpose flour
> 2 cups instant nonfat dry milk powder
> 1 cup sugar
> 7-1/2 teaspoons salt

ADDITIONAL INGREDIENTS FOR BASIC LOAF:
> 1 package (1/4 ounce) quick-rise yeast
> 1 cup warm water (120° to 130°)
> 1 egg
> 2 tablespoons butter *or* margarine, melted

In a large bowl, combine bread mix ingredients with a wire whisk. Store in an airtight container in a cool dry place for up to 6 months. **Yield:** 20 cups (enough to make about 5 basic loaves or Cinnamon Nut Loaves *or* 10 Homemade Pizza crusts). **To prepare a basic loaf:** In a mixing bowl, combine 1 cup bread mix and yeast. Add water, egg and butter; beat until smooth. Stir in 2-1/2 to 3 cups additional bread mix to form a soft dough. Turn onto a floured surface; knead until smooth and elastic, about 4-6 minutes. Cover and let rest for 10 minutes. Shape into a loaf; place in a greased 9-in. x 5-in. x 3-in. loaf pan. Place a heatproof bowl on work surface; fill half full with boiling water. Cover bowl with a baking sheet. Place loaf pan on baking sheet; cover and let rise for 20

Cinnamon Nut Loaf

(Pictured above left)

I also use my bread mix to create this beautiful breakfast loaf swirled with cinnamon and nuts and topped with a sweet and simple icing. —Lois Fleming

> 3-1/2 to 4 cups Shortcut Bread Mix (recipe on this page)
> 1 package (1/4 ounce) quick-rise yeast
> 1 cup warm water (120° to 130°)
> 1 egg
> 3 tablespoons butter *or* margarine, melted and *divided*
> 1/4 cup sugar
> 1/4 cup chopped nuts
> 1-1/2 teaspoons ground cinnamon

ICING:
> 1/2 cup confectioners' sugar
> 1 tablespoon milk
> 1/2 teaspoon vanilla extract

In a mixing bowl, combine 1 cup bread mix and yeast. Add water, egg and 2 tablespoons butter; beat until smooth. Stir in enough remaining bread mix to form a soft dough. Turn onto a floured surface; knead until smooth and elastic, about 4-6 minutes. Cover and let rest for 10 minutes. On a floured surface, roll dough into an 18-in. x 8-in. rectangle. Brush with remaining butter. Combine sugar, nuts and cinnamon; sprinkle over

Rapid Reference

Attach the recipe for your homemade mixes to their storage containers. You won't have to hunt for the recipe when your supply needs replenishing.
—Bonnie Harcey, Hill City, Minnesota

dough. Roll up, jelly-roll style, starting with a short side; seal edges. Place seam side down in a greased 9-in. x 5-in. x 3-in. loaf pan. Place a heatproof bowl on work surface; fill half full with boiling water. Cover bowl with a baking sheet. Place loaf pan on baking sheet; cover and let rise for 20 minutes. Bake at 350° for 30-35 minutes or until golden brown. Remove from pan and cool on a wire rack. Combine icing ingredients; drizzle over loaf. **Yield:** 1 loaf.

Fresh Lemonade Syrup

(Pictured below right)

This is a refreshing summer drink to enjoy on those lazy dog days of summer. With the simple syrup in the fridge, it's a breeze to stir up this thirst-quenching beverage by the glass or pitcher. —Kathy Kittell, Lenexa, Kansas

> 3 cups sugar
> 1 cup boiling water
> 3 cups lemon juice (about 16 lemons)
> 2 tablespoons grated lemon peel

In a 1-1/2-qt. heatproof container, dissolve sugar in boiling water. Cool. Add lemon juice and peel; mix well. Cover and store in the refrigerator for up to 1 week. **Yield:** 5-1/2 cups syrup (number of batches varies depending on concentration of lemonade). **To prepare lemonade:** For 1 serving, combine 1/4 to 1/3 cup syrup and 3/4 cup cold water in a glass; stir well. For 8 servings, combine 2-2/3 cups syrup and 5 cups cold water in a 2-qt. pitcher; stir well.

Sand Castle Brownie Mix

(Pictured at right)

The home economics teacher at the school where I work shared these moist, fudgy brownies with me. Attach the recipe to a jar of the lovely layered mix, and you have a super-easy gift for any occasion. —Carin Rounds Boonville, New York

> 1/3 cup chopped nuts
> 1/2 cup semisweet chocolate chips
> 1/3 cup flaked coconut
> 2/3 cup packed brown sugar
> 3/4 cup sugar
> 1/3 cup baking cocoa
> 1-1/2 cups all-purpose flour
> ADDITIONAL INGREDIENTS:
> 2 eggs
> 2/3 cup vegetable oil
> 1 teaspoon vanilla extract

In a 1-qt. glass container, layer the first seven ingredients in order listed, packing well between each layer.

Cover and store in a cool dry place for up to 6 months. **Yield:** 1 batch (4-1/4 cups total). **To prepare brownies:** In a bowl, combine eggs, oil, vanilla and brownie mix; mix well. Spread into a greased 8-in. square baking pan. Bake at 350° for 30 minutes or until a toothpick inserted near the center comes out clean. Cool on a wire rack. **Yield:** about 2 dozen.

Bakery Frosting

Mom used this sweet frosting for all of our family's birthday cakes. Now I use it on cakes for our three preschoolers. A big batch keeps for quite a while in the refrigerator and is cheaper than canned frosting. —Barbara Jones Pana, Illinois

> 2 cups shortening
> 1/2 cup nondairy creamer
> 1 teaspoon almond extract
> 1 package (32 ounces) confectioners' sugar
> 1/2 to 3/4 cup water
> Food coloring, optional

In a mixing bowl, beat the shortening, creamer and extract. Gradually beat in sugar. Add enough water until frosting reaches desired consistency. If desired, add food coloring. Store in the refrigerator for up to 3 months. Bring to room temperature before spreading. **Yield:** 8 cups.

Fresh Lemonade Syrup
Sand Castle Brownie Mix

Classic Onion Soup Mix

(Pictured below)

You can prepare soup, make dips and even season meats with this handy mix. My grandchildren really enjoy it as a coating on oven-roasted potatoes.
—June Mullins
Livonia, Missouri

✓ Uses less fat, sugar or salt. Includes Nutritional Analysis and Diabetic Exchanges.

3/4 cup dried minced onion
1/3 cup beef bouillon granules
1/4 cup onion powder
1/4 teaspoon sugar
1/4 teaspoon celery seed
FOR ROASTED POTATOES
(pictured below):
    6 medium potatoes (about 2 pounds), cut into 1/2-inch cubes
1/3 cup olive *or* vegetable oil
FOR ONION SOUP:
    4 cups water
FOR ONION DIP:
    2 cups (16 ounces) sour cream
Assorted raw vegetables, chips *or* crackers

Combine the first five ingredients. Store in an airtight container in a cool dry place for up to 1 year. **Yield:** 4 batches (20 tablespoons total). **To prepare roasted potatoes:** In a bowl, toss potatoes and oil. Sprinkle with 5 tablespoons onion soup mix; toss to coat. Transfer to an ungreased 15-in. x 10-in. x 1-in. baking pan. Bake, uncovered, at 450° for 35-40 minutes or until tender, stirring occasionally. **Yield:** 6 servings. **To prepare onion soup:** In a saucepan, combine water and 5 tablespoons onion soup mix. Bring to a boil over medium-high heat, stirring occasionally. Reduce heat; simmer, uncovered, for 10 minutes, stirring occasionally. **Yield:** 3 servings. **To prepare onion dip:** In a bowl, combine sour cream and 5 tablespoons onion soup mix; mix well. Refrigerate for at least 2 hours. Serve with vegetables, chips

Roasted Potatoes with Classic Onion Soup Mix

or crackers. **Yield:** 2 cups. **Nutritional Analysis:** 1 tablespoon of soup mix (prepared with low-sodium bouillon) equals 15 calories, 3 mg sodium, 0 cholesterol, 3 gm carbohydrate, trace protein, trace fat. **Diabetic Exchange:** Free food.

Chocolate Chip Cookie Mix

This mix comes in handy when you need to bake a batch of cookies in a hurry. Add two ingredients, and soon you'll be serving warm-from-the-oven cookies as an after-school snack or for drop-in company.
—Patti Wolfe Bailey, Chanute, Kansas

4-1/2 cups all-purpose flour
1-1/2 cups sugar
1-1/2 cups packed brown sugar
    2 teaspoons baking soda
1-1/2 teaspoons salt
    2 cups shortening
    2 cups chopped pecans
    2 packages (12 ounces *each*) semisweet chocolate chips
ADDITIONAL INGREDIENTS:
    2 eggs
    2 teaspoons vanilla extract

In a large bowl, combine the first five ingredients. Cut in shortening until crumbly. Stir in pecans and chocolate chips. Store in an airtight container in a cool dry place for up to 6 months. **Yield:** 2 batches (14 cups total). **To prepare cookies:** In a mixing bowl, beat eggs and vanilla. Stir in 7 cups cookie mix until well blended (if dough is dry, add 1-2 tablespoons water). Drop by teaspoonfuls 2 in. apart onto greased baking sheets. Bake at 375° for 7-9 minutes or until golden brown. Cool 1-2 minutes before removing to wire racks. **Yield:** about 6 dozen per batch.

Fruit Crisp Topping Mix

I keep this sweet mixture on hand to use as a time-saving topping for many desserts. Sprinkle over muffins or pies, or use it to create this quick fruit crisp with convenient canned pie filling.
—Wendy Masters
Grand Valley, Ontario

    5 cups quick-cooking oats
    5 cups packed brown sugar
    5 cups all-purpose flour
    2 teaspoons ground cinnamon
1-1/2 teaspoons baking powder
1-1/2 teaspoons baking soda
1/2 teaspoon salt
ADDITIONAL INGREDIENTS:
    1 can (21 ounces) cherry pie filling *or* pie filling of your choice
1/4 cup cold butter *or* margarine
Vanilla ice cream, optional

Combine first seven ingredients. Store in an airtight container in a cool dry place for up to 1 year. **Yield:** 13 batches (13 cups total). **To prepare fruit crisp:** Place pie filling in an 8-in. square baking dish. Cut butter into 1

Vegetable Rice Mix

1/2 cup instant coffee
  granules
1/2 cup baking cocoa
Dash salt
1/4 teaspoon vanilla extract
1/4 teaspoon almond extract
ADDITIONAL INGREDIENTS:
  3/4 cup boiling water
Whipped cream, optional

In a bowl, combine the first five ingredients; mix well. Divide mixture in half; add vanilla to one portion and almond extract to the other. Mix well. Store in airtight containers in a cool dry place for up to 1 year. **Yield:** 14-16 batches (7-8 batches vanilla mocha mix; 7-8 batches almond mocha mix), about 3 cups total. **To prepare beverage:** Dissolve about 3 tablespoons mix in water; stir well. Top with whipped cream if desired. **Yield:** 1 serving per batch.

cup topping mix until crumbly; sprinkle over fruit. Bake at 350° for 30-40 minutes or until lightly browned. Serve warm with ice cream if desired. **Yield:** 6-8 servings.

Vegetable Rice Mix

(Pictured above)

Each batch of this easy rice mixture flavored with vegetable soup mix makes a pretty side dish when you're in a hurry. —Marjorie Carey, Freeport, Florida,

  4 cups uncooked instant rice
  1 package (1.4 ounces) vegetable soup mix
  2 tablespoons dried minced onion
  2 tablespoons dried celery flakes
  2 tablespoons dried sweet red *or* green pepper
1-1/2 teaspoons salt
ADDITIONAL INGREDIENTS:
  2 cups water
  1 tablespoon butter *or* margarine

In a bowl, combine the first six ingredients; mix well. Store in an airtight container in a cool dry place for up to 1 year. **Yield:** 4 batches (4 cups total). **To prepare rice:** In a saucepan, combine water, butter and 1 cup rice mix. Bring to a boil; reduce heat. Cover and simmer for 10-15 minutes or until the water is absorbed. **Yield:** 2-3 servings per batch.

Flavored Mocha Drink Mix

Vanilla and almond extracts give two great flavors to this hot beverage mix. At Christmastime, you can package these fun mixes in pretty jars, decorative tins or holiday mugs to make great-tasting gifts. —Edna Hoffman, Hebron, Indiana

1-1/2 cups nondairy creamer
  1 cup sugar

Instant Stuffing Mix

I assemble this mix when I want to save bread that's starting to get stale. This nicely seasoned stuffing is great with any type of poultry and costs a fraction of the store-bought version. —Darlene Markel, Sublimity, Oregon

✓ Uses less fat, sugar or salt. Includes Nutritional Analysis and Diabetic Exchanges.

1/2 cup plus 1 tablespoon dried celery flakes
  3 tablespoons dried minced onion
  3 tablespoons dried parsley flakes
  2 tablespoons chicken bouillon granules
1-1/2 teaspoons poultry seasoning
  3/4 teaspoon rubbed sage
10-1/2 cups dried bread cubes (about 24 slices) *or* unseasoned croutons
ADDITIONAL INGREDIENTS:
  1 cup water
  2 tablespoons butter *or* margarine

In a small resealable plastic bag, combine the first six ingredients; mix well. Place the bread cubes in a large resealable plastic bag; add the small seasoning bag. Store in a cool dry place for up to 1 year. **Yield:** 3 batches. **To prepare stuffing:** In a large saucepan, combine water, butter and 1/3 cup seasoning mix. Bring to a boil; reduce heat. Cover and simmer for 10 minutes. Remove from the heat. Add 3-1/2 cups bread cubes; stir just to moisten. Cover and let stand for 5 minutes. Fluff with a fork before serving. **Yield:** 2-4 servings per batch. **Nutritional Analysis:** One 1/2-cup serving (prepared with low-sodium bouillon and reduced-fat margarine) equals 188 calories, 427 mg sodium, 1 mg cholesterol, 29 gm carbohydrate, 8 gm protein, 7 gm fat. **Diabetic Exchanges:** 2 starch, 1 fat.

Chapter 7

Look Ahead for Lively Leftovers

COOKING up a little extra on weekends can be the key to made-in-minutes meals during the rest of the week.

But instead of simply reheating the same food over and over again, turn these "planned overs" into a whole different dish or two.

For example, first treat your family to Pork Chop Potato Casserole on the next page. (Like all the weekend dishes that supply the main ingredient for the weekday ones, its title is highlighted in a colored box.) Later, surprise them with such lively leftovers as Italian Pork and Rice and Country Skillet Supper.

Your family will never again look at leftovers the same way!

SECOND HELPINGS. Clockwise from lower right: Garden Fish Packets, Gone Fishin' Chowder and Fried Fish Nuggets (all recipes on pp. 102 and 103).

Pork Chop Potato Casserole
Italian Pork and Rice

Pork Chop Potato Casserole

(Pictured above)

This rich dish features tender pork chops, hearty hash browns and a golden topping of cheese and french-fried onions. —Norma Shepler, Charlotte, Michigan

- 8 pork chops (1/2 inch thick)
- 1 teaspoon seasoned salt
- 1 tablespoon vegetable oil
- 1 can (10-3/4 ounces) condensed cream of celery soup, undiluted
- 2/3 cup milk
- 1/2 cup sour cream
- 1/2 teaspoon salt
- 1/4 teaspoon pepper
- 1 package (26 ounces) frozen shredded hash brown potatoes
- 1 cup (4 ounces) shredded cheddar cheese, *divided*
- 1 can (2.8 ounces) french-fried onions, *divided*

Sprinkle pork chops with seasoned salt. In a skillet, brown chops on both sides in oil. In a large bowl, combine the soup, milk, sour cream, salt and pepper; stir in hash browns, 3/4 cup cheese and half of the onions. Spread into a greased 13-in. x 9-in. x 2-in. baking dish. Arrange pork chops on top. Cover and bake at 350° for 40 minutes. Uncover; sprinkle with the remaining cheese and onions. Bake, uncovered, 5-10 minutes longer or until

potatoes are tender, cheese is melted and meat juices run clear. **Yield:** 8 servings.

Italian Pork and Rice

(Pictured above)

I always prepare a few extra pork chops for this colorful stovetop meal. I serve it with garlic bread and a tossed salad. —Loreen McAllister, Elsie, Michigan

✓ Uses less fat, sugar or salt. Includes Nutritional Analysis and Diabetic Exchanges.

- 1 cup sliced fresh mushrooms
- 1/3 cup chopped onion
- 1 garlic clove, minced
- 1 tablespoon butter *or* margarine
- 1 can (14-1/2 ounces) Italian diced tomatoes, undrained
- 1 cup cubed cooked pork (about 2 pork chops)
- 1/2 cup chopped green pepper
- 1/2 cup chopped sweet red pepper
- 1 teaspoon Italian seasoning
- 1/2 teaspoon salt, optional
Pinch sugar
- 1/2 cup uncooked instant rice

In a saucepan, saute the mushrooms, onion and garlic in butter until tender. Stir in tomatoes, pork, peppers, Italian seasoning, salt if desired and sugar; bring to a boil.

Stir in rice. Cover and remove from the heat; let stand for 5 minutes. Stir before serving. **Yield:** 3 servings. **Nutritional Analysis:** One 1-cup serving (prepared with margarine and without salt) equals 245 calories, 341 mg sodium, 41 mg cholesterol, 25 gm carbohydrate, 18 gm protein, 7 gm fat. **Diabetic Exchanges:** 2 lean meat, 1-1/2 starch, 1/2 vegetable.

Country Skillet Supper

This casserole, with pork, potatoes and peas, is great served alongside biscuits.
—Arlene Snyder
Ephrata, Pennsylvania

    1 small onion, chopped
    1 tablespoon vegetable oil
    1 can (10-3/4 ounces) condensed cream of
      celery soup, undiluted
  1/2 cup milk
    1 teaspoon Worcestershire sauce
  1/4 teaspoon salt
  1/8 teaspoon pepper
    1 cup cubed cooked pork (about 2 pork chops)
    1 cup cubed cooked potatoes
    1 cup frozen peas, thawed

In a skillet, saute onion in oil until tender. Stir in soup, milk, Worcestershire, salt and pepper; mix well. Add pork, potatoes and peas; heat through. **Yield:** 2-3 servings.

Basic Cooked Rice

Rice is a quick-to-fix accompaniment to any entree. Leftovers can easily be turned into tasty second-day dishes.

    2 cups water
    1 cup long grain rice
    1 teaspoon salt
    1 tablespoon butter *or* margarine

In a large saucepan, combine all ingredients. Bring to a boil. Reduce heat, cover and simmer for 15 minutes. Remove from heat; let stand for 5 minutes. **Yield:** 3 cups.

Peachy Rice Dessert

I make extra servings of rice with this old-fashioned dessert in mind. Beneath its cinnamon and peach topping is a saucy rice pudding-like layer. —Monica Staff, Nada, Texas

    2 cups cooked rice
1-1/2 cups milk
  1/4 cup sugar
  1/8 teaspoon salt
    2 eggs, lightly beaten
  1/2 teaspoon vanilla extract
    1 can (15 ounces) sliced peaches, drained
  1/3 cup packed brown sugar
  1/2 teaspoon ground cinnamon
  1/4 cup sour cream, optional

In a saucepan, combine rice, milk, sugar and salt. Bring to a boil. Reduce heat; simmer, uncovered, for 10 min-

utes, stirring occasionally. Stir a small amount of rice mixture into eggs; return all to the pan. Cook and stir for 2-3 minutes or until a thermometer reads 160°. Remove from the heat; stir in vanilla. Pour into a greased shallow 1-qt. baking pan. Top with peaches. Combine brown sugar and cinnamon; sprinkle 1 tablespoonful over peaches. Broil for 3-5 minutes or until browned. Let stand for 5-10 minutes. Serve in bowls; sprinkle with remaining cinnamon-sugar. Top with sour cream if desired. **Yield:** 4 servings.

Vegetable Rice Salad

This mixture blends rice and crisp vegetables in a cool, creamy ranch-flavored dressing. —Cathy Sestak
Freeburg, Missouri

✓ Uses less fat, sugar or salt. Includes Nutritional Analysis and Diabetic Exchanges.

1-1/2 cups cooked rice
    1 cup broccoli florets
    1 cup cauliflowerets
    3 green onions, thinly sliced
  1/2 cup mayonnaise
    2 tablespoons ranch salad dressing mix
    2 tablespoons milk
    1 tablespoon vinegar
    2 teaspoons sugar

In a bowl, combine rice and vegetables. In a small bowl, combine the remaining ingredients; mix well. Stir into rice mixture. Cover and refrigerate for 1 hour or until serving. **Yield:** 6 servings. **Nutritional Analysis:** One 1/2-cup serving (prepared with fat-free mayonnaise and skim milk) equals 96 calories, 341 mg sodium, trace cholesterol, 21 gm carbohydrate, 2 gm protein, trace fat. **Diabetic Exchanges:** 1 vegetable, 1 starch.

Beef 'n' Rice Bake

Chow mein noodles provide the nice crunch in this hearty dish.
—Deborah Schermerhorn
Colorado Springs, Colorado

    1 pound ground beef
    3 celery ribs, thinly sliced
    1 medium onion, chopped
    2 cups cooked rice
  1/2 cup chopped green pepper
  1/2 cup chopped sweet red pepper
    1 jar (4-1/2 ounces) sliced mushrooms, drained
  1/2 cup soy sauce
    2 tablespoons butter *or* margarine
    1 tablespoon brown sugar
    1 can (3 ounces) chow mein noodles

In a skillet, cook beef, celery and onion until the meat is browned and vegetables are tender; drain. Stir in rice, peppers, mushrooms, soy sauce, butter and brown sugar; heat through. Transfer to a greased 2-qt. baking dish. Cover and bake at 350° for 25-30 minutes. Sprinkle with chow mein noodles. Bake, uncovered, 5-10 minutes longer or until the noodles are crisp. **Yield:** 4-6 servings.

Supreme Roast Beef

This fix-and-forget roast is one of our family's favorite Sunday meals. With just five ingredients, it's simple to prepare and leaves plenty of leftovers to enjoy later in the week. —Jackie Holland, Gillette, Wyoming

    1 large onion, sliced into rings
    2 tablespoons Worcestershire sauce
    4 to 5 teaspoons coarsely ground pepper
    1 boneless rump roast (4 to 5 pounds)
    6 to 8 bay leaves

Place onion in a greased shallow roasting pan. Rub Worcestershire sauce and pepper over the roast. Place over the onion; top with bay leaves. Cover and bake at 325° for 1-3/4 to 2-1/4 hours or until meat reaches desired doneness. Discard bay leaves. Let stand for 10-15 minutes before carving. Thicken pan juices if desired. **Yield:** 8 servings.

Spicy Beef Burritos

Green chilies, salsa and jalapeno peppers add lots of zip to these meaty burritos. Instead of cooking the filling on the stove, it can be simmered in a slow cooker. —Deb Poitz, Fort Morgan, Colorado

    2 to 3 cups julienned cooked roast beef
    1 jar (16 ounces) salsa
    1 jar (8 ounces) green chili salsa *or regular salsa*
    1 can (4 ounces) chopped green chilies
    1 to 3 teaspoons diced jalapenos,* optional
    6 to 8 flour tortillas (8 inches)
Shredded cheddar *or* Colby cheese
Sour cream, chopped tomatoes and additional salsa, optional

In a saucepan, combine the beef, salsa, chilies and jalapenos if desired. Bring to a boil; reduce heat. Simmer, uncovered, for 15-20 minutes or until mixture reaches desired thickness. Spoon 1/3 to 1/2 cup off-center on each tortilla; sprinkle with cheese. Fold the sides and ends of tortilla over filling and roll up. Serve with sour cream, tomatoes and additional salsa if desired. **Yield:** 6-8 servings. ***Editor's Note:** When cutting or seeding hot peppers, use rubber or plastic gloves to protect your hands. Avoid touching your face.

Roast Beef Pizza

A crust made from convenient frozen bread dough is the key to this easy second-day main dish. Leftover roast beef and fresh vegetables get a boost from a mild marinade. —Janet Fitzpatrick, Essex Junction, Vermont

    1/4 cup olive *or* vegetable oil
    2 tablespoons cider *or* red wine vinegar
    2 garlic cloves, minced
    3/4 teaspoon salt
    1/4 teaspoon pepper
    2 cups chopped fully cooked roast beef
    1 medium onion, sliced
    1 medium green *or* sweet red pepper, julienned
    1 cup sliced mushrooms
    1 loaf (16 ounces) frozen white bread dough, thawed

In a large resealable plastic bag or shallow glass dish, combine oil, vinegar, garlic, salt and pepper. Add beef, onion, green pepper and mushrooms; toss to coat. Refrigerate for at least 2 hours. Meanwhile, let dough rise at room temperature for 1 hour. Punch dough down and roll into a 14-in. circle. Transfer to a greased 14-in. pizza pan. Drain and discard marinade; arrange beef and vegetables over crust. Bake at 375° for 30-40 minutes. **Yield:** 8 slices.

Cinnamon Swirl Bread

(Pictured at right)

Your family will be impressed with the soft texture and appealing swirls of cinnamon in these lovely breakfast loaves. —Diane Armstrong, Elm Grove, Wisconsin

    2 packages (1/4 ounce *each*) active dry yeast
    1/3 cup warm water (110° to 115°)
    1 cup warm milk (110° to 115°)
    2 eggs, lightly beaten
    1 cup sugar, *divided*
    6 tablespoons butter *or* margarine, softened
1-1/2 teaspoons salt
5-1/2 to 6 cups all-purpose flour
    2 tablespoons ground cinnamon

In a mixing bowl, dissolve yeast in water. Add milk, eggs, 1/2 cup sugar, butter, salt and 2-1/2 cups flour; beat until smooth. Stir in enough remaining flour to form a soft dough. Turn onto a floured surface; knead until smooth and elastic, about 6-8 minutes. Place in a greased bowl, turning once to grease top. Cover and let rise in a warm place until doubled, about 1 hour. Punch dough down; divide in half. Roll each half into an 18-in. x 8-in. rectangle. Combine cinnamon and remaining sugar; sprinkle over the dough. Roll up each rectangle from a short side; pinch seam to seal. Place seam side down in two greased 9-in. x 5-in. x 3-in. loaf pans. Cover and let rise until doubled, about 1-1/2 hours. Bake at 350° for 30-35 minutes or until golden brown. Remove from pans and cool on wire racks. **Yield:** 2 loaves.

Orange French Toast

(Pictured at right)

I use leftover slices of cinnamon bread in creating this awesome overnight brunch dish. With a hint of orange flavor, it's a special way to wake up the taste buds of weekend guests. —Kristy Martin, Circle Pine, Minnesota

6 eggs, lightly beaten
3/4 cup orange juice
1/2 cup half-and-half cream
2 tablespoons sugar
1 teaspoon vanilla extract
1/2 teaspoon grated orange peel
8 thick slices cinnamon bread
1/4 cup butter *or* margarine, melted

In a shallow bowl, combine the first six ingredients. Dip both sides of bread into egg mixture; let soak for 5 minutes. Place in a greased 15-in. x 10-in. x 1-in. baking pan. Cover and refrigerate overnight. Uncover; drizzle with butter. Bake at 325° for 35-40 minutes or until browned. **Yield:** 8 servings.

Rhubarb Betty

Try this speedy fruit dessert once and you'll rave about its taste and convenience. The cinnamony flavor of the leftover bread complements the tart, tender rhubarb quite nicely.   —Sharon Keys, Spencerport, New York

5 cups diced fresh *or* frozen rhubarb, thawed
3/4 to 1 cup sugar
1/2 teaspoon ground cinnamon
4 cups cubed cinnamon bread
1/4 cup butter *or* margarine, melted
Vanilla ice cream *or* whipped cream, optional

In a bowl, combine rhubarb, sugar and cinnamon. Add half of the bread cubes; toss gently. Transfer to an ungreased 2-qt. microwave-safe dish. Top with remaining bread cubes; drizzle with butter. Microwave, uncovered, on high for 10-12 minutes or until rhubarb is tender. Serve warm with ice cream or whipped cream if desired. **Yield:** 8 servings. **Editor's Note:** This recipe was tested in an 850-watt microwave. It can also be prepared in a conventional oven. Use an ungreased 2-qt. baking dish. Cover and bake at 350° for 40 minutes; uncover and bake 10 minutes longer or until the rhubarb is tender.

Cinnamon Swirl Bread
Orange French Toast

Fried Fish Nuggets
Gone Fishin' Chowder
Garden Fish Packets

Garden Fish Packets

(Pictured above and on page 97)

I frequently serve this flavorful combination of fish, vegetables and cheese over a bed of rice. It's quick to assemble, and the foil packets make cleanup a breeze. For fun family time, have everyone help assemble the pockets.
—Sally Davis, Warren, Pennsylvania

  3 tablespoons butter *or* margarine, melted
  3 pounds frozen cod *or* haddock fillets, thawed
  2 teaspoons seasoned salt
3/4 teaspoon lemon-pepper seasoning
  1 medium tomato, thinly sliced
  1 medium green pepper, thinly sliced
1/4 cup thinly sliced green onions
1/4 pound fresh mushrooms, sliced
  1 cup (4 ounces) shredded mozzarella cheese

Drizzle the butter over eight pieces of heavy-duty foil (about 18 in. x 12 in.). Cut fish into eight portions; place one portion on each piece of foil. Sprinkle all with seasoned salt and lemon-pepper. Top only four pieces of fish with vegetables and cheese (leave four plain). Loosely wrap foil around fish; seal top and sides. Place in an ungreased 15-in. x 10-in. x 1-in. baking pan. Bake at 350° for 23-25 minutes or until fish flakes easily with a fork. Carefully open foil; transfer fish and vegetables to serving plates. Refrigerate the plain fish to use for the Gone Fishin' Chowder and Fried Fish Nuggets. **Yield:** 4 servings plus 3 cups cooked fish. **Editor's Note:** To make 8 servings, double the amount of vegetables and cheese and add to all fish packets.

Gone Fishin' Chowder

(Pictured above and on page 96)

My grandpa and his brother (they're twins) love to fish. For years, they've made this colorful chowder. It's so good that when I entered it in our 4-H Food Show, I received a top award.
—Jasmina Kocurek, Palacios, Texas

✓ Uses less fat, sugar or salt. Includes Nutritional Analysis and Diabetic Exchanges.

  4 bacon strips
  1 cup chopped onion
  1 teaspoon dried thyme
  5 cups water
  3 cups diced peeled potatoes
1-1/2 cups coarsely chopped carrots
1/2 cup chopped celery
  2 teaspoons salt, optional
1/8 to 1/4 teaspoon pepper
  1 can (28 ounces) diced tomatoes, undrained
  1 tablespoon dried parsley flakes
1-1/2 cups cubed cooked fish*

In a Dutch oven or soup kettle over medium heat, cook bacon until crisp. Drain, reserving 1 teaspoon drippings. Crumble bacon and set aside. Saute onion and thyme in drippings. Add the water, potatoes, carrots, celery, salt if desired and pepper. Cover and simmer for 20-25 minutes or until vegetables are tender. Add tomatoes, parsley and bacon; cook for 10 minutes. Add fish; heat through. **Yield:** 12 servings (about 3 quarts). **Nutritional Analysis:** One 1-cup serving (prepared without salt) equals 65 calories, 175 mg sodium, 15 mg cholesterol, 6 gm carbohydrate, 7 gm protein, 1 gm fat. **Diabetic Exchanges:** 1 very lean meat, 1 vegetable. *Editor's Note:* To prepare with fresh fish, dice 3/4 pound fresh fish and add to chowder at the same time as the tomatoes. Cook for 10-15 minutes or until fish is opaque.

Fried Fish Nuggets

(Pictured at left and on page 97)

My family always requests these cheesy fish bites during our annual fishing trip in Canada. You can use most any leftover fish with tasty results.
—Lynn Negaard
Litchfield, Minnesota

    2 eggs, beaten
1/2 cup dry bread crumbs
1/2 cup shredded cheddar cheese
1/4 cup finely chopped onion
    1 garlic clove, minced
1-1/2 teaspoons minced fresh parsley
1/4 teaspoon dill weed
1/4 teaspoon pepper
1-1/2 cups flaked cooked fish
Oil for deep-fat frying
Tartar sauce, optional

In a bowl, combine the first eight ingredients; mix well. Stir in the fish. Roll into 1-in. balls. Heat oil in a deep-fat fryer to 375°. Fry fish nuggets for 2 minutes or until golden brown; drain on paper towels. Serve with tartar sauce if desired. **Yield:** about 2-1/2 dozen.

Rosemary Chicken

A fast-to-fix overnight marinade with dried rosemary gives wonderful herb flavor to this tender chicken. The leftovers are delicious in a chicken salad and other dishes.
—Marcia Morgan, Chevy Chase, Maryland

✓ Uses less fat, sugar or salt. Includes Nutritional Analysis and Diabetic Exchanges.

    1 cup orange juice
1/4 cup olive or vegetable oil
    3 garlic cloves, minced
    1 tablespoon dried rosemary, crushed
    1 tablespoon dried thyme
    8 boneless skinless chicken breast halves
       (2 pounds)

Combine the first five ingredients; pour half into a large resealable plastic bag. Refrigerate the remaining marinade for basting. Add chicken to bag; seal and toss to coat. Refrigerate for 8 hours or overnight. Drain and discard marinade. Grill chicken, uncovered, over medium heat or broil 4 in. from the heat for 3 minutes on each side. Baste with reserved marinade. Continue cooking for 6-8 minutes or until meat juices run clear. **Yield:** 8 servings. **Nutritional Analysis:** One serving equals 200 calories, 64 mg sodium, 73 mg cholesterol, 3 gm carbohydrate, 27 gm protein, 8 gm fat. **Diabetic Exchanges:** 4 very lean meat, 1 fat.

Chicken Salad Pie

A creamy chicken salad mixture chock-full of celery, walnuts and pineapple looks special enough for company when chilled in a flaky pie crust.
—Lois McAtee
Oceanside, California

    1 unbaked pastry shell (9 inches)
2/3 cup shredded cheddar cheese, *divided*
    1 cup (8 ounces) sour cream
2/3 cup mayonnaise
    2 boneless skinless chicken breast halves,
       cooked and cubed (about 1-1/2 cups)
    1 cup pineapple tidbits
    1 cup plus 2 tablespoons chopped walnuts,
       divided
1/2 cup chopped celery

Prick the bottom and sides of pastry shell several times with a fork. Sprinkle with 1/3 cup cheese. Bake at 375° for 15-16 minutes or until the crust is lightly browned. Cool on a wire rack. Meanwhile, combine sour cream and mayonnaise in a bowl. Stir in the chicken, pineapple, 1 cup walnuts and celery. Pour into cooled crust. Top with remaining cheese and walnuts. Refrigerate for 1 hour before cutting. **Yield:** 6-8 servings.

Chicken Alfredo

Bright broccoli, zucchini and sweet red pepper lend fresh taste to this rich chicken and pasta entree. Cream cheese makes the smooth sauce a snap to stir up.
—Jody Stewart, Goldsboro, North Carolina

    1 package (8 ounces) cream cheese, cubed
    6 tablespoons butter *or* margarine
1/2 cup milk
1/2 teaspoon garlic powder
Salt and pepper to taste
    2 boneless skinless chicken breast halves,
       cooked and cubed (about 1-1/2 cups)
    2 cups frozen chopped broccoli, thawed
    2 small zucchini, julienned
1/2 cup julienned sweet red pepper
    6 ounces fettuccine, cooked and drained

In a skillet over low heat, melt cream cheese and butter; stir until smooth. Add milk, garlic powder, salt and pepper. Cook and stir for 3 minutes or until thickened. Add chicken, broccoli, zucchini and red pepper. Cook over medium heat for 3 minutes. Reduce heat; cover and cook 5 minutes longer or until vegetables are tender. Serve over fettuccine. **Yield:** 4-6 servings.

Taco-Seasoned Meat

This seasoned meat is tasty in traditional tacos. By browning all the ground beef at once, you save time and cleanup when using the leftovers.

        4 pounds ground beef
        4 medium onions, chopped
        4 envelopes taco seasoning mix
ADDITIONAL INGREDIENTS:
    2/3 cup water
      8 taco shells
OPTIONAL INGREDIENTS:
Shredded lettuce, shredded cheddar cheese, sliced
    ripe olives, sour cream *and/or* chopped tomatoes

In a Dutch oven, cook beef and onions until meat is no longer pink; drain. Add the taco seasoning and mix well. Cool. Spoon 2-1/2 cups into four resealable freezer bags. Freeze for up to 3 months. **Yield:** 4 batches (10 cups total). **To prepare tacos:** In a saucepan or skillet, combine water and 2-1/2 cups of seasoned meat. Bring to a boil; reduce heat. Simmer, uncovered, for 8-10 minutes, stirring occasionally. Spoon 1/3 cupful into each taco shell. Top with lettuce, cheese, olives, sour cream and/or tomatoes if desired. **Yield:** 8 tacos.

Taco Twist Bake

People of all ages enjoy this Mexican-flavored noodle bake. When my sister-in-law cooked for a youth camp several years ago, she multiplied the recipe. It was an instant success.
—Karen Buhr, Gasport, New York

2-1/2 cups cooked Taco-Seasoned Meat (recipe on
        this page)
      2 cans (8 ounces *each*) tomato sauce
    1/4 cup chopped green pepper
      1 package (8 ounces) spiral pasta, cooked and
        drained
      1 cup (8 ounces) sour cream
      1 cup (4 ounces) shredded cheddar cheese,
        divided

In a saucepan, combine the taco meat, tomato sauce and green pepper; bring to a boil. Meanwhile, combine pasta and sour cream; place in a greased 8-in. square baking dish. Sprinkle with 1/2 cup of cheese. Top with meat mixture. Bake, uncovered, at 350° for 25 minutes. Sprinkle with remaining cheese. Bake 5-10 minutes longer or until the cheese is melted. **Yield:** 4-6 servings.

Taco Corn Bread Squares

Corn bread makes a delicious crust for this hearty meal. I cut it into bite-size squares so it's less messy to eat. My family loves it! —Denise Hughes, Waynesville, Missouri

      1 package (8-1/2 ounces) corn bread/muffin
        mix
      1 egg
    1/3 cup milk

2-1/2 cups cooked Taco-Seasoned Meat (recipe on
        this page)
      1 can (1 pound) refried beans
      1 cup (8 ounces) sour cream
1-1/2 cups (6 ounces) shredded Mexican cheese
        blend *or* cheddar cheese, *divided*
    1/4 cup chopped onion
      1 medium tomato, chopped
      1 cup shredded lettuce
      1 can (2-1/4 ounces) sliced ripe olives, drained

In a bowl, combine corn bread mix, egg and milk until blended. Spread into a greased 9-in. square baking dish. Bake at 350° for 15 minutes. Combine taco meat and beans; spread over corn bread. Combine sour cream, 1 cup cheese and onion; spread over meat mixture. Bake for 20-25 minutes or until heated through and cheese is melted. Sprinkle with tomato, lettuce, olives and remaining cheese. **Yield:** 4-6 servings.

Basic Elbow Macaroni

The next time you make macaroni, cook up a double batch. Then turn the leftovers into a delightful new dish.

      2 quarts water
      8 ounces uncooked elbow macaroni

In a large kettle, bring water to a boil. Add macaroni; return to boil. Cook, uncovered, for 6-8 minutes or until tender, stirring frequently. Rinse and drain. **Yield:** about 4 cups. **Editor's Note:** Cooked pasta will keep for 3 days in a covered container in the fridge.

Hearty Macaroni Salad

(Pictured at right)

This refreshing salad is a complete meal served with bread and a fruit dessert.
—Andrea Bolden
Unionville, Tennessee

✓ Uses less fat, sugar or salt. Includes Nutritional Analysis
  and Diabetic Exchanges.

      2 cups cubed cooked ham *or* chicken
      4 cups cooked elbow macaroni
      1 cup frozen cooked small shrimp, thawed
      1 celery rib, chopped
    1/4 cup *each* chopped onion, green pepper and
        sweet red pepper
    1/2 cup shredded cheddar cheese
DRESSING:
    1/3 cup sour cream
    1/3 cup mayonnaise
      4 teaspoons vinegar
      1 teaspoon snipped fresh dill *or* 1/4 teaspoon
        dill weed
    1/2 teaspoon salt, optional
    1/4 teaspoon pepper
    1/4 teaspoon sugar

In a bowl, combine the ham, macaroni, shrimp, celery,

onion, peppers and cheese. In another bowl, combine the dressing ingredients until blended. Pour over salad and toss to coat. Cover and chill for several hours before serving. **Yield:** 8 servings. **Nutritional Analysis:** One 3/4-cup serving (prepared with chicken, reduced-fat cheese and nonfat sour cream and without salt) equals 188 calories, 136 mg sodium, 49 mg cholesterol, 14 gm carbohydrate, 12 gm protein, 9 gm fat. **Diabetic Exchanges:** 1-1/2 meat, 1 starch, 1/2 fat.

Cheesy Broccoli Macaroni

(Pictured below)

You'll need just four ingredients to fix this macaroni and cheese that gets extra flavor from broccoli and bacon.
—Dorothy Pritchett, Wills Point, Texas

   1 cup frozen chopped broccoli
   8 ounces process American cheese, cubed
2-1/2 cups cooked elbow macaroni
   3 bacon strips, cooked and crumbled

In a large saucepan, cook broccoli according to package directions until crisp-tender; drain. Add the cheese; cook and stir over medium-low heat until cheese is melted. Add macaroni; heat through. Sprinkle with bacon. **Yield:** 4 servings.

Beefy Barbecue Macaroni

(Pictured below)

I developed this dish while visiting a friend. She came home late from work and didn't have time to grocery shop. So I threw together this all-in-one skillet dish using pantry staples. —Mary Petrara, Lancaster, Pennsylvania

  3/4 pound ground beef
  1/2 cup chopped onion
    3 garlic cloves, minced
3-1/2 cups cooked elbow macaroni
  3/4 cup barbecue sauce
  1/4 teaspoon pepper
Dash cayenne pepper
  1/4 cup milk
    1 tablespoon butter *or* margarine
    1 cup (4 ounces) shredded sharp cheddar cheese
Additional cheddar cheese, optional

In a skillet, cook beef, onion and garlic until meat is no longer pink; drain. Add macaroni, barbecue sauce, pepper and cayenne; mix well. In a saucepan, heat milk and butter over medium heat until butter is melted. Stir in cheese until melted. Pour over the macaroni mixture and mix gently. Sprinkle with cheese if desired. **Yield:** 4 servings.

Hearty Macaroni Salad
Beefy Barbecue Macaroni
Cheesy Broccoli Macaroni

Browned Bulk Pork Sausage

To save time when making meals, brown several pounds of bulk sausage at a time. Drain well and store in a covered container in the refrigerator for no more than 2 days. Use in a variety of dishes for truly tasty meals!

2 pounds bulk pork sausage

In a large skillet, crumble sausage. Cook over medium heat until no longer pink; drain. **Yield:** 5 cups.

Sausage Rice Scramble

This inexpensive skillet meal can be served any time of day, but we like it as a quick supper. It's a family favorite...and a great way to use up leftover rice and sausage.
—JoAnn Moseman, Blair, Oklahoma

2 cups cooked rice
1-1/4 cups cooked bulk pork sausage (1/2 pound uncooked)
1/4 cup thinly sliced green onions
4 eggs
3/4 cup milk
1/2 teaspoon dried oregano
1/2 teaspoon salt
1/8 teaspoon pepper

In a large skillet over medium heat, combine rice, cooked sausage and onions; heat through. In a bowl, beat eggs, milk, oregano, salt and pepper; add to rice mixture. Cook and stir until the eggs are completely set. **Yield:** 4 servings.

Pork Sausage Puff

I like to serve this special brunch dish to overnight guests because I can prepare it the night before. The recipe, which I changed a bit to suit our family's tastes, came from a dear lady at our church.
—Christina French
Elkhart, Indiana

1 cup biscuit/baking mix
6 eggs, beaten
2 cups milk
2-1/2 cups cooked bulk pork sausage (1 pound uncooked)
1 cup (4 ounces) shredded cheddar cheese
1/2 teaspoon dried oregano

In a bowl, combine the biscuit mix, eggs and milk until blended. Add the cooked sausage, cheese and oregano.

Heavenly Angel Food Cake
Caramelized Angel Dessert
Cranberry Ribbon Loaf

Transfer to a greased 13-in. x 9-in. x 2-in. baking dish. Bake, uncovered, at 350° for 50-55 minutes or until a knife inserted near the center comes out clean. **Yield:** 6 servings. **Editor's Note:** This recipe can be prepared and refrigerated overnight. Remove from the refrigerator 30 minutes before baking.

Hearty Black-Eyed Peas

Even my sister, who doesn't like black-eyed peas, can't get enough of this hearty herb-seasoned combination of sausage, black-eyed peas, tomatoes and green pepper.
—*Pauletta Anderson, Simpsonville, South Carolina*

    1-1/4 cups cooked bulk pork sausage (1/2 pound uncooked)
        1 can (15-1/2 ounces) black-eyed peas, rinsed and drained
        1 can (14-1/2 ounces) diced tomatoes, undrained
      1/2 cup chopped green pepper
      1/4 cup chopped onion
        2 garlic cloves, minced
      1/2 teaspoon salt
      1/2 teaspoon dried oregano
      1/4 to 1/2 teaspoon dried rosemary, crushed
      1/4 teaspoon pepper
      1/4 to 1/2 cup shredded cheddar cheese

In a skillet, combine the first 10 ingredients. Bring to a boil. Reduce heat; cover and simmer for 10-15 minutes. Sprinkle with cheese. **Yield:** 2-4 main-dish servings (4-6 side-dish servings).

Heavenly Angel Food Cake

(Pictured at left)

This light, moist cake is my favorite. It tastes heavenly and is special enough for most any occasion.
—*Fayrene De Koker Auburn, Washington*

☑ Uses less fat, sugar or salt. Includes Nutritional Analysis and Diabetic Exchanges.

       12 eggs
    1-1/4 cups confectioners' sugar
        1 cup all-purpose flour
    1-1/2 teaspoons cream of tartar
    1-1/2 teaspoons vanilla extract
      1/2 teaspoon almond extract
      1/4 teaspoon salt
        1 cup sugar

Separate eggs; discard yolks or refrigerate for another use. Measure egg whites, adding or removing whites as needed to equal 1-1/2 cups. Place in a mixing bowl; let stand at room temperature for 30 minutes. Meanwhile, sift confectioners' sugar and flour together three times; set aside. Add cream of tartar, extracts and salt to egg whites; beat on high speed. Gradually add sugar, beat-

ing until sugar is dissolved and stiff peaks form. Fold in flour mixture, 1/4 cup at a time. Gently spoon into an ungreased 10-in. tube pan. Cut through batter with a knife to remove air pockets. Bake at 350° for 40-45 minutes or until cake springs back when lightly touched. Immediately invert pan; cool completely before removing cake from pan. **Yield:** 20 servings. **Nutritional Analysis:** One slice equals 101 calories, 59 mg sodium, 0 cholesterol, 23 gm carbohydrate, 3 gm protein, trace fat. **Diabetic Exchange:** 1-1/2 starch.

Caramelized Angel Dessert

(Pictured below left)

This quick-and-easy treat is wonderful. Cake slices, spread with a sweet caramel-like sauce and broiled, get an elegant treatment when topped with sour cream and mandarin oranges.
—*Sharon Bickett Chester, South Carolina*

      1/2 cup butter *or* margarine, softened
      1/2 cup packed brown sugar
        1 tablespoon lemon juice
      1/4 teaspoon ground cinnamon
    Dash ground nutmeg
        6 slices angel food cake
        1 cup mandarin oranges
    Sour cream, optional

In a mixing bowl, cream butter, brown sugar, lemon juice, cinnamon and nutmeg. Spread about 1 tablespoonful on the top and sides of each cake slice. Place on a baking sheet. Broil 4-6 in. from the heat for 1-2 minutes or until bubbly. Top with oranges and sour cream if desired. **Yield:** 6 servings.

Cranberry Ribbon Loaf

(Pictured at far left)

I use leftover angel food cake to create a refreshing cranberry dessert perfect for holiday gatherings. It's convenient, too, because it can be assembled ahead and kept in the freezer. —*Patricia Kile, Greentown, Pennsylvania*

        1 package (3 ounces) cream cheese, softened
      1/4 cup sugar
    Dash salt
        1 can (16 ounces) whole-berry cranberry sauce
        1 cup whipping cream, whipped
        6 slices angel food cake (1/2 inch thick)

Line the bottom and sides of a 9-in. x 5-in. x 3-in. loaf pan with heavy-duty foil; set aside. In a mixing bowl, beat cream cheese, sugar and salt. Beat in cranberry sauce. Fold in the whipped cream. Spread one-third of the mixture in prepared pan; top with three cake slices (cut cake if needed to fit). Repeat layers. Top with remaining cranberry mixture. Cover and freeze. Remove from the freezer 15 minutes before serving. Use foil to remove loaf from pan, then discard foil. Cut into slices. **Yield:** 8 servings.

Pepper Steak Sandwiches
Broiled Sirloin
Sirloin Stir-Fry

Broiled Sirloin

(Pictured above)

A mild marinade prepared with lemon juice, thyme and oregano seasons this steak. It feeds a family of four with lots left over to enjoy in satisfying second-day dishes later in the week. —Sue Ross, Casa Grande, Arizona

       3 pounds sirloin *or* round steak (about 1 inch thick)
       1 medium onion, chopped
     1/2 cup lemon juice
     1/4 cup vegetable oil
       1 teaspoon garlic salt
       1 teaspoon dried thyme
       1 teaspoon dried oregano
     1/2 teaspoon celery salt
     1/2 teaspoon pepper
       2 tablespoons butter *or* margarine, melted

With a meat fork, pierce holes in both sides of steak. Place in a shallow glass container or large resealable bag. Combine onion, lemon juice, oil, garlic salt, thyme, oregano, celery salt and pepper; pour over meat. Cover and refrigerate for 6 hours or overnight. Discard marinade. Place steak on a broiler pan. Broil 6 in. from the heat for 8 minutes. Brush with butter and turn. Broil 6 minutes longer or until meat reaches desired doneness (for rare, a meat thermometer should read 140°; medium, 160°; well-done, 170°). **Yield:** 8-10 servings.

Pepper Steak Sandwiches

(Pictured above)

You'll want to make plenty of these speedy sandwiches because they're unbelievably delicious. Garlic flavors a mixture of leftover steak, green pepper strips and sliced onion heaped on crisp rolls. —Ruby Williams Bogalusa, Louisiana

✓ Uses less fat, sugar or salt. Includes Nutritional Analysis and Diabetic Exchanges.

       2 medium green peppers, julienned
       1 small onion, sliced
       4 garlic cloves, minced, *divided*
       1 tablespoon olive *or* vegetable oil
       2 cups cooked sirloin *or* round steak (3/4 pound), thinly sliced
     1/2 teaspoon salt, optional
     1/8 teaspoon pepper
     1/4 cup butter *or* margarine, softened

4 French *or* **Italian sandwich rolls, split and toasted**

In a skillet, saute green peppers, onion and half of the garlic in oil until vegetables are tender. Add steak, salt if desired and pepper; heat through. Blend butter and remaining garlic; spread over cut side of rolls. Place steak mixture on bottom halves; replace roll tops. **Yield:** 4 servings. **Nutritional Analysis:** One serving (prepared with reduced-fat margarine and without salt; calculated without roll) equals 252 calories, 175 mg sodium, 58 mg cholesterol, 7 gm carbohydrate, 21 gm protein, 16 gm fat. **Diabetic Exchanges:** 3 meat, 1 vegetable.

Sirloin Stir-Fry

(Pictured at left)

For a tasty main dish that's ready in minutes, I jazz up leftovers with colorful fresh peppers and convenient canned tomatoes. The slightly sweet combination looks appealing over rice. —Kim Shea, Wethersfield, Connecticut

✓ Uses less fat, sugar or salt. Includes Nutritional Analysis and Diabetic Exchanges.

1 medium onion, chopped
1 medium green pepper, chopped
1 medium sweet red pepper, chopped
3 garlic cloves, minced
2 tablespoons butter *or* **margarine**
1 can (14-1/2 ounces) Italian stewed tomatoes
2 to 3 teaspoons dried basil
2 teaspoons sugar
1 teaspoon garlic salt *or* **1/8 teaspoon garlic powder**
1/4 teaspoon pepper
2 cups cooked sirloin *or* **round steak (3/4 pound), cut into thin strips**
Hot cooked rice

In a skillet or wok, stir-fry the onion, peppers and garlic in butter until vegetables are tender. Add tomatoes, basil, sugar, garlic salt and pepper. Bring to a boil. Reduce heat; cover and simmer for 5 minutes. Add steak; cover and simmer until heated through. Serve over rice. **Yield:** 4 servings. **Nutritional Analysis:** One serving (prepared with reduced-fat margarine, no-salt-added stewed tomatoes and garlic powder; calculated without rice) equals 273 calories, 168 mg sodium, 77 mg cholesterol, 16 gm carbohydrate, 28 gm protein, 11 gm fat. **Diabetic Exchanges:** 3-1/2 lean meat, 1 starch.

Thanksgiving Stuffing

This nicely seasoned homemade stuffing is our favorite for holiday turkeys. It doesn't require a lot of prep time, which I like, and it tastes good whether stuffed in the bird or baked separately. —Denise Goedeken
Platte Center, Nebraska

3 large onions, chopped
6 celery ribs, chopped

3 garlic cloves, minced
1/2 cup butter *or* **margarine**
4-1/2 cups chicken broth
1/2 cup minced fresh parsley
1 tablespoon rubbed sage
1-1/2 teaspoons poultry seasoning
1-1/2 teaspoons salt
3/4 teaspoon pepper
1-1/2 pounds day-old French bread, cubed (27 cups)

In a large skillet, saute onions, celery and garlic in butter until tender. Transfer to a large bowl; add broth, parsley, sage, poultry seasoning, salt and pepper. Gently stir in bread cubes until mixed. Spoon into a greased 13-in. x 9-in. x 2-in. baking dish (dish will be full). Bake, uncovered, at 350° for 30-35 minutes or until lightly browned and heated through. **Yield:** about 12 cups.

Stuffed Pasta Shells

This is a different way to use up leftovers. A casserole of pasta shells filled with moist stuffing, tender chicken chunks and green peas is covered with an easy sauce. —Judy Memo, New Castle, Pennsylvania

1-1/2 cups cooked stuffing
2 cups diced cooked chicken *or* **turkey**
1/2 cup frozen peas, thawed
1/2 cup mayonnaise*
18 jumbo pasta shells, cooked and drained
1 can (10-3/4 ounces) condensed cream of chicken soup, undiluted
2/3 cup water
Paprika
Minced fresh parsley

Combine the stuffing, chicken, peas and mayonnaise; spoon into pasta shells. Place in a greased 13-in. x 9-in. x 2-in. baking dish. Combine soup and water; pour over shells. Sprinkle with paprika. Cover and bake at 350° for 30 minutes or until heated through. Sprinkle with parsley. **Yield:** 6 servings. ***Editor's Note:** Light or fat-free mayonnaise may not be substituted for regular mayonnaise.

Turkey Day Bake

After Thanksgiving, I make room in my fridge by putting together this hearty cheese-topped casserole. A jar of prepared gravy works fine when you run out of homemade gravy. —Lisa Stepanski, Munnsville, New York

4 cups cooked stuffing
2-1/2 cups cubed cooked turkey
2 cups cooked broccoli florets
2 cups turkey gravy
4 slices process American cheese, halved

Press the stuffing onto the bottom of a greased 2-1/2-qt. baking dish. Top with turkey and broccoli. Pour gravy over all. Bake, uncovered, at 350° for 25-30 minutes or until edges are bubbly. Top with cheese; bake 2-4 minutes longer or until cheese is melted. **Yield:** 6-8 servings.

Chapter 8

IT'S EASY to offer your family a hearty home-cooked meal at the end of the day—even when you can only muster enough energy to open the freezer door and switch on the stove.

By simply taking some time on your more leisurely days, you can prepare delicious main courses, side dishes and desserts, then pop them into the freezer for fast-to-fix future meals.

These savory make-ahead recipes—and host of hints for stocking your freezer—will help you keep your cool on hurried, hectic days...and give hunger the cold shoulder!

KEEP YOUR COOL. Top to bottom: Sausage-Stuffed Loaf (p. 118) and Frozen Berry Fluff (p. 119).

YOU CAN toss together a wholesome meal in minutes when you have the ingredients for fast-to-fix foods in the freezer.

● I keep a heavy-duty resealable plastic bag in the freezer to store soup ingredients. When we have corn, beans or other vegetables left over at dinner, I put them in the bag. I do the same with leftover beef or chicken—even broth. In no time, I have everything I need to simmer up a nice soup. Since the vegetables are already cooked, I just add rice or noodles and it's ready in a jiffy. —*Lee Deneau, Lansing, Michigan*

● When I buy chickens, I immediately cut them up and coat them with my family's favorite seasoning mix. I freeze the individual pieces on waxed paper-lined baking sheets. When the pieces are frozen, I place them in a heavy-duty resealable plastic bag. On mornings when I know I'll have a busy day, I take out as many pieces of chicken as needed and thaw them in the fridge. When I get home, it's a snap to pop them in the oven to bake while I prepare the rest of the meal. —*Lise Thomson, Magrath, Alberta*

● I rarely have time to fix French toast, our children's favorite breakfast, on school mornings. So on weekends, I make an entire loaf of bread into French toast and freeze the leftovers. On hectic school mornings, it's a snap to warm a few slices—with delicious results. —*Rita French, Jefferson City, Missouri*

● I keep a container in my freezer to hold ingredients for my next pot of chili. I dump in leftover taco meat, sloppy joes and cooked meats as well as tomato-based dishes such as spaghetti sauce, marinara sauce, etc. When the container is full, it's time to make chili. I just add kidney beans, extra tomato sauce and meat if needed, then season it. Although it's never the same twice, the chili tastes terrific. —*Lynn Adams, Petoskey, Michigan*

● When we have juice left over from a can of pineapple, I refrigerate or freeze it and use it to make an easy homemade marinade for chicken breasts. I combine the thawed juice with a little oil, soy sauce and minced garlic. Then I pour the mixture over the chicken in a baking dish and let it marinate in the refrigerator overnight. The next day, I bake it in the marinade. —*Lenora Cuccia, Tallahassee, Florida*

● Whenever I have some leftover mashed potatoes, I freeze small portions in freezer containers or resealable plastic bags. Later, I use them in place of flour to thicken soups and stews. —*Violet Bernard, Salinas, California*

● I often make double batches of a recipe and freeze half to enjoy later. But I used to forget I had these meals in the freezer. Now I jot a note on my calendar indicating the day of the week sometime in the future I'd like to serve the dish. This helps in meal planning, and I no longer "lose" meals in the freezer. —*Carol Loveland, Williamsport, Pennsylvania*

● When I buy ground beef for burgers, I place the amounts I'll need for a meal in heavy-duty resealable plastic bags. Then I flatten the beef in the bags into squares and press out all the air. The packages stack well in the freezer to conserve space, and I find that they defrost faster, too. —*Patricia Brown, Smyrna, Georgia*

Cheesy Chicken Casserole

This cheesy chicken and pasta dish freezes well, so you can take one casserole to a potluck and save the second for another time. It makes a quick, comforting meal.
—*Debbi Smith, Crossett, Arkansas*

    4 cups cubed cooked chicken
    2 cans (10-3/4 ounces *each*) condensed cream of mushroom soup, undiluted
2-1/2 cups chicken broth
    1 medium green pepper, chopped
    1 medium onion, chopped
    3 celery ribs, chopped
    2 tablespoons dried parsley flakes
1/2 teaspoon salt
1/2 teaspoon pepper
    1 pound process American cheese, cubed
    1 package (12 ounces) spaghetti, cooked and drained
    1 can (2-1/4 ounces) sliced ripe olives, drained, optional

In a soup kettle or Dutch oven, combine the first nine ingredients. Bring to a boil. Reduce heat; cover and simmer for 15-20 minutes. Stir in cheese until melted. Add the spaghetti and olives if desired. Transfer to two greased 11-in. x 7-in. x 2-in. baking dishes. Cover and freeze one casserole for up to 3 months. Cover and bake the second casserole at 325° for 40 minutes. Uncover and bake 10 minutes longer. **To use the frozen casserole:** Thaw in the refrigerator for 24 hours. Bake as directed. **Yield:** 2 casseroles (5 servings each).

Chocolate Creme Cakes

(Pictured at right)

Moist layers of chocolate cake sandwich a sweet and creamy filling. The yummy treats are handy to keep in the freezer for lunches and after-school snacks.
—*Faith Sommers, Beckwourth, California*

    1 package (18-1/4 ounces) chocolate cake mix
    1 package (3.9 ounces) instant chocolate pudding mix
3/4 cup vegetable oil
3/4 cup water
    4 eggs
FILLING:
    3 tablespoons all-purpose flour
    1 cup milk
1/2 cup butter *or* margarine, softened
1/2 cup shortening
    1 cup sugar
    1 teaspoon vanilla extract

In a mixing bowl, combine cake and pudding mixes, oil, water and eggs; mix well. Pour into a greased and floured 13-in. x 9-in. x 2-in. baking pan. Bake at 350° for 30-35 minutes or until a toothpick inserted near the center comes out clean. Cool for 10 minutes; invert onto a wire rack to cool completely. In a small saucepan, com-

**Make-Ahead Sloppy Joes
Chocolate Creme Cakes**

bine flour and milk until smooth. Bring to a boil; cook and stir for 2 minutes or until thickened. Cool. In a mixing bowl, cream the butter, shortening, sugar and vanilla; beat in milk mixture until sugar is dissolved, about 5 minutes. Split cake into two horizontal layers. Spread filling over the bottom layer; cover with top layer. Cut into serving-size pieces. Freeze in an airtight container for up to 1 month. Remove from the freezer 1 hour before serving. **Yield:** 12-18 servings.

Make-Ahead Sloppy Joes

(Pictured above)

I frequently made big batches of these flavorful filled buns when our six children were growing up. Having the zesty sandwiches in the freezer was such a time-saver on busy days. Now my kids make them for their families.
—Alyne Fuller, Odessa, Texas

1 pound bulk pork sausage

1 pound ground beef
1 medium onion, chopped
14 to 16 sandwich buns, split
2 cans (8 ounces *each*) tomato sauce
2 tablespoons prepared mustard
1 teaspoon dried parsley flakes
1 teaspoon garlic powder
1 teaspoon salt
1/4 teaspoon pepper
1/4 teaspoon dried oregano

In a skillet, brown sausage, beef and onion. Remove from the heat; drain. Remove the centers from the tops and bottoms of each bun. Tear removed bread into small pieces; add to skillet. Set buns aside. Stir remaining ingredients into sausage mixture. Spoon about 1/3 cupful onto the bottom of each bun; replace tops. Wrap individually in heavy-duty foil. Bake at 350° for 20 minutes or until heated through or freeze for up to 3 months. **To use frozen sandwiches:** Bake at 350° for 35 minutes or until heated through. **Yield:** 14-16 servings.

Parmesan Knots
Crab Bisque

Crab Bisque

(Pictured above)

I love to try new recipes, especially when they're easy and delicious. This hearty chowder has a rich creamy broth that's swimming with tasty chunks of crab and crunchy corn. —Sherrie Manton, Folsom, Louisiana

    1 celery rib, thinly sliced
    1 small onion, chopped
  1/2 cup chopped green pepper
    3 tablespoons butter *or* margarine
    2 cans (14-3/4 ounces *each*) cream-style corn
    2 cans (10-3/4 ounces *each*) condensed cream of potato soup, undiluted
1-1/2 cups milk
1-1/2 cups half-and-half cream
    2 bay leaves
    1 teaspoon dried thyme
  1/2 teaspoon garlic powder
  1/4 teaspoon white pepper
  1/8 teaspoon hot pepper sauce
    3 cans (6 ounces *each*) crabmeat, drained, flaked and cartilage removed

In a large saucepan or soup kettle, saute celery, onion and green pepper in butter until tender. Add the next nine ingredients; mix well. Stir in crab; heat through. Discard bay leaves. Transfer to a freezer container; cover and freeze for up to 3 months. **To use frozen soup:** Thaw in the refrigerator; place in a saucepan and heat through. **Yield:** 10 servings.

Parmesan Knots

(Pictured above)

I use refrigerated biscuits to make a big batch of these buttery snacks. They're handy to keep in the freezer and a snap to reheat and serve with a meal. —Cathy Adams Parkersburg, West Virginia

1/2 cup vegetable oil
1/4 cup grated Parmesan cheese
1-1/2 teaspoons dried parsley flakes
1-1/2 teaspoons dried oregano
1 teaspoon garlic powder
Dash pepper
3 cans (12 ounces *each*) refrigerated
buttermilk biscuits

In a small bowl, combine oil, cheese, parsley, oregano, garlic powder and pepper; set aside. Cut each biscuit in half. Roll each portion into a 6-in. rope; tie in a loose knot. Place on greased baking sheets. Bake at 450° for 6-8 minutes or until golden brown. Immediately brush with the Parmesan mixture, then brush again. Serve warm or freeze for up to 2 months. **To use frozen rolls:** Bake at 350° for 6-8 minutes or until heated through. **Yield:** 5 dozen.

Rhubarb Ice Cream

You don't need an ice cream freezer to make this rich refreshing treat. Years ago, we had a big rhubarb patch and were looking for new ways to use it up. A neighbor who knew I loved ice cream shared this recipe with me.
—Jan Douglas, Dent, Minnesota

4 cups sliced rhubarb
2 cups sugar
2 cups water
3 cups miniature marshmallows
3 tablespoons lemon juice
5 to 7 drops red food coloring, optional
2 cups whipping cream, whipped

A Bounty of Baked Goods

MOST BREADS AND COOKIES freeze beautifully, so they're great to bake and keep on hand for last-minute meals.

● When I bake bread, I usually make several loaves at once, slice the cooled loaves and freeze them. That way, I can pull out a few slices of bread at a time instead of thawing the whole loaf.   —Katie Koziolek
Hartland, Minnesota

● Whenever I make chocolate chip cookies, I prepare a double batch of dough. I bake half of the dough into treats for my family and shape the other half into a roll. I double-wrap it in clear plastic wrap and foil, attach baking instructions to the foil for convenience and store in the freezer for up to 6 months. When I have drop-in company, I just slice and bake the frozen dough for warm-from-the-oven cookies.
—Ann Lutka, Welland, Ontario

● Frozen bread dough is quite a time-saver for busy cooks. If you take it out of the freezer at lunchtime, set it on the counter and cover it with plastic wrap coated with nonstick cooking spray, it will be ready to pop in the oven when you come home before dinner. You can break off small portions, roll them into balls and have fresh-baked rolls in no time.
—Jan Roat, Red Lodge, Montana

In a saucepan, bring rhubarb, sugar and water to a boil. Reduce heat; cover and simmer for 10-12 minutes or until the rhubarb is soft. Stir in marshmallows, lemon juice and food coloring if desired; cook and stir until marshmallows are melted. Cover and refrigerate for 1 hour. Fold in whipped cream. Transfer to a freezer container; cover and freeze for up to 2 months. Remove from the freezer 20 minutes before serving. **Yield:** about 2 quarts.

Chocolate Almond Velvet

Good food is best when shared with family and friends. But I'm tempted to make an exception with this cool and creamy make-ahead frozen dessert. It's so smooth and chocolaty I could eat it all by myself!
—Lise Thomson, Magrath, Alberta

2 pints whipping cream
1 can (16 ounces) chocolate syrup
1 can (14 ounces) sweetened condensed milk
2 teaspoons vanilla extract
1/2 cup slivered almonds, toasted

In a mixing bowl, combine the first four ingredients; beat until stiff peaks form. Fold in almonds. Spread into an ungreased 13-in. x 9-in. x 2-in. dish. Cover and freeze for at least 4 hours or until firm. May be frozen for up to 2 months. Remove from the freezer 5 minutes before serving. **Yield:** 16-20 servings.

Beef Enchiladas

Canned soups make the sauce in this spicy entree easy to prepare. It's a good dish to feed a large group of people...or freeze half for a fuss-free supper later.   *—Rosemary Gonser
Clay Center, Kansas*

2-1/2 pounds ground beef
1 medium onion, chopped
2 cans (15 ounces *each*) enchilada sauce
1 can (10-3/4 ounces) condensed cream of mushroom soup, undiluted
1 can (10-3/4 ounces) condensed tomato soup, undiluted
20 flour tortillas (7 inches)
2-1/2 cups (10 ounces) shredded cheddar cheese
Additional shredded cheddar cheese

In a skillet, cook beef and onion until meat is no longer pink; drain. Combine enchilada sauce and soups; pour about 1 cup each into two ungreased 13-in. x 9-in. x 2-in. baking dishes. Stir 1-1/2 cups sauce into beef mixture; set remaining sauce aside. Spoon 1/4 cupfuls of beef mixture down the center of tortillas; top with 2 tablespoons cheese. Roll up tightly; place 10 tortillas seam side down in each dish. Top with remaining sauce. Cover and freeze one pan for up to 3 months. Cover and bake second pan at 350° for 25-30 minutes. Uncover; sprinkle with additional cheese. Bake 5-10 minutes longer or until cheese is melted. **To use frozen enchiladas:** Thaw in the refrigerator overnight and bake as directed. **Yield:** 2 pans (6-8 servings each).

Pizza Pasta Casserole

(Pictured below)

Pepperoni provides the zip in this pizza-flavored casserole that kids of all ages will enjoy. Serve it with a tossed salad and garlic toast, and you'll have a winner every time.
—Nancy Scarlett, Graham, North Carolina

2 pounds ground beef
1 large onion, chopped
2 jars (28 ounces *each*) spaghetti sauce
1 package (16 ounces) spiral pasta, cooked and drained
4 cups (16 ounces) shredded mozzarella cheese
8 ounces sliced pepperoni

In a large skillet, cook beef and onion until meat is no longer pink; drain. Stir in spaghetti sauce and pasta. Transfer to two greased 13-in. x 9-in. x 2-in. baking dishes. Sprinkle with cheese. Arrange pepperoni over the top. Cover and freeze one casserole for up to 3 months. Bake the second casserole, uncovered, at 350° for 25-30 minutes or until heated through. **To use frozen casserole:** Thaw in the refrigerator overnight. Bake at 350° for 35-40 minutes or until heated through. **Yield:** 2 casseroles (8-10 servings each).

Puddingwiches

(Pictured below)

Our daughter loves these fun chocolate and peanut butter snacks. I often defrost them in the microwave so they're a bit softer.
—Joanne Zimmerman
Ephrata, Pennsylvania

1-1/2 cups cold milk
1 package (3.9 ounces) instant chocolate pudding mix
1/4 to 1/2 cup peanut butter
15 whole graham crackers

In a mixing bowl, combine milk, pudding mix and peanut butter. Beat on low speed for 2 minutes. Let stand 5 minutes. Break or cut graham crackers in half. Spread pudding mixture over half of the crackers; top with the remaining crackers. Wrap and freeze until firm. May be frozen for up to 1 month. **Yield:** 15 servings.

Frosty Orange Pie

The night before I'm expecting company, I whip together this rich creamy pie with pleasant orange flavor. It's also refreshing made with lemonade concentrate.
—Jo Magic, Worth, Illinois

Pizza Pasta Casserole
Puddingwiches

1 package (8 ounces) cream cheese, softened
1 can (14 ounces) sweetened condensed milk
1 can (6 ounces) frozen orange juice concentrate, thawed
1 carton (8 ounces) frozen whipped topping, thawed
1 graham cracker crust (9 inches)

In a mixing bowl, beat cream cheese and condensed milk until smooth. Beat in orange juice concentrate. Fold in whipped topping. Spoon into crust. Cover and freeze for up to 3 months. **Yield:** 6-8 servings.

Chocolate Ice Cream Dessert

I took the best parts of two ice cream dessert recipes and added my own touches to come up with this chocolaty layered treat. At our family gatherings and quilting parties, it never fails to draw compliments. —Ruth Yoder
Grantsville, Maryland

2 squares (1 ounce *each*) unsweetened chocolate
1 cup sugar
1 can (5 ounces) evaporated milk
1 package (1 pound 4 ounces) chocolate sandwich cookies, crushed
1/2 cup butter *or* margarine, melted
1 quart vanilla ice cream, softened
1 quart chocolate ice cream, softened
Whipped topping, optional

In a saucepan over low heat, combine chocolate, sugar and milk. Bring to a boil, stirring constantly; boil for 1 minute. Remove from the heat; cool for 10 minutes. Meanwhile, combine the cookie crumbs and butter; set aside 2 cups. Press remaining crumb mixture into a greased 13-in. x 9-in. x 2-in. pan. Carefully spoon vanilla ice cream over crust; spread evenly. Spoon chocolate sauce over top. Sprinkle with reserved crumb mixture. Carefully spread chocolate ice cream over crumbs. Cover and freeze overnight. Serve with whipped topping if desired. May be frozen for up to 2 months. **Yield:** 16-20 servings.

Frozen Fruit Salad Ring

This tasty make-ahead salad is an appealing addition to a buffet table. For pretty presentation, I serve it on a bed of lettuce and garnish it with fresh strawberries.
—Carol Heath, Fayetteville, Georgia

1 package (8 ounces) cream cheese, softened
1 cup mayonnaise
1/3 cup sugar
1 teaspoon vinegar
3 to 4 drops green food coloring, optional
1 can (30 ounces) fruit cocktail, drained
1-1/2 cups miniature marshmallows
1/2 cup chopped pecans
1 cup whipping cream, whipped

In a mixing bowl, beat the cream cheese, mayonnaise and sugar. Add vinegar and food coloring if desired; mix

well. Fold in fruit cocktail, marshmallows, pecans and whipped cream. Spoon into a 2-qt. ring mold or fluted tube pan that has been coated with nonstick cooking spray. Cover and freeze for up to 2 months. Just before serving, invert onto a platter. Cut into 1-in. slices. **Yield:** 12-14 servings.

Cheesy Chili

My six grandchildren enjoy feasting on big bowls of this zesty chili. It's so creamy and tasty you can even serve it as a dip at parties. —Codie Ray, Tallulah, Louisiana

2 pounds ground beef
2 medium onions, chopped
2 garlic cloves, minced
3 cans (10 ounces *each*) diced tomatoes and green chilies, undrained
1 can (28 ounces) diced tomatoes, undrained
2 cans (4 ounces *each*) chopped green chilies
1/2 teaspoon pepper
2 pounds process American cheese, cubed

In a large saucepan, cook beef, onions and garlic until meat is no longer pink; drain. Stir in tomatoes, chilies and pepper; bring to a boil. Reduce heat; simmer, uncovered, for 10-15 minutes. Stir in cheese until melted. Serve immediately or allow to cool before freezing. May be frozen for up to 3 months. **To use frozen chili:** Thaw in the refrigerator; heat in a saucepan or microwave. **Yield:** 12 servings (about 3 quarts).

Diane Catau

Just Like Fresh Corn

This is a good way to extend the garden-fresh flavor of summer corn. It remains crunchy, buttery and delicious, whether warmed in the microwave or on the stovetop.
—Denise Goedeken, Platte Center, Nebraska

 1 pound butter (no substitutes)
20 cups fresh-cut sweet corn kernels (about 24 large ears)
 2 cups half-and-half cream

Place butter in a roasting pan; place in a 325° oven until melted. Stir in corn and cream. Bake, uncovered, for 75 minutes or until the corn is tender, stirring occasionally. Immediately place the roaster in ice water to cool quickly, stirring frequently. Transfer corn to heavy-duty plastic freezer bags; freeze. May be frozen for up to 1 month. To serve, reheat in a microwave or on the stove. **Yield:** 16 cups.

Chilly Coconut Pie

Everyone loves this creamy coconut pie. I keep several in the freezer for when I need a quick dessert.
—Jeannette Mack, Rushville, New York

 1 package (3 ounces) cream cheese, softened
 2 tablespoons sugar
1/2 cup milk
1/4 teaspoon almond extract
 1 cup flaked coconut
 1 carton (8 ounces) frozen whipped topping, thawed
 1 graham cracker crust (9 inches)

In a mixing bowl, beat cream cheese and sugar until smooth. Gradually beat in milk and extract. Fold in coconut and whipped topping. Spoon into crust. Cover and freeze for at least 4 hours. Remove from the freezer 30 minutes before serving. **Yield:** 6-8 servings.

Hamburger Stroganoff

I've been making this simple yet satisfying dish for more than 25 years. Just last year, I tried freezing the ground beef mixture so I'd have a head start on a future dinner. It works great! —*Aline Christenot, Chester, Montana*

 1 pound ground beef
1/4 cup chopped onion
 1 garlic clove, minced

Towel Trick

To keep from losing some of the ground beef when draining grease, I remove the pan from the heat, then take a few paper towels and place them over the browned meat. They absorb the drippings quickly so I can just pick up the paper towels by the corner and throw them away. —*Lee Goodrich, Bend, Oregon*

 1 can (10-1/2 ounces) condensed beef consomme, undiluted
 1 can (4 ounces) mushroom stems and pieces, undrained
 3 tablespoons lemon juice
1/4 teaspoon pepper
ADDITIONAL INGREDIENTS (for each dish):
 2 cups cooked spiral pasta
1/2 cup sour cream
 2 tablespoons water

In a skillet over medium heat, cook beef, onion and garlic until meat is no longer pink; drain. Stir in consomme, mushrooms, lemon juice and pepper. Place half of the mixture in a freezer container; cover and freeze for up to 3 months. To the remaining meat mixture, add pasta, sour cream and water; heat through (do not boil). **To use frozen meat mixture:** Thaw in the refrigerator overnight. Place in a saucepan or skillet and prepare as directed. **Yield:** 2 main dishes (2 servings each).

Dreamy Cherry Torte

A purchased pound cake makes this show-stopping dessert a breeze to prepare ahead of time. Cream cheese frosting gives this torte a rich taste that will have guests thinking you spent hours making it. —*Valerie Putsey, Winamac, Indiana*

 1 loaf (10-3/4 ounces) frozen pound cake, thawed
 1 pint cherry ice cream, softened
 2 packages (3 ounces *each*) cream cheese, softened
1/4 cup butter *or* margarine, softened
 1 teaspoon almond extract
 3 cups confectioners' sugar
1/4 cup chopped pecans
Maraschino cherries, optional

With a serrated knife, slice pound cake horizontally into two layers. Place bottom layer on a freezer-safe serving platter; spread with ice cream. Replace cake top; cover and freeze for at least 3 hours. For frosting, beat cream cheese, butter and extract in a mixing bowl until smooth. Gradually add sugar; beat until fluffy. Set aside 1/2 cup. Remove torte from freezer; frost the top and sides. Cut a small hole in the corner of a plastic or pastry bag; insert a #20 star tip. Fill bag with reserved frosting; pipe around the bottom edge of torte. Cover and freeze for at least 1 hour. May be frozen up to 3 months. Remove from the freezer 10 minutes before serving. Sprinkle with pecans. Garnish with cherries if desired. **Yield:** 8 servings.

Sausage-Stuffed Loaf

(Pictured above right and on page 111)

This bread is filled with cheese, spinach and sausage, making it a real crowd-pleaser. Tasty slices are great as a snack, served with a bowl of soup or as a fun appetizer at your next pizza party. —*Suzanne Hansen, Arlington Heights, Illinois*

Sausage-Stuffed Loaf
Frozen Berry Fluff

2 loaves (1 pound *each*) frozen bread dough
1 pound bulk Italian sausage
1 package (10 ounces) frozen chopped
    spinach, thawed and squeezed dry
4 cups (1 pound) shredded mozzarella cheese
1/4 cup grated Parmesan cheese
1 teaspoon dried oregano
1/2 teaspoon garlic powder
2 tablespoons butter *or* margarine, cubed
1 egg, lightly beaten

Thaw bread dough on a greased baking sheet according to package directions; let rise until doubled. Meanwhile, in a skillet over medium heat, cook the sausage until no longer pink. Drain and place in a bowl. Add spinach, cheeses, oregano and garlic powder; set aside. Roll each loaf of bread into a 14-in. x 12-in. rectangle. Spread sausage mixture lengthwise down the center of each rectangle. Gently press the filling down; dot with butter. Bring edges of dough to the center over filling; pinch to seal. Return to the baking sheet, placing seam side down; tuck ends under and form into a crescent shape. Brush with egg. Bake at 350° for 20-25 minutes or until golden brown. Let stand for 5-10 minutes before cutting. Cool remaining loaf on a wire rack; wrap in foil and freeze for up to 3 months. **To use frozen loaf:** Thaw at room temperature for 2 hours. Unwrap and place on a greased baking sheet. Bake at 350° for 15-20 minutes or until heated through. **Yield:** 2 loaves.

Frozen Berry Fluff

(Pictured above and on page 110)

My family loves this cool, refreshing dessert no matter what flavor pie filling I use, but I must admit raspberry is their favorite.
—*Donetta Brunner, Savanna, Illinois*

2 cans (21 ounces *each*) raspberry *or*
    strawberry pie filling
1 can (14 ounces) sweetened condensed milk
1 can (8 ounces) crushed pineapple,
    undrained, optional
1 carton (12 ounces) frozen whipped topping,
    thawed
Fresh berries and mint, optional

In a bowl, combine pie filling, milk and pineapple if desired. Fold in whipped topping. Spread into an ungreased 13-in. x 9-in. x 2-in. pan. Cover and freeze for 8 hours or overnight. Remove from the freezer 10-15 minutes before serving. Cut into squares. Garnish each with berries and mint if desired. **Yield:** 12-15 servings.

Pumpkin Ice Cream Pie
Apricot Pork Chops

Cook-Ahead Pork Chops

I found the recipe for these moist make-ahead pork chops in a magazine years ago and adapted a couple of our favorite recipes to work with them. It's handy to have them in the freezer for quick dinners. —Marge Anderson
Fergus Falls, Minnesota

4 pork loin chops (1 to 1-1/4 inches thick)
3/4 cup chicken broth

Place pork chops in an ungreased 9-in. square baking pan. Pour chicken broth over chops. Cover and bake at 350° for 45-55 minutes or until meat juices run clear. Cool. Wrap in heavy-duty foil or place in freezer bags; freeze for up to 4 months. **Yield:** 4 servings.

Apricot Pork Chops

(Pictured above)

I often give this sweet apricot treatment to the tender chops I pull out of the freezer the night before. Then supper can be on the table in less than a half hour.

—Marge Anderson

2 cooked pork chops
Salt and pepper to taste
1 can (8-1/4 ounces) apricot halves, undrained

Thaw pork chops if frozen. Place in an ungreased 8-in. square baking dish. Sprinkle with salt and pepper. Pour apricots over the chops. Cover and bake at 350° for 25-30 minutes or until heated through. **Yield:** 2 servings.

Chops with Potato Gravy

For a completely different taste, I simmer the chops in a creamy sauce I make with a can of cream of potato soup. Served with noodles, it's a satisfying meal for two.
—Marge Anderson

2 cooked pork chops
1/2 teaspoon garlic salt
1/2 teaspoon poultry seasoning
1/8 to 1/4 teaspoon pepper
 1 can (10-3/4 ounces) condensed cream of
  potato soup, undiluted

Thaw pork chops if frozen. Place in a skillet; sprinkle with garlic salt, poultry seasoning and pepper. Spread soup over chops. Cover and cook over low heat for 20-25 minutes or until heated through. **Yield:** 2 servings.

Pumpkin Ice Cream Pie

(Pictured at left)

Although it looks like you fussed, this pretty layered pie is easy to assemble with convenient canned pumpkin, store-bought candy bars and a prepared crust.
—Suzanne McKinley, Lyons, Georgia

3 English toffee candy bars (1.4 ounces *each*),
  crushed, *divided*
3 cups vanilla ice cream, softened, *divided*
1 chocolate crumb crust (9 inches)
1/2 cup canned *or* cooked pumpkin
2 tablespoons sugar
1/2 teaspoon ground cinnamon
1/4 teaspoon ground nutmeg

Combine two-thirds of the crushed candy bars and 2 cups ice cream. Spoon into crust; freeze for 1 hour or until firm. In a bowl, combine the pumpkin, sugar, cinnamon, nutmeg and remaining ice cream. Spoon over ice cream layer in crust. Sprinkle with remaining crushed candy bars. Cover and freeze for 8 hours or up to 2 months. Remove from the freezer 10-15 minutes before serving. **Yield:** 8 servings.

Save-the-Day Soup

I created this pureed vegetable soup from what was left in the refrigerator before we went on an extended vacation. I kept the mixture in the freezer of our RV, so it made supper a snap to prepare at the campground.
—Agnes Davis, Las Animas, Colorado

✔ Uses less fat, sugar or salt. Includes Nutritional Analysis and Diabetic Exchanges.

6 cups chopped broccoli
6 cups chopped cauliflower
4 celery ribs with leaves, cut into 1-inch pieces
3 medium carrots, cut into chunks
1 medium onion, cut into chunks
2 cans (14-1/2 ounces *each*) chicken broth
1/2 to 1 teaspoon seasoned salt or salt-free
  seasoning blend

1/2 to 1 teaspoon ground cumin
1/4 to 1/2 teaspoon garlic powder
1/4 to 1/2 teaspoon Cajun seasoning
1/4 to 1/2 teaspoon lemon-pepper seasoning
1/4 teaspoon crushed red pepper flakes
1/4 teaspoon pepper
1/4 teaspoon hot pepper sauce
ADDITIONAL INGREDIENTS (for each batch):
 2 cups half-and-half cream *or* skim milk
Shredded cheddar cheese, optional

In a large saucepan or Dutch oven, combine the first 14 ingredients. Bring to a boil. Reduce heat; cover and simmer for 20 minutes or until vegetables are tender. Cool. Process in small batches in a blender or food processor until smooth. Freeze in 2-cup portions in freezer containers. May be frozen up to 3 months. **Yield:** 4 batches (8 cups total). **To prepare soup:** Thaw soup base in the refrigerator. Transfer to a saucepan; stir in cream and heat through. Sprinkle with cheese if desired. **Yield:** 4 servings per batch. **Nutritional Analysis:** One 1-cup serving (prepared with low-sodium broth, salt-free seasoning, salt-free lemon-pepper and skim milk and served without cheese) equals 76 calories, 129 mg sodium, 3 mg cholesterol, 12 gm carbohydrate, 7 gm protein, 1 gm fat. **Diabetic Exchange:** 1 starch.

Storing Seasonings

SPICES, herbs and vegetables are used in a variety of recipes to add homemade flavor. By storing these invaluable items in your freezer, meal preparation is a snap.

● To prevent fresh parsley from spoiling before I get a chance to use it all, I place washed sprigs in an ice cube tray, then fill the tray with water. After the cubes are frozen, I store them in a freezer bag. This makes it easy to pull out as many as needed and drop them in soups and stews.
—Sherri Keim
Grand Junction, Colorado

● I buy half a pound of garlic at a time and chop it up in my food processor. Then I put it all in a heavy-duty resealable bag and lay it flat in the freezer. Once it's frozen, I can break it into small pieces and take out just the right amount of fresh-tasting garlic anytime I need it. This also works with onions and green peppers. —Agnes Toenjes, St. Paul, Minnesota

● I love fresh ginger, but I hate throwing so much away when a recipe calls for a small amount. A friend told me how to save the leftover ginger and help it retain its fresh taste. She suggested peeling the whole root and freezing it. When a recipe calls for ginger, I pull it out of the freezer, grate the amount needed and return the unused portion. It works great.
—Jennifer Cobb, London, Ohio

● When I have a bit of extra time, I chop a few stalks of celery or a few onions. After sauteing them in margarine, I spoon them into ice cube trays, freeze, then pop the frozen "veggie cubes" into a labeled freezer bag to store. They are an invaluable addition to soups or casseroles when I'm in a hurry.
—Sally Morgan, Neligh, Nebraska

Peppermint Ice Cream Cake

This fancy-looking cake can be prepared in a flash and stored in the freezer for later use. It's light, minty and a real hit with guests who think you're showing off!
—Nancy Horsburgh, Everett, Ontario

✓ Uses less fat, sugar or salt. Includes Nutritional Analysis and Diabetic Exchanges.

- 1 round angel food cake (10 inches)
- 1 quart vanilla ice cream, slightly softened
- 6 chocolate-covered peppermint patties (1.5 ounces *each*), chopped
- 1/2 cup chopped pecans
- 1/8 teaspoon peppermint extract
- Green food coloring, optional

Split cake into three horizontal layers; place bottom layer on a serving plate. In a bowl, combine ice cream, peppermint patties, pecans, extract and a few drops of food coloring if desired. Spread a third of the mixture over bottom cake layer. Top with a second cake layer and another portion of ice cream mixture; repeat layers. Cover and freeze for up to 1 month. Remove from the freezer just before serving. **Yield:** 16 servings. **Nutritional Analysis:** One serving (prepared with nonfat frozen vanilla yogurt) equals 224 calories, 228 mg sodium, 1 mg cholesterol, 44 gm carbohydrate, 5 gm protein, 4 gm fat. **Diabetic Exchanges:** 2-1/2 starch, 1 fat.

Rich Mashed Potatoes

These nicely seasoned potatoes are so fresh-tasting and creamy that there's no need for extra butter or gravy. I freeze them in individual and family servings for added convenience.
—Natalie Warf
Spring Lake, North Carolina

- 5 pounds potatoes, peeled and cubed
- 5 tablespoons butter *or* margarine, *divided*
- 1 package (8 ounces) cream cheese, cubed
- 1 cup (8 ounces) sour cream
- 2 teaspoons onion salt
- 1/4 teaspoon garlic powder
- 1/4 teaspoon pepper

Cook potatoes in boiling salted water until very tender, about 20-25 minutes; drain well. Mash with 3 tablespoons of butter. Add cream cheese, sour cream, onion

Convenient Cooked Bacon

I always fry 2 pounds or more of bacon at a time, drain the slices well, then freeze them in freezer bags. The slices don't stick together, so it's easy to remove a few from the bag for a sandwich or to crumble small amounts for a recipe.
—Shirley Murphy
Goldsboro, North Carolina

salt, garlic powder and pepper; mix well. Spoon into a greased 13-in. x 9-in. x 2-in. baking dish. Melt remaining butter; drizzle over the top. Cover and freeze for up to 1 month. Or bake, uncovered, at 350° for 30-35 minutes or until heated through. **To use frozen potatoes:** Thaw in the refrigerator. Bake as directed. **Yield:** 12-14 servings.

Onion Rye Appetizers

I take these hearty appetizers to every party we attend and always bring home an empty tray. I also keep a supply in the freezer for a speedy snack that gets rave reviews—even from children. —Vicki Wolf, Aurora, Ohio

- 1 can (2.8 ounces) french-fried onions, crushed
- 1 jar (2 ounces) crumbled bacon *or* 3/4 cup cooked crumbled bacon
- 1/2 cup mayonnaise *or* salad dressing
- 3 cups (12 ounces) shredded Swiss cheese
- 1 jar (14 ounces) pizza sauce
- 1 loaf (16 ounces) snack rye bread

In a bowl, combine the onions, bacon, mayonnaise and Swiss cheese. Spread about 1 teaspoon of pizza sauce on each slice of bread. Top with about 1 tablespoon of the cheese mixture. Cover and freeze in a single layer for up to 2 months, or bake on an ungreased baking sheet at 350° for 12-14 minutes or until heated through and cheese is melted. **To use frozen appetizers:** Place on an ungreased baking sheet. Bake at 350° for 14-16 minutes or until heated through and cheese is melted. **Yield:** 20 appetizers.

Two-Tone Butter Cookies

(*Pictured at right*)

During the hectic holiday season, you'll appreciate the ease of these irresistible butter cookies. It's wonderful to pull the two-tone dough from the freezer and bake a festive batch in no time.
—Kathy Kittell
Lenexa, Kansas

- 1 cup butter (no substitutes), softened
- 1 cup confectioners' sugar
- 1 teaspoon vanilla extract
- 2 cups all-purpose flour
- Red and green liquid *or* paste food coloring
- Red colored sugar, optional

In a mixing bowl, cream butter and confectioners' sugar. Beat in vanilla. Add flour and mix well. Divide dough in half; with food coloring, tint half red and half green. Shape each portion into an 8-in. log. Wrap in plastic wrap and refrigerate for at least 1 hour. Cut each log in half lengthwise. Press red and green halves together. Tightly wrap each roll in plastic wrap; freeze for up to 6 months. To prepare cookies: Let dough stand at room temperature for 15 minutes. Cut into 1/4-in. slices; place 2 in. apart on ungreased baking sheets. Sprinkle with colored sugar if desired. Bake at 350° for 12-14 minutes or until set. Cool on wire racks. **Yield:** about 5 dozen.

Make-Ahead Holiday Cake

(Pictured below)

This impressive make-ahead dessert really pleases a crowd. For my granddaughter's birthday, my daughter placed slivered almonds artfully to decorate this cake as a bear instead. It was a big hit. —Julia Kinard
Dallastown, Pennsylvania

　1 can (14 ounces) sweetened condensed milk
2/3 cup chocolate syrup
　2 cups whipping cream, whipped
　1 package (18-1/4 ounces) white cake mix
　1 carton (12 ounces) frozen whipped topping, thawed
Additional chocolate syrup

Mint leaves and candied cherries

Line a 13-in. x 9-in. x 2-in. pan with foil; set aside. In a bowl, combine milk and chocolate syrup; fold in whipped cream. Pour into the prepared pan; cover and freeze for 6 hours. Prepare and bake the cake according to package directions, using a greased and floured 13-in. x 9-in. x 2-in. baking pan. Cool for 10 minutes; invert cake onto a wire rack to cool completely. Transfer to a serving platter. Remove cream mixture from the freezer; carefully invert onto cake and remove foil. Spread whipped topping over top and sides. Return to the freezer for 2 hours. May be frozen for up to 2 months. Just before serving, drizzle with additional chocolate syrup; garnish with mint and cherries. **Yield:** 16-20 servings.

Two-Tone Butter Cookies
Make-Ahead Holiday Cake

THESE DAYS, people wake up and rush to work, school and other activities, often leaving little or no time to fix and eat a good breakfast. Unfortunately, folks either forgo a morning meal altogether or head to the nearest fast-food drive-thru.

With the sunny selections in this chapter, it's a snap to offer your on-the-go family wholesome and hearty breakfasts at home.

From easy egg dishes, beverages and fruit to fast-to-fix French toast, pancakes and waffles, you can get your family's day off to a rise-and-shine start in a matter of minutes.

MORNING MEALS. Top to bottom: Deluxe Scrambled Eggs, Breakfast Pizza Skillet and Strawberry Syrup (all recipes on p. 132).

Scrambled Egg Muffins

(Pictured at right)

After enjoying scrambled egg muffins at a local restaurant, I came up with this version that my husband likes even better. They're pretty, hearty and fun to serve, too.
—Cathy Larkins, Marshfield, Missouri

1/2 pound bulk pork sausage
12 eggs
1/2 cup chopped onion
1/4 cup chopped green pepper
1/2 teaspoon salt
1/4 teaspoon pepper
1/4 teaspoon garlic powder
1/2 cup shredded cheddar cheese

In a skillet, brown the sausage; drain. In a bowl, beat the eggs. Add onion, green pepper, salt, pepper and garlic powder. Stir in sausage and cheese. Spoon by 1/3 cupfuls into greased muffin cups. Bake at 350° for 20-25 minutes or until a knife inserted near the center comes out clean. **Yield:** 1 dozen.

Herbed Chicken Omelet

Tender chunks of leftover chicken provide a nice change of pace from the usual ham in this omelet. Served with toast and tomato slices, it's a special breakfast for two that takes minutes to make. —Sonja Blow
Groveland, California

4 eggs
1 green onion, sliced
2 tablespoons minced fresh parsley
1/4 teaspoon dried tarragon
1/4 teaspoon salt
1/4 teaspoon pepper
1 tablespoon butter *or* margarine
1/2 cup cubed cooked chicken
1/2 teaspoon celery seed

In a bowl, beat eggs, onion, parsley, tarragon, salt and pepper. Melt butter in a skillet over medium heat; add egg mixture. As eggs set, lift edges, letting uncooked portion flow underneath. Sprinkle with chicken and celery seed. When the eggs are set, remove from the heat; fold omelet in half. **Yield:** 2 servings.

Blueberry Fruit Salad

(Pictured at right)

I toss together both fresh and canned fruit to create this quick and colorful salad. A tangy dressing made with instant pudding mix and powdered orange drink provides refreshing flavor. —Ruth Hastings, Louisville, Illinois

1 can (20 ounces) pineapple chunks
1 can (15-1/4 ounces) sliced peaches
4 cups fresh *or* frozen blueberries
3 medium firm bananas, sliced
1 cup green grapes, halved
1 cup sliced fresh strawberries
1 package (3.4 ounces) instant vanilla pudding mix
3 tablespoons powdered orange drink mix

Drain pineapple and peaches, reserving juices; set aside. Combine fruit in a large bowl. In another bowl, combine fruit juices with pudding and drink mixes; mix well. Pour over fruit; toss to coat. **Yield:** 20-24 servings.

Overnight Pancakes

(Pictured at right)

I keep a big batch of this pancake batter in the fridge to ease the morning rush. The golden, fluffy pancakes are great for Sunday brunch. And during the week, they get our two kids off to a good start before school.
—Lisa Sammons, Cut Bank, Montana

1 package (1/4 ounce) active dry yeast
1/4 cup warm water (110° to 115°)
4 cups all-purpose flour
2 tablespoons baking powder
2 teaspoons baking soda
2 teaspoons sugar
1 teaspoon salt
6 eggs
1 quart buttermilk
1/4 cup vegetable oil

In a small bowl, dissolve yeast in water; let stand for 5 minutes. Meanwhile, in a large bowl, combine the dry ingredients. Beat eggs, buttermilk and oil; stir into dry ingredients just until moistened. Stir in yeast mixture. Cover and refrigerate for 8 hours or overnight. To make pancakes, pour batter by 1/4 cupfuls onto a greased hot griddle; turn when bubbles form on top of pancakes. Cook until second side is golden brown. **Yield:** about 2-1/2 dozen.

Ruby Breakfast Sauce

(Pictured at right)

You can easily brighten a special breakfast with this delicious cherry sauce on French toast, pancakes or waffles. With a hint of cranberry flavor, the mixture also is nice served over ham, pork or chicken. —Edie DeSpain
Logan, Utah

1 can (21 ounces) cherry pie filling
1 can (8 ounces) jellied cranberry sauce
1/4 cup maple syrup
1/4 cup orange juice
3 tablespoons butter *or* margarine
Pancakes *or* French toast

In a microwave-safe bowl, combine pie filling, cranberry sauce, syrup, orange juice and butter. Microwave on high for 3 minutes; stir. Microwave 2-3 minutes longer or until butter is melted and mixture is heated through; stir. Serve over pancakes or French toast. **Yield:** about 4 cups. **Editor's Note:** This recipe was tested in an 850-watt microwave.

Scrambled Egg Muffins
Blueberry Fruit Salad
Overnight Pancakes
Ruby Breakfast Sauce

Ham 'n' Cheese Potato Bake
Pineapple Cooler
Olé Omelet

Olé Omelet

(Pictured at left)

My family loves omelets after church on Sundays. These cook quickly and satisfy big appetites in a hurry.
—Karen Stephens, Noble, Illinois

3 eggs
1/8 teaspoon salt
Dash pepper
2 slices process American cheese, halved
2 tablespoons salsa
2 tablespoons chopped green chilies, optional
2 tablespoons chopped mushrooms, optional
Additional salsa and sour cream, optional

In a small bowl, beat eggs, salt and pepper. Coat a 10-in. skillet with nonstick cooking spray and place over medium heat. Add egg mixture. As the eggs set, lift the edges, letting uncooked portion flow underneath. When eggs are nearly set, place cheese, salsa, and chilies and mushrooms if desired over half of the eggs; fold in half. Cover and let stand for 1-2 minutes or until cheese is melted. Serve with additional salsa and sour cream if desired. **Yield:** 1-2 servings.

Pineapple Cooler

(Pictured at left)

This mild and refreshing beverage stirs up in a jiffy. Lemon juice cuts the sweetness you might expect from pineapple juice and lemon-lime soda.
—Michelle Blumberg
Littlerock, California

✓ Uses less fat, sugar or salt. Includes Nutritional Analysis and Diabetic Exchanges.

1 cup unsweetened pineapple juice, chilled
1 to 2 tablespoons lemon juice
1 can (12 ounces) lemon-lime soda, chilled

Combine all ingredients in a pitcher; shake or stir well. Serve over ice. **Yield:** 2-2/3 cups. **Nutritional Analysis:** One 1-cup serving (prepared with diet soda) equals 48 calories, 13 mg sodium, 0 cholesterol, 12 gm carbohydrate, trace protein, trace fat. **Diabetic Exchange:** 1 fruit.

Ham 'n' Cheese Potato Bake

(Pictured at left)

This rich ham and hash brown casserole is frequently requested at family gatherings. I include it in my brunch buffets and sometimes serve it as a meal in itself along with juice and toast. It offers fix-and-forget-it ease.
—Barbara Larson, Rosemount, Minnesota

1 package (24 ounces) frozen O'Brien hash brown potatoes
2 cups cubed fully cooked ham
3/4 cup shredded cheddar cheese, *divided*
1 small onion, chopped
2 cups (16 ounces) sour cream
1 can (10-3/4 ounces) condensed cheddar cheese soup, undiluted
1 can (10-3/4 ounces) condensed cream of potato soup, undiluted
1/4 teaspoon pepper

In a large bowl, combine potatoes, ham, 1/2 cup cheese and onion. In another bowl, combine sour cream, soups and pepper; add to potato mixture and mix well. Transfer to a greased 3-qt. baking dish. Sprinkle with remaining cheese. Bake, uncovered, at 350° for 60-65 minutes or until bubbly and potatoes are tender. Let stand for 10 minutes before serving. **Yield:** 10-12 servings.

Apple-Oat Breakfast Treats

Our three grandsons gobble up these soft, chewy oatmeal cookies at breakfast with some yogurt and a glass of juice.
—Dolores Kastello, Waukesha, Wisconsin

3/4 cup butter *or* margarine, softened
3/4 cup packed brown sugar
2 eggs
1 teaspoon vanilla extract
2-1/2 cups old-fashioned oats
3/4 cup all-purpose flour
1/2 cup instant nonfat dry milk powder
1 teaspoon salt
1/2 teaspoon baking powder
1/2 teaspoon ground cinnamon
1 to 1-1/4 cups apple pie filling

In a mixing bowl, cream the butter and brown sugar. Add the eggs and vanilla. Combine dry ingredients; add to the creamed mixture and mix well. Drop by 1/4 cupfuls 6 in. apart onto ungreased baking sheets. Flatten into 3-in. circles. Make a slight indentation in the center of each; top with a rounded tablespoonful of pie filling. Bake at 350° for 16-20 minutes or until edges are lightly browned. Cool for 5 minutes; remove to wire racks to cool completely. **Yield:** 10 servings.

Omelets Made Easy

1. Coat a 10-inch skillet with nonstick cooking spray; warm over medium heat. Add egg mixture. As eggs set, gently lift edges with a heatproof spatula, allowing uncooked portion to flow underneath. Tilt pan slightly if needed.

2. When eggs are set but still moist, place filling ingredients on one side of the omelet. Carefully fold in half. Cover and let stand until eggs are completely set (and, if you added cheese, until it's melted).

Southwestern Hash with Eggs
Peppy Ham Tortillas

Peppy Ham Tortillas

(Pictured at left)

This hearty breakfast can be made ahead of time and refrigerated. In the morning, just pop the pan in the oven.
—*Donna Freeland, Upland, California*

- 12 thin slices fully cooked ham
- 1 block (16 ounces) Monterey Jack cheese, cut into 1/2-inch strips
- 2 cans (4 ounces *each*) chopped jalapenos *or* chilies, drained
- 12 flour tortillas (6 inches)

SAUCE:
- 1/4 cup butter *or* margarine
- 1/2 cup all-purpose flour
- 1 teaspoon salt
- 1 teaspoon ground mustard
- 4 cups milk
- 3 cups (12 ounces) shredded cheddar cheese

Place a ham slice, cheese strip and 2 teaspoons jalapenos down the center of each tortilla. Roll up and place seam side down in a greased 13-in. x 9-in. x 2-in. baking dish; set aside. In a saucepan over medium heat, melt butter. Stir in the flour, salt and mustard until smooth. Gradually add milk; bring to a boil. Cook and stir for 2 minutes. Add cheese; cook and stir until melted. Spoon sauce evenly over tortillas. Bake, uncovered, at 350° for 45 minutes or until heated through. **Yield:** 6 servings.

Southwestern Hash with Eggs

(Pictured at left)

Before I retired, this all-in-one skillet dish was often requested at office brunches. I'd leave out the eggs, double or triple the recipe and wrap the zippy pork mixture in warm tortillas. —*Barbara Beasley, Beaumont, Texas*

- 1-1/2 pounds pork steak, cubed
- 1 teaspoon vegetable oil
- 1 large potato, peeled and cubed
- 1 medium onion, chopped
- 1 garlic clove, minced
- 1/2 cup chopped green pepper
- 1 can (10 ounces) tomatoes with green chilies, undrained
- 1 beef bouillon cube
- 1/2 teaspoon ground cumin
- 1/2 teaspoon salt
- 1/4 teaspoon pepper
- 1/8 teaspoon cayenne pepper
- 4 eggs
- 3/4 cup shredded cheddar cheese
- 4 corn tortillas, warmed

In a 10-in. ovenproof skillet, cook pork in oil until browned, about 4 minutes. Add potato, onion, garlic and green pepper; cook and stir for 4 minutes. Stir in tomatoes, bouillon, cumin, salt, pepper and cayenne. Cover and cook over low heat for 30 minutes or until potatoes are tender, stirring occasionally. Make four wells in the hash; break an egg into each. Bake, uncovered, at 350° for 10-12 minutes or until the eggs are completely set. Sprinkle with cheese; cover and let stand for 5 minutes. Serve over tortillas. **Yield:** 4 servings.

Apple Orange Syrup

You're sure to like the fruity flavor of this simple syrup. With just three ingredients, it's an effortless alternative to traditional maple syrup. —*Mavis Diment, Marcus, Iowa*

✓ Uses less fat, sugar or salt. Includes Nutritional Analysis and Diabetic Exchanges.

- 1 to 2 tablespoons cornstarch
- 1 cup apple juice
- 1/3 cup orange juice

In a saucepan, stir cornstarch and juices until smooth. Bring to a boil; boil and stir for 2 minutes. **Yield:** about 1 cup. **Nutritional Analysis:** One serving (2 tablespoons) equals 23 calories, 1 mg sodium, 0 cholesterol, 6 gm carbohydrate, trace protein, trace fat. **Diabetic Exchange:** 1/2 fruit.

Avocado Scrambled Eggs

Bacon and avocado blend nicely in these easy eggs. While great for breakfast, I prefer to whip them together after a church meeting or football game.
—*Sundra Lewis, Bogalusa, Louisiana*

- 8 eggs
- 1/2 cup milk
- 1/2 teaspoon salt
- 1/4 teaspoon pepper
- 1 medium ripe avocado, peeled and cubed
- 2 tablespoons butter *or* margarine
- 6 bacon strips, cooked and crumbled

In a bowl, beat eggs. Add milk, salt and pepper; stir in avocado. In a skillet over medium heat, melt butter. Add egg mixture; cook and stir gently until the eggs are completely set. Sprinkle with bacon. **Yield:** 6 servings.

Bacon Cheese Frittata

I serve this attractive frittata to overnight guests in our home. To save time, I keep cooked bacon in the freezer.
—*Diana Bullock, Hanover, Maryland*

- 6 eggs
- 1 cup milk
- 2 tablespoons butter *or* margarine, melted
- 1/2 teaspoon salt
- 1/4 teaspoon pepper
- 1/4 cup chopped green onions
- 5 bacon strips, cooked and crumbled
- 1 cup (4 ounces) shredded cheddar cheese

In a bowl, beat eggs, milk, butter, salt and pepper. Pour into a greased 11-in. x 7-in. x 2-in. baking dish. Sprinkle with onions, bacon and cheese. Bake, uncovered, at 350° for 25-30 minutes or until a knife inserted near the center comes out clean. **Yield:** 6 servings.

Deluxe Scrambled Eggs

(Pictured at right and on page 125)

Corn, peppers, zucchini and green onions add fresh flavor and color to these dill-seasoned eggs. They're also great served as a nice light supper. —Diane Hixon, Niceville, Florida

    1/2 cup *each* chopped green onions, zucchini,
        green pepper and sweet red pepper
      1 tablespoon vegetable oil
      1 cup fresh *or* frozen corn
    1/2 to 3/4 teaspoon salt
    1/2 teaspoon dill weed
      8 eggs, beaten
      1 cup (4 ounces) shredded sharp cheddar
        cheese
Pepper to taste

In a large skillet, saute onions, zucchini and peppers in oil until tender, about 5 minutes. Add corn, salt and dill; mix well. Add eggs; sprinkle with cheese. Cook and stir gently until eggs are completely set. Sprinkle with pepper. **Yield:** 4 servings.

Strawberry Syrup

(Pictured at right and on page 125)

This pretty berry-flavored syrup is scrumptious, especially on homemade waffles. Our three children prefer it over maple syrup. —Sarah Carpenter, Trumansburg, New York

      1 pint fresh strawberries, halved
    3/4 cup sugar
      2 tablespoons corn syrup
  1-1/2 teaspoons lemon juice
    1/2 teaspoon butter *or* margarine
Waffles *or* pancakes

Place strawberries in a blender or food processor; cover and process until smooth. Transfer to a saucepan; add sugar, corn syrup, lemon juice and butter. Bring to a boil; boil and stir for 1 minute. Skim off foam. Strain seeds if desired. Serve warm over waffles or pancakes. Refrigerate leftovers; reheat before serving. **Yield:** about 1-1/2 cups.

Savory Baked Eggs

A flavorful mixture of green pepper and onion makes a savory bed for these baked eggs. —Judy Robertson
Russell Springs, Kentucky

      1 medium onion, chopped
      1 medium green pepper, chopped
      5 tablespoons butter *or* margarine, *divided*
      6 eggs
      1 cup dry bread crumbs
    1/4 teaspoon salt
Pepper to taste

In a small saucepan, saute onion and green pepper in 3 tablespoons butter until tender. Transfer to a greased 8-in. square baking dish. Break eggs over the onion mixture. Melt remaining butter; toss with bread crumbs, salt

and pepper. Sprinkle over eggs. Place dish in a larger baking pan; pour boiling water into larger pan to a depth of 1 in. Bake, uncovered, at 375° for 12-15 minutes or until the eggs are firm. **Yield:** 4-6 servings.

Breakfast Pizza Skillet

(Pictured at right and on page 124)

I found the recipe for this hearty stovetop dish several years ago and changed it to fit our tastes. When I served it at a Christmas brunch, it was an instant hit.
—Marilyn Hash, Enumclaw, Washington

      1 pound bulk Italian sausage
      5 cups frozen hash brown potatoes
    1/2 cup chopped onion
    1/2 cup chopped green pepper
    1/4 to 1/2 teaspoon salt
Pepper to taste
    1/2 cup sliced mushrooms
      4 eggs
      1 medium tomato, thinly sliced
      1 cup (4 ounces) shredded cheddar cheese
Sour cream and salsa, optional

In a large skillet, cook sausage until no longer pink. Add potatoes, onion, green pepper, salt and pepper. Cook over medium-high heat for 18-20 minutes or until the potatoes are browned. Stir in mushrooms. Beat eggs; pour over the potato mixture. Arrange tomato slices on top. Sprinkle with cheese. Cover and cook over medium-low heat for 10-15 minutes or until eggs are completely set (do not stir). Serve with sour cream and salsa if desired. **Yield:** 6 servings.

Family-Style French Toast

I can serve a crowd by baking a big batch of this sweet, cinnamony French toast. Leftovers are good warmed in the microwave. —Hennie Scholten, Edgerton, Minnesota

    2/3 cup packed brown sugar
    1/2 cup butter *or* margarine, melted
      2 teaspoons ground cinnamon
      6 eggs, lightly beaten
  1-3/4 cups milk
      1 loaf (1 pound) French bread, cut into 1-inch
        slices
Confectioners' sugar

Combine brown sugar, butter and cinnamon; spread evenly in a greased 15-in. x 10-in. x 1-in. baking pan; set aside. Combine eggs and milk in a shallow dish; place bread in dish and soak for 5 minutes, turning once. Place bread over sugar mixture. Bake, uncovered, at 350° for 25-30 minutes or until golden brown. Serve brown sugar side up; dust with confectioners' sugar. **Yield:** 6-8 servings.

Juice in a Jiffy

To save seconds when making juice from frozen concentrate, process the concentrate and cold water in a blender for a minute or so. —Dorothy Pritchett
Wills Point, Texas

Deluxe Scrambled Eggs
Breakfast Pizza Skillet
Strawberry Syrup

Breakfast Cookies
Berry Smoothie
Sausage Egg Subs

Berry Smoothie

(Pictured at left)

With two busy teenage boys in our house, getting everyone to eat well before school is a challenge. This thick fruity beverage is quick to fix and delicious, too.
—*Patricia Mahoney, Presque Isle, Maine*

☑ Uses less fat, sugar or salt. Includes Nutritional Analysis and Diabetic Exchanges.

  1 cup milk
  1 cup frozen unsweetened strawberries
1/2 cup frozen unsweetened raspberries
  3 tablespoons sugar
  1 cup ice cubes

Place the milk, berries and sugar in a blender; cover and process until smooth. Add ice cubes; cover and process until smooth. **Yield:** 3 servings. **Nutritional Analysis:** One 1-cup serving (prepared with skim milk) equals 113 calories, 44 mg sodium, 1 mg cholesterol, 26 gm carbohydrate, 3 gm protein, trace fat. **Diabetic Exchanges:** 1 fruit, 1/2 skim milk.

Sausage Egg Subs

(Pictured at left)

Spicy chunks of sausage give winning flavor to this scrambled egg mixture. Served in a bun, it's a satisfying all-in-one sandwich for breakfast or lunch. —*Dee Pasternak Goshen, Indiana*

1-1/4 pounds bulk pork sausage
  1/4 cup chopped onion
   12 eggs, lightly beaten
  1/2 cup chopped fresh mushrooms
    1 to 2 tablespoons finely chopped green pepper
    1 to 2 tablespoons finely chopped sweet red pepper
    6 submarine sandwich buns (about 6 inches), split

In a large skillet over medium heat, cook sausage and onion until the meat is no longer pink; drain. Remove with a slotted spoon and keep warm. In the same skillet, cook and stir the eggs until nearly set, about 7 minutes. Add mushrooms, peppers and the sausage mixture. Cook until eggs are completely set and mixture is heated through. Serve on buns. **Yield:** 6 servings.

Breakfast Cookies

(Pictured at left)

I tried this recipe when I was a 4-H leader. Before morning chores, the young members would grab a glass of milk or juice and a handful of these crisp cookies. Chock-full of bacon, cornflakes and raisins, they're a handy breakfast on the go. —*Louise Gangwish Shelton, Nebraska*

1/2 cup butter *or* margarine, softened
3/4 cup sugar
  1 egg
  1 cup all-purpose flour
1/4 teaspoon baking soda
 10 bacon strips, cooked and crumbled
  2 cups cornflakes
1/2 cup raisins

In a mixing bowl, cream butter and sugar. Beat in egg. Add flour and baking soda; mix well. Stir in bacon, cornflakes and raisins. Drop by rounded tablespoonfuls 2 in. apart onto ungreased baking sheets. Bake at 350° for 15-18 minutes or until lightly browned. Cool for 2 minutes before removing to wire racks. Store in the refrigerator. **Yield:** 2 dozen.

Potato Omelet

This is an old German dish that was served to the threshers and us kids when I was growing up. With toast and jam, this flavorful omelet will make four people very happy. —*Katherine Stallwood, Kennewick, Washington*

  2 large potatoes, thinly sliced
  3 tablespoons butter *or* margarine
1/2 cup sliced green onions
  8 eggs
1/4 cup milk
Salt and pepper to taste

In a large skillet, cook potatoes in butter until browned and tender, about 15 minutes. Sprinkle with onions. Beat the eggs, milk, salt and pepper; pour over potatoes. As the eggs set, lift edges, letting uncooked portion flow underneath. Continue cooking until the eggs are completely set. Fold in half or cut into wedges. **Yield:** 4 servings.

Ham Floret Strata

This fluffy egg bake is a snap to prepare the night before using frozen vegetables. In the morning, the aroma is wonderful while it bakes. —*Elizabeth Montgomery Taylorville, Illinois*

  2 cups frozen broccoli florets
  2 cups frozen cauliflowerets
  1 cup cubed fully cooked ham
  8 slices bread, crusts removed and cubed
  8 eggs
1-1/2 cups milk
  1 to 2 teaspoons ground mustard
1/4 to 1/2 teaspoon garlic powder
1/4 to 1/2 teaspoon onion powder
1-1/2 cups (6 ounces) shredded cheddar cheese

Place the broccoli and cauliflower in a greased 13-in. x 9-in. x 2-in. baking dish. Top with ham and bread. In a bowl, beat eggs, milk, mustard, garlic powder and onion powder. Pour over bread. Sprinkle with cheese. Cover and refrigerate for 8 hours or overnight. Remove from the refrigerator 30 minutes before baking. Bake, uncovered, at 350° for 40-50 minutes or until a knife inserted near the center comes out clean. Let stand 10 minutes before serving. **Yield:** 8 servings.

Chicken Brunch Bake
Chilled Fruit Cups
Yogurt Waffles

Chicken Brunch Bake

(Pictured at left)

Chunks of tender chicken add heartiness to this appealing brunch casserole. —DeLee Jochum, Dubuque, Iowa

9 slices day-old bread, cubed
3 cups chicken broth
4 cups cubed cooked chicken
1/2 cup uncooked instant rice
1/2 cup diced pimientos
2 tablespoons minced fresh parsley
1-1/2 teaspoons salt, optional
4 eggs, beaten

In a large bowl, toss bread cubes and broth. Add chicken, rice, pimientos, parsley and salt if desired; mix well. Transfer to a greased 13-in. x 9-in. x 2-in. baking dish. Pour eggs over all. Bake, uncovered, at 325° for 1 hour or until a knife inserted near the center comes out clean. **Yield:** 8 servings.

Chilled Fruit Cups

(Pictured at left)

This refreshing frozen salad is easy to assemble ahead and serve to a group at breakfast—or any time of day. —Andrea Hawthorne, Bozeman, Montana

1 can (12 ounces) frozen pineapple juice concentrate, thawed
1 can (6 ounces) frozen orange juice concentrate, thawed
1 cup water
1 cup sugar
2 tablespoons lemon juice
3 medium firm bananas, sliced
1 package (16 ounces) frozen unsweetened strawberries
1 can (15 ounces) mandarin oranges, drained
1 can (8 ounces) crushed pineapple
18 clear plastic cups (9 ounces)

In a large bowl, prepare pineapple juice concentrate according to package directions. Add orange juice concentrate, water, sugar, lemon juice and fruit. Spoon 3/4 cupful into each plastic cup. Place cups in a pan and freeze. Remove from the freezer 40-50 minutes before serving. **Yield:** 18 servings.

Omelet for Two

I give a little zip to my family's breakfast omelets with a rich and satisfying sausage filling. —Sandi Pichon, Slidell, Louisiana

1/2 cup sliced fresh mushrooms
2 tablespoons butter *or* margarine, *divided*
1/4 pound bulk pork sausage
1 tablespoon all-purpose flour
1/4 cup milk
1/8 teaspoon salt
Pepper to taste
1/2 cup sour cream

OMELET:
4 eggs
1/4 cup milk
1/2 teaspoon salt
1/4 teaspoon pepper
2 tablespoons butter *or* margarine

In a large saucepan, saute mushrooms in 1 tablespoon butter. Remove mushrooms and keep warm. In the same pan, cook sausage until no longer pink; drain. Add remaining butter. Stir in flour until blended. Gradually add milk, salt and pepper. Bring to a boil; cook and stir for 2 minutes or until thickened and bubbly. Remove from the heat. Stir in sour cream and mushrooms; set aside and keep warm. In a bowl, beat eggs, milk, salt and pepper. In a skillet, melt butter. Pour egg mixture into skillet. As eggs set, lift edges, letting uncooked portion flow underneath. Cook until eggs are completely set. Transfer to a serving plate. Spoon sausage mixture over one side of the omelet; fold in half. **Yield:** 2 servings.

Yogurt Waffles

(Pictured at left)

Yogurt lends the flavorful difference to these soft waffles. They look tempting topped with additional yogurt and fresh fruit. —Margaret Wilson, Hemet, California

1-1/4 cups all-purpose flour
1-1/2 teaspoons baking powder
1 teaspoon baking soda
1/4 teaspoon salt
2 cups (16 ounces) plain yogurt
1/4 cup butter *or* margarine, melted
2 eggs
2 tablespoons honey
Raspberry, peach *or* strawberry yogurt
Raspberries, blueberries *and/or* sliced peaches

In a mixing bowl, combine the flour, baking powder, baking soda and salt. Beat in plain yogurt, butter, eggs and honey until smooth. Bake in a preheated waffle iron according to manufacturer's directions until golden brown. Top with flavored yogurt and fruit. **Yield:** 6 waffles.

Thin Egg Pancakes

When I was young, my grandmother made these crepe-like pancakes and spread them with fresh honey. —Helen Wiese, Michigan City, Indiana

5 eggs
1 cup milk
1/2 cup all-purpose flour
1/2 cup confectioners' sugar
1/4 cup butter *or* margarine, melted
Salt and pepper to taste

In a bowl, beat eggs until foamy. Add milk. Stir in flour and sugar just until blended. Add butter, salt and pepper. Pour 1/4 cup of batter into a hot greased 8-in. skillet. Cook 2-3 minutes on each side or until lightly browned. Remove and keep warm. Repeat; stack pancakes with waxed paper in between. **Yield:** 1 dozen.

Chapter 10

⏱ *Casseroles and Skillet Suppers*

ARE YOU looking to fill up your hungry family with true comfort food? You'll find that nothing satisfies like a convenient casserole. These one-dish dinners are quick to fix and simple to make and bake.

And when your time's at a premium, you'll appreciate this chapter's slew of skillet suppers that require just a single pan and only a few minutes of cooking time. (Cleanup's a snap, too!)

From meaty meals to savory side dishes, comforting casseroles and speedy skillet suppers are sure to satisfy.

ONE-DISH DINNERS. Clockwise from upper right: Squash Stuffing Casserole (p. 142), Meatball Sub Casserole (p. 141), Tasty Meat Pie (p. 143) and Creamy Chicken and Rice (p. 149).

Catchall Casseroles

YOU'LL welcome these hearty and hot dishes that are proven favorites with other families. Just toss the ingredients together and turn on the oven. (Most of these casseroles can be ready in an hour or under!)

French Country Casserole

(Pictured below)

This delicious dish is great for busy nights when you don't have much time to devote to dinner. It's a quick-to-fix version of a traditional French cassoulet that was an instant hit with my husband, who enjoys smoked sausage.
—Kim Lowe, Coralville, Iowa

✓ Uses less fat, sugar or salt. Includes Nutritional Analysis and Diabetic Exchanges.

  1 **pound fully cooked kielbasa *or* Polish sausage, halved and cut into 1/4-inch slices**
  1 **can (16 ounces) kidney beans, rinsed and drained**
  1 **can (15-1/2 ounces) great northern beans, rinsed and drained**
  1 **can (15 ounces) black beans, rinsed and drained**
  1 **can (15 ounces) tomato sauce**
  3 **medium carrots, thinly sliced**
  2 **small onions, sliced into rings**
1/2 **cup red wine *or* beef broth**
  2 **tablespoons brown sugar**
  2 **garlic cloves, minced**
1-1/2 **teaspoons dried thyme**

French Country Casserole

Combine all ingredients in a bowl; transfer to an ungreased 3-qt. baking dish. Cover and bake at 375° for 60-70 minutes or until the carrots are tender. **Yield:** 9 servings. **Nutritional Analysis:** One 1-cup serving (prepared with low-fat turkey kielbasa and low-sodium broth) equals 268 calories, 894 mg sodium, 33 mg cholesterol, 39 gm carbohydrate, 19 gm protein, 5 gm fat. **Diabetic Exchanges:** 2 starch, 2 vegetable, 1-1/2 lean meat.

Hearty Barley Bake

Barley is a nice change of pace from the usual pasta or rice in this colorful casserole. It's chock-full of spicy sausage and vegetables. —Jenny Browning, Cypress, Texas

  2 **cups sliced fresh mushrooms**
  1 **cup thinly sliced carrots**
1/2 **cup chopped onion**
  1 **garlic clove, minced**
  2 **teaspoons vegetable oil**
12 **ounces bulk pork sausage**
1-1/2 **cups cooked pearl barley**
  1 **can (14-3/4 ounces) cream-style corn**
  1 **package (10 ounces) frozen chopped spinach, thawed and drained**
  3 **green onions, sliced**
  1 **teaspoon dried savory**
  1 **teaspoon dried thyme**
1/2 **teaspoon dried marjoram**
1/8 **teaspoon pepper**
1/2 **cup shredded Parmesan cheese**

In a skillet, saute mushrooms, carrots, onion and garlic in oil until tender; remove to a large bowl. In the same skillet, cook sausage until no longer pink; drain. Add to mushroom mixture. Add barley, corn, spinach, onions, savory, thyme, marjoram and pepper; mix well. Transfer to a greased shallow 2-qt. baking dish. Cover and bake at 350° for 40 minutes. Sprinkle with cheese. Bake, uncovered, 5 minutes longer or until the cheese is melted. **Yield:** 6 servings.

Mom's Ground Beef Casserole

This is a favorite passed down from my mom, who got the recipe from a friend. Served with a green vegetable, it's a tasty, satisfying meal. —Julie Gillespie, Kirklin, Indiana

  2 **pounds ground beef**
  1 **medium green pepper, chopped**
  1 **medium onion, chopped**
  9 **cups cooked wide egg noodles**
  1 **pound process American cheese, cubed**
  1 **can (15-1/4 ounces) whole kernel corn, drained**
  1 **can (11-1/2 ounces) condensed chicken with rice soup, undiluted**
  1 **can (10-3/4 ounces) condensed cream of mushroom soup, undiluted**
1/2 **cup milk**
  1 **teaspoon salt**
1/4 **teaspoon pepper**

Fish Stick Supper

In a Dutch oven, cook beef, green pepper and onion until meat is no longer pink and vegetables are tender; drain. Remove from the heat; stir in remaining ingredients. Transfer to two greased 2-1/2-qt. baking dishes. Cover and bake at 350° for 45-50 minutes or until bubbly. **Yield:** 16-18 servings.

Fish Stick Supper

(Pictured above)

Dill adds fresh flavor to this comforting combination of foods you likely keep in your freezer. When our children were growing up, they loved this meal.
—Ruth Andrewson, Leavenworth, Washington

    1 package (12 ounces) frozen shredded hash
      brown potatoes, thawed
    4 eggs
    2 cups milk
    1 tablespoon dried minced onion
    1 tablespoon snipped fresh dill *or* 1 teaspoon
      dill weed
 1-1/4 teaspoons seasoned salt
    1/8 teaspoon pepper
    1 cup (4 ounces) shredded cheddar cheese
    1 package (12 ounces) frozen fish sticks
      (about 18)

Break apart hash browns with a fork; set aside. In a large bowl, beat eggs and milk. Add onion, dill, seasoned salt and pepper. Stir in hash browns and cheese. Transfer to a greased 11-in. x 7-in. x 2-in. baking dish; arrange fish sticks over the top. Bake, uncovered, at 350° for 50 minutes or until top is golden brown and fish flakes with a fork. Let stand for 5 minutes before cutting. **Yield:** 6 servings.

Meatball Sub Casserole

(Pictured on page 139)

This tangy casserole has all the rich flavor of meatball subs with none of the mess.   *—Gina Harris*
Seneca, South Carolina

    1/3 cup chopped green onions
    1/4 cup seasoned bread crumbs
    3 tablespoons grated Parmesan cheese
    1 pound ground beef
    1 loaf (1 pound) Italian bread, cut into 1-inch
      slices
    1 package (8 ounces) cream cheese, softened
    1/2 cup mayonnaise*
    1 teaspoon Italian seasoning
    1/4 teaspoon pepper
    2 cups (8 ounces) shredded mozzarella cheese,
      divided
    1 jar (28 ounces) spaghetti sauce
    1 cup water
    2 garlic cloves, minced

In a bowl, combine onions, crumbs and Parmesan cheese. Add beef and mix well. Shape into 1-in. balls; place on a rack in a shallow baking pan. Bake at 400° for 15-20 minutes or until no longer pink. Meanwhile, arrange bread in a single layer in an ungreased 13-in. x 9-in. x 2-in. baking dish (all of the bread might not be used). Combine cream cheese, mayonnaise, Italian seasoning and pepper; spread over the bread. Sprinkle with 1/2 cup mozzarella. Combine sauce, water and garlic; add meatballs. Pour over cheese mixture; sprinkle with remaining mozzarella. Bake, uncovered, at 350° for 30 minutes or until heated through. **Yield:** 6-8 servings.
***Editor's Note:** Do not use light or fat-free mayonnaise.

Pizza Tot Casserole

(Pictured at right)

You need just seven ingredients to make this upside-down pizza casserole. Since I cook for two, I often divide it into two smaller dishes—one for dinner and one to freeze. I thaw the frozen portion in the fridge overnight before baking. —Chris Stukel, Des Plaines, Illinois

- 1 pound ground beef
- 1 medium green pepper, chopped
- 1 medium onion, chopped
- 1 can (11-1/8 ounces) condensed Italian tomato soup, undiluted
- 1 jar (4-1/2 ounces) sliced mushrooms, drained
- 2 cups (8 ounces) shredded mozzarella cheese
- 1 package (32 ounces) frozen Tater Tots

In a skillet, cook the beef, pepper and onion until meat is no longer pink; drain. Add soup and mushrooms. Transfer to a greased 13-in. x 9-in. x 2-in. baking dish. Top with cheese and potatoes. Bake, uncovered, at 400° for 30-35 minutes or until golden brown. **Yield:** 6-8 servings.

Pizza Tot Casserole

Picante Biscuit Bake

(Pictured below)

This tasty Mexican-flavored casserole is a breeze to put together. To make it heartier, you can add a pound of browned ground beef. Or try a pizza variation using pizza sauce, pepperoni and mozzarella cheese. —Lanita Anderson, Jacksonville, North Carolina

- 2 tubes (12 ounces *each*) refrigerated buttermilk biscuits
- 1 jar (16 ounces) picante sauce *or* salsa
- 1 medium green pepper, chopped
- 1 medium onion, chopped
- 1 can (2-1/4 ounces) sliced ripe olives, drained

Picante Biscuit Bake

- 2 cups (8 ounces) shredded Monterey Jack cheese

Quarter the biscuits; place in a greased 13-in. x 9-in. x 2-in. baking dish. Top with picante sauce, green pepper, onion and olives. Bake, uncovered, at 350° for 20 minutes. Sprinkle with cheese. Bake 10 minutes longer or until the cheese is melted. **Yield:** 6 servings.

Squash Stuffing Casserole

(Pictured on page 139)

The recipe for this zippy side dish was given to me by my husband's grandmother. Convenient corn bread stuffing mix and a can of green chilies give fast flavor to summer squash. I often freeze the leftovers for another day. —Tara Kay Cottingham, Munday, Texas

- 3/4 cup water
- 1/4 teaspoon salt
- 6 cups sliced yellow summer squash (1/4 inch thick)
- 1 small onion, halved and sliced
- 1 can (10-3/4 ounces) condensed cream of mushroom soup, undiluted
- 1 cup (8 ounces) sour cream
- 1 package (6 ounces) instant corn bread stuffing mix
- 1 can (4 ounces) chopped green chilies
- Salt and pepper to taste
- 1 cup (4 ounces) shredded cheddar cheese

In a large saucepan, bring water and salt to a boil. Add squash and onion. Reduce heat; cover and cook until squash is crisp-tender, about 6 minutes. Drain well; set aside. In a bowl, combine soup, sour cream, stuffing and the contents of seasoning packet, chilies, salt and pepper; mix well. Fold in squash mixture. Pour into a greased shallow 2-qt. baking dish. Sprinkle with cheese. Bake, uncovered, at 350° for 25-30 minutes or until heated through. **Yield:** 8-10 servings.

Tasty Meat Pie

(Pictured on page 138)

I work full-time as a nurse, so I like meals that are quick and easy. This comforting all-in-one pie is filled with ground beef and tender vegetables. At my sister's suggestion, I replaced the prepared gravy I had been using with canned soups for better flavor. —Cheryl Cattane
Lapeer, Michigan

    1 pound ground beef
    1 small onion, chopped
    1 can (11 ounces) condensed beef with
      vegetables and barley soup, undiluted
    1 can (10-3/4 ounces) condensed golden
      mushroom soup, undiluted
    3 medium uncooked potatoes, cut into
      1/2-inch cubes
    4 medium carrots, sliced 1/8 inch thick
  1/4 teaspoon salt
  1/8 teaspoon pepper
Pastry for double-crust pie (9 inches)

In a skillet, cook beef and onion until meat is no longer pink; drain. Add the soups, potatoes, carrots, salt and pepper; mix well. Divide between two ungreased 9-in. pie plates. On a floured surface, roll pastry to fit the top of each pie; place over filling. Seal and flute edges; cut slits in top. Bake at 350° for 45-50 minutes or until golden brown. Let stand on a wire rack for 15 minutes before serving. **Yield:** 2 pies (6 servings each).

Spinach Tuna Casserole

After a busy day of bookkeeping for our family contracting business, I count on this rapid recipe my mother passed along to me. I double it if I need to feed unexpected guests who stop by at mealtime.
—Nancy Adams
Hancock, New Hampshire

    1 package (10 ounces) frozen
      chopped spinach, thawed and
      squeezed dry
    1 can (6 ounces) tuna, drained
  1/3 cup seasoned bread crumbs
    3 tablespoons crushed seasoned
      stuffing
  1/4 teaspoon salt
  1/2 cup mayonnaise
  1/4 cup sour cream
    2 to 3 teaspoons lemon juice
    2 to 3 tablespoons Parmesan
      cheese

In a bowl, combine the first five ingredients; mix well. Combine the mayonnaise, sour cream and lemon juice; add to tuna mixture and mix well. Transfer to a greased 2-cup baking dish. Sprinkle with Parmesan cheese. Cover and bake at 350° for 20-25 minutes or until heated through. **Yield:** 2 servings.

Pepperoni Pizzazz

(Pictured below)

With this hearty entree, all you'll need to round out the meal is garlic bread and a tossed salad. I've fixed it for buffets, for potluck dinners and even for company.
—Marge Unger, La Porte, Indiana

    8 ounces medium tube pasta
    1 jar (28 ounces) spaghetti sauce, *divided*
    1 jar (4-1/2 ounces) sliced mushrooms, drained
    1 package (8 ounces) sliced pepperoni
  1/2 cup chopped green pepper
  1/2 cup chopped onion
  1/2 cup grated Parmesan cheese
  1/2 teaspoon garlic powder
  1/2 teaspoon salt
  1/8 teaspoon pepper
  1/8 teaspoon crushed red pepper flakes
    1 can (8 ounces) tomato sauce
    2 cups (8 ounces) shredded mozzarella cheese

Cook pasta according to package directions. Meanwhile, combine 2-1/3 cups spaghetti sauce, mushrooms, pepperoni, green pepper, onion, Parmesan cheese, garlic powder, salt, pepper and red pepper flakes in a bowl. Drain pasta; add to sauce mixture and mix well. Transfer to a greased 3-qt. baking dish. Combine the tomato sauce and remaining spaghetti sauce; pour over top. Cover and bake at 350° for 40-45 minutes or until bubbly. Sprinkle with mozzarella cheese. Bake, uncovered, 5-10 minutes longer or until cheese is melted. Let stand 5 minutes before serving. **Yield:** 9-12 servings.

Pepperoni Pizzazz

Crowned Beef Bake

Because this comforting casserole looks so special, I enjoy serving it to company and bringing it to church suppers. It's simple to put together but looks like I spent a lot of time preparing it. —Linda Parker, Covington, Georgia

- 1 pound ground beef
- 1 can (4 ounces) mushroom stems and pieces, drained
- 1 can (2.8 ounces) french-fried onions, crumbled, *divided*
- 2 cups frozen mixed vegetables
- 1 can (10-3/4 ounces) condensed cream of celery soup, undiluted
- 1 cup (8 ounces) sour cream, *divided*
- 1 tube (7-1/2 ounces) refrigerated buttermilk biscuits
- 1 egg, lightly beaten
- 1 teaspoon celery seed
- 1/2 teaspoon salt

In a skillet, cook the beef until no longer pink; drain. Place half in a greased 2-qt. baking dish. Layer with mushrooms, two-thirds of the onions and all of the vegetables. Top with remaining beef. In a saucepan, combine soup and 1/2 cup of sour cream; cook over low heat until heated through. Pour over the beef. Cut each biscuit in half; arrange cut side down around edge of dish. Sprinkle with remaining onions. Combine egg, celery seed, salt and remaining sour cream; drizzle over biscuits. Bake, uncovered, at 375° for 25-30 minutes or until golden brown. **Yield:** 4-6 servings.

Corn Tortilla Quiche

(Pictured below)

A corn tortilla crust makes this tasty quiche a snap to assemble. Cheesy wedges are great for breakfast, lunch or dinner. —Leicha Welton, Fairbanks, Alaska

- 3/4 pound bulk pork sausage
- 5 corn tortillas (6 inches)
- 1 cup (4 ounces) shredded Monterey Jack cheese
- 1 cup (4 ounces) shredded cheddar cheese
- 1/4 cup chopped canned green chilies
- 6 eggs, beaten
- 1/2 cup whipping cream
- 1/2 cup small-curd cottage cheese
- 1/2 teaspoon chili powder
- 1/4 cup minced fresh cilantro *or* parsley

In a skillet, cook the sausage until no longer pink; drain. Place four tortillas in a greased 9-in. pie plate, overlapping and extending 1/2 in. beyond rim. Place remaining tortilla in the center. Layer with sausage, Monterey Jack and cheddar cheeses and chilies. Combine eggs, cream, cottage cheese and chili powder; slowly pour over chilies. Bake at 350° for 45 minutes or until the center is set and puffed. Sprinkle with cilantro. **Yield:** 6 servings.

Corn Tortilla Quiche

Apple-a-Day Casserole

Apple-a-Day Casserole

(Pictured above)

This sweet-tart casserole is a fun change of pace from traditional vegetable side dishes. It's super-quick to prepare if you use a food processor to slice the apples and carrots.
—Elizabeth Erwin, Syracuse, New York

  6 medium tart apples, peeled and sliced
  6 medium carrots, thinly sliced
1/2 cup orange juice
1/3 cup all-purpose flour
1/3 cup sugar
1/2 teaspoon ground nutmeg
  2 tablespoons cold butter *or* margarine

Combine apples and carrots; place in a greased shallow 2-qt. baking dish. Drizzle with orange juice. Cover and bake at 350° for 40-45 minutes or until carrots are crisp-tender. In a bowl, combine the flour, sugar and nutmeg; cut in butter until crumbly. Sprinkle over apple mixture. Bake, uncovered, 10-15 minutes longer or until the carrots are tender. **Yield:** 6-8 servings.

Hearty Ham Casserole

I like to fix this saucy dish when we have leftover ham and potatoes. I often make it during wheat harvest. All our helpers really seem to enjoy it.   *—Debbie Leininger*
Carpenter, Wyoming

  2 cups cubed fully cooked ham
  2 cups diced cooked potatoes
  1 can (15-1/4 ounces) whole kernel corn,
     drained
1/4 cup minced fresh parsley
  1 tablespoon chopped onion
1/4 cup butter *or* margarine
1/3 cup all-purpose flour
1-3/4 cups milk
1/8 teaspoon pepper
  1 cup (4 ounces) shredded cheddar cheese *or*
    process American cheese

In a large bowl, combine the first four ingredients; set aside. In a saucepan, saute onion in butter for 2 minutes; stir in flour until blended. Gradually add milk and pepper. Bring to a boil; cook and stir for 2 minutes. Remove from the heat; pour over the ham mixture and stir until combined. Transfer to a greased 11-in. x 7-in. x 2-in. baking dish. Cover and bake at 350° for 25 minutes. Uncover and sprinkle with cheese. Bake 5-10 minutes longer or until cheese is melted. **Yield:** 4-6 servings.

Cajun Cabbage

(Pictured below)

Looking for a different treatment for cabbage? Try this spicy cheese-topped dish that I adapted from a friend's recipe. I added a little of this and that until it tasted the way I wanted. Not only do my husband and kids like it, I get rave reviews when I make it for company.
—Bobbie Soileau, Opelousas, Louisiana

  1 pound ground beef
  1 medium green pepper, chopped
  1 medium onion, chopped
  2 garlic cloves, minced
  1 can (10 ounces) diced tomatoes and green
    chilies
  1 can (8 ounces) tomato sauce
1/2 cup uncooked long grain rice
  1 teaspoon salt
1/2 teaspoon dried basil
1/2 teaspoon dried oregano
1/4 to 1/2 teaspoon *each* white, black and
    cayenne pepper
  4 to 6 drops hot pepper sauce
  1 small head cabbage, chopped
  1 cup (4 ounces) shredded Colby cheese

In a skillet, cook the beef, green pepper, onion and garlic until meat is no longer pink; drain. Stir in the tomatoes, tomato sauce, rice and seasonings. Spread into an ungreased 13-in. x 9-in. x 2-in. baking dish. Top with the cabbage and cheese. Cover and bake at 350° for 65-75 minutes or until the rice is tender. **Yield:** 6-8 servings.

Cajun Cabbage

California Chicken Casserole

Salmon Broccoli Bake

A good friend gave me this quick-and-easy recipe that uses canned salmon, wild rice and frozen broccoli. I often serve this casserole with a wilted spinach salad for a complete meal. —Brigitte Schaller, Flemington, Missouri

    1 cup chopped onion
    1 tablespoon butter *or* margarine
1-1/2 cups cooked wild rice
    1 can (7-1/2 ounces) salmon, drained, flaked
      and bones removed
    1 egg
  1/2 cup mayonnaise*
  1/2 cup grated Parmesan cheese
    1 package (10 ounces) frozen chopped
      broccoli, thawed and drained
1-1/2 cups (6 ounces) shredded cheddar cheese,
      divided

In a skillet, saute onion in butter until tender. Remove from the heat; stir in rice and salmon. Combine egg and mayonnaise; add to the salmon mixture. Spoon half into a greased 2-qt. baking dish; top with half of the Parmesan cheese and broccoli. Sprinkle with 1 cup cheddar cheese. Top with the remaining salmon mixture, Parmesan and broccoli. Bake, uncovered, at 350° for 30 minutes. Sprinkle with remaining cheddar. Bake 5 minutes longer or until cheese is melted. **Yield:** 4 servings. ***Editor's Note:** Light or fat-free mayonnaise may not be substituted for regular mayonnaise.

California Chicken Casserole

(Pictured above)

I love to try new recipes, and this chicken and vegetable combo passed my family's taste test. If there are leftovers, I package them for my husband to reheat in the microwave. —Debbie Kokes, Tabor, South Dakota

    1 can (10-3/4 ounces) condensed cream of
      mushroom soup, undiluted
  1/3 cup milk
    1 package (16 ounces) frozen California blend
      vegetables, thawed
1-1/2 cups cubed cooked chicken
1-1/2 cups (6 ounces) shredded Swiss cheese,
      divided
    1 jar (2 ounces) diced pimientos, drained
Salt and pepper to taste
Hot cooked rice

In a bowl, combine soup and milk. Stir in vegetables, chicken, 1-1/4 cups cheese, pimientos, salt and pepper. Transfer to a greased 9-in. square baking dish. Cover and bake at 350° for 40 minutes. Uncover; top with remaining cheese. Bake 5-10 minutes longer or until bubbly. Let stand for 5 minutes. Serve over rice. **Yield:** 4 servings.

Almond Chicken and Rice

The recipe for this almond-topped casserole has been in

our family for years. It's as comforting as chicken rice soup, so it's on our dinner table often. —Sharon Skildum
Maple Grove, Minnesota

   1 cup uncooked long grain rice
   1 broiler-fryer chicken (3-1/2 to 4 pounds), cut up
   1 can (10-3/4 ounces) condensed cream of mushroom soup, undiluted
   1 cup milk
   1 celery rib, chopped
 1/2 cup chopped onion
   2 tablespoons minced fresh parsley
 1/4 teaspoon salt
 1/4 teaspoon pepper
 1/2 cup slivered almonds, *divided*

Place the rice in a greased 13-in. x 9-in. x 2-in. baking dish; top with chicken. In a bowl, combine soup, milk, celery, onion, parsley, salt, pepper and 1/4 cup of almonds. Pour over chicken. Cover and bake at 350° for 45 minutes. Sprinkle with remaining almonds. Bake, uncovered, 15 minutes longer or until meat juices run clear. **Yield:** 4 servings.

Southwestern Veggie Bake

(Pictured below right)

Refrigerated corn bread twists create an appealing lattice top on this zippy main dish. The original recipe contained cooked chicken instead of kidney beans and celery, but my family prefers my meatless version, which is spicier, too. —Julie Zeager, Kent, Ohio

✓ Uses less fat, sugar or salt. Includes Nutritional Analysis and Diabetic Exchanges.

   3 medium carrots, peeled and sliced
   2 celery ribs, chopped
   1 small onion, chopped
   2 to 3 teaspoons chili powder
   1 teaspoon ground cumin
 1/4 teaspoon cayenne pepper
   2 tablespoons butter *or* margarine
   3 tablespoons all-purpose flour
 1/2 cup milk
   1 can (16 ounces) kidney beans, rinsed and drained
   1 can (15 ounces) black beans, rinsed and drained
   1 can (15-1/4 ounces) whole kernel corn, drained
   1 can (14-1/2 ounces) diced tomatoes, undrained
   1 can (4 ounces) chopped green chilies
   1 tube (11-1/2 ounces) refrigerated corn bread twists

In a large skillet, saute the carrots, celery, onion and seasonings in butter until vegetables are crisp-tender. Stir in flour until blended. Gradually add the milk. Bring to a boil; cook and stir for 2 minutes or until thickened and bubbly. Remove from the heat; add beans, corn, tomatoes and chilies. Spoon into an ungreased 13-in. x

9-in. x 2-in. baking dish. Separate corn bread twists; make a lattice crust over filling. Bake, uncovered, at 350° for 20-25 minutes or until corn bread is done. **Yield:** 8 servings. **Nutritional Analysis:** One 1-cup serving (prepared with margarine and skim milk) equals 350 calories, 713 mg sodium, trace cholesterol, 54 gm carbohydrate, 13 gm protein, 10 gm fat. **Diabetic Exchanges:** 2 starch, 2 vegetable, 2 fat.

Zippy Beef Supper

I rely on two cans of soup and zippy canned tomatoes with chilies to make this spicy and satisfying casserole. Shredded cheddar cheese and crunchy tortilla chips create a tasty topping. —Ruth Foster, Crooksville, Ohio

   2 pounds ground beef
   1 medium onion, chopped
   1 cup cubed cooked potatoes
   1 can (11 ounces) condensed nacho cheese soup, undiluted
   1 can (10-3/4 ounces) condensed cream of onion soup, undiluted
   1 can (10 ounces) tomatoes and green chilies, undrained
   2 to 3 teaspoons ground cumin
 1/2 to 1 teaspoon garlic powder
   3 cups crushed tortilla chips
   1 cup (4 ounces) shredded cheddar cheese

In a large saucepan over medium heat, cook beef and onion until meat is no longer pink; drain. Add potatoes; cook and stir until heated through. Stir in the soups, tomatoes, cumin and garlic powder; mix well. Transfer to a greased 13-in. x 9-in. x 2-in. baking dish. Cover and bake at 350° for 30 minutes. Uncover; sprinkle with tortilla chips and cheese. Bake, uncovered, for 5-10 minutes or until cheese is melted. **Yield:** 6-8 servings.

Southwestern Veggie Bake

Great Pork Chop Bake

(Pictured at right)

A friend brought this hearty meat-and-potatoes dish to our home when I returned from the hospital with our youngest child. Since then, we have enjoyed it many times. It's a snap to throw together on a busy day, then pop in the oven to bake. —Rosie Glenn, Los Alamos, New Mexico

- 6 bone-in pork chops (3/4 inch thick)
- 1 tablespoon vegetable oil
- 1 can (10-3/4 ounces) condensed cream of chicken soup, undiluted
- 3 tablespoons ketchup
- 2 tablespoons Worcestershire sauce
- 1/2 teaspoon salt
- 1/4 teaspoon pepper
- 4 medium potatoes, cut into 1/2-inch wedges
- 1 medium onion, sliced into rings

In a skillet, brown pork chops in oil. Transfer to a greased 13-in. x 9-in. x 2-in. baking dish. In a bowl, combine the soup, ketchup, Worcestershire sauce, salt and pepper. Add potatoes and onion; toss to coat. Pour over the chops. Cover and bake at 350° for 55-60 minutes or until meat juices run clear and potatoes are tender. **Yield:** 6 servings.

Great Pork Chop Bake

Chicken 'n' Chips

(Pictured below)

My husband, Chad, is always ready to try a new recipe, so I surprised him with this creamy chicken casserole sprinkled with crushed tortilla chips. He loves the flavor, and I like that it's the perfect size for our small family. —Kendra Schneider, Grifton, North Carolina

- 1 can (10-3/4 ounces) condensed cream of chicken soup, undiluted
- 1 cup (8 ounces) sour cream
- 2 tablespoons taco sauce
- 1/4 cup chopped green chilies
- 3 cups cubed cooked chicken
- 12 slices process American cheese
- 4 cups broken tortilla chips

In a bowl, combine the soup, sour cream, taco sauce and chilies. In an ungreased shallow 2-qt. baking dish, layer half of the chicken, soup mixture, cheese and tortilla chips. Repeat layers. Bake, uncovered, at 350° for 25-30 minutes or until bubbly. **Yield:** 4-6 servings.

Chicken 'n' Chips

Meal-in-One Casserole

My husband and I are retired and enjoy vegetable gardening and fishing. This meat-and-potatoes casserole that I created makes a satisfying supper. —Madge Watkins Ontario, Oregon

✓ Uses less fat, sugar or salt. Includes Nutritional Analysis and Diabetic Exchanges.

- 1 pound ground beef
- 3 medium unpeeled potatoes, thinly sliced
- 1 medium onion, sliced and separated into rings
- 1 cup frozen peas
- 1-1/2 cups sliced mushrooms
- 1-1/2 teaspoons salt, optional
- 1/4 teaspoon pepper
- 1 teaspoon sesame seeds
- 3 tablespoons butter *or* margarine, melted

In a skillet over medium heat, cook beef until no longer pink; drain. Place potatoes in a greased 2-qt. baking dish. Top with beef and onion. Place peas in the center; arrange mushrooms around the peas. Sprinkle with the salt, pepper and sesame seeds; drizzle with butter. Cover and bake at 375° for 50-60 minutes or until potatoes are tender. **Yield:** 4 servings. **Nutritional Analysis:** One serving (prepared with lean ground beef and reduced-fat margarine and without salt) equals 391 calories, 231 mg sodium, 41 mg cholesterol, 33 gm carbohydrate, 29 gm protein, 16 gm fat. **Diabetic Exchanges:** 2 starch, 1 meat, 1 vegetable.

Creamy Chicken and Rice

(Pictured on page 138)

When my mom asked me to prepare a speedy supper to feed our family, I used leftover chicken to create this casserole. Cheese and sour cream make the chicken and rice so creamy and tasty. I recently got married, and my husband, Doug, loves it, too. —Jennifer Biggs Cassel
Mediapolis, Iowa

      4 cups cooked rice
  1/2 cup butter *or* margarine, *divided*
  1/4 cup all-purpose flour
      2 cups milk
      2 teaspoons chicken bouillon granules
  1/2 to 1 teaspoon seasoned salt
  1/2 teaspoon garlic powder
  1/4 teaspoon pepper
      4 to 5 cups cubed cooked chicken
    12 ounces process American cheese, cubed
      2 cups (16 ounces) sour cream
  1-1/4 cups crushed butter-flavored crackers
      (about 32)

Spread rice into a greased shallow 3-qt. or 13-in. x 9-in. x 2-in. baking dish; set aside. In a saucepan, melt 1/4 cup butter; stir in flour until smooth. Gradually add milk, bouillon, seasoned salt, garlic powder and pepper. Bring to a boil; cook and stir for 2 minutes or until thickened and bubbly. Reduce heat; add chicken, cheese and sour cream; stir until the cheese is melted. Pour over rice. Melt the remaining butter; toss with cracker crumbs. Sprinkle over casserole. Bake, uncovered, at 425° for 10-15 minutes or until heated through. **Yield:** 6-8 servings.

Scalloped Potatoes 'n' Franks

This kid-pleasing combination was requested often when our children were young. Now that they're grown, they like to make it for their families. —Sandra Scheirer
Mertztown, Pennsylvania

      2 tablespoons chopped onion
      3 tablespoons butter *or* margarine
  1/4 cup all-purpose flour
  1-1/2 teaspoons salt
  1/8 teaspoon pepper
      2 cups milk
      1 cup (4 ounces) shredded Swiss cheese
      2 tablespoons minced fresh parsley
      5 medium potatoes, peeled and thinly sliced
      8 hot dogs, halved and sliced

In a saucepan, saute onion in butter until tender. Stir in flour, salt and pepper until blended. Gradually add milk. Bring to a boil over medium heat; cook and stir for 2 minutes. Remove from the heat; stir in cheese until melted. Add parsley. Place half of the potatoes in a greased 2-qt. baking dish; top with half of the sauce. Arrange hot dogs over the sauce. Top with remaining potatoes and sauce. Cover and bake at 350° for 1-1/2 hours or until bubbly. Uncover and bake 10 minutes longer or until lightly browned. **Yield:** 4-6 servings.

Chicken Hot Dish

Chicken Hot Dish

(Pictured at left)

When my brother and his wife came over to visit after our third child was born, they brought this comforting creamy dish for supper. It's become a favorite since then.
—Amber Dudley, New Prague, Minnesota

      1 package (26 ounces) frozen
          shredded hash brown potatoes,
          thawed
      1 package (24 ounces) frozen
          California-blend vegetables
      3 cups cubed cooked chicken
      1 can (10-3/4 ounces) condensed
          cream of chicken soup, undiluted
      1 can (10-3/4 ounces) condensed
          cream of mushroom soup,
          undiluted
      1 cup chicken broth
  3/4 cup french-fried onions

In a greased 13-in. x 9-in. x 2-in. baking dish, layer the potatoes, vegetables and chicken. In a bowl, combine soups and broth; pour over the chicken (dish will be full). Cover and bake at 375° for 1 hour. Uncover; sprinkle with onions. Bake 10 minutes longer or until heated through. **Yield:** 6 servings.

Dash in the Pan

YOU'VE come to the right place if "going steady" with your stovetop doesn't fit into your—or your family's—active lifestyle. File these speedy skillet suppers under "F" for filling, flavorful...and flat-out fast!

Smoky Macaroni

(Pictured below)

Our two grandsons love macaroni and cheese. When they are hungry, I can have this tasty variation—with little sausages that are just their size—ready in about 20 minutes.
—*Perlene Hoekema, Lynden, Washington*

    1/4 cup chopped sweet red pepper
      2 tablespoons chopped onion
      1 can (10-3/4 ounces) condensed cheddar
        cheese soup, undiluted
      1 cup milk
      1 package (16 ounces) miniature smoked
        sausage links
      8 ounces process American cheese, cut into
        1/2-inch cubes
      1 cup frozen peas
      4 cups cooked elbow macaroni

In a nonstick skillet, saute red pepper and onion until tender. Combine soup and milk; stir into skillet. Add sausage, cheese and peas. Reduce heat; simmer, uncovered, for 5-10 minutes or until the cheese is melted, stirring occasionally. Add the macaroni; cook 5-10 minutes longer or until heated through. **Yield:** 6-8 servings.

Smoky Macaroni

Spicy Chicken Stir-Fry

This zesty dish served over rice tastes so special we save it for family birthdays. It's simple, and it doesn't keep me in the kitchen all day.   —*Debbie Long, Elburn, Illinois*

      6 tablespoons vegetable oil, *divided*
      2 tablespoons soy sauce, *divided*
      3 teaspoons cornstarch, *divided*
      1 pound boneless skinless chicken breasts, cut
        into cubes
    1/2 teaspoon crushed red pepper flakes
      1 pound broccoli florets
  1-1/2 cups sliced onion
      1 garlic clove, minced
  1-1/2 cups chicken broth
    1/2 to 1 teaspoon ground ginger
    1/2 cup chopped walnuts

In a bowl, stir 1 tablespoon oil, 1 tablespoon soy sauce and 1 teaspoon cornstarch until smooth. Add chicken; toss to coat. Cover and refrigerate 15 minutes. In a large skillet or wok, heat 2 tablespoons of oil over medium-high heat. Add chicken and pepper flakes; stir-fry for 5 minutes or until meat juices run clear. Remove and keep warm. Heat remaining oil; stir-fry broccoli, onion and garlic for 5-8 minutes or until tender. Combine broth, ginger and remaining soy sauce and cornstarch; stir until smooth. Add to the skillet; bring to a boil, stirring constantly. Cook 2 minutes or until thickened. Add chicken and walnuts; heat through. **Yield:** 4 servings.

Ground Turkey and Hominy

Hominy is a real favorite of mine, so when I saw this fast-to-fix recipe, I had to try it.   —*Esther Hoff-Sherrow Denver, Colorado*

 Uses less fat, sugar or salt. Includes Nutritional Analysis and Diabetic Exchanges.

  1-1/2 pounds ground turkey
      1 large onion, chopped
      2 garlic cloves, minced
      2 tablespoons olive *or* vegetable oil
      2 cans (14-1/2 ounces *each*) diced tomatoes,
        undrained
      1 tablespoon chili powder
  1-1/2 teaspoons ground cumin
      1 teaspoon salt, optional
    1/2 teaspoon ground mustard
    1/2 teaspoon dried thyme
    1/4 teaspoon ground cinnamon
    1/4 teaspoon ground allspice
    1/4 teaspoon pepper
      1 can (15-1/2 ounces) yellow hominy, rinsed
        and drained
      1 can (15-1/2 ounces) white hominy, rinsed
        and drained

In a large skillet or saucepan, cook turkey, onion and garlic in oil until meat is no longer pink. Stir in tomatoes and seasonings; heat through. Add hominy and heat through. **Yield:** 8 servings. **Nutritional Analysis:** One 1-

cup serving (prepared with ground turkey breast and without salt) equals 271 calories, 526 mg sodium, 73 mg cholesterol, 23 gm carbohydrate, 19 gm protein, 11 gm fat. **Diabetic Exchanges:** 2 meat, 1 starch, 1 vegetable, 1 fat.

Chicken Cacciatore

(Pictured at right)

Not only is this satisfying main dish easy to fix, it tastes fantastic. And it has plenty of nicely spiced sauce.
—*Susan Adair, Muncie, Indiana*

1-1/2 pounds boneless skinless chicken breasts, cut into 1/2-inch strips
1 medium onion, sliced into rings
1 medium green pepper, julienned
2 tablespoons vegetable oil
1 can (15 ounces) tomato sauce
1 can (14-1/2 ounces) stewed tomatoes
2 teaspoons garlic powder
1/2 teaspoon dried oregano
1/2 teaspoon salt
1/2 teaspoon pepper
Hot cooked rice

In a skillet, cook the chicken, onion and green pepper in oil until chicken is lightly browned and vegetables are tender. Add tomato sauce, stewed tomatoes and seasonings; bring to a boil. Reduce heat; simmer, uncovered, for 5 minutes or until heated through. Serve over rice. **Yield:** 6 servings.

Chicken Cacciatore

1 tablespoon cornstarch
1 tablespoon cold water
1 jar (4 ounces) diced pimientos, drained

Place flour in a large resealable plastic bag; add pork and shake to coat. In a large skillet or wok over medium heat, brown pork in oil; drain. Add the next 11 ingredients; bring to a boil. Reduce heat; cover and simmer for 20 minutes. Combine cornstarch and cold water until smooth; stir into skillet. Simmer 10 minutes longer. Just before serving, add pimientos. **Yield:** 6 servings. **Nutritional Analysis:** One 1-cup serving (prepared with low-sodium broth and without salt) equals 310 calories, 84 mg sodium, 90 mg cholesterol, 14 gm carbohydrate, 34 gm protein, 13 gm fat. **Diabetic Exchanges:** 4 lean meat, 1-1/2 vegetable, 1/2 starch.

Gingered Pork Stir-Fry

I fall back on this tasty stir-fry often when time's short. It's wonderful with a combination of white and brown rice.
—*Dorothy Bateman, Carver, Massachusetts*

✓ Uses less fat, sugar or salt. Includes Nutritional Analysis and Diabetic Exchanges.

1/3 cup all-purpose flour
2 pounds pork chop suey meat *or* cubed pork tenderloin
3 tablespoons vegetable oil
1 large onion, sliced
1 medium green pepper, sliced
2 celery ribs, sliced
1 cup water
1/4 cup chicken broth
1 tablespoon lemon juice
1 teaspoon sugar
1 teaspoon ground ginger
1 garlic clove, minced
1/2 teaspoon salt, optional
1/4 teaspoon pepper

Pasta with Greens 'n' Beans

It takes mere minutes to get this fast and flavorful pasta combination on the table. It's a snap to prepare when you brown the sausage while the noodles are cooking.
—*Kathleen Majewski, East Rochester, New York*

8 ounces uncooked spiral pasta (3 cups)
1/2 pound bulk Italian sausage
1 small onion, chopped
2 garlic cloves, minced
1 bunch escarole *or* spinach, trimmed and coarsely chopped (about 4 cups)
1 can (15 ounces) white kidney *or* cannellini beans, rinsed and drained
1 cup chicken broth
1/3 cup grated Parmesan *or* Romano cheese

Cook pasta according to package directions. Meanwhile, in a large skillet, cook sausage, onion and garlic until sausage is no longer pink and onion is tender; drain. Stir in escarole, beans and broth. Cover and simmer for 6-8 minutes or until escarole is wilted and tender. Drain pasta; add to vegetable mixture. Sprinkle with cheese. **Yield:** 4-6 servings.

Spaghetti Skillet

(Pictured at right)

No one can believe you don't cook the spaghetti before adding it to this family-pleasing fare. I love to make it for company to show them how easy it is. —Margery Bryan
Royal City, Washington

1/2 pound ground beef
1/4 pound bulk Italian sausage
1 can (15 ounces) tomato sauce
1 can (14-1/2 ounces) stewed tomatoes
1 cup water
1 can (4 ounces) mushroom stems and pieces, drained
2 celery ribs, sliced
4 ounces uncooked spaghetti, broken in half
1/4 teaspoon dried oregano
Salt and pepper to taste

In a skillet over medium heat, cook beef and sausage until no longer pink; drain. Add the remaining ingredients. Bring to a boil. Reduce heat; cover and simmer for 14-16 minutes or until spaghetti is tender. **Yield:** 4-6 servings.

Spaghetti Skillet

Meatballs and Beans

I pair meatballs with sweet baked beans to create this quick-and-easy dish. Serve it with a tossed green salad and dinner rolls to make a complete meal. —Bernice Morris
Marshfield, Missouri

2/3 cup soft bread crumbs
1/2 cup evaporated milk
1 teaspoon salt
1/4 teaspoon pepper
1 pound lean ground beef
1 small onion, diced
1 can (16 ounces) baked beans, undrained
2 to 3 tablespoons ketchup
1 tablespoon brown sugar
1/4 to 1/2 teaspoon ground mustard

Combine bread crumbs, milk, salt and pepper. Add beef; mix well. Shape into 1-1/2-in. balls. In a skillet, cook meatballs and onion until meatballs are browned; drain. Add beans, ketchup, brown sugar and mustard; mix well. Bring to a boil. Reduce heat; cover and simmer for 20-25 minutes or until meatballs are no longer pink. **Yield:** 4-6 servings.

Italian Sausage and Spuds

I collect recipes, especially ones that are quick. This hearty sausage and potato supper is great when we're camping in our motor home because it requires only one pot. —Pam Sprowl, Thousand Oaks, California

1 pound uncooked Italian sausage links, cut into 1/2-inch pieces

10 small red potatoes, cut into 1/4-inch wedges
1 teaspoon salt
1/2 teaspoon dried thyme
1/4 teaspoon pepper
1 cup thinly sliced yellow *or* red onion
1 medium green pepper, cut into 1-inch pieces
1/4 cup minced fresh parsley

In a skillet, combine sausage, potatoes, salt, thyme and pepper. Cover and cook until the sausage is no longer pink and the potatoes are tender, about 30-40 minutes. Add onion, green pepper and parsley. Cook, uncovered, until vegetables are crisp-tender. **Yield:** 4-6 servings.

Tasty Eggs for Two

I found this tasty stovetop recipe while looking for something quick to fix for dinner. My teenage son, who can be a picky eater, really likes the combination of ingredients. —Deb Cornelius, Grant, Nebraska

1 cup frozen cubed hash brown potatoes, thawed
1/4 cup chopped onion
2 tablespoons butter *or* margarine
1 cup fresh *or* frozen broccoli florets
1/2 cup julienned fully cooked ham
4 eggs
1 tablespoon milk
1/4 to 1/2 teaspoon lemon-pepper seasoning
1/4 teaspoon dill weed, optional

In a skillet, cook the potatoes and onion in butter over medium heat until lightly browned, about 10 minutes. Add broccoli; cook until tender. Stir in ham. In a bowl, beat eggs, milk, lemon-pepper and dill if desired. Pour over potato mixture; cook for 3-5 minutes or until eggs are completely set, stirring occasionally. **Yield:** 2 servings.

Artichoke Chicken Saute

This is a fast but elegant entree that is perfect for company. I've also made it with shrimp in place of chicken and asparagus or broccoli instead of artichokes.
—Nancy Dreher, Birmingham, Alabama

   1 small onion, thinly sliced
   1 medium sweet red pepper, julienned
   2 tablespoons butter *or* margarine
   2 cups cubed cooked chicken
   1 can (8-1/2 ounces) artichoke hearts, drained and quartered
  1/2 cup sliced fresh mushrooms
  1/2 cup white wine *or* chicken broth
1-1/2 teaspoons Italian seasoning
   1 teaspoon chicken bouillon granules
  1/2 teaspoon salt
  1/4 teaspoon pepper
   2 tablespoons cornstarch
   1 cup whipping cream, *divided*
Hot cooked rice *or* noodles

In a skillet, saute onion and red pepper in butter for 2-3 minutes. Add chicken, artichokes, mushrooms, wine or broth, Italian seasoning, bouillon, salt and pepper. Cook and stir for 3 minutes. Combine cornstarch and 1/4 cup cream until smooth; stir into skillet. Add remaining cream. Bring to a boil; cook and stir for 2 minutes or until thickened. Serve over rice or noodles. **Yield:** 4 servings.

Chicken Olé

The recipe for this zesty stovetop dinner came from a grocery store demonstration several years ago. It goes together in the time it takes to set the table.
—Robi Huggins, Anchorage, Alaska

✓ Uses less fat, sugar or salt. Includes Nutritional Analysis and Diabetic Exchanges.

   1 pound boneless skinless chicken breasts, cut into 1/2-inch cubes
   1 tablespoon vegetable oil
   1 can (15-1/4 ounces) whole kernel corn, drained
   1 can (15 ounces) tomato sauce
   1 can (4 ounces) chopped green chilies
1-1/2 teaspoons chili powder
   1 teaspoon onion powder
Tortilla chips *or* hot cooked rice
Shredded cheddar cheese

In a large skillet, cook chicken in oil for 5-6 minutes or until no longer pink. Add corn, tomato sauce, chilies, chili powder and onion powder; bring to a boil. Reduce heat; cover and simmer for 10-12 minutes, stirring occasionally. Serve over tortilla chips or rice and sprinkle with cheese. **Yield:** 4 servings. **Nutritional Analysis:** One serving (calculated without chips, rice or cheese) equals 274 calories, 1,024 mg sodium, 63 mg cholesterol, 28 gm carbohydrate, 27 gm protein, 7 gm fat. **Diabetic Exchanges:** 3 very lean meat, 1-1/2 starch, 1 vegetable.

Fiesta Fry Pan Dinner

(Pictured below)

Taco seasoning mix adds fast flavor to this speedy skillet dish. It's so easy to make that I fix it frequently. All I need is salad and dessert, and the meal is ready.
—Leota Shaffer, Sterling, Virginia

✓ Uses less fat, sugar or salt. Includes Nutritional Analysis and Diabetic Exchanges.

   1 pound ground turkey *or* beef
  1/2 cup chopped onion
   1 envelope taco seasoning
1-1/2 cups water
1-1/2 cups sliced zucchini
   1 can (14-1/2 ounces) stewed tomatoes, undrained
   1 cup frozen corn
1-1/2 cups uncooked instant rice
   1 cup (4 ounces) shredded cheddar cheese

In a skillet, cook turkey and onion until meat is no longer pink; drain if necessary. Stir in taco seasoning, water, zucchini, tomatoes and corn; bring to a boil. Add rice. Reduce heat; cover and simmer for 5 minutes or until rice is tender and liquid is absorbed. Sprinkle with cheese; cover and let stand until the cheese is melted. **Yield:** 8-10 servings. **Nutritional Analysis:** One 3/4-cup serving (prepared with ground turkey breast and reduced-sodium taco seasoning) equals 310 calories, 647 mg sodium, 57 mg cholesterol, 33 gm carbohydrate, 27 gm protein, 8 gm fat. **Diabetic Exchanges:** 3 lean meat, 2 starch.

Fiesta Fry Pan Dinner

Carrot Pepper Skillet

You can prepare stuffed peppers on the stove-top, cooked alongside nicely seasoned carrots, with this creative recipe. This dish is attractive, delicious and goes together in a hurry.
—Esther Shank, Harrisonburg, Virginia

✓ Uses less fat, sugar or salt. Includes Nutritional Analysis and Diabetic Exchanges.

    6 medium green peppers
1-1/2 cups cooked rice
    1 medium onion, chopped
  1/3 cup tomato juice
1-1/4 cups water, *divided*
    2 tablespoons Worcestershire sauce
    2 teaspoons salt *or* salt-free seasoning blend,
      divided
    2 teaspoons sugar, *divided*
    1 pound lean ground beef
    4 cups sliced carrots
    1 tablespoon butter *or* margarine, melted
Dash ground ginger
Dash ground nutmeg
    1 tablespoon corn syrup

Cut tops off peppers and remove seeds and membranes; set aside. In a bowl, combine the rice, onion, tomato juice, 1/4 cup water, Worcestershire sauce, 1 teaspoon salt and 1 teaspoon sugar. Add beef; mix well. Spoon into peppers. Place around the edge of a 10-in. skillet. Combine the carrots, butter, ginger, nutmeg and remaining salt and sugar. Place in the center of the skillet. Pour remaining water around peppers; cover and simmer for 30 minutes or until meat is no longer pink. Drizzle corn syrup over the carrots. **Yield:** 6 servings. **Nutritional Analysis:** One serving (prepared with low-sodium tomato juice, salt-free seasoning and reduced-fat margarine) equals 297 calories, 176 mg sodium, 28 mg cholesterol, 37 gm carbohydrate, 19 gm protein, 8 gm fat. **Diabetic Exchanges:** 2 starch, 1-1/2 meat, 1 vegetable.

Kielbasa and Kidney Beans

Kielbasa and Kidney Beans

(Pictured below left)

This hearty meal-in-one is one of my family's favorites. It keeps well in a slow cooker as I'm often asked to bring it to numerous gatherings. —Doreen Kelly
Roslyn, Pennsylvania

    1 pound fully cooked kielbasa *or* Polish
      sausage, cut into 1/2-inch pieces
    1 small onion, chopped
  1/2 cup chopped sweet red pepper
  1/2 cup chopped green pepper
  1/4 cup packed brown sugar
    2 tablespoons steak sauce
    1 tablespoon cider vinegar
    1 teaspoon Worcestershire sauce
    1 can (15 ounces) white kidney *or*
      cannelini beans, rinsed and drained

In a skillet, cook sausage for 2-3 minutes. Stir in onion and peppers. Cook and stir until sausage is lightly browned and vegetables are tender; drain. Combine brown sugar, steak sauce, vinegar and Worcestershire sauce; stir into skillet. Add beans. Cook and stir until heated through. **Yield:** 4 servings.

Quick Tomato Mac 'n' Beef

This one-skillet supper satisfies big appetites with its hearty mix of ingredients. For variety, add a cup of frozen vegetables or drained canned vegetables during the last 5-7 minutes of cooking.

    1 pound ground beef
    1 cup chopped onion
Salt and pepper to taste
    1 can (14-1/2 ounces) diced tomatoes with
      garlic and onion,* undrained
    1 cup water
    1 cup uncooked elbow macaroni
    1 cup (4 ounces) shredded cheddar cheese
Sliced green onions and sour cream, optional

In a skillet over medium heat, cook beef and onion until meat is no longer pink; drain. Season with salt and pepper. Add tomatoes and water; bring to a boil. Stir in macaroni. Cover and simmer for 10 minutes or until macaroni is tender. Stir in cheese. Garnish with onions and sour cream if desired. **Yield:** 4 servings. ***Editor's Note:** For a spicier flavor, substitute a can of diced tomatoes with green chilies.

Italian Stew

To create this tasty chili-like stew, I started with a pound of Italian sausage and just kept adding different ingredients that I knew would appeal to me and my family. Everyone who tries this savory stew enjoys it.
—Joann Schultz, Stevens Point, Wisconsin

    1 pound bulk Italian sausage
    1 medium onion, chopped
  1/2 cup chopped celery

- 2 medium carrots, sliced 1/8 inch thick
- 1/4 to 1/2 teaspoon Italian seasoning
- 1/4 teaspoon dried basil
- 1/4 teaspoon salt
- 1/4 teaspoon pepper
- 2 cups water
- 1 can (14-1/2 ounces) Italian stewed tomatoes
- 1 can (10-3/4 ounces) condensed tomato soup, undiluted
- 3/4 cup uncooked instant rice

In a skillet, cook the sausage until no longer pink; drain. Add the onion, celery, carrots, Italian seasoning, basil, salt and pepper. Cook and stir over medium heat for 5 minutes or until the vegetables are crisp-tender. Stir in the water, tomatoes and soup; bring to a boil. Reduce heat; cover and simmer for 30 minutes or until vegetables are tender. Stir in the rice; cover and cook for 10 minutes or until tender. **Yield:** 6 servings.

Lemon Chicken and Rice

Cabbage Sausage Stew

Because we live an hour's drive from work, I want something fast and easy to prepare for dinner when I get home. This flavorful combination of sausage, potatoes and cabbage makes a filling supper served with a garden salad and fresh rolls. —Pauline Rye, Titus, Alabama

 Uses less fat, sugar or salt. Includes Nutritional Analysis and Diabetic Exchanges.

- 1 pound fully cooked kielbasa *or* Polish sausage, cut into 3/4-inch pieces
- 6 medium red potatoes, cut into 3/4-inch chunks
- 1 small head cabbage, cubed
- 1 medium onion, cut into 8 wedges
- 1 teaspoon dried oregano
- 1 teaspoon brown sugar, optional
- 1 teaspoon salt, optional
- 1/8 teaspoon pepper
- 1 can (14-1/2 ounces) stewed tomatoes, undrained

In a skillet, cook sausage until lightly browned. Add potatoes, cabbage and onion. Sprinkle with the oregano, brown sugar and salt if desired and pepper. Pour tomatoes over all. Bring to a boil. Reduce heat; cover and simmer for 30-35 minutes or until potatoes and cabbage are tender. Serve in bowls. **Yield:** 8 servings. **Nutritional Analysis:** One serving (prepared with low-fat turkey kielbasa and no-salt-added stewed tomatoes and without brown sugar and salt) equals 152 calories, 524 mg sodium, 37 mg cholesterol, 16 gm carbohydrate, 12 gm protein, 5 gm fat. **Diabetic Exchanges:** 1 starch, 1 meat.

Lemon Chicken and Rice

(Pictured above)

On our ranch, we often need meals we can put on the table in a hurry. This chicken dish, with its delicate lemon flavor, fits the bill. —Kat Thompson, Prineville, Oregon

Uses less fat, sugar or salt. Includes Nutritional Analysis and Diabetic Exchanges.

- 1 pound boneless skinless chicken breasts, cut into strips
- 1 medium onion, chopped
- 1 large carrot, thinly sliced
- 2 garlic cloves, minced
- 2 tablespoons butter *or* margarine
- 1 tablespoon cornstarch
- 1 can (14-1/2 ounces) chicken broth
- 2 tablespoons lemon juice
- 1/2 teaspoon salt, optional
- 1-1/2 cups uncooked instant rice
- 1 cup frozen peas

In a skillet, cook chicken, onion, carrot and garlic in butter for 5-7 minutes or until chicken is no longer pink. In a bowl, combine cornstarch, broth, lemon juice and salt if desired until smooth. Add to skillet; bring to a boil. Cook and stir for 2 minutes or until thickened. Stir in rice and peas. Remove from the heat; cover and let stand for 5 minutes. **Yield:** 6 servings. **Nutritional Analysis:** One serving (prepared with reduced-fat margarine and low-sodium broth and without salt) equals 235 calories, 156 mg sodium, 43 mg cholesterol, 27 gm carbohydrate, 20 gm protein, 5 gm fat. **Diabetic Exchanges:** 2 lean meat, 1-1/2 starch, 1 vegetable.

Chapter 11

WHEN minutes count, you can round out meals with breads, rolls, biscuits, muffins and more in record time.

Whether you rely on traditional quick breads that don't require yeast or rising time, or you get a head start from such convenience items as biscuit mix, frozen bread dough or refrigerated crescent, pizza and biscuit doughs, the irresistible aroma of home-baked goods can soon be wafting through your house.

And with today's bread machines, old-fashioned home-made yeast breads can be easy, too. They promise fresh-from-the-oven flavor without all the work.

FUSS-FREE BREADS. Clockwise from upper right: Savory Italian Rounds, Bacon Swiss Bread, Sweet Raspberry Muffins and Gingerbread Loaf (all recipes on pp. 172 and 173).

Oven-Fresh Quick Breads

YOU need not worry about kneading—or spending hours in the kitchen—when you make these quick loaves, muffins, sweet rolls and biscuits. Whether you want sweet or savory, you're sure to find a recipe to suit your taste and time.

Three-Cheese Twists

(Pictured below)

My daughter has given me many great recipes, but this is one of my favorites. Although these tasty twists look like you fussed, convenient frozen dinner rolls hurry along the preparation. I usually serve them with chili, but they're great with a salad, too. —June Poepping, Quincy, Illinois

  1/2 cup butter *or* margarine, melted
  1/4 teaspoon garlic salt
1-1/2 cups (6 ounces) finely shredded cheddar
     cheese
1-1/2 cups (6 ounces) finely shredded mozzarella
     cheese
  3/4 cup grated Parmesan cheese
    1 tablespoon dried parsley flakes
  24 frozen dinner rolls, thawed

In a shallow bowl, combine butter and garlic salt. In another shallow bowl, combine cheeses and parsley. On a lightly floured surface, roll each dinner roll into a 10-in.

Three-Cheese Twists

rope. Dip in butter mixture, then in cheese mixture. Fold each rope in half and twist twice; pinch ends together to seal. Place 2 in. apart on greased baking sheets. Cover and let rise in a warm place until almost doubled, about 30 minutes. Bake at 350° for 15 minutes or until golden brown. **Yield:** 2 dozen.

Lemon Streusel Muffins

These delicate lemon muffins are wonderful served with bacon and eggs on Sunday mornings...or with a shrimp soup and garden salad for lunch. —Mary Kelly
Hopland, California

  1 cup butter *or* margarine, softened
  1 cup sugar
  4 eggs, *separated*
  2 cups all-purpose flour
  2 teaspoons baking powder
1/2 teaspoon salt
1/2 cup lemon juice
STREUSEL TOPPING:
1/4 cup finely chopped nuts
  2 tablespoons all-purpose flour
  2 tablespoons brown sugar
1/4 teaspoon ground nutmeg

In a mixing bowl, cream butter and sugar. Beat in egg yolks. Combine flour, baking powder and salt; add to the creamed mixture alternately with lemon juice. In a small bowl, beat egg whites until stiff; fold into batter. Fill greased or paper-lined muffin cups two-thirds full. Combine topping ingredients; sprinkle over muffins. Bake at 375° for 15-20 minutes or until muffins test done. Cool for 5 minutes before removing from pan to a wire rack. **Yield:** about 1 dozen.

Apple Pumpkin Muffins

If you like pumpkin, you'll love these moist muffins. With an appealing streusel topping and tender apple bits throughout, they make a great accompaniment to a harvest meal or a handy breakfast on the run.
—Mary Ann Taylor, Rockwell, Iowa

2-1/2 cups all-purpose flour
  2 cups sugar
  1 tablespoon pumpkin pie spice
  1 teaspoon baking soda

Less Elbow Grease

I don't like to spend time greasing and flouring pans, so I've come up with a speedy one-step method. When I have a little time, I blend together 1/3 cup of flour, 1/3 cup of shortening and 1/3 cup of vegetable oil, then use a pastry brush to spread a light coat of the mixture in the pan. It's especially handy for hard-to-coat bundt pans. The mixture keeps in a glass jar in the refrigerator for about 6 weeks. —*Mildred Naef*
Merced, California

Aloha Quick Bread

1 cup milk
2/3 cup honey
1/4 cup butter *or* margarine
1-1/2 cups all-purpose flour
1 cup whole wheat flour
1/2 cup wheat germ
1/2 cup chopped walnuts, toasted, optional
1 tablespoon baking powder
1/2 teaspoon salt

In a saucepan or microwave-safe bowl, combine milk, honey and butter. Heat just until the butter is melted. Cool for 10 minutes. In a bowl, combine the remaining ingredients; stir in milk mixture just until combined. Pour into a greased 9-in. x 5-in. x 3-in. loaf pan. Bake at 325° for 1 hour or until a toothpick inserted near the center comes out clean. Cool for 10 minutes before removing from pan to a wire rack. Serve warm. **Yield:** 1 loaf (16 slices). **Nutritional Analysis:** One slice (prepared with skim milk and reduced-fat margarine and without nuts) equals 145 calories, 206 mg sodium, trace cholesterol, 29 gm carbohydrate, 4 gm protein, 2 gm fat. **Diabetic Exchange:** 2 starch.

Aloha Quick Bread

(Pictured at left)

This one-of-a-kind quick bread recipe has been a favorite around our house for several years. The addition of flaked coconut, grated orange peel, crushed pineapple and chopped nuts gives a new tropical twist to a loaf of basic banana bread. It's so good I sometimes serve slices of it to friends and family for dessert.
—Lanita Anderson, Chesapeake, Virginia

1/2 cup butter *or* margarine, softened
1 cup sugar
2 eggs
1 cup mashed ripe bananas (about 2 medium)
1/4 cup milk
1 tablespoon grated orange peel
1 teaspoon vanilla extract
1/2 teaspoon almond extract
2 cups all-purpose flour
1 teaspoon baking soda
1/2 teaspoon salt
1 cup flaked coconut
1/2 cup chopped nuts
1/2 cup crushed pineapple

In a mixing bowl, cream butter and sugar. Add the eggs, one at a time, beating well after each addition. Beat in banana, milk, orange peel and extracts. Combine flour, baking soda and salt; add to the creamed mixture just until moistened. Fold in the coconut, nuts and pineapple. Transfer to a greased 9-in. x 5-in. x 3-in. loaf pan. Bake at 350° for 1 hour and 20 minutes or until a toothpick inserted near the center comes out clean. Cool for 10 minutes before removing from pan to a wire rack. **Yield:** 1 loaf.

1/2 teaspoon salt
2 eggs
1 cup canned *or* cooked pumpkin
1/2 cup vegetable oil
2 cups finely chopped peeled apples
STREUSEL:
1/4 cup sugar
2 tablespoons all-purpose flour
1/2 teaspoon ground cinnamon
4 teaspoons cold butter *or* margarine

In a bowl, combine the first five ingredients. In another bowl, combine the eggs, pumpkin and oil; stir into dry ingredients just until moistened. Fold in apples. Fill paper-lined muffin cups two-thirds full. In a small bowl, combine sugar, flour and cinnamon. Cut in butter until crumbly. Sprinkle over batter. Bake at 350° for 35-40 minutes or until golden brown. Cool for 5 minutes before removing from pans to wire racks. **Yield:** 1-1/2 dozen.

Milk 'n' Honey Bread

When you cut into this wholesome-tasting bread, you can hardly believe it's not a yeast bread. I think it tastes best warm from the oven…however, leftovers are also great toasted and buttered the next day. —Wendy Skipper
Cornelius, Oregon

✓ Uses less fat, sugar or salt. Includes Nutritional Analysis and Diabetic Exchanges.

Mini Cheddar Loaves
Cheesy Flat Bread

Cheesy Flat Bread

(Pictured above)

With its pretty color and cheesy topping, this buttery bread is delicious with soups. Our daughter loves to help press out the thawed bread dough and sprinkle it with cheese.
—*Sue Burton, Frankfort, Kansas*

   1 loaf (1 pound) frozen bread dough, thawed
   3 tablespoons butter *or* margarine, softened
   2 tablespoons finely chopped onion
   2 to 3 teaspoons paprika
1/2 teaspoon dried oregano *or* basil
1/2 teaspoon garlic powder
   1 cup (4 ounces) shredded cheddar cheese

Pat dough onto the bottom and up the sides of a greased 14-in. pizza pan or 15-in. x 10-in. x 1-in. baking pan, forming a crust. Spread with butter. Sprinkle with onion, paprika, oregano and garlic powder. Prick the crust several times with a fork; sprinkle with cheese. Cover and let rise in a warm place for 30 minutes. Bake at 375° for 20-25 minutes or until golden brown. **Yield:** 8 servings.

Mini Cheddar Loaves

(Pictured above)

It's hard to believe you need only four ingredients to bake up a batch of these beautiful miniature loaves. Sliced warm from the oven, this golden bread is simple and delicious. —*Melody Rowland, Chattanooga, Tennessee*

3-1/2 cups biscuit/baking mix
2-1/2 cups (10 ounces) shredded sharp cheddar
       cheese
   2 eggs
1-1/4 cups milk

In a large bowl, combine biscuit mix and cheese. Beat eggs and milk; stir into cheese mixture just until moistened. Pour into four greased and floured 5-3/4-in. x 3-

in. x 2-in. loaf pans. Bake at 350° for 35-40 minutes or until a toothpick inserted near the center comes out clean. Cool for 10 minutes. Remove from pans; slice and serve warm. **Yield:** 4 mini loaves. **Editor's Note:** Bread can also be made in one 9-in. x 5-in. x 3-in. loaf pan. Bake for 50-55 minutes.

Sweetheart Scones

I've made these tender heart-shaped scones many times for my family and for special occasions. They are especially pretty when split and filled with colorful jam.
—*Debbie Graham, Creston, British Columbia*

    4 cups all-purpose flour
  1/2 cup sugar
    1 tablespoon baking powder
  1/2 teaspoon baking soda
  1/2 teaspoon salt
  2/3 cup cold butter *or* margarine
1-1/2 cups buttermilk
Red colored sugar, optional
Cherry, raspberry *or* strawberry jam

In a large bowl, combine the dry ingredients; cut in butter until crumbly. Stir in buttermilk just until moistened. Turn onto a lightly floured surface; knead 10-12 times. Roll out to 2/3-in. thickness; cut with a 3-1/2-in. heart-shaped cookie cutter. Place on a lightly greased baking sheet. Sprinkle with sugar if desired. Bake at 425° for 15-18 minutes or until lightly browned. Remove to a wire rack. Split scones in half. Spread bottom halves with jam; replace the tops. Serve warm. **Yield:** 10 scones.

Cheddar Biscuits

I often serve my family these warm cheese biscuits with a hearty breakfast of bacon and eggs. They freeze well, too.
—*Colleen Horudko, Warman, Saskatchewan*

  2 cups all-purpose flour
  2 teaspoons baking powder
  1 teaspoon baking soda
1/2 teaspoon salt
3/4 cup shredded cheddar cheese
1/3 cup shortening
  1 cup buttermilk

Baking Biscuits

- To make biscuits in a hurry, I pat or roll the dough into a rectangle and cut out square biscuits with a pizza cutter. The dough only needs to be rolled out once since there are no little leftover pieces. This method is a great time-saver. —*Konnie Locke Grove, Oklahoma*

- I love sweet potato biscuits. When I have the time, I make large batches of mashed sweet potatoes and measure 2-cup amounts into heavy-duty freezer bags. Then, when I want to whip up the biscuits in a hurry, I just pop a bag into the microwave to thaw. —*Marcia Porter, Greensboro, Maryland*

In a bowl, combine flour, baking powder, baking soda and salt. Cut in cheese and shortening until crumbly. Add buttermilk; stir just until moistened. Turn onto a lightly floured surface; knead 8-10 times. Roll out to 1/2-in. thickness; cut with a 2-1/2-in. biscuit cutter. Place on an ungreased baking sheet. Bake at 425° for 10-12 minutes or until golden brown. **Yield:** 16 biscuits.

Chocolate Chip Coffee Cake

With chocolate chips and cinnamon in the middle and on top, this special breakfast treat never fails to please all ages. —*Trish Quinn, Middletown, Pennsylvania*

  1/2 cup butter *or* margarine, softened
    1 cup sugar
    2 eggs
    1 cup (8 ounces) sour cream
    1 teaspoon vanilla extract
2-1/2 cups all-purpose flour
1-1/2 teaspoons baking powder
    1 teaspoon baking soda
TOPPING:
    1 cup (6 ounces) semisweet chocolate chips
  1/2 cup sugar
    1 teaspoon ground cinnamon

In a mixing bowl, cream butter and sugar. Add eggs, sour cream and vanilla; mix well. Combine the flour, baking powder and soda; add to creamed mixture (batter will be thick). Spread half of the batter into a greased 13-in. x 9-in. x 2-in. baking pan. Combine chocolate chips, sugar and cinnamon; sprinkle half over batter. Repeat layers. Bake at 350° for 25-30 minutes or until a toothpick inserted near the center comes out clean. **Yield:** 12-16 servings.

Cucumber Quick Bread

Move over, zucchini—I have replaced you with cucumbers in this moist, cinnamony loaf. When we have lots of cucumbers in our garden, I use them in my favorite zucchini recipes. —*Darlene Kamis, Romeoville, Illinois*

    3 eggs
    2 cups sugar
    2 cups grated seeded peeled cucumbers
    1 cup vegetable oil
1-1/2 teaspoons vanilla extract
    3 cups all-purpose flour
    1 cup chopped nuts
1-1/2 teaspoons ground cinnamon
    1 teaspoon baking soda
    1 teaspoon salt
  1/4 teaspoon baking powder

In a mixing bowl, beat eggs. Beat in sugar, cucumbers, oil and vanilla until well blended. Combine the remaining ingredients; add to cucumber mixture and beat just until combined. Pour into two greased 9-in. x 5-in. x 3-in. loaf pans. Bake at 350° for 60-65 minutes or until a toothpick inserted near the center comes out clean. Cool for 10 minutes before removing from pans to wire racks. **Yield:** 2 loaves.

Upside-Down Orange Puffs

These delicious citrusy morsels are quick to make with refrigerated biscuits. They're our teenage son's favorite, so I make them often. —Rosa Griffith
Christiansburg, Virginia

1/4 cup butter *or* margarine
1/4 cup sugar
2 tablespoons orange juice
1 teaspoon grated orange peel
1 can (7-1/2 ounces) refrigerated buttermilk biscuits

In a saucepan, combine butter, sugar, orange juice and peel. Cook and stir over medium heat until sugar is dissolved. Divide among 10 muffin cups. Make a hole in the center of each biscuit; place over orange mixture. Bake at 450° for 8-10 minutes or until golden brown. Immediately invert onto a wire rack to cool. **Yield:** 10 puffs.

Nutmeg Sour Cream Muffins

I stir up these moist, fluffy muffins as a speedy accompaniment to a salad lunch. A sprinkling of sugar and nutmeg creates the tempting topping. —Pat Walter
Pine Island, Minnesota

1 egg
1 cup (8 ounces) sour cream
1/2 cup plus 1 teaspoon sugar, *divided*
2 tablespoons shortening
1-1/3 cups all-purpose flour
1 teaspoon baking powder
1/2 teaspoon baking soda
1/2 teaspoon salt
1/2 teaspoon ground nutmeg

In a mixing bowl, beat egg until light and fluffy. Add sour cream, 1/2 cup sugar and shortening; beat well. Combine the flour, baking powder, baking soda and salt; stir into sour cream mixture just until moistened. Fill greased or paper-lined muffin cups three-fourths full. Combine nutmeg and remaining sugar; sprinkle over muffins. Bake at 400° for 15 minutes or until muffins test done. Cool for 10 minutes; remove from pan to a wire rack. **Yield:** 9 muffins.

Hearty Morning Muffins

(Pictured above right)

These delicious muffins are loaded with goodies. I got the recipe from our pastor's wife. We like them for Sunday breakfast, but it's a good idea to double the recipe and keep some in the freezer for brown-bag lunches during the week. —Elaine Kauffman, Tofield, Alberta

2 cups whole wheat flour
1 cup sugar
2 teaspoons baking soda
2 teaspoons ground cinnamon
2 cups shredded carrots

1/3 cup chopped dried apricots
1/3 cup sunflower kernels
1/3 cup flaked coconut
1/3 cup semisweet chocolate chips
1 medium ripe banana, mashed
3 eggs
1 cup vegetable oil
2 teaspoons vanilla extract

In a mixing bowl, combine flour, sugar, baking soda and cinnamon. Add the carrots, apricots, sunflower kernels, coconut and chocolate chips. Stir in the banana. Beat eggs, oil and vanilla; stir into carrot mixture just until moistened. Fill greased or paper-lined muffin cups two-thirds full. Bake at 375° for 18-22 minutes. Cool for 5 minutes; remove from pans to wire racks. **Yield:** 1-1/2 dozen.

Sunshine Muffins

(Pictured at right)

I use two convenient mixes to create these sweet corn bread muffins. The yellow cake mix gives them a smoother texture than traditional corn bread. —Linnea Rein, Topeka, Kansas

2 eggs
1/2 cup water
1/3 cup milk
2 tablespoons vegetable oil
1 package (9 ounces) yellow cake mix
1 package (8-1/2 ounces) corn bread/muffin mix

In a bowl, combine the eggs, water, milk and oil. Stir in mixes and mix well. Fill greased and floured muffin cups half full. Bake at 350° for 18-22 minutes or until muffins test done. Cool for 5 minutes; remove from pans to wire racks. **Yield:** 14 muffins.

Cheddar Chive Muffins

(Pictured above right)

These savory muffins have been a favorite since I made the first batch several years ago. I usually have all of the ingredients on hand, so they're easy to mix up at the last minute. —Donna Royer, Largo, Florida

1-1/4 cups milk
3/4 cup mashed potato flakes
1 egg
1/3 cup vegetable oil
1 cup (4 ounces) shredded cheddar cheese
1-2/3 cups all-purpose flour
3 tablespoons sugar
2 tablespoons snipped chives
1 tablespoon dried parsley flakes
1 tablespoon baking powder
1 teaspoon salt

Hearty Morning Muffins
Sunshine Muffins
Cheddar Chive Muffins

In a saucepan, bring milk to a boil. Remove from the heat; stir in potato flakes. Let stand for 2 minutes. Whip with a fork until smooth; cool slightly. Beat in egg, oil and cheese. Combine remaining ingredients; stir into potato mixture just until moistened (batter will be thick). Fill greased muffin cups three-fourths full. Bake at 400° for 20-25 minutes or until muffins test done. Cool for 5 minutes; remove from pan to a wire rack. Serve warm. **Yield:** 1 dozen.

Oat-Chip Banana Bread

Banana bread has always been a favorite in our home. As I was mixing up a batch one afternoon, I decided to add a cup of oatmeal and some chocolate chips. The result was a hit! —Lisa Green, Kunkletown, Pennsylvania

1/2 cup shortening
1 cup sugar
2 eggs
1-1/2 cups mashed ripe bananas (3 to 4 medium)
2 cups all-purpose flour
1 cup quick-cooking oats
1 teaspoon baking soda
1 teaspoon baking powder
1 teaspoon salt
1/2 cup miniature semisweet chocolate chips

In a mixing bowl, cream shortening and sugar. Add eggs, one at a time, beating well after each addition. Add bananas; mix well. Combine flour, oats, baking soda, baking powder and salt; add to the creamed mixture, stirring just until moistened. Stir in chocolate chips. Pour into a greased 9-in. x 5-in. x 3-in. loaf pan. Bake at 350° for 60-65 minutes or until a toothpick inserted near the center comes out clean. Cool for 10 minutes; remove from pan to a wire rack. **Yield:** 1 loaf.

Poppy Seed Lemon Scones

160° and is thickened. Cover and refrigerate until chilled (may be stored in the refrigerator for up to 1 week). For scones, combine the first five ingredients in a bowl. Cut in butter until mixture resembles fine crumbs. Combine milk and lemon juice; stir into crumb mixture just until blended (dough will be soft). Turn onto a floured surface; knead gently six times. Shape into a ball. Pat dough into an 8-in. circle. Using a sharp knife, cut into eight wedges. Separate wedges and transfer to a greased baking sheet. Sprinkle with additional sugar. Bake at 425° for 12-15 minutes or until lightly browned. Serve with the lemon curd. **Yield:** 8 scones (1-1/2 cups lemon curd). **Nutritional Analysis:** One scone (prepared with margarine and skim milk and calculated without lemon curd) equals 221 calories, 357 mg sodium, trace cholesterol, 32 gm carbohydrate, 4 gm protein, 8 gm fat. **Diabetic Exchanges:** 2 starch, 1-1/2 fat.

Orange Nut Bread

This recipe from my grandma is an oldie but a goodie. The peel of an orange (not the juice) provides the sunny flavor in these nut-studded loaves. Slices are especially yummy spread with cream cheese. —Sue Gronholz Columbus, Wisconsin

        1 large navel orange
        3 cups all-purpose flour
        1 cup sugar
        1 tablespoon baking powder
    1/2 teaspoon salt
        1 egg, beaten
        1 cup milk
    1/2 cup chopped nuts

Peel orange (save fruit for another use). Place the peel in a small saucepan and cover with water; cook over medium-high heat for 5 minutes. Drain. Cover peel again with water and cook for 3 minutes; drain. Finely chop peel; set aside. In a bowl, combine flour, sugar, baking powder and salt. Combine egg and milk; stir into dry ingredients just until combined. Fold in nuts and orange peel. Pour batter into three greased and floured 5-3/4-in. x 3-in. x 2-in. loaf pans. Bake at 350° for 35-40 minutes or until a toothpick inserted near the center comes out clean. Cool for 10 minutes; remove from pans to a wire rack. **Yield:** 3 mini loaves.

Poppy Seed Lemon Scones

(Pictured above)

You'll love the appealing look and delicate texture of these lightly sweet scones. For the best results, work quickly to mix and cut them. The less you handle the dough, the more tender the scones are. They're delightful served warm with homemade lemon curd for breakfast or with a salad for lunch. —Linda Murray, Allenstown, New Hampshire

✓ Uses less fat, sugar or salt. Includes Nutritional Analysis and Diabetic Exchanges.

LEMON CURD:
        2 eggs
        1 cup sugar
        6 tablespoons butter *or* margarine, melted
    1/4 cup lemon juice
        2 tablespoons grated lemon peel
SCONES:
        2 cups all-purpose flour
    1/4 cup sugar
        1 tablespoon baking powder
        1 tablespoon poppy seeds
    1/4 teaspoon salt
    1/3 cup cold butter *or* margarine
    3/4 cup milk
        2 tablespoons lemon juice
Additional sugar

In the top of a double boiler, beat eggs and sugar. Stir in butter, lemon juice and peel. Cook and stir over simmering water for 15 minutes or until mixture reaches

Candy Bar Coffee Cake

A sweet, nutty topping is the crowning touch to this dessert-like coffee cake. It tastes especially good when warm. —Mrs. Eugene Plager, Grundy Center, Iowa

        2 cups all-purpose flour
        1 cup packed brown sugar
    1/2 cup sugar
    1/2 cup cold butter *or* margarine
        1 teaspoon baking soda
        1 teaspoon salt
        1 egg
        1 cup buttermilk

1 teaspoon vanilla extract
3 Heath candy bars (1.4 ounces *each*), crushed
1 cup chopped pecans

In a large bowl, combine the flour and sugars; cut in butter until the mixture resembles coarse crumbs. Set aside 1/2 cup for topping. To the remaining crumb mixture, add baking soda and salt. Beat egg, buttermilk and vanilla; add to the crumb mixture and mix well. Pour into a greased 11-in. x 7-in. x 2-in. baking pan. Combine the candy bars, pecans and reserved crumb mixture; sprinkle over the top. Bake at 350° for 40 minutes or until a toothpick inserted near the center comes out clean. **Yield:** 8-10 servings.

Onion Sandwich Rolls

(Pictured at right)

These tempting rolls have a mild onion flavor from handy dry soup mix. They are great with Italian meals or as sandwich rolls or hamburger buns. Plus, they freeze well, so you can prepare them ahead and take them out when needed.
—*Josie-Lynn Belmont, Woodbine, Georgia*

✓ Uses less fat, sugar or salt. Includes Nutritional Analysis and Diabetic Exchanges.

1 envelope onion soup mix
1/2 cup boiling water
1 tablespoon butter *or* margarine
3-1/2 to 4 cups all-purpose flour, *divided*
2 packages (1/4 ounce *each*) quick-rise yeast
1 tablespoon sugar
1 cup warm water (120° to 130°)

In a bowl, combine the soup mix, boiling water and butter; cool to 120°-130°. In a mixing bowl, combine 1 cup flour, yeast and sugar. Add the warm water; beat un-

Onion Sandwich Rolls

til smooth. Stir in 1 cup flour. Beat in onion soup mixture and enough remaining flour to form a soft dough. Turn onto a floured surface; knead until smooth and elastic, about 6 minutes. Cover and let stand for 10 minutes. Divide dough into 12 portions and shape each into a ball. Place on greased baking sheets; flatten slightly. Place two large shallow pans on the work surface; fill half full with boiling water. Place baking pans with rolls over water-filled pans. Cover and let rise for 15 minutes. Bake at 375° for 16-19 minutes or until golden brown. Remove from pans to a wire rack. **Yield:** 1 dozen. **Nutritional Analysis:** One roll (prepared with margarine and reduced-sodium soup mix) equals 160 calories, 168 mg sodium, 0 cholesterol, 32 gm carbohydrate, 5 gm protein, 1 gm fat. **Diabetic Exchange:** 2 starch.

Flaky Dill Biscuits

(Pictured at left)

The dill weed in these lovely golden biscuits really comes through. My friends like them because they're fluffy, tender and delicious. I like them because they don't take as much time to make as yeast rolls. —*Audrey Lockau*
Kitchener, Ontario

2 cups all-purpose flour
3 teaspoons baking powder
2 to 3 teaspoons dill weed
3/4 teaspoon salt
1/4 teaspoon pepper
1/2 cup cold butter *or* margarine
2 eggs, lightly beaten
1/2 cup plus 1 tablespoon half-and-half cream, *divided*

In a bowl, combine the flour, baking powder, dill, salt and pepper. Cut in butter until the mixture resembles coarse crumbs. With a fork, stir in eggs and 1/2 cup cream just until moistened. Drop by 1/4 cupfuls onto an ungreased baking sheet. Brush tops with remaining cream. Bake at 450° for 10-12 minutes or until golden brown. **Yield:** 9 servings.

Flaky Dill Biscuits

Peaches and Cream Muffins

(Pictured below)

Fresh or frozen peaches star in these pretty crumb-topped muffins. Breakfast muffins are a must at our house. Our two girls love these not-too-sweet treats.

—Deanne Bagley, Bath, New York

    1 egg
1/2 cup milk *or* sour cream
1/4 cup vegetable oil
1-1/2 cups all-purpose flour
1/2 cup sugar
    2 teaspoons baking powder
1/2 teaspoon salt
    1 cup chopped fresh *or* frozen peaches, thawed

In a bowl, beat egg; add milk and oil. Combine flour, sugar, baking powder and salt; stir into the egg mixture just until moistened. Stir in the peaches. Fill greased or paper-lined muffin cups three-fourths full. Bake at 400° for 20-25 minutes or until muffins test done. Cool for 5 minutes before removing from pan to a wire rack. **Yield:** 10 muffins.

Blueberry Mini Muffins

(Pictured below)

These bite-size muffins are popular in our family. They're especially nice for potlucks since they leave enough room on your plate to try all the other dishes.

—Suzanne Fredette, Littleton, Massachusetts

Blueberry Mini Muffins
Peaches and Cream Muffins

1 cup butter *or* margarine, softened
2 cups sugar
5 eggs
1 cup buttermilk
2 teaspoons vanilla extract
5 cups all-purpose flour
1 teaspoon baking soda
1 teaspoon baking powder
3/4 teaspoon salt
3 cups fresh *or* frozen blueberries
Additional sugar, optional

In a mixing bowl, cream butter and sugar. Add eggs, buttermilk and vanilla; mix well. Combine flour, baking soda, baking powder and salt; stir into the creamed mixture just until moistened. Fold in blueberries (batter will be thick). Fill greased or paper-lined miniature muffin cups with about a tablespoon of batter. Sprinkle with sugar if desired. Bake at 400° for 10-15 minutes or until muffins test done. Cool for 5 minutes before removing from pan to a wire rack. **Yield:** 7 dozen.

Orange Pecan Muffins

The ladies in my church circle really enjoy the refreshing orange flavor of these moist muffins. We like all the raisins and crunchy pecans, too.
—Amelia Nowack
Peshtigo, Wisconsin

1-1/4 cups all-purpose flour
3/4 cup sugar
1-1/2 teaspoons baking soda
1 teaspoon salt
4 medium navel oranges
2 eggs, lightly beaten
1/2 cup vegetable oil
4-1/2 cups Raisin Bran cereal
1 cup chopped pecans

In a bowl, combine flour, sugar, baking soda and salt; set aside. Remove peel and white membrane from three oranges; cut all four oranges into eight wedges. Place in a blender or food processor; cover and process until pureed. Measure 2 cups of puree (discard the remaining puree or save for another use). Add puree, eggs and oil to dry ingredients; stir just until moistened. Fold in cereal and pecans. Fill greased or paper-lined muffin cups three-fourths full. Bake at 375° for 20-25 minutes or until the muffins test done. **Yield:** about 1-1/2 dozen.

Sesame Zucchini Bread

We were treated to this delicious zucchini-flecked bread when we went to visit a friend one evening. We couldn't get enough! Each healthy slice is dotted with goodies like raisins, sesame seeds and nuts.
—Dawn Fagerstrom, Warren, Minnesota

✓ Uses less fat, sugar or salt. Includes Nutritional Analysis and Diabetic Exchanges.

3/4 cup buttermilk

1/2 cup sugar
1/2 cup packed brown sugar
1 egg
1 egg white
2 tablespoons vegetable oil
2 to 3 teaspoons maple flavoring
1-1/2 cups all-purpose flour
1/2 cup whole wheat flour
1/4 cup wheat germ, toasted
1 teaspoon baking powder
1 teaspoon baking soda
1/4 teaspoon salt
1/2 cup raisins
1/4 cup chopped walnuts
4 teaspoons sesame seeds, *divided*
1-1/2 cups shredded zucchini

In a mixing bowl, combine the first seven ingredients; beat until smooth. In another bowl, combine the flours, wheat germ, baking powder, baking soda and salt. Add raisins, walnuts and 3 teaspoons sesame seeds. Stir into sugar mixture just until moistened. Stir in zucchini. Pour into a greased 9-in. x 5-in. x 3-in. loaf pan. Sprinkle with the remaining sesame seeds. Bake at 350° for 55-60 minutes or until a toothpick inserted near the center comes out clean. Cool for 10 minutes before removing from pan to a wire rack. **Yield:** 1 loaf (16 slices). **Nutritional Analysis:** One slice equals 168 calories, 170 mg sodium, 14 mg cholesterol, 31 gm carbohydrate, 4 gm protein, 4 gm fat. **Diabetic Exchanges:** 2 starch, 1/2 fat.

Green Chili Corn Muffins

Green Chili Corn Muffins

(Pictured above)

While visiting a local Mexican restaurant, I sampled a spicy corn muffin with a surprising sweetness. This recipe is a result of numerous attempts to recreate that treat using convenient mixes. These moist muffins are tasty with Mexican dishes, chili and soup.
—Melissa Cook, Chico, California

  1 package (8-1/2 ounces) corn bread/muffin mix
  1 package (9 ounces) yellow cake mix
  2 eggs
1/2 cup milk
1/3 cup water
  2 tablespoons vegetable oil
  1 can (4 ounces) chopped green chilies, drained
  1 cup (4 ounces) shredded cheddar cheese, *divided*

In a bowl, combine the dry corn bread and cake mixes. In another bowl, combine the eggs, milk, water and oil. Stir into the dry ingredients just until moistened. Add the chilies and 3/4 cup cheese. Fill greased or paper-lined muffin cups two-thirds full. Bake at 350° for 20-22 minutes or until muffins test done. Immediately sprinkle with the remaining cheese. Cool for 5 minutes before removing from pans to wire racks. Serve warm. **Yield:** 16 servings.

Olive Cheese Bread

The recipe for this rich cheesy bread was given to me by a co-worker's wife, and I've used it often. With the tasty addition of ripe olives and onions, it's a perfect complement to seafood, Italian food or barbecue fare.
—Nancy McWhorter, Bridge City, Texas

1/2 cup butter *or* margarine, melted
1/2 cup mayonnaise*
  1 can (2-1/4 ounces) sliced ripe olives, drained
  2 green onions, chopped
1-1/2 cups (6 ounces) shredded Monterey Jack cheese
  1 loaf (1 pound) unsliced French bread

In a bowl, combine the first five ingredients. Slice bread in half widthwise and lengthwise; place on a baking sheet. Spread cheese mixture over cut sides of bread. Bake at 350° for 15-20 minutes or until the cheese is melted. **Yield:** 12-16 servings. ***Editor's Note:** Light or fat-free mayonnaise may not be substituted for regular mayonnaise.

Peppery Cheddar Muffins

It takes just minutes to stir up a dozen of these savory muffins. The cheddar cheese and pepper flavors come through in each bite.
—Joanie Elbourn
Gardner, Massachusetts

  2 cups all-purpose flour
  2 teaspoons baking powder
  1 teaspoon pepper
1/2 teaspoon salt
  1 egg
  1 cup buttermilk
1/4 cup vegetable oil
  1 tablespoon honey
  1 cup (4 ounces) shredded cheddar cheese

In a bowl, combine the flour, baking powder, pepper and salt. Combine the egg, buttermilk, oil and honey; stir into dry ingredients just until moistened. Fold in cheese. Fill greased or paper-lined muffin cups two-thirds full. Bake at 400° for 18-22 minutes or until muffins test done. Cool for 5 minutes before removing from pan to a wire rack. **Yield:** 1 dozen.

Oat Cinnamon Rolls

(Pictured at right)

Dried cranberries add holiday flair to these special rolls made from convenient frozen bread dough. My husband loves marmalade, so when I spotted this recipe that used it as icing, I knew I had to try it. Now it's one of his favorites. *—Margaret Wilson, Hemet, California*

  1 cup quick-cooking oats
1/3 cup packed brown sugar
  2 teaspoons ground cinnamon
  1 cup dried cranberries *or* raisins
1/3 cup butter *or* margarine, melted
  1 pound frozen bread dough, thawed
1/4 cup orange marmalade

In a bowl, combine oats, brown sugar and cinnamon. Stir in cranberries and butter; set aside. On a lightly floured surface, roll the dough into a 12-in. x 10-in. rectangle. Sprinkle with oat mixture. Roll up, jelly-roll style, starting with a long side; seal seam. Cut into nine slices; place in a greased 9-in. square baking pan. Cover and let rise in a warm place until doubled, about 30 minutes. Bake at 350° for 30-35 minutes or until golden brown. Remove to a wire rack. Brush with marmalade. Serve warm. **Yield:** 9 rolls.

Fresh Pear Bread

(Pictured below)

When our tree branches are loaded with ripe juicy pears, I treat my family and friends to loaves of this cinnamony bread that's richly studded with walnuts and pears.
—Linda Patrick, Houston, Texas

   3 **eggs**
1-1/2 **cups sugar**
  3/4 **cup vegetable oil**
   1 **teaspoon vanilla extract**

   3 **cups all-purpose flour**
   2 **teaspoons baking powder**
   2 **teaspoons ground cinnamon**
   1 **teaspoon baking soda**
   1 **teaspoon salt**
   4 **cups finely chopped peeled ripe pears (about 4 medium)**
   1 **teaspoon lemon juice**
   1 **cup chopped walnuts**

In a mixing bowl, combine the eggs, sugar, oil and vanilla; mix well. Combine flour, baking powder, cinnamon, baking soda and salt; stir into the egg mixture just until moistened. Toss pears with lemon juice. Stir pears and walnuts into batter (batter will be thick). Spoon into two greased 9-in. x 5-in. x 3-in. loaf pans. Bake at 350° for 55-60 minutes or until a toothpick inserted near the center comes out clean. Cool for 10 minutes before removing from pans to wire racks. **Yield:** 2 loaves.

Fresh Pear Bread
Oat Cinnamon Rolls

Potato Scones

These pretty biscuit-like wedges are very moist and flavorful. They're tasty slathered with butter, honey or jam...or use them as a base for creamed dishes.
—Judie Anglen
Riverton, Wyoming

2 cups all-purpose flour
1 tablespoon baking powder
1 teaspoon salt
3 tablespoons cold butter *or* margarine
1 cup mashed potatoes (prepared with milk and butter)
1/3 cup milk
1 egg

In a bowl, combine the flour, baking powder and salt. Cut in butter until mixture resembles coarse crumbs. Combine potatoes, milk and egg; stir into the crumb mixture until a soft dough forms. Turn onto a floured surface; knead gently 10-12 times or until no longer sticky. Gently pat or roll dough into a 9-in. circle about 3/4 in. thick. Cut into 10-12 wedges. Separate wedges and place on an ungreased baking sheet. Bake at 400° for 15-18 minutes or until golden brown. **Yield:** 10-12 servings.

Lemon Coconut Loaf

This lemony loaf is so luscious it's almost a dessert! The bread's pound cake-like texture gets an unexpected twist from sweet chewy coconut.
—Donna Carper
South Jordan, Utah

Measuring Techniques

FOR BEST RESULTS when baking, always measure liquid ingredients in measuring cups designed for liquids and dry ingredients in measuring cups designed for dry measure. Then follow these suggestions:

● When measuring liquids, place the measuring cup on a level surface. Pour in the liquid to the desired measurement while viewing it from eye level.

● When measuring dry ingredients, spoon fine dry ingredients into the measuring cup until it is overflowing. Level off along the top of the cup with a metal spatula or knife. Bulky ingredients can be spooned into the cup until they are level with the rim.

1/2 cup butter *or* margarine, softened
1 cup sugar
4-1/2 teaspoons lemon juice
2 eggs
1-1/2 cups all-purpose flour
1 teaspoon baking powder
1/4 teaspoon salt
1/2 cup milk
1/4 cup flaked coconut
1 teaspoon grated lemon peel
GLAZE:
1/4 cup confectioners' sugar
2 tablespoons lemon juice

In a mixing bowl, cream butter, sugar and lemon juice. Add the eggs, one at a time, beating well after each addition. Combine flour, baking powder and salt; add to creamed mixture alternately with milk. Stir in the coconut and lemon peel. Pour into a greased 8-in. x 4-in. x 2-in. loaf pan. Bake at 350° for 60-70 minutes or until a toothpick inserted near the center comes out clean. Cool for 10 minutes; remove from pan to a wire rack. Combine glaze ingredients; brush over loaf. **Yield:** 1 loaf.

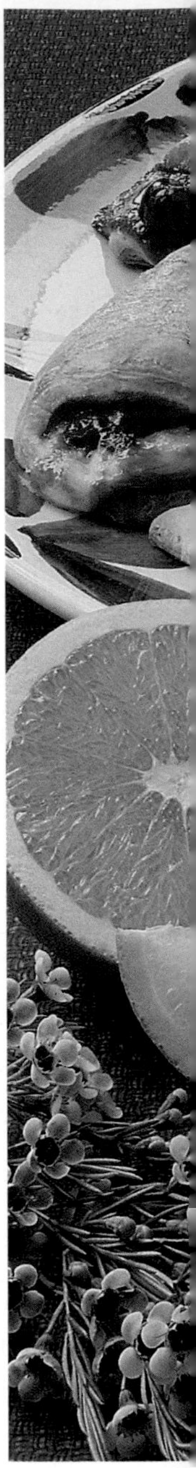

Orange Pull-Apart Bread

(Pictured at right)

The recipe for this appealing breakfast loaf came from my sister, who's an excellent cook. Brushed with a sweet orange glaze, the bread is so popular I usually double or triple the recipe.
—Kristin Salzman, Fenton, Illinois

1 tube (8 ounces) refrigerated crescent rolls
2 tablespoons butter *or* margarine, softened
2 tablespoons honey
1/2 to 1 teaspoon grated orange peel

Open tube of crescent rolls; do not unroll. Place on a greased baking sheet, forming one long roll. Cut into 12 slices to within 1/8 in. of bottom, being careful not to cut all the way through. Fold down alternating slices from left to right to form a loaf. Bake at 375° for 20-25 minutes or until golden brown. Combine butter, honey and orange peel; brush over the loaf. Serve warm. **Yield:** 6 servings.

Cherry Cream Crescents

(Pictured above right)

You'll need refrigerated crescent dough and just four more ingredients to assemble these fruity filled rolls. My family and friends love them. I never have any left over.
—Elouise Bullion, Kingsville, Texas

1 package (8 ounces) cream cheese, softened
1 cup confectioners' sugar
1 egg, *separated*

Cherry Cream Crescents
Orange Pull-Apart Bread

2 tubes (8 ounces *each*) refrigerated crescent rolls
1 can (21 ounces) cherry pie filling

In a mixing bowl, beat cream cheese, sugar and egg yolk. Separate dough into 16 triangles; place on lightly greased baking sheets. Spread 1 tablespoon of cream cheese mixture near the edge of the short side of each triangle. Top with 1 tablespoon pie filling. Fold long point of triangle over filling and tuck under dough. Lightly beat egg white; brush over rolls. Bake at 350° for 15-20 minutes or until golden brown. **Yield:** 16 rolls.

Buttermilk Nut Bread

Brown sugar and buttermilk give pleasing flavor to this no-fuss quick bread. Nuts provide the tasty crunch.
—Sue Ross, Casa Grande, Arizona

1 egg
1 cup packed brown sugar
2 tablespoons shortening, melted
2 cups all-purpose flour
3/4 teaspoon baking powder
1/2 teaspoon baking soda
1/2 teaspoon salt
1 cup buttermilk
1/2 cup chopped nuts

In a mixing bowl, beat the egg. Gradually beat in brown sugar and shortening. Combine flour, baking powder, baking soda and salt; add to egg mixture alternately with buttermilk. Beat just until moistened. Stir in nuts. Pour into a greased 9-in. x 5-in. x 3-in. loaf pan. Bake at 350° for 45-55 minutes or until a toothpick inserted near the center comes out clean. Cool for 10 minutes; remove from pan to a wire rack. **Yield:** 1 loaf.

Savory Italian Rounds
Bacon Swiss Bread
Sweet Raspberry Muffins
Gingerbread Loaf

Gingerbread Loaf

(Pictured above and on page 156))

Enjoy the old-fashioned appeal of gingerbread in a loaf with this recipe originally from Holland. This moist spicy bread smells delicious while it's baking...and slices are wonderful spread with cream cheese. The recipe makes two big loaves, so we have one to eat and one to freeze for later...or to give away.
—Martina Biemond
Rosedale, British Columbia

　 4 cups all-purpose flour
　 2 cups sugar
　 4 teaspoons baking powder
　 2 teaspoons ground cinnamon
1-1/4 teaspoons ground cloves
1-1/4 teaspoons ground nutmeg
　 1 teaspoon baking soda
　 1 teaspoon ground ginger
　 2 eggs
　 2 cups milk
　 1 cup maple syrup
　 2 tablespoons vegetable oil

In a large bowl, combine dry ingredients. In another bowl, combine the eggs, milk, syrup and oil. Stir into the dry ingredients just until moistened (batter will be thin). Pour into two greased 9-in. x 5-in. x 3-in. loaf pans. Bake at 325° for 60-70 minutes or until a toothpick inserted near the center comes out clean. Cool for 10 minutes before removing from pans to wire racks. **Yield:** 2 loaves.

Sweet Raspberry Muffins

(Pictured above and on page 156)

I like to linger over a cup of coffee and a warm sweet treat on weekend mornings. These moist muffins are perfect because making them ties up so little time in the kitchen. I also serve them with holiday meals for something different.　　—Teresa Raab, Tustin, Michigan

　 2 cups biscuit/baking mix
　 2 tablespoons sugar
1/4 cup cold butter *or* margarine
2/3 cup milk

1/4 cup raspberry jam
GLAZE:
  1/2 cup confectioners' sugar
    2 teaspoons warm water
  1/4 teaspoon vanilla extract

In a bowl, combine biscuit mix and sugar. Cut in butter until the mixture resembles coarse crumbs. Stir in milk just until moistened (batter will be thick). Spoon about 1 tablespoon of batter into 12 paper-lined muffin cups. Top with 1 teaspoon jam. Spoon the remaining batter (about 1 tablespoon each) over jam. Bake at 425° for 12-14 minutes or until lightly browned. Cool in pans for 5 minutes. Meanwhile, in a small bowl, combine glaze ingredients until smooth. Remove muffins to a wire rack. Drizzle with glaze. **Yield:** 1 dozen.

Bacon Swiss Bread

(Pictured at left and on page 157)

I'm a busy PTA and pom-pom mom, so I'm always looking for fast and easy recipes. Savory slices of jazzed-up French bread are great with soup and salad. My daughter and her friends like to snack on them instead of pizza.
    —Shirley Mills, Tulsa, Oklahoma

  1 loaf (1 pound) French bread (20 inches)
2/3 cup butter *or* margarine, softened
1/3 cup chopped green onions
  4 teaspoons prepared mustard
  5 slices process Swiss cheese
  5 bacon strips

Cut bread into 1-in.-thick slices, leaving slices attached at bottom. In a bowl, combine butter, onions and mustard; spread on both sides of each slice of bread. Cut each cheese slice diagonally into four triangles; place between the slices of bread. Cut bacon in half widthwise and then lengthwise; drape a piece over each slice. Place the loaf on a double thickness of heavy-duty foil. Bake at 400° for 20-25 minutes or until bacon is crisp. **Yield:** 10 servings.

Savory Italian Rounds

(Pictured above left and on page 157)

A friend gave me the recipe for these cheesy golden rounds years ago. She said her dad used to make them for her when she was little. Because they're a snap to put together, I frequently fix them for my family during the week...and for company on weekends.   *—Donna Ebert*
    Jackson, Wisconsin

2/3 cup grated Parmesan cheese
1/2 cup mayonnaise*
1/4 teaspoon dried basil
1/8 teaspoon garlic powder
1/8 teaspoon garlic salt
1/8 teaspoon dried oregano
Dash onion salt
  1 tube (12 ounces) refrigerated buttermilk
    biscuits

In a small bowl, combine the first seven ingredients. Separate biscuits and place on two ungreased baking sheets. Let stand for 5 minutes. Flatten biscuits into 4-in. circles. Spread about 1 tablespoon mayonnaise mixture over each circle to within 1/2 in. of edge. Bake at 400° for 10-13 minutes or until golden brown. Serve immediately. **Yield:** 10 servings. ***Editor's Note:** Light or fat-free mayonnaise may not be substituted for regular mayonnaise.

Tomato Pizza Bread

(Pictured below)

Refrigerated pizza crust dough gets a tasty treatment from pleasant seasonings and easy cheese and tomato toppings. This basic recipe can be modified to suit individual tastes. My husband loves to add sliced ripe olives just before baking. We think it's best when served fresh out of the oven.
    —Kimberly McFarland
    Broken Arrow, Oklahoma

  1 tube (10 ounces) refrigerated pizza crust
  2 garlic cloves, minced
1/2 teaspoon dried oregano
  1 cup (4 ounces) shredded mozzarella cheese,
    divided
  1 plum tomato, halved lengthwise and thinly
    sliced
1/2 teaspoon Italian seasoning, optional

On a greased baking sheet, roll pizza crust into a 12-in. x 8-in. rectangle. Bake at 425° for 6-8 minutes or until the edges are lightly browned. Sprinkle with garlic, oregano and half of the cheese. Arrange tomato slices in a single layer over cheese. Top with remaining cheese and Italian seasoning if desired. Bake 6-8 minutes longer or until cheese is melted and crust is lightly browned. **Yield:** 8 servings.

Tomato Pizza Bread

Rhubarb Oatmeal Muffins

A crisp oatmeal topping adds a different twist to these spring favorites. Friends with a big rhubarb patch often share their bounty with us. But you can use frozen rhubarb with the same tasty results. —Diane Gagnon-Fee
Tupper Lake, New York

    1 cup all-purpose flour
    3/4 cup quick-cooking oats
    1/2 cup packed brown sugar
    2 teaspoons baking powder
    1/2 teaspoon baking soda
    1/4 teaspoon salt
    1/4 teaspoon ground nutmeg
    1 egg
    1/3 cup vegetable oil
    1/3 cup orange juice *or* white grape juice
    1 teaspoon grated orange peel
    1 cup diced fresh *or* frozen rhubarb, thawed
        and drained
TOPPING:
    1/4 cup quick-cooking oats
    1/4 cup packed brown sugar
    2 tablespoons chopped pecans
    2 tablespoons butter *or* margarine, softened
    1/8 teaspoon ground ginger
    1/8 teaspoon ground cinnamon

In a mixing bowl, combine the first seven ingredients; set aside. In another bowl, combine egg, oil, orange juice and peel. Stir into dry ingredients just until moistened. Fold in rhubarb. Fill greased or paper-lined muffin cups two-thirds full. Combine topping ingredients; sprinkle over tops. Bake at 350° for 18-20 minutes or until muffins test done. Cool for 5 minutes; remove from the pan to a wire rack. **Yield:** 1 dozen.

Sticky Bun Coffee Ring

Cherry Chip Muffins

When Valentine's Day rolls around, I like to bake these cute muffins in small heart-shaped tins to give to family and friends as gifts. Drizzled with pink icing, they look adorable and taste wonderful.
—Shirley Glaab, Hattiesburg, Mississippi

1-1/2 cups all-purpose flour
    1/2 cup sugar
    2 teaspoons baking powder
    1/2 teaspoon salt
    1 egg
    1/2 cup milk
    1/4 cup vegetable oil
    1 jar (10 ounces) red maraschino cherries
    3/4 cup miniature semisweet chocolate chips
    1/2 cup chopped pecans
    1 cup confectioners' sugar
Softened cream cheese, optional

In a bowl, combine flour, sugar, baking powder and salt. In another bowl, whisk egg, milk and oil; stir into dry ingredients just until moistened. Drain cherries, reserving 2 tablespoons of juice for glaze (discard remaining juice or save for another use). Chop cherries; fold into the batter with chocolate chips and pecans. Spoon the batter by tablespoonfuls into greased or paper-lined heart-shaped or miniature muffin cups. Bake at 375° for 10-13 minutes or until muffins test done. Cool for 10 minutes; remove from pans to wire racks. Combine confectioners' sugar and reserved cherry juice to make a thin glaze; drizzle over muffins. Serve with cream cheese if desired. **Yield:** about 4 dozen.

Sticky Bun Coffee Ring

(Pictured at left)

Guests will think you went to a lot of trouble when you bring out this pretty nut-topped ring of scrumptious caramel rolls. In fact, these tasty treats are easy to put together using refrigerated biscuits. They taste best when warm and chewy. —Viola Shephard, Bay City, Michigan

    3 tablespoons butter *or* margarine, melted,
        divided
    3 tablespoons maple syrup
    1/4 cup packed brown sugar
    1/4 cup chopped pecans
    1/4 cup chopped almonds
    1/2 teaspoon ground cinnamon
    1 tube (12 ounces) refrigerated buttermilk
        biscuits

Brush a 10-in. fluted tube pan with 1 tablespoon butter. In a small bowl, combine syrup and remaining butter. Drizzle 2 tablespoons into pan. Combine brown sugar, nuts and cinnamon; sprinkle 1/3 cupful over syrup mixture. Separate biscuits; place in prepared pan with edges overlapping. Top with remaining syrup and nut mixtures. Bake at 375° for 15 minutes or until golden brown. Cool for 1-2 minutes; invert onto a serving platter. Serve warm. **Yield:** 10 servings.

Spaghetti Bread

Bread at The Touch Of a Button

EVEN the best store-bought loaf can't compare with fresh homemade bread. But who has time anymore to bake it from scratch? You do!

Bread machines actually make it more convenient to bake bread at home than pick it up at the supermarket. As you'll see in these recipes, it takes only minutes to put your ingredients in the pan, flick a few switches and make a simple check. Then about all you need to do is wait for the aroma to fill the kitchen.

Editor's Note: All of these recipes were tested in a Regal brand bread machine *and* in a West Bend or Black & Decker bread machine.

Measuring Up

TO ASSURE the best results from bread machines, always measure accurately.

- Measure water by pouring it into a transparent liquid measuring cup; read the measurement at eye level.
- Measure flour by spooning it into a standard dry measuring cup; level with a straight-edged knife.
- Measure yeast, salt or spices by filling a standard measuring spoon to overflowing; level with a straight-edged knife.

Spaghetti Bread

(Pictured above)

You're sure to love the heavenly aroma and pleasant herb flavor of this tender bread. It's great with spaghetti and meatballs or most any Italian pasta dish. —Lois Gelzer
Oak Bluffs, Massachusetts

✓ Uses less fat, sugar or salt. Includes Nutritional Analysis and Diabetic Exchanges.

    1 cup water (70° to 80°)
    2 tablespoons olive *or* vegetable oil
    3 cups bread flour
    1/3 cup grated Parmesan cheese
    1 tablespoon sugar
    1 to 2 teaspoons garlic powder
    1 teaspoon salt
    1/4 teaspoon dried oregano
    1/8 teaspoon *each* dried basil, marjoram, savory
        and thyme
    1/8 teaspoon rubbed sage
    1/8 teaspoon dried rosemary, crushed
    1 package (1/4 ounce) active dry yeast

In bread machine pan, place all ingredients in order suggested by manufacturer. Select basic bread setting. Choose crust color and loaf size if available. Bake according to bread machine directions. (Check dough after 5 minutes of mixing; this dough should appear dry. If it looks wet, add 1 to 2 tablespoons of flour.) **Yield:** 1 loaf, 16 slices (1-1/2 pounds). **Nutritional Analysis:** One slice equals 122 calories, 185 mg sodium, 2 mg cholesterol, 20 gm carbohydrate, 4 gm protein, 3 gm fat. **Diabetic Exchange:** 1-1/2 starch. **Editor's Note:** Use of the timer feature is not recommended for this recipe.

Choose crust color and loaf size if available. Bake according to bread machine directions (check dough after 5 minutes of mixing; add 1 to 2 tablespoons of water or flour if needed). **Yield:** 1 loaf (about 2 pounds). **Editor's Note:** Use of the timer feature is not recommended for this recipe.

Ricotta Bread

This moist, slightly sweet bread is one of my favorites to prepare in my bread machine. The recipe produces a smaller loaf, which is especially nice for households with one or two people. —Jenet Cattar Neptune Beach, Florida

> 3 tablespoons warm milk (70° to 80°)
> 2/3 cup ricotta cheese
> 4 teaspoons butter *or* margarine, softened
> 1 egg
> 2 tablespoons sugar
> 1/2 teaspoon salt
> 1-1/2 cups bread flour
> 1 teaspoon active dry yeast

In bread machine pan, place all ingredients in order suggested by manufacturer. Select basic bread setting. Choose crust color and loaf size if available. Bake according to bread machine directions (check dough after 5 minutes of mixing; add 1 to 2 tablespoons of water or flour if needed). **Yield:** 1 loaf (1 pound). **Editor's Note:** Use of the timer feature is not recommended for this recipe.

Mexican Sunset Bread

(Pictured above)

I always serve this tasty taco-seasoned bread with chili or cream soups. With its slightly chewy crust and wonderful texture inside, I'm sure you'll love it, too.
—Bobbie Hruska, Montgomery, Minnesota

> 2/3 cup water (70° to 80°)
> 1/2 cup sour cream
> 3 tablespoons chunky salsa
> 2 tablespoons plus 1-1/2 teaspoons taco seasoning
> 4-1/2 teaspoons sugar
> 1-1/2 teaspoons dried parsley flakes
> 1 teaspoon salt
> 3-1/3 cups bread flour
> 1-1/2 teaspoons active dry yeast

In bread machine pan, place all ingredients in order suggested by manufacturer. Select basic bread setting.

Potato Bread

I use our bread machine at least three times a week. This basic loaf made with easy instant potato flakes is so soft and delicious. I've shared the recipe with many people.
—Jane Hutfles, Omaha, Nebraska

> 1-1/4 cups water (70° to 80°)
> 3 tablespoons vegetable oil
> 7-1/2 teaspoons sugar
> 1 teaspoon salt
> 2 tablespoons mashed potato flakes
> 3 cups bread flour
> 1-1/2 teaspoons active dry yeast

In bread machine pan, place all ingredients in order suggested by manufacturer. Select basic bread setting. Choose crust color and loaf size if available. Bake according to bread machine directions (check dough af-

Mexican Sunset Bread

ter 5 minutes of mixing; add 1 to 2 tablespoons of water or flour if needed). **Yield:** 1 loaf (1-1/2 pounds).

Three-Seed Bread

I sampled a wonderful gourmet bread during an out-of-town trip. When I got home, I tried to recreate it in my bread machine and came up with this hearty whole wheat bread chock-full of sunflower kernels, and poppy and sesame seeds. —Melissa Vannoy, Childress, Texas

- 2/3 cup plus 2 teaspoons water (70° to 80°)
- 1 tablespoon butter *or* margarine, softened
- 1 tablespoon honey
- 2 tablespoons sesame seeds
- 2 tablespoons sunflower kernels
- 2 tablespoons poppy seeds
- 3/4 teaspoon salt
- 1 cup bread flour
- 1 cup whole wheat flour
- 3 tablespoons instant nonfat dry milk powder
- 2 teaspoons active dry yeast

In bread machine pan, place all ingredients in order suggested by manufacturer. Select basic bread setting. Choose crust color and loaf size if available. Bake according to bread machine directions (check dough after 5 minutes of mixing; add 1 to 2 tablespoons of water or flour if needed). **Yield:** 1 loaf (about 1 pound).

Fruit-Filled Kolaches

(Pictured below)

In our Czech community, these tender pastries are served at weddings and family dinners. The bread machine saves you from kneading the dough by hand.
—Mary Pecinovsky, Calmar, Iowa

Fruit-Filled Kolaches

- 1-1/4 cups water (70° to 80°)
- 1/2 cup butter *or* margarine, softened
- 1 egg
- 1 egg yolk
- 1 teaspoon lemon juice
- 1/3 cup instant nonfat dry milk powder
- 1/4 cup mashed potato flakes
- 1/4 cup sugar
- 1 teaspoon salt
- 3-3/4 cups plus 3 tablespoons bread flour
- 2 teaspoons active dry yeast
- 1 can (12 ounces) apricot *or* raspberry pastry filling*

Additional butter *or* margarine, melted

In bread machine pan, place the first 11 ingredients in order suggested by manufacturer. Select dough setting (check dough after 5 minutes of mixing; add 1 to 2 tablespoons of water or flour if needed). When the cycle is completed, turn dough onto a lightly floured surface. Pat or roll into a 16-in. x 10-in. rectangle. Cover with plastic wrap; let rest for 10 minutes. Cut dough into 24 squares. Place a heaping teaspoonful of pastry filling in the center of each square. Overlap two opposite corners of dough over filling; pinch tightly to seal. Place at least 2 in. apart on greased baking sheets. Cover and let rise in a warm place until doubled, about 1 hour. Bake at 425° for 8-10 minutes or until lightly browned. Remove from the oven; brush with butter. Remove to paper towels to cool. **Yield:** 2 dozen. **Editor's Note:** Use of the timer feature is not recommended for the dough. *This recipe was tested with Solo brand fruit filling.

Jalapeno Bread

Grilled cheese sandwiches are especially good made with moist slices from this pretty corn-flecked loaf. For a milder chili taste, use green chilies in place of the jalapenos.
—Lola Gangwer, Burgoon, Ohio

- 1/2 cup water (70° to 80°)
- 1 tablespoon butter *or* margarine, softened
- 1 tablespoon sugar
- 1 teaspoon salt
- 1/2 cup whole kernel corn
- 2 tablespoons chopped jalapenos *or* green chilies
- 1 teaspoon chopped fresh cilantro *or* parsley
- 2 cups bread flour
- 1/3 cup cornmeal
- 1-1/2 teaspoons active dry yeast

In bread machine pan, place all ingredients in order suggested by manufacturer. Select basic bread setting. Choose crust color and loaf size if available. Bake according to bread machine directions (check dough after 5 minutes of mixing; add 1 to 2 tablespoons of water or flour if needed). **Yield:** 1 loaf (1 pound). **Editor's Note:** Use of the timer feature is not recommended for this recipe.

Bread Machine Basics

- Bread machines vary somewhat, depending on the manufacturer. It will be easier for you to use your machine if you first become very familiar with it. Before trying new recipes, make a variety of those provided in your manual—they were developed specifically for your machine.

- When trying any new recipe, be sure to stay within the limits of the maximum flour amounts listed in the recipes in your machine's manual.

- Canadian cooks should use 3 to 4 tablespoons less flour than called for in the bread recipes published in this chapter.

- Add the ingredients only in the order recommended by the manufacturer (which isn't always how they may appear in a recipe here).

- Your bread machine does the mixing and kneading for you. Because of that, you must learn to judge the bread with your eyes and ears to decide whether a recipe is right for your machine or needs a little adjusting.

    Listen to your bread machine as it's kneading the dough. If the machine sounds labored, the dough might be too dry. After 5 minutes of mixing, take a look at it. It should be forming a smooth satiny ball. If the dough looks dry or cracked, add 1 to 2 tablespoons of water. If the dough is flat and wet-looking, add 1 to 2 tablespoons of flour.

- The crispness of bread machine crusts varies depending on the manufacturer. If you don't care for a crisp crust, use your machine's lightest crust setting and remove the loaf from the machine as soon as the baking cycle is complete. If the loaf is still too crusty for your liking, brush the loaf with melted butter while it's warm for a softer texture.

Banana Raisin Bread

Toasted slices of this moist banana bread are wonderful for breakfast. For a special treat, I sometimes substitute chocolate chips for half or all of the raisins.
—Jackie Kew, Grand Island, New York

 1/2 cup plus 2 tablespoons water (70° to 80°)
 3 tablespoons honey
4-1/2 teaspoons vegetable oil
 1 egg yolk, lightly beaten
 1 medium ripe banana, mashed
 3/4 teaspoon salt
 3/4 teaspoon ground cinnamon
 3 cups bread flour
1-1/2 teaspoons active dry yeast
 1/2 cup raisins
 1/3 cup chopped walnuts

In bread machine pan, place the first nine ingredients in order suggested by manufacturer. Select basic bread setting. Choose crust color and loaf size if available. Bake according to bread machine directions (check dough after 5 minutes of mixing; add 1 to 2 tablespoons of water or flour if needed). Just before the final kneading (your machine may audibly signal this), add raisins and walnuts. **Yield:** 1 loaf (2 pounds). **Editor's Note:** Use of the timer feature is not recommended for this recipe.

Golden Honey Bread

This slightly sweet bread has a crispy crust and tender interior. It's simply delicious. —Regina Lindgren
Natrona Heights, Pennsylvania

✓ Uses less fat, sugar or salt. Includes Nutritional Analysis and Diabetic Exchanges.

 1 cup plus 2 tablespoons water (70° to 80°)
 2 tablespoons honey
 2 tablespoons vegetable oil
1-1/2 teaspoons sugar
 1 teaspoon salt
3-1/2 cups bread flour
 2 teaspoons active dry yeast

In bread machine pan, place all ingredients in order suggested by manufacturer. Select basic bread setting. Choose crust color and loaf size if available. Bake according to bread machine directions (check dough after 5 minutes of mixing; add 1 to 2 tablespoons of water or flour if needed). **Yield:** 1 loaf, 16 slices (2 pounds). **Nutritional Analysis:** One slice equals 134 calories, 146 mg sodium, 0 cholesterol, 25 gm carbohydrate, 4 gm protein, 2 gm fat. **Diabetic Exchanges:** 1-1/2 starch, 1/2 fat.

Poppy Seed Yeast Bread

This yeast bread features just the right amount of poppy seeds and almond extract for a unique and flavorful treat. We enjoy eating tender slices of this lovely loaf, which I frequently give as gifts to family and friends. Everyone loves it as much as we do. —Loretta Hill
Westminster, Maryland

✓ Uses less fat, sugar or salt. Includes Nutritional Analysis and Diabetic Exchanges.

 1 cup water (70° to 80°)
 1/4 cup vegetable oil
 1 teaspoon vanilla extract
 1 teaspoon almond extract
 1 teaspoon butter flavoring
 2 tablespoons sugar
 1 teaspoon salt
 3 cups bread flour
 2 tablespoons poppy seeds
 2 teaspoons active dry yeast

In bread machine pan, place all ingredients in order suggested by manufacturer. Select basic bread setting. Choose crust color and loaf size if available. Bake according to bread machine directions (check dough after 5 minutes of mixing; add 1 to 2 tablespoons of water or flour if needed). **Yield:** 1 loaf, 16 slices (about 1-1/2 pounds). **Nutritional Analysis:** One slice equals 131 calories, 146 mg sodium, 0 cholesterol, 19 gm carbohydrate, 4 gm protein, 4 gm fat. **Diabetic Exchanges:** 1 starch, 1 fat.

Cranberry Oat Bread

This is my favorite bread machine recipe. Dried cranberries add a sweet touch to this moist oatmeal bread.
—Dorothy Gilmore, Elburn, Illinois

　1 cup water (70° to 80°)
　1 tablespoon butter *or* margarine, softened
　2 tablespoons honey
3/4 teaspoon salt
1/2 teaspoon ground cinnamon
1/3 cup old-fashioned oats
2-1/2 cups bread flour
1-3/4 teaspoons active dry yeast
1/3 cup dried cranberries *or* raisins

In bread machine pan, place the first eight ingredients in order suggested by manufacturer. Select basic bread setting. Choose crust color and loaf size if available. Bake according to bread machine directions (check dough after 5 minutes of mixing; add 1 to 2 tablespoons of water or flour if needed). Just before final kneading (your machine may audibly signal this), add cranberries. **Yield:** 1 loaf (1-1/2 pounds). **Editor's Note:** Use of the timer feature is not recommended for this recipe.

Cocoa Almond Bread

(Pictured below)

With its subtle cocoa and almond flavors, this bread is heavenly. Serve slices with hot chocolate for a scrumptious snack. —*Wilma Maly, Fort Lauderdale, Florida*

　1 cup warm milk (70° to 80°)
1/4 cup butter *or* margarine, softened
　1 egg
1/2 teaspoon almond extract
1/2 cup sugar
1/4 cup baking cocoa
1/2 teaspoon salt
　3 cups plus 2 tablespoons bread flour
2-1/2 teaspoons active dry yeast

In bread machine pan, place all ingredients in order suggested by manufacturer. Select basic bread setting. Choose crust color and loaf size if available. Bake according to bread machine directions (check dough after 5 minutes of mixing; add 1 to 2 tablespoons of water or flour if needed). **Yield:** 1 loaf (about 1-1/2 pounds). **Editor's Note:** Use of the timer feature is not recommended for this recipe.

Cocoa Almond Bread

Pumpkin Yeast Bread

(Pictured below)

This lightly spiced pumpkin bread has a crisp brown crust and appealing golden-orange interior.
                    —*Alicyn Swift, Greenfield, Indiana*

✓ Uses less fat, sugar or salt. Includes Nutritional Analysis and Diabetic Exchanges.

     1/2 cup plus 2 tablespoons water (70° to 80°)
     1/2 cup cooked *or* canned pumpkin
     1/4 cup butter *or* margarine, softened
     1/4 cup instant nonfat dry milk powder
     1/4 cup packed brown sugar
       1 teaspoon ground cinnamon
     1/2 to 1 teaspoon ground nutmeg
     3/4 teaspoon salt
     1/8 teaspoon ground ginger
   2-3/4 cups bread flour
       1 package (1/4 ounce) active dry yeast

In bread machine pan, place all ingredients in order suggested by manufacturer. Select basic bread setting.

Choose crust color and loaf size if available. Bake according to bread machine directions (check dough after 5 minutes of mixing; add 1 to 2 tablespoons of water or flour if needed). **Yield:** 1 loaf, 16 slices (about 1-1/2 pounds). **Nutritional Analysis:** One slice (prepared with reduced-fat margarine) equals 121 calories, 150 mg sodium, trace cholesterol, 22 gm carbohydrate, 3 gm protein, 2 gm fat. **Diabetic Exchanges:** 1-1/2 starch, 1/2 fat.

Walnut Bread

(Pictured below)

The walnut flavor really comes through in this nicely textured loaf. It's delicious, moist and excellent for toasting.
                    —*Ginny Rice, Oshkosh, Wisconsin*

       1 cup water (70° to 80°)
   4-1/2 teaspoons butter *or* margarine, softened
       1 egg
       2 tablespoons instant nonfat dry milk powder
       2 tablespoons sugar
       1 teaspoon salt

Walnut Bread
Pumpkin Yeast Bread

3 cups bread flour
3/4 cup chopped walnuts, toasted
1-1/2 teaspoons active dry yeast

In bread machine pan, place all ingredients in order suggested by manufacturer. Select basic bread setting. Choose crust color and loaf size if available. Bake according to bread machine directions (check dough after 5 minutes of mixing; add 1 to 2 tablespoons of water or flour if needed). **Yield:** 1 loaf (1-1/2 pounds). **Editor's Note:** Use of the timer feature is not recommended for this recipe.

Bread Machine Roll Mix

(Pictured at right)

I usually triple this recipe so I have the mix on hand when I want to make a batch of these soft rolls. This mix also makes a nice gift. —Alberta Anderson Finke
Denair, California

Bread Machine Roll Mix

3 cups bread flour
3 tablespoons sugar
3 tablespoons instant nonfat dry milk powder
1-1/2 teaspoons salt
ADDITIONAL INGREDIENTS:
1 cup water (70° to 80°)
2 tablespoons butter *or* margarine, softened
1-1/2 teaspoons active dry yeast
Beaten egg white and sesame seeds, optional

Combine the first four ingredients. Store in a resealable plastic bag. **Yield:** 1 batch (3-1/3 cups total). **To prepare rolls:** Place water in bread machine pan. Add roll mix. Top with butter and yeast. Select dough setting (check dough after 5 minutes of mixing; add 1 to 2 tablespoons of water or flour if needed). When cycle is completed, turn dough onto a lightly floured surface. Punch down; cover and let stand for 10 minutes. Divide into 12 portions; shape each into a ball. Place on lightly greased baking sheets. Cover and let rise in a warm place for 1 hour. If desired, brush tops with egg white and sprinkle with sesame seeds. Bake at 350° for 12-15 minutes or until lightly browned. **Yield:** 1 dozen.

Peppery Onion Bread

This bread gets a flavor boost from minced onion and black pepper. It's very good toasted and served with steak or spaghetti. —Dale Rosenthal, Austin, Minnesota

1 cup plus 1 tablespoon water (70° to 80°)
2 tablespoons butter *or* margarine, softened
1-1/2 teaspoons salt
3 cups bread flour
3 tablespoons instant nonfat dry milk powder
1 tablespoon sugar
1 teaspoon pepper

1/4 teaspoon garlic powder
2 teaspoons active dry yeast
1 tablespoon dried minced onion

In bread machine pan, place all ingredients in order suggested by manufacturer. Select basic bread setting. Choose crust color and loaf size if available. Bake according to bread machine directions (check dough after 5 minutes of mixing; add 1 to 2 tablespoons of water or flour if needed). **Yield:** 1 loaf (1-1/2 pounds).

Grandma's Molasses Bread

We converted some bread recipes from my husband's grandmother for use in the bread machine. This dark, slightly sweet bread is great toasted. —Jeannie Thomas
Kokomo, Indiana

1 cup warm milk (70° to 80°)
2 tablespoons butter *or* margarine, softened
2 tablespoons molasses
1 egg
1-1/2 teaspoons salt
2-1/2 cups bread flour
4-1/2 teaspoons sugar
1/2 cup rye flour
1/4 cup whole wheat flour
2-1/4 teaspoons active dry yeast

In bread machine pan, place all ingredients in order suggested by manufacturer. Select basic bread setting. Choose crust color and loaf size if available. Bake according to bread machine directions (check dough after 5 minutes of mixing; add 1 to 2 tablespoons of water or flour if needed). **Yield:** 1 loaf (about 1-1/2 pounds). **Editor's Note:** Use of the timer feature is not recommended for this recipe.

Chapter 12

YOUR family won't have to wait long to hear "Soup's on!" when you add one or more of these simple-to-make soups, salads and sandwiches to your recipe collection.

And your brood will like what they'll find at the table—delicious down-home dishes that will fill 'em up fast and that can be made in a snap.

Whether you prepare a taste-tempting trio for a hearty dinner or an individual soup, salad or sandwich for a light lunch, you'll come to rely on their fast-to-fix convenience even when you're not hurried.

SOUPED-UP SUPPER. Clockwise from upper right: Chicken Salad Croissants, Black Bean Gazpacho and Melon Cucumber Medley (all recipes on p. 199).

Creamy Swiss Onion Soup

(Pictured at right)

It was a cool spring day when I came up with this sweet and creamy variation of traditional baked French onion soup. I top individual bowls with toasty buttered croutons and a sprinkling of Swiss cheese, then pop them under the broiler. The rich results are delightful!
—I. MacKay Starr, North Saanich, British Columbia

        7 tablespoons butter *or* margarine, *divided*
1-1/2 cups day-old bread cubes
        3 large onions, quartered and thinly sliced
1-1/2 cups water
4-1/2 teaspoons chicken bouillon granules
        1/4 cup all-purpose flour
1-3/4 cups milk, *divided*
1-1/2 cups (6 ounces) shredded Swiss cheese,
        divided
Pepper to taste
Fresh minced chives *or* parsley

Melt 3 tablespoons of butter; toss with bread cubes. Place on a lightly greased baking sheet. Bake at 350° for 7 minutes; turn and bake 7 minutes longer or until toasted. Meanwhile, in a large saucepan, saute onions in remaining butter until lightly browned, about 12 minutes. Stir in water and bouillon; bring to a boil. Reduce heat; cover and simmer for 15 minutes. Combine flour and 1/2 cup milk until smooth; gradually stir into onion mixture. Stir in remaining milk. Bring to a boil; boil for 2 minutes, stirring until thickened. Reduce heat to low; stir in 3/4 cup Swiss cheese and pepper. Ladle into four ovenproof bowls; sprinkle with reserved croutons and remaining cheese. Broil 4 in. from the heat until cheese is melted and bubbly. Garnish with chives. **Yield:** 4 servings.

Hearty Hamburger Soup

(Pictured at right)

At family get-togethers, our children always request this spirit-warming soup along with a fresh loaf of homemade bread and tall glasses of milk. It has robust flavor, plenty of fresh-tasting vegetables and is easy to make.
—Barbara Brown, Janesville, Wisconsin

        1 pound ground beef
        4 cups water
        1 can (14-1/2 ounces) diced tomatoes,
            undrained
        3 medium carrots, sliced
        2 medium potatoes, peeled and cubed
        1 medium onion, chopped
        1/2 cup chopped celery
        4 beef bouillon cubes
1-1/2 teaspoons salt
        1/4 teaspoon pepper
        1/4 teaspoon dried oregano
        1 cup cut fresh *or* frozen green beans

In a large saucepan, brown beef; drain. Add the next 10 ingredients; bring to a boil. Reduce heat; cover and simmer for 15 minutes or until potatoes and carrots are ten-

der. Add beans. Cover and simmer 15 minutes longer or until the beans are tender. **Yield:** 8 servings (2 quarts).

Halibut Chowder

(Pictured at right)

This rich, creamy chowder is so good you won't believe it starts with canned soup and frozen vegetables. It showcases tender chunks of halibut, but salmon or most any type of whitefish will do. I double the recipe for large gatherings.
—Mary Davis, Palmer, Alaska

        8 to 10 green onions, thinly sliced
        2 garlic cloves, minced
        2 tablespoons butter *or* margarine
        4 cans (10-3/4 ounces *each*) condensed cream
            of potato soup, undiluted
        2 cans (10-3/4 ounces *each*) condensed cream
            of mushroom soup, undiluted
        4 cups milk
        2 packages (8 ounces *each*) cream cheese,
            cubed
1-1/2 pounds halibut *or* salmon fillets, cubed
1-1/2 cups frozen sliced carrots
1-1/2 cups frozen corn
        1/8 to 1/4 teaspoon cayenne pepper, optional

In a Dutch oven or soup kettle, saute onions and garlic in butter until tender. Add soups, milk and cream cheese; cook and stir until cheese is melted. Bring to a boil. Stir in fish, carrots and corn. Reduce heat; simmer, uncovered, for 5-10 minutes or until fish flakes easily and the vegetables are tender. Add cayenne pepper if desired. **Yield:** 16 servings (about 4 quarts).

Pronto Taco Soup

(Pictured at right)

When out-of-state friends dropped by, I invited them to stay for dinner, knowing that I could put together this mild, chili-flavored soup in a jiffy. I served it with cornmeal muffins and a crisp salad for a filling meal everyone loved.
—Priscilla Gilbert, Indian Harbour Beach, Florida

        1 pound ground beef
        1 medium onion, chopped
        2 garlic cloves, minced
        2 cans (14-1/2 ounces *each*) beef broth
        1 can (14-1/2 ounces) diced tomatoes,
            undrained
1-1/2 cups picante sauce
        1 cup uncooked spiral *or* small shell pasta
        1 medium green pepper, chopped
        2 teaspoons chili powder
        1 teaspoon dried parsley flakes
Shredded cheddar cheese and tortilla chips

In a large saucepan, cook beef, onion and garlic until meat is no longer pink; drain. Add the broth, tomatoes, picante sauce, pasta, green pepper, chili powder and parsley. Bring to a boil, stirring occasionally. Reduce heat; cover and simmer for 10-15 minutes or until pasta is tender. Garnish with cheese and tortilla chips. **Yield:** 8 servings (2 quarts).

Pronto Taco Soup
Halibut Chowder
Hearty Hamburger Soup
Creamy Swiss Onion Soup

Lemon Chicken Soup
Toasted Cheese Supreme
Apple Coleslaw

Apple Coleslaw

(Pictured at left)

Chopped apple, celery and green pepper add extra crunch to this crisp cabbage salad. The lemony homemade dressing has plenty of celery seed and a hint of honey. —Ann Main
Moorefield, Ontario

  2 cups coleslaw mix
  1 unpeeled tart apple, chopped
  1/2 cup chopped celery
  1/2 cup chopped green pepper
  1/4 cup vegetable oil
  2 tablespoons lemon juice
  2 tablespoons honey
  1 teaspoon celery seed

In a bowl, combine the coleslaw mix, apple, celery and green pepper. In a small bowl, whisk the remaining ingredients. Pour over coleslaw; toss to coat. **Yield:** 4-6 servings.

Lemon Chicken Soup

(Pictured at left)

For years, I made Greek chicken soup from scratch. My daughter devised this super-simple version that she and her family can enjoy when time's short. Lemon juice makes the delicious difference. —Joan Fotopoulos
Turah, Montana

  1 can (11-1/2 ounces) condensed chicken with
    rice soup, undiluted
  1 can (10-3/4 ounces) condensed cream of
    chicken soup, undiluted
2-1/4 cups water
  1 cup diced cooked chicken, optional
  1 to 2 tablespoons lemon juice
Pepper to taste
Minced fresh parsley, optional

In a 3-qt. saucepan, combine soups and water; mix well. Heat through. Add the chicken if desired. Stir in lemon juice and pepper. Garnish with parsley if desired. **Yield:** 4-5 servings.

Toasted Cheese Supreme

(Pictured at left)

I serve these flavorful hot ham and cheese sandwiches by themselves for lunch or with steaming bowls of my homemade clam chowder for a heartier meal.
—Wanda Evans, Tacoma, Washington

  8 slices white bread
  2 tablespoons mayonnaise
  6 ounces thinly sliced fully cooked ham
  4 slices cheddar cheese
  2 slices red onion, separated into rings
  2 tablespoons horseradish sauce
  1/4 cup butter *or* margarine, softened

Spread four slices of bread with mayonnaise. Layer each with ham, cheese and onion. Spread horseradish

sauce on remaining bread; place bread with horseradish side down over onion. Spread butter on the outside of each sandwich. In a skillet over medium heat, toast sandwiches until bread is lightly browned on both sides and cheese is melted. **Yield:** 4 servings.

Kitchen Sink Salad

Once or twice each week, we enjoy a main-dish salad for our evening meal. With ham, cheese, pineapple and a variety of vegetables, this tasty 'kitchen sink' version is one of our favorites. —Ed Wolak, Moreland, Georgia

  1 cup (4 ounces) shredded Co-Jack cheese
  1 cup chopped fully cooked ham
  1 celery rib, thinly sliced
 10 baby carrots, thinly sliced
  1 medium tart apple, chopped
  1/2 cup pineapple tidbits
  1/4 cup thinly sliced green pepper
  1/4 cup chopped onion
  5 cups torn salad greens
  1/2 cup sour cream
  1/4 cup mayonnaise

In a large bowl, combine the first nine ingredients. In a small bowl, whisk the sour cream and mayonnaise. Pour over salad and toss to coat. Serve immediately. **Yield:** 8-10 servings.

Crunchy Tuna Sandwiches

I put a unique twist on tuna salad sandwiches by seasoning the creamy mixture with ginger and soy sauce. A can of sliced water chestnuts provides the tasty crunch.
—Charlotte Baillargeon
Hinsdale, Massachusetts

  1 can (8 ounces) sliced water chestnuts,
    drained and chopped
  1 can (6 ounces) tuna, drained and flaked
  1/3 cup mayonnaise
  1 tablespoon minced fresh parsley
  1 teaspoon soy sauce
  1/4 teaspoon salt
  1/8 to 1/4 teaspoon ground ginger
  2 sandwich rolls, split
Lettuce leaves

In a bowl, combine the first seven ingredients; mix well. Cover and refrigerate for 1 hour. Just before serving, spoon onto rolls and top with a lettuce leaf. **Yield:** 2 servings.

Keep Them Crisp

When storing salad greens, carrots or cabbage, I add a few dry paper towels to the plastic bag before sealing the bag and putting it in the refrigerator. When the towels become wet, I replace them with dry ones. I find this helps the vegetables stay crisp longer.
—Alma Dalinsky, Lancaster, Pennsylvania

Comforting Chicken Noodle Soup

Comforting Chicken Noodle Soup

(Pictured above)

A good friend made us this rich, comforting soup after the birth of our son. It was such a help to have dinner taken care of until I was back on my feet. This yummy dish is so simple to fix that now I give a pot of it (along with the recipe) to other new mothers. —Joanna Sargent
Sandy, Utah

 2 quarts water
 8 chicken bouillon cubes
6-1/2 cups uncooked wide egg noodles
 2 cans (10-3/4 ounces *each*) condensed cream
  of chicken soup, undiluted
 3 cups cubed cooked chicken
 1 cup (8 ounces) sour cream
Minced fresh parsley

In a large saucepan, bring water and bouillon to a boil. Add noodles; cook, uncovered, until tender, about 10 minutes. Do not drain. Add soup and chicken; heat through. Remove from heat; stir in sour cream. Sprinkle with parsley. **Yield:** 10-12 servings (about 2-1/2 quarts).

Tangy Pork Sandwiches

Lemon and a hint of cayenne flavor the sauce in these tasty pork sandwiches. They're so warm and satisfying on a cool day. —Glennis Stuart Liles, Greenup, Kentucky

1/4 cup butter *or* margarine
1/4 cup Worcestershire sauce

Save the Soup

Mom shared this handy hint for rescuing homemade soup when I've added too much salt or garlic powder. Peel a whole potato and drop it into the simmering soup for 30 minutes to an hour. The potato absorbs the salt or garlic powder. Remove and discard the potato before serving. —Angie Aull, Perry Hall, Maryland

 2 tablespoons lemon juice
 2 tablespoons sugar
1/4 teaspoon paprika
1/8 teaspoon salt
1/8 teaspoon cayenne pepper
1/2 pound thinly sliced fully cooked pork
 4 hamburger buns, split

In a saucepan, combine the first seven ingredients. Bring to a boil, stirring frequently. Add the pork; simmer just until heated through, stirring frequently. Divide meat among buns; top each with 1 tablespoon sauce. Serve with the remaining sauce. **Yield:** 4 servings.

Sausage Potato Soup

(Pictured below)

After a full day of teaching and coaching, I'm often too tired to spend a lot of time preparing dinner. So I rely on this thick, chunky blend that I can have on the table in 30 minutes. The whole family enjoys the wonderful flavor of the smoked sausage. —Jennifer LeFevre
Hesston, Kansas

1/2 pound fully cooked kielbasa *or* Polish
  sausage, diced
 6 medium potatoes, peeled and cubed
 2 cups frozen corn
1-1/2 cups chicken broth
 1 celery rib, sliced
1/4 cup sliced carrot
1/2 teaspoon garlic powder
1/2 teaspoon onion powder
1/2 teaspoon salt
1/4 teaspoon pepper
1-1/2 cups milk
2/3 cup shredded cheddar cheese
 1 teaspoon minced fresh parsley

In a large saucepan, brown sausage; drain. Set sausage aside. In the same pan, combine potatoes, corn, broth, celery, carrot and seasonings. Bring to a boil. Reduce

Sausage Potato Soup

Meatball Mushroom Soup

mushrooms and Parmesan cheese; heat through. **Yield:** 6 servings.

Best-Ever Potato Soup

(Pictured below)

You'll be surprised at the taste of this rich, cheesy concoction—it's not a typical potato soup. I came up with the recipe after enjoying baked potato soup at one of our favorite restaurants. I added bacon, and we think that makes it even better.
—Coleen Morrissey
Sweet Valley, Pennsylvania

   6 bacon strips, diced
   3 cups cubed peeled potatoes
   1 can (14-1/2 ounces) chicken broth
   1 small carrot, grated
1/2 cup chopped onion
   1 tablespoon dried parsley flakes
1/2 teaspoon *each* celery seed, salt and pepper
   3 tablespoons all-purpose flour
   3 cups milk
   8 ounces process American cheese, cubed
   2 green onions, thinly sliced, optional

In a large saucepan, cook bacon until crisp; drain. Add potatoes, broth, carrot, onion, parsley, celery seed, salt and pepper. Cover and simmer until potatoes are tender, about 15 minutes. Combine flour and milk until smooth; add to soup. Bring to a boil; boil and stir for 2 minutes. Add cheese; stir until cheese is melted and the soup is heated through. Garnish with green onions if desired. **Yield:** 8 servings (2 quarts).

heat; cover and simmer for 15 minutes or until vegetables are tender. Add milk, cheese, parsley and sausage. Cook and stir over low heat until cheese is melted and soup is heated through. **Yield:** 6 servings.

Meatball Mushroom Soup

(Pictured above)

This creamy, super-thick soup is hearty with meatballs, mushrooms, barley, macaroni and rice. With dinner rolls or breadsticks, it's a simple and satisfying meal for my husband and me on a rainy day. Leftovers easily reheat for a fast, filling lunch or dinner.
—JoAnn Abbott
Kerhonkson, New York

1/2 pound ground beef
   2 cans (10-3/4 ounces *each*) condensed cream
        of mushroom soup, undiluted
1-1/3 cups milk
1-1/3 cups water
   1 teaspoon Italian seasoning
   1 teaspoon dried minced onion
1/2 teaspoon dried minced garlic
1/4 cup quick-cooking barley
1/4 cup uncooked elbow macaroni
1/4 cup uncooked long grain rice
   1 medium carrot, shredded
   1 jar (4-1/2 ounces) sliced mushrooms, drained
   2 tablespoons grated Parmesan cheese

Shape beef into 1-in. balls; set aside. In a large saucepan, combine soup, milk and water; bring to a boil. Add Italian seasoning, onion, garlic, barley, macaroni and rice. Reduce heat; simmer, uncovered, for 15 minutes. Meanwhile, brown meatballs in a nonstick skillet until no longer pink. Stir carrot into soup; cover and simmer for 5 minutes. Use a slotted spoon to transfer meatballs to soup. Stir in

Best-Ever Potato Soup

Creamy Lemon Chicken Soup

I think it's the addition of lemon juice that gives this creamy soup its special taste. Hearty bowlfuls are heaping with lots of chicken and rice. Add a green salad and crusty rolls, and you have a crowd-pleasing meal on the table in minutes.
—Elissa Armbruster, Medford Lakes, New Jersey

✓ Uses less fat, sugar or salt. Includes Nutritional Analysis and Diabetic Exchanges.

 5 cups chicken broth
 5 cups water
 5 teaspoons chicken bouillon granules
 3 medium carrots, cut into small chunks
 1 large onion, chopped
 4 cups cubed cooked chicken
 1 cup uncooked long grain rice
 3 eggs
 1/3 cup lemon juice
1-1/2 teaspoons dried oregano
Pepper to taste

In a Dutch oven or soup kettle, combine the first five ingredients; bring to a boil. Add the chicken and rice. Reduce heat. Cover and simmer for 15 minutes or until rice is tender. Whisk together eggs and lemon juice; quickly stir into soup. Add oregano and pepper. Serve immediately. **Yield:** 14 servings. **Nutritional Analysis:** One 1-cup serving (prepared with low-sodium broth and bouillon) equals 133 calories, 64 mg sodium, 71 mg cholesterol, 16 gm carbohydrate, 10 gm protein, 3 gm fat. **Diabetic Exchanges:** 1 starch, 1 lean meat.

Picnic Chicken Pitas

(Pictured at right)

A mustard-flavored dressing coats the colorful combination of chicken, broccoli, tomatoes and bacon in this tasty sandwich filling. It's great for a picnic because you can prepare the filling ahead and assemble the pitas at the picnic site. —Marla Brenneman, Goshen, Indiana

✓ Uses less fat, sugar or salt. Includes Nutritional Analysis and Diabetic Exchanges.

 1 package (10 ounces) frozen broccoli florets, cooked and drained
 2 cups shredded cooked chicken
 1 cup (4 ounces) shredded cheddar cheese
 1 medium tomato, chopped
1/4 cup mayonnaise
 2 tablespoons prepared mustard
1/2 teaspoon salt, optional
1/8 teaspoon pepper
 4 pita breads (6 inches), halved
 4 bacon strips, cooked and crumbled, optional

In a large bowl, combine the broccoli, chicken, cheese and tomato. In a small bowl, combine the mayonnaise, mustard, salt if desired and pepper; pour over the broccoli mixture and toss to coat. Spoon about 3/4 cup into each pita half; top with bacon if desired. **Yield:** 4 servings. **Nutritional Analysis:** One serving (prepared with reduced-fat cheese and fat-free mayonnaise and without salt and bacon) equals 320 calories, 725 mg sodium, 48 mg cholesterol, 41 gm carbohydrate, 26 gm protein, 5 gm fat. **Diabetic Exchanges:** 3 lean meat, 2-1/2 starch.

Fresh 'n' Fruity Salad

(Pictured at right)

We love all types of melons, so I'm always experimenting with different ways to serve them. A light dressing brings out the refreshing fruit flavors in this cool salad that's so delightful in warm weather.
—Bernice Morris
Marshfield, Missouri

✓ Uses less fat, sugar or salt. Includes Nutritional Analysis and Diabetic Exchanges.

 1 can (20 ounces) unsweetened pineapple chunks, drained
 1 can (15 ounces) unsweetened dark sweet cherries, drained
1-1/2 cups cubed cantaloupe
1-1/2 cups cubed seeded watermelon
1-1/2 cups cubed honeydew
DRESSING:
 3 tablespoons vegetable oil
 3 tablespoons orange juice
 3 tablespoons lemon juice
 2 tablespoons sugar
1/4 teaspoon paprika

Combine the fruit in a large bowl. In a small bowl, combine the dressing ingredients; pour over fruit and toss to coat. Serve immediately with a slotted spoon. **Yield:** 8 servings. **Nutritional Analysis:** One 1/2-cup serving equals 140 calories, 8 mg sodium, 0 cholesterol, 24 gm carbohydrate, 1 gm protein, 6 gm fat. **Diabetic Exchanges:** 1-1/2 fruit, 1 fat.

Summer Squash Soup

(Pictured at right)

Fresh dill pleasantly seasons this rich, delicious soup. With its delicate taste, the creamy concoction makes an easy but elegant first course for a company dinner.
—Sandi Pichon, Slidell, Louisiana

 5 small yellow summer squash, seeded and cubed
 2 green onions, cut into 3-inch pieces
 2 tablespoons butter *or* margarine
 1 can (14-1/2 ounces) chicken broth
1/2 teaspoon salt
1/8 to 1/4 teaspoon white pepper
1-1/2 cups whipping cream

In a large saucepan, saute squash and onions in butter until tender. Stir in broth, salt and pepper; bring to a boil. Reduce heat; cover and simmer for 20-25 minutes or until vegetables are tender. Cool slightly. Process in batches in a blender or food processor; return all to the pan. Stir in cream and heat through. **Yield:** 6 servings.

Summer Squash Soup
Fresh 'n' Fruity Salad
Picnic Chicken Pitas

Sausage Kale Soup
Pickled Carrot Salad
Cheesy Walnut Burgers

Sausage Kale Soup

(Pictured at left)

This zesty Italian soup is sure to become a favorite with your guests—just as it has with mine. The spicier the seasoning in the sausage, the better the soup. —Nancy Dyer
Grove, Oklahoma

      1 pound uncooked Italian sausage links
  3/4 cup chopped onion
      1 bacon strip, diced
      2 garlic cloves, minced
      2 cups water
      1 can (14-1/2 ounces) chicken broth
      2 cups diced potatoes
      2 cups thinly sliced fresh kale *or* spinach
  1/3 cup whipping cream

Place the sausages in an ungreased 15-in. x 10-in. x 1-in. baking pan; pierce casings. Bake at 300° for 20-25 minutes or until fully cooked. Drain; set aside to cool. Meanwhile, in a saucepan, saute onion and bacon for 3 minutes or until onion is tender. Add garlic; saute for 1 minute. Add water, broth and potatoes; bring to a boil. Reduce heat; cover and simmer for 20 minutes or until potatoes are tender. Cut sausages in half lengthwise, then into 1/4-in. slices. Add kale, cream and sausage to soup; heat through (do not boil). **Yield:** 8 servings (2 quarts).

Cheesy Walnut Burgers

(Pictured at left)

I serve these crisp meatless burgers with ketchup or plain yogurt to create an unusual taste sensation. The sharp cheddar brings a little zip to each bite. —Janet Chappell
Almonte, Ontario

  1-1/2 cups (6 ounces) shredded sharp cheddar
          cheese
      1 cup finely chopped walnuts
      1 cup soft bread crumbs
  1/2 cup finely chopped onion
      1 egg, beaten
      1 tablespoon ketchup
      2 teaspoons minced fresh basil *or* thyme
  1/4 teaspoon salt
  1/8 teaspoon lemon-pepper seasoning
      6 hamburger buns, split
Ketchup *or* plain yogurt, optional

In a bowl, combine the first nine ingredients; shape into six 3/4-in.-thick patties. Fry in a greased skillet until golden brown on both sides, or bake on a greased baking sheet at 350° for 25 minutes or until browned, turning once. Serve on buns with ketchup or yogurt if desired. **Yield:** 6 servings.

Grilled Pizza Sandwiches

I've been fixing this jazzed-up grilled cheese sandwich for years. Kids of all ages think its pizza-like flavor is the best. —Janice Mitchell, Aurora, Colorado

  1/3 cup pizza sauce
      8 slices Italian bread (1/2 inch thick)
      4 slices salami
      4 slices mozzarella cheese
      1 small green pepper, thinly sliced
  1/4 cup butter *or* margarine, melted

Spread about 2 teaspoons pizza sauce on one side of each slice of bread. Top four slices with the salami, cheese and green pepper. Top with remaining bread; brush the outsides of bread with butter. Grill sandwiches on a hot griddle or in a skillet over medium heat until both sides are golden brown and cheese is melted. **Yield:** 4 servings.

Pickled Carrot Salad

(Pictured at left)

Years ago, we enjoyed chilled pickled carrots in a restaurant. They were so good I hunted through my cookbooks until I found a similar recipe. It's a refreshing change from traditional picnic fare. —Pat Walter, Pine Island, Minnesota

      1 pound carrots, julienned
  1/2 cup vegetable oil
  1/2 cup vinegar
  1/3 cup water
      1 tablespoon sugar
      2 garlic cloves, minced
      2 teaspoons dried oregano
      1 teaspoon salt
  1/2 teaspoon pepper
  1/2 teaspoon ground mustard

In a saucepan, cook carrots in a small amount of water until crisp-tender; drain. Transfer to a serving dish. Combine remaining ingredients in a jar with a tight-fitting lid; shake well. Pour over carrots; cover and refrigerate for several hours or overnight. Serve with a slotted spoon. **Yield:** 4 servings.

Success with Salads

- To save time when preparing potato salad, put the peeled cooked potatoes and peeled hard-cooked eggs into a bowl and use a pastry cutter to chop them. It works great. —Marilyn Lowe, Kerman, California
- I use kitchen shears to cut green onions for salads and to use in recipes. It's safer than using a knife, and I finish in a flash. —Mary Peek, Hillsboro, Indiana
- Before inverting a gelatin mold onto a serving plate, I wet the surface of the dish. This allows the gelatin to slide and makes it easy to center on the plate. —Elaine Cooley, Louisville, Kentucky
- When making a fruit salad, I use the juice from a small can of pineapple to keep my apples and bananas from browning. —Fran Avery, Rohnert Park, California
- Before boiling red potatoes for potato salad, cut a circle around each potato, just piercing the skin. Once boiled, the potatoes are much easier to peel. —Mrs. Ishmael Hayes, Rocklin, California

Three-Bean Soup

Marinated Mushroom Salad

I'm a cook on a tour boat for a month at a time and never leave home without this recipe. This marinated salad is a snap to serve when you're rushed. —Rita Evans
Evansville, Indiana

    2 pounds fresh mushrooms, quartered
    3 medium tomatoes, cut into wedges
    1 cup Italian salad dressing
    1 teaspoon dried parsley flakes
 1/2 teaspoon garlic powder
 1/2 teaspoon onion salt, optional
 1/2 teaspoon dried basil
    2 cups torn fresh spinach
    3 bacon strips, cooked and crumbled, optional

Place mushrooms and tomatoes in a large shallow dish. Combine the next five ingredients; drizzle over mushrooms and tomatoes. Cover and refrigerate overnight, stirring once. Line a serving platter or bowl with spinach. Using a slotted spoon, arrange vegetables over spinach. Sprinkle with bacon if desired. **Yield:** 18-20 servings. **Nutritional Analysis:** One 3/4-cup serving (prepared with fat-free Italian dressing and without onion salt and bacon) equals 20 calories, 122 mg sodium, 0 cholesterol, 4 gm carbohydrate, 1 gm protein, trace fat. **Diabetic Exchange:** 1 vegetable.

Three-Bean Soup

(Pictured above)

When I was growing up, my mother prepared many different soups, each seasoned just right. She often made this colorful combination that's chock-full of harvest-fresh goodness. It showcases an appealing assortment of beans, potatoes, carrots and spinach. —Valerie Lee
Snellville, Georgia

    1 medium onion, chopped
    1 tablespoon vegetable oil
    3 small potatoes, peeled and cubed
    2 medium carrots, sliced
    3 cans (14-1/2 ounces *each*) chicken broth
    3 cups water
    2 tablespoons parsley flakes
    2 teaspoons dried basil
    1 teaspoon dried oregano
    1 garlic clove, minced
 1/2 teaspoon pepper
    1 can (15-1/2 ounces) great northern beans,
      rinsed and drained
    1 can (15 ounces) pinto beans, rinsed and
      drained
    1 can (15 ounces) garbanzo beans, rinsed and
      drained
    3 cups chopped fresh spinach

In a Dutch oven, saute onion in oil. Add the next nine ingredients. Simmer, uncovered, until vegetables are tender. Add beans and spinach; heat through. **Yield:** 12 servings (about 3 quarts). **Nutritional Analysis:** One 1-cup serving (prepared with low-sodium broth) equals 169 calories, 276 mg sodium, 2 mg cholesterol, 29 gm carbohydrate, 9 gm protein, 3 gm fat. **Diabetic Exchanges:** 2 starch, 1-1/2 meat.

Tasty Reuben Soup

(Pictured below)

I'm a working mom with limited time to feed my hungry family, so I'm always looking for quick recipes. This speedy soup (which may remind you of a Reuben sandwich) is a favorite of ours. I frequently stir up a batch of apple muffins to complete this meal. —Terry Ann Brandt
Tobias, Nebraska

Tasty Reuben Soup

Uses less fat, sugar or salt. Includes Nutritional Analysis and Diabetic Exchanges.

- 4 cans (14-1/2 ounces *each*) chicken broth
- 4 cups shredded cabbage
- 2 cups uncooked medium egg noodles
- 1 pound fully cooked kielbasa *or* Polish sausage, halved and cut into 1-inch slices
- 1/2 cup chopped onion
- 1 teaspoon caraway seeds
- 1/4 teaspoon garlic powder
- 1 cup (4 ounces) shredded Swiss cheese

In a large saucepan, combine the first seven ingredients; bring to a boil. Reduce heat; cover and simmer for 15 minutes or until cabbage and noodles are tender. Garnish with cheese. **Yield:** 10 servings (2-1/2 quarts). **Nutritional Analysis:** One 1-cup serving (prepared with low-sodium chicken broth, low-fat turkey kielbasa and reduced-fat cheese) equals 125 calories, 455 mg sodium, 41 mg cholesterol, 9 gm carbohydrate, 12 gm protein, 5 gm fat. **Diabetic Exchanges:** 1 meat, 1 vegetable, 1/2 starch.

Chicken Tomato Soup

Chicken Tomato Soup

(Pictured at right)

While creating this crowd-pleasing soup, I was trying to keep in mind a variety of textures, colors and flavors. Its sweet tomato base brims with chicken, broccoli, corn and a couple kinds of beans. —Connie Johnson Springfield, Missouri

- 1-1/2 cups water
- 1 package (10 ounces) frozen chopped broccoli
- 3/4 cup chopped onion
- 1 garlic clove, minced
- 3/4 pound boneless skinless chicken breast, cut into 1-inch chunks
- 1/2 teaspoon seasoned salt
- 1/4 teaspoon pepper
- 1 can (46 ounces) tomato juice
- 1 can (15-1/2 ounces) great northern beans, rinsed and drained
- 1 can (15 ounces) black beans, rinsed and drained
- 1 can (11 ounces) whole kernel corn, drained
- 1 tablespoon ketchup
- 1 teaspoon brown sugar

Crumbled bacon and shredded cheddar cheese, optional

In a Dutch oven or soup kettle, combine water, broccoli, onion and garlic. Bring to a boil; boil for 8-10 minutes, stirring frequently. Meanwhile, in a nonstick skillet, cook chicken until no longer pink, about 6 minutes. Sprinkle with seasoned salt and pepper. Add to broccoli mixture. Stir in tomato juice, beans, corn, ketchup and brown sugar; bring to a boil. Reduce heat; cover and simmer for 10-15 minutes, stirring occasionally. Garnish with bacon and cheese if desired. **Yield:** 12 servings (about 3 quarts).

Macaroni Ham Salad

I like to make this hearty main-dish salad in summer when it's too hot to turn on the oven. My husband and children like the unexpected flavor of the dill pickle. —Lori Thompson, New London, Texas

 Uses less fat, sugar or salt. Includes Nutritional Analysis and Diabetic Exchanges.

- 4 cups cooked elbow macaroni
- 1 block (7 ounces) sharp cheddar cheese, diced
- 1 cup diced fully cooked ham
- 1 cup chopped dill pickles
- 3 hard-cooked eggs, chopped
- 1 small onion, finely chopped
- 3/4 cup mayonnaise
- 1 tablespoon Dijon mustard

In a bowl, combine the first six ingredients. Combine mayonnaise and mustard; add to macaroni mixture and toss. Cover and chill until serving. Refrigerate leftovers. **Yield:** 12 servings. **Nutritional Analysis:** One 3/4-cup serving (prepared with low-fat ham, reduced-fat cheddar cheese and fat-free mayonnaise) equals 130 calories, 576 mg sodium, 27 mg cholesterol, 16 gm carbohydrate, 9 gm protein, 3 gm fat. **Diabetic Exchanges:** 1 starch, 1 lean meat.

Turkey Cranwich

My mother-in-law and I are always dreaming up new sandwiches. When we put these Thanksgiving leftovers between slices of sourdough bread, we knew we had a family favorite. —Judy Benson, Capron, Illinois

2 tablespoons cream cheese, softened
4 slices sourdough bread
1/4 cup chopped walnuts
1/3 pound thinly sliced cooked turkey
1/4 cup whole-berry cranberry sauce
2 slices Swiss cheese
Lettuce leaves

Spread cream cheese on two slices of bread. Sprinkle with walnuts. Top with turkey; spread cranberry sauce over turkey. Top with Swiss cheese, lettuce and remaining bread. **Yield:** 2 servings.

Echo Valley Bean Soup

I came up with this recipe after sampling some excellent bean soup at a sandwich shop in a neighboring town. —Patricia Crandall, Echo Valley Farm Inchelium, Washington

10 bacon strips, diced
1 medium onion, diced
2 garlic cloves, minced
1 can (14-1/2 ounces) stewed tomatoes
2 cans (15 ounces *each*) pork and beans
2 cans (14-1/2 ounces *each*) beef broth

In a saucepan, cook bacon until crisp. Set bacon aside; drain, reserving 1-2 tablespoons drippings. In the drippings, saute the onion and garlic until tender. Meanwhile, in a blender or food processor, process tomatoes until smooth. Add to the onion mixture. Stir in pork and beans and broth. Bring to a boil. Reduce heat; simmer, uncovered, for 15 minutes or until heated through. Stir in bacon. **Yield:** 6 servings.

Summer Sub Sandwich

(Pictured at right)

Being originally from the Northeast, we love submarine sandwiches. So I came up with this hearty ham-and-cheese combination that's good either hot or cold. —Jennifer Beck, Concord, Ohio

1 loaf (1 pound) unsliced French bread
1 package (3 ounces) cream cheese, softened
8 slices fully cooked ham
6 slices provolone cheese
1 jar (4 ounces) sliced mushrooms, drained
1-1/2 cups shredded lettuce
2 medium tomatoes, thinly sliced
1 small onion, thinly sliced
2 banana peppers, thinly sliced

Cut the loaf of bread in half horizontally. Spread bottom half with cream cheese; layer with ham, provolone and mushrooms. Replace top. Cut loaf in half; wrap in paper towels. Microwave on high for 45-60 seconds. Remove top; add lettuce, tomatoes, onion and peppers. Replace top. Cut into serving-size pieces. **Yield:** 4 servings.

BLT Soup

(Pictured at right)

I'm always inventing new recipes or improving on old ones. Since the BLT is a family favorite, I created a soup with all the fabulous flavors of the sandwich. But I gave it extra zip by adding picante sauce. —Sharon Richardson Dallas, Texas

3 tablespoons butter *or* margarine
2 teaspoons vegetable oil
3 cups cubed French bread
1 pound sliced bacon, diced
2 cups finely chopped celery
1 medium onion, finely chopped
2 tablespoons sugar
6 tablespoons all-purpose flour
5 cups chicken broth
1 jar (16 ounces) picante sauce
1 can (8 ounces) tomato sauce
1/8 teaspoon pepper
3 cups shredded lettuce

In a Dutch oven or large saucepan over medium, heat butter and oil. Add the bread cubes; stir until crisp and golden brown. Remove and set aside. In the same pan, cook bacon until crisp. Drain, reserving 1/4 cup drippings; set bacon aside. Saute celery and onion in drippings until tender. Add sugar; cook and stir for 1 minute. Stir in flour; cook and stir for 1 minute. Add broth, picante sauce, tomato sauce and pepper; bring to a boil. Boil and stir for 2 minutes. Just before serving, add lettuce and heat through. Garnish with the croutons and bacon. **Yield:** 8 servings (2 quarts).

Layered Roast Beef Salad

(Pictured at right)

I've prepared this fast-to-fix salad for my bridge club several times, and I always get requests for the recipe. If I don't have leftover roast beef on hand, I use sliced roast beef from the deli with equally tasty results. —Susan Graham Cherokee, Iowa

8 cups torn salad greens
1 pound cooked roast beef, cut into 3/4-inch strips
1 cup grated carrots
1/2 cup thinly sliced red onion
3 hard-cooked eggs, sliced
1 cup (8 ounces) sour cream *or* plain yogurt
1/2 cup mayonnaise
1 tablespoon minced fresh parsley
1 tablespoon minced fresh basil

In a 3-qt. salad bowl, layer a third of the greens, beef, carrots, onion and eggs. Repeat layers twice. Combine remaining ingredients; spread over salad. Toss just before serving. **Yield:** 6-8 servings.

Layered Roast Beef Salad
BLT Soup
Summer Sub Sandwich

Chicken Salad Croissants
Melon Cucumber Medley
Black Bean Gazpacho

Chilled Cantaloupe Soup

(Pictured at right)

A friend in New York shared the recipe for this chilled melon soup that's pleasantly spiced with cinnamon. Most people are skeptical when I describe it, but after one spoonful, they're hooked. It's easy to prepare, pretty to serve and so refreshing.
—Margaret McNeil
Memphis, Tennessee

Chilled Cantaloupe Soup

✓ Uses less fat, sugar or salt. Includes Nutritional Analysis and Diabetic Exchanges.

> 1 medium cantaloupe, peeled, seeded and cubed
> 2 cups orange juice, *divided*
> 1 tablespoon lime juice
> 1/4 to 1/2 teaspoon ground cinnamon
Fresh mint, optional

Place cantaloupe and 1/2 cup orange juice in a blender or food processor; cover and process until smooth. Transfer to a large bowl; stir in lime juice, cinnamon and remaining orange juice. Cover and refrigerate for at least 1 hour. Garnish with mint if desired. **Yield:** 6 servings. **Nutritional Analysis:** One 3/4-cup serving equals 70 calories, 9 mg sodium, 0 cholesterol, 17 gm carbohydrate, 1 gm protein, trace fat. **Diabetic Exchange:** 1 fruit.

Chicken Salad Croissants

(Pictured at left and on page 183)

This tempting chicken salad gets its special taste from Swiss cheese and pickle relish. It's a favorite of my brother, who insists I make it whenever he visits.
—Laura Koziarski, Battle Creek, Michigan

> 2 cups cubed cooked chicken
> 1 cup cubed Swiss cheese
> 1/2 cup dill pickle relish
> 2/3 cup mayonnaise
> 1 tablespoon minced fresh parsley
> 1 teaspoon lemon juice
> 1/2 teaspoon seasoned salt
> 1/8 teaspoon pepper
Lettuce leaves
> 6 croissants, split

In a bowl, combine the chicken, cheese and pickle relish. Combine mayonnaise, parsley, lemon juice, seasoned salt and pepper; add to chicken mixture and mix well. Place a lettuce leaf on each croissant; top with about 1/2 cup of the chicken mixture. **Yield:** 6 servings.

Melon Cucumber Medley

(Pictured at left and on page 182)

A light lemony dressing complements a beautiful mixture of melons and sliced cucumber. This delightful summer salad is especially good served at a brunch or luncheon.
—Edie DeSpain, Logan, Utah

> 1/2 cup vegetable oil

> 1/4 cup lemon juice
> 1 teaspoon sugar
> 1/2 teaspoon salt
Dash pepper
> 6 cups melon balls *or* cubes (cantaloupe, honeydew *and/or* watermelon)
> 3 medium cucumbers, thinly sliced
Lettuce leaves, optional

In a jar with a tight-fitting lid, combine the oil, lemon juice, sugar, salt and pepper; shake until sugar is dissolved. In a bowl, combine melon and cucumbers; drizzle with dressing. Cover and refrigerate for at least 1 hour. Serve in a lettuce-lined bowl if desired. **Yield:** 12 servings.

Black Bean Gazpacho

(Pictured at left and on page 183)

I first tried this colorful chilled soup at my best friend's house during one of the hottest summers I can remember. Its garden-fresh flavor really hit the spot!
—Shelley Graff, Philo, Illinois

> 3 cans (11-1/2 ounces *each*) picante V-8 juice
> 4 medium tomatoes, seeded and chopped*
> 1 can (15 ounces) black beans, rinsed and drained
> 1 cup cubed fully cooked ham
> 1/2 cup *each* chopped green, sweet yellow and red pepper
> 1/2 cup chopped cucumber
> 1/2 cup chopped zucchini
> 1/4 cup finely chopped green onions
> 2 tablespoons Italian salad dressing
> 3/4 teaspoon salt
> 1/8 to 1/4 teaspoon hot pepper sauce

Combine all of the ingredients in a large bowl. Cover and refrigerate for at least 2 hours. **Yield:** 10 servings.
*Editor's Note: Two 14-1/2-ounce cans of diced tomatoes, drained, can be substituted for the fresh tomatoes.

Sausage Broccoli Bread

(Pictured at right)

My husband is in the Air Force, so we move often. This lifestyle lets me make friends—and share wonderful recipes like this one—with people from all over the United States.
—Kelly Praska, Bellevue, Nebraska

- 2 loaves (1 pound *each*) frozen bread dough
- 1 pound bulk pork sausage
- 2-1/2 cups chopped fresh broccoli
- 1 can (14-1/2 ounces) Italian diced tomatoes, drained
- 1 large onion, chopped
- 2 cups (8 ounces) shredded Monterey Jack cheese
- 1 egg, beaten

Thaw dough and let rise according to package directions. Meanwhile, in a skillet over medium heat, cook sausage until no longer pink. Remove sausage with a slotted spoon and set aside. In the drippings, saute the broccoli, tomatoes and onion until crisp-tender; drain and cool. On a lightly floured surface, roll each loaf of dough into a 12-in. x 10-in. rectangle. Spread sausage lengthwise down the center third of each rectangle. Top with broccoli mixture and cheese. Fold the short sides in 1 in.; pinch to seal. Fold long sides over filling; pinch to seal. Place seam side down on a greased baking sheet. Brush egg over top and sides of each loaf. Bake, uncovered, at 350° for 25-30 minutes or until golden brown. **Yield:** 2 loaves.

Italian Sandwich Loaf

Served with a green salad, slices of this pizza-flavored sandwich make a terrific lunch or dinner. The crispy bread is loaded with a hearty filling. *—Eleanor Dunbar, Peoria, Illinois*

- 2 unsliced loaves (8 ounces *each*) Italian bread
- 6 tablespoons olive *or* vegetable oil, *divided*
- 1 can (14-1/2 ounces) Italian diced tomatoes, drained
- 1 can (6 ounces) tomato paste
- 1 package (6 ounces) Canadian bacon, chopped
- 1 package (3-1/2 ounces) sliced pepperoni
- 1 garlic clove, minced
- 1/2 teaspoon dried basil
- 1/2 teaspoon dried oregano
- 1/8 teaspoon pepper
- 1 cup (4 ounces) shredded mozzarella cheese
- 1/2 cup grated Parmesan *or* Romano cheese

Cut 1/2 in. from the top of each loaf of bread; set aside. Hollow out bottom portion, leaving a 1/2-in. shell (discard removed bread or save for another use). Brush insides of shells and crust with 4 tablespoons oil. Place on a baking sheet. Bake at 350° for 5-10 minutes or until toasted. In a 3-qt. saucepan, combine tomatoes, tomato paste, bacon, pepperoni, garlic, basil, oregano and pepper. Bring to a boil over medium heat. Reduce heat; simmer for 10 minutes. Remove from the heat and stir in cheeses. Spoon into bread shells; replace tops and brush with remaining oil. Bake 15 minutes longer. **Yield:** 10-12 servings.

Vegetable Crab Soup

(Pictured at right)

This recipe, rich with cheese and crab, is a quick and different way to dress up canned soup. *—Amy Lingren, Des Peres, Missouri*

- 1 can (19 ounces) ready-to-serve New England clam chowder
- 1 can (11 ounces) condensed cheddar cheese soup, undiluted
- 2-1/2 to 3 cups half-and-half cream
- 1/4 cup white wine *or* chicken broth
- 1 tablespoon Worcestershire sauce
- 1 package (16 ounces) frozen stir-fry vegetable blend
- 2 cans (6 ounces *each*) crabmeat, drained, flaked and cartilage removed
- 1 medium tomato, seeded and chopped
- 2/3 cup shredded cheddar cheese
- 2 tablespoons minced fresh parsley
- 1/4 to 1/2 teaspoon pepper

In a large saucepan, combine chowder, soup, cream, wine or broth and Worcestershire sauce. Bring to a boil. Stir in vegetables; return to a boil. Reduce heat; cover and simmer for 6-8 minutes or until vegetables are crisp-tender. Stir in crab, tomato, cheese, parsley and pepper. Cook and stir until heated through. **Yield:** 8 servings.

Cranberry Salad Dressing

(Pictured at right)

Cranberries add color to this tangy dressing that coats salad greens nicely. *—Suzanne McKinley, Lyons, Georgia*

- 1 cup cranberries
- 1 medium navel orange, peeled and sectioned
- 2/3 cup sugar
- 1/2 cup vinegar
- 1 teaspoon salt
- 1 teaspoon ground mustard
- 1 teaspoon grated onion
- 1 cup vegetable oil

In a blender or food processor, combine cranberries, orange, sugar, vinegar, salt, mustard and onion. While processing, gradually add oil in a steady stream. Refrigerate. **Yield:** about 2-1/2 cups.

Sloppy Soup Solution

To help kids get thin soup or broth from their bowls to their mouths without a mess, I give them a straw.
—Brenda Schrag, Farmington, New Mexico

Cranberry Salad Dressing
Vegetable Crab Soup
Sausage Broccoli Bread

Chapter 13

⏱ *Delectable Desserts*

WHETHER you're looking for a fantastic finale to serve at a special-occasion supper or for a tasty take-along treat to share at a potluck, you can rely on this chapter's appealing assortment of cookies, cakes, candies, pies and more.

Folks will think you fussed all day when these impressive-looking delights make an appearance on the table.

But all of these sweet treats are easy to prepare, so you can quickly whip them up for your family, unexpected company and even dinner guests with time to spare.

SWEET INSPIRATION. Clockwise from top: Angel Berry Tunnel Cake, Diamond Bars and Banana Snack Cake (all recipes on page 212).

Chocolate Dream Dessert

(Pictured at right)

I make this crowd-pleasing dessert simply with cake cubes, instant pudding, whipped topping, chocolate syrup and nuts. It's a surefire way to satisfy chocolate lovers.
—Kathleen Gordon, Treadway, Tennessee

- 1 package (18-1/4 ounces) chocolate cake mix
- 1 package (3.4 ounces) instant vanilla pudding mix
- 1 cup chocolate syrup, *divided*
- 1 carton (12 ounces) frozen whipped topping, thawed
- 1/2 cup chopped pecans

Prepare and bake the cake according to package directions, using a greased 13-in. x 9-in. x 2-in. baking pan. Cool on a wire rack. Meanwhile, prepare pudding according to package directions; pour into a 13-in. x 9-in. x 2-in. dish. Tear cake into small pieces and gently push down into the pudding. Drizzle with 3/4 cup of chocolate syrup. Spread with whipped topping. Drizzle with remaining chocolate syrup. Sprinkle with pecans. Refrigerate until serving. **Yield:** 16-20 servings.

Mocha Layer Cake

(Pictured at right)

My family often requests this delightful layer cake. They love the mocha flavor and extra chocolate surprise hidden beneath the taste-tempting frosting. —Terry Gilbert
Orlean, Virginia

- 1 package (18-1/4 ounces) devil's food *or* chocolate cake mix*
- 1-1/3 cups brewed coffee, room temperature
- 1/2 cup vegetable oil
- 3 eggs
- 1/2 cup semisweet chocolate chips
- FROSTING:
- 1/2 cup butter *or* margarine, softened
- 1/2 cup shortening
- 4 cups confectioners' sugar
- 3/4 cup baking cocoa
- 1/4 teaspoon almond extract
- 7 tablespoons brewed coffee, room temperature, *divided*
- 1/2 cup semisweet chocolate chips

In a mixing bowl, combine dry cake mix, coffee, oil and eggs; beat on low speed for 30 seconds. Beat on medium for 2 minutes. Pour into two greased and floured 8-in. round cake pans. Bake at 350° for 30-35 minutes or until a toothpick inserted near the center comes out clean. Cool in pans for 5 minutes; invert onto a wire rack. Sprinkle each cake with 1/4 cup chocolate chips; when melted, gently spread chocolate over cakes. Place cakes in the freezer. Meanwhile, for frosting, cream butter, shortening and sugar in a mixing bowl. Beat in cocoa and extract. Add 5 tablespoons coffee, 1 tablespoon at a time, beating until light and fluffy. Spread between layers and over the top and sides of cake. In a saucepan,

heat chocolate chips and remaining coffee until melted; stir until smooth. Pour over cake; carefully spread over the top, allowing it to drizzle down the sides. **Yield:** 10-12 servings. ***Editor's Note:** This recipe was tested with Duncan Hines devil's food cake mix.

German Chocolate Cookies

(Pictured at right)

A handy boxed cake mix hurries along the preparation of these chewy cookies studded with chips and raisins. I make them for our family reunion each year, and they always get rave reviews. —Leslie Henke, Louisville, Colorado

- 1 package (18-1/4 ounces) German chocolate cake mix
- 2 eggs
- 1/2 cup butter *or* margarine, melted
- 1/2 cup quick-cooking oats
- 1 cup (6 ounces) semisweet chocolate chips
- 1/2 cup raisins

In a mixing bowl, combine dry cake mix, eggs, butter and oats; mix well. Stir in the chocolate chips and raisins. Drop by heaping tablespoonfuls 2 in. apart onto ungreased baking sheets. Bake at 350° for 9-11 minutes or until set. Cool for 5 minutes; remove to wire racks. **Yield:** about 3-1/2 dozen.

Minty Chocolate Snowballs

If you like chocolate and mint, you'll love the winning flavor of these sweet make-ahead treats. Everyone enjoys their light and fluffy texture. I like that the recipe calls for five ingredients! —Julia Powell, Jerome, Idaho

- 2 cups whipping cream, whipped
- 1 package (16 ounces) miniature marshmallows
- 1/2 cup crushed peppermint candy
- 1/2 cup chopped pecans
- 1 package (9 ounces) chocolate wafers, crushed

In a bowl, combine the whipped cream, marshmallows, candy and pecans. Cover and chill for 3 hours or overnight. Place wafer crumbs in a shallow dish. Stir marshmallow mixture; shape by 1/2 cupfuls into balls. Roll in crumbs until coated. Chill until serving. **Yield:** 20 servings.

Leveling Cake Layers

Stacking layers for a layered cake is easier when the layers are level. When the cake is cool, use a long serrated knife to slice the high spot from the bottom layer of a two-layer cake or the bottom and middle layers of a three-layer cake. You can trim off the crown of the top layer or leave it for a domed effect.

Mocha Layer Cake
Chocolate Dream Dessert
German Chocolate Cookies

Munchable Snack Mix

My family loves to take along individual bags of this colorful fast-to-fix mixture when we go on long car trips. The sweet and salty flavors really taste good together.
—Lisa Keylor, Louisville, Kentucky

1 package (16 ounces) M&M's
1 can (12 ounces) salted peanuts
1 package (11 ounces) butterscotch chips
2 cups raisins
1 cup cashews

In a large bowl, combine all ingredients; mix well. Place in resealable plastic bags. **Yield:** about 10 cups.

Oatmeal Animal Crackers

(Pictured below)

When I was a child, we kids helped Mom cut these crispy crackers into all sorts of shapes. They're not too sweet, but sweet enough that we always wanted more.
—Bob Dittmar, Trout Run, Pennsylvania

2 cups sugar
2 cups old-fashioned oats
1 teaspoon baking soda
1/4 teaspoon salt
1/2 cup shortening
1/2 cup hot water

1 tablespoon vanilla extract
2 to 2-1/2 cups all-purpose flour

In a bowl, combine sugar, oats, baking soda and salt. Cut in shortening until crumbly. Add water and vanilla; stir until blended. Add enough flour to form a stiff dough. On a lightly floured surface, roll dough to 1/8-in. thickness. Cut into rectangles or use cookie cutters dipped in flour. Using a floured spatula, transfer to greased baking sheets. Bake at 350° for 8-10 minutes or until lightly browned. Cool on wire racks. **Yield:** about 4 dozen.

Rocky Road Brownies

(Pictured below)

Anyone who likes rocky road ice cream will like these moist, fudgy brownies loaded with goodies. They're great for children's parties. —Rita Lenes, Renton, Washington

3/4 cup butter *or* margarine
4 squares (1 ounce *each*) unsweetened chocolate
4 eggs
2 cups sugar
1 teaspoon vanilla extract
1 cup all-purpose flour
2 cups miniature marshmallows
1 cup (6 ounces) semisweet chocolate chips
1 cup chopped walnuts

Oatmeal Animal Crackers
Rocky Road Brownies

In a saucepan over low heat, melt butter and chocolate; cool for 10 minutes. In a mixing bowl, beat eggs, sugar and vanilla. Stir in chocolate mixture. Add flour and mix well. Spread into a greased 13-in. x 9-in. x 2-in. baking pan. Bake at 350° for 25-30 minutes or until a toothpick inserted near the center comes out clean. Sprinkle with marshmallows, chocolate chips and walnuts; bake 4 minutes longer. Cool on a wire rack. **Yield:** 2 dozen.

Sour Cream Chip Muffins
Chocolate Chip Oat Bars

Chocolate Chip Oat Bars

(Pictured at right)

I love to stir up a big panful of these chewy oat squares loaded with nuts and chocolate chips. The sweet bars are easy to prepare, and they cut cleanly when cool to make serving a breeze.
—Kim Wills, Sagamore Hills, Ohio

- 1 cup all-purpose flour
- 1 cup quick-cooking oats
- 3/4 cup packed brown sugar
- 1/2 cup cold butter *or* margarine
- 1 can (14 ounces) sweetened condensed milk
- 1 cup chopped pecans
- 1 cup (6 ounces) semisweet chocolate chips

In a bowl, combine the flour, oats and brown sugar. Cut in the butter until crumbly. Press half of the mixture into a greased 13-in. x 9-in. x 2-in. baking pan. Bake at 350° for 8-10 minutes. Remove from the oven. Spread condensed milk evenly over the crust. Sprinkle with pecans and chocolate chips. Top with remaining oat mixture and pat lightly. Bake for 25-30 minutes or until lightly browned. Cool in pan on a wire rack. **Yield:** about 2-1/2 dozen.

Sour Cream Chip Muffins

(Pictured above right)

Take one bite and you'll see why these tender muffins are the best I've ever tasted. Sour cream lends to their rich, moist flavor, while semisweet or mint chocolate chips make them a big hit with my family and friends. I hope you try them soon.
—Stephanie Moon
Green Bay, Wisconsin

- 1-1/2 cups all-purpose flour
- 2/3 cup sugar
- 3/4 teaspoon baking soda
- 3/4 teaspoon baking powder
- 1/4 teaspoon salt
- 1 egg
- 1 cup (8 ounces) sour cream
- 5 tablespoons butter *or* margarine, melted
- 1 teaspoon vanilla extract
- 3/4 cup mint *or* semisweet chocolate chips

In a bowl, combine the first five ingredients. In another bowl, combine the egg, sour cream, butter and vanilla. Stir into dry ingredients just until moistened. Fold in chocolate chips. Fill greased or paper-lined muffin cups three-fourths full. Bake at 350° for 18-20 minutes or until muffins test done. Cool for 10 minutes; remove from pan to a wire rack to cool completely. **Yield:** 1 dozen.

Crunchy No-Bake Bites

Chow mein noodles put the crunch in these easy no-bake bars. Their pretty golden coating gets plenty of flavor from honey, vanilla and cinnamon. They always disappear whenever I make them for bake sales.
—Peggy Key
Grant, Alabama

- 1 cup packed brown sugar
- 1/3 cup butter *or* margarine
- 1/3 cup honey
- 1/2 teaspoon ground cinnamon
- 1 teaspoon vanilla extract
- 2 cans (5 ounces *each*) chow mein noodles
- 1 can (6-1/2 ounces) salted peanuts (1-1/4 cups)

In a large saucepan, combine brown sugar, butter, honey and cinnamon. Bring to a boil over medium heat; cook and stir for 1 minute. Remove from the heat; stir in vanilla. Add noodles and peanuts; gently stir to coat. Transfer to a greased 9-in. square pan. Cover with waxed paper; press into an even layer. Let stand for at least 1 hour before cutting. **Yield:** 1-1/2 dozen.

Chocolate Peanut Supreme
Lime Cheesecake Pie
Citrus Mini Cakes

Lime Cheesecake Pie

(Pictured at left)

This light citrus pie combines two of our favorite dessert flavors—lime and cheesecake. It's the perfect treat on a hot day—and all the more inviting because you don't have to heat up the kitchen to prepare it. —*Vivian Eagleson Cumming, Georgia*

1 package (8 ounces) cream cheese, softened
1 can (14 ounces) sweetened condensed milk
1/3 cup lime juice
1-1/2 teaspoons vanilla extract
1 graham cracker crust (8 inches)
1 carton (8 ounces) frozen whipped topping, thawed
Lime slices and fresh mint, optional

In a mixing bowl, beat cream cheese until smooth. Add milk, lime juice and vanilla; beat until smooth. Pour into the crust. Refrigerate for 2 hours. Spread with whipped topping; refrigerate 1 hour longer. Garnish with lime and mint if desired. **Yield:** 6-8 servings.

Citrus Mini Cakes

(Pictured at left)

These moist, bite-size muffins are melt-in-your-mouth good. With their appealing look, they really dress up a party table. The recipe makes a big batch, so there's plenty to please a crowd. —*Linda Terrell, Palatka, Florida*

1 package (18-1/4 ounces) yellow cake mix
1-1/4 cups water
3 eggs
1/3 cup vegetable oil
3-1/2 cups confectioners' sugar
1/2 cup orange juice
1/4 cup lemon juice
Toasted chopped almonds

In a mixing bowl, combine cake mix, water, eggs and oil; beat on low speed for 30 seconds. Beat on medium for 2 minutes. Fill well-greased miniature muffin cups two-thirds full. Bake at 350° for 10-12 minutes or until a toothpick inserted near the center comes out clean. Meanwhile, in a bowl, combine sugar and juices until smooth. Cool cakes for 2 minutes; remove from pans. Immediately dip cakes into glaze, coating well. Place top down on wire racks; sprinkle with almonds. **Yield:** about 6 dozen.

Easy German Chocolate Cake

There's no need to frost this yummy chocolate cake. After baking, just turn the cake upside down onto a pretty platter—the coconut and pecan topping is already in place. —*Dawn Glenn, Johnson City, Tennessee*

1-1/3 cups flaked coconut
1 cup chopped pecans
1 package (18-1/4 ounces) German chocolate cake mix

1 package (8 ounces) cream cheese, softened
1/2 cup butter *or* margarine, softened
1 egg
4 cups confectioners' sugar

Sprinkle the coconut and pecans into a greased and floured 13-in. x 9-in. x 2-in. baking pan. Prepare cake mix according to package directions. Pour batter into prepared pan. In a mixing bowl, beat cream cheese and butter until smooth. Add egg and sugar; beat until smooth. Drop by tablespoonfuls over the batter. Carefully spread to within 1 in. of edges. Bake at 325° for 55-60 minutes or until a toothpick inserted near the center comes out clean. Cool for 10 minutes; invert onto a serving plate. **Yield:** 12-16 servings.

Chocolate Peanut Supreme

(Pictured at left)

One of our sons asked the cooks at his school to share the recipe for his favorite cafeteria dessert. With its peanutty crust and chocolate filling, it's still a favorite years later. —*Carole Ostlie, Chisago City, Minnesota*

1/2 cup chunky peanut butter
1/3 cup butter *or* margarine, melted
1-1/2 cups graham cracker crumbs (about 24 squares)
1/2 cup sugar
1 package (5.9 ounces) instant chocolate pudding mix
3 cups cold milk
1 carton (12 ounces) frozen whipped topping, thawed
1 cup chopped peanuts

In a bowl, combine peanut butter and butter. Stir in cracker crumbs and sugar; mix well. Press into a greased 13-in. x 9-in. x 2-in. dish. Prepare pudding with milk according to package directions; spoon over crust. Spread with whipped topping; sprinkle with peanuts. Cover and refrigerate for at least 1 hour or until set. Refrigerate leftovers. **Yield:** 12-16 servings.

Blueberry Parfaits

These cool and lightly sweet parfaits put a new twist on berries and cream. My guests marvel at the simple ingredients that go into this elegant dessert. —*Adeline Piscitelli, Sayreville, New Jersey*

1-1/2 cups (12 ounces) sour cream
1/2 cup packed brown sugar
1 tablespoon lemon juice
1 teaspoon grated lemon peel
1-1/2 cups fresh *or* frozen blueberries, thawed
Whipped cream

In a bowl, combine sour cream, brown sugar, lemon juice and peel. Cover and refrigerate. Just before serving, place half of the berries in dessert dishes or parfait glasses; top with half of the sour cream mixture. Repeat layers. Top with whipped cream. **Yield:** 4 servings.

Pretzel Sparklers

(Pictured at right)

These irresistible treats are simple enough for kids to make, and they sell well at bazaars. You can use different candy sprinkles to reflect other holiday themes. —Renee Schwebach
Dumont, Minnesota

8 squares (1 ounce *each*) white baking chocolate
1 package (10 ounces) pretzel rods
Colored candy stars *or* sprinkles

Place chocolate in a microwave-safe bowl; heat until melted. Dip each pretzel rod about halfway into chocolate; sprinkle with stars. Place on waxed paper to dry. **Yield:** about 2 dozen.

Peanut Butter Brownies

(Pictured at right)

I came up with these fudgy peanut butter brownies when I ran out of ingredients I needed for my usual recipe. They take less than 10 minutes to mix up. —Marcella Cremer
Decatur, Illinois

1 package (17-1/2 ounces) peanut butter cookie mix*
1/2 cup baking cocoa
2/3 cup chocolate syrup
1/4 cup butter *or* margarine, melted
1 egg
1/2 cup chopped walnuts *or* peanuts
FROSTING:
2 cups plus 2 tablespoons confectioners' sugar
1/2 cup chocolate syrup
1/4 cup baking cocoa
1/4 cup butter *or* margarine, melted
1/2 teaspoon vanilla extract

In a mixing bowl, combine the cookie mix and cocoa. Add chocolate syrup, butter and egg; beat until combined. Stir in the nuts. Spread into a greased 13-in. x 9-in. x 2-in. baking pan. Bake at 350° for 28-32 minutes or until a toothpick inserted near the center comes out clean. Cool on a wire rack. Meanwhile, combine the frosting ingredients in a bowl; stir until smooth. Spread over brownies. Cut into squares. **Yield:** 2 dozen. ***Editor's Note:** This recipe was tested with Betty Crocker peanut butter cookie mix.

Butterscotch Popcorn Bars

Dotted with peanuts and raisins, these chewy squares are easy to mix up on the stovetop when I know the grandchildren are on the way. —Carol Stone
Waverly, Tennessee

2 quarts unsalted popped popcorn
1 cup salted peanuts

Pretzel Sparklers
Peanut Butter Brownies

1 cup raisins
1/2 cup butter *or* margarine
1 package (10-1/2 ounces) miniature marshmallows
1 cup butterscotch chips

In a large bowl, combine the popcorn, peanuts and raisins. In a large saucepan over low heat, melt butter. Stir in the marshmallows and chips until melted and smooth. Pour over popcorn mixture and stir until evenly coated. Immediately pour into a greased 13-in. x 9-in. x 2-in. pan and press down evenly. Cool before cutting. **Yield:** 3 dozen.

Couldn't Be Simpler Bars

Every time I take these sweet, chewy bars to a gathering or serve them to guests, I get lots of compliments. They're easy to make, too—just sprinkle a few ingredients in a pan and bake. —Kerry Bouchard, Augusta, Montana

1/2 cup butter (no substitutes), melted
1 cup graham cracker crumbs (about 16 squares)
1 cup flaked coconut
1 cup semisweet chocolate chips
1 cup butterscotch chips
1 can (14 ounces) sweetened condensed milk
1 cup chopped walnuts

Pour butter into a greased 13-in. x 9-in. x 2-in. baking pan. Sprinkle with crumbs and coconut. Top with chips. Pour milk over all. Sprinkle with walnuts. Bake at 350° for 23-28 minutes or until browned and bubbly. Cool completely before cutting. **Yield:** about 3-1/2 dozen.

Bake 2-3 minutes longer or until the marshmallows begin to melt. Cool on a wire rack before cutting. **Yield:** 3-1/2 dozen.

Fun Marshmallow Bars

(Pictured below)

These colorful kid-tested treats go fast at bake sales. Cake mix really cuts your prep time. —Debbie Brunssen
Randolph, Nebraska

> 1 package (18-1/4 ounces) devil's food cake mix
> 1/4 cup butter *or* margarine, melted
> 1/4 cup water
> 1 egg
> 3 cups miniature marshmallows
> 1 cup plain M&M's
> 1/2 cup chopped peanuts

In a mixing bowl, combine dry cake mix, butter, water and egg; mix well. Press into a greased 13-in. x 9-in. x 2-in. baking pan. Bake at 375° for 20-22 minutes or until a toothpick inserted near the center comes out clean. Sprinkle with marshmallows, M&M's and peanuts.

Snickers Cookies

(Pictured below)

Though you wouldn't know by looking, you'll find a sweet surprise inside these cookies. My mother got this recipe from a fellow teacher at her school. It's a great way to dress up refrigerated cookie dough. —Kari Pease
Conconully, Washington

> 1 tube (18 ounces) refrigerated chocolate chip cookie dough*
> 24 to 30 bite-size Snickers candy bars

Cut dough into 1/4-in.-thick slices. Place a candy bar on each slice and wrap dough around it. Place 2 in. apart on ungreased baking sheets. Bake at 350° for 8-10 minutes or until lightly browned. Cool on wire racks. **Yield:** 2 to 2-1/2 dozen. ***Editor's Note:** 2 cups of any chocolate chip cookie dough can be substituted for the refrigerated dough. Use 1 tablespoon of dough for each cookie.

**Snickers Cookies
Fun Marshmallow Bars**

Banana Snack Cake

(Pictured at right and on page 202)

I often make this moist banana cake for birthdays. The recipe is good for making cupcakes, too—they taste great even without the frosting. —Dawn Fagerstrom
Warren, Minnesota

  1/2 cup shortening
  3/4 cup packed brown sugar
  1/2 cup sugar
    2 eggs
    1 cup mashed ripe bananas (2 to 3 medium)
    1 teaspoon vanilla extract
    2 cups all-purpose *or* whole wheat flour
    1 teaspoon baking soda
    1 teaspoon salt
  1/2 cup buttermilk
  1/2 cup chopped nuts
FROSTING (optional):
  1/2 cup packed brown sugar
  1/4 cup butter *or* margarine
    6 tablespoons milk
2-1/2 to 3 cups confectioners' sugar

In a mixing bowl, cream the shortening and sugars. Add eggs, one at a time, beating well after each addition. Beat in bananas and vanilla. Combine the flour, baking soda and salt; add to the creamed mixture alternately with buttermilk. Stir in nuts. Pour into a greased 13-in. x 9-in. x 2-in. baking pan. Bake at 350° for 25-30 minutes or until a toothpick inserted near the center comes out clean. Cool on a wire rack. If desired for frosting, combine the brown sugar, butter and milk in a saucepan. Bring to a boil over medium heat; boil and stir for 2 minutes. Remove from the heat; cool to lukewarm. Gradually beat in confectioners' sugar until frosting reaches spreading consistency. Frost the cooled cake. **Yield:** 12 servings.

Diamond Bars

(Pictured at right and on page 203)

You'll need just seven basic ingredients to stir up a batch of these delicious diamond-shaped bars. They're simple to fix for a bake sale or when your kids want a snack. —Lois Lipker, Ormond Beach, Florida

    1 cup butter *or* margarine, softened
    1 cup packed brown sugar
    2 egg yolks
    2 cups all-purpose flour
    2 cups (12 ounces) semisweet chocolate chips
    1 cup chopped walnuts
    1 cup flaked coconut

In a mixing bowl, cream the butter and brown sugar. Add egg yolks; beat well. Stir in flour and mix well. Spread into a greased 15-in. x 10-in. x 1-in. baking pan. Bake at 325° for 20-25 minutes or until golden brown. Sprinkle with chocolate chips. Return to the oven until chips are melted, about 1 minute. Spread chocolate with an icing knife. Sprinkle with walnuts and co-

conut. Cool on a wire rack. Cut into diamond shapes. **Yield:** 5 dozen.

Frosty Cranberry Pie

It's nice to have this light, not-too-sweet pie in the freezer when unexpected guests stop over for coffee. It's so easy to put together, and everyone always asks for the recipe. —Mildred Skrha, Oak Brook, Illinois

    1 package (8 ounces) cream cheese, softened
    1 cup confectioners' sugar
    1 can (16 ounces) whole-berry cranberry sauce
    1 carton (8 ounces) frozen whipped topping, thawed
    2 pastry shells (9 inches), baked*
Additional whipped topping, optional
Slivered almonds, toasted, optional

In a mixing bowl, beat the cream cheese and sugar. Stir in cranberry sauce. Fold in the whipped topping. Spoon into crusts. Cover and freeze for up to 3 months. Remove from the freezer 10-15 minutes before serving. Garnish with whipped topping and almonds if desired. **Yield:** 2 pies (6-8 servings each). ***Editor's Note:** Shortbread or graham cracker crusts may be substituted for the pastry shells.

Angel Berry Tunnel Cake

(Pictured at right and on page 203)

This tasty cake with berries is a light family favorite for summer. To save myself time, I rely on a purchased angel food cake and frozen whipped topping. —Ruth Marie Lyons
Boulder, Colorado

    1 prepared angel food cake (10 inches)
1-1/2 cups fresh *or* frozen raspberries, thawed
       and drained
1-1/2 cups fresh *or* frozen blueberries
    8 cups whipped topping
Additional berries, optional

With a serrated knife, slice off the top 1/2 in. of the cake; set aside. Cut a tunnel about 2 in. deep in the cake, leaving a 3/4-in. shell. Remove cake from tunnel; cut into 1-in. cubes. Combine cake cubes, berries and half of the whipped topping; spoon into tunnel. Replace cake top. Frost with remaining whipped topping. Garnish with berries if desired. Refrigerate until serving. **Yield:** 12 servings.

Chilled and Chopped

When a recipe calls for cranberries and you're using frozen ones, there's no need to take the time to thaw them first. In fact, if the berries must be chopped, it's even easier to chop them right from the freezer using a knife or a food processor before adding them to the recipe.

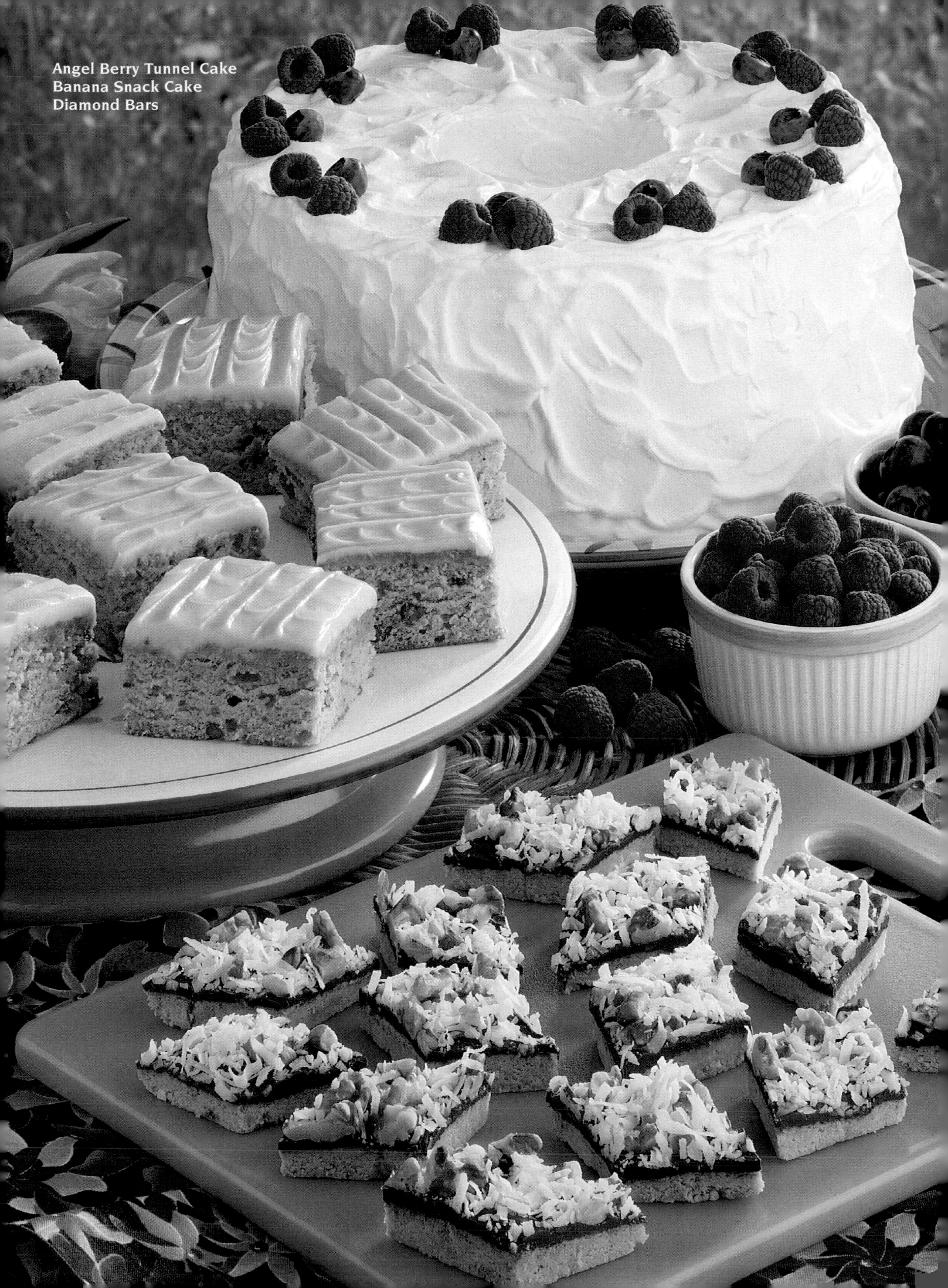

Angel Berry Tunnel Cake
Banana Snack Cake
Diamond Bars

**Peanut Butter Cocoa Fudge
Easy Gingerbread Cutouts**

Peanut Butter Cocoa Fudge

(Pictured above)

My brother-in-law gave me the recipe for this fast five-ingredient fudge that combines two classic flavors. It makes a great gift. —Georgianna Thompson
Boothwyn, Pennsylvania

    1 cup plus 3 tablespoons chunky peanut butter
    1 cup butter (no substitutes)
3-1/2 cups confectioners' sugar
    3 tablespoons baking cocoa
    1 tablespoon vanilla extract

In a saucepan, combine the peanut butter and butter. Cook and stir over medium heat until blended. Remove from the heat; stir in confectioners' sugar, cocoa and vanilla. Spread into a buttered 8-in. square pan. Freeze for 30 minutes or just until firm before cutting into squares. Store at room temperature. **Yield:** about 2 pounds.

Easy Gingerbread Cutouts

(Pictured above)

I rely on this tried-and-true recipe during the holidays. The cream cheese frosting complements the cookies' gingery flavor and sets up nicely for easy packaging and stacking. —Sandy McKenzie, Braham, Minnesota

    1 package (18-1/4 ounces) spice cake mix
3/4 cup all-purpose flour
    2 eggs

1/3 cup vegetable oil
1/3 cup molasses
    2 teaspoons ground ginger
3/4 cup canned cream cheese frosting, warmed
    slightly
Red-hot candies

In a mixing bowl, combine dry cake mix, flour, eggs, oil, molasses and ginger; mix well. Refrigerate for 30 minutes or until easy to handle. On a floured surface, roll out dough to 1/8-in. thickness. Cut with 5-in. cookie cutters

Packing Cookies for Shipping

1 Drop cookies pass the "drop test" when two cookies are placed with their bottoms together and wrapped in plastic wrap. They stay fresher and are less likely to crumble when wrapped this way or individually.

2 Line a tin or a box with crumpled waxed paper to help cushion the cookies. Fill the container with cookies to within 1 inch of the top. Add more crumpled waxed paper or bubble wrap at the top to cushion the cookies and prevent them from shifting during shipping.

dipped in flour. Place 3 in. apart on ungreased baking sheets. Bake at 375° for 7-10 minutes or until edges are firm and bottom is lightly browned. Remove to wire racks to cool. Decorate with cream cheese frosting as desired. Use red-hots for eyes, nose and buttons. **Yield:** about 2-1/2 dozen.

Candy Corn Cupcakes

(Pictured below right)

These moist tender white cupcakes are perfect for any occasion. For fast yet fabulous results anytime of year, choose candy decorations appropriate to the season.
—Renee Schwebach, Dumont, Minnesota

1/2 cup shortening
1-1/2 cups sugar
  1 teaspoon vanilla extract
  2 cups all-purpose flour
3-1/2 teaspoons baking powder
  1 teaspoon salt
  1 cup milk
  4 egg whites
Frosting of your choice
Candy corn *or* other decorations

In a mixing bowl, cream shortening and sugar. Beat in vanilla. Combine flour, baking powder and salt; add to the creamed mixture alternately with milk. Beat in the egg whites. Fill greased or paper-lined muffin cups half full. Bake at 350° for 18-22 minutes or until a toothpick inserted near the center comes out clean. Cool for 10 minutes before removing from pans to wire racks. Frost cooled cupcakes; decorate as desired. **Yield:** 2 dozen.

Pumpkin Chip Drops

With a combination of pumpkin, oats and chocolate chips, these soft drop cookies make delightful fall treats. I sometimes make them into bars and increase the baking time. —Regina Stock
Topeka, Kansas

  1 cup butter *or* margarine, softened
  1 cup sugar
  1 cup packed brown sugar
  1 egg
  1 teaspoon vanilla extract
  2 cups all-purpose flour
  1 cup quick-cooking oats
  1 teaspoon baking soda
  1 teaspoon ground cinnamon
1/2 teaspoon salt
  1 cup cooked *or* canned pumpkin
  1 cup (6 ounces) semisweet chocolate chips

In a mixing bowl, cream the butter and sugars. Beat in egg and vanilla. Combine flour, oats, baking soda, cinnamon and salt; add to the creamed mixture alternately with pumpkin. Stir in the chocolate chips. Drop by tablespoonfuls

2 in. apart onto greased baking sheets. Bake at 350° for 9-12 minutes or until golden brown. Cool on wire racks. **Yield:** 4 dozen.

Cookie Sticks

(Pictured below)

If you have a craving for cookies and you want them now, these yummy strips take just a few minutes to make from start to finish. Nothing could be quicker!
—Kathy Zielicke, Fond du Lac, Wisconsin

1/2 cup vegetable oil
1/2 cup sugar
1/2 cup packed brown sugar
  1 egg
  1 teaspoon vanilla extract
1-1/2 cups all-purpose flour
1/2 teaspoon baking soda
1/2 teaspoon salt
  1 cup (6 ounces) semisweet chocolate chips
1/2 cup chopped walnuts, optional

In a mixing bowl, combine the oil, sugars, egg and vanilla; mix well. Combine flour, baking soda and salt; gradually add to sugar mixture. Divide dough in half. On a greased baking sheet, shape each portion into a 15-in. x 3-in. rectangle about 3 in. apart. Sprinkle chocolate chips and nuts if desired over dough; press lightly. Bake at 375° for 6-7 minutes. (Bake for 8-9 minutes for crispier cookies.) Cool for 5 minutes. Cut with a serrated knife into 1-in. strips; remove to wire racks to cool. **Yield:** about 3 dozen.

Cookie Sticks
Candy Corn
Cupcakes

Banana Cream Cheese Pie
Peanut Butter Cup Cupcakes
Brownie Mounds

Peanut Butter Cup Cupcakes

(Pictured at left)

Kids love these rich, yummy cupcakes in school lunches or at parties. They're so easy to make because the mini peanut butter cups eliminate the need to frost them.
—Heidi Harrington, Steuben, Maine

1/3 cup shortening
1/3 cup peanut butter
1-1/4 cups packed brown sugar
2 eggs
1 teaspoon vanilla extract
1-3/4 cups all-purpose flour
1-3/4 teaspoons baking powder
1 teaspoon salt
1 cup milk
16 miniature peanut butter cups

In a mixing bowl, cream the shortening, peanut butter and brown sugar. Add eggs and vanilla; mix well. Combine flour, baking powder and salt; add to creamed mixture alternately with milk. Fill paper-lined muffin cups with 1/4 cup of batter. Press a peanut butter cup into the center of each until top edge is even with batter. Bake at 350° for 22-24 minutes or until a toothpick inserted on an angle toward the center comes out clean. **Yield:** 16 cupcakes.

Brownie Mounds

(Pictured at left)

If you crave brownies but not the longer baking time, try these quick chocolaty cookies. They're good any time of year.
—Mary Turner, Blountville, Tennessee

1/3 cup butter *or* margarine, softened
3/4 cup sugar
1/3 cup light corn syrup
1 egg
3 squares (1 ounce *each*) unsweetened chocolate, melted
1 teaspoon vanilla extract
1-2/3 cups all-purpose flour
1/2 teaspoon baking powder
1/4 teaspoon salt
1/2 cup chopped walnuts

In a mixing bowl, cream butter and sugar. Add corn syrup and egg; beat well. Stir in chocolate and vanilla. Combine flour, baking powder and salt; add to chocolate mixture. Stir in walnuts. Drop by tablespoonfuls 2 in. apart onto greased baking sheets. Bake at 350° for

---

Making Cupcakes

To make the same-size cupcakes, I use a solid plastic ice cream scoop to dip into the batter. It prevents having pans of cupcakes with some cups half full and others overflowing. —Beth Lytle, Old Fort, North Carolina

---

10-12 minutes or until edges are firm. Remove to wire racks to cool. **Yield:** 3 dozen.

Banana Cream Cheese Pie

(Pictured at left)

Whenever I make this creamy banana pie topped with a thick strawberry sauce, everyone looks forward to dessert.
—Zahra Sulemanji, Houston, Texas

1 package (8 ounces) cream cheese, softened
1/2 cup sugar
1 cup mashed ripe bananas (2 to 3 medium)
1 teaspoon lemon juice
1 carton (8 ounces) frozen whipped topping, thawed
1 graham cracker crust (9 inches)
STRAWBERRY TOPPING:
2 tablespoons sugar
1 teaspoon cornstarch
1-1/4 cups sliced fresh strawberries
5 drops red food coloring, optional

In a bowl, beat cream cheese and sugar until smooth. Combine bananas and lemon juice; add to cream cheese mixture. Fold in whipped topping. Pour into crust. Cover and refrigerate for 1 hour or until set. In a saucepan, combine sugar and cornstarch. Stir in strawberries and food coloring if desired. Let stand for 5 minutes. Bring to a boil. Reduce heat; cook and stir for 2 minutes or until thickened. Cool. Drizzle some over pie. Cut into wedges; serve with remaining topping. **Yield:** 6-8 servings.

Grape Pear Crisp

You'll be pleasantly surprised by this unusual fruit combination. Over the years, we have enjoyed this dessert topped with whipped cream or ice cream. In fact, I've worn out the recipe card several times.
—Donna Mosher, Augusta, Montana

1-1/2 cups halved seedless grapes
1 can (16 ounces) sliced pears, drained
1/2 cup plus 2 tablespoons all-purpose flour, *divided*
1/4 teaspoon almond extract
1/3 cup packed brown sugar
1/2 teaspoon salt
1/4 teaspoon ground cinnamon
1/4 teaspoon ground nutmeg
1/4 cup cold butter *or* margarine
1/2 cup finely chopped walnuts

In a bowl, combine the grapes, pears, 2 tablespoons flour and extract until blended. Spoon into a lightly greased 8-in. square baking dish. In another bowl, combine brown sugar, salt, cinnamon, nutmeg and remaining flour; cut in butter until mixture resembles coarse crumbs. Stir in walnuts; sprinkle over fruit. Bake at 375° for 30 minutes or until lightly browned. **Yield:** 6-8 servings.

Walnut Dessert Sauce

(Pictured at right)

We have two walnut trees in our front yard, so I always have plenty of nuts for this sweet sauce. It's one of my son's favorites. —Susan Zeidler, Lancaster, Pennsylvania

3/4 cup light corn syrup
1/2 cup maple syrup
1/4 cup sugar
1/4 cup water
1-1/4 cups coarsely chopped walnuts
Ice cream *or* pound cake

In a heavy saucepan, combine the first four ingredients; bring to a boil, stirring constantly. Stir in walnuts. Reduce heat; simmer, uncovered, for 25 minutes. Serve warm over ice cream or pound cake. **Yield:** 2 cups.

Snow-Covered Crescents

These tasty almond cookies coated in powdered sugar are quick, easy and delicious. —Dorothy Smith
El Dorado, Arkansas

1 cup butter (no substitutes), softened
3/4 cup confectioners' sugar
1 teaspoon almond extract
1-3/4 cups all-purpose flour
1 cup old-fashioned oats
1/2 cup finely chopped almonds
1/4 teaspoon salt
Additional confectioners' sugar

In a mixing bowl, cream butter and confectioners' sugar. Beat in extract. Combine flour, oats, almonds and salt; gradually add to the creamed mixture. Roll level tablespoonfuls of dough into ropes. Place 2 in. apart on ungreased baking sheets and curve into crescents. Bake at 325° for 14-16 minutes or until lightly browned. Remove to wire racks to cool; roll in additional confectioners' sugar. **Yield:** about 3 dozen.

Favorite Bundt Cake

(Pictured at right)

To satisfy all of the chocolate lovers I know, I made some changes to a recipe I clipped out from the newspaper. The result is this simple-to-fix cake that always turns out very moist and tasty every time. —Karen Swanson
McHenry, Illinois

1 package (18-1/4 ounces) yellow cake mix
1 package (3.9 ounces) instant chocolate pudding mix
1/2 cup sugar
1 cup (8 ounces) sour cream
3/4 cup vegetable oil
3/4 cup water
4 eggs
1 cup (6 ounces) semisweet chocolate chips
2 squares (1 ounce *each*) white baking chocolate

In a mixing bowl, combine dry cake and pudding mixes and sugar. Add the sour cream, oil and water; mix well. Add eggs, one at a time, beating well after each addition. Stir in chocolate chips. Pour into a greased and floured 12-cup fluted tube pan. Bake at 350° for 50-55 minutes or until a toothpick inserted near the center comes out clean. Cool for 10 minutes; remove from pan to a wire rack to cool completely. In a microwave or double boiler, melt the white chocolate; drizzle over cake. **Yield:** 12-16 servings.

Cranberry Icebox Cookies

(Pictured at right)

These crisp cookies are especially popular at Thanksgiving and Christmas with a cup of hot tea or coffee. It's convenient to bake a batch, too, because you can store the dough in the fridge until needed. —Gloria Anderson
Paso Robles, California

1-1/4 cups butter (no substitutes), softened
1 cup packed brown sugar
2/3 cup sugar
2 eggs
1 teaspoon vanilla extract
1/4 teaspoon almond extract
3-1/4 cups all-purpose flour
1 teaspoon baking powder
1/2 teaspoon salt
1/4 teaspoon baking soda
1 cup chopped walnuts
2 cups chopped fresh *or* frozen cranberries

In a mixing bowl, cream butter and sugars. Add eggs, one at a time, beating well after each addition. Beat in extracts. Combine the flour, baking powder, salt and baking soda; gradually add to the creamed mixture. Stir in walnuts. Carefully stir in cranberries. Shape into three 7-in. rolls; wrap each roll in plastic wrap and refrigerate for 4 hours or overnight. Cut into 1/4-in. slices and place 1 in. apart on ungreased baking sheets. Bake at 375° for 10-12 minutes or until golden brown. Cool on wire racks. **Yield:** 5-1/2 dozen.

Cookie and Bar Basics

- My family enjoys several cookie recipes that call for coating the treats with confectioners' sugar. To save time and eliminate the mess, I place the sugar in a resealable plastic bag, add the cooled cookies and turn the bag a couple of times. I can sugar-coat the cookies without getting my fingers sticky.
—Cheryl Polen, Raleigh, North Carolina

- When making bar cookies such as oatmeal layer bars or marshmallow treats, I use waxed paper to press the mixture into the pan. It produces an even layer and keeps your hands clean. —Laura Johnson
Largo, Florida

- A pizza cutter makes cutting brownies a breeze. You can cut the pieces more evenly, and the brownies won't stick to the cutter. It works well with fudge, too. —Edna Caldwell, Mont Vernon, New Hampshire

Favorite Bundt Cake
Cranberry Icebox Cookies
Walnut Dessert Sauce

COOKIES

Raspberry Trifle
Fudge-Topped Shortbread
Cream Cheese Candies

Cream Cheese Candies

(Pictured at left)

This four-ingredient recipe was recommended by friends and shared throughout our neighborhood. The rich, simple mints are often seen at wedding receptions and graduation parties, and they make a perfect last-minute addition to holiday candy trays.
—Katie Koziolek, Hartland, Minnesota

  1 package (3 ounces) cream cheese, softened
1/4 teaspoon peppermint *or* almond extract
  3 cups confectioners' sugar
Green and red colored sugar, optional

In a small mixing bowl, combine cream cheese and extract. Beat in 1-1/2 cups confectioners' sugar. Knead in remaining confectioners' sugar until smooth. Shape into 1/2-in. balls. Roll in colored sugar if desired. Place on ungreased baking sheets and flatten with a fork. Let stand for 1 hour to harden. Store in an airtight container in the refrigerator. **Yield:** 6 dozen.

Fudge-Topped Shortbread

(Pictured at left)

This combination of buttery shortbread and sweet chocolate is wonderful. Whenever I make it, only the crumbs are left behind. Be sure to cut these into small squares because they're very rich. —Valarie Wheeler, De Witt, Michigan

  1 cup butter (no substitutes), softened
1/2 cup confectioners' sugar
1/4 teaspoon salt
1-1/4 cups all-purpose flour
  1 can (14 ounces) sweetened condensed milk
  2 cups (12 ounces) semisweet chocolate chips
1/2 teaspoon almond extract
1/3 cup sliced almonds, toasted

In a mixing bowl, cream butter, sugar and salt until fluffy. Gradually beat in flour. Spread into a greased 13-in. x 9-in. x 2-in. baking pan. Bake at 350° for 16-20 minutes or until lightly browned. In a microwave-safe bowl, combine condensed milk and chocolate chips. Microwave, uncovered, on high for 1-2 minutes or until chips are melted; stir until smooth. Stir in extract. Spread over the shortbread. Sprinkle with almonds and press down. Refrigerate until firm. Cut into squares. **Yield:** 4 dozen.

Pecan Grahams

Years ago, I was eager to enter a recipe contest I'd read about. I went to my pantry and threw together these nutty cookies. Although they didn't win, they've been a hit with my family and friends ever since! —June Russell
Green Cove Springs, Florida

1/2 cup shortening
1/2 cup sugar
1/2 cup packed brown sugar
  1 egg
  1 cup all-purpose flour
1/2 teaspoon baking powder
1/2 teaspoon baking soda
1/4 teaspoon salt
  1 cup graham cracker crumbs (about 16 squares)
  1 cup ground pecans
54 to 60 pecan halves

In a mixing bowl, cream shortening and sugars. Add egg and mix well. Combine flour, baking powder, baking soda and salt; add to the creamed mixture. Stir in cracker crumbs and ground pecans; mix well. Drop by rounded teaspoonfuls 2 in. apart onto ungreased baking sheets. Place a pecan half in the center of each cookie; press down lightly. Bake at 350° for 9-11 minutes or until lightly browned. Cool for 2 minutes before removing to wire racks. **Yield:** about 4-1/2 dozen.

Raspberry Trifle

(Pictured at left)

This lovely layered dessert is my husband's favorite. I always make it for our Christmas dinner, but it's excellent after any special meal.
—Karen Bourne, Magrath, Alberta

  1 loaf (10-3/4 ounces) frozen pound cake
1-1/2 cups whipping cream
3/4 cup sugar, *divided*
  2 packages (8 ounces *each*) cream cheese, softened
  2 teaspoons lemon juice
1-1/2 teaspoons vanilla extract
  2 packages (10 ounces *each*) frozen sweetened raspberries, thawed
  2 tablespoons baking cocoa
Fresh raspberries, optional

Slice cake into 18-20 slices about 1/2 in. thick; set aside. In a mixing bowl, beat cream with 1/4 cup sugar until stiff peaks form. In another mixing bowl, beat cream cheese, lemon juice, vanilla and the remaining sugar. Fold in 2 cups of the whipped cream; set remaining whipped cream aside for topping. Drain raspberries, reserving juice; set berries aside. Line the bottom of a 3-qt. glass bowl with a third of the cake slices. Drizzle with some of the raspberry juice. Spread with a fourth of the cream cheese mixture. Sift a fourth of the cocoa over the top. Sprinkle with a third of the berries. Repeat layers twice. Top with the remaining cream cheese mixture, whipped cream and sifted cocoa. Cover and refrigerate for 4 hours or overnight. Garnish with fresh raspberries if desired. **Yield:** 12-15 servings.

Crumbly Advice

To make crumbs from graham crackers, I place them in a shallow pan, then use a potato masher to crush a small section at a time. No muss, no fuss!
—Rene Zummo, Waukesha, Wisconsin

Chapter 14

Fast, Delicious...and Nutritious

LOOKING for fast-to-fix dishes that fit today's healthy lifestyle? The lighter fare featured here fits right in if you're counting calories or trying to reduce sugar or fat in your diet (*and* if you're doing all this while keeping an eye on the clock).

That's because each of these rapid recipes is lower in fat, sugar or salt and includes Nutritional Analysis and Diabetic Exchanges.

Anyone on a special diet—and even those who aren't—will enjoy these delicious and nutritious dishes.

(For a complete listing of foods that are lower in fat, sugar or salt, refer to the Nutritional Analysis Recipes Index on page 354.)

GOOD-FOR-YOU FOODS. Clockwise from bottom: Applesauce Gelatin Squares, Hearty Brunch Potatoes and Hash Brown Cheese Omelet (all recipes on pp. 234 and 235).

Soft Chicken Tacos

(Pictured below)

I came up with this chicken and bean filling for tacos since my husband needs to watch his cholesterol level. Sliced radishes are unique. —Ruth Peterson, Jenison, Michigan

- 1 pound boneless skinless chicken breasts, cut into cubes
- 1 can (15 ounces) black beans, rinsed and drained
- 1 cup salsa
- 1 tablespoon taco seasoning
- 6 fat-free flour tortillas (8 inches), warmed
- OPTIONAL TOPPINGS: Shredded lettuce, reduced-fat shredded cheddar cheese, sliced radishes, diced tomatoes, sliced green onions and non-fat sour cream

In a skillet that has been coated with nonstick cooking spray, cook chicken until juices run clear. Add beans, salsa and taco seasoning; heat through. Spoon the chicken mixture down the center of each tortilla. Garnish with toppings of your choice. **Yield:** 6 servings. **Nutritional Analysis:** One taco (calculated without toppings) equals 271 calories, 1,077 mg sodium, 42 mg cholesterol, 39 gm carbohydrate, 23 gm protein, 2 gm fat. **Diabetic Exchanges:** 2-1/2 starch, 2 very lean meat.

Southwestern Hominy

(Pictured below)

This colorful cheese-topped dish gets its great flavor from green chilies and a variety of seasonings. It's sure to add pizzazz to most any meal. —Martha Holland Reno, Nevada

- 1 cup chopped onion
- 2 garlic cloves, minced
- 2 cans (15-1/2 ounces *each*) yellow hominy, drained
- 2 cups chopped tomatoes
- 1 can (4 ounces) chopped green chilies
- 1 teaspoon chili powder
- 1/2 teaspoon ground cumin
- 1/4 teaspoon pepper
- 1/2 cup reduced-fat shredded cheddar cheese

In a large skillet that has been coated with nonstick cooking spray, saute onion and garlic until tender. Add the hominy, tomatoes, chilies, chili powder, cumin and pepper; mix gently. Transfer to a 2-qt. baking dish that has been coated with nonstick cooking spray. Bake, uncovered, at 350° for 25 minutes. Sprinkle with cheese; bake 5 minutes longer or until the cheese is melted. **Yield:** 12 servings. **Nutritional Analysis:** One 1/2-cup

Cappuccino Pudding
Southwestern Hominy
Soft Chicken Tacos

serving equals 76 calories, 223 mg sodium, 1 mg cholesterol, 14 gm carbohydrate, 3 gm protein, 1 gm fat. **Diabetic Exchange:** 1 starch.

Gingered Pepper Steak

This wonderfully tender steak is a treat even for folks not watching their diet. When my mother-in-law shared the recipe, she said it cooks up in no time...and she was right! —Susan Adair, Muncie, Indiana

- 1/4 cup light soy sauce
- 1 tablespoon cider *or* white wine vinegar
- 2 teaspoons sugar
- 2 teaspoons cornstarch
- 1/4 teaspoon ground ginger
- 1 pound flank steak, thinly sliced
- 2 medium green peppers, julienned
- 1 teaspoon vegetable oil

Hot cooked rice

In a large bowl, combine soy sauce, vinegar, sugar, cornstarch and ginger until smooth. Add steak; toss to coat. In a skillet or wok, stir-fry green peppers in oil until crisp-tender, about 3 minutes. Remove with a slotted spoon and keep warm. Add beef with marinade to pan; stir-fry for 3 minutes or until the meat reaches desired doneness. Return peppers to pan; heat through. Serve over rice. **Yield:** 4 servings. **Nutritional Analysis:** One 1-cup serving (calculated without rice) equals 236 calories, 579 mg sodium, 59 mg cholesterol, 10 gm carbohydrate, 26 gm protein, 10 gm fat. **Diabetic Exchanges:** 3 lean meat, 2 vegetable.

Double Chili Cheese Dip

Cappuccino Pudding

(Pictured at left)

With its fun combination of chocolate, coffee and cinnamon, this smooth dessert is one of my favorites. A garnish of whipped topping and chocolate wafer crumbs provides additional appeal.
—Cindy Bertrand
Floydada, Texas

- 4 teaspoons instant coffee granules
- 1 tablespoon boiling water
- 1-1/2 cups cold skim milk
- 1 package (1.4 ounces) instant sugar-free chocolate pudding mix
- 1/2 teaspoon ground cinnamon
- 1 cup light whipped topping

Additional whipped topping and chocolate wafer crumbs, optional

Dissolve coffee in water; set aside. In a mixing bowl, combine milk, pudding mix and cinnamon. Beat on low speed for 2 minutes. Stir in coffee. Fold in whipped topping. Spoon into serving dishes. Garnish with whipped topping and wafer crumbs if desired. **Yield:** 4 servings. **Nutritional Analysis:** One 1/2-cup serving (calculated without garnish) equals 105 calories, 48 mg sodium, 2 mg cholesterol, 17 gm carbohydrate, 3 gm protein, 2 gm fat. **Diabetic Exchanges:** 1/2 fat, 1/2 fruit, 1/2 skim milk.

Double Chili Cheese Dip

(Pictured above)

This rich and zesty dip for tortilla chips can be made in a jiffy when the munchies strike. My husband and I often have it as a late-night snack after the kids are all in bed.
—Linda Keller, Sylvania, Ohio

- 1 package (8 ounces) light cream cheese, softened
- 1 can (15 ounces) turkey chili without beans
- 4 green onions, thinly sliced
- 3 tablespoons chopped green chilies
- 1/4 cup sliced ripe olives, optional
- 1 cup (4 ounces) shredded reduced-fat cheddar cheese

Baked tortilla chips

Spread cream cheese into a 9-in. pie plate or quiche dish that has been coated with nonstick cooking spray. Top with chili, onions, chilies and olives if desired. Sprinkle with cheese. Bake, uncovered, at 350° for 15-20 minutes or until the cheese is melted. Serve with tortilla chips. **Yield:** 8 servings. **Nutritional Analysis:** One serving (calculated without olives and tortilla chips) equals 189 calories, 502 mg sodium, 35 mg cholesterol, 5 gm carbohydrate, 12 gm protein, 14 gm fat. **Diabetic Exchanges:** 1-1/2 fat, 1 meat, 1/2 starch.

Low-Fat Cherry Cobbler

I love to cook and especially enjoy sharing the results with family and friends. This is a lighter version of my cherry cobbler. —Mary Dudek, Alliance, Ohio

> 1 cup fat-free vanilla yogurt
> 1-1/2 cups sugar
> 6 egg whites
> 2 cups all-purpose flour
> 2 teaspoons baking powder
> 1 can (20 ounces) light cherry pie filling

In a mixing bowl, beat yogurt and sugar. Add egg whites; mix well. Combine flour and baking powder; stir into yogurt mixture. Pour into a 13-in. x 9-in. x 2-in. baking pan coated with nonstick cooking spray. Spoon cherry filling on top. Bake at 350° for 40-50 minutes or until filling is bubbly and a toothpick inserted near the center comes out clean. **Yield:** 15 servings. **Nutritional Analysis:** One serving equals 190 calories, 100 mg sodium, trace cholesterol, 43 gm carbohydrate, 4 gm protein, trace fat. **Diabetic Exchanges:** 1-1/2 starch, 1-1/2 fruit.

Kiwi Ice

(Pictured below)

I need just five ingredients to blend together this tart, refreshing frozen treat. A serving is especially pretty garnished with kiwi and orange slices. —Shirley Glaab
Hattiesburg, Mississippi

Kiwi Ice

> 2 cups unsweetened apple juice
> 1 tablespoon lemon juice
> 4 kiwifruit, peeled and sliced
> Artificial sweetener equivalent to 6 teaspoons sugar
> 1/2 teaspoon grated orange peel
> Sliced orange and additional kiwifruit, optional

In a blender, combine the first three ingredients; cover and process just until smooth. Add artificial sweetener. Stir in orange peel. Pour into an ungreased 8-in. square pan. Cover and freeze for 1-1/2 to 2 hours or until partially set. Spoon into a mixing bowl; beat on medium speed for 1-1/2 minutes. Return to pan; freeze for 2-3 hours or until firm. Let stand 10 minutes before serving. Spoon into small bowls; garnish with orange and additional kiwi if desired. **Yield:** 8 servings. **Nutritional Analysis:** One 1/2-cup (calculated without garnish) serving equals 56 calories, 2 mg sodium, 0 cholesterol, 14 gm carbohydrate, 1 gm protein, trace fat. **Diabetic Exchange:** 1 fruit.

Zippy Turkey Tortilla Bake

This hearty casserole is so well seasoned your family won't realize it's good for them. It can be prepared ahead of time, then baked right before serving. —Joy Maynard
St. Ignatius, Montana

> 1 small onion, finely chopped
> 1/2 teaspoon garlic powder
> 1 teaspoon vegetable oil
> 1 pound ground turkey breast
> 1 tablespoon vinegar
> 2 teaspoons chili powder
> 1-1/2 teaspoons dried oregano
> 1/2 teaspoon ground cumin
> 1/4 teaspoon cayenne pepper
> 1 can (15 ounces) black beans, rinsed and drained
> 1 jar (16 ounces) salsa
> 3/4 cup low-sodium chicken broth
> 8 fat-free flour tortillas (7 inches)
> 1/2 cup shredded reduced-fat Monterey Jack cheese
> 1/3 cup light sour cream

In a skillet, saute onion and garlic powder in oil until the onion is tender. Add turkey, vinegar, chili powder, oregano, cumin and cayenne; cook and stir over medium heat until turkey is no longer pink. Stir in beans. Remove from the heat. Combine salsa and broth; spread a thin layer in a 2-1/2-qt. baking dish coated with nonstick cooking spray. Cut tortillas into 1-in. strips and then into thirds; arrange half over salsa mixture. Top with half of the turkey mixture and half of the remaining salsa mixture. Repeat layers. Sprinkle with cheese. Cover and bake at 350° for 25 minutes or until bubbly. Top servings with sour cream. **Yield:** 8 servings. **Nutritional Analysis:** One 1-cup serving equals 279 calories, 886 mg sodium, 37 mg cholesterol, 37 gm carbohydrate, 23 gm protein, 4 gm fat. **Diabetic Exchanges:** 2 starch, 2 lean meat, 1 vegetable.

Tomato-Topped Chicken
Colorful Pea Salad

Tomato-Topped Chicken

(Pictured above)

The Italian salad dressing makes this chicken moist and tender, while tomato slices and basil give garden-fresh flavor. I conveniently keep a resealable bag of individually frozen chicken breasts in my freezer, so it's easy to take out just two for this recipe.
—Ruth Andrewson
Leavenworth, Washington

2 boneless skinless chicken breast halves (1/2 pound)
1/2 cup fat-free Italian salad dressing, *divided*
4 tomato slices, 1/4 inch thick
4 teaspoons seasoned bread crumbs
1 teaspoon minced fresh basil *or* 1/4 teaspoon dried basil
1 teaspoon grated Parmesan cheese

Place chicken in a shallow bowl; pour 1/4 cup dressing over chicken. Cover and refrigerate for 2 hours. Transfer chicken to a shallow baking dish; discard marinade. Drizzle with remaining dressing. Cover and bake at 400° for 10 minutes. Top each chicken breast with tomato slices, crumbs, basil and cheese. Cover and bake for 10 minutes. Uncover and bake 10-15 minutes longer or until chicken juices run clear. **Yield:** 2 servings. **Nutritional Analysis:** One serving equals 173 calories, 790 mg sodium, 64 mg cholesterol, 9 gm carbohydrate, 24 gm protein, 3 gm fat. **Diabetic Exchanges:** 3-1/2 very lean meat, 1/2 starch.

Colorful Pea Salad

(Pictured above)

A light buttermilk and herb dressing coats this colorful combination of green peas, carrots and mozzarella cheese cubes.
—Marlene Muckenhirn, Delano, Minnesota

2 medium carrots, chopped
1 package (16 ounces) frozen peas
1 celery rib, thinly sliced
1/4 cup cubed reduced-fat part-skim mozzarella cheese
2 green onions, thinly sliced
3 tablespoons buttermilk
1 tablespoon plain nonfat yogurt
1-1/2 teaspoons fat-free mayonnaise
1/2 teaspoon cider *or* red wine vinegar
1/2 to 1 teaspoon dried basil
1/4 teaspoon sugar
1/8 teaspoon pepper

In a saucepan, cook carrots in a small amount of boiling water for 2 minutes. Add peas; cook 5 minutes longer. Drain; rinse in cold water and drain again. Place in a bowl; add celery, cheese and onions. Combine remaining ingredients; pour over pea mixture and toss to coat. Cover and refrigerate for at least 1 hour. **Yield:** 9 servings. **Nutritional Analysis:** One 1/2-cup serving equals 61 calories, 103 mg sodium, 2 mg cholesterol, 10 gm carbohydrate, 4 gm protein, 1 gm fat. **Diabetic Exchanges:** 1 vegetable, 1/2 starch.

Light Berry Mousse
Shrimp Scampi

Light Berry Mousse

(Pictured at left)

Members of my family are diabetic, so I'm always looking for sugar-free recipes. This light, fluffy dessert flavored with fresh strawberries is a refreshing ending to a summer meal. It chills for 2 hours, so it's a nice make-ahead treat. —Peggy Key Grant, Alabama

    3/4 cup boiling water
       1 package (.3 ounce) sugar-free
          strawberry gelatin
       1 cup ice cubes
 1-1/2 cups sliced fresh strawberries
    3/4 cup light whipped topping

In a blender, combine water and gelatin. Cover and process until gelatin is dissolved. Blend in ice cubes until partially melted. Add strawberries; process well. Pour into a bowl; fold in whipped topping. Chill for 2 hours. **Yield:** 4 servings. **Nutritional Analysis:** One serving equals 57 calories, 55 mg sodium, 0 cholesterol, 8 gm carbohydrate, 2 gm protein, 2 gm fat. **Diabetic Exchanges:** 1/2 fruit, 1/2 fat.

Pineapple Upside-Down Cake

I dole out slices of this sunny-colored dessert while it's still warm from the oven. The moist cake gets fruity flavor from crushed pineapple and lemon gelatin. —Anna Polhemus North Merrick, New York

       1 can (20 ounces) unsweetened crushed
          pineapple
       1 package (.3 ounce) sugar-free lemon gelatin
Egg substitute equivalent to 2 eggs
       1 egg white
    3/4 cup sugar
       1 teaspoon vanilla extract
    3/4 cup all-purpose flour
       1 teaspoon baking powder

Drain pineapple, reserving 1/3 cup juice (discard or save remaining juice for another use). Line a 9-in. round baking pan with waxed paper; coat with nonstick cooking spray. Spread pineapple over waxed paper; sprinkle with gelatin. In a mixing bowl, beat egg substitute and egg white. Beat in sugar, reserved pineapple juice and vanilla. Combine flour and baking powder; add to egg mixture and stir well. Pour over gelatin. Bake at 350° for 25-30 minutes or until a toothpick inserted near the center comes out clean. Cool for 5 minutes; invert onto a serving plate. Serve warm. **Yield:** 10 servings. **Nutritional Analysis:** One serving equals 158 calories, 282 mg sodium, trace cholesterol, 27 gm carbohydrate, 7 gm protein, 1 gm fat. **Diabetic Exchange:** 2 starch.

Shrimp Scampi

(Pictured above)

I frequently prepare this simple seafood entree that looks fancy enough for company or special occasions. I've been serving this delicious dish for years, and everyone likes it. —Lori Watkins, Burien, Washington

       8 ounces angel hair pasta
 1-3/4 cups low-sodium chicken broth
       2 garlic cloves, minced
    1/4 teaspoon salt-free lemon-pepper seasoning
    1/4 cup chopped green onions, *divided*
    1/4 cup minced fresh parsley, *divided*
       1 pound uncooked shrimp, peeled and
          deveined

Cook pasta according to package directions. Meanwhile, in a large saucepan, combine the broth, garlic, lemon-pepper and 3 tablespoons each green onions and parsley. Bring to a boil. Add shrimp; cook for 3-5 minutes or until shrimp turn pink. Drain pasta and place in a serving bowl. Top with shrimp mixture and remaining onions and parsley. **Yield:** 4 servings. **Nutritional Analysis:** One serving equals 250 calories, 398 mg sodium, 136 mg cholesterol, 33 gm carbohydrate, 23 gm protein, 2 gm fat. **Diabetic Exchanges:** 2 starch, 2 very lean meat, 1/2 vegetable.

Applesauce Cake

When I make this mild apple dessert for our church's fellowship refreshment hour, people comment on how moist and tasty it is. Often they ask for seconds—and for the recipe! —Tom Hall, Montrose, Pennsylvania

Egg substitute equivalent to 3 eggs
  2 cups unsweetened applesauce
  1/3 cup milk
  1/3 cup vegetable oil
  4 teaspoons vanilla extract
  1 package (18-1/4 ounces) white cake mix
  1 package (.8 ounce) sugar-free vanilla cook-and-serve pudding mix
  2 tablespoons brown sugar substitute
  1 teaspoon ground cinnamon
  1/4 teaspoon ground nutmeg

In a mixing bowl, beat egg substitute for 1 minute on medium speed. Add applesauce, milk, oil and vanilla; mix well. Combine remaining ingredients; gradually add to applesauce mixture. Beat on medium speed for 3 minutes. Pour into a 13-in. x 9-in. x 2-in. baking pan coated with nonstick cooking spray. Bake at 350° for 35-40 minutes or until a toothpick inserted near the center comes out clean. **Yield:** 15 servings. **Nutritional Analysis:** One serving equals 224 calories, 261 mg sodium, trace cholesterol, 32 gm carbohydrate, 3 gm protein, 9 gm fat. **Diabetic Exchanges:** 2 fat, 1 starch, 1 fruit.

Aloha Chicken
(Pictured below right)

I'm always on the lookout for low-fat recipes that are scrumptious, too, like this one. Quick-cooking chicken breasts get wonderful sweet flavor from pineapple, honey and teriyaki sauce. —Jenny Reece, Lowry, Minnesota

  4 boneless skinless chicken breast halves (1 pound)
  1 tablespoon all-purpose flour
  1 tablespoon vegetable oil
  2 cans (8 ounces *each*) unsweetened pineapple chunks
  1 teaspoon cornstarch
  1 tablespoon honey
  1 tablespoon light teriyaki sauce *or* light soy sauce
  1/8 teaspoon pepper
Hot cooked rice

Flatten the chicken to 1/4-in. thickness. Place flour in a large resealable plastic bag; add chicken and shake to coat. In a skillet over medium heat, brown chicken in oil for 3-5 minutes on each side or until juices run clear. Remove and keep warm. Drain pineapple, reserving 1/4 cup juice. (discard or save remaining juice for another use). In a small bowl, combine cornstarch and reserved juice until smooth. Add to skillet. Stir in honey, teriyaki sauce and pepper. Boil for 30 seconds or until thickened. Add pineapple and chicken; heat through. Serve over rice. **Yield:** 4 servings. **Nutritional Analysis:** One serving (prepared with light teriyaki sauce; calculated without rice) equals 238 calories, 145 mg sodium, 73 mg cholesterol, 17 gm carbohydrate, 28 gm protein, 7 gm fat. **Diabetic Exchanges:** 4 very lean meat, 1 fruit, 1/2 fat.

Chocolate Muffins

I first made these fancy nut-topped muffins for a Valentine's Day breakfast for my husband and son. Applesauce keeps them moist and eliminates the need for oil. —Carol Gaus, Itasca, Illinois

1-1/4 cups all-purpose flour
  1/2 cup sugar
  1/3 cup baking cocoa
  1 teaspoon baking powder
  1 teaspoon baking soda
  1 cup unsweetened applesauce
  1/2 cup skim milk
Egg substitute equivalent to 2 eggs
  1 teaspoon vanilla extract
  1/4 cup sliced almonds

In a bowl, combine the flour, sugar, cocoa, baking powder and baking soda. In another bowl, whisk the applesauce, milk, egg substitute and vanilla until smooth. Stir into dry ingredients just until moistened. Coat muffin cups with nonstick cooking spray; fill three-fourths full with batter. Sprinkle with almonds. Bake at 400° for 20-25 minutes or until muffins test done. Cool for 10 minutes; remove from pan to a wire rack. **Yield:** 1 dozen. **Nutritional Analysis:** One muffin equals 119 calories, 171 mg sodium, trace cholesterol, 23 gm carbohydrate, 4 gm protein, 2 gm fat. **Diabetic Exchange:** 1-1/2 starch.

Aloha Chicken

Cantaloupe Cooler
Dilly Potato Salad
Crispy Chicken Strips

Crispy Chicken Strips

(Pictured above)

This is an easy method for dressing up chicken. I roll strips in a quick coating made with potato flakes and bread crumbs, then cook them for a couple minutes in a skillet.
—Dawn Hart, Lake Havasu City, Arizona

3/4 pound boneless skinless chicken breasts
1/2 cup mashed potato flakes
1/2 cup seasoned bread crumbs
Egg substitute equivalent to 1 egg
   2 tablespoons olive *or* vegetable oil

Flatten chicken to 1/2-in. thickness; cut into 1-in. strips. In a shallow bowl, combine the potato flakes and bread crumbs. Dip chicken in egg substitute, then in potato mixture. In a skillet, cook chicken in oil for 4-5 minutes or until golden. **Yield:** 3 servings. **Nutritional Analysis:** One serving equals 327 calories, 629 mg sodium, 63 mg cholesterol, 19 gm carbohydrate, 28 gm protein, 14 gm fat. **Diabetic Exchanges:** 3 meat, 1-1/2 starch.

Dilly Potato Salad

(Pictured above)

Curry, dill and Dijon mustard provide the tangy flavor in this creamy potato salad. —Rosemarie Kondrk
Old Bridge, New Jersey

2 pounds red potatoes
1 cup nonfat yogurt
3 tablespoons fat-free mayonnaise
1/4 cup thinly sliced green onions
1 teaspoon Dijon mustard
1 teaspoon dill weed
1/2 teaspoon curry powder
1/8 teaspoon pepper

Place the potatoes in a large saucepan and cover with water; cover and bring to a boil. Cook until tender, about 25-30 minutes; drain. In a large bowl, combine the remaining ingredients. Thinly slice potatoes; add to the yogurt mixture and toss gently until coated. Refrigerate until serving. **Yield:** 8 servings. **Nutritional Analysis:** One 2/3-cup serving equals 101 calories, 84 mg sodium, 1 mg cholesterol, 21 gm carbohydrate, 4 gm protein, trace fat. **Diabetic Exchange:** 1-1/2 starch.

Cantaloupe Cooler

(Pictured above)

Strawberries, grapes and cantaloupe combine in this delightful drink that takes just seconds to whip up in the blender. It's a good beverage for diabetics.
—Ruth Andrewson, Leavenworth, Washington

1 cup cubed cantaloupe
1 cup frozen unsweetened strawberries

1 cup green grapes
1/2 cup ice cubes
Artificial sweetener equivalent to 4 teaspoons sugar

Place all ingredients in the order listed in a blender. Cover and process until smooth. Pour into glasses; serve immediately. **Yield:** 4 servings. **Nutritional Analysis:** One 3/4-cup serving equals 64 calories, 6 mg sodium, 0 cholesterol, 16 gm carbohydrate, 1 gm protein, trace fat. **Diabetic Exchange:** 1 fruit.

Zippy Vegetable Soup

A blend of tender vegetables adds garden-fresh goodness to this hearty soup. You can give it extra zip by using spicier salsa. —Michelle Nichol, Bedford, Nova Scotia

1/2 cup chopped onion
1/2 cup chopped green pepper
1/2 cup thinly sliced carrot
1 teaspoon vegetable oil
1 can (16 ounces) kidney beans, rinsed and drained
1 can (14-1/2 ounces) diced tomatoes, undrained
1 cup water
1/4 cup salsa
4 teaspoons nonfat sour cream

In a saucepan, saute onion, green pepper and carrot in oil until tender. Add beans, tomatoes, water and salsa; mix well. Bring to a boil; reduce heat. Cover and simmer for 20-25 minutes or until vegetables are tender. Top each serving with a teaspoon of sour cream. **Yield:** 4 servings. **Nutritional Analysis:** One 1-cup serving equals 195 calories, 290 mg sodium, trace cholesterol, 35 gm carbohydrate, 10 gm protein, 2 gm fat. **Diabetic Exchanges:** 2 starch, 1 vegetable, 1/2 fat.

Low-Fat Fudge Pops

I changed the original recipe for these fudgy treats by replacing some of the sugar with a sugar substitute. The kids in the neighborhood love them so much I can't keep enough on hand. —Jeanie Castor, Decatur, Illinois

1 can (14 ounces) fat-free sweetened condensed milk
1/2 cup sugar
1/2 cup baking cocoa
2-1/2 cups skim milk
Artificial sweetener equivalent to 1/2 cup sugar
1 teaspoon vanilla extract
12 disposable plastic cups (3 ounces)
12 Popsicle sticks

In a heavy saucepan, combine the condensed milk, sugar and cocoa; stir until smooth. Bring to a boil over medium-low heat; cook and stir for 1 minute. Gradually whisk in skim milk, whisking until cocoa and sugar are dissolved. Remove from the heat; stir in the sweetener and vanilla. Pour into cups. Cover each cup with heavy-duty foil; insert sticks through foil (foil will hold sticks upright). Place in a 13-in. x 9-in. x 2-in. pan. Freeze until firm, about 5 hours. Remove the foil and cups before serving. **Yield:** 12 servings. **Nutritional Analysis:** One serving equals 155 calories, 62 mg sodium, 3 mg cholesterol, 34 gm carbohydrate, 5 gm protein, 1 gm fat. **Diabetic Exchange:** 2 starch.

Melon Mousse

(Pictured below)

This unique summer dessert is low in fat and a creative way to use cantaloupe. It's best when made with very ripe melon to give the sweetest flavor. —Sandy McKenzie Braham, Minnesota

2 envelopes unflavored gelatin
3 tablespoons lemon juice
4 cups cubed ripe cantaloupe
1 tablespoon sugar
1 carton (8 ounces) nonfat lemon yogurt
Fresh raspberries, optional

In a small saucepan, sprinkle gelatin over lemon juice; let stand for 1 minute. Cook over low heat until gelatin is dissolved. Place cantaloupe, sugar and gelatin mixture in a blender; cover and process until smooth. Transfer to a bowl; stir in yogurt. Spoon into individual dishes; chill until firm. Garnish with raspberries if desired. **Yield:** 6 servings. **Nutritional Analysis:** One 1/2-cup serving (without garnish) equals 90 calories, 40 mg sodium, 1 mg cholesterol, 18 gm carbohydrate, 5 gm protein, trace fat. **Diabetic Exchanges:** 1 fruit, 1/2 skim milk.

Melon Mousse

Garden Pork Stir-Fry

(Pictured below)

This easy all-in-one skillet supper is brimming with fresh-from-the-garden flavor. It's a tasty way to make the most of seasonal produce—from your backyard veggie patch or the farmer's market. —Kim Marie Van Rheenen Mendota, Illinois

1 pound boneless pork loin, cut into 3/4-inch cubes
2 cups julienned zucchini
1/2 pound fresh mushrooms, sliced
1 medium onion, cut into wedges
1 cup julienned green pepper
1 tablespoon cornstarch
3 tablespoons light soy sauce
1 tablespoon cold water
1/4 teaspoon garlic powder
Hot cooked rice

In a skillet or wok coated with nonstick cooking spray, stir-fry the pork until no longer pink, about 4 minutes. Add zucchini, mushrooms, onion and green pepper; stir-fry for 3 minutes or until crisp-tender. In a small bowl, combine cornstarch, soy sauce, water and garlic powder until smooth. Add to the skillet. Bring to a boil; cook and stir for 1-2 minutes or until thickened and bubbly. Serve over rice. **Yield:** 6 servings. **Nutritional Analysis:** One serving (calculated without rice) equals 152 calories, 491 mg sodium, 45 mg cholesterol, 9 gm carbohydrate, 17 gm protein, 5 gm fat. **Diabetic Exchanges:** 2 lean meat, 2 vegetable.

Apricot Squash Soup

(Pictured below)

This unusual golden soup combines two of our family's favorite foods—nutritious butternut squash and canned apricots. It's thick, rich and dresses up any meal. —Jean Hennessey Klein, New Berlin, Wisconsin

1 medium onion, chopped
1 tablespoon olive *or* vegetable oil
2 cups cubed peeled butternut squash
1 can (15 ounces) apricot halves in extra light syrup, drained
1 can (14-1/2 ounces) low-sodium chicken broth
1/8 teaspoon pepper
1 green onion, thinly sliced

In a saucepan, saute the onion in oil until tender. Add the squash; cook and stir for 2 minutes. Add the apricots,

Apricot Squash Soup
Garden Pork Stir-Fry

broth and pepper; bring to a boil. Reduce heat; cover and simmer for 15-20 minutes or until the squash is tender. Cool slightly. Process in small batches in a blender or food processor until smooth. Return to the pan and heat through. Garnish with green onion. **Yield:** 4 servings. **Nutritional Analysis:** One 1-cup serving equals 117 calories, 75 mg sodium, 2 mg cholesterol, 19 gm carbohydrate, 4 gm protein, 4 gm fat. **Diabetic Exchanges:** 1 fat, 1/2 fruit, 1/2 starch.

Cilantro Lime Cod

My daughter loves to cook and especially likes dishes with Mexican flair. She bakes these wonderfully seasoned fish fillets in foil to keep them moist and cut down on cleanup. —Donna Hackman
Huddleston, Virginia

Fudgy Brownie Dessert

      4 cod *or* flounder fillets (2 pounds)
   1/4 teaspoon pepper
      1 tablespoon dried minced onion
      1 garlic clove, minced
      1 tablespoon olive *or* vegetable oil
 1-1/2 teaspoons ground cumin
   1/4 cup minced fresh cilantro *or* parsley
      2 limes, thinly sliced
      2 tablespoons reduced-fat margarine, melted

Place each fillet on a 15-in. x 12-in. piece of heavy-duty foil. Sprinkle with pepper. In a small saucepan, saute onion and garlic in oil; stir in cumin. Spoon over fillets; sprinkle with cilantro. Place lime slices over each; drizzle with margarine. Fold foil around fish and seal tightly. Place on a baking sheet. Bake at 375° for 35-40 minutes or until fish flakes easily with a fork. **Yield:** 8 servings. **Nutritional Analysis:** One serving (prepared with cod) equals 96 calories, 77 mg sodium, 30 mg cholesterol, 3 gm carbohydrate, 13 gm protein, 4 gm fat. **Diabetic Exchanges:** 2 very lean meat, 1/2 fat.

Fudgy Brownie Dessert

(Pictured above right)

I came up with this recipe when searching for a low-fat dessert for my chocolate-loving family. My husband's and son's eyes light up whenever I serve these fudgy brownies topped with a fluffy mousse. —Karen Yoder
Bremerton, Washington

   1/2 cup sugar
   1/4 cup cornstarch
   1/4 cup baking cocoa
      1 can (12 ounces) evaporated skim milk
Egg substitute equivalent to 2 eggs
BROWNIE CRUST:
 1-1/4 cups baking cocoa
      1 cup sugar
   3/4 cup all-purpose flour

      1 teaspoon baking powder
      1 cup unsweetened applesauce
Egg substitute equivalent to 4 eggs
   1/4 cup vegetable oil
      2 teaspoons vanilla extract
      1 carton (8 ounces) frozen light whipped topping, thawed

In a saucepan, combine sugar, cornstarch and cocoa. Stir in the milk until smooth. Cook and stir over low heat just until boiling. Remove from the heat; stir a small amount into egg substitute. Return all to pan; cook for 1 minute or until thickened. Refrigerate. Meanwhile, for crust, combine cocoa, sugar, flour and baking powder in a bowl. Combine applesauce, egg substitute, oil and vanilla; add to the dry ingredients and mix just until blended. Pour into a 13-in. x 9-in. x 2-in. baking pan coated with nonstick cooking spray. Bake at 350° for 20 minutes or until a toothpick inserted near the center comes out clean. Cool on a wire rack. In a mixing bowl, beat the chilled chocolate mixture until light. Fold in whipped topping; carefully spread over crust. Refrigerate for 2 hours. **Yield:** 15 servings. **Nutritional Analysis:** One serving equals 220 calories, 106 mg sodium, 1 mg cholesterol, 33 gm carbohydrate, 7 gm protein, 8 gm fat. **Diabetic Exchanges:** 2 starch, 1-1/2 fat.

Monster Squash?

This is one of the tasty ways I use up those end-of-the-summer "monster" zucchini. I cut the squash into 1/2-inch-thick slices, then marinate them in my favorite Italian salad dressing for a half hour. I drain the slices, saving the dressing. Then I cook the slices on the grill, turning them with a tongs and brushing them once or twice with the reserved dressing. The results are yummy.
—Ruth Randolph
Orefield, Pennsylvania

Raisin Spice Cake

This moist spiced dessert with plenty of raisins is my aunt's recipe. It's so satisfying you won't know the sugar was replaced with sweetener. —Bernice Morris
Marshfield, Missouri

1-1/2 cups raisins
1-1/2 cups water
   1 cup unsweetened applesauce
  3/4 cup vegetable oil
Egg substitute equivalent to 2 eggs
Liquid artificial sweetener equivalent to 1 cup sugar
   1 teaspoon vanilla extract
   2 cups all-purpose flour
1-1/2 teaspoons ground cinnamon
   1 teaspoon baking soda
  1/2 teaspoon ground nutmeg

In a saucepan over medium heat, cook raisins and water until water is absorbed. Transfer to a bowl; add applesauce, oil, egg substitute, sweetener and vanilla. Combine the remaining ingredients; add to applesauce mixture and stir well. Pour into a 9-in. square baking pan coated with nonstick cooking spray. Bake at 350° for 20-25 minutes or until a toothpick inserted near the center comes out clean. **Yield:** 16 servings. **Nutritional Analysis:** One serving equals 221 calories, 182 mg sodium, trace cholesterol, 27 gm carbohydrate, 3 gm protein, 12 gm fat. **Diabetic Exchanges:** 2 fat, 1 fruit, 1 starch.

Crunchy Dessert Bars

My son-in-law is diabetic and loves these five-ingredient frozen dessert bars. With their nutty crunch from Grape Nuts cereal, we think they taste like the inside of a Snickers candy bar. —Shirley Reed, San Angelo, Texas

   1 pint sugar-free nonfat ice cream, softened
   1 cup light whipped topping
  1/2 cup reduced-fat peanut butter
   1 package (1 ounce) instant sugar-free
     butterscotch pudding mix
   1 cup Grape Nuts cereal

In a mixing bowl, combine the first four ingredients; beat until smooth. Stir in cereal. Transfer to a foil-lined 8-in. square pan. Cover and freeze for 3-4 hours or until firm. Use foil to lift out of pan; discard foil. Cut into bars. **Yield:** 2 dozen. **Nutritional Analysis:** One bar equals 67 calories, 122 mg sodium, 0 cholesterol, 10 gm carbohydrate, 3 gm protein, 2 gm fat. **Diabetic Exchange:** 1 starch.

Cinnamon Raisin Chicken

Orange juice and cinnamon lend a pleasant spicy taste to these quick-cooking boneless chicken breasts. I frequently serve this unusual combination over rice with broccoli or green beans on the side. —Connie Moore, Medway, Ohio

  1/2 cup chopped onion
   3 garlic cloves, minced

  3/4 teaspoon ground cinnamon
  1/8 teaspoon pepper
   1 tablespoon vegetable oil
   4 boneless skinless chicken breast halves (1
     pound)
  3/4 cup orange juice
  1/4 cup raisins

In a skillet, saute onion, garlic, cinnamon and pepper in oil until onion is tender. Add chicken; turn to coat. Cook, uncovered, for 10 minutes or until juices run clear. Add orange juice and raisins. Cook over low heat for 5-10 minutes or until heated through. **Yield:** 4 servings. **Nutritional Analysis:** One serving equals 232 calories, 66 mg sodium, 73 mg cholesterol, 15 gm carbohydrate, 28 gm protein, 7 gm fat. **Diabetic Exchanges:** 4 very lean meat, 1 fruit, 1/2 fat.

Hash Brown Cheese Omelet

(Pictured below right and on page 223)

This fluffy omelet filled with potatoes, onion and green pepper makes a family-pleasing meal. Serve it with toast and fruit. It's also good with sliced tomatoes.
—Jennifer Reisinger, Sheboygan, Wisconsin

   1 medium onion, chopped
  1/2 cup chopped green pepper
1-3/4 cups frozen cubed hash brown potatoes,
     thawed
Egg substitute equivalent to 8 eggs
  1/4 cup water
  1/8 teaspoon pepper
   3 slices light process American cheese

In a large skillet coated with nonstick cooking spray, saute onion and green pepper. Add potatoes; cook and stir over medium heat for 5 minutes or until heated through. In a bowl, beat egg substitute, water and pepper; pour over vegetables. As eggs set, lift edges, letting uncooked portion flow underneath. Just before eggs are completely set, place cheese slices over half of the omelet. Fold the omelet in half and transfer to a warm serving platter. **Yield:** 4 servings. **Nutritional Analysis:** One serving equals 239 calories, 457 mg sodium, 9 mg cholesterol, 23 gm carbohydrate, 21 gm protein, 7 gm fat. **Diabetic Exchanges:** 2-1/2 lean meat, 1-1/2 starch.

Hearty Brunch Potatoes

(Pictured at right and on page 222)

Our family of five enjoys this hearty dish with salad or green beans and crusty bread for lunch or supper. Leftovers are delicious reheated with eggs and toast for breakfast the next morning. —Madonna McCollough
Harrison, Arkansas

   7 medium potatoes, peeled and cut into
     1/2-inch cubes
  1/2 cup chopped green pepper
  1/2 cup chopped sweet red pepper

1/2 cup fresh *or* frozen corn
1 small onion, chopped
1 to 2 garlic cloves, minced
1/2 pound low-fat smoked turkey sausage links
2 tablespoons olive *or* vegetable oil
1/4 teaspoon pepper

Place potatoes in a saucepan and cover with water. Bring to a boil; reduce heat. Cook, uncovered, just until tender, about 10 minutes. Meanwhile, in a skillet coated with nonstick cooking spray, saute the peppers, corn, onion and garlic until tender. Cut sausage into small chunks; add to the vegetable mixture. Cook, uncovered, for 6-8 minutes or until heated through. Drain potatoes; add to the vegetable mixture. Add oil and pepper; mix well. Transfer to an ungreased 13-in. x 9-in. x 2-in. baking dish. Bake, uncovered, at 350° for 35 minutes or until heated through. **Yield:** 12 servings. **Nutritional Analysis:** One serving equals 141 calories, 178 mg sodium, 12 mg cholesterol, 22 gm carbohydrate, 5 gm protein, 4 gm fat. **Diabetic Exchanges:** 1-1/2 starch, 1 fat.

Applesauce Gelatin Squares

(Pictured below and on page 223)

I make this attractive soft-set salad during the holidays and garnish it with ranch dressing that's tinted green. Or spoon on a dollop of whipped topping for a light sweet dessert anytime. —Judy Ernst, Montague, Michigan

4 packages (.3 ounce *each*) sugar-free raspberry gelatin *or* flavor of your choice
4 cups boiling water
2 cups cold water
1 jar (46 ounces) unsweetened applesauce

In a bowl, dissolve the gelatin in boiling water. Stir in cold water and applesauce. Pour into a 13-in. x 9-in. x 2-in. dish coated with nonstick cooking spray. Refrigerate for 8 hours or overnight. Cut into squares. **Yield:** 16 servings. **Nutritional Analysis:** One serving equals 42 calories, 48 mg sodium, 0 cholesterol, 10 gm carbohydrate, 1 gm protein, trace fat. **Diabetic Exchange:** 1/2 fruit.

Hash Brown Cheese Omelet
Hearty Brunch Potatoes
Applesauce Gelatin Squares

Spinach Minestrone

(Pictured at right)

Sprinkle grated Parmesan on bowls of this flavorful soup that's seasoned with garlic and oregano. Each spoonful is chock-full of spinach, beans and pasta. Breadsticks are an easy accompaniment.
— *Gladys De Boer*
Castleford, Idaho

1 large onion, chopped
1 garlic clove, minced
4 cups low-sodium chicken broth
1 can (16 ounces) kidney beans, rinsed and drained
1 can (14-1/2 ounces) no-salt-added diced tomatoes, undrained
2 medium carrots, sliced
1/2 cup uncooked elbow macaroni
1/4 teaspoon dried oregano
1 package (10 ounces) frozen chopped spinach, thawed

In a saucepan coated with nonstick cooking spray, saute onion and garlic until tender. Add broth, beans, tomatoes, carrots, macaroni and oregano. Cook until vegetables and macaroni are tender, about 20 minutes. Stir in spinach; bring to a boil. Remove from the heat; let stand for 5-10 minutes. **Yield:** 8 servings (2 quarts). **Nutritional Analysis:** One 1-cup serving equals 143 calories, 109 mg sodium, 2 mg cholesterol, 26 gm carbohydrate, 8 gm protein, 1 gm fat. **Diabetic Exchanges:** 1-1/2 starch, 1 vegetable.

Spinach Minestrone

Lentil Burritos

I'm constantly trying to incorporate healthy but tasty meals into our menu. Both kids and adults love these mildly spiced burritos that combine filling lentils with crisp zucchini. — *Pam Masters, Derby, Kansas*

2 cups water
1 cup dry lentils
2 tablespoons dried minced onion
1/2 teaspoon dried minced garlic
1/2 teaspoon ground cumin
1/8 teaspoon hot pepper sauce
1 small zucchini, chopped
1 cup taco sauce
1 cup (4 ounces) shredded reduced-fat mozzarella cheese
8 fat-free flour tortillas (7 inches)

In a saucepan, combine the first six ingredients; bring to a boil. Reduce heat; cover and simmer for 15-20 minutes or until lentils are tender. Drain if necessary. Stir in zucchini, taco sauce and cheese. Place about 1/2 cupfuls down the center of each tortilla. Fold sides and ends over filling and roll up. **Yield:** 8 burritos. **Nutritional Analysis:** One burrito equals 237 calories, 608 mg sodium, 7 mg cholesterol, 40 gm carbohydrate, 13 gm protein, 3 gm fat. **Diabetic Exchanges:** 2 starch, 2 lean meat, 1 vegetable.

Fettuccine with Chicken

I stir up this tender chicken and pasta entree to feed my husband and three teenagers in a hurry. It features spinach fettuccine for a colorful change of pace.
— *Gwynne Fleener, Coeur d'Alene, Idaho*

8 ounces spinach fettuccine
1/2 pound boneless skinless chicken breast, cut into cubes
1 cup skim milk
1/4 cup reduced-fat margarine
3/4 cup nonfat Parmesan cheese topping
3/4 teaspoon garlic powder
1/4 teaspoon pepper

Cook fettuccine according to package directions. Meanwhile, in a large skillet that has been coated with nonstick cooking spray, cook chicken until juices run clear. Drain fettuccine; add to skillet. Add milk and margarine. Stir in cheese topping, garlic powder and pepper; heat through. **Yield:** 6 servings. **Nutritional Analysis:** One 1-cup serving equals 282 calories, 403 mg sodium, 28 mg cholesterol, 36 gm carbohydrate, 21 gm protein, 7 gm fat. **Diabetic Exchanges:** 2-1/2 starch, 2 lean meat.

Soft Raisin Cookies

I modified a recipe for cake mix cookies to make it healthier. My family likes my version, with its mild spice flavor and touch of sweetness from raisins, even better than the original. —Ray Amet, Kansas City, Missouri

    1 package (9 ounces) yellow cake mix
    1 cup quick-cooking oats
    6 tablespoons unsweetened applesauce
Egg substitute equivalent to 1 egg
    2 tablespoons margarine, melted
    1/2 teaspoon apple pie spice
    1/2 cup raisins

In a mixing bowl, combine the first six ingredients; beat until blended. Stir in raisins. Drop by tablespoonfuls 2 in. apart onto baking sheets coated with nonstick cooking spray. Bake at 375° for 10-12 minutes or until the edges are lightly browned. Cool for 5 minutes before removing to wire racks to cool completely. **Yield:** 2 dozen. **Nutritional Analysis:** One cookie equals 126 calories, 166 mg sodium, trace cholesterol, 22 gm carbohydrate, 2 gm protein, 3 gm fat. **Diabetic Exchanges:** 1 starch, 1/2 fruit, 1/2 fat.

Turkey Burger Pie

This recipe saved the day when I came home from the hospital after delivering our son. It requires just six ingredients and bakes in less than half an hour, so I can have this hearty dinner on the table in a jiffy. —Danielle Monai, Brooklyn Heights, Ohio

    1 pound ground turkey breast
    1 cup chopped onion
    1 cup reduced-fat shredded cheddar cheese
Egg substitute equivalent to 2 eggs
    1 cup skim milk
    1/2 cup reduced-fat biscuit/baking mix

In a skillet over medium heat, cook turkey and onion until meat is no longer pink; drain. Transfer to a 9-in. pie plate coated with nonstick cooking spray. Sprinkle with cheese. In a bowl, combine egg substitute, milk and baking mix; mix well. Pour over cheese. Bake at 400° for 20-25 minutes or until golden brown and a knife inserted near the center comes out clean. **Yield:** 6 servings. **Nutritional Analysis:** One serving equals 221 calories, 226 mg sodium, 51 mg cholesterol, 12 gm carbohydrate, 30 gm protein, 6 gm fat. **Diabetic Exchanges:** 3 very lean meat, 1 starch, 1/2 fat.

Brown Rice Veggie Stir-Fry

My husband and I first tasted this colorful combination while visiting my sister in Grants Pass, Oregon. We enjoyed it so much that now I often make it for family and friends. —Maxine Driver, Littleton, Colorado

    2 tablespoons water
    2 tablespoons light soy sauce
    1 tablespoon olive *or* vegetable oil
    1 cup sliced zucchini
    1 cup shredded cabbage
    1/2 cup sliced fresh mushrooms
    1/2 cup chopped onion
    1 cup cooked brown rice

    1/4 cup diced fresh tomato
    1/4 cup grated carrot
    2 tablespoons slivered almonds, optional

In a skillet, combine water, soy sauce and oil; add zucchini, cabbage, mushrooms and onion. Stir-fry for 4-5 minutes or until vegetables are crisp-tender. Add rice, tomato and carrot. Stir-fry for 2-3 minutes or until heated through. Sprinkle with almonds if desired. **Yield:** 4 servings. **Nutritional Analysis:** One 3/4-cup serving (prepared without almonds) equals 107 calories, 461 mg sodium, 0 cholesterol, 16 gm carbohydrate, 2 gm protein, 4 gm fat. **Diabetic Exchanges:** 1 starch, 1 fat.

Tangy Peas And Cauliflower

My family loves vegetables, so I'm always looking for new and different ways to fix them. This pretty side dish gets its pleasant tangy flavor from creamy yogurt. —Marie Hoyer, Hodgenville, Kentucky

    4 cups cauliflowerets
    1 package (16 ounces) frozen peas
    3/4 cup plain nonfat yogurt
    3 tablespoons minced fresh cilantro *or* parsley
    1 tablespoon lemon juice
    1/4 teaspoon ground cumin
Dash salt-free lemon-pepper seasoning

Place cauliflower in a saucepan with a small amount of water. Bring to a boil; cook for 6-8 minutes. Add peas; cook 2-4 minutes longer or until the vegetables are crisp-tender; drain. Combine remaining ingredients; pour over vegetables and toss to coat. **Yield:** 8-10 servings. **Nutritional Analysis:** One 1/2-cup serving equals 70 calories, 96 mg sodium, trace cholesterol, 12 gm carbohydrate, 5 gm protein, trace fat. **Diabetic Exchanges:** 1 vegetable, 1/2 starch.

Waist Not, Want Not

• To cut the fat in my recipes, I sometimes substitute applesauce for some of the shortening in baked goods. It's very convenient to buy the applesauce packed in individual servings, which stay fresh on the cupboard shelf until I need them. Plus, I don't have to worry about using up the rest of a jar before it spoils. —Brenda Busek, Dillsboro, Indiana

• Canned chicken broth adds excellent flavor to most any vegetable. Use low-sodium broth (which also contains less fat) instead of water when cooking.

• When I need to take the skin off of chicken, I use a paper towel to grip it. It comes off in a breeze. —Edna Ivey, Graham, North Carolina

• Nonstick cooking spray is terrific to have on hand because it doesn't saturate the foods you're cooking with unwanted fat. For best flavor, store nonstick cooking spray at room temperature for 2 years from the date of purchase. (With a crayon, write the purchase date on the bottom of the can when you bring it home from the grocery store.)

Chapter 15

Centsible Foods—Fast and Frugal

ALTHOUGH carryout restaurant meals and store-bought packaged entrees save you time in the kitchen, they don't save you money. In fact, if you always rely on them when in a pinch, these costly convenience foods could likely break the family's budget.

So if you're counting pennies as well as minutes, look here for "centsible" express-eating alternatives that are not only easy on the wallet, but delectable as well.

Our test kitchen staff has figured the cost per serving for each delicious dish. So these fast and frugal recipes are sure to result in prompt meals and a plumper pocketbook!

EATING ECONOMICALLY. Minestrone Stew (p. 242).

Chicken Biscuit Potpie

1/4 cup chopped green pepper
2 tablespoons butter *or* margarine
2 tablespoons all-purpose flour
1/2 teaspoon sugar
1/2 teaspoon salt
1/8 teaspoon pepper
1/3 cup milk
1 can (14-1/2 ounces) stewed tomatoes
1 can (6 ounces) tuna, drained and flaked
1 teaspoon Creole seasoning*

In a saucepan, saute green pepper in butter until tender. Stir in flour, sugar, salt and pepper until blended. Gradually add milk, stirring constantly. Stir in tomatoes. Bring to a boil; cook and stir for 2 minutes. Add tuna and Creole seasoning; heat through. **Yield:** 4 servings (48¢ per serving). ***Editor's Note:** The following spices may be substituted for the Creole seasoning: 1/2 teaspoon each paprika and garlic powder and 1/8 teaspoon each cayenne pepper, dried thyme and ground cumin.

Piggies in Blankies

Franks nestled in sauerkraut and wrapped in tender biscuit blankets make for a pretty presentation. They're easy to assemble, too. —Iola Egle, McCook, Nebraska

2 cups biscuit/baking mix
1/2 cup water
1 can (14 ounces) sauerkraut, rinsed and drained, *divided*
1 pound hot dogs

In a bowl, combine biscuit mix and water until a soft dough forms. Turn onto a floured surface; knead 5-10 times. Roll dough into a 13-in. circle; cut into 10 wedges. Place 1 tablespoon sauerkraut on each wedge. Place a hot dog at the wide end; roll up each wedge tightly. Place on an ungreased baking sheet. Bake at 450° for 12-15 minutes or until golden brown. Heat remaining sauerkraut; serve with the hot dogs. **Yield:** 10 servings (33¢ per serving).

Chicken Biscuit Potpie

(Pictured above)

This hearty meal-in-one takes just 10 minutes to assemble before popping it in the oven. —Dorothy Smith, El Dorado, Arkansas

1-2/3 cups frozen mixed vegetables, thawed
1-1/2 cups cubed cooked chicken
1 can (10-3/4 ounces) condensed cream of chicken soup, undiluted
1/4 teaspoon dried thyme
1 cup biscuit/baking mix
1/2 cup milk
1 egg

In a bowl, combine vegetables, chicken, soup and thyme. Pour into an ungreased deep-dish 9-in. pie plate. Combine biscuit mix, milk and egg; pour over chicken mixture. Bake at 400° for 25-30 minutes or until golden brown. **Yield:** 6 servings (54¢ per serving).

Creole Tuna

This speedy recipe has been in my family for as long as I can remember. Because it relies on pantry staples, it's easy to make when you can't decide what to fix for dinner. I sometimes serve it over rice. —Betty Bernat
Bethlehem, New Hampshire

Cabbage Saute

My husband and I love this mildly sweet cabbage alongside chicken or turkey. I think you'll agree it's a nice change from a plain tossed salad. —Dorothy Phillips
Sun Prairie, Wisconsin

1 medium onion, chopped
2 tablespoons butter *or* margarine
4 medium carrots, thinly sliced
6 cups chopped cabbage
1/2 cup chicken broth
1 teaspoon salt
1 teaspoon sugar

In a large skillet, saute onion in butter until tender. Add carrots; cook and stir for 2-3 minutes. Stir in the remaining ingredients; bring to a boil. Reduce heat; cover and simmer for 5-7 minutes or until vegetables are tender. Serve with a slotted spoon. **Yield:** 8 servings (17¢ per serving).

Flaky Fruit Dessert

Craving an old-fashioned crisp? I use cornflakes to create the yummy topping on this quick and comforting dessert.
—Clara Honeyager, Mukwonago, Wisconsin

1 can (21 ounces) fruit pie filling of your choice
1 teaspoon lemon juice
1/4 cup packed brown sugar
2 tablespoons butter *or* margarine, softened
1 teaspoon ground cinnamon
2 cups cornflakes

In a bowl, combine pie filling and lemon juice. Transfer to a lightly greased 1-qt. baking dish. In another bowl, combine brown sugar, butter and cinnamon; add cornflakes. Spread over filling. Bake at 350° for 15-20 minutes or until heated through. Serve warm. **Yield:** 6 servings (36¢ per serving).

Mushroom Rice

A co-worker shared the recipe for this tasty rice side dish more than 30 years ago, and I've been taking it to potlucks ever since. It's a snap to throw together. *—Iris Hubbard North Fort Myers, Florida*

1 can (10-1/2 ounces) beef broth
3/4 cup uncooked long grain rice
1 jar (4-1/2 ounces) sliced mushrooms, undrained
1/4 cup butter *or* margarine, melted
1/2 teaspoon garlic powder
1/2 teaspoon onion salt

In a 2-qt. microwave-safe dish, combine all ingredients. Cover and microwave on high for 5 minutes. Microwave on 50% power for 15 minutes. Let stand for 5-10 minutes. Stir before serving. **Yield:** 4 servings (41¢ per serving). **Editor's Note:** This recipe was tested in an 850-watt microwave.

Meatball Skillet Meal

(Pictured below)

With colorful vegetables and nicely seasoned meatballs, this tasty meal-in-one offers a lot of flavor for a little cash.
—Donna Smith, Victor, New York

1/2 cup finely chopped fresh mushrooms
1/3 cup quick-cooking oats
2 tablespoons finely chopped green pepper
2 tablespoons finely chopped onion
2 tablespoons dried parsley flakes
1 teaspoon dried basil
1 teaspoon dried oregano
1/2 teaspoon dried thyme
1/2 teaspoon salt
1/4 teaspoon pepper
1 pound ground beef
4 medium carrots, sliced
1 small zucchini, sliced
1 can (14-1/2 ounces) diced tomatoes, undrained
4 cups hot cooked rice

In a bowl, combine the first 10 ingredients. Add beef and mix well. Shape into 1-1/4-in. balls. In a skillet over medium heat, brown meatballs; drain. Add carrots and zucchini; cook for 5 minutes or until tender. Stir in tomatoes; heat through. Serve over rice. **Yield:** 6 servings (77¢ per serving).

Meatball Skillet Meal

Marshmallow Fruit Bowl

I dress up canned fruit with marshmallows and a home-cooked pudding-like dressing to make this light, refreshing salad. It's an economical addition to most any meal.
—Patricia Staudt, Marble Rock, Iowa

    1 can (20 ounces) pineapple tidbits
    1 can (15 ounces) chunky mixed fruit
  1/4 cup lemon juice
  1/4 cup sugar
    2 tablespoons all-purpose flour
    2 eggs, lightly beaten
  1/2 cup whipped topping
    1 cup miniature marshmallows

Drain pineapple and mixed fruit, reserving 1 cup of juice. Set fruit aside. In a saucepan, combine lemon juice, sugar, flour and reserved fruit juice; stir until smooth. Cook and stir until heated through. Add a small amount of hot liquid to eggs; return all to pan. Bring to a boil; boil and stir for 2 minutes. Cool completely. Fold in whipped topping. Fold in marshmallows, pineapple and mixed fruit. Transfer to a serving bowl. **Yield:** 10 (1/2-cup) servings (31¢ per serving).

Minestrone Stew

(Pictured below and on page 238)

I add green chilies to this slow-cooked stew made from convenient pantry ingredients. You're sure to like the taste.
—Janie Hoskins, Red Bluff, California

    1 pound ground beef
    1 small onion, chopped
    1 can (19 ounces) ready-to-serve minestrone
      soup
    1 can (15 ounces) pinto beans, rinsed and
      drained
    1 can (14-1/2 ounces) stewed tomatoes

Minestrone Stew

    1 can (11 ounces) whole kernel corn, drained
    1 can (4 ounces) chopped green chilies
    1 teaspoon salt
  1/2 teaspoon garlic powder
  1/2 teaspoon onion powder

In a skillet, cook beef and onion until meat is no longer pink; drain. Transfer to a slow cooker. Add the remaining ingredients; mix well. Cover and cook on low for 4-6 hours or until heated through. **Yield:** 8 servings (66¢ per serving).

Cajun-Fried Rice

I put leftover pork to good use as a side or main dish. The colorful combination is a family favorite. As you can see, it's a budget favorite, too.
—Karen Combs
Union Bridge, Maryland

✓ Uses less fat, sugar or salt. Includes Nutritional Analysis and Diabetic Exchanges.

        2 cups uncooked long grain rice
        3 tablespoons vegetable oil
        1 medium green pepper, diced
        1 small onion, chopped
        1 celery rib, thinly sliced
    2-1/4 cups water
        1 can (14-1/2 ounces) chicken broth
        1 medium tomato, diced
    1-1/2 teaspoons salt, optional
      1/2 to 1 teaspoon ground cumin
      1/4 teaspoon pepper
        1 cup cubed cooked pork

In a large skillet, saute rice in oil until lightly browned. Add the green pepper, onion and celery; saute for 2-3 minutes. Stir in water, broth, tomato, salt if desired, cumin and pepper. Bring to a boil. Reduce heat; cover and simmer for 18-20 minutes or until rice is tender. Stir in pork; heat through. **Yield:** 8 servings (49¢ per serving). **Nutritional Analysis:** One 1-cup serving (prepared with low-sodium broth and without salt) equals 285 calories, 46 mg sodium, 14 mg cholesterol, 43 gm carbohydrate, 10 gm protein, 8 gm fat. **Diabetic Exchanges:** 3 starch, 1-1/2 fat.

One-Pot Dinner

My family always comes back for seconds when this nicely seasoned skillet supper is on the table.
—Bonnie Morrow, Spencerport, New York

✓ Uses less fat, sugar or salt. Includes Nutritional Analysis and Diabetic Exchanges.

    1/2 pound ground beef
      1 medium onion, chopped
      1 cup chopped celery
    3/4 cup chopped green pepper
      2 teaspoons Worcestershire sauce
      1 teaspoon salt, optional
    1/2 teaspoon dried basil
    1/4 teaspoon pepper

Roasted Vegetables

2 cups uncooked medium egg noodles
1 can (16 ounces) kidney beans, rinsed and drained
1 can (14-1/2 ounces) stewed tomatoes
3/4 cup water
1 beef bouillon cube

In a large saucepan or skillet, cook meat until no longer pink; drain. Add onion, celery and green pepper; cook for 5 minutes or until vegetables are crisp-tender. Add Worcestershire sauce, salt if desired, basil and pepper. Stir in noodles, beans, tomatoes, water and bouillon. Bring to a boil. Reduce heat; cover and simmer for 20 minutes or until noodles are tender, stirring occasionally. **Yield:** 5 servings (72¢ per serving). **Nutritional Analysis:** One 1-cup serving (prepared with lean ground beef, no-yolk egg noodles, no-salt-added tomatoes and low-sodium bouillon and without salt) equals 282 calories, 91 mg sodium, 29 mg cholesterol, 39 gm carbohydrate, 19 gm protein, 5 gm fat. **Diabetic Exchanges:** 2-1/2 starch, 1 meat, 1 vegetable.

Garlic Spaghetti

I make this family favorite at least two or three times a month. It's wonderful with a salad and fresh Italian bread. Besides being extremely easy to prepare, this meatless main dish is easy on the pocketbook. —Jackie Messina
Chardon, Ohio

1 package (16 ounces) spaghetti
10 garlic cloves, minced
1/4 cup olive *or* vegetable oil
1/4 cup minced fresh parsley
2 teaspoons dried oregano *or* 2 tablespoons minced fresh oregano
1 teaspoon salt
1/4 teaspoon pepper
1/2 cup grated Parmesan cheese

Cook spaghetti according to package directions. Meanwhile, in a skillet over low heat, cook garlic in oil until lightly browned. Remove from the heat; stir in parsley, oregano, salt and pepper. Drain spaghetti; place in a large bowl. Add garlic mixture and Parmesan cheese; toss to coat. **Yield:** 4 servings (61¢ per serving).

Roasted Vegetables

(Pictured above)

Garlic and other seasonings give great flavor to this medley of vegetables. —Sally Domark, Orland Hills, Illinois

✓ Uses less fat, sugar or salt. Includes Nutritional Analysis and Diabetic Exchanges.

2 medium potatoes, peeled and cut into 1/2-inch cubes
2 medium carrots, cut into 1/2-inch slices
1 large zucchini, cut into 1/2-inch slices
1 large sweet red pepper, cut into 1-inch pieces
1 tablespoon olive *or* vegetable oil
1 teaspoon *each* dried basil and oregano *or* 1 tablespoon minced fresh basil and oregano
1/2 teaspoon salt, optional
1/4 teaspoon pepper
2 garlic cloves, minced

In a mixing bowl, combine the potatoes, carrots, zucchini and red pepper. Combine the remaining ingredients; drizzle over vegetables. Stir to coat. Transfer to an ungreased 13-in. x 9-in. x 2-in. baking dish. Bake, uncovered, at 375° for 30-35 minutes or until tender. **Yield:** 6 servings (33¢ per serving). **Nutritional Analysis:** One 3/4-cup serving (prepared without salt) equals 80 calories, 13 mg sodium, 0 cholesterol, 14 gm carbohydrate, 2 gm protein, 3 gm fat. **Diabetic Exchanges:** 1 vegetable, 1/2 starch, 1/2 fat.

Chicken-Baked Chops

Chicken-Baked Chops

(Pictured above)

Even my husband, who doesn't care for pork, enjoys these tender chops covered with an easy sauce.
—Debbie Smith, Broken Arrow, Oklahoma

    4 bone-in pork chops (1/2 inch thick)
    1 tablespoon vegetable oil
    1 can (10-3/4 ounces) condensed cream of chicken soup, undiluted
  1/2 cup water
    3 tablespoons Worcestershire sauce
  1/4 teaspoon salt
  1/8 teaspoon pepper

In a skillet, brown the pork chops in oil. Transfer to a greased 13-in. x 9-in. x 2-in. baking dish. Combine the remaining ingredients; pour over chops. Cover and bake at 350° for 1 hour or until meat juices run clear. **Yield:** 4 servings (98¢ per serving).

Creamed Ham on Corn Bread

I top pieces of corn bread with a cheesy sauce chock-full of ham to make a satisfying and economical supper. This is one budget meal our family loves. —Denise Hershman
Cromwell, Indiana

    1 package (8-1/2 ounces) corn bread/muffin mix
    1 egg
  1/3 cup milk
CREAMED HAM:
    2 tablespoons butter *or* margarine
    2 tablespoons all-purpose flour
  1/2 teaspoon ground mustard
  1/4 teaspoon salt
1-1/2 cups milk
  3/4 cup shredded cheddar cheese
1-1/2 cups cubed fully cooked ham

In a bowl, combine corn bread mix, egg and milk until blended. Spread into a greased 8-in. square baking pan. Bake at 400° for 18-20 minutes. Meanwhile, in a saucepan, melt butter; stir in flour, mustard and salt until smooth. Add milk. Bring to a boil; boil and stir for 2 minutes. Stir in cheese until melted. Add ham and heat through. Cut corn bread into squares; top with creamed ham. **Yield:** 6 servings (45¢ per serving).

Fruity Tapioca

Folks who like tapioca will enjoy this fast and fruity variation. Convenient canned peaches and mandarin oranges give refreshing flavor.
—Louise Martin
Denver, Pennsylvania

    4 cups water
    1 cup sugar
  1/3 cup quick-cooking tapioca
    1 can (6 ounces) frozen orange juice concentrate, thawed
    1 can (29 ounces) sliced peaches, drained and diced
    1 can (11 ounces) mandarin oranges, drained

In a saucepan, combine the water, sugar and tapioca; let stand for 5 minutes. Bring to a full rolling boil. Remove from the heat; stir in orange juice concentrate. Cool for 20 minutes. Stir in the peaches and oranges. Transfer to a serving bowl. Refrigerate until serving. **Yield:** 10 servings (36¢ per serving).

Broccoli and Rice

A short list of ingredients helps keep the cost down for this quick-to-cook side dish.
—Betty Janway, Ruston, Louisiana

    1 package (10 ounces) frozen chopped broccoli
    1 cup cooked rice
  1/2 teaspoon celery salt
1-1/2 cups cubed process American cheese

Cook broccoli according to package directions; drain. Stir in rice and celery salt. Stir in cheese until melted. Serve immediately. **Yield:** 4 servings (47¢ per serving).

Cold Day Chili

I like to make chili from beans I've soaked overnight, but this speedier version, featuring a mildly sweet mixture of beef and beans, tastes just as good on a winter day.
—Lucile Proctor, Panguitch, Utah

    1 pound ground beef
    1 medium onion, halved and thinly sliced
    2 cans (16 ounces *each*) kidney beans, rinsed and drained
    1 can (14-1/2 ounces) diced tomatoes, undrained
  1/2 to 3/4 cup water
    1 to 2 tablespoons brown sugar

1 tablespoon chili powder
1 tablespoon vinegar
2 teaspoons prepared mustard
1 teaspoon salt
1/8 teaspoon pepper

In a large saucepan over medium heat, cook beef and onion until the meat is no longer pink; drain. Add the remaining ingredients. Bring to a boil; reduce heat. Cover and simmer for 10 minutes or until heated through. **Yield:** 4 servings (90¢ per serving).

Ground Beef 'n' Biscuits

(Pictured below)

This recipe was given to me by a good friend when I got married, and I have used it many times since. The saucy meal is family-pleasing. —Lois Hill
Trinity, North Carolina

1-1/2 pounds ground beef
1/2 cup chopped celery
1/2 cup chopped onion
2 tablespoons all-purpose flour
1 teaspoon salt
1/4 teaspoon dried oregano
1/8 teaspoon pepper
2 cans (8 ounces *each*) tomato sauce
1 package (10 ounces) frozen peas
1 tube (7-1/2 ounces) refrigerated buttermilk biscuits
1 cup (4 ounces) shredded cheddar cheese

In a skillet over medium heat, cook beef, celery and onion until meat is no longer pink and celery is tender; drain. Stir in the flour, salt, oregano and pepper until blended. Add tomato sauce and peas; simmer for 5 minutes. Transfer to a greased 13-in. x 9-in. x 2-in. baking dish. Separate biscuits; arrange over beef mixture. Sprinkle with cheese. Bake, uncovered, at 350° for 20 minutes or until biscuits are golden and cheese is melted. **Yield:** 6 servings (98¢ per serving).

Harvard Onions

These sweet-sour onions are similar to Harvard beets. I frequently made them when our three sons were growing up.
—Frances Thompson, Freeport, Maine

4 medium onions, cut into 1/2-inch slices
1/2 cup water
1/2 cup sugar
2 tablespoons all-purpose flour
1/2 teaspoon salt
1/2 cup cider vinegar
2 tablespoons butter *or* margarine
1/2 teaspoon dried parsley flakes

Place onions and water in a saucepan. Cover and cook over medium heat until tender, about 12 minutes. Meanwhile, in another saucepan, combine sugar, flour, salt and vinegar; stir until smooth. Bring to a boil; cook and stir for 2 minutes. Stir in butter until melted. Drain onions and add to the sauce; sprinkle with parsley. Heat through. **Yield:** 5 servings (16¢ per serving).

Ground Beef 'n' Biscuits

IF YOUR KIDS are picky eaters, ask them to join you in the kitchen and make some of these tasty kid-approved treats!

From speedy snacks and basic breads to hearty main dishes and delectable desserts, younger children can mix and measure ingredients while older ones help you get a head start on dinner. (Toddlers can also help with the "cleanup" by licking the bowl!)

With such rapid recipes, cooking can be a family activity that's as fun as it is delicious. Best of all, kids and parents will be pleased (and proud) to sit down to a dinner that they all helped create.

FAMILY FUN. Clockwise from upper right: Fourth of July Jell-O, Lunch Box Pizzas and Taco Dogs (all recipes on p. 251).

**Fruity Oatmeal
Brunch Punch
Peanut Butter Syrup**

2 cans (46 ounces *each*) tropical punch-
    flavored soft drink
1 cup pineapple juice
3/4 cup lemonade concentrate
1 can (12 ounces) ginger ale, chilled

In a punch bowl or large container, combine the first three ingredients. Cover and refrigerate. Stir in ginger ale just before serving. **Yield:** about 3 quarts.

Peanut Butter Syrup

(Pictured at left)

This is the perfect topping for pancakes. It's thick, peanutty and can be zapped in the microwave.
            —Janice Nightingale, Cedar Rapids, Iowa

1/2 cup maple syrup
1/4 cup peanut butter
Waffles, pancakes *or* French toast

In a saucepan over low heat, heat syrup and peanut butter until peanut butter is melted. Stir until smooth. Serve warm over waffles, pancakes or French toast. **Yield:** about 2/3 cup.

Thick Turkey Bean Chili

When our daughters wouldn't eat the spicy chili beans I prepared, I came up with this milder, slightly sweet version. They love eating the hearty chili as a dip with tortilla chips. I never have leftovers.
            —Keri Scofield Lawson, Fullerton, California

1 pound ground turkey
2 cans (16 ounces *each*) baked beans,
    undrained
1 can (16 ounces) kidney beans, rinsed and
    drained
1 can (15-1/2 ounces) sloppy joe sauce
1 can (14-1/2 ounces) diced tomatoes,
    undrained
1 tablespoon brown sugar
1/4 teaspoon *each* garlic powder, salt and pepper
**Shredded cheddar cheese, sour cream and tortilla
    chips, optional**

In a large saucepan, brown the turkey; drain. Stir in beans, sloppy joe sauce, tomatoes, brown sugar and seasonings. Simmer, uncovered, for 30 minutes or until heated through. Serve with cheese, sour cream and tortilla chips if desired. **Yield:** 8-10 servings.

Chicken in a Haystack

This is probably one of the quickest meals in my recipe file and a wonderful way to please picky eaters. Youngsters will love "stacking" their favorite toppings over this creamy chicken and rice combo.   —Helle Watson
                            Thornton, Colorado

1 can (10-3/4 ounces) condensed cream of
    chicken soup, undiluted
2 cups cubed cooked chicken

Fruity Oatmeal

(Pictured above)

I never liked oatmeal until my mom found this wonderful combination of uncooked oats and fresh fruit. Now I often make it myself for breakfast or an after-school snack.
            —Sarah Hunt, Everett, Washington

✓ Uses less fat, sugar or salt. Includes Nutritional Analysis and Diabetic Exchanges.

1/3 cup old-fashioned oats
1 teaspoon oat bran
1/3 cup diced unpeeled tart apple
1 medium firm banana, diced
1/4 cup halved seedless grapes
2 tablespoons raisins
1 tablespoon sliced almonds
Milk *or* yogurt, optional

Toss the first seven ingredients; divide between two bowls. Top with milk or yogurt if desired. Serve immediately. **Yield:** 2 servings. **Nutritional Analysis:** One 1/2-cup serving (calculated without milk or yogurt) equals 182 calories, 5 mg sodium, 0 cholesterol, 37 gm carbohydrate, 4 gm protein, 4 gm fat. **Diabetic Exchanges:** 1-1/2 fruit, 1 starch, 1/2 fat.

Brunch Punch

(Pictured above)

Kids will love the sweet, tropical taste of this pretty party punch.   —Rosa Griffith, Christiansburg, Virginia

1/2 cup water
Hot cooked rice
TOPPINGS:
Cooked peas, raisins, pineapple tidbits, shredded
cheddar cheese, sliced ripe olives, chow mein
noodles *and/or* mandarin oranges

In a microwave-safe bowl, combine soup, chicken and
water; mix well. Cover and microwave on high for 3-
5 minutes or until heated through. Serve over rice.
Top with toppings of your choice. **Yield:** 4-6 servings.

Crispy Peanut Butter Treats

*I don't make these crispy bars very often because it's
hard to stop eating them! The peanut buttery ribbon
in the middle makes them an eye-catcher at bake
sales.*
—Lisa Hornish
Grand Forks Air Force Base, North Dakota

 2 cups (12 ounces) semisweet chocolate
   chips
 3/4 cup peanut butter
 7 cups crisp rice cereal
 1 package (10 ounces) peanut butter chips
 1/4 cup butter *or* margarine
 2 tablespoons water
 1/2 teaspoon vanilla extract
 1 cup confectioners' sugar

In a large microwave-safe bowl, heat chocolate chips
and peanut butter, uncovered, on high for 1 minute;
stir. Microwave 30-45 seconds longer or until chips
are melted; stir until smooth. Stir in cereal until
evenly coated. Pat half into a greased 13-in. x 9-in. x
2-in. dish. In a microwave-safe bowl, heat peanut butter chips and butter, uncovered, on high for 1 minute;
stir. Microwave 10-20 seconds longer or until chips
are melted; stir until smooth. Stir in water, vanilla
and confectioners' sugar until smooth. Carefully
spread over the cereal layer. Carefully press remaining
cereal mixture over peanut butter layer. Cover and
chill for at least 1 hour. Cut into squares. **Yield:** 3
dozen. **Editor's Note:** This recipe was tested in an
850-watt microwave.

Strawberry Cream Freeze

*Youngsters need to gather just four ingredients to fix this
fruity dessert. It's delicious, fast and easy to throw together.* —Ruth Ann Stelfox, Raymond, Alberta

 1 package (8 ounces) cream cheese,
   softened
 1 package (10 ounces) frozen sweetened
   strawberries, thawed
 1/2 cup sugar
 1 cup whipping cream, whipped

Place cream cheese in a bowl; mash with a fork. Add
berries and sugar; mix well. Fold in whipped cream.
Spoon into foil-lined muffin tins. Freeze until firm,
about 2 hours. **Yield:** 12 servings.

Kid-Pleasing Pops Are Fun

WHAT could be better than soft marshmallows, sweet
chocolate and crunchy nuts? A sweet snack made
from those ingredients that's conveniently placed
on a stick for easy eating!

Marcia Porch of Winter Park, Florida shares the idea
for mouth-watering Marshmallow Pops that she frequently makes with son Nicholas.

"Making the pops is a fun activity for a children's
party because any age can participate," says the pastry chef and cooking instructor.

Youngsters simply place the marshmallows on
wooden sticks, dip them in melted chocolate, then
roll them in their favorite goodies, such as coconut,
nuts or candy sprinkles.

"The pops can be customized for holidays or special occasions by rolling them in coordinating colored
sprinkles, such as red and green for Christmas or orange and white for Halloween," Marcia notes.

Marshmallow Pops
(Pictured below)

 2 cups (12 ounces) semisweet chocolate chips
 4-1/2 teaspoons vegetable oil
 36 to 40 large marshmallows
 18 to 20 wooden sticks
 1 cup flaked coconut
 1 cup ground walnuts *or* pecans
 3/4 cup colored *or* chocolate sprinkles

Combine chocolate chips and oil in a shallow microwave-safe bowl; heat until melted. Stir until smooth.
Thread two marshmallows onto each wooden stick.
Roll marshmallows in melted chocolate, turning to
coat. Allow excess to drip off. Roll in coconut, walnuts or
sprinkles. Place on waxed paper-lined baking sheets. Refrigerate until firm. **Yield:** 18-20 servings.

Bunny Dessert Delight to Decorate

CAN'T pull a rabbit out of a hat? Don't worry—you won't need a magic wand to make these effortless treats appear at your table.

Kids can help transform dishes of instant pudding into cute bunnies simply by adding store-bought sweets.

Oval sandwich cookies decorated with pink frost-ing make the rabbit's munchable ears, while colorful jelly beans and black licorice create its fetching face.

"This dessert never fails to delight my grandchildren," writes Flo Burtnett from Gage, Oklahoma.

"You'll want to wait and add the candy right before you're ready to serve the bunnies," Flo notes. "Otherwise the color from the candies may bleed into the pudding."

Bunny in a Cup

(Pictured at left)

2 cups cold milk
1 package (3.4 ounces) instant vanilla pudding mix
2 sticks black licorice
1/4 cup vanilla frosting
Red liquid *or* paste food coloring
8 oval cream-filled vanilla sandwich cookies
8 green jelly beans
4 pink jelly beans

In a bowl, beat milk and pudding mix for 2 minutes or until thickened. Pour into four small bowls; refrigerate. Cut licorice widthwise into fourths, then lengthwise into thirds; set aside. Combine frosting and red food coloring; frost top of cookies to within 1/2 in. of edge. Just before serving, insert two cookies into each bowl of pudding for ears. Add green jelly beans for eyes and a pink jelly bean for nose. Place three pieces of licorice on each side of the nose for whiskers. **Yield:** 4 servings.

Ham and Swiss Snacks

Following a ball game or for a fun after-school treat, ravenous teenagers can prepare this satisfying snack in a jiffy. It's an unusual but delicious combination of ham, cheese and apples on a no-fuss crust. —Beth Gambro
Yorkville, Illinois

2 tubes (8 ounces *each*) refrigerated crescent rolls
2 tablespoons prepared mustard
2 tablespoons dried parsley flakes
2 tablespoons finely chopped onion
1 tablespoon butter *or* margarine, softened
1 cup chopped peeled tart apple
1 cup chopped fully cooked ham
3/4 cup shredded Swiss cheese
2 tablespoons grated Parmesan cheese

Unroll crescent dough; pat onto the bottom and up the sides of an ungreased 15-in. x 10-in. x 1-in. baking pan. Seal seams and perforations. Bake at 375° for 10-12 minutes or until lightly browned. Combine mustard, parsley, onion and butter; spread over crust. Sprinkle with apple, ham and cheeses. Bake 5-10 minutes longer or until cheese is melted. Cut into squares. **Yield:** 2 dozen.

Kids' Favorite Biscuits

I combine two kid-favorite flavors—peanut butter and jelly—in a new way. Refrigerated biscuits with a warm, gooey filling make a yummy lunch or snack. —Dustin Chasteen, Weaverville, North Carolina

1 tube (7-1/2 ounces) refrigerated buttermilk biscuits (10 biscuits)
1/2 cup peanut butter
1/2 cup jelly

Separate biscuits; pat onto the bottom and up the sides of greased muffin cups. In a small bowl, combine peanut butter and jelly until smooth; place a rounded tablespoonful into each biscuit cup. Bake at 450° for 8-10 minutes or until golden brown. **Yield:** 10 servings.

Taco Dogs

(Pictured below right and on page 246)

A taco shell makes a good holder for a hot dog dressed up with a tasty combination of baked beans and cheese. When our children were young, they asked for this meal at least once a week. —Kat Thompson, Prineville, Oregon

      1 package (1 pound) hot dogs
     10 slices process American cheese
     10 hard taco shells, warmed
      1 can (16 ounces) baked beans, warmed

Prepare hot dogs according to package directions. Place a cheese slice and hot dog in each taco shell; top with beans. **Yield:** 10 tacos.

Lunch Box Pizzas

(Pictured below right and on page 247)

It's a challenge finding lunch fare that both our children enjoy. These mini pizzas are fun to make. They pack nicely in plastic sandwich bags and travel well, so there's no mess. —Rhonda Cliett, Belton, Texas

      1 tube (7-1/2 ounces) refrigerated
         buttermilk biscuits (10 biscuits)
    1/4 cup tomato sauce
      1 teaspoon Italian seasoning
     10 slices pepperoni
    3/4 cup shredded Monterey Jack cheese

Flatten each biscuit into a 3-in. circle and press into a greased muffin cup. Combine the tomato sauce and Italian seasoning; spoon 1 teaspoonful into each cup. Top each with a slice of pepperoni and about 1 tablespoon of cheese. Bake at 425° for 10-15 minutes or until golden brown. Serve immediately or store in the refrigerator. **Yield:** 10 servings.

Fourth of July Jell-O

(Pictured at right and on page 247)

With six children, I'm always looking for wholesome quick recipes. This colorful salad can be fixed by school-age children and looks so pretty served in a glass bowl. —Mabel Yoder
Bonduel, Wisconsin

      1 package (3 ounces) berry blue
         gelatin
      2 cups boiling water, *divided*
    1/2 cup cold water, *divided*
      1 package (3 ounces) strawberry
         gelatin
      1 can (15 ounces) pear halves,
         drained and cubed

In a bowl, dissolve blue gelatin in 1 cup boiling water. Stir in 1/4 cup cold water. Pour into an ungreased 9-in. x 5-in. x 3-in. loaf pan. Refrigerate until firm. Repeat with strawberry gelatin

and remaining boiling and cold water. When gelatin is set, cut into cubes. Just before serving, gently combine gelatin cubes and pears in a large glass bowl or individual dishes. **Yield:** 6-8 servings.

Four-Food-Group Shakes

We created this thick peanut butter and banana shake while teaching our son about the four basic food groups. It's a quick and delicious breakfast or snack that he enjoys making for family and friends. —Heather Fortney
Gahanna, Ohio

    1/2 cup milk
      1 cup vanilla ice cream, softened
      1 medium ripe banana, cut into chunks
      2 graham cracker squares
      2 tablespoons peanut butter
      2 tablespoons chocolate syrup
    Cinnamon-sugar, optional

Combine the first six ingredients in a blender; cover and process until smooth. Pour into glasses; sprinkle with cinnamon-sugar if desired. Serve immediately. **Yield:** 2 servings.

**Fourth of July Jell-O
Taco Dogs
Lunch Box Pizzas**

Get Creative With Cute Caterpillar

THIS SHOWSTOPPING sandwich from Iola Egle of McCook, Nebraska is a delightful addition to a children's birthday party or summer picnic.

Packed with a favorite sandwich filling, the French bread loaf is coated with cream cheese, then decorated with green pepper and carrot trims. (You can also make individual caterpillars by dressing up submarine sandwich buns or hoagie rolls.)

Just cut this big sandwich into slices and let kids get their fingers gooey in the colorful frosting as they nibble away.

Cute Caterpillar Sandwich

(Pictured below)

> 1 loaf (1 pound) French bread
> 4 cups chicken, ham *or* tuna salad
> 1 package (8 ounces) cream cheese, softened
> Yellow liquid *or* paste food coloring
> 2 ripe olive slices
> 3 pimiento strips
> 1 medium green pepper, sliced into rings
> 2 medium carrots, shredded

Cut the top fourth off the loaf of bread. Carefully hollow out top and bottom of loaf, leaving a 1/2-in. shell (discard removed bread or save for another use). Fill shell with salad mixture. Replace bread top. Combine cream cheese and food coloring; spread over top and sides of loaf. Place olives at one end for caterpillar's eyes. Arrange pimiento strips to form a mouth. Cut one pepper ring into two 3-in. pieces; insert above eyes for antennae. Cut each remaining pepper ring in one place; place over loaf a few inches apart, trimming ends if necessary. Sprinkle carrots next to the rings. Serve immediately. **Yield: 6 servings.**

Peanut Butter Snack Cups

When our kids were little, they loved this cool and creamy summertime treat. We'd keep several batches in the freezer so there were plenty when their neighborhood friends came over to play.
—Nancy Clark
Cochranton, Pennsylvania

✓ Uses less fat, sugar or salt. Includes Nutritional Analysis and Diabetic Exchanges.

> 12 vanilla wafers
> 1 carton (8 ounces) frozen whipped topping, thawed, *divided*
> 1 cup cold milk
> 1/2 cup peanut butter
> 1 package (3.9 ounces) instant chocolate pudding mix

Place wafers in paper- or foil-lined muffin cups. Top each with 1 tablespoon whipped topping. In a mixing bowl, combine milk and peanut butter. Add pudding mix; beat on low speed for 2 minutes. Fold in remaining whipped topping. Spoon into prepared cups. Cover and freeze. Remove from the freezer 10 minutes before serving. **Yield: 12 servings. Nutritional Analysis:** One serving (prepared with light frozen whipped topping, skim milk, reduced-fat peanut butter and sugar-free chocolate pudding) equals 154 calories, 184 mg sodium, 1 mg cholesterol, 19 gm carbohydrate, 5 gm protein, 7 gm fat. **Diabetic Exchanges:** 1-1/2 starch, 1/2 fat.

Cookies and Cream

(Pictured at right)

This rich and fluffy no-bake dessert has a proven track record in our family. It's easy to make the night before a reunion or church supper. Then just take it out of the fridge and go.
—Teena Lang
Mt. Vernon, Ohio

> 1 package (12 ounces) rocky road *or* chocolate chocolate chip cookies
> 1 carton (8 ounces) frozen whipped topping, thawed
> 1/2 cup milk

Crumble one cookie and set aside. Spoon a fourth of the whipped topping into an 8-in. square pan. Place milk in a shallow bowl. Break the remaining cookies in half; dip seven or eight halves into milk for about 30 seconds each. Place over whipped topping. Repeat layers twice. Top with the remaining whipped topping; sprinkle with the reserved cookie crumbs. Cover and refrigerate for 4 hours or overnight. **Yield: 4-6 servings.**

Cola Chicken

(Pictured above right)

Our daughters, Tricia and Kristin, love to serve this tender chicken with instant mashed potatoes and peas

Cookies and Cream
Cola Chicken

when they have friends over for dinner. A can of cola gives the savory barbecue sauce a flavor boost.
—Keri Scofield Lawson, Fullerton, California

  1/2 cup chopped onion
    2 tablespoons vegetable oil
    4 boneless skinless chicken breast halves
    1 can (12 ounces) cola
    1 cup ketchup
  1/8 teaspoon garlic powder
  1/8 teaspoon salt
  1/8 teaspoon pepper
4-1/2 teaspoons cornstarch
    3 tablespoons cold water

In a skillet, saute onion in oil until tender. Add chicken; brown on all sides. Carefully add cola, ketchup, garlic powder, salt and pepper. Cover and simmer for 25-30 minutes or until chicken juices run clear. Remove the chicken and keep warm. Combine the cornstarch and cold water until smooth; add to the skillet. Bring to a boil; cook and stir for 2 minutes or until thickened. Return chicken to the pan and heat through. **Yield:** 4 servings.

Volcano Pancake

Our daughter Charity enjoys making this cheesy puff pancake, then peeking in the oven to see how high it's risen. You can eliminate the cheese and serve it with confectioners' sugar or syrup instead.
—Kay Curtis
Guthrie, Oklahoma

    6 eggs
    1 cup milk
    1 cup all-purpose flour
  1/2 teaspoon salt
  1/2 cup butter *or* margarine, melted
  3/4 cup shredded cheddar cheese

In a bowl, beat eggs. Add milk, flour and salt; stir until smooth. Pour butter into a 13-in. x 9-in. x 2-in. baking pan. Add batter. Bake at 400° for 30-35 minutes or until a knife inserted near the center comes out clean. Sprinkle with cheese. Serve immediately. **Yield:** 8 servings.

Kool-Aid Sherbet

(Pictured below)

The recipe for this frosty treat is more than 30 years old, and kids love it. You'd never guess that powdered soft drink mix provides the yummy flavor. —Elizabeth Stanton
Mt. Vernon, Washington

1 cup sugar
1 envelope unsweetened orange Kool-Aid *or* flavor of your choice
3 cups milk

In a bowl, stir sugar, Kool-Aid mix and milk until sugar is dissolved. Pour into a shallow freezer container; cover and freeze for 1 hour or until slightly thickened. Transfer to a mixing bowl; beat until smooth. Return to freezer container; cover and freeze until firm. Remove from the freezer 20 minutes before serving. **Yield:** about 3 cups.

Meat-za Pie

(Pictured below)

Our young daughter loves to help in the kitchen. This pizza-shaped meat loaf is so easy to make that she can do several of the steps by herself. —Denise Albers
Freeburg, Illinois

1 can (5 ounces) evaporated milk
1/2 cup plain *or* seasoned dry bread crumbs

3/4 teaspoon garlic salt
1 pound lean ground beef
1/4 cup ketchup
1 teaspoon sugar
1/2 cup canned sliced mushrooms
3 slices process American cheese, cut into thin strips
1/4 teaspoon dried oregano
2 tablespoons grated Parmesan cheese

In a bowl, combine milk, bread crumbs and garlic salt; add beef. Stir with a fork just until mixed. Press onto the bottom and 1/2 in. up the sides of an ungreased 9-in. pie plate. Combine the ketchup and sugar; spread over beef mixture. Sprinkle with mushrooms. Arrange cheese in a lattice pattern on top. Sprinkle with oregano and Parmesan cheese. Bake at 400° for 20 minutes or until meat is no longer pink and the cheese is lightly browned. Drain. Cut into wedges. **Yield:** 4 servings.

Golden Veggie Dip

This snack is sure to encourage kids to eat their vegetables. It's a thick, mild-tasting dip that's easy to prepare and has always been my favorite. —Evelyn Hill
Marion Station, Maryland

1 package (8 ounces) cream cheese, softened
1/4 cup steak sauce
1 tablespoon chili sauce
1/4 teaspoon garlic salt
1/2 teaspoon celery salt
1/4 teaspoon paprika

In a small bowl, combine all ingredients. Refrigerate until serving. **Yield:** 1-1/2 cups.

Chicken Egg Pie

My son, Will, has been making this breakfast quiche since he was 5. He thought quiche was a funny name and said it should be named "chicken egg pie", which is what we've called it ever since. —Judy Bedell
San Miguel, California

1 tube (8 ounces) refrigerated crescent roll dough
2 cups (8 ounces) shredded cheddar cheese, *divided*
1/2 pound bacon, cooked and crumbled
1 cup cubed fully cooked ham
4 eggs
1/3 cup milk
Salt and pepper to taste

Unroll crescent dough; separate into triangles. Arrange in a greased 9-in. pie plate, forming a crust; seal seams and perforations. Sprinkle with 1 cup cheese, bacon and ham. In a bowl, beat eggs, milk, salt and pepper. Pour over the ham. Sprinkle with remaining cheese. Cover edges of crust loosely with foil. Bake at 350° for 20-25 minutes. Remove foil. Bake 20 minutes longer or until a knife inserted near the center comes out clean. **Yield:** 6-8 servings.

Meat-za Pie
Kool-Aid Sherbet

Sweet Snacks On a Stick

A DIP and a drizzle turn crunchy creme-filled sandwich cookies into a deliciously different treat!

"Kids love Cookie Lollipops because they taste as good as they look," reports Jessie Wiggers from Halstead, Kansas. "You need just four ingredients and Popsicle sticks, so these fun snacks make great party favors," she notes.

For special occasions, they're a snap to assemble ahead of time. Or let young guests make their own "cookie pops" as a party activity.

"For an easy variation, reverse the process, dipping the cookies in semisweet chocolate and drizzling them with vanilla instead," Jessie adds.

Cookie Lollipops

(Pictured above right)

1 package (12 ounces) vanilla chips
2 tablespoons shortening, *divided*
1 package (16 ounces) double-stuffed
    chocolate cream-filled sandwich cookies
32 wooden Popsicle *or* craft sticks
1 cup (6 ounces) semisweet chocolate chips

In a microwave or double boiler, melt vanilla chips and 1 tablespoon shortening; stir until smooth. Twist apart sandwich cookies. Dip the end of each Popsicle stick into melted chips; place on a cookie half and top with another half. Place cookies on a waxed paper-lined baking sheet; freeze for 15 minutes. Reheat vanilla chip mixture again if necessary; dip frozen cookies into mixture until completely covered. Return to the baking sheet; freeze 30 minutes longer. Melt the chocolate chips and remaining shortening; stir until smooth. Drizzle over cookies. Store in an airtight container. **Yield:** 32 servings.

Count on Domino Brownies!

IT doesn't take a mathematician to figure out that these cleverly calculated creations won't last long around hungry youngsters.

The fast five-ingredient brownies get their fun domino look with a topping of prepared frosting and mini chocolate chips.

"I've been fixing these brownies with my children for years," writes Cathy Drew of Monroe, Michigan.

"I first made them with my son when he was 7; he's now in his 20's. He entered them in a 4-H exhibit at our county fair and won a blue ribbon," she recalls.

"Kids have so much fun making and decorating these tasty treats," Cathy adds. "They're easy and they're so good!"

Chocolate Dominoes

(Pictured below left)

1/4 cup butter *or* margarine, softened
1/2 cup sugar
  2 eggs
3/4 cup chocolate syrup
2/3 cup all-purpose flour
1/2 cup vanilla frosting
Miniature chocolate chips

In a mixing bowl, cream the butter and sugar. Add eggs and chocolate syrup; mix well. Gradually add flour. Spread into a greased 8-in. square baking pan. Bake at 350° for 30-35 minutes or until a toothpick inserted near the center comes out clean. Cool completely. Frost brownies; cut into 18 rectangles (2-1/3 in. x 1-1/8 in.). With a toothpick, draw a line dividing each rectangle in half widthwise. Decorate with chocolate chips. **Yield:** 1-1/2 dozen.

Holiday Treats Are a Hit

THESE ADORABLE peanut butter cookies resemble the most famous reindeer of all.

"When the holidays came around one year, my son Eric said he wanted to buy every one of the 30 students in his class a Christmas present," relates Gretchen Vandenberghe of Toledo, Ohio. "Not wanting to discourage his generous heart, I suggested he make a treat for everyone instead.

"These Reindeer Cookies were easy to make using a boxed cookie mix. Eric enjoyed creating the faces with pretzels, chocolate chips and red-hots," Gretchen adds.

Reindeer Cookies

(Pictured above)

    1 package (17-1/2 ounces) peanut butter
      cookie mix
1/3 cup vegetable oil
    1 egg
   60 miniature pretzel twists
   60 semisweet chocolate chips
   30 red-hot candies

In a mixing bowl, combine dry cookie mix, oil and egg. Beat until well mixed. Shape into a 7-1/2-in. roll; wrap in plastic wrap. Refrigerate for 1 hour. Unwrap and cut into 1/4-in. slices. Place 2 in. apart on ungreased baking sheets. Using thumb and forefinger, make a slight indention one-third of the way down the sides of each slice. Press in pretzels for antlers, chocolate chips for eyes and a red-hot for the nose. Bake at 350° for 9-11 minutes or until light brown. Remove to wire racks to cool. **Yield:** 2-1/2 dozen. **Editor's Note:** You may substitute any peanut butter cookie recipe for the cookie mix, oil and egg.

Banana Split Muffins

(Pictured below)

My daughter Elizabeth and I pack all the goodies that kids love in a banana split into moist muffins. Her favorite part is adding the cherries at the end. —Elaine Anderson
Aliquippa, Pennsylvania

1-1/2 cups all-purpose flour
    1 cup sugar
  1/2 cup miniature semisweet chocolate chips
  1/2 cup chopped walnuts
    1 teaspoon baking soda
    1 teaspoon salt
    3 medium ripe bananas, mashed
  1/2 cup mayonnaise*
    6 maraschino cherries, halved

In a bowl, combine flour, sugar, chocolate chips, walnuts, baking soda and salt. In another bowl, combine bananas and mayonnaise. Stir into the dry ingredients just until moistened. Fill greased or paper-lined muffin cups three-fourths full. Bake at 375° for 20-25 minutes or until muffins test done. Press a cherry half, cut side down, into the top of each muffin. Cool for 5 minutes before removing from pan to a wire rack. **Yield:** 1 dozen. ***Editor's Note:** Light or fat-free mayonnaise may not be substituted for regular mayonnaise.

Crispy Chocolate Log

(Pictured below)

Our teacher challenged our class to use the microwave for more than defrosting and reheating leftovers. This crispy jelly roll is one of our favorite microwave recipes.
—Michael Saunders and Andy Lyness
West Delaware Middle School in Manchester, Iowa

    1 package (10 ounces) large marshmallows
  1/4 cup butter *or* margarine

Banana Split Muffins
Crispy Chocolate Log

Cinnamon Apples
Cheesy Potato Beef Bake

1/4 cup peanut butter
5-1/2 cups crisp rice cereal
1-1/3 cups semisweet chocolate chips
3/4 cup butterscotch chips

Line a 15-in. x 10-in. x 1-in. pan with waxed paper; grease the paper and set aside. In a large microwave-safe bowl, combine the marshmallows, butter and peanut butter. Cover and microwave on high for 2 minutes; stir until well blended. Stir in cereal until well coated. Spread into prepared pan. In a microwave-safe bowl, combine chocolate and butterscotch chips. Microwave, uncovered, on high for 2 minutes. Stir; spread over cereal mixture to within 1 in. of edges. Roll up jelly-roll style, starting with a short side, peeling waxed paper away while rolling. Place seam side down on a serving plate. Refrigerate for 1 hour or until set. Cut into 1-in. slices. **Yield:** 10 servings. **Editor's Note:** This recipe was tested in an 850-watt microwave.

Cinnamon Apples

(Pictured above)

Teenagers will have fun melting the red cinnamon candies that give bright color to these tender apples. I serve this with pork. —Alma Dinsmore, Lebanon, Indiana

2 cups water
3/4 cup red-hot candies
1/3 cup sugar
6 medium tart apples, peeled and quartered

In a large saucepan over medium heat, bring water, candies and sugar to a boil, stirring constantly until candies and sugar are dissolved. Reduce heat; carefully add ap-ples. Cook, uncovered, until apples are tender. Cool slightly. With a slotted spoon, transfer apples to a serving dish; pour sugar syrup over apples. Cover and refrigerate for at least 3 hours. **Yield:** 6-8 servings.

Cheesy Potato Beef Bake

(Pictured above)

I created this layered meat-and-potatoes casserole a few years ago when my mother asked me what I wanted for supper. —Nicole Rute, Fall River, Wisconsin

1 pound ground beef
2 cans (4 ounces *each*) mushroom stems and pieces, drained, optional
2 packages (5-1/4 ounces *each*) au gratin potatoes
4 cups boiling water
1-1/3 cups milk
2 teaspoons butter *or* margarine
1 teaspoon salt
1/2 teaspoon seasoned salt
1/2 teaspoon pepper
1 cup (4 ounces) shredded cheddar cheese

In a skillet over medium heat, cook beef until no longer pink; drain. Place in a greased 13-in. x 9-in. x 2-in. baking pan. Top with mushrooms. Combine potatoes and contents of sauce mix packets, water, milk, butter, salt, seasoned salt and pepper. Pour over beef and mushrooms. Cover and bake at 400° for 30 minutes or until heated through. Sprinkle with cheese. Bake, uncovered, for 5 minutes or until cheese is melted. Let stand 10 minutes before serving. **Yield:** 8 servings.

Chapter 17

MOST COOKS agree it's fun and rewarding to spend time in the kitchen preparing a comforting, homemade meal for the family.

Unfortunately, you can't always afford to spend a day in the kitchen.

In this chapter, readers share their favorite old-fashioned dishes. Then our test kitchen home economists streamline those recipes into speedier forms by trimming ingredients and preparation time—but not taste.

The home-style flavors of these "recipe redos" are so appealing you might even fool Grandma!

RECIPE "REHAB". Top to bottom: Eclair Torte and Traditional Eclairs (both recipes on p. 263).

259

WHEN she has free time, Kris Hernandez of Oneida, Wisconsin enjoys making from-scratch meals for her husband, Bill. One of the newlywed couple's favorites is baked pork chops over mounds of moist homemade stuffing.

"Although we enjoy the hearty home-cooked flavor of this oven meal, I usually fix it only on weekends," Kris relates. "Bill and I both work full-time. Often we get home late, and there's not enough time to make a dish like this."

To achieve that old-fashioned flavor faster, our test kitchen staff came up with Quicker Pork Chops Over Stuffing that's so easy to prepare Kris can make it during the week.

Boxed stuffing mix eliminates the need to cube bread and chop onion and celery, yet provides homemade flavor.

Using tender boneless chops instead of bone-in chops cuts down on the cooking time, too, without sacrificing flavor. So this tasty dish can be out of the oven and on the table 20 minutes sooner.

Pork Chops Over Stuffing

6 cups cubed day-old bread (1/2-inch cubes)
1 small onion, chopped
1 cup chopped celery
2 tablespoons butter
1 cup hot water
1 tablespoon rubbed sage
1-1/2 teaspoons chicken bouillon granules
1/2 teaspoon salt
1/2 teaspoon pepper
8 bone-in pork loin chops
Worcestershire sauce, optional
Minced fresh parsley, optional

Place bread cubes in a large bowl; set aside. In a saucepan, saute onion and celery in butter until tender. Add water, sage, bouillon, salt and pepper. Pour over bread and toss. Spoon stuffing into eight mounds in a greased 13-in. x 9-in. x 2-in. baking dish. Place a pork chop over each mound. Sprinkle with Worcestershire sauce if desired. Cover and bake at 325° for 25 minutes. Uncover; bake 30 minutes longer or until meat juices run clear. Garnish with parsley if desired. **Yield:** 8 servings.

Quicker Pork Chops Over Stuffing

Quicker Pork Chops Over Stuffing

(Pictured below left)

    2 packages (6 ounces *each*) instant
      stuffing mix
3-1/3 cups chicken broth
  1/2 cup butter
    8 boneless pork loin chops (1/2 to
      3/4 inch thick)
Worcestershire sauce, optional
Minced fresh parsley, optional

In a large saucepan, combine the veg-etable/seasoning packets from stuffing mix with broth and butter. Bring to a boil. Reduce heat; cover and simmer for 5 min-utes. Stir in stuffing. Cover and remove from the heat; let stand for 5 minutes. Spoon stuffing into eight mounds in a greased 13-in. x 9-in. x 2-in. baking dish. Place a pork chop over each mound. Sprin-kle with Worcestershire sauce if desired. Cover and bake at 425° for 15 minutes. Un-cover; bake 20 minutes longer or until meat juices run clear. Garnish with parsley if de-sired. **Yield:** 8 servings.

Quicker Barbecued
Chicken 'n' Rice

TANGY barbecued chicken and rice is a special week-end meal for Patricia Kaliska's family. "Our three daughters like to help out in the kitchen, especially on Sundays," reports the Phillips, Wisconsin cook.

"For this recipe, they enjoy measuring the rice and stirring together the spices and other ingredi-ents that go into the homemade barbecue sauce," she adds.

"The moist, tender chicken is one of their dad's favorites, so they're always proud to have played a part in making it. Once we get the pan in the oven, they can hardly wait an hour until it's time to eat!"

To help Patricia and her family enjoy this tasty meal sooner, our home economists created Quicker Barbecued Chicken 'n' Rice.

They trimmed the list of ingredients to six by us-ing bottled barbecue sauce. This nearly eliminates preparation time without sacrificing the dish's tangy flavor.

Baking time also was cut by substituting instant rice for long grain rice and using quicker-cooking boneless chicken breasts in place of bone-in chicken pieces.

Barbecued Chicken 'n' Rice

1/3 cup chopped onion
  2 tablespoons chopped celery
  1 tablespoon butter *or* margarine
  1 cup ketchup
1/3 cup packed brown sugar

  3 tablespoons vinegar
  2 tablespoons water
  1 tablespoon Worcestershire sauce
  2 teaspoons prepared mustard
1/2 teaspoon salt
  2 garlic cloves, minced
Few drops hot pepper sauce, optional
1-1/2 cups uncooked long grain rice
1-1/4 cups chicken broth
  1 broiler/fryer chicken (3-1/2 to 4 pounds),
    cut up

In a saucepan, saute onion and celery in butter until ten-der. Add the next nine ingredients. Simmer, uncovered, for 30 minutes, stirring occasionally. Meanwhile, com-bine rice and broth in a greased 13-in. x 9-in. x 2-in. bak-ing dish. Top with chicken and barbecue sauce. Bake, un-covered, at 400° for 55-60 minutes or until the rice is ten-der and meat juices run clear. **Yield:** 4 servings.

Quicker Barbecued Chicken 'n' Rice

(Pictured above)

1-1/2 cups uncooked instant rice
  1 cup chicken broth
  6 boneless skinless chicken breast halves
1-1/4 cups barbecue sauce
  1 tablespoon dried minced onion
1/4 teaspoon celery seed

Combine rice and broth in a greased 11-in. x 7-in. x 2-in. baking dish. Top with chicken. Combine barbecue sauce, onion and celery seed; pour over chicken. Bake, uncovered, at 375° for 25-30 minutes or until the rice is tender and meat juices run clear. **Yield:** 4-6 servings.

Quicker
Comforting Chicken

WHEN Sally Hook's family craves a supper with old-fashioned flavor, the Houston, Texas cook prepares Comforting Chicken. This tasty combination of chicken and vegetables is simmered in a creamy sauce that's rich from whipping cream and butter.

"This hearty meal-in-one-pot is an all-time favorite," Sally says. "I like to fix it when I know our children will be stopping home after work or college classes," she notes. "But I don't make it as often as I'd like, because it takes a while to cook on the stove."

To get the special flavor of the original main dish in less time, our test kitchen staff came up with Quicker Comforting Chicken.

This faster makeover version uses convenient canned potatoes and frozen baby carrots to eliminate much of the prep work.

Along with quicker-cooking boneless chicken breasts, the canned and frozen vegetables reduce the simmering time, so Sally can have dinner on the table in less than half an hour.

Comforting Chicken

  1 **medium onion, sliced and separated into rings**
1/2 **cup butter *or* margarine**
  1 **broiler/fryer chicken (3 to 4 pounds), cut up**
  4 **medium potatoes, peeled and quartered**
  4 **medium carrots, quartered widthwise**
  1 **cup whipping cream**

  1 **tablespoon minced fresh parsley**
1/2 **teaspoon salt**
1/4 **teaspoon pepper**

In a large skillet or Dutch oven, saute onion in butter until tender. Remove with a slotted spoon and set aside. In the same pan, brown chicken pieces on all sides. Return onion to pan; add potatoes and carrots. Cover and cook over medium-low heat for 30 minutes or until the vegetables are tender. Stir in cream, parsley, salt and pepper. Reduce heat. Simmer, uncovered, for 15 minutes or until slightly thickened. **Yield:** 4 servings.

Quicker Comforting Chicken

(Pictured at left)

    1 **pound boneless skinless chicken breasts, cut into strips**
    1 **medium onion, sliced and separated into rings**
1-1/2 **cups frozen baby carrots, thawed**
  1/2 **cup butter *or* margarine**
    1 **can (15 ounces) small whole potatoes, drained**
    1 **cup whipping cream**
    1 **tablespoon dried parsley flakes**
  1/2 **teaspoon salt**
  1/4 **teaspoon pepper**

In a large skillet or Dutch oven, cook chicken, onion and carrots in butter until chicken is lightly browned. Add potatoes. Cover and cook over medium heat for 10 minutes or until the carrots are tender. Add the cream, parsley, salt and pepper. Reduce heat. Simmer, uncovered, for 10 minutes or until slightly thickened. **Yield:** 4 servings.

DO YOU RECALL the old-fashioned taste of sweet eclairs like Grandma used to make? She baked the puffed pastries to a beautiful golden brown, filled them with creamy vanilla pudding and frosted them with chocolaty icing.

If you have the time, you can still enjoy the homemade goodness of these traditional treats using this from-scratch recipe from our test kitchen.

But even busy bakers can serve up that wonderful flavor by fixing quicker Eclair Torte. Kathy Shepard of Shepherd, Michigan sent in the time-saving recipe.

"Over the years, family, friends, co-workers and students have enjoyed this tried-and-true dessert," she writes. "For birthdays, our sons prefer it over birthday cake!"

The pastry part of this torte bakes into one big crust, which eliminates filling individual eclairs. The homemade pudding is replaced with a rich vanilla layer that's a snap to blend together using convenient instant pudding and cream cheese.

Frozen whipped topping and purchased chocolate syrup add the fast final touches to this delicious dessert.

Traditional Eclairs

(Pictured below and on page 258)

- 1 cup water
- 1/2 cup butter (no substitutes)
- 1 teaspoon sugar
- 1/4 teaspoon salt
- 1 cup all-purpose flour
- 4 eggs

FILLING:
- 1/3 cup sugar
- 3 tablespoons cornstarch
- 2-1/2 cups milk
- 2 egg yolks
- 1 tablespoon butter (no substitutes)
- 1-1/2 teaspoons vanilla extract
- Confectioners' sugar *or* chocolate frosting

In a saucepan over medium heat, bring water, butter, sugar and salt to a boil. Add flour all at once; stir until a smooth ball forms. Remove from the heat; let stand for 5 minutes. Add eggs, one at a time, beating well with a wooden spoon after each addition. Beat until smooth. Cut a 1/2-in. hole in the corner of a heavy-duty plastic bag; add batter. Pipe into 12 strips (about 3 in. long) 3 in. apart on a greased baking sheet. Bake at 400° for 30-35 minutes or until golden brown. Remove to a wire rack. Immediately cut a slit in each for steam to escape; cool. In a saucepan, combine the sugar and cornstarch; gradually add milk until smooth. Cook and stir over medium-high heat until thickened and bubbly. Reduce heat; cook and stir 2 minutes longer. Remove from the heat. Stir 1 cup hot filling into egg yolks; return all to pan. Bring to a gentle boil; cook for 2 minutes, stirring constantly. Remove from the heat; stir in butter and vanilla. Cool. Split puffs; remove and discard soft dough from inside. Spoon filling into puffs. Replace tops; dust with confectioners' sugar or spread with frosting. Refrigerate until serving. **Yield:** 1 dozen.

Eclair Torte

(Pictured below and on page 259)

- 1 cup water
- 1/2 cup butter (no substitutes)
- 1/4 teaspoon salt
- 1 cup all-purpose flour
- 4 eggs
- 1 package (8 ounces) cream cheese, softened
- 2 packages (3.4 ounces *each*) instant vanilla pudding mix
- 3 cups cold milk
- 1 carton (12 ounces) frozen whipped topping, thawed
- Chocolate syrup

In a saucepan over medium heat, bring water, butter and salt to a boil. Add flour all at once; stir until a smooth ball forms. Remove from the heat; let stand for 5 minutes. Add eggs, one at a time, beating well with a wooden spoon after each addition. Beat until smooth. Spread into a greased 13-in. x 9-in. x 2-in. baking pan. Bake at 400° for 30-35 minutes or until puffed and golden brown. Cool completely on a wire rack. If desired, remove puff from pan and place on a serving platter. In a mixing bowl, beat cream cheese, pudding mix and milk until smooth. Spread over puff; refrigerate for 20 minutes. Spread with whipped topping; refrigerate. Drizzle with chocolate syrup just before serving. Refrigerate leftovers. **Yield:** 12 servings.

Traditional Eclairs
Eclair Torte

Chapter 18

Timeless Recipes with Kitchen Tools

WHEN every minute counts, on-the-go cooks appreciate time-saving appliances like slow cookers, grills and microwaves to get them out of the kitchen in a hurry.

With just a little preparation, you can assemble all the ingredients for terrific recipes in your slow cooker. Then just pop on the lid and switch on the pot as you head out the door.

Grilling is "hot" no matter the season. Fire up the grill throughout the year for a sizzling selection of fast, fuss-free fare and capture that great outdoor flavor.

Time-conscious cooks use microwave ovens for more than just defrosting foods and warming leftovers. Microwaves are marvelous for preparing all kinds of delicious dishes.

MICROWAVE MARVELS. Clockwise from upper left: Casserole Carrot Cake (p. 292), Coffee Shop Fudge (p. 289), Quick Chicken Cordon Bleu (p. 295) and Broccoli Ham Stroganoff (p. 288).

Slow-Cooked Specialties

EVEN THOUGH it simmers foods ever so slowly, a slow cooker can be an indispensable time-saver. After a busy day, a "from-scratch" meal can be cooked to perfection when you walk in the door.

Chicken a la King

(Pictured below)

When I know I'll be having a busy day with little time for cooking, I prepare this tasty main dish. Brimming with tender chicken and colorful vegetables, it smells so good while cooking. —Eleanor Mielke, Snohomish, Washington

✓ Uses less fat, sugar or salt. Includes Nutritional Analysis and Diabetic Exchanges.

    1 can (10-3/4 ounces) condensed cream of
      chicken soup, undiluted
    3 tablespoons all-purpose flour
    1/4 teaspoon pepper
    Dash cayenne pepper
      1 pound boneless skinless chicken breasts, cut
        into cubes
      1 celery rib, chopped
    1/2 cup chopped green pepper
    1/4 cup chopped onion
      1 package (10 ounces) frozen peas, thawed
      2 tablespoons diced pimientos, drained
    Hot cooked rice

In a slow cooker, combine soup, flour, pepper and cayenne until smooth. Stir in chicken, celery, green pepper and onion. Cover and cook on low for 7-8 hours or until meat juices run clear. Stir in peas and pimientos. Cook 30 minutes longer or until heated through. Serve over rice. **Yield:** 6 servings. **Nutritional Analysis:** One 1-cup serving (prepared with low-fat soup; calculated without rice) equals 183 calories, 284 mg sodium, 52 mg cholesterol, 16 gm carbohydrate, 22 gm protein, 3 gm fat. **Diabetic Exchanges:** 2-1/2 very lean meat, 1 starch.

Hot Fruit Salad

(Pictured below)

This spicy fruit mixture is a breeze to make—just open the cans and empty them into the slow cooker. With its pretty color from cherry pie filling, this salad is nice around the holidays...or for any special occasion.
—Barb Vande Voort, New Sharon, Iowa

Hot Fruit Salad
Chicken a la King

Uses less fat, sugar or salt. Includes Nutritional Analysis and Diabetic Exchanges.

- 1 jar (25 ounces) chunky applesauce
- 1 can (21 ounces) cherry pie filling
- 1 can (20 ounces) pineapple chunks, undrained
- 1 can (15-1/4 ounces) sliced peaches, undrained
- 1 can (15-1/4 ounces) apricot halves, undrained
- 1 can (15 ounces) mandarin oranges, undrained
- 1/2 cup packed brown sugar
- 1 teaspoon ground cinnamon

Place the first six ingredients in a slow cooker and stir gently. Combine brown sugar and cinnamon; sprinkle over fruit mixture. Cover and cook on low for 3-4 hours. **Yield:** 16 servings. **Nutritional Analysis:** One 3/4-cup serving (prepared with reduced-sugar pie filling, unsweetened applesauce and pineapple, and no-sugar-added peaches and apricots) equals 124 calories, 12 mg sodium, 0 cholesterol, 32 gm carbohydrate, 1 gm protein, trace fat. **Diabetic Exchange:** 2 fruit.

Creamy Red Potatoes

I can please a crowd with this rich and creamy potato side dish. It's easy to double, and I always receive compliments when I take it to potlucks. —*Sheila Schmitt Topeka, Kansas*

- 2 pounds small red potatoes, quartered
- 1 package (8 ounces) cream cheese, softened
- 1 can (10-3/4 ounces) condensed cream of potato soup, undiluted
- 1 envelope ranch salad dressing mix

Place potatoes in a slow cooker. In a small mixing bowl, beat cream cheese, soup and salad dressing mix until blended. Stir into potatoes. Cover and cook on low for 8 hours or until potatoes are tender. **Yield:** 4-6 servings.

Artichoke Beef Stew

The recipe for this special stew was given to me by a dear friend before she moved to another state. She served it with dumplings, but my husband prefers noodles. —*Janell Schmidt, Athelstane, Wisconsin*

- 1/3 cup all-purpose flour
- 1 teaspoon salt
- 1/2 teaspoon pepper
- 2-1/2 pounds lean beef stew meat, cut into 1-inch cubes
- 3 tablespoons vegetable oil
- 1 can (10-1/2 ounces) condensed beef consomme, undiluted
- 2 medium onions, halved and sliced
- 1 cup red wine *or* beef broth
- 1 garlic clove, minced
- 1/2 teaspoon dill weed
- 2 jars (6-1/2 ounces *each*) marinated artichoke hearts, drained and chopped
- 20 small fresh mushrooms, halved

Hot cooked noodles

In a shallow bowl or large resealable plastic bag, combine the flour, salt and pepper. Add beef and toss to coat. In a skillet, brown beef in oil. Transfer to a slow cooker with a slotted spoon. Gradually add consomme to the skillet. Bring to a boil; stir to loosen browned bits from pan. Stir in onions, wine or broth, garlic and dill. Pour over beef. Cover and cook on low for 7-8 hours or until the meat is nearly tender. Stir in the artichokes and mushrooms. Cook 30 minutes longer or until heated through. Serve over noodles. **Yield:** 6-8 servings.

Spiced Acorn Squash

Working full-time, I didn't always have time to cook the meals my family loved. So I recreated many of our favorites in the slow cooker. This cinnamony treatment for squash is one of them. —*Carol Greco, Centereach, New York*

- 3/4 cup packed brown sugar
- 1 teaspoon ground cinnamon
- 1 teaspoon ground nutmeg
- 2 small acorn squash, halved and seeded
- 3/4 cup raisins
- 4 tablespoons butter *or* margarine
- 1/2 cup water

Combine brown sugar, cinnamon and nutmeg; spoon into the squash halves. Sprinkle with raisins. Top each with 1 tablespoon of butter. Wrap each squash half individually in heavy-duty foil; seal tightly. Pour water into a slow cooker. Place the squash, cut side up, in slow cooker (packets may be stacked). Cover and cook on high for 4 hours or until the squash is tender. Open foil packets carefully to allow steam to escape. **Yield:** 4 servings.

Reuben Spread

You'll need only five ingredients to stir up this hearty dip that tastes like a Reuben sandwich. It's requested at all the gatherings we attend. —*Pam Rohr, Troy, Ohio*

- 2-1/2 cups cubed cooked corned beef
- 1 jar (16 ounces) sauerkraut, rinsed and well drained
- 2 cups (8 ounces) shredded Swiss cheese
- 2 cups (8 ounces) shredded cheddar cheese
- 1 cup mayonnaise

Snack rye bread

In a slow cooker, combine the first five ingredients and mix well. Cover and cook on low for 3 hours, stirring occasionally. Serve warm with rye bread. **Yield:** about 5 cups. **Editor's Note:** Reduced-fat cheese and mayonnaise are not recommended for this recipe.

No Peeking!

Resist the temptation to take a peek at your meal while it's cooking in the slow cooker. Heat escapes each time the cover is removed, which can lengthen the cooking time. —*Edna Hoffman, Hebron, Indiana*

Smoky Beef 'n' Beans

Liquid smoke gives a unique taste to this thick and hearty combination of beef and beans. I like to serve it with a crisp salad to make a complete meal. —Anita Curtis
Camarillo, California

   1 pound ground beef
   1 cup chopped onion
  12 bacon strips, cooked and crumbled
   2 cans (16 ounces *each*) pork and beans
   1 can (16 ounces) kidney beans, rinsed and drained
   1 can (16 ounces) butter beans, drained
   1 cup ketchup
 1/4 cup packed brown sugar
   3 tablespoons vinegar
   1 teaspoon liquid smoke, optional
 1/2 teaspoon salt
 1/4 teaspoon pepper

In a skillet, cook the beef and onion until meat is no longer pink; drain. Transfer to a slow cooker. Stir in the remaining ingredients. Cover and cook on low for 6-7 hours or until heated through. **Yield:** 8 servings.

Corned Beef and Cabbage

I first tried this fuss-free way to cook traditional corned beef and cabbage for St. Patrick's Day a few years ago. Now it's a regular in my menu planning. This is terrific with Dijon mustard and crusty bread. —Karen Waters
Laurel, Maryland

   1 medium onion, cut into wedges
   4 medium potatoes, peeled and quartered
   1 pound baby carrots
   3 cups water
   3 garlic cloves, minced
   1 bay leaf
   2 tablespoons sugar
   2 tablespoons cider vinegar
 1/2 teaspoon pepper
   1 corned beef brisket with spice packet (2-1/2 to 3 pounds), cut in half
   1 small head cabbage, cut into wedges

Place the onion, potatoes and carrots in a 5-qt. slow cooker. Combine water, garlic, bay leaf, sugar, vinegar, pepper and contents of spice packet; pour over the vegetables. Top with brisket and cabbage. Cover and cook on low for 8-9 hours or until the meat and vegetables are tender. Remove bay leaf before serving. **Yield:** 6-8 servings.

Manhattan Clam Chowder

I came up with this simple, delicious soup years ago when my husband and I both worked. It's easy to dump all the ingredients into the slow cooker in the morning...and wonderful to come home to the aroma of dinner ready. —Mary Dixon, Northville, Michigan

 Uses less fat, sugar or salt. Includes Nutritional Analysis and Diabetic Exchanges.

   3 celery ribs, sliced
   1 large onion, chopped
   1 can (14-1/2 ounces) sliced potatoes, drained
   1 can (14-1/2 ounces) sliced carrots, drained
   2 cans (6-1/2 ounces *each*) chopped clams
   2 cups tomato juice
 1-1/2 cups water
 1/2 cup tomato puree
   1 tablespoon dried parsley flakes
 1-1/2 teaspoons dried thyme
   1 teaspoon salt, optional
   1 bay leaf
   2 whole black peppercorns

In a slow cooker, combine all ingredients; stir. Cover and cook on low for 8-10 hours or until the vegetables are tender. Remove bay leaf and peppercorns before serving. **Yield:** 9 servings. **Nutritional Analysis:** One 1-cup serving (prepared with no-salt-added tomato juice and without salt) equals 123 calories, 330 mg sodium, 27 mg cholesterol, 17 gm carbohydrate, 12 gm protein, 1 gm fat. **Diabetic Exchanges:** 1 starch, 1 very lean meat, 1 vegetable.

Spiced Apricot Cider

(Pictured at right)

You'll need just six ingredients to simmer together this hot spiced beverage. Each delicious mugful is rich with apricot flavor. —Connie Cummings
Gloucester, New Jersey

   2 cans (12 ounces *each*) apricot nectar
   2 cups water
 1/4 cup lemon juice
 1/4 cup sugar
   2 whole cloves
   2 cinnamon sticks (3 inches)

In a slow cooker, combine all ingredients; mix well. Cover and cook on low for 2 hours or until cider reaches desired temperature. Remove cloves and cinnamon sticks before serving. **Yield:** 6 servings.

Strawberry Rhubarb Sauce

(Pictured above right)

This tart and tangy fruit sauce is excellent over pound cake or ice cream. I've served this rosy-colored mixture many times and gotten rave reviews from friends and family. —Judith Waxman, Harkers Island, North Carolina

✓ Uses less fat, sugar or salt. Includes Nutritional Analysis and Diabetic Exchanges.

   6 cups chopped rhubarb (1/2-inch pieces)
   1 cup sugar
 1/2 teaspoon grated orange peel
 1/2 teaspoon ground ginger
   1 cinnamon stick (3 inches)

Strawberry Rhubarb Sauce
Spiced Apricot Cider
Herb-Stuffed Chops

1/2 cup white grape juice
2 cups halved unsweetened strawberries
Pound cake *or* vanilla ice cream

Place rhubarb in a slow cooker. Combine sugar, orange peel and ginger; sprinkle over rhubarb. Add cinnamon stick and grape juice. Cover and cook on low for 5-6 hours or until rhubarb is tender. Stir in strawberries; cook 1 hour longer. Discard cinnamon stick. Serve over cake or ice cream. **Yield:** 10 servings. **Nutritional Analysis:** One 1/2-cup serving (calculated without cake or ice cream) equals 115 calories, 4 mg sodium, 0 cholesterol, 29 gm carbohydrate, 1 gm protein, trace fat. **Diabetic Exchange:** 2 fruit.

Herb-Stuffed Chops

(Pictured above)

Guests will think you stayed home all day when you serve these tender stuffed chops. I often share this recipe with new brides because I know it will become one of their favorites. —Diane Seeger, New Springfield, Ohio

3/4 cup chopped onion
1/4 cup chopped celery
2 tablespoons butter *or* margarine
2 cups day-old bread cubes
1/2 cup minced fresh parsley
1/3 cup evaporated milk
1 teaspoon fennel seed, crushed
1-1/2 teaspoons salt, *divided*
1/2 teaspoon pepper, *divided*
6 rib *or* loin pork chops (1 inch thick)
1 tablespoon vegetable oil
3/4 cup white wine *or* chicken broth

In a skillet, saute onion and celery in butter until tender. Add bread cubes, parsley, milk, fennel, 1/4 teaspoon salt and 1/8 teaspoon pepper; toss to coat. Cut a pocket in each chop by slicing from the fat side almost to the bone. Spoon about 1/4 cup stuffing into each pocket. Combine the remaining salt and pepper; rub over chops. In a skillet, brown the chops in oil; transfer to a slow cooker. Pour wine or broth over the chops. Cover and cook on low for 8-9 hours or until meat juices run clear. **Yield:** 6 servings.

Hearty Black Bean Soup

Cumin and chili powder give spark to this thick, hearty soup. If you have leftover meat—smoked sausage, browned ground beef or roast—toss it in for the last 30 minutes of cooking. —Amy Chop, Eufaula, Alabama

✔ Uses less fat, sugar or salt. Includes Nutritional Analysis and Diabetic Exchanges.

   3 medium carrots, halved and thinly sliced
   2 celery ribs, thinly sliced
   1 medium onion, chopped
   4 garlic cloves, minced
   1 can (30 ounces) black beans, rinsed and drained
   2 cans (14-1/2 ounces *each*) chicken broth
   1 can (15 ounces) crushed tomatoes
1-1/2 teaspoons dried basil
  1/2 teaspoon dried oregano
  1/2 teaspoon ground cumin
  1/2 teaspoon chili powder
  1/2 teaspoon hot pepper sauce
Hot cooked rice

In a slow cooker, combine the first 12 ingredients. Cover and cook on low for 9-10 hours or until vegetables are tender. Serve over rice. **Yield:** 8 servings. **Nutritional Analysis:** One 1-cup serving (prepared with low-sodium broth; calculated without rice) equals 141 calories, 477 mg sodium, 2 mg cholesterol, 24 gm carbohydrate, 9 gm protein, 2 gm fat. **Diabetic Exchanges:** 1-1/2 starch, 1-1/2 very lean meat.

Herbed Chicken and Veggies

(Pictured below right)

This subtly seasoned chicken and vegetable combination is a snap to prepare on a hectic working day. A dessert is all that's needed to complete this satisfying supper.
—Dorothy Pritchett, Wills Point, Texas

   1 broiler-fryer chicken (3 to 4 pounds), cut up and skin removed
   2 medium tomatoes, chopped
   1 medium onion, chopped
   2 garlic cloves, minced
  1/2 cup chicken broth
   2 tablespoons white wine *or* additional chicken broth
   1 bay leaf
1-1/2 teaspoons salt
   1 teaspoon dried thyme
  1/4 teaspoon pepper
   2 cups broccoli florets
Hot cooked rice

Place chicken in a slow cooker. Top with tomatoes, onion and garlic. Combine broth, wine or additional broth, bay leaf, salt, thyme and pepper; pour over chicken. Cover and cook on low for 7-8 hours. Add broccoli; cook 45-60 minutes longer or until the chicken juices run clear and the broccoli is tender. Discard bay leaf. Thicken pan juices if desired. Serve over rice. **Yield:** 4-6 servings.

Four-Bean Medley

This bean side dish always draws compliments. Because it's easy to fix ahead and simmer in the slow cooker, it's convenient to take to potlucks and church meals.
—Susanne Wasson, Montgomery, New York

   8 bacon strips, diced
   2 medium onions, quartered and sliced
  3/4 cup packed brown sugar
  1/2 cup vinegar
   1 teaspoon salt
   1 teaspoon ground mustard
  1/2 teaspoon garlic powder
   1 can (16 ounces) baked beans, undrained
   1 can (16 ounces) kidney beans, rinsed and drained
   1 can (15-1/2 ounces) butter beans, rinsed and drained
   1 can (14-1/2 ounces) cut green beans, drained

In a skillet, cook bacon until crisp. Drain, reserving 2 tablespoons drippings; set bacon aside. Saute onions in drippings until tender. Stir in brown sugar, vinegar, salt, mustard and garlic powder. Simmer, uncovered, for 15 minutes or until onions are golden brown. Combine the beans in a slow cooker. Add onion mixture and bacon; mix well. Cover and cook on low for 6-7 hours or until the beans are tender. Serve with a slotted spoon. **Yield:** 8-10 servings.

Gone-All-Day Casserole

Even less expensive cuts of meat become deliciously tender when cooked slowly in this savory casserole. Wild rice and almonds give this meal a special look and taste.
—Janet Haak Aarness, Pelican Rapids, Minnesota

   1 cup uncooked wild rice, rinsed and drained
   1 cup chopped celery
   1 cup chopped carrots
   2 cans (4 ounces *each*) mushroom stems and pieces, drained
   1 large onion, chopped
   1 garlic clove, minced
  1/2 cup slivered almonds
   3 beef bouillon cubes
2-1/2 teaspoons seasoned salt
   2 pounds boneless round steak, cut into 1-inch cubes
   3 cups water

Place ingredients in order listed in a slow cooker (do not stir). Cover and cook on low for 6-8 hours or until rice is tender. Stir before serving. **Yield:** 12 servings.

Quick Cleanup

I lightly coat the inside of my slow cooker with non-stick cooking spray before filling it with ingredients. This simple tip makes cleanup a breeze.
—Caroline Thompson, Louisville, Tennessee

Saucy Italian Roast

This tender roast is one of my favorite fix-and-forget meals. I thicken the juices with a little flour and add ketchup, then serve the sauce and beef slices over pasta.
—Jan Roat, Red Lodge, Montana

    1 boneless rump roast (3 to 3-1/2 pounds)
1/2 to 1 teaspoon salt
1/2 teaspoon garlic powder
1/4 teaspoon pepper
    1 jar (4-1/2 ounces) sliced mushrooms, drained
    1 medium onion, diced
    1 jar (14 ounces) spaghetti sauce
1/4 to 1/2 cup red wine *or* beef broth
Hot cooked pasta

Cut the roast in half. Combine salt, garlic powder and pepper; rub over roast. Place in a 5-qt. slow cooker. Top with mushrooms and onion. Combine the spaghetti sauce and wine or broth; pour over meat and vegetables. Cover and cook on low for 8-9 hours or until meat is tender. Slice roast; serve over pasta with pan juices. **Yield:** 8-10 servings.

Spiced Coffee

(Pictured below)

Even those who usually don't drink coffee will find this spiced blend with a hint of chocolate appealing. I keep a big batch simmering at a brunch or open house.
—Joanne Holt, Bowling Green, Ohio

    8 cups brewed coffee
1/3 cup sugar
1/4 cup chocolate syrup
1/2 teaspoon anise extract
    4 cinnamon sticks (3 inches), halved
1-1/2 teaspoons whole cloves
Additional cinnamon sticks, optional

In a slow cooker, combine the first four ingredients; mix well. Place cinnamon sticks and cloves in a double thickness of cheesecloth; bring up corners of cloth and tie with string to form a bag. Add to slow cooker. Cover and cook on low for 2-3 hours. Discard spice bag. Ladle coffee into mugs; garnish each with a cinnamon stick if desired. **Yield:** 8 cups.

Spiced Coffee
Herbed Chicken and Veggies

Stuffed Sweet Peppers
Slow-Cooked Salsa

Slow-Cooked Salsa

(Pictured above)

I love the fresh taste of homemade salsa, but as a working mother, I don't have much time to make it. So I came up with this slow-cooked version that practically makes itself! —Toni Menard, Lompoc, California

✓ Uses less fat, sugar or salt. Includes Nutritional Analysis and Diabetic Exchanges.

 10 plum tomatoes, cored
  2 garlic cloves
  1 small onion, cut into wedges
  2 jalapeno peppers*
 1/4 cup cilantro *or* parsley leaves
 1/2 teaspoon salt, optional

Cut a small slit in two tomatoes; insert a garlic clove into each slit. Place tomatoes and onion in a slow cooker. Cut stem off jalapenos; remove seeds if a milder salsa is desired. Place jalapenos in the slow cooker. Cover and cook on high for 2-1/2 to 3 hours or until vegetables are softened (some may brown slightly); cool. In a blender or food processor, combine the tomato mixture, cilantro and salt if desired; cover and process until smooth. Refrigerate leftovers. **Yield:** about 2 cups. **Nutritional Analysis:** One 1/4-cup serving (prepared without salt) equals 24 calories, 9 mg sodium, 0 cholesterol, 5 gm carbohydrate, 1 gm protein, trace fat. **Diabetic Exchange:** 1 vegetable. ***Editor's Note:** When cutting or seeding hot peppers, use rubber or plastic gloves to protect your hands. Avoid touching your face.

Stuffed Sweet Peppers

(Pictured above)

Italian sausage gives zest to the rice filling in these tender peppers. When I married in 1970, slow cookers were the rage. In our home, it's one appliance that's never gone out of style. —Judy Earl, Sarasota, Florida

  3 medium sweet red peppers
  2 medium sweet yellow peppers
  1 jar (14 ounces) spaghetti sauce, *divided*
 3/4 pound uncooked bulk Italian turkey sausage
 3/4 cup uncooked instant rice

1/2 cup crumbled feta *or* blue cheese
1/2 cup chopped onion
1/4 cup chopped tomato
1/4 cup minced fresh parsley
  2 tablespoons sliced ripe olives
1/4 to 1/2 teaspoon garlic powder
1/2 teaspoon salt
1/2 teaspoon Italian seasoning
1/2 teaspoon crushed red pepper flakes

Cut tops off peppers; chop tops and set aside. Discard stems and seeds; set pepper cups aside. Reserve 3/4 cup spaghetti sauce; pour the remaining sauce into a slow cooker. Combine the sausage, rice, cheese, onion, tomato, parsley, olives, garlic powder, salt, Italian seasoning, red pepper flakes and reserved chopped peppers and spaghetti sauce. Spoon into pepper cups; place in slow cooker. Cover and cook on low for 4-5 hours or until peppers are tender. **Yield:** 5 servings.

Fruit Compote Dessert

This is one of the first desserts I learned to make in the slow cooker, and it's the one guests still enjoy most. It tastes like it came from a fancy restaurant.
—*Laura Bryant German, West Warren, Massachusetts*

✓ Uses less fat, sugar or salt. Includes Nutritional Analysis and Diabetic Exchanges.

  2 medium tart apples, peeled
  2 medium fresh peaches, peeled and cubed
  2 cups unsweetened pineapple chunks
1-1/4 cups unsweetened pineapple juice
1/4 cup honey
  2 lemon slices (1/4 inch)
  1 cinnamon stick (3-1/2 inches)
  1 medium firm banana, thinly sliced
Whipped cream, sliced almonds and maraschino
  cherries, optional

Cut apples into 1/4-in. slices and then in half; place in a slow cooker. Add the peaches, pineapple, pineapple juice, honey, lemon and cinnamon. Cover and cook on low for 3-4 hours. Just before serving, stir in banana slices. Serve with a slotted spoon if desired. Garnish with whipped cream, almonds and cherries if desired. **Yield:** 8 servings. **Nutritional Analysis:** One 3/4-cup serving (without garnish) equals 117 calories, 2 mg sodium, 0 cholesterol, 30 gm carbohydrate, 1 gm protein, trace fat. **Diabetic Exchange:** 2 fruit.

Sweet and Tangy Chicken

Spicy barbecue sauce blends with sweet pineapple in this quick-to-fix chicken dish. It's tasty enough for a company dinner...just add a salad and rolls. —*Mary Zawlocki Gig Harbor, Washington*

  8 boneless skinless chicken breast halves
  2 bottles (18 ounces *each*) barbecue sauce
  1 can (20 ounces) pineapple chunks,
    undrained
  1 medium green pepper, chopped

  1 medium onion, chopped
  2 garlic cloves, minced
Hot cooked rice

Place four chicken breasts in a 5-qt. slow cooker. Combine barbecue sauce, pineapple, green pepper, onion and garlic; pour half over the chicken. Top with remaining chicken and sauce. Cover and cook on low for 8-9 hours or until chicken is tender. Thicken sauce if desired. Serve the chicken and sauce over rice. **Yield:** 8 servings.

Shredded Beef Sandwiches

I find it easy to feed a crowd with this tender and tasty beef on hamburger buns. The recipe came from my children's third-grade teacher, and it remains one of our favorites.
—*Myra Innes, Auburn, Kansas*

✓ Uses less fat, sugar or salt. Includes Nutritional Analysis and Diabetic Exchanges.

  1 boneless beef roast (3 pounds)
  1 medium onion, chopped
1/3 cup vinegar
  3 bay leaves
1/2 teaspoon salt, optional
1/4 teaspoon ground cloves
1/8 teaspoon garlic powder
  12 hamburger buns, split

Cut roast in half; place in a slow cooker. Combine onion, vinegar, bay leaves, salt if desired, cloves and garlic powder; pour over roast. Cover and cook on low for 10-12 hours or until the meat is very tender. Discard bay leaves. Remove meat and shred with a fork. Serve on buns. **Yield:** 12 servings. **Nutritional Analysis:** One 1/2-cup serving (prepared without salt; calculated without bun) equals 173 calories, 52 mg sodium, 78 mg cholesterol, 2 gm carbohydrate, 26 gm protein, 6 gm fat. **Diabetic Exchange:** 3 lean meat.

Slow-Cooker Bread Pudding

I use my slow cooker to turn day-old cinnamon rolls into a comforting, old-fashioned dessert. It tastes wonderful topped with lemon or vanilla sauce or whipped cream.
—*Edna Hoffman, Hebron, Indiana*

  8 cups cubed day-old unfrosted cinnamon rolls*
  2 cups milk
  4 eggs
1/4 cup sugar
1/4 cup butter *or* margarine, melted
1/2 teaspoon vanilla extract
1/4 teaspoon ground nutmeg
  1 cup raisins

Place cubed cinnamon rolls in a slow cooker. In a mixing bowl, combine the next six ingredients; beat until smooth. Stir in raisins. Pour over cinnamon rolls; stir gently. Cover and cook on low for 3 hours. **Yield:** 6 servings. ***Editor's Note:** 8 slices of cinnamon or white bread, cut into 1-inch cubes, may be substituted for the cinnamon rolls.

Hobo Meatball Stew

(Pictured below)

Basic ingredients make this hearty stew a favorite. I usually have everything on hand for this recipe, so it's simple to load up the slow cooker at noon. When I get home, dinner's ready and waiting.   —Margery Bryan
Royal City, Washington

✓ Uses less fat, sugar or salt. Includes Nutritional Analysis and Diabetic Exchanges.

     1 pound ground beef
1-1/2 teaspoons salt *or* salt-free seasoning blend,
     divided
   1/2 teaspoon pepper, *divided*
     4 medium potatoes, peeled and cut into chunks
     4 medium carrots, cut into chunks
     1 large onion, cut into chunks
   1/2 cup ketchup
   1/2 cup water
1-1/2 teaspoons vinegar
   1/2 teaspoon dried basil

In a bowl, combine beef, 1 teaspoon salt and 1/4 teaspoon pepper; mix well. Shape into 1-in. balls. In a skillet over medium heat, brown meatballs on all sides; drain. Place potatoes, carrots and onion in a slow cooker; top with meatballs. Combine the ketchup, water, vinegar, basil, and remaining salt and pepper; pour over meatballs. Cover and cook on high for 4-5 hours or until the vegetables are tender. **Yield:** 4 servings. **Nutritional Analysis:** One serving (prepared with lean ground beef, salt-free seasoning and no-salt-added ketchup) equals 401 calories, 124 mg sodium, 41 mg cholesterol, 49 gm carbohydrate, 28 gm protein, 11 gm fat. **Diabetic Exchanges:** 3 starch, 3 lean meat, 1 vegetable.

Pumpkin Pie Pudding

(Pictured below)

My husband loves any foods that contain pumpkin, and this creamy, comforting no-hassle dessert is one of his favorites. We make this super easy pudding year-round, but it's especially nice in fall.   —Andrea Schaak
Bloomington, Minnesota

     1 can (15 ounces) solid-pack pumpkin
     1 can (12 ounces) evaporated milk
   3/4 cup sugar

Pumpkin Pie Pudding
Hobo Meatball Stew

When using canned pumpkin in a recipe, remember that a 15-ounce can contains about 1-3/4 cups of mashed pumpkin. When cooking fresh pumpkin, you'll find that a 5-pound pumpkin will yield about 4-1/2 cups mashed cooked pumpkin.

1/2 cup biscuit/baking mix
2 eggs, beaten
2 tablespoons butter *or* margarine, melted
2-1/2 teaspoons pumpkin pie spice
2 teaspoons vanilla extract
Whipped topping, optional

In a large bowl, combine the first eight ingredients. Transfer to a slow cooker coated with nonstick cooking spray. Cover and cook on low for 6-7 hours or until a thermometer reads 160°. Serve in bowls with whipped topping if desired. **Yield:** 6-8 servings.

Pizza in a Pot

Since most kids will try anything to do with pizza, I rely on this recipe when one of my two teenage sons has a friend stay for dinner. It's frequently a hit.
—Anita Doughty, West Des Moines, Iowa

1 pound bulk Italian sausage
1 can (28 ounces) crushed tomatoes
1 can (15-1/2 ounces) chili beans
1 can (15 ounces) black beans, rinsed and drained
1 can (2-1/4 ounces) sliced ripe olives, drained
1 medium onion, chopped
1 small green pepper, chopped
2 garlic cloves, minced
1/4 cup grated Parmesan cheese
1 tablespoon quick-cooking tapioca
1 tablespoon dried basil
1 bay leaf
1 teaspoon salt
1/2 teaspoon sugar
Hot cooked pasta
Shredded mozzarella cheese, optional

In a skillet over medium heat, cook the sausage until no longer pink; drain. Transfer to a slow cooker. Add the next 13 ingredients; mix well. Cover and cook on low for 8-9 hours or until slightly thickened. Discard bay leaf. Stir before serving over pasta. Sprinkle with mozzarella cheese if desired. **Yield:** 6-8 servings.

Apple Granola Dessert

I would be lost without my slow cooker. Besides using it to prepare our evening meal, I often make desserts in it, including these tender apples that get a tasty treatment from granola cereal. —Janis Lawrence, Childress, Texas

4 medium tart apples, peeled and sliced
2 cups granola cereal with fruit and nuts

1/4 cup honey
2 tablespoons butter *or* margarine, melted
1 teaspoon ground cinnamon
1/2 teaspoon ground nutmeg
Vanilla ice cream *or* whipped topping, optional

In a slow cooker, combine apples and cereal. In a bowl, combine honey, butter, cinnamon and nutmeg; pour over apple mixture and mix well. Cover and cook on low for 6-8 hours. Serve with ice cream or whipped topping if desired. **Yield:** 4-6 servings.

Minister's Delight

You'll need just four common ingredients to put together this comforting dessert. A friend gave me this recipe several years ago. She said a local minister's wife fixed it every Sunday, so she named it accordingly. —Mary Ann Potter Blue Springs, Missouri

1 can (21 ounces) cherry *or* apple pie filling
1 package (18-1/4 ounces) yellow cake mix
1/2 cup butter *or* margarine, melted
1/3 cup chopped walnuts, optional

Place pie filling in a slow cooker. Combine dry cake mix and butter (mixture will be crumbly); sprinkle over filling. Sprinkle with walnuts if desired. Cover and cook on low for 2-3 hours. Serve in bowls. **Yield:** 10-12 servings.

Spicy Beef Vegetable Stew

This zesty ground beef and vegetable soup is flavorful and fast to fix. It makes a complete meal when served with warm corn bread, sourdough bread or French bread.
—Lynnette Davis, Tullahoma, Tennessee

✓ Uses less fat, sugar or salt. Includes Nutritional Analysis and Diabetic Exchanges.

1 pound ground beef
1 cup chopped onion
1 jar (30 ounces) meatless spaghetti sauce
3-1/2 cups water
1 package (16 ounces) frozen mixed vegetables
1 can (10 ounces) diced tomatoes and green chilies
1 cup sliced celery
1 teaspoon beef bouillon granules
1 teaspoon pepper

In a skillet over medium heat, cook beef and onion until meat is no longer pink; drain. Transfer to a slow cooker. Stir in the remaining ingredients. Cover and cook on low for 8 hours or until the vegetables are tender. **Yield:** 12 servings (3 quarts). **Nutritional Analysis:** One serving (prepared with lean ground beef, reduced-sodium spaghetti sauce and low-sodium bouillon) equals 159 calories, 159 mg sodium, 14 mg cholesterol, 14 gm carbohydrate, 10 gm protein, 7 gm fat. **Diabetic Exchanges:** 1-1/2 meat, 1 vegetable, 1/2 starch.

Pineapple Sweet Potatoes

Pineapple and pecans make a pretty topping for this no-fuss fall side dish. It's light, tasty and not too sweet. Making it in the slow cooker leaves extra space in the oven when preparing a holiday turkey and other dishes.
—Bette Fulcher, Lexington, Texas

    6 to 6-1/2 cups mashed sweet potatoes
      (without added milk or butter)
    4 eggs
    1 cup milk
    1/2 cup butter *or* margarine, softened
    1 teaspoon vanilla extract
    1/2 teaspoon lemon extract
    1 teaspoon salt
    1 teaspoon ground cinnamon
    1/2 teaspoon ground nutmeg
    1 can (8 ounces) pineapple slices, drained
    1/4 cup chopped pecans

In a mixing bowl, combine the first nine ingredients; mix well. Transfer to a slow cooker. Top with pineapple slices and pecans. Cover and cook on low for 4-5 hours or until a thermometer reads 160°. **Yield:** 12-14 servings.

Cranberry Pork Roast

I love to serve guests this moist flavorful pork. You don't have to slave away in the kitchen to prepare it, yet it tastes like a gourmet meal.
—Kimberley Scasny
Douglasville, Georgia

    1 boneless rolled pork loin roast (2-1/2 to 3
      pounds)
    1/2 teaspoon salt
    1/4 teaspoon pepper
    1 can (16 ounces) whole-berry cranberry sauce
    1/4 cup honey
    1 teaspoon grated orange peel
    1/8 teaspoon ground cloves
    1/8 teaspoon ground nutmeg

Cut roast in half and place in a slow cooker; sprinkle with salt and pepper. Combine the remaining ingredients; pour over roast. Cover and cook on low for 4-5 hours or until a meat thermometer reads 160°. Let stand 10 minutes before slicing. **Yield:** 6-8 servings.

Cheesy Spinach

My daughter often serves this cheese and spinach blend at church suppers. Even people who don't usually eat spinach like this flavorful treatment once they try it. There is never any left. —Frances Moore, Decatur, Illinois

    2 packages (10 ounces *each*) frozen chopped
      spinach, thawed and well drained
    2 cups (16 ounces) small-curd cottage cheese
    1-1/2 cups cubed process American cheese
    3 eggs, lightly beaten
    1/4 cup butter *or* margarine, cubed
    1/4 cup all-purpose flour
    1 teaspoon salt

In a large bowl, combine all ingredients. Pour into a greased slow cooker. Cover and cook on high for 1 hour. Reduce heat to low; cook 4-5 hours longer or until a knife inserted near the center comes out clean. **Yield:** 6-8 servings.

Hot Crab Dip

(Pictured below right)

I have six children and one grandchild, work full-time, and coach soccer and football. So I appreciate recipes like this one that are easy to assemble.
—Teri Rasey-Bolf
Cadillac, Michigan

✓ Uses less fat, sugar or salt. Includes Nutritional Analysis and Diabetic Exchanges.

    1/2 cup milk
    1/3 cup salsa
    3 packages (8 ounces *each*) cream cheese,
      cubed
    2 packages (8 ounces *each*) imitation
      crabmeat, flaked
    1 cup thinly sliced green onions
    1 can (4 ounces) chopped green chilies
Assorted crackers

Combine milk and salsa. Transfer to a slow cooker coated with nonstick cooking spray. Stir in cream cheese, crab, onions and chilies. Cover and cook on low for 3-4 hours, stirring every 30 minutes. Serve with crackers. **Yield:** about 5 cups. **Nutritional Analysis:** One 1/4-cup serving (prepared with skim milk and light cream cheese; calculated without crackers) equals 80 calories, 385 mg sodium, 23 mg cholesterol, 5 gm carbohydrate, 7 gm protein, 3 gm fat. **Diabetic Exchanges:** 1 lean meat, 1 vegetable.

Hearty Pork Stew

This spicy slow-cooked stew combines tender chunks of pork with colorful tomatoes and green peppers. I garnish bowls of it with chopped hard-cooked eggs and green onions.
—Rebecca Overy, Evanston, Wyoming

    1-1/2 to 2 pounds boneless pork, cut into 1-inch
      cubes
    4 cups water
    1 can (14-1/2 ounces) stewed tomatoes
    1 medium onion, chopped
    1 medium green pepper, chopped
    1/3 cup soy sauce
    1 to 2 tablespoons chili powder
    1 tablespoon dried celery flakes
    1/2 teaspoon garlic powder
    1/2 teaspoon pepper
    1/3 cup cornstarch
    1/3 cup cold water
Hot cooked noodles

In a slow cooker, combine the first 10 ingredients. Cover and cook on low for 8 hours. Combine cornstarch and water until smooth; gradually stir into slow cooker. Cover and cook on high for 30 minutes or until slightly thickened. Serve in bowls over noodles. **Yield:** 8-10 servings.

chicken juices run clear. Serve over rice or noodles. **Yield:** 4 servings.

Creamy Italian Chicken

My recipe for tender chicken in a creamy sauce gets fast flavor from salad dressing mix. Served over rice or pasta, it's rich, delicious and special enough for company.
—*Maura McGee, Tallahassee, Florida*

4 boneless skinless chicken breast halves
1 envelope Italian salad dressing mix
1/4 cup water
1 package (8 ounces) cream cheese, softened
1 can (10-3/4 ounces) condensed cream of chicken soup, undiluted
1 can (4 ounces) mushroom stems and pieces, drained
Hot cooked rice *or* noodles

Place the chicken in a slow cooker. Combine salad dressing mix and water; pour over chicken. Cover and cook on low for 3 hours. In a small mixing bowl, beat the cream cheese and soup until blended. Stir in the mushrooms. Pour over chicken. Cook 1 hour longer or until

Slow Cooker Party Mix

(Pictured below)

This mildly seasoned snack mix is always a party favorite. Served warm from a slow cooker, the munchable mixture is very satisfying. —*Dana Hughes, Gresham, Oregon*

4 cups Wheat Chex
4 cups Cheerios
3 cups pretzel sticks
1 can (12 ounces) salted peanuts
1/4 cup butter *or* margarine, melted
2 to 3 tablespoons grated Parmesan cheese
1 teaspoon celery salt
1/2 to 3/4 teaspoon seasoned salt

In a 5-qt. slow cooker, combine cereals, pretzels and peanuts. Combine butter, Parmesan cheese, celery salt and seasoned salt; drizzle over cereal mixture and mix well. Cover and cook on low for up to 3 hours, stirring every 30 minutes. Serve warm or at room temperature. **Yield:** about 3 quarts.

Slow Cooker Party Mix
Hot Crab Dip

Great Grilling Recipes

WANT to spend a lot less time in the kitchen? Step outdoors anytime of year and fix a meal on the grill! It's easy to cook an entire menu at once...plus there's less mess and cleanup.

Summertime Chicken Tacos

(Pictured below)

Try these tempting tacos when you're looking for a change of pace from regular tacos. A mild zing from the lime juice in the marinade for the chicken comes through after grilling. I like to serve them with salsa, cheese, lettuce and tomatoes.
—Susan Scott
Asheville, North Carolina

✓ Uses less fat, sugar or salt. Includes Nutritional Analysis and Diabetic Exchanges.

1/3 cup olive *or* vegetable oil
1/4 cup lime juice
4 garlic cloves, minced
1 tablespoon minced fresh parsley *or* 1 teaspoon dried parsley flakes
1 teaspoon ground cumin
1 teaspoon dried oregano
1/2 teaspoon salt, optional
1/4 teaspoon pepper
4 boneless skinless chicken breast halves (1-1/4 pounds)
6 flour tortillas (8 inches) *or* taco shells, warmed
Toppings of your choice

In a large resealable plastic bag or shallow glass container, combine the first eight ingredients. Add chicken and turn to coat. Seal or cover and refrigerate 8 hours or overnight, turning occasionally. Drain and discard marinade. Grill chicken, uncovered, over medium heat for 5-7 minutes on each side or until juices run clear. Cut into thin strips; serve in tortillas or taco shells with desired toppings. **Yield:** 6 servings. **Nutritional Analysis:** One serving (prepared with flour tortillas and without salt; calculated without toppings) equals 338 calories, 289 mg sodium, 63 mg cholesterol, 28 gm carbohydrate, 27 gm protein, 12 gm fat. **Diabetic Exchanges:** 3 lean meat, 2 starch, 1/2 fat.

Cool-Kitchen Meat Loaf
Summertime Chicken Tacos
Garden Turkey Burgers
Gingered Honey Salmon

Garden Turkey Burgers

(Pictured below left)

These moist burgers get plenty of color and flavor from onion, zucchini and red pepper. I often make the mixture ahead of time and put it in the refrigerator. Later, after helping my husband with farm chores, I can put the burgers on the grill while whipping up a salad or side dish.
—Sandy Kitzmiller, Unityville, Pennsylvania

✓ Uses less fat, sugar or salt. Includes Nutritional Analysis and Diabetic Exchanges.

  1 cup old-fashioned oats
3/4 cup chopped onion
3/4 cup finely chopped sweet red *or* green pepper
1/2 cup shredded zucchini
1/4 cup ketchup
  2 garlic cloves, minced
1/4 teaspoon salt, optional
  1 pound ground turkey
  6 whole wheat hamburger buns, split and toasted

Coat grill rack with nonstick cooking spray before starting the grill. In a bowl, combine the first seven ingredients. Add turkey and mix well. Shape into six 1/2-in.-thick patties. Grill, covered, over indirect medium heat for 6 minutes on each side or until a meat thermometer reads 165°. Serve on buns. **Yield:** 6 burgers. **Nutritional Analysis:** One serving (prepared with ground turkey breast and without salt; calculated without the bun) equals 156 calories, 174 mg sodium, 37 mg cholesterol, 15 gm carbohydrate, 21 gm protein, 2 gm fat. **Diabetic Exchanges:** 2 very lean meat, 1 starch.

Cool-Kitchen Meat Loaf

(Pictured at left)

Juicy slices of this tender meat loaf are wonderful served with a homemade sweet-and-sour sauce. It's an easy way to fix supper, especially when the weather is too hot to turn on the oven. Plus, cleanup is a breeze because you just toss out the foil pans. —Susan Taul, Birmingham, Alabama

    1 cup soft bread crumbs
    1 medium onion, chopped
  1/2 cup tomato sauce
    1 egg
1-1/2 teaspoons salt
  1/4 teaspoon pepper
1-1/2 pounds lean ground beef
SAUCE:
  1/2 cup ketchup
    3 tablespoons brown sugar
    3 tablespoons Worcestershire sauce
    2 tablespoons vinegar
    2 tablespoons prepared mustard

In a bowl, combine the first six ingredients. Add beef and mix well. Shape into two loaves; place each loaf in a disposable 8-in. x 4-in. x 2-in. loaf pan. Cover with foil.

Grill, covered, over indirect medium heat for 30 minutes or until the meat is no longer pink and a meat thermometer reads 160°. Meanwhile, in a saucepan, combine the sauce ingredients. Cook and stir over low heat until sugar is dissolved. Spoon over meat loaves before serving. **Yield:** 2 loaves (3 servings each).

Gingered Honey Salmon

(Pictured below left)

Ginger, garlic powder and green onion blend nicely in an easy marinade that gives pleasant flavor to salmon. We also like to use this versatile mixture when grilling chicken, but we've found it tastes even better when marinated in the fridge overnight.
—Dan Strumberger
Farmington, Minnesota

  1/3 cup orange juice
  1/3 cup soy sauce
  1/4 cup honey
    1 green onion, chopped
    1 teaspoon ground ginger
    1 teaspoon garlic powder
    1 salmon fillet (1-1/2 pounds and 3/4 inch thick)

Coat grill rack with nonstick cooking spray before starting the grill. In a bowl, combine the first six ingredients; mix well. Set aside 1/3 cup for basting; cover and refrigerate. Pour remaining marinade into a large resealable plastic bag or shallow glass container; add salmon and turn to coat. Seal or cover and refrigerate for 30 minutes, turning once or twice. Drain and discard marinade. Place salmon skin side down on grill. Grill, covered, over medium-hot heat for 5 minutes. Baste with reserved marinade. Grill 10-15 minutes longer or until fish flakes easily with a fork, basting frequently. **Yield:** 4-6 servings.

Sweet Onions with Radish Sauce

I stir up this light creamy sauce to complement sweet grilled onions. The side dish is a special treat in spring, when Vidalia onions are in season.   —Phyllis Schmalz
Kansas City, Kansas

    2 large sweet onions, cut into 1/2-inch slices
  1/4 cup olive *or* vegetable oil
  1/2 teaspoon salt
  1/8 teaspoon pepper
  1/2 cup plain yogurt
    1 tablespoon mayonnaise
  1/4 cup chopped radishes
    2 tablespoons snipped fresh dill *or* 2 teaspoons dill weed

Brush both sides of onion slices with oil; sprinkle with salt and pepper. Place the onions directly on grill rack. Grill, covered, over indirect heat for 8 minutes on each side or until crisp-tender. In a small bowl, combine the yogurt, mayonnaise, radishes and dill. Serve with the onions. **Yield:** 4 servings.

Decked-Out Burgers

(Pictured at right)

This is an easy way to make ordinary burgers taste exceptionally good. Guests always enjoy the flavorful topping that's made with bacon, cheese, mushrooms and mayonnaise. —Karen Bourne
Magrath, Alberta

  1 cup (4 ounces) shredded cheddar
    cheese
  1 jar (4-1/2 ounces) sliced mushrooms,
    drained
  1/3 cup mayonnaise
  6 bacon strips, cooked and crumbled
1-1/2 pounds lean ground beef
  1/4 cup finely chopped onion
  1 teaspoon salt
  1/2 teaspoon pepper
  1/4 teaspoon garlic powder
  1/8 teaspoon hot pepper sauce
  6 hamburger buns, split
Lettuce leaves and tomato slices, optional

Decked-Out Burgers

In a bowl, combine cheese, mushrooms, mayonnaise and bacon; cover and refrigerate. In another bowl, combine the beef, onion, salt, pepper, garlic powder and hot pepper sauce. Shape into six 1/2-in.-thick patties. Grill, covered, over medium-hot heat for 4-5 minutes on each side. Spoon cheese mixture on top of each burger. Grill 1-2 minutes longer or until the cheese begins to melt. Serve on buns with lettuce and tomato if desired. **Yield:** 6 servings.

Marinated Flank Steak

(Pictured below)

I first grilled this appetizing flank steak for my father on a special occasion. We loved it so much that I now make it this way all the time. The steak marinates overnight, so there's little last-minute preparation to worry about.
—Ann Fox, Austin, Texas

Marinated Flank Steak

  2/3 cup olive *or* vegetable oil
  1/4 cup lemon juice
  2 tablespoons cider *or* red wine vinegar
  1 tablespoon Worcestershire sauce
  1 tablespoon soy sauce
  1 tablespoon Dijon mustard
  1 teaspoon dried basil
  1/2 teaspoon dried oregano
  1/4 teaspoon dried thyme
  1 flank steak (about 1-1/2 pounds)

In a large resealable plastic bag or shallow glass container, combine the first nine ingredients; mix well. Add steak and turn to coat. Seal or cover and refrigerate for 8 hours or overnight, turning occasionally. Drain and discard marinade. Grill, covered, over medium-hot heat for 6-10 minutes on each side or until meat reaches desired doneness (for rare, a meat thermometer should read 140°; medium, 160°; well-done, 170°). **Yield:** 4-6 servings.

Cookout Potatoes

The recipe for this comforting potato side dish came from my mother. It's a snap to prepare with convenient frozen hash browns. —Wanda Holoubek, Omaha, Nebraska

  4 cups cubed hash brown potatoes, thawed
  1/2 cup chopped celery
  1/2 cup chopped green pepper
  1/3 cup butter *or* margarine, melted
  2 tablespoons finely chopped onion
  1 tablespoon minced fresh parsley
  1 teaspoon salt

Combine all of the ingredients. Place on a double thickness of heavy-duty foil (about 28 in. x 18 in.). Fold foil around the potato mixture and seal tightly. Grill, covered, over medium heat for 45-50 minutes or until the potatoes are tender. **Yield:** 6-8 servings.

Barbecued Hot Wings

(Pictured below)

My husband can't get enough of these spicy chicken wings. They're excellent appetizers at cookouts. We serve them with blue cheese dressing and celery sticks.
—Anita Carr, Cadiz, Ohio

    12 whole chicken wings (about 2-1/2 pounds)*
     1 bottle (8 ounces) Italian salad dressing
    1/2 to 3/4 cup hot pepper sauce
    1/8 to 1/2 teaspoon cayenne pepper
     2 tablespoons butter *or* margarine, melted

Cut chicken wings into three sections; discard wing tips. In a bowl, combine salad dressing, hot pepper sauce and cayenne. Remove 1/2 cup for basting; cover and refrigerate. Place remaining sauce in a large resealable plastic bag or shallow glass container; add chicken and turn to coat. Seal or cover and refrigerate overnight. Drain and discard marinade. Grill wings, covered, over medium heat for 12-16 minutes, turning occasionally. Add butter to the reserved sauce; brush over wings. Grill, uncovered, 8-10 minutes longer or until juices run clear, basting and turning several times. **Yield:** 6-8 servings. ***Editor's Note:** 2-1/2 pounds of uncooked chicken wing sections may be substituted for the whole chicken wings. Omit the first step of the recipe.

Grilled Pizza Bread

(Pictured below)

These fun French bread pizzas are great picnic fare for both kids and adults. Although they're tasty on the grill, they can just as easily be baked in the oven. —Edna Hoffman
Hebron, Indiana

     1 pound ground beef
    1/2 cup chopped onion
     1 can (8 ounces) tomato sauce
    1/2 teaspoon salt
    1/2 teaspoon dried oregano
     1 loaf (1 pound) French bread
     1 cup (4 ounces) shredded mozzarella cheese
     1 can (2-1/4 ounces) sliced ripe olives, drained
Sliced pepperoni, optional

In a skillet over medium heat, cook beef and onion until meat is browned and onion is tender; drain. Stir in the tomato sauce, salt and oregano; simmer for 5-10 minutes. Cut bread in half lengthwise and then widthwise. Spread meat mixture on the cut side of bread; sprinkle with the cheese, olives and pepperoni if desired. Loosely wrap bread individually in pieces of heavy-duty foil (about 24 in. x 18 in.); seal. Grill, covered, over medium heat for 15-20 minutes or until heated through. **Yield:** 4-6 servings.

Grilled Pizza Bread
Barbecued Hot Wings

Grilled Game Hens

2 garlic cloves, minced
1 teaspoon dill seed
1/2 teaspoon salt, optional
1/2 teaspoon curry powder
1/2 teaspoon pepper
1 broiler/fryer chicken (3 to 3-1/2 pounds), cut up

In a large resealable plastic bag or shallow glass container, combine the first 10 ingredients. Add chicken and turn to coat. Seal or cover and refrigerate for 4-6 hours. Drain and discard marinade. Grill chicken, covered, over low heat for 50-60 minutes or until juices run clear, turning several times. **Yield:** 4 servings. **Nutritional Analysis:** One serving (prepared with low-sodium Worcestershire sauce and without salt) equals 219 calories, 132 mg sodium, 96 mg cholesterol, 3 gm carbohydrate, 36 gm protein, 6 gm fat. **Diabetic Exchange:** 4 lean meat.

Meatball Shish Kabobs

(Pictured below)

Convenience foods make this hearty entree a snap to prepare. Purchased meatballs are easy to thread onto skewers. And since they're precooked, you just need to grill the kabobs until the fresh veggies are tender. Basting with bottled barbecue sauce adds fast flavor.
—Shawn Solley, Lawton, Oklahoma

1 package (16 ounces) frozen fully cooked meatballs, thawed (about 30 meatballs)
2 medium zucchini, cut into 1/2-inch slices
2 medium yellow summer squash, cut into 1/2-inch slices
12 cherry tomatoes
12 pearl onions
1 cup barbecue sauce
Hot cooked rice

On metal or soaked bamboo skewers, alternate meatballs, zucchini, summer squash, tomatoes and onions. Grill, uncovered, over medium heat for 6 minutes,

Grilled Game Hens

(Pictured above)

An easy overnight marinade spiced with cinnamon and cumin adds wonderful flavor to these game hens. My family enjoys them often during the grilling season.
—Marcia Bland, North Platte, Nebraska

1 cup lime juice
1/2 cup olive *or* vegetable oil
4 garlic cloves, minced
4 teaspoons ground cumin
1/2 to 1 teaspoon ground cinnamon
Salt and pepper to taste
4 Cornish game hens (22 ounces *each*), halved

In a large resealable plastic bag or shallow glass container, combine lime juice, oil, garlic, cumin, cinnamon, salt and pepper; mix well. Add hens and turn to coat. Seal or cover and refrigerate for several hours or overnight, turning once. Drain and discard marinade. Grill hens, covered, over medium heat for 20-25 minutes or until juices run clear, turning occasionally. **Yield:** 4 servings.

Moist Lemon Chicken

I originally developed this marinade for seafood, but it's wonderful with chicken, too. It adds mild lemon zing and keeps the meat moist and tender.
—Nancy Schickling, Bedford, Virginia

✓ Uses less fat, sugar or salt. Includes Nutritional Analysis and Diabetic Exchanges.

3/4 cup water
1/4 cup lemon juice
2 tablespoons dried minced onion
1 tablespoon dried parsley flakes
1 tablespoon Worcestershire sauce

Meatball Shish Kabobs

Cola Burgers

turning once. Baste with barbecue sauce. Grill 8-10 minutes longer or until meatballs are heated through and vegetables are tender, turning and basting frequently. Serve over rice. **Yield:** 5 servings.

Cola Burgers

(Pictured above)

A friend who's an excellent cook shared this hamburger recipe with me, and it has since become a family favorite. The unusual combination of cola and French salad dressing added to the ground beef gives it fabulous flavor. The mixture is also used as a basting sauce on the moist burgers. —Melva Baumer, Millmont, Pennsylvania

　　 1 egg
　1/2 cup cola,* *divided*
　1/2 cup crushed saltines (about 15)
　　 6 tablespoons French salad dressing, *divided*
　　 2 tablespoons grated Parmesan cheese
　1/4 teaspoon salt
1-1/2 pounds ground beef
　　 6 hamburger buns, split

In a bowl, combine the egg, 1/4 cup cola, cracker crumbs, 2 tablespoons salad dressing, Parmesan cheese and salt. Add beef and mix well. Shape into six 3/4-in.-thick patties (the mixture will be moist). In a bowl, combine the remaining cola and salad dressing; set aside. Grill patties, uncovered, over medium-hot heat for 3 minutes on each side. Brush with cola mixture. Grill 8-10 minutes longer or until juices run clear, basting and turning occasionally. Serve on buns. **Yield:** 6 servings.
*****Editor's Note:** Diet cola is not recommended for this recipe.

Marinated Chops 'n' Onion

The first time I made this spicy dish, my husband commented on how moist the pork was, so I knew it was a keeper. It gets eye-appeal from red onion slices.
　　　　　　　—Connie Brueggeman, Sparta, Wisconsin

　3/4 cup lime juice
　　 1 teaspoon salt, optional
　1/4 to 1/2 teaspoon cayenne pepper
　　 4 pork chops (1/2 inch thick)
　　 1 large red onion, sliced

In a large resealable plastic bag or shallow glass container, combine lime juice, salt if desired and cayenne. Add pork chops and onion; turn to coat. Seal or cover and refrigerate for at least 2 hours. Drain and reserve marinade and onion. Grill chops, covered, over medium-hot heat for 8-10 minutes on each side or until no longer pink. Place the marinade and onion in a saucepan; bring to a rolling boil. Serve with the chops. **Yield:** 4 servings. **Nutritional Analysis:** One serving (prepared without salt) equals 171 calories, 45 mg sodium, 59 mg cholesterol, 7 gm carbohydrate, 22 gm protein, 6 gm fat. **Diabetic Exchanges:** 3 lean meat, 1/2 fruit.

Mushroom Bacon Bites

(Pictured below)

This is the perfect appetizer for most any occasion. The tasty bites are easy to assemble and brush with prepared barbecue sauce. When we have a big cookout, they're always a hit...but they make a nice little "extra" for a family dinner, too. —Gina Roesner, Ashland, Missouri

　24 medium fresh mushrooms
　12 bacon strips, halved
　　 1 cup barbecue sauce

Wrap each mushroom with a piece of bacon; secure with a toothpick. Thread onto metal or soaked bamboo skewers; brush with barbecue sauce. Grill, uncovered, over indirect medium heat for 10-15 minutes or until the bacon is crisp and the mushrooms are tender, turning and basting occasionally with remaining barbecue sauce. **Yield:** 2 dozen.

Mushroom Bacon Bites

Oregano Onions

My dad, who loves onions, invented this tasty side dish. The tender seasoned onions go well with all types of grilled meat, so we enjoy them frequently. Cleanup is a breeze, too. —Marcia Preston, Clear Lake, Iowa

✓ Uses less fat, sugar or salt. Includes Nutritional Analysis and Diabetic Exchanges.

　　5 large onions, sliced
　　6 teaspoons butter *or* margarine
1-1/2 teaspoons dried oregano
Pepper to taste

Divide onions between two pieces of double-layered heavy-duty foil (about 22 in. x 18 in.) coated with non-stick cooking spray. Top each with butter, oregano and pepper. Fold foil around the mixture and seal tightly. Grill, covered, over indirect heat for 30-40 minutes or until onions are tender. **Yield:** 10 servings. **Nutritional Analysis:** One serving (prepared with reduced-fat margarine) equals 41 calories, 28 mg sodium, 0 cholesterol, 7 gm carbohydrate, 1 gm protein, 2 gm fat. **Diabetic Exchanges:** 1 vegetable, 1/2 fat.

Cabbage on the Grill

My father first fixed these bacon-wrapped cabbage wedges a few years ago. Now I make them for my family when we put steak and potatoes on the grill. Even our three daughters like them. —Demi Rice, Macks Creek, Missouri

　　1 medium head cabbage (about 2 pounds)
　　4 teaspoons butter *or* margarine, softened
　　1 teaspoon salt
1/2 teaspoon garlic powder
1/4 teaspoon pepper
　　2 tablespoons grated Parmesan cheese
　　4 bacon strips

Cut cabbage into four wedges; place each on a piece of double-layered heavy-duty foil (about 18 in. square). Spread cut sides with butter. Sprinkle with salt, garlic powder, pepper and Parmesan cheese. Wrap a bacon strip around each wedge. Fold foil around cabbage and seal tightly. Grill, covered, over medium heat for 40 minutes or until the cabbage is tender, turning twice. **Yield:** 4 servings.

Grilled Turkey Breast

(Pictured below left)

I combined several recipes to come up with this entree that our family loves any time of year. After marinating overnight, the turkey is grilled, then dressed up with a fast fruity sauce. —Ravonda Mormann Raleigh, North Carolina

✓ Uses less fat, sugar or salt. Includes Nutritional Analysis and Diabetic Exchanges.

　　2 boneless skinless turkey breast halves (about 2-1/2 pounds *each*)
　　1 cup cranberry juice
1/4 cup orange juice
1/4 cup olive *or* vegetable oil
　　1 teaspoon salt, optional
　　1 teaspoon pepper
SAUCE:
　　1 can (16 ounces) jellied cranberry sauce
1/4 cup lemon juice
　　3 tablespoons brown sugar
　　1 teaspoon cornstarch

Place turkey in a large resealable plastic bag. Combine the next five ingredients; pour over turkey. Seal and refrigerate for 8 hours or overnight, turning occasionally. Drain and discard marinade. Grill turkey, covered, over indirect heat for 1-1/4 to 1-1/2 hours or until juices run clear and a meat thermometer reads 170°. Meanwhile, combine the sauce ingredients in a saucepan; cook and stir over medium heat until thickened, about 5 minutes. Serve with the turkey. **Yield:** 10 servings. **Nutritional Analysis:** One serving (prepared with unsweetened cranberry and orange juices; calculated without the sauce) equals 110 calories, 149 mg sodium, 51 mg cholesterol, 1 gm carbohydrate, 18 gm protein, 3 gm fat. **Diabetic Exchange:** 2 very lean meat.

Flavorful Flounder

When my grandparents lived in the Florida Keys, Grandpop went fishing every day. They ate fish often, so Grandmom had to find creative ways to serve it. The Parmesan cheese in this fast recipe adds just the right flavor. —Tammy Sanborn, Alto, Michigan

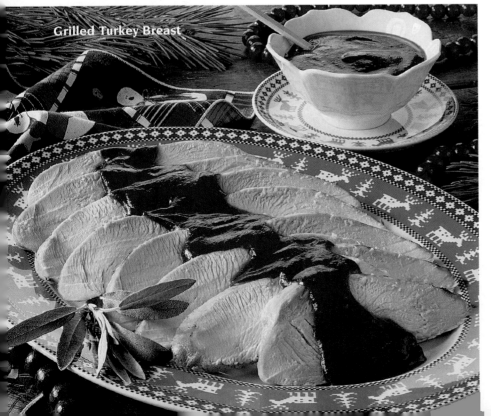

Grilled Turkey Breast

Peanutty Pork Kabobs

ing occasionally. Drain and discard the marinade. On metal or soaked bamboo skewers, alternate pork and green peppers. Grill, uncovered, over medium heat for 6 minutes, turning once. Baste with reserved marinade. Grill 8-10 minutes longer or until meat juices run clear, turning and basting frequently. **Yield:** 4 servings.

Glazed Country Ribs

(Pictured below)

When I take these mouth-watering ribs to our frequent potlucks at work, they're a hit. I like them basted only with the mildly sweet glaze, but you can serve your favorite barbecue sauce on the side, too. They taste as good reheated as they do right off the grill. —*Tamrah Bird Gaines, Michigan*

    3 pounds boneless country-style ribs
  3/4 cup pineapple juice
  1/2 cup vegetable oil
  1/2 cup white wine *or* chicken broth
  1/4 cup packed brown sugar
    1 tablespoon Worcestershire sauce
    6 garlic cloves, minced
    1 teaspoon salt
    1 teaspoon pepper
    1 teaspoon dried rosemary, crushed

Place ribs in a large shallow glass container. Pierce several times with a fork. In a bowl, combine the remaining ingredients; set aside 1/2 cup for basting. Pour the remaining marinade over ribs. Cover and refrigerate for 8 hours or overnight, turning once. Drain and discard marinade. Grill ribs, covered, over indirect medium heat for 10 minutes on each side. Baste with some of the reserved marinade. Grill 20-25 minutes longer or until juices run clear and meat is tender, turning and basting occasionally. **Yield:** 6 servings.

    2 pounds flounder *or* sole fillets
    2 tablespoons lemon juice
  1/2 cup grated Parmesan cheese
  1/4 cup butter *or* margarine, melted
    3 tablespoons mayonnaise
    3 tablespoons chopped green onions
  1/4 teaspoon salt

Coat a piece of heavy-duty foil (about 14 in. x 14 in.) with nonstick cooking spray. Place fillets on foil; brush with lemon juice. Crimp foil, forming edges. Place foil flat on the grill (do not seal). Grill, covered, over medium-hot heat for 4 minutes. Combine Parmesan cheese, butter, mayonnaise, onions and salt; brush over the fillets. Grill 3-4 minutes longer or until fish flakes easily with a fork. **Yield:** 4-6 servings.

Peanutty Pork Kabobs

(Pictured above)

Cubes of pork tenderloin and green pepper chunks get a spicy treatment from a combination of peanut butter, brown sugar, ginger and red pepper flakes. Reserving half of this mixture to use as a basting sauce adds an extra boost of flavor. —*Ellen Koch, St. Martinville, Louisiana*

  1/2 cup soy sauce
  1/4 cup lime *or* lemon juice
  1/4 cup peanut butter
    2 tablespoons brown sugar
    2 garlic cloves, minced
    1 teaspoon crushed red pepper flakes
  1/4 teaspoon ground ginger
    1 pork tenderloin (about 1 pound), cut into
      1-inch cubes
    2 medium green peppers, cut into 1-inch
      pieces

In a large bowl, combine the first seven ingredients; mix well. Set aside 1/2 cup for basting; cover and refrigerate. Pour remaining marinade into a large resealable plastic bag or shallow glass container; add pork and turn to coat. Seal or cover and refrigerate for 2-3 hours, turn-

Glazed Country Ribs

Grilled Potato Fans

Grilled Potato Fans

(Pictured above)

If you're looking for a change from plain baked potatoes, try these tender and buttery potato fans seasoned with oregano, garlic powder, celery and onion. To cut down on grilling time, I sometimes microwave the potatoes for 5-6 minutes before slicing them. —Jennifer Black-Ortiz
San Jose, California

6 medium baking potatoes
2 medium onions, halved and thinly sliced
6 tablespoons butter *or* margarine, cubed
1/4 cup finely chopped celery
1 teaspoon salt
1 teaspoon dried oregano
1/4 teaspoon garlic powder
1/4 teaspoon pepper

With a sharp knife, make cuts 1/2 in. apart in each potato, leaving slices attached at the bottom. Fan the potatoes slightly. Place each on a piece of heavy-duty foil (about 12 in. square). Insert onions and butter between potato slices. Sprinkle with celery, salt, oregano, garlic powder and pepper. Fold foil around potatoes and seal tightly. Grill, covered, over medium-hot heat for 40-45 minutes or until tender. **Yield:** 6 servings.

Chocolate Dessert Wraps

(Pictured at right)

I came up with this chocolate and peanut butter treat when I needed a unique, fast dessert for a special dinner. The filled tortillas take just minutes on the grill and get a chewy consistency from marshmallows.
—Laurie Gwaltney, Indianapolis, Indiana

1/2 cup creamy peanut butter*
4 flour tortillas (8 inches)
1 cup miniature marshmallows
1/2 cup miniature semisweet chocolate chips
Vanilla ice cream
Chocolate shavings, optional

Spread 2 tablespoons of peanut butter on each tortilla. Sprinkle 1/4 cup marshmallows and 2 tablespoons chocolate chips on half of each tortilla. Roll up, beginning with the topping side. Wrap each tortilla in heavy-duty foil; seal tightly. Grill, covered, over low heat for 5-10 minutes or until heated through. Unwrap tortillas and place on dessert plates. Serve with ice cream. Garnish with chocolate shavings if desired. **Yield:** 4 servings. ***Editor's Note:** Crunchy peanut butter is not recommended for this recipe.

Apricot Sausage Kabobs

Basted with a simple sweet-sour sauce, these tasty kabobs make a quick meal that's elegant enough for company.
—Susie Lindquist, Ellijay, Georgia

3/4 cup apricot preserves
3/4 cup Dijon mustard
1 pound fully cooked kielbasa *or* Polish sausage, cut into 12 pieces
12 dried apricots
12 medium fresh mushrooms
Hot cooked rice

In a small bowl, combine preserves and mustard; mix well. Remove 1/2 cup for serving; set aside. Alternate sausage, apricots and mushrooms on four metal or soaked bamboo skewers. Grill, covered, over indirect heat for 15-20 minutes or until meat juices run clear. Turn frequently and baste with remaining apricot sauce. Warm the reserved sauce; serve with kabobs and rice. **Yield:** 4 servings.

Curry Grilled Chicken

(Pictured at far right)

Chicken marinated in this fuss-free mixture comes out tender and tangy. Its mild curry flavor is equally good on pork.
—Nancy Ode, Sherman, South Dakota

1/2 cup sugar
1/2 cup vinegar

Chocolate Dessert Wraps

- 1/3 cup ketchup
- 1 tablespoon Worcestershire sauce
- 1/2 teaspoon ground mustard
- 1/2 teaspoon paprika
- 1/2 teaspoon curry powder
- 1/2 teaspoon garlic salt
- 1/2 teaspoon salt
- 1/8 teaspoon pepper
- 4 boneless skinless chicken breast halves

In a blender, combine the first 10 ingredients; cover and process until blended. Pour into a large resealable plastic bag or shallow glass container; add the chicken. Seal or cover and refrigerate for 1-2 hours. Drain and discard marinade. Grill the chicken, covered, over medium heat for 6 minutes on each side or until juices run clear. **Yield:** 4 servings.

Red Potato Skewers
Bundle of Veggies
Curry Grilled Chicken

Bundle of Veggies

(Pictured at right)

I came across the recipe for this grilled vegetable medley at a nurses' station at the hospital where I work. It's a big hit at home and while camping. The foil packet makes cleanup easy, too. —Sheila Dedman
New Dundee, Ontario

✓ Uses less fat, sugar or salt. Includes Nutritional Analysis and Diabetic Exchanges.

- 8 ounces whole fresh mushrooms
- 8 ounces cherry tomatoes
- 1 cup sliced zucchini
- 1 tablespoon olive *or* vegetable oil
- 1 tablespoon butter *or* margarine, melted
- 1/2 teaspoon salt *or* salt-free seasoning blend
- 1/2 teaspoon onion powder
- 1/2 teaspoon Italian seasoning
- 1/8 teaspoon garlic powder

Dash pepper

Place mushrooms, tomatoes and zucchini on a double thickness of heavy-duty foil (about 18 in. square). Combine the remaining ingredients; drizzle over vegetables. Fold the foil around vegetables and seal tightly. Grill, covered, over medium heat for 20-25 minutes or until tender. **Yield:** 6 servings. **Nutritional Analysis:** One serving (prepared with reduced-fat margarine and salt-free seasoning) equals 52 calories, 27 mg sodium, 0 cholesterol, 5 gm carbohydrate, 1 gm protein, 4 gm fat. **Diabetic Exchanges:** 1 vegetable, 1/2 fat.

Red Potato Skewers

(Pictured above right)

As a busy mother of three boys, I love to find good grilling recipes that my husband can use. A seasoned mayonnaise mixture keeps these quartered potatoes moist and heavenly. —Dawn Finch, Prosser, Washington

✓ Uses less fat, sugar or salt. Includes Nutritional Analysis and Diabetic Exchanges.

- 2 pounds red potatoes (about 6 medium), quartered
- 1/2 cup water
- 1/2 cup mayonnaise *or* salad dressing
- 1/4 cup chicken broth
- 2 teaspoons dried oregano
- 1/2 teaspoon garlic salt
- 1/2 teaspoon onion powder

Place the potatoes in an ungreased microwave-safe 2-qt. dish. Cover and microwave on high for 12-14 minutes, stirring once; drain. Combine remaining ingredients in a bowl; add potatoes. Cover and refrigerate for 1 hour. Drain, reserving mayonnaise mixture. Thread the potatoes onto metal or soaked bamboo skewers. Grill, uncovered, over medium heat for 4 minutes. Turn; brush with reserved mayonnaise mixture. Grill 4 minutes longer or until golden brown. **Yield:** 6 servings. **Nutritional Analysis:** One serving (prepared with low-sodium broth and light mayonnaise) equals 167 calories, 307 mg sodium, trace cholesterol, 21 gm carbohydrate, 4 gm protein, 7 gm fat. **Diabetic Exchanges:** 1-1/2 starch, 1-1/2 fat. **Editor's Note:** This recipe was tested in an 850-watt microwave.

Microwave Magic

Microwave Frittata

TRY the made-in-minutes microwave recipes here and you'll never again use your "zapper" just for heating up coffee or warming leftovers.

Editor's Note: All of these recipes were tested in an 850-watt microwave.

Microwave Frittata

(Pictured at right)

This quick, filling dish is good anytime of day. I often make it when we come in from gardening, hunting or fishing and don't feel like preparing a big dinner. —Delia Kennedy
Deer Park, Washington

> 1 tablespoon butter *or* margarine
> 1 cup cubed fully cooked ham
> 1/2 cup chopped onion
> 1/4 cup chopped green pepper
> 4 eggs, beaten
> Salt and pepper to taste

Place butter in a microwave-safe 9-in. pie plate. Cover with waxed paper; microwave on high for 30-40 seconds or until melted. Add ham, onion and green pepper. Cover and cook on high for 2 minutes. Stir in eggs, salt and pepper. Cover and cook on high for 1-1/2 to 2-1/2 minutes or until a knife inserted near the center comes out clean. Let stand for 3 minutes or until completely set. Cut into wedges. **Yield:** 4 servings.

Spiced Mixed Nuts

Everyone who tastes these glazed nuts loves them. They're quick, easy and a unique addition to a holiday cookie tray.
—Julie Gesicki, Tracyton, Washington

> 1/2 cup packed brown sugar
> 1/2 teaspoon salt
> 1/2 teaspoon ground cinnamon
> 1/4 teaspoon ground allspice
> 1/8 teaspoon ground nutmeg
> 1/8 teaspoon ground cloves
> 4-1/2 teaspoons water
> 2 cups mixed nuts

In a microwave-safe bowl, combine the first six ingredients. Stir in the water. Microwave, uncovered, on high for 1 minute; stir. Add nuts and stir until well-coated. Cook, uncovered, on high for 4-5 minutes or until syrup begins to harden, stirring after each minute. Immediately pour onto a greased foil-lined baking sheet and separate nuts. Cool completely. Store in an airtight container. **Yield:** 2-1/2 cups.

Broccoli Ham Stroganoff

(Pictured on page 264)

This tasty main dish is a snap to prepare in the microwave and takes just minutes to make. It's a great way to use up extra ham...and it works equally well with leftover chicken or turkey. The white sauce gets added creaminess from sour cream. —Amanda Denton, Barre, Vermont

> 2 cups frozen chopped broccoli
> 1 tablespoon water
> 1 tablespoon butter *or* margarine
> 1/4 cup chopped onion
> 3 tablespoons all-purpose flour
> 1 can (10-1/2 ounces) chicken broth
> 2 cups cubed fully cooked ham
> 1 cup (8 ounces) sour cream
> 1 jar (4-1/2 ounces) sliced mushrooms, drained
> Hot cooked noodles

Place broccoli and water in a 1-qt. microwave-safe bowl. Cover and microwave on high for 3-5 minutes or until the broccoli is tender, stirring once. Drain; set aside and keep warm. In another microwave-safe bowl, heat butter, uncovered, on high for 20 seconds or until melted. Add onion; cover and microwave on high for 2 minutes or until tender. Stir in flour until blended. Gradually stir in broth; mix well. Microwave, uncovered, on high for 4-6 minutes or until thickened and bubbly, stirring once. Add the ham, sour cream, mushrooms and reserved broccoli; mix well. Cook, uncovered, on high for 3-5 minutes or until heated through, stirring once. Serve over noodles. **Yield:** 4 servings.

Coffee Shop Fudge

(Pictured on page 265)

This recipe is one that my son, Jackson, and I worked on together. After several efforts, we decided this version was a winner. It is smooth, creamy and has an irresistible crunch from pecans. The coffee and cinnamon blend nicely to provide subtle flavor.
—Beth Osborne Skinner, Bristol, Tennessee

  1 cup chopped pecans
  3 cups (18 ounces) semisweet chocolate chips
  1 can (14 ounces) sweetened condensed milk
  2 tablespoons strong brewed coffee, room
     temperature
  1 teaspoon ground cinnamon
1/8 teaspoon salt
  1 teaspoon vanilla extract

Line an 8-in. square pan with foil and butter the foil; set aside. Place pecans in a microwave-safe pie plate. Microwave, uncovered, on high for 4 minutes, stirring after each minute; set aside. In a 2-qt. microwave-safe bowl, combine chocolate chips, milk, coffee, cinnamon and salt. Microwave, uncovered, on high for 1-1/2 minutes. Stir until smooth. Stir in vanilla and pecans. Immediately spread into the prepared pan. Cover and refrigerate until firm, about 2 hours. Remove from pan; cut into 1-in. squares. Cover and store at room temperature (70°-80°). **Yield:** 2 pounds.

Teriyaki Potatoes

Simple seasonings turn red potatoes into a special side dish that's attractive, too. They're so easy to prepare that you can have them on the table in about 15 minutes.
—Sue Jent, Golconda, Illinois

✓ Uses less fat, sugar or salt. Includes Nutritional Analysis and Diabetic Exchanges.

1-1/2 pounds small red potatoes, quartered
    1 tablespoon butter *or* margarine
    1 tablespoon teriyaki *or* soy sauce
  1/4 teaspoon garlic salt, optional
  1/4 teaspoon Italian seasoning
Dash *each* pepper and cayenne pepper

Place potatoes in an ungreased 1-1/2-qt. microwave-safe dish. Dot with butter. Add remaining ingredients; toss to coat. Cover and microwave on high for 12-15 minutes or until potatoes are tender, stirring twice. **Yield:** 6 servings. **Nutritional Analysis:** One serving (prepared without garlic salt) equals 93 calories, 26 mg sodium, 0 cholesterol, 15 gm carbohydrate, 3 gm protein, 2 gm fat. **Diabetic Exchanges:** 1 starch, 1/2 fat.

Caramel-Chocolate Oat Squares

(Pictured below)

In the summer, we often have weekend guests who go boating with us. These sweet, chewy bars are the perfect treat to take along. Since I can use my microwave to prepare a batch, I don't have to heat up the oven—and my kitchen.
—Kellie Ochsner, Newton, Iowa

   3/4 cup butter *or* margarine
1-1/4 cups all-purpose flour
1-1/4 cups quick-cooking oats
   3/4 cup packed brown sugar
   1/2 teaspoon baking soda
   1/4 teaspoon salt
   24 caramels
   1/4 cup milk
     1 cup (6 ounces) semisweet chocolate chips
   1/2 cup chopped walnuts, optional

In a microwave-safe bowl, heat butter, uncovered, on high for 30-45 seconds or until softened. Combine flour, oats, brown sugar, baking soda and salt; stir into butter until blended. Set a third of the mixture aside for topping. Press remaining mixture into an 8-in. square microwave-safe dish. Cook, uncovered, on high for 2-3 minutes or until crust is raised and set (crust will be uneven), rotating a half turn after each minute. In a 1-qt. microwave-safe dish, heat the caramels and milk, uncovered, on high for 3-4 minutes or until melted and smooth, stirring every minute. Sprinkle chips and nuts if desired over crust. Pour caramel mixture over all. Sprinkle with reserved oat mixture; press down lightly. Microwave, uncovered, on high for 3-4 minutes or until the caramel is bubbly, rotating a quarter turn every minute. Cool before cutting. **Yield:** 16 servings.

Carmel-Chocolate Oat Squares

Reuben Casserole

You'll find all the flavor of a Reuben sandwich (and none of the mess) in this satisfying casserole. It's prepared lickety-split, so you can serve your hungry family fast.
—Terri Holmgren, Swanville, Minnesota

   1 can (14 ounces) sauerkraut, rinsed and
      drained
   1 teaspoon caraway seeds
   2 cups (8 ounces) shredded Monterey Jack *or*
      Swiss cheese, *divided*
 1/2 cup Thousand Island salad dressing
1-1/4 cups cubed turkey pastrami
   5 slices rye bread, cubed
 1/3 cup butter *or* margarine, melted

Place the sauerkraut in a greased 2-qt. microwave-safe dish; sprinkle with caraway seeds and half of the cheese. Top with the salad dressing, pastrami and remaining cheese. Toss bread cubes with butter; sprinkle over the top. Cover and microwave at 60% power for 8-10 minutes or until heated through. **Yield:** 4-6 servings.

Confetti Salmon Steaks

(Pictured below)

I rely on my microwave to cook this tender fish in a jiffy. With its sprinkling of bright peppers, the mildly seasoned dish makes a pretty entree for two. —*Mary Kay Dixson Decatur, Alabama*

✓ Uses less fat, sugar or salt. Includes Nutritional Analysis and Diabetic Exchanges.

   2 salmon steaks (1 inch thick)
 1/2 teaspoon Worcestershire sauce
 1/2 teaspoon lemon juice
 1/2 teaspoon Cajun *or* Creole seasoning

Confetti Salmon Steaks

 1/4 teaspoon salt, optional
 1/2 cup diced green pepper
 1/2 cup diced sweet red pepper

Place the salmon in an ungreased 8-in. square microwave-safe dish. Rub with Worcestershire sauce and lemon juice; sprinkle with Cajun seasoning and salt if desired. Sprinkle peppers on top. Cover and microwave on high for 5-1/2 to 6 minutes, turning once, or until fish flakes easily with a fork. Let stand, covered, for 2 minutes. **Yield:** 2 servings. **Nutritional Analysis:** One serving (prepared without salt) equals 192 calories, 185 mg sodium, 68 mg cholesterol, 5 gm carbohydrate, 22 gm protein, 9 gm fat. **Diabetic Exchanges:** 3 lean meat, 1 vegetable.

Micro-Roasted Potatoes

For a tasty change from baked potatoes, try this versatile side dish. —*Janet Machulcz, Westminster, Maryland*

✓ Uses less fat, sugar or salt. Includes Nutritional Analysis and Diabetic Exchanges.

   2 tablespoons vegetable oil
   1 garlic clove, minced
 1/2 teaspoon salt, optional
 1/8 teaspoon paprika
 1/2 teaspoon browning sauce
   4 medium potatoes, cut lengthwise into 6
      wedges
Pepper to taste

In an ungreased 11-in. x 7-in. x 2-in. microwave-safe dish, combine the first four ingredients. Microwave on high for 30-45 seconds or until the garlic is soft. Stir in browning sauce. Add potatoes and pepper; stir to coat. Cover and microwave on high for 13-16 minutes, turning and stirring twice. **Yield:** 4 servings. **Nutritional Analysis:** One serving (prepared without salt) equals 192 calories, 26 mg sodium, trace cholesterol, 30 gm carbohydrate, 3 gm protein, 7 gm fat. **Diabetic Exchanges:** 2 starch, 1 fat.

Chicken Breast Cacciatore

(Pictured above right)

I make this moist chicken often in summer when we want something quick and yummy. With its golden coating, this entree is special enough for company.
—Roni Goodell, Spanish Fork, Utah

   1 can (8 ounces) tomato sauce
   1 teaspoon Italian seasoning
 1/4 teaspoon garlic powder
 1/2 cup cornflake crumbs
 1/4 cup grated Parmesan cheese
   1 teaspoon dried parsley flakes
   6 boneless skinless chicken breast halves
   1 egg, beaten
 2/3 cup shredded mozzarella cheese

In a microwave-safe bowl, combine tomato sauce, Italian seasoning and garlic powder. Cover and microwave

Chicken Breast Cacciatore
Marble Brownies
Parmesan Corn on the Cob

on high for 2 minutes; stir. Cook at 50% power for 3-5 minutes or until mixture simmers, stirring once; set aside. In a bowl, combine crumbs, Parmesan and parsley. Dip chicken into egg, then roll in crumb mixture. Place in a lightly greased shallow 3-qt. microwave-safe dish. Cover and microwave on high for 10-12 minutes, rotating a half turn after 5 minutes. Pour tomato mixture over chicken; sprinkle with mozzarella. Cook, uncovered, at 50% power for 3-5 minutes or until meat juices run clear. **Yield:** 6 servings.

Marble Brownies

(Pictured above)

I like to cook and enjoy trying new recipes. Here a cream cheese topping flavors the moist chocolaty brownies.
—Diana Coppernoll, Linden, North Carolina

    5 tablespoons butter (no substitutes)
    2 squares (1 ounce *each*) unsweetened
       chocolate
2/3 cup sugar
    2 eggs
    1 teaspoon vanilla extract
2/3 cup all-purpose flour
1/2 teaspoon baking powder
CHEESECAKE LAYER:
    1 package (8 ounces) cream cheese
1/2 cup sugar
    1 egg
    1 teaspoon vanilla extract
    1 cup (6 ounces) semisweet chocolate chips

In a large microwave-safe bowl, combine the butter and chocolate. Cover and microwave on high for 1-2 minutes; stir until smooth. Beat in sugar, eggs and vanilla. Add the flour and baking powder until blended. Spread into a greased microwave-safe 8-in. square dish; set aside. In a microwave-safe bowl, heat cream cheese on high for 45-60 seconds or until softened; stir until smooth. Beat in sugar, egg and vanilla. Spoon over brownie batter; cut through batter with a knife to swirl. Sprinkle with the chocolate chips. Shield corners of dish with triangles of foil.* Place the dish on an inverted microwave-safe saucer. Cook, uncovered, at 70% power for 11-13 minutes or until a toothpick comes out clean, rotating a half turn after 5 minutes. Heat on high for 1 minute. Cool on a wire rack. Store in the refrigerator. **Yield:** 1 dozen. ***Editor's Note:** Shielding with small pieces of foil prevents overcooking of food in the corners of a square or rectangular dish. Secure foil firmly to dish and do not allow it to touch insides of oven.

Parmesan Corn on the Cob

(Pictured above)

This seasoned butter is an easy way to dress up fresh corn on the cob.   *—Suzanne McKinley, Lyons, Georgia*

1/4 cup butter *or* margarine, melted
1/4 cup grated Parmesan cheese
1/2 teaspoon Italian seasoning
    4 ears corn on the cob
1/4 cup water
Salt to taste

In a bowl, combine the butter, Parmesan cheese and Italian seasoning; set aside. Remove husks and silk from corn; place in a shallow microwave-safe dish. Add water. Cover and microwave on high for 10-13 minutes, turning once. Let stand for 5 minutes; drain. Brush with butter mixture; sprinkle with salt. **Yield:** 4 servings.

Scalloped Apples

Scalloped Apples

(Pictured above)

When I was a child, I loved eating at my grandma's house, especially when she baked this comforting apple dish. As a busy mother of seven, I'm often short on time, so I use the microwave to fix it quickly. My family enjoys its "apple pie" flavor. —Sandy Daniels, Grandville, Michigan

✓ Uses less fat, sugar or salt. Includes Nutritional Analysis and Diabetic Exchanges.

  10 **cups sliced peeled tart apples (about 8 medium)**
1/3 **cup sugar**
  2 **tablespoons cornstarch**
1/2 **to 1 teaspoon ground cinnamon**
1/4 **teaspoon ground nutmeg**
  2 **tablespoons butter *or* margarine, cubed**

Place apples in a 2-1/2-qt. microwave-safe bowl. Combine the sugar, cornstarch, cinnamon and nutmeg; sprinkle over apples and toss to coat. Dot with butter. Cover and microwave on high for 15 minutes or until apples are tender, stirring every 5 minutes. **Yield:** 8 servings. **Nutritional Analysis:** One 1/2-cup serving (prepared with artificial sweetener equivalent to 1/3 cup sugar and reduced-fat margarine) equals 116 calories, 33 mg sodium, 0 cholesterol, 30 gm carbohydrate, trace protein, 2 gm fat. **Diabetic Exchange:** 2 fruit.

Mushroom Salisbury Steak

(Pictured at right and on front cover)

My family really looks forward to supper when these tasty beef patties with gravy are on the menu. I served this effortless entree to our preacher when he came to dinner, and I often bring it to covered-dish gatherings. I keep the recipe typed and ready to hand out because it's always requested. —Louise Miller, Westminster, Maryland

1/4 **cup cornstarch**
  2 **cans (10-1/2 ounces *each*) beef consomme, undiluted**

  1 **jar (6 ounces) sliced mushrooms, drained**
  4 **teaspoons Worcestershire sauce**
  1 **teaspoon dried basil**
  1 **egg, beaten**
1/2 **cup soft bread crumbs**
  1 **medium onion, finely chopped**
1/2 **to 1 teaspoon seasoned salt**
1/4 **teaspoon pepper, optional**
1-1/2 **pounds ground beef**
Hot mashed potatoes *or* cooked noodles

In a bowl, combine cornstarch and consomme until smooth. Stir in mushrooms, Worcestershire sauce and basil; set aside. In another bowl, combine egg, bread crumbs, onion, seasoned salt and pepper if desired. Add beef and mix well. Shape into six oval patties; place in a shallow 1-1/2-qt. microwave-safe dish. Cover and microwave on high for 6 minutes; drain. Turn patties, moving the ones in the center to the outside of dish. Pour consomme mixture over patties. Cover and microwave on high for 8-10 minutes or until meat is no longer pink. Let stand for 5 minutes. Serve with potatoes or noodles. **Yield:** 6 servings.

Casserole Carrot Cake

(Pictured on page 264)

I learned to make this yummy cake in a microwave cooking class more than 15 years ago. I keep cans of cream cheese frosting in the cupboard and usually have the rest of the ingredients on hand. It's nice to invite company for dinner at the last minute and have a great homemade dessert in no time. —Judie Arnold, East Peoria, Illinois

  1 **cup all-purpose flour**
  1 **cup sugar**
1-1/4 **teaspoons ground cinnamon**
  1 **teaspoon baking powder**
  1 **teaspoon baking soda**
1/2 **teaspoon salt**

Mushroom Salisbury Steak

1/4 teaspoon ground cloves
1/4 teaspoon ground ginger
1/2 cup vegetable oil
  2 eggs
1-1/2 cups grated *or* finely chopped
      carrots (about 4 medium)
  1 can (8 ounces) crushed
      pineapple, well drained
3/4 cup chopped pecans
  1 can (16 ounces) cream cheese
      frosting

In a mixing bowl, combine the first eight ingredients. Add oil; mix well. Add eggs, one at a time, beating well after each. Stir in carrots, pineapple and pecans. Transfer to a greased 8-in. round microwave-safe casserole dish. Microwave, uncovered, at 70% power for 12-14 minutes, rotating a half turn once or until a moist area about 1-1/2 in. in diameter remains in the center (when touched, cake will cling to your finger while area underneath will be almost dry). Cool completely on a wire rack. Invert onto a serving plate. Frost cake. Store in the refrigerator. **Yield:** 6-8 servings. **Editor's Note:** This recipe was tested in a 2-qt. round Pyrex casserole dish.

Microwave Corn Chowder

Pork 'n' Pea Stir-Fry

You don't need a wok to make this simple stir-fry. A fast-to-fix sauce coats strips of pork, pretty green onions and crisp-tender snow peas.
—*Verona Koehlmoos*
Pilger, Nebraska

✓ Uses less fat, sugar or salt. Includes Nutritional Analysis and Diabetic Exchanges.

  2 tablespoons vegetable oil
  1 pound boneless pork, cut into 1/4-inch strips
  2 tablespoons soy sauce
1/8 teaspoon garlic powder
  1 package (6 ounces) frozen snow peas,
      thawed
  1 cup thinly sliced green onions
  2 tablespoons cornstarch
  1 cup beef broth
Hot cooked rice

In a 2-qt. microwave-safe dish, heat oil at 70% power for 2 minutes. Add pork, soy sauce and garlic powder; toss to coat. Cover and microwave on high for 7-8 minutes or until meat is no longer pink. Stir in peas and onions. Cover and microwave at 70% power for 3 minutes. Combine the cornstarch and broth until smooth; stir into pork mixture. Cover and microwave on high for 2 minutes; stir. Cover and microwave 4-5 minutes longer or until thickened, stirring every minute. Serve over rice. **Yield:** 4 servings. **Nutritional Analysis:** One 1-cup serving (prepared with light soy sauce and low-sodium broth; calculated without rice) equals 288 calories, 333 mg sodium, 67 mg cholesterol, 10 gm carbohydrate, 27

gm protein, 15 gm fat. **Diabetic Exchanges:** 3 meat, 2 vegetable.

Microwave Corn Chowder

(Pictured above)

I used to cook for a tearoom, and this rich, sunny-colored chowder was a customer favorite. It's a snap to make in the microwave because there's no scorching.
—*Isabel Kublik, Saskatoon, Saskatchewan*

  2 cups water
  2 cups diced peeled potatoes
1/2 cup sliced carrots
1/2 cup sliced celery
1/4 cup chopped onion
  1 teaspoon salt
1/4 teaspoon pepper
1/4 cup butter *or* margarine
1/4 cup all-purpose flour
  2 cups milk
  3 cups (12 ounces) shredded cheddar cheese
  2 cans (14-3/4 ounces *each*) cream-style corn

Place water in a 2-qt. microwave-safe dish; cover and heat until boiling. Add potatoes, carrots, celery, onion, salt and pepper. Cook, uncovered, on high for 8-10 minutes or until vegetables are crisp-tender; set aside (do not drain). Meanwhile, in a 3-qt. dish, microwave butter on high for 50-60 seconds or until melted. Stir in flour until smooth. Gradually stir in milk. Cook, uncovered, on high for 6-7 minutes or until thickened, stirring every 2 minutes. Add the cheese. Heat for 1 to 1-1/2 minutes or until the cheese is melted. Stir in the corn and reserved vegetables. Cook on high for 2-3 minutes or until heated through. **Yield:** 10 servings (2-1/2 quarts).

Hash Brown Egg Dish

(Pictured below)

I cook the bacon and chop up the vegetables for this hearty casserole the night before, so it only takes a few minutes to finish in the morning. When we have overnight guests, I serve it for breakfast along with blueberry muffins. My family also thinks it's good for dinner. —Diann Sivley
Signal Mountain, Tennessee

    3/4 to 1 pound sliced bacon
      6 cups frozen shredded hash brown potatoes
      1 small onion, chopped
      1 medium green pepper, chopped
      1 jar (4-1/2 ounces) sliced mushrooms, drained
      3 tablespoons butter *or* margarine
      6 eggs
    1/4 cup milk
    3/4 teaspoon salt
    1/4 teaspoon dried basil
    1/8 teaspoon pepper
      2 cups (8 ounces) shredded cheddar cheese

Layer paper towels on a microwave-safe plate. Top with four bacon strips; cover with more paper towels. Microwave on high for 4 minutes. Repeat with remaining bacon. Cool; crumble and set aside. In a 2-1/2-qt. microwave-safe dish, combine potatoes, onion, green pepper, mushrooms and butter. Cover and microwave on high for 7-8 minutes or until the vegetables are tender, stirring once. Beat eggs, milk, salt, basil and pepper; stir into vegetable mixture. Cover and cook at 70% power for 6-8 minutes or until eggs are almost set, stirring every 2 minutes. Sprinkle with cheese and bacon. Cook, uncovered, on high for 1-2 minutes or until cheese is melted. Let stand for 5 minutes before serving. **Yield:** 6-8 servings.

Colorful Stuffed Peppers

Colorful Stuffed Peppers

(Pictured above)

You're sure to enjoy this tasty twist on traditional stuffed peppers. Crisp-tender pepper cups hold a colorful filling that gets south-of-the-border flavor from salsa and cumin. They're fast to assemble using convenience items such as instant rice and frozen corn. —Angie Dierikx
State Center, Iowa

      1 pound ground beef
      2 cups salsa
      1 cup frozen corn
    1/4 cup water
    3/4 teaspoon ground cumin
    3/4 teaspoon dried oregano
      1 teaspoon salt
    1/2 teaspoon pepper
    1/2 cup uncooked instant rice
      1 cup (4 ounces) shredded cheddar cheese,
        divided
      4 medium green peppers, halved lengthwise
Sliced canned jalapeno peppers, optional

Crumble beef into a 2-qt. microwave-safe dish. Cover and microwave on high for 2 minutes; stir. Cook on high 1-2 minutes longer or until the meat is no longer pink; drain. Stir in salsa, corn, water, cumin, oregano, salt and pepper. Cover and microwave on high for 3 minutes or until mixture bubbles around the edges. Stir in rice and 1/2 cup cheese. Cover and let stand for 5 minutes; stir. Spoon 1/2 cupful into each pepper half. Place on a 12-in. round microwave-safe plate. Cover loosely and cook on high for 8-10 minutes or until peppers are tender, rotating a half turn once. Cover and let stand for 4 minutes. Sprinkle with remaining cheese; top with jalapenos if desired. **Yield:** 4 servings.

Hash Brown Egg Dish

Enchilada Stack

I tried this fast flavorful casserole when I bought my first microwave more than 15 years ago. With a tossed salad and French bread, it's a hearty meal my family has enjoyed often. —Doreen Adams, Sacramento, California

    1 pound ground beef
1/4 cup chopped onion
    1 garlic clove, minced
    1 can (8 ounces) tomato sauce
1/4 cup water
    1 to 2 teaspoons chili powder
1/2 teaspoon salt
1/4 teaspoon pepper
    4 corn tortillas (6 inches)
    2 cups (8 ounces) shredded cheddar cheese

In an ungreased 2-qt. microwave-safe dish, combine the beef, onion and garlic. Cover and cook on high for 5 minutes or until meat is no longer pink, stirring once; drain. Stir in tomato sauce, water, chili powder, salt and pepper. Cover and cook on high for 8 minutes, stirring once. In an ungreased 1-1/2-qt. round dish, layer one tortilla, 1/2 cup meat sauce and 1/2 cup cheese. Repeat layers three times. Heat, uncovered, on high for 1 minute or until the cheese is melted. **Yield:** 4 servings.

Quick Chicken Cordon Bleu

(Pictured on page 265)

I used this speedy microwave recipe the first time I made chicken cordon bleu. Although I've since tried other recipes that bake in the oven, this remains the quickest...and the best. The moist chicken and flavorful cheese sauce make this entree perfect for a special occasion.
—Shirley Jackson, Elkton, Virginia

    4 boneless skinless chicken breast halves
    2 teaspoons Dijon mustard
1/2 teaspoon paprika
    4 thin slices fully cooked ham
    1 cup soft bread crumbs
1/4 cup grated Parmesan cheese
1/4 teaspoon pepper
1/4 cup mayonnaise
SAUCE:
    1 tablespoon butter *or* margarine
    1 tablespoon all-purpose flour
    1 cup milk
1/4 teaspoon salt
1/2 cup shredded Swiss cheese
    2 tablespoons white wine *or* chicken broth

Flatten the chicken to 1/2-in. thickness. Spread mustard on one side; sprinkle with paprika. Top with a ham slice. Roll up tightly; secure with toothpicks. In a bowl, combine the bread crumbs, Parmesan cheese and pepper. Brush chicken with mayonnaise; roll in crumb mixture. Place in a shallow 2-qt. microwave-safe dish; cover loosely. Microwave on high for 7 minutes. Turn the chicken; cook 7 minutes longer or until juices run clear. Remove toothpicks; set aside and keep warm. In a 1-qt. microwave-safe dish, heat the butter on high for 30 seconds; stir in the flour until smooth. Cook, uncovered, on high for 30 seconds. Add milk and salt. Cook 3-4 minutes longer or until thickened. Stir in cheese until smooth. Add the wine or broth. Serve over chicken. **Yield:** 4 servings.

Microwave Mac 'n' Cheese

(Pictured below)

My family prefers homemade macaroni and cheese over the kind you get out of a box. This recipe is an easy way to keep them happy. Whenever we have a family get-together, I bring this comforting dish. Its "from-scratch" taste can't be beat.
—Linda Gingrich
Freeburg, Pennsylvania

    2 cups uncooked elbow macaroni
    2 cups hot water
1/3 cup butter *or* margarine
1/4 cup chopped onion
3/4 teaspoon salt
1/4 teaspoon pepper
1/4 teaspoon ground mustard
1/3 cup all-purpose flour
1-1/4 cups milk
    8 ounces process American cheese, cubed

In a 2-qt. microwave-safe dish, combine the first seven ingredients. Cover and microwave on high for 3-1/2 minutes; stir. Cover and cook at 50% power for 4 minutes or until mixture comes to a boil, rotating a half turn once. Combine flour and milk until smooth; stir into macaroni mixture. Add cheese. Cover and cook on high for 6-8 minutes or until the macaroni is tender and sauce is bubbly, rotating a half turn once and stirring every 3 minutes. **Yield:** 4 servings.

Microwave Mac 'n' Cheese

Ham with Apricots

Ham with Apricots

(Pictured above)

A very good friend made this special main dish when I visited for dinner. I really like the spiced fruit glaze.
—*Nancy King, Greenfield, Indiana*

  1 can (15 ounces) apricot halves
  1 ham slice (about 1-1/2 pounds)
  1/4 cup packed brown sugar
  2 tablespoons cornstarch
  1/4 teaspoon ground nutmeg
  2 tablespoons vinegar

Drain apricots, reserving 1 cup syrup; set aside. Cut apricots in half; set aside. Score edges of ham; place in a shallow 2-qt. microwave-safe dish. In a small bowl, combine brown sugar, cornstarch and nutmeg; stir in vinegar and reserved syrup until smooth. Pour over ham. Cover and microwave at 70% power for 5 minutes. Turn ham; arrange apricots on top. Cover and microwave at 70% power for 8-10 minutes or until the sauce is thickened. Let stand for 2 minutes. **Yield:** 4-6 servings.

Chocolate Chews

I'm always searching for good recipes to use in the microwave. These thick, rich and chocolaty bars are oh-so-good served warm.
—*Sharan Williams*
Spanish Fork, Utah

  1 can (14 ounces) sweetened condensed milk
  1/2 cup chunky peanut butter
  2 teaspoons vanilla extract, *divided*
  1/2 teaspoon salt
  1/2 teaspoon ground cinnamon
  1/4 teaspoon ground nutmeg
  2 cups (12 ounces) semisweet chocolate chips, *divided*
1-1/2 cups quick-cooking oats
4-1/2 teaspoons milk

In a bowl, combine the condensed milk, peanut butter, 1 teaspoon vanilla, salt, cinnamon, nutmeg, 1-1/2 cups chocolate chips and oats; mix well. Spread into an 8-in. square microwave-safe dish; shield corners with small triangles of foil.* Microwave, uncovered, at 50% power for 10 minutes. Microwave on high for 3-4 minutes or until top springs back when lightly touched. Cool slightly; remove foil. In a microwave-safe bowl, combine milk and the remaining vanilla and chocolate chips. Microwave on high for 30-40 seconds or until chocolate is melted. Stir; spread over bars. **Yield:** 16 bars. ***Editor's Note:** Shielding with small pieces of foil prevents overcooking of food in the corners of a square or rectangular dish. This is the only time foil should be used in the microwave, but you should check your manufacturer's instructions before doing so. Secure foil firmly to dish and do not allow it to touch insides of oven.

Rhubarb Dumplings

Tender dumplings and a sweet, tangy rhubarb sauce combine to make this quick and comforting dessert. We love it alone or with ice cream. If you prefer, replace the rhubarb with blueberries.
—*Doris Peterson*
Mesa, Arizona

3/4 cup packed brown sugar
1/4 cup sugar
 2 tablespoons cornstarch
 1 cup water
 3 cups sliced fresh *or* frozen rhubarb
 3 tablespoons butter *or* margarine
DUMPLINGS:
1-1/4 cups all-purpose flour
 1/4 cup sugar
1-1/2 teaspoons baking powder
 1/3 cup milk
 1/4 cup butter *or* margarine, melted
 2 teaspoons sugar
 1/2 teaspoon ground cinnamon

In a 2-qt. microwave-safe dish, combine sugars and cornstarch. Stir in water until smooth. Add rhubarb and butter. Cover and microwave on high for 5 minutes; stir. Microwave 3 minutes longer or until rhubarb is tender and the sauce is thickened. Meanwhile, for dumplings, combine flour, sugar, baking powder, milk and butter. Drop batter in eight mounds around the edge of dish. Cover and microwave on high for 2 minutes (do not lift cover). Rotate a quarter-turn; microwave 3 minutes longer or until a toothpick inserted in a dumpling comes out clean. Combine sugar and cinnamon; sprinkle over top. Serve warm. **Yield:** 8 servings.

Hot Kielbasa Dip

(Pictured below)

My husband and I are retired, and I like to look for simple, speedy ways to cook. This thick cheesy dip, with the unusual addition of sausage, goes together in a jiffy. Accompanied by crackers or fresh veggies, it's a hearty appetizer for a football party or family gathering.
—Mary Bondegard, Brooksville, Florida

 1 package (8 ounces) cream cheese
 1/2 cup sour cream
 1/3 cup milk
 1 tablespoon mayonnaise

Hot Kielbasa Dip

Cinnamon Peanut Brittle

 1/2 teaspoon Worcestershire sauce
 8 ounces fully cooked kielbasa *or* Polish
 sausage, finely chopped
 1/2 cup sliced green onions, *divided*
 1/4 cup grated Parmesan cheese
Assorted crackers *or* raw vegetables

In a 1-1/2-qt. microwave-safe bowl, heat cream cheese, uncovered, on high for 1 minute. Stir in the sour cream, milk, mayonnaise and Worcestershire sauce. Add the kielbasa, 1/4 cup of onions and Parmesan cheese; mix well. Microwave, uncovered, on high for 3-4 minutes or until heated through, stirring once. Sprinkle with remaining onions. Serve with crackers or vegetables. Store in the refrigerator. **Yield:** about 3 cups.

Cinnamon Peanut Brittle

(Pictured above)

I made this sweet and crunchy candy for Christmas and sent some with my husband to work. His co-workers liked it so much they asked for more. —Grace Miller
Mansfield, Ohio

 1 cup sugar
 1/2 cup light corn syrup
 2 cups salted peanuts
 1 teaspoon butter (no substitutes)
 1/2 teaspoon ground cinnamon
 1 teaspoon baking soda
 1 teaspoon vanilla extract

In a 2-qt. microwave-safe bowl, combine sugar and corn syrup. Heat, uncovered, on high for 4 minutes; stir. Heat 3 minutes longer. Stir in peanuts, butter and cinnamon. Microwave, uncovered, on high for 30-60 seconds or until mixture turns a light amber color (mixture will be very hot). Quickly stir in baking soda and vanilla until light and foamy. Immediately pour onto a greased baking sheet and spread with a metal spatula. Refrigerate for 20 minutes or until firm; break into small pieces. Store in an airtight container. **Yield:** 1-1/4 pounds.

Chapter 19

HERE'S a collection of reliable theme-related recipes that are tops for taste and time-saving.

We've rounded up a host of favorite recipes for flavorful lamb entrees, pretty freezer jams and seasonal zucchini.

If rapid recipes that serve large households aren't convenient for your smaller one, you'll appreciate the perfectly portioned recipes that are great for just the two of you.

The next time you gather the gang and head to the great outdoors, turn to the simple picnic fare featuring make-ahead recipes.

SUCCESS WITH SQUASH. Top to bottom: Sweet-Sour Zucchini Salad and Baked Chicken and Zucchini (both recipes on p. 305).

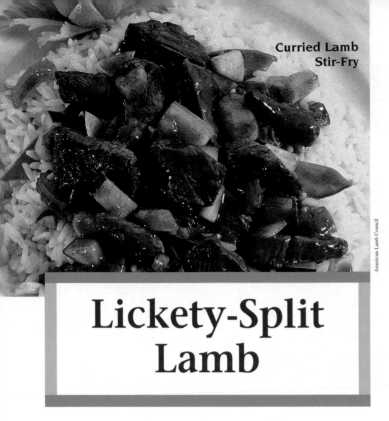
Curried Lamb
Stir-Fry

Lickety-Split Lamb

ADD these creative, quick-cooking entrees from the American Lamb Council to your recipe file.

Pasta Lamb Skillet

Ground lamb provides an interesting change from ground beef in this speedy stovetop dinner.

12 ounces ground lamb
1 cup chopped onion
2 garlic cloves, minced
1 tablespoon olive *or* vegetable oil
1 medium zucchini, quartered and thinly sliced (1-1/4 cups)
1 can (14-1/2 ounces) diced tomatoes, undrained
1 cup sliced fresh mushrooms
3 tablespoons minced fresh basil *or* 1 tablespoon dried basil
1/2 teaspoon pepper
1/4 to 1/2 teaspoon seasoned salt
1 package (8 ounces) small pasta, cooked and drained
1/4 cup sliced ripe olives

In a large skillet, cook lamb, onion and garlic in oil until meat is no longer pink and vegetables are tender; drain. Set aside. Add the vegetables and seasonings to skillet; cover and cook for 5 minutes or until vegetables are tender. Add pasta, olives and lamb mixture; heat through. **Yield:** 8 servings.

Grilled Lamb with Veggies

Lean lamb chops teamed with a colorful medley of vegetables make a special grilled meal.

1/2 cup apple juice
1/2 cup honey

2 tablespoons dried minced onion
2 tablespoons cider *or* red wine vinegar
2 tablespoons tomato paste
2 garlic cloves, minced
1 teaspoon Worcestershire sauce
1/2 teaspoon pepper
3 medium potatoes
1 *each* medium green, sweet red and yellow pepper, julienned
2 sirloin lamb chops (about 1-1/2 pounds), trimmed

In a saucepan, combine the first eight ingredients; bring to a boil. Reduce heat; simmer, uncovered, for 5 minutes. Cut each potato into 16 wedges. Divide potatoes and peppers between two pieces of heavy-duty foil (about 18 in. square). Top each with 1/2 cup sauce; set remaining sauce aside. Seal foil tightly. Grill vegetable packets and lamb chops, covered, over medium-hot heat for 5 minutes. Turn chops; baste with remaining sauce. Grill 5 minutes longer. Turn and baste again. Grill for 2 minutes or until a meat thermometer reads 140° for rare, 150° for medium or 160° for well-done. Serve with vegetables. **Yield:** 2 servings.

Curried Lamb Stir-Fry

(Pictured above left)

Tender strips of lamb contrast nicely with the crunchy apples, snow peas and water chestnuts.

✓ Uses less fat, sugar or salt. Includes Nutritional Analysis and Diabetic Exchanges.

1 teaspoon cornstarch
1/4 cup chicken broth
1 tablespoon soy sauce
1/4 teaspoon curry powder
12 ounces boneless lamb, cut into 1/8-inch strips
1 small onion, chopped
2 garlic cloves, minced
2 tablespoons vegetable oil, *divided*
1 small red apple, chopped
1/2 cup chopped green pepper
1/2 cup sliced celery
1 can (8 ounces) sliced water chestnuts, drained
6 ounces fresh *or* frozen snow peas
1/4 teaspoon ground ginger
Hot cooked rice

In a bowl, combine cornstarch, broth, soy sauce and curry powder; stir until smooth. Set aside. In a large skillet or wok, saute lamb, onion and garlic in 1 tablespoon oil until meat is browned. Remove and keep warm. In the same skillet, stir-fry apple, green pepper, celery, water chestnuts, peas and ginger in remaining oil until crisp-tender. Add lamb mixture. Stir broth mixture and add to skillet. Bring to a boil; cook and stir for 2 minutes or until thickened. Serve over rice. **Yield:** 4 servings. **Nutritional Analysis:** One 1-cup serving (prepared with low-sodium broth and light soy sauce; calculated without rice) equals 264 calories, 198 mg sodium, 55 mg cholesterol, 19 gm carbohydrate, 20 gm protein, 12 gm fat. **Diabetic Exchanges:** 2 meat, 1 starch, 1 vegetable, 1/2 fat.

Dinner for Two

FOR THOSE OCCASIONS when you don't need to feed a crowd, try this scaled-down fancy, no fuss menu cooked up by our test kitchen.

Peppercorn Steaks

(Pictured below right)

These tender peppered steaks get plenty of zip from a quick-to-fix sauce flavored with mustard and Worcestershire.

> 1 tablespoon whole black peppercorns, crushed
> 2 strip *or* top loin steaks* (about 8 ounces *each*)
> 2 to 3 tablespoons butter *or* margarine, melted
> 1 to 2 garlic cloves, minced
> 1 tablespoon Worcestershire sauce
> 1/2 cup red wine *or* beef broth
> 1 teaspoon ground mustard
> 1/2 teaspoon sugar
> 2 teaspoons cornstarch
> 1 tablespoon water

Rub pepper over both sides of steaks. Refrigerate for 15 minutes. In an ungreased skillet over medium-high heat, brown steaks on both sides. Add butter and garlic; cook for 4-6 minutes, turning steaks once. Add Worcestershire sauce; cook 4-6 minutes longer, turning once, or until meat reaches desired doneness (for rare, a meat thermometer should read 140°; medium, 160°; well-done, 170°). Remove steaks and keep warm. Combine wine or broth, mustard and sugar; add to the pan. Stir to loosen browned bits. Combine cornstarch and water until smooth; add to pan. Bring to a boil; cook and stir for 2 minutes or until thickened. Serve with the steaks. **Yield:** 2 servings. ***Editor's Note:** Steak may be known as New York strip steak, Kansas City strip steak, Ambassador Steak or boneless Club Steak in your region.

Two-Cheese Linguine

(Pictured at right)

An easy cheese sauce turns ordinary pasta into a special side dish that's the perfect accompaniment to the steaks.

> 1 package (7 ounces) linguine
> 2 tablespoons butter *or* margarine
> 3 tablespoons all-purpose flour
> 1/4 teaspoon salt
> 1/8 teaspoon pepper
> 1-1/2 cups milk
> 3/4 cup (6 ounces) shredded mozzarella cheese
> 1/4 cup shredded Parmesan cheese
> 2 tablespoons lemon juice

Cook linguine according to package directions. Meanwhile, in a skillet over low heat, melt butter. Stir in flour, salt and pepper until smooth. Gradually stir in milk. Bring to a boil; boil and stir for 2 minutes or until thickened. Remove from the heat. Combine cheeses; toss with lemon juice. Add to the sauce; stir until cheese begins to melt. Drain linguine; add the cheese sauce and toss to coat. **Yield:** 2 servings.

French Green Beans

(Pictured below)

Frozen green beans get tasty flavor from rosemary and basil.

> 1 package (9 ounces) frozen French-style green beans
> 1 jar (4-1/2 ounces) sliced mushrooms, drained
> 3 tablespoons butter *or* margarine, melted
> 1/4 teaspoon dried rosemary, crushed
> 1/4 teaspoon dried basil
> Toasted slivered almonds

Cook green beans according to package directions; drain. Add mushrooms and keep warm. Combine butter, rosemary and basil; drizzle over bean mixture and toss to coat. Sprinkle with almonds. **Yield:** 2 servings.

Trifle for Two

(Pictured below)

This delightful dessert combines chocolate chips, cubed pound cake and a rich cappuccino-flavored topping.

> 1 package (3 ounces) cream cheese, softened
> 4 teaspoons instant cappuccino powder *or* other flavored sweetened instant coffee powder
> 2 teaspoons sugar
> 1 cup whipped topping
> 2 slices pound cake, cut into cubes
> 1/4 cup semisweet chocolate chips
> Additional whipped topping and chocolate chips, optional

In a mixing bowl, beat cream cheese, coffee powder and sugar until smooth. Beat in whipped topping until blended. Divide cake cubes between two dessert dishes; top with cream cheese mixture and chocolate chips. Garnish with additional whipped topping and chocolate chips if desired. **Yield:** 2 servings.

Savor a Cool Summer Picnic

Super Italian Sub
Make-Ahead Vegetable Salad
Double Chip Bars

TO FULLY enjoy outdoor dining, plan a day in advance and prepare this pleasing picnic fare.

Super Italian Sub

(Pictured at right)

I like recipes like this flavorful sandwich that can be made ahead because they let me relax with family and friends. Just unwrap, slice and enjoy.
—Patricia Lomp, Middleboro, Massachusetts

  1 loaf (1 pound) unsliced Italian bread
1/3 cup olive *or* vegetable oil
1/4 cup cider *or* red wine vinegar
  8 garlic cloves, minced
  1 teaspoon dried oregano
1/4 teaspoon pepper
1/2 pound thinly sliced fully cooked ham
1/2 pound thinly sliced cooked turkey
1/4 pound thinly sliced salami
1/4 pound sliced provolone cheese
1/4 pound sliced mozzarella cheese
  1 medium green pepper, thinly sliced into rings

Cut bread in half lengthwise; hollow out top and bottom, leaving a 1/2-in. shell (discard removed bread or save for another use). Combine oil, vinegar, garlic, oregano and pepper; brush on cut sides of bread top and bottom. On the bottom half, layer half of the meats, cheeses and green pepper. Repeat layers. Replace bread top. Wrap tightly in plastic wrap; refrigerate for up to 24 hours. **Yield:** 10-12 servings.

Make-Ahead Vegetable Salad

(Pictured above right)

I make this tangy salad that's chock-full of garden-fresh goodies. Storing it in the fridge overnight helps blend the flavors.   *—Kathy Berndt, El Campo, Texas*

  6 medium tomatoes, cut into eighths
  1 medium green pepper, thinly sliced
  1 medium red onion, thinly sliced
  1 medium cucumber, thinly sliced
3/4 cup cider vinegar
1/4 cup water
  2 tablespoons sugar
1-1/2 teaspoons celery salt
1-1/2 teaspoons mustard seed
1/4 teaspoon salt
1/8 to 1/4 teaspoon cayenne pepper
1/8 teaspoon pepper

In a large bowl, combine the tomatoes, green pepper, onion and cucumber; set aside. In a saucepan, combine the remaining ingredients. Bring to a boil; boil for 1 minute. Pour over vegetables and toss to coat. Cover and refrigerate for 8 hours or overnight. Serve with a slotted spoon. **Yield:** 10-12 servings.

Double Chip Bars

(Pictured above)

Our two children love these rich dessert bars. They go together quickly.   *—Victoria Lowe, Lititz, Pennsylvania*

1/2 cup butter (no substitutes)
1-1/2 cups graham cracker crumbs (about 24 squares)
  1 can (14 ounces) sweetened condensed milk
  2 cups semisweet chocolate chips
  1 cup peanut butter chips

Place butter in a 13-in. x 9-in. x 2-in. baking pan; place in a 350° oven until melted. Remove from oven. Sprinkle cracker crumbs evenly over butter. Pour milk evenly over crumbs. Sprinkle with chips; press down firmly. Bake at 350° for 25-30 minutes or until golden brown. Cool on a wire rack before cutting. **Yield:** 3 dozen.

No-Bake Party Mix

A packet of ranch salad dressing mix makes this a breeze to prepare.   *—Regina Stock, Topeka, Kansas*

  8 cups Crispix cereal
2-1/2 cups miniature pretzels *or* pretzel sticks
2-1/2 cups bite-size cheddar cheese crackers
  3 tablespoons vegetable oil
  1 envelope ranch salad dressing mix

In a heavy-duty resealable 2-gal. plastic bag, combine the cereal, pretzels and crackers; drizzle with oil. Seal and toss gently to mix. Sprinkle with dressing mix; seal and toss until well-coated. Store in an airtight container. **Yield:** about 12 cups.

Make Note of Dinner Duets

Chicken Red Pepper Saute

SPEEDY SUPPERS that feed a crowd can hit the right note for large households, family get-togethers and church potlucks. But for some folks, like newlywed Cathy McMahon of Bloomingdale, Illinois, those meals are not always in harmony with her lifestyle.

"My husband and I both work crazy hours, so rapid recipes are just what we need," Cathy explains. "But since there's just the two of us, I'd like to see recipes that serve two."

For Cathy and readers like her, our test kitchen came up with two recipes for two main dishes that serve two people.

Nut-Crusted Fried Fish

(Pictured below)

The nutty taste of this simple coating complements flaky fish fillets quite nicely. Complete the meal with parsley new potatoes and corn on the cob in season. Or, for a faster finish, serve with frozen French fries and mixed vegetables

- 3 tablespoons seasoned bread crumbs
- 3 tablespoons finely chopped pecans *or* pistachios
- 1/4 teaspoon salt
- Dash pepper
- 3 tablespoons all-purpose flour
- 3 tablespoons milk

Nut-Crusted Fried Fish

- 1/2 pound fish fillets (about 1/2 inch thick)
- 2 tablespoons vegetable oil

In a shallow bowl, combine the bread crumbs, pecans or pistachios, salt and pepper. Place the flour in a shallow bowl and the milk in another bowl. Cut fish fillets into serving-size pieces if necessary. Dredge fish in flour, dip in milk, then coat with the crumb mixture. Heat oil in a nonstick skillet over medium heat. Fry the fish for 4-5 minutes on each side or until it flakes easily with a fork. **Yield:** 2 servings.

Chicken Red Pepper Saute

(Pictured above)

The garlic and lemon-pepper really come through in this quick stir-fry. Serve the colorful combination on a bed of rice or over chow mein noodles for fun crunch. For dessert, pour cream over sliced fresh peaches or serve easy fudge brownies.

- 1 tablespoon cornstarch
- 1/2 cup chicken broth, *divided*
- 1 garlic clove, minced
- 1/2 teaspoon lemon-pepper seasoning
- 1/2 pound boneless skinless chicken breasts, cut into 1/2-inch strips
- 1 tablespoon vegetable oil
- 1 medium sweet red pepper, julienned
- Green onion strips *or* fresh chives

In a bowl, combine the cornstarch, 1/4 cup of broth, garlic and lemon-pepper seasoning; stir until smooth. Add the chicken strips and toss to coat. Heat oil in a nonstick skillet over medium-high heat. Add the chicken mixture and remaining broth; cook and stir for 2 minutes. Add red pepper strips; cook and stir until the chicken is no longer pink and the peppers are crisp-tender, about 6-8 minutes. Garnish with green onions or chives. **Yield:** 2 servings.

Pretty Peach Jam
Pineapple Kiwi Jam
Freezer Berry Jam

1 can (8 ounces) crushed pineapple, undrained
1/4 cup lime juice
1 pouch (3 ounces) liquid fruit pectin
3 drops green food coloring, optional

In a 2-qt. microwave-safe bowl, combine kiwi, sugar, pineapple and lime juice. Microwave, uncovered, on high for 10-13 minutes or until mixture comes to a full rolling boil, stirring every 2 minutes. Stir in pectin. Add food coloring if desired. Pour into jars or freezer containers and cool to room temperature, about 1 hour. Cover and let stand overnight or until set, but not longer than 24 hours. Refrigerate or freeze. **Yield:** 4 cups. **Editor's Note:** This recipe was tested in an 850-watt microwave.

Pretty Peach Jam

(Pictured at left)

This jam has a delicious medley of fruits, including peaches, cherries, pineapple and orange.
—Theresa Beckman, Canton, South Dakota

8 medium peaches, cut into wedges
1 small unpeeled navel orange, cut into wedges
2 cans (8 ounces *each*) crushed pineapple, undrained
12 maraschino cherries
3 tablespoons maraschino cherry juice
2 packages (1-3/4 ounces *each*) powdered fruit pectin
10 cups sugar

In a blender or food processor, cover and process fruits and cherry juice in batches until smooth. Transfer to a large kettle; stir in pectin. Bring to a rolling boil over high heat, stirring constantly. Add sugar; boil for 2 minutes. Remove from the heat. Pour into jars or freezer containers; cool to room temperature, about 1 hour. Cover and let stand overnight or until set, but not longer than 24 hours. Refrigerate or freeze. **Yield:** 13 cups.

Plum-Kissed Pear Jam

I won the grand prize in a recipe contest with this thick tasty jam! —*Margaret Zickert, Deerfield, Wisconsin*

3 cups chopped *or* coarsely ground peeled pears
1 cup chopped *or* coarsely ground pitted plums
1 package (1-3/4 ounces) powdered fruit pectin
5-1/2 cups sugar

In a kettle, combine pears and plums. Stir in pectin. Bring to a full rolling boil over high heat, stirring constantly. Stir in sugar; return to a full rolling boil. Boil for 1 minute, stirring constantly. Remove from the heat; skim off foam. Pour into jars or freezer containers and cool to room temperature, about 1 hour. Cover and let stand overnight or until set, but not longer than 24 hours. Refrigerate or freeze. **Yield:** 6 cups.

Freezer Jams

DOES a jam-packed summer calendar keep you from preserving the fresh taste of ripe summer fruits? Try these jam recipes that bypass the canning method and go straight to the freezer.

Freezer Berry Jam

(Pictured above)

Whenever we find wild blueberries nearby, I make this gorgeous ruby-red jam. —*Rita Pischke*
Whitemouth, Manitoba

4 cups blueberries
2 cups raspberries
5 cups sugar
2 tablespoons lemon juice
3/4 cup water
1 package (1-3/4 ounces) powdered fruit pectin

In a large bowl, crush the blueberries. Add raspberries and crush. Stir in sugar and lemon juice. Let stand for 10 minutes. In a small saucepan, bring water and pectin to a boil. Boil for 1 minute, stirring constantly. Add to fruit mixture; stir for 3 minutes. Pour into jars or freezer containers; cool to room temperature, about 30 minutes. Cover and let stand overnight or until set, but not longer than 24 hours. Refrigerate or freeze. **Yield:** 7 cups.

Pineapple Kiwi Jam

(Pictured above)

Pineapple, kiwi and a hint of lime blend nicely in this unique jam. —*Sondra Rogers, Columbus, Indiana*

4 kiwifruit, peeled and thinly sliced
3 cups sugar

Zesty Zucchini

WHETHER you have a bumper crop in your garden or receive some from neighbors, these recipes will help you make the most of plentiful squash.

Sweet-Sour Zucchini Salad

(Pictured below right and on page 298)

This make-ahead mixture can be served as a condiment or a salad. —*Jan Koppri, Mancos, Colorado*

    1/2 cup cider *or* white wine vinegar
    4-1/2 teaspoons dried minced onion
      7 small zucchini, thinly sliced
    1/2 cup chopped celery
    1/4 cup chopped green pepper
    1/4 cup chopped sweet red pepper
DRESSING:
    3/4 cup sugar
    2/3 cup cider vinegar
    1/3 cup vegetable oil
      1 teaspoon salt
      1 teaspoon pepper

In a large bowl, combine vinegar and onion. Add zucchini, celery and peppers. In a jar with a tight-fitting lid, combine dressing ingredients; shake well. Pour over vegetables and stir gently. Cover and refrigerate for 8 hours or overnight. Serve with a slotted spoon. **Yield:** 10 servings.

Frosted Brownies

These moist fudgy brownies disappear fast at potluck dinners. —*Ruth Bramble, Rushville, Missouri*

      2 cups all-purpose flour
    1/3 cup baking cocoa
    1-1/2 teaspoons baking soda
      1 teaspoon salt
      2 cups shredded zucchini
    1-1/2 cups sugar
    3/4 cup vegetable oil
    1/2 cup chopped walnuts
      2 teaspoons vanilla extract
FROSTING:
    1/4 cup butter *or* margarine
      1 cup sugar
    1/4 cup milk
    1/2 cup semisweet chocolate chips
    1/2 cup miniature marshmallows
      1 teaspoon vanilla extract
    1/2 cup chopped walnuts, optional

In a bowl, combine flour, cocoa, baking soda and salt. Combine zucchini, sugar and oil; add to dry ingredients. Mix well. Stir in walnuts and vanilla. Pour into a greased 13-in. x 9-in. x 2-in. baking pan. Bake at 350° for 35-40 minutes or until a toothpick inserted near the center comes out clean. Cool on a wire rack for 30 minutes. In a saucepan, melt butter; stir in sugar and milk. Bring to a boil over medium heat, stirring frequently. Boil and stir 1 minute. Remove from heat. Stir in chips and marshmallows until melted; add vanilla. Spread over brownies. Sprinkle with walnuts if desired. **Yield:** 2 dozen.

Baked Chicken and Zucchini

(Pictured below and on page 299)

I love zucchini, so this colorful dish is one of my favorites. I make it often in summer. It's especially good with tomatoes fresh from the garden. —*Sheryl Goodnough Eliot, Maine*

      1 egg
      1 tablespoon water
    3/4 teaspoon salt, *divided*
    1/8 teaspoon pepper
      1 cup dry bread crumbs
      4 boneless skinless chicken breast halves
      4 tablespoons olive *or* vegetable oil, *divided*
      5 medium zucchini, sliced
      4 medium tomatoes, sliced
      1 cup (4 ounces) shredded mozzarella cheese, *divided*
      2 teaspoons minced fresh basil

In a shallow bowl, beat egg, water, 1/2 teaspoon salt and pepper. Set aside 2 tablespoons bread crumbs. Place the remaining crumbs in a large resealable plastic bag. Dip chicken in egg mixture, then place in bag and shake to coat. In a skillet, cook chicken in 2 tablespoons oil for 2-3 minutes on each side or until golden brown; remove and set aside. In the same skillet, saute zucchini in remaining oil until crisp-tender; drain. Transfer to a greased 13-in. x 9-in. x 2-in. baking dish. Sprinkle reserved bread crumbs over zucchini. Top with tomato slices; sprinkle with 2/3 cup mozzarella cheese, basil and remaining salt. Top with chicken. Cover and bake at 400° for 25 minutes. Uncover; sprinkle with remaining cheese. Bake 10 minutes longer or until cheese is melted. **Yield:** 4 servings.

Sweet-Sour Zucchini Salad
Baked Chicken and Zucchini

NO TIME for entertaining? Think again! An elaborate meal can have time-easing elements that make hosting a get-together a snap...and a lot more fun for the hostess. You can even offer unexpected company a memorable brunch on a moment's notice.

With this chapter's step-saving recipes, you can spend more time visiting with your guests, instead of slaving away in the kitchen. So you'll feel like a guest at your own party!

Plus, easy and inexpensive garnishes, table decorations and food presentation ideas provide special touches.

ENTERTAINING IS EASY! Clockwise from lower right: Special Pork Tenderloin, Garlic Mashed Potatoes, Pleasing Peas and Asparagus and Chocolate Raspberry Torte (all recipes on p. 313).

Meaty Magical Meal

ENTERTAIN effortlessly during the holidays with this timely menu featuring a tasty stuffed tenderloin. (See page 320 for festive table toppers.)

Twice-Baked Potato Casserole

This casserole is loaded with many palate-pleasing flavors.
—Betty Miars, Anna, Ohio

> 6 medium unpeeled potatoes, baked
> 1/4 teaspoon salt
> 1/4 teaspoon pepper
> 1 pound sliced bacon, cooked and crumbled
> 3 cups (24 ounces) sour cream
> 2 cups (8 ounces) shredded mozzarella cheese
> 2 cups (8 ounces) shredded cheddar cheese
> 2 green onions, chopped

Cut baked potatoes into 1-in. cubes. Place half in a greased 13-in. x 9-in. x 2-in. baking dish. Sprinkle with half of the salt, pepper and bacon. Top with half of the sour cream and cheeses. Repeat layers. Bake, uncovered, at 350° for 20 minutes or until cheese is melted. Sprinkle with onions. **Yield:** 6-8 servings.

Mushroom-Stuffed Tenderloin

Tender slices of beef are filled with a savory mixture of mushrooms, bacon and bread crumbs. —Marie Steeber Mishicot, Wisconsin

> 3 bacon strips
> 1 cup chopped fresh mushrooms
> 2 tablespoons chopped onion
> 1 garlic clove, minced
> 3/4 cup dry bread crumbs, *divided*
> 2 tablespoons minced fresh parsley
> 1 beef tenderloin (about 2 pounds), trimmed
> 1 tablespoon butter *or* margarine, melted
> 1 tablespoon grated Parmesan cheese

In a skillet, cook bacon until crisp. Remove bacon; crumble and set aside. Drain, reserving 1 tablespoon drippings. In the drippings, saute the mushrooms, onion and garlic until tender. Remove from the heat; stir in 1/2 cup of bread crumbs, parsley and bacon. Cut a slit lengthwise three-quarters of the way through the tenderloin (see below left). Lightly place stuffing in the pocket; close with toothpicks. Combine butter and Parmesan cheese; spread over top and sides of meat. Press the remaining bread crumbs onto butter mixture. Place meat on a rack in a shallow roasting pan. Bake, uncovered, at 350° for 15 minutes. Cover and bake for 1 hour or until meat reaches desired doneness (for medium-rare, a meat thermometer should read 145°; medium, 160°; well-done, 170°). Let stand for 10 minutes and remove toothpicks before slicing. **Yield:** 6-8 servings.

Elegant Chocolate Cake

My mom fixed this dressed-up chocolate cake for me when I came home from college. Now I serve it to my family. They love the yummy pecan-packed caramel sauce.
—Laura German, West Warren, Massachusetts

> 3 eggs
> 1 cup sugar
> 3/4 cup vegetable oil
> 1/4 cup milk
> 3/4 cup all-purpose flour
> 1/2 cup cocoa
> 1/2 teaspoon baking powder
> 1/2 teaspoon salt
> 1/2 teaspoon vanilla extract
> 1 package (14 ounces) caramels
> 1/4 cup water
> 1 cup chopped pecans
> Whipped cream and additional chopped pecans, optional

In a mixing bowl, beat eggs, sugar, oil and milk. Combine the flour, cocoa, baking powder and salt; gradually add to egg mixture and mix well. Stir in vanilla. Transfer to a greased 8-in. square baking pan. Bake at 350° for 30-35 minutes or until a toothpick comes out clean. Cool on a wire rack. In a heavy saucepan, combine caramels and water. Cook and stir over low heat until smooth. Add pecans. Cool slightly. Cut the cake into squares; drizzle with warm caramel sauce. Top with whipped cream and pecans if desired. **Yield:** 9 servings.

Baked Cranberry Relish

(Not pictured)

Orange marmalade and walnuts make this cranberry sauce delightful. —Anita Curtis, Camarillo, California

> 4-1/2 cups cranberries
> 1-1/2 cups sugar
> 1 cup chopped walnuts, toasted
> 1 cup orange marmalade
> 2 tablespoons lemon juice

Toss cranberries and sugar; place in a lightly greased 2-qt. baking dish. Cover and bake at 350° for 1 hour. Stir in walnuts, marmalade and lemon juice. Refrigerate. **Yield:** 6-8 servings.

Stuffing a Beef Tenderloin

STUFFING beef tenderloin with a savory filling and coating it with bread crumbs gives it an appealing look yet won't keep you in the kitchen for hours.

1 Begin by cutting a pocket down the length of the tenderloin, three-quarters of the way through meat. Lightly stuff with mushroom-bread crumb mixture.

2 Pinch meat together to enclose stuffing and insert toothpicks through meat along the seam. Brush with butter mixture and pat with remaining crumbs. Bake as directed.

South-of-the-Border Supper

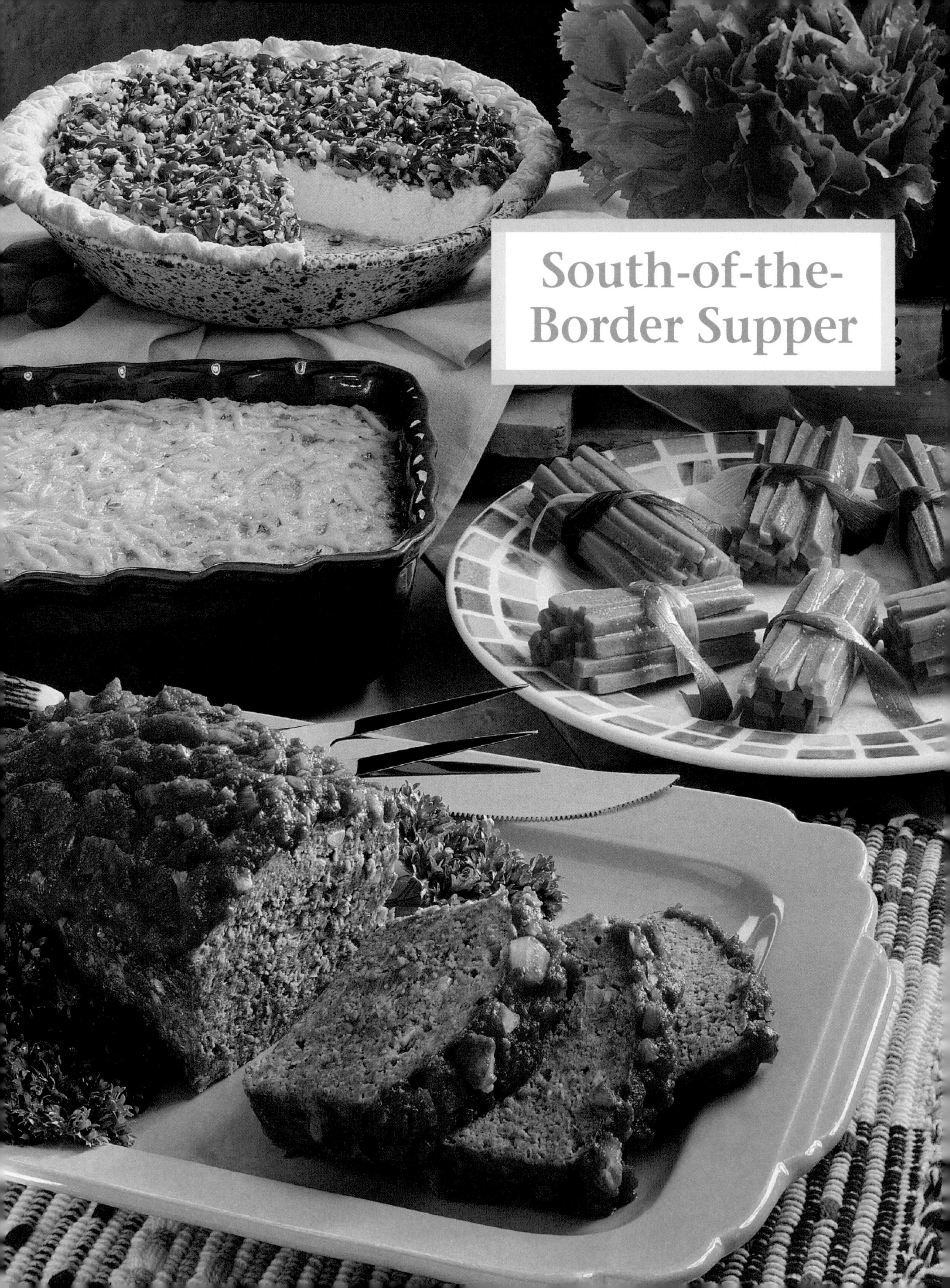

WARM UP with this fast fiesta seasoned with full flavor. (Turn to page 321 for tips on bringing color to your table.)

Mexican Meat Loaf

Chili powder gives my meat loaf a fun Mexican flavor that's complemented by zesty picante sauce poured over the top. —Debra Jane Webb, Muskogee, Oklahoma

   3/4 cup milk
   2 eggs, beaten
   1/2 cup dry bread crumbs
   1/4 cup finely chopped onion
   1/2 teaspoon salt
   1/2 teaspoon pepper
   1/2 teaspoon chili powder
1-1/2 pounds lean ground beef
   1 jar (16 ounces) picante sauce, warmed

In large bowl, combine first seven ingredients. Add beef; mix well. Pat into greased 8-in. x 4-in. x 2-in. loaf pan. Bake, uncovered, at 350° for 1 hour or until juices run clear; drain. Top with picante sauce. **Yield:** 6 servings.

Cheddar Rice Casserole

With its blend of garlic, parsley and cheese, this casserole makes a savory side dish. It's one of my favorite ways to serve rice. —Nancy Baylor, Holiday Island, Arkansas

1/4 cup chopped onion
   2 garlic cloves, minced
1/4 cup butter *or* margarine
   3 cups cooked long grain rice
   2 cups (8 ounces) shredded cheddar cheese
   1 cup minced fresh parsley
   1 cup milk
   4 eggs, lightly beaten
   2 teaspoons Worcestershire sauce
   1 teaspoon salt

In a large saucepan, saute onion and garlic in butter until tender. Add remaining ingredients; mix well. Transfer to a greased shallow 1-qt. baking dish. Bake, uncovered, at 350° for 40-45 minutes or until a knife inserted near the center comes out clean. **Yield:** 6-8 servings.

Citrus Carrot Sticks

These julienned carrots pick up a pleasant tang from orange juice and cumin. This tasty treatment is kid-tested and approved. —Amy Volk, Geneva, Illinois

✓ Uses less fat, sugar or salt. Includes Nutritional Analysis and Diabetic Exchanges.

   3 tablespoons orange juice
   1 teaspoon butter *or* margarine, melted
1/2 teaspoon ground cumin
   1 pound carrots
   6 cups water

Combine orange juice, butter and cumin; set aside. Cut carrots into 3-in. chunks, then into matchstick strips. In a large saucepan, bring water to a boil. Add carrots; cook for about 2 minutes or until crisp-tender. Drain; place in a serving bowl. Drizzle with orange juice mixture. **Yield:** 6 servings. **Nutritional Analysis:** One serving (prepared with margarine) equals 44 calories, 35 mg sodium, 0 cholesterol, 9 gm carbohydrate, 1 gm protein, 1 gm fat. **Diabetic Exchange:** 1-1/2 vegetable. **Editor's Note:** See page 320 for tips on cutting and bundling the carrots as shown in the photo.

Pecan Cream Cheese Pie

Toasted coconut, nuts and caramel sauce top a cream cheese layer in this special pie. —Mildred Troupe Wartrace, Tennessee

   1 cup chopped pecans
1/2 cup flaked coconut
1/4 cup butter *or* margarine, melted
   4 ounces cream cheese, softened
1/4 cup confectioners' sugar
1-3/4 cups whipped topping
   1 pastry shell (9 inches), baked and cooled
1/2 cup caramel ice cream topping

In a bowl, combine pecans, coconut and butter. Pour onto an ungreased 15-in. x 10-in. x 1-in. baking pan. Bake at 350° for 5-10 minutes or until golden brown, stirring occasionally. Cool. In a mixing bowl, beat the cream cheese and sugar until smooth. Fold in whipped topping. Spoon into pastry shell. Sprinkle with coconut mixture. Drizzle with caramel topping. Refrigerate for 2 hours. **Yield:** 6-8 servings.

Party Bean Dip

(Not pictured)

This colorful, crowd-pleasing dip is full of flavor. A cousin made it for a family get-together, and we finished off every bite! —Darnele West, Lancaster, South Carolina

   6 bacon strips
   2 garlic cloves, minced
   1 can (15 ounces) black beans, drained, rinsed and mashed
1-1/2 cups (6 ounces) shredded cheddar *or* Monterey Jack cheese
2/3 cup picante sauce
1/3 cup sliced green onions
   1 teaspoon ground cumin
Chopped sweet red and yellow peppers, optional
Minced fresh cilantro *or* parsley, optional
Fresh vegetables *or* tortilla chips

In a skillet over medium heat, cook bacon until crisp. Drain, reserving 1 tablespoon drippings. Crumble bacon and set aside. In the drippings, saute garlic for 1-2 minutes. Stir in beans, cheese, picante sauce, onions and cumin; mix well. Cook over low heat until cheese is melted, stirring occasionally. Stir in bacon. Transfer to a serving bowl. Garnish with peppers and cilantro if desired. Serve with vegetables or chips. **Yield:** 2-1/2 cups.

Easy Easter Dinner

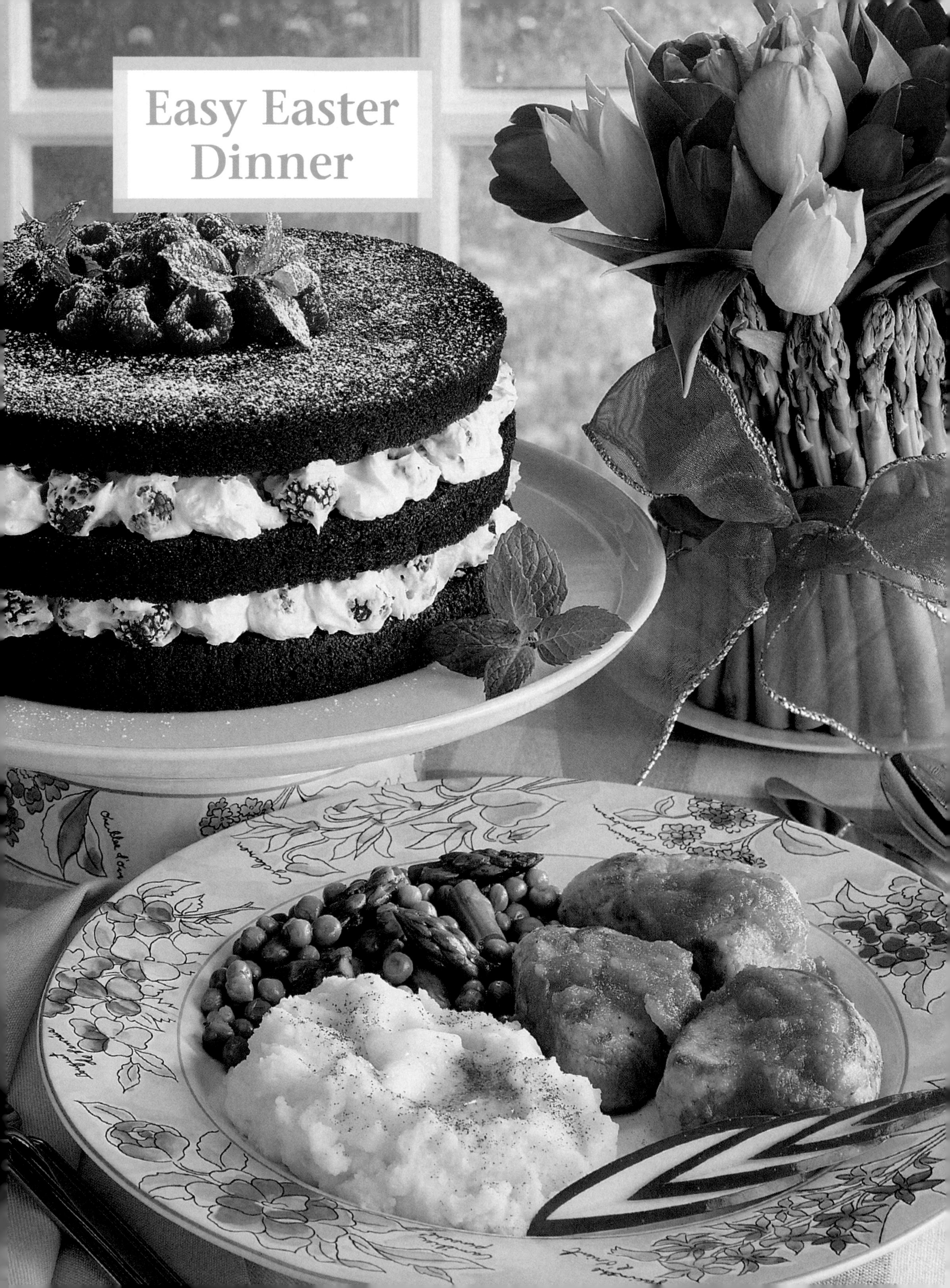

HERE'S a fast feast that's perfect for Easter dinner or most any special occasion. The savory pork tenderloin can be popped in the oven before guests arrive, while both side dishes cook in no time on the stovetop. The elegant torte is a snap to make earlier in the day. (To create apple accents and add color to your table, see page 322.)

Special Pork Tenderloin

(Also pictured on page 307)

This is my family's all-time favorite pork recipe. The moist tenderloin, beautifully complemented by a jazzy applesauce, bakes to melt-in-your-mouth tenderness.
—*Ruth Harrow, Bristol, New Hampshire*

✓ Uses less fat, sugar or salt. Includes Nutritional Analysis and Diabetic Exchanges.

    1/3 cup all-purpose flour
    1/2 teaspoon salt, optional
    1/2 teaspoon pepper
      2 pork tenderloins (1 pound *each*)
      2 tablespoons butter *or* margarine
      1 cup chopped onion
      1 garlic clove, minced
      2 cups unsweetened applesauce
    1/4 cup packed brown sugar
    1/4 cup soy sauce
    1/4 cup apple juice
    1/2 teaspoon ground ginger

In a shallow bowl, combine flour, salt if desired and pepper. Cut each tenderloin into six pieces; flatten to about 1-in. thickness. Melt butter in a large skillet. Dip pork into flour mixture; add to skillet and brown on both sides. Place in an ungreased 11-in. x 7-in. x 2-in. baking pan. In the same skillet, saute onion and garlic until tender. Add remaining ingredients; bring to a boil. Pour over pork. Cover and bake at 350° for 1 hour or until the juices run clear and a meat thermometer reads 160°. **Yield:** 6 servings. **Nutritional Analysis:** One serving (prepared with margarine and light soy sauce and without salt) equals 341 calories, 451 mg sodium, 90 mg cholesterol, 29 gm carbohydrate, 34 gm protein, 9 gm fat. **Diabetic Exchanges:** 4 lean meat, 1 starch, 1 fruit.

Pleasing Peas and Asparagus

(Also pictured on page 307)

Guests won't be able to resist the fresh flavor and color of this springtime vegetable combination. —*Nina Hall Citrus Heights, California*

✓ Uses less fat, sugar or salt. Includes Nutritional Analysis and Diabetic Exchanges.

    1/2 cup water
      2 packages (10 ounces *each*) frozen peas
    3/4 pound fresh asparagus, cut into 1-inch pieces
         or frozen asparagus tips
      3 tablespoons butter *or* margarine
      1 tablespoon minced fresh parsley
    3/4 teaspoon garlic salt, optional
Dash pepper

In a large saucepan, bring water to a boil. Add the peas, asparagus, butter, parsley, garlic salt if desired and pepper. Return to a boil. Reduce heat; cover and simmer until the asparagus is crisp-tender, about 10 minutes. Drain and serve immediately. **Yield:** 6 servings. **Nutritional Analysis:** One 3/4-cup serving (prepared with margarine and without garlic salt) equals 136 calories, 179 mg sodium, 0 cholesterol, 15 gm carbohydrate, 6 gm protein, 6 gm fat. **Diabetic Exchanges:** 1 starch, 1 vegetable, 1 fat.

Garlic Mashed Potatoes

(Also pictured on page 307 and front cover)

I cook these rich, creamy mashed potatoes frequently. Garlic cloves are boiled and then mashed right along with the potatoes.
—*Myra Innes, Auburn, Kansas*

      5 large potatoes, peeled and cut into 1/2-inch cubes
     15 garlic cloves, peeled and halved
      2 teaspoons salt, *divided*
    1/2 cup butter *or* margarine, softened
    1/2 cup whipping cream

Place potatoes, garlic and 1 teaspoon salt in a large saucepan; add enough water to cover. Bring to a boil; reduce heat. Cover and simmer until potatoes are tender, about 10 minutes; drain. Transfer potatoes and garlic to a mixing bowl; mash. Add butter, cream and remaining salt; beat until smooth. **Yield:** 6 servings.

Chocolate Raspberry Torte

(Also pictured on page 306 and front cover)

When our daughter requested this fancy cake for her birthday, I thought it would be difficult to make. But it's easy!
—*Rosemary Ford Vinson, El Cajon, California*

      1 package (18-1/4 ounces) chocolate cake mix
      1 package (3 ounces) cream cheese, softened
    3/4 cup cold milk
      1 package (3.4 ounces) instant vanilla pudding mix
      1 carton (8 ounces) frozen whipped topping, thawed
      2 cups fresh raspberries
Confectioners' sugar
Fresh mint and additional raspberries, optional

Prepare the cake according to package directions, using three greased and floured 9-in. round cake pans. Bake at 350° for 25-30 minutes or until a toothpick inserted near the center comes out clean. Cool for 10 minutes; remove from pans to wire racks to cool completely. In a mixing bowl, beat cream cheese until fluffy. Combine milk and pudding mix; add to cream cheese and mix well. Fold in whipped topping and raspberries. Place one cake layer on a serving plate. Spread with half of the filling. Repeat layers. Top with remaining cake; dust with confectioners' sugar. Garnish with mint and raspberries if desired. Store in the refrigerator. **Yield:** 12 servings.

Brunch on a Moment's Notice

SOMETIMES the only warning you get when unexpected guests drop by is a knock on the door. Invite them in for this late-morning meal that uses ingredients you likely have on hand. (Turn to page 323 for simple preparation pointers and table decorating ideas.)

Colorful Frittata

This pretty egg bake is a great way to get your family to eat vegetables. —Julie Watson, Anderson, Indiana

- 1 cup broccoli florets
- 3/4 cup sliced fresh mushrooms
- 2 green onions, finely chopped
- 1 tablespoon butter *or* margarine
- 1 cup cubed fully cooked ham
- 8 eggs
- 1/4 cup water
- 1/4 cup Dijon mustard
- 1/2 teaspoon Italian seasoning
- 1/4 teaspoon garlic salt
- 1-1/2 cups (6 ounces) shredded cheddar cheese
- 1/2 cup chopped tomatoes

In a skillet, saute the broccoli, mushrooms and onions in butter until tender. Add ham; heat through. Remove from the heat and keep warm. In a mixing bowl, beat eggs, water, mustard, Italian seasoning and garlic salt until foamy. Stir in cheese, tomatoes and broccoli mixture. Pour into a greased shallow 1-1/2-qt. baking dish. Bake at 375° for 22-27 minutes or until a knife inserted near the center comes out clean. **Yield:** 4-6 servings.

Black Forest Crepes

These fancy, make-ahead crepes are a sweet ending to a special-occasion meal. —Lisa Tanner
Warner Robins, Georgia

- 1-1/4 cups buttermilk
- 3 eggs
- 3 tablespoons butter *or* margarine, melted
- 1 cup all-purpose flour
- 2 tablespoons sugar
- 2 tablespoons baking cocoa
CHOCOLATE SAUCE:
- 3/4 cup sugar
- 1/3 cup baking cocoa
- 1 can (5 ounces) evaporated milk
- 1/4 cup butter *or* margarine
- 1 teaspoon vanilla extract
- 1 can (21 ounces) cherry pie filling

In a mixing bowl, combine buttermilk, eggs and butter. Combine flour, sugar and cocoa; add to milk mixture and mix well. Cover and chill for 1 hour. Heat a lightly greased 8-in. nonstick skillet; add 2 tablespoons batter. Lift and tilt pan to evenly coat bottom. Cook until top appears dry; turn and cook 15-20 seconds longer. Remove to a wire rack. Repeat with remaining batter. When cool, stack crepes with waxed paper or paper towels in between. For sauce, combine sugar and cocoa in a saucepan. Whisk in milk; add butter. Bring to a boil over medium heat, stirring constantly. Remove from

the heat; stir in vanilla. To serve, spoon about 2 tablespoons pie filling down the center of each crepe. Fold sides of crepe over filling; place in a greased 13-in. x 9-in. x 2-in. baking pan. Bake, uncovered, at 225° for 15 minutes. Transfer to serving plates; drizzle with warm chocolate sauce. **Yield:** 10 servings (20 crepes). **Editor's Note:** Unfilled crepes may be covered and refrigerated for 2 to 3 days or frozen for 4 months.

Brunch Fruit Salad

Convenient canned and fresh fruits are tossed with a quick-to-cook sauce. —Millie Vickery, Lena, Illinois

- 1 can (20 ounces) pineapple chunks
- 2 large firm bananas, cut into 1/4-inch chunks
- 1 cup green grapes
- 1 can (15 ounces) mandarin oranges, drained
- 1 Golden Delicious apple, sliced
- 1 Red Delicious apple, sliced
- 1/2 cup sugar
- 2 tablespoons cornstarch
- 1/3 cup orange juice
- 1 tablespoon lemon juice

Drain pineapple, reserving juice. Combine the pineapple, bananas, grapes, oranges and apples in a large bowl; set aside. In a saucepan, combine sugar and cornstarch. Add the orange juice, lemon juice and reserved pineapple juice; stir until smooth. Bring to a boil; reduce heat. Cook and stir for 2 minutes. Pour over fruit; mix gently. Cover and refrigerate until serving. **Yield:** 10 servings.

Mini Coffee Cakes

These moist, buttery muffins with their nutty topping are so easy to make and bake alongside the frittata. —Dena Engelland, Sterling, Kansas

- 1/3 cup butter *or* margarine, softened
- 1/4 cup sugar
- 1 egg
- 1-1/2 cups all-purpose flour
- 1 package (3.4 ounces) instant vanilla pudding mix
- 1 tablespoon baking powder
- 1/4 teaspoon salt
- 1-1/4 cups milk
- 1/2 cup chopped walnuts
TOPPING:
- 1/2 cup chopped walnuts
- 1/3 cup packed brown sugar
- 2 tablespoons butter *or* margarine, melted
- 1/4 teaspoon ground cinnamon

In a mixing bowl, cream the butter and sugar. Beat in egg. Combine the flour, pudding mix, baking powder and salt; add to the creamed mixture alternately with milk. Beat until blended. Stir in walnuts. Fill paper-lined muffin cups two-thirds full. Combine topping ingredients; sprinkle over batter. Bake at 375° for 20-25 minutes or until a toothpick inserted near the center comes out clean. Cool for 10 minutes; remove from pan to a wire rack. **Yield:** about 1 dozen.

Easy Outdoor Dining

PLANNING an outside summer gathering on the deck or in the backyard? Outdoor entertaining is a breeze with this no-fuss menu. (See ideas for presenting dishes and special table touches on page 324.)

French Dip Sandwiches

When I want to impress company, I put these satisfying sandwiches on the menu. I serve the au jus sauce in individual bowls for dipping. It's delicious.
—Florence Robinson, Lenox, Iowa

    2 large onions, cut into 1/4-inch slices
  1/4 cup butter *or* margarine
    1 boneless bottom round roast (3 to 4 pounds)
    5 cups water
  1/2 cup soy sauce
    1 envelope onion soup mix
1-1/2 teaspoons browning sauce, optional
    1 garlic clove, minced
  12 to 14 French rolls, split
    1 cup (4 ounces) shredded Swiss cheese

In a skillet, saute onions in butter until tender; transfer to a slow cooker. Cut the roast in half; place over onions. Combine water, soy sauce, soup mix, browning sauce if desired and garlic; pour over roast. Cover and cook on low for 7-9 hours or until the meat is tender. Remove roast with a slotted spoon and let stand for 15 minutes. Thinly slice meat across the grain. Place on rolls; sprinkle with Swiss cheese. Broil 3 to 4 in. from the heat for 1 minute or until the cheese is melted. Skim fat from the cooking juices; strain and serve as a dipping sauce. **Yield:** 12-14 servings.

Curried Pineapple Rice

Rice, curry, garlic and pineapple blend together to create this distinctive side dish. It's so pretty served in a pineapple shell. And it tastes as good as it looks.
—Cecelia Bodden, Burnaby, British Columbia

✓ Uses less fat, sugar or salt. Includes Nutritional Analysis and Diabetic Exchanges.

    1 whole pineapple *or* 1 can (20 ounces) unsweetened pineapple chunks
  1/2 cup finely chopped onion
    2 tablespoons butter *or* margarine
2-1/2 cups uncooked long grain rice
    2 garlic cloves, minced
    1 tablespoon curry powder
    5 cups chicken broth
    1 tablespoon soy sauce
    1 jalapeno pepper, seeded and chopped,* optional
    4 green onions, chopped

Cut fresh pineapple to form a serving bowl if desired (see page 324). Cut removed fruit into bite-size chunks; set aside. If using canned pineapple, drain and set aside (discard juice or save for another use). In a large saucepan, saute onion in butter until tender. Stir in rice, garlic and curry powder. Add broth, soy sauce and jalapeno if de-

sired. Bring to a boil. Reduce heat; cover and simmer for 20 minutes. Remove from the heat and let stand for 5 minutes or until liquid is absorbed. Stir in green onions and pineapple chunks. Spoon into pineapple shell. Replenish as needed or place remaining rice in another serving bowl. **Yield:** 12-14 servings. **Nutritional Analysis:** One 3/4-cup serving (prepared with low-sodium broth and light soy sauce) equals 178 calories, 96 mg sodium, 1 mg cholesterol, 34 gm carbohydrate, 4 gm protein, 3 gm fat. **Diabetic Exchanges:** 1 starch, 1 vegetable, 1 fruit, 1/2 fat. ***Editor's Note:** When cutting hot peppers, use rubber or plastic gloves to protect your hands. Avoid touching your face.

Hot Mustard Pretzel Dip

With its hint of honey, this zippy mixture is great with pretzels...or try it anywhere you'd use a hot-and-spicy sauce.
—Kim Barrick, Lincoln, Illinois

  1/4 cup ground mustard
  1/4 cup vinegar
  1/4 cup sugar
    1 egg yolk
    2 tablespoons honey
Pretzels

In a small saucepan, combine mustard and vinegar; let stand for 30 minutes. Whisk in the sugar and egg yolk until smooth. Cook over medium heat, whisking constantly, until mixture just begins to simmer and is thickened, about 7 minutes. Remove from the heat; whisk in honey. Chill. Serve with pretzels. Store in the refrigerator. **Yield:** 1/2 cup.

Fluffy Cheesecake Dessert

I prepare a light, creamy filling with mild citrus flavor, then spoon it over a simple vanilla wafer crust. The yummy result makes an appealing ending to a summer meal.
—Rhonda Miller, Bethalto, Illinois

    4 cups miniature marshmallows
  1/3 cup orange juice
    2 packages (8 ounces *each*) cream cheese, softened
    1 carton (12 ounces) frozen whipped topping, thawed
2-1/2 cups crushed vanilla wafers (about 60 wafers)
  1/2 cup butter *or* margarine, melted

In a large microwave-safe bowl, combine marshmallows and orange juice. Microwave, uncovered, on high for 1-1/2 minutes. Stir until smooth. In a mixing bowl, beat cream cheese. Add marshmallow mixture; beat just until smooth. Fold in whipped topping. Combine wafer crumbs and butter; set aside 3/4 cup for topping. Press remaining crumbs into an ungreased 13-in. x 9-in. x 2-in. pan. Spoon cream cheese filling over crust. Sprinkle with reserved crumbs. Cover and refrigerate for 1 hour or until set. Store in the refrigerator. **Yield:** 12-16 servings. **Editor's Note:** This recipe was tested in an 850-watt microwave.

Italian Fare With Flair

ADD SPARK to your daily dining with this Italian-style supper. It's a memorable meal that will become a family favorite. (Turn to page 325 for pointers on giving rolls different looks—and for table topper tips.)

Garlic Lover's Chicken

This super easy coating for flavorful chicken is a great recipe if you like garlic. I've shared it with several friends who say their families went wild over it.
—Janice Steinmetz, Somers, Connecticut

✓ Uses less fat, sugar or salt. Includes Nutritional Analysis and Diabetic Exchanges.

```
1/2 cup dry bread crumbs
1/3 cup grated Parmesan cheese
  2 tablespoons minced fresh parsley
1/2 teaspoon salt, optional
1/8 teaspoon pepper
1/4 cup milk
  6 boneless skinless chicken breast halves (1-1/2
    pounds)
1/4 cup butter or margarine, melted
  1 to 2 garlic cloves, minced
  2 tablespoons lemon juice
Paprika
```

In a large resealable plastic bag, combine the first five ingredients. Place milk in a shallow bowl. Dip chicken in milk, then shake in the crumb mixture. Place in a greased 13-in. x 9-in. x 2-in. baking dish. Combine the butter, garlic and lemon juice; drizzle over the chicken. Sprinkle with paprika. Bake, uncovered, at 350° for 25-30 minutes or until the juices run clear. **Yield:** 6 servings. **Nutritional Analysis:** One serving (prepared with nonfat Parmesan cheese topping, skim milk and reduced-fat margarine and without salt) equals 234 calories, 331 mg sodium, 75 mg cholesterol, 8 gm carbohydrate, 30 gm protein, 8 gm fat. **Diabetic Exchanges:** 4 very lean meat, 1 fat, 1/2 starch.

Pesto Pasta

My husband loves this fresh-tasting side dish that's as good as it is easy. The appetizing aroma of basil is sure to whet guests' appetites.
—Karen Behrend
Newport, Washington

```
  1 package (8 ounces) spiral pasta
1/3 cup minced fresh basil
1/4 cup minced fresh parsley
1/4 cup grated Parmesan cheese
1/2 teaspoon salt
  1 garlic clove, quartered
1/8 teaspoon ground nutmeg
1/3 cup olive or vegetable oil
```

Cook pasta according to package directions. Meanwhile, in a blender or food processor, place the basil, parsley, Parmesan cheese, salt, garlic and nutmeg. Cover and process on low for 1 minute or until very finely chopped. While processing, gradually add the oil in a steady stream. Drain pasta; top with the pesto and toss to coat. **Yield:** 6 servings.

Refrigerator Rolls

These rolls are golden and crusty on the outside and sweet and tender on the inside. The easy-to-handle dough rises in the refrigerator overnight for added convenience.
—Martha Sue Stroud, Clarksville, Texas

✓ Uses less fat, sugar or salt. Includes Nutritional Analysis and Diabetic Exchanges.

```
    1 package (1/4 ounce) active dry yeast
2-1/2 cups warm water (110° to 115°), divided
  1/2 cup shortening
  1/2 cup sugar
    1 egg
1-1/2 teaspoons salt
    7 cups all-purpose flour
```

In a bowl, dissolve yeast in 1/2 cup water; set aside. In a mixing bowl, cream shortening and sugar. Add egg, salt, 4 cups flour, yeast mixture and remaining water; beat until smooth. Add enough remaining flour to form a soft dough. Turn onto a floured surface and knead until smooth and elastic, about 6-8 minutes. Place in a greased bowl, turning once to grease top. Cover and refrigerate for 8 hours or overnight. Punch dough down and divide into thirds; shape each portion into 12 rolls in desired shape. Place on greased baking sheets. Cover and let rise in a warm place until doubled, about 1 hour. Bake at 400° for 12-14 minutes or until lightly browned. **Yield:** 3 dozen. **Nutritional Analysis:** One roll (prepared with egg substitute equivalent to one egg) equals 126 calories, 101 mg sodium, trace cholesterol, 21 gm carbohydrate, 3 gm protein, 3 gm fat. **Diabetic Exchanges:** 1-1/2 starch, 1/2 fat.

Mocha Mousse Pie

Coffee and chocolate are perfectly paired in this lovely layered dessert. A convenient chocolate crumb crust holds the cool, fluffy filling.
—Beverly Gottfried
Candler, North Carolina

```
1-1/2 cups semisweet chocolate chips, melted and
      slightly cooled
    2 cups whipping cream
    2 tablespoons instant coffee granules
    2 tablespoons sugar
    1 teaspoon vanilla extract
    1 chocolate crumb or graham cracker crust
      (9 inches)
Chocolate shavings, optional
```

In a large microwave-safe bowl, melt the chocolate chips; set aside to cool. In a mixing bowl, beat the cream, coffee granules, sugar and vanilla on low until coffee and sugar are dissolved. Beat on high just until stiff peaks form. Set aside 1-1/2 cups for topping. Gradually fold remaining cream mixture into the cooled chocolate until well blended. Pour into pie crust. Spread with reserved cream mixture. Refrigerate for 3 hours. Garnish with chocolate shavings if desired. Store in the refrigerator. **Yield:** 6-8 servings.

Table Toppers

FOR special meals, add the perfect finishing touches with tasteful table toppers, pretty folded napkins and appealing food presentation. Our kitchen staff came up with these inexpensive eye-pleasing ideas.

Add a Warm Glow with Berry Bowl

RUBY-RED cranberries lend festive color to many holiday recipes. Their brilliant color can brighten your table as well as part of this simple centerpiece. It's "berry" easy to assemble because it requires just a few supplies.

First, choose a shallow glass dish. The fluted serving bowl we used has a decorative rim and measured 10 inches in diameter (see above right).

You may want to pick one with a pedestal to give your arrangement some height. (Because our bowl didn't have a pedestal, we created one by inverting a smaller bowl.)

Fill the serving bowl partway with water—we used about 2 cups. Then add the cranberries until you have enough floating to almost cover the surface (about 1-1/2 cups).

Gently place a few floating candles or tea lights into the bowl among the cranberries. Light the candles right before dinner.

Folded Napkin Polishes Plate Setting

A SOPHISTICATED napkin fold can add elegance to place settings without a lot of fuss.

To start, place an ironed cloth napkin open on a flat surface. Fold the napkin in half diagonally by bringing the two opposite corners together to form a large triangle.

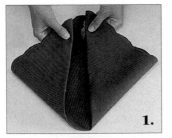
1.

1. Bring the two outside points created by the fold together to meet at the open point, forming a square.

2. Fold the open point underneath the napkin to create a triangle. Lift the napkin at the center; arrange it on the plate (as pictured above right).

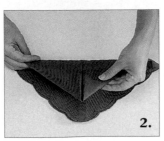
2.

Bundle Your Carrots

HERE'S an inviting way to serve the Citrus Carrot Sticks on page 311.

1 Cut a thin slice from each carrot chunk to create a flat bottom that makes cutting easier. With the flat side down, cut each chunk lengthwise into thin slices.

2 Stack a few slices and cut lengthwise to create matchstick-like strips. Repeat with remaining carrots. Drop julienned carrots into boiling water for 30 seconds. Remove with a slotted spoon; drain on paper towels. Divide into individual servings.

3 Cut green onion tops into narrow strips and soften in boiling water. Wrap a strip around each serving of carrots; gently tie in a half-knot. Carefully lower bundles into boiling water for 1 minute. Drain; serve as directed.

Picture-Perfect Place Markers

INSTEAD OF making place markers with paper, purchase miniature picture frames to display each guest's photo (as shown above).

Folding Napkin Pockets

COLORFUL cloth napkins can be simply folded into eye-pleasing pockets that hold each guest's silverware. Begin with a square napkin folded in half with the fold at the bottom.

1 Use both hands to pick up the two corners of the top layer of the napkin. Fold down cloth in three folds (about 1 inch each) to create a band that runs from left to right across  the middle of the napkin. Then carefully flip napkin over without disturbing the band.

2 With napkin turned over, bring the right side of napkin into the center. Repeat with the left side of the napkin so the two edges meet in the middle.

Now fold the napkin in half where the two edges meet. This will form a rectangle with a pocket on each side. Place fork, knife and spoon in one of the pockets and place the whole package on each guest's plate (as shown in the photo below right) or next to each place setting.

Paper Flowers Bloom

TISSUE PAPER is the key to the bright bouquet of handmade flowers pictured at right. To make this cheerful centerpiece, you'll need several sheets of tissue paper and some pipe cleaners.

Choose any combination of colored tissue paper that coordinates with your table setting. To continue the feel of our Mexican-inspired menu and casual tabletop on page 310, we picked orange, blue, green and yellow.

For a single flower, start with one sheet of tissue paper (ours measured 20 x 30 inches). Fold the tissue in half widthwise to create a rectangle (15 x 20 inches). Trim off the folded edge to create two rectangular pieces (12 x 20 inches). Then cut those pieces in half lengthwise so you end up with four strips measuring 6 x 20 inches each.

You can stick with a single color of tissue paper for each flower you make or combine two or more colors to create multicolored paper blooms.

1. Place four pieces of tissue paper on top of one another. Starting with a short side, fold layers accordion-style (like you're creating a fan) with about 1-inch folds.

2. When the paper is folded, place a pipe cleaner around the center of it, taking care not to bunch the paper as you secure it. If you don't have a pipe cleaner, a twist-tie or piece of florist's wire will work. Use scissors to even out the layers of paper at each end. Or trim with pinking shears to give the finished flower a "fluffier" look.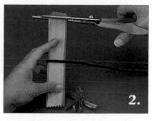

3. Starting with one half, separate the top layer of tissue from the other layers very gently to prevent the paper from ripping. Repeat with the remaining layers of paper on that half. Then repeat with the other half of the flower.

When the layers are fully separated, use your fingers to arrange and fluff the flower. (You can use a scissors or pinking shears to trim the flowers evenly if necessary.)

If needed, wrap the ends of the pipe cleaners, twist-ties or wire around wooden skewers to create sturdier flower stems. Then place several of your completed blooms in a festive bowl, vase or other container to create an eye-catching centerpiece.

Vegetable Vase Made in a Snap

DINNER GUESTS can't help but smile when you display a bright bouquet in this whimsical vase surrounded by fresh asparagus spears.

First, gather your supplies. You'll need a clean empty aluminum can, a rubber band, some ribbon and fresh asparagus spears.

We bought a little more asparagus than we needed—about 1-1/2 pounds—so we could choose the most uniform spears. Trim the bottoms of the asparagus so spears measure an inch taller than the height of the can. (A large fruit cocktail or baked bean can works well for this project.)

Place a thick rubber band around the middle of the can. Begin tucking spears into the rubber band so the trimmed ends are flush with the bottom of the can (see the photo below). Rotate the can as you add spears until the can is completely hidden (we needed about 30 spears).

Conceal the rubber band with a length of attractive

ribbon that coordinates with your table decorations. We used a 2-inch-wide ribbon with wire edges to make it easy to shape the bow.

Place the vase on a saucer to prevent the cut ends of asparagus from discoloring the table's cloth or finish.

To complete this sunny centerpiece, fill the vase with water and your favorite bright flowers, such as daffodils or tulips as shown at left.

Pedestal from Pantry Takes the Cake

MOST ANY dessert will dazzle guests when displayed on a pretty cake pedestal. If you don't own one, you can assemble it in a wink using dishes from your cupboard.

To form the pedestal, invert a soup bowl, custard cup, footed dessert dish, ice cream sundae dish or similar bowl (see the photo below for examples).

When choosing this dish, one with a wider base will be more sturdy. If the dish is footed, be sure the stem is not too delicate; it will need to support the weight of the plate and dessert.

Then select a coordinating cake plate, dinner plate or round serving plate that's proportional in size to the pedestal dish (see photo at left for examples).

A few pieces of florist's clay can help make the cake pedestal more stable. Evenly space the clay on the inverted dish where it will meet the plate.

Place your cake or torte on the plate and carefully center the plate on the inverted dish or bowl.

Since this setup is for display only, it's best to remove the cake plate from the pedestal dish before cutting and serving your dessert.

Apple 'Leaves' Add Wedges of Color

SIMPLE slices with a sharp knife can turn an ordinary apple into appealing apple leaves that make an easy and elegant garnish for main dishes, salads and even desserts.

1 To begin, cut an apple in half from stem to base. Place cut side down on work surface. Make a shallow V-shaped cut in the center of the apple to form a small wedge.

2 Remove wedge. Following the lines of the first wedge, make three or four additional cuts so each wedge is slightly larger than the previous one, removing each wedge as you cut it. Dip wedges in lemon juice to prevent browning.

To complete the garnish, reassemble the cut wedges. Create the layered effect by gently pushing and sliding apple wedges, separating each by 1/8 to 1/4 inch. One apple will yield two apple leaves.

Arrange a few apple leaves on a serving plate with the entree or place one on every guest's dinner plate.

Spur-of-the-Moment Centerpiece

BRIGHTENING your table with a cheery centerpiece doesn't require a lot of time or fuss.

One key to an effortless arrangement is to take advantage of everyday items, like the houseplants that flourish in your home.

An appealing grouping of flowering plants, trailing vines, green ferns or variegated ivy can lend a lighthearted touch to an impromptu gathering.

For example, we placed three African violets on decorative saucers and set them side by side (see photo below). The saucers add color and help keep water from dripping on your table and marring its finish.

A length of wide ribbon or lace can be used beneath the saucers to unite the arrangement and give it a finished appearance.

Don't have any flowering plants? No lace or ribbon on hand? Experiment with whatever is available.

Perhaps you have a colorful teacup and bright teapot you could arrange with a green plant on a coordinating place mat. (See photo above for an example.) If the plant has trailing foliage, tuck it around the teacup and pot.

Another option is to make the most of the fresh herbs or tender seedlings sprouting on your kitchen windowsill. Set the plants in miniature clay pots tied with matching ribbons and place them on attractive trivets or coasters.

Crepes Are Fabulous Finale

DELECTABLE dessert crepes are an elegant ending for most any special meal.

Made ahead and frozen, the paper-thin pancakes thaw in minutes and can be filled with a variety of simple ingredients with spectacular results.

Try fuss-free fillings such as ice cream, jam, sliced fruit or a blend of instant pudding and whipped topping. Drizzle the filled crepes with a sweet sauce, syrup or ice cream topping, then sprinkle with chopped nuts, chocolate sprinkles or toasted coconut. The combinations are endless!

Whether you prepare a basic batter or the chocolaty version featured in the Black Forest Crepes (see pages 314-315 for photo and recipe), each crepe takes just seconds to cook.

1 Heat a lightly greased 8-inch nonstick skillet over medium-high. Lift skillet off the heat and pour in 2 tablespoons of crepe batter.

2 Immediately tilt skillet and swirl the batter so it evenly and completely covers the bottom with a very thin layer. Return to heat.

3 When the top of the crepe appears dry and the bottom is lightly browned, carefully turn with a spatula. Cook 15 seconds longer or until lightly browned. Cool on a wire rack.

You'll be a Fan of Fast Napkin Fold

ADD a decorative touch to your table with fun napkin fans that can be assembled in a snap.

Start with a square cloth napkin that coordinates with your dishes and centerpiece. Open it all the way and lay it flat on a table or countertop.

Begin folding it accordion-style to form pleats that are about an inch wide.

When it's completely folded, fold the stack of pleats in half to form a fan and cinch the center with a ribbon or a decorative napkin ring.

Place a completed fan on each guest's dinner plate and spread out folds to create a pretty effect as shown in the photo at left.

Napkins made from a stiffer fabric will have sharp creases and give your finished fan a more formal look. A softer fabric will produce a casual look.

Pretty Twist on Paper Napkin Stack

YOU CAN bring quick color to a casual buffet dinner without folding individual napkins. All you need to do is put a fun spin on the way you present a stack of convenient paper napkins. Try this speedy suggestion for displaying ordinary napkins.

First, simply stack the napkins in a pile and place a drinking glass (or coffee mug) on top as shown. Holding the glass firmly and pressing down on the stack, turn the glass slightly in a circular motion to begin fanning the napkins.

You'll need to lift the glass and repeat this step several times to fan the napkins into a pretty swirl (see photo at top left).

This quick trick is easy enough to use at picnics, too. Don't have a glass handy? Use the flat side of your fist as shown in the photo at bottom left. (Be sure to take off any rings first or you might tear the napkins.)

This swirled stack also is an attractive way to arrange smaller appetizer or beverage napkins at a party.

Pineapple Shell Adds Tropical Flair

FRESH CHUNKS from a whole pineapple give a tropical taste to side dishes and salads. If you're careful when removing the fruit, you can save the shell to use as a distinctive serving dish.

It's especially appropriate for serving the Curried Pineapple Rice pictured below left (the recipe is on page 317). But it would also be an uncommon way to show off a medley of fresh fruit at a buffet or most any hot or cold salad or side dish that features pineapple.

1 To begin, stand the pineapple upright and vertically cut about a third from one side, leaving top attached. Set the cut piece aside.

2 Using a paring knife or grapefruit knife, remove strips of pineapple, leaving a 1/2-inch shell. Cut the strips into bite-size chunks. Invert shell onto paper towels to drain. Remove fruit from reserved piece and cut into chunks; discard peel.

3 Put the shell right on your dinner or buffet table and fill it with your favorite pineapple recipe. Or place the filled shell on a serving plate or platter and arrange flowers around it. Then it becomes a striking centerpiece. Cleanup is a snap, too. Just toss out the shell when dinner is over, and there's no serving bowl to wash!

Knot Hard to Keep Tablecloth in Place

A LIGHT BREEZE can add a cool and refreshing touch to an outdoor meal. But it can also set the tablecloth on a picnic table to flapping.

To prevent those loose corners from fluttering in the wind, tie a simple knot at each corner of the cloth (as shown below right).

For a little bit dressier look, bunch the fabric at each corner and then tie the bunches with short lengths of complementary colored ribbon.

For a fun touch at a garden party, tuck some fresh flowers (or perhaps a few sprigs of herbs) into the bunched fabric as you tie the ribbons.

Plants Become Pretty Place Markers

BASIL is a common ingredient in many Italian dishes, so it's natural to incorporate this aromatic herb into your table decorations when serving Italian fare.

Here, we set small potted basil plants at each guest's place setting. Transplanted into miniature clay pots with matching saucers, the seedlings add a fresh look to your tabletop.

To use them as place markers, pick up blank plant markers available at most greenhouses and garden centers. Write guests' names on the markers and insert them into the pots. A pretty ribbon adds a quick and colorful finishing touch.

Green thumbs can take the tender seedlings home to add to their vegetable patches, while novices can start their own windowsill herb gardens.

If you don't have or can't find mini clay pots, you can disguise the plastic nursery containers with wrapping paper to look like a small wrapped present.

First, cover the piece of wrapping paper with plastic wrap that's the same size. (This will protect the paper and your table from water leaking out of the pot.)

Then, set the plant in the middle of the layers and draw the edges up and around the pot to the rim, bunching them as you go. Secure the paper and plastic with a ribbon around the rim.

Pasta Makes Speedy Swirl Centerpiece

YOU MIGHT not think of using dry pasta in place of flowers in a table centerpiece. But for an Italian meal, this arrangement is simple, suitable and a snap to put together.

To display the pasta, we selected a clear glass jar that's about 5 inches high. We filled it with about 1-1/2 pounds of fettuccine, then arranged the noodles to create a swirled effect inside the jar and a bouquet-like effect above the rim (see photo at top).

Experiment with a glass vase, a clean jar from prepared spaghetti sauce or any clear container that's the appropriate height to show off the pasta.

Of course, any straight dry pasta (spaghetti, linguine, etc.) can be used in this arrangement with good results. The amount you'll need depends on the size of your container.

If you'd like to continue the Italian theme, tie ribbons in the colors of Italy's flag (which are red, green and white) around the jar's neck.

Another centerpiece option is to display shaped pasta in clear glass containers of varying heights (see photo above).

There are dozens of small fun shapes available (both plain and tricolor) that would add just the right touch to your table.

Tempting Rolls Rise to the Occasion

THE AROMA of tender dinner rolls as they come out of the oven is sure to draw guests to your table. They're likely to be even more tempted when they discover the fresh-baked rolls are fashioned into appealing shapes.

It takes just seconds to form dough into one of the easy variations shown here. Using the dough for Refrigerator Rolls (see pages 318-319 for photo and recipe), each portion will make a dozen shaped rolls. Or try with similar amounts of your favorite yeast dough or frozen bread dough.

- To make S-shaped rolls, divide one portion of dough into 12 pieces. Roll each into a 9-in. rope. On a greased baking sheet, coil the ends of each rope toward the center in opposite directions to form an S shape.

- To make crescent rolls, roll one portion of dough into a 12-in. circle. Cut into 12 wedges and roll up each wedge, starting at the wide end. Place point side down on a greased baking sheet

DURING the week, most folks barely have an extra moment to sit and relax, much less spend time cooking.

So on those more leisurely weekend days when you do have a few minutes to spare, why not head to the kitchen for a refresher on basic cooking techniques or for an opportunity to tackle more challenging and time-consuming recipes?

Whether you need to enhance your knowledge of kitchen cutlery and reacquaint yourself with the grill or you'd like to learn the proper way of making homemade gravy, candy and meringues, these helpful hints and easy-to-follow recipes will sharpen your culinary skills in a snap!

MAKE MERINGUE! Top to bottom: Lemon Meringue Pie and Swiss Meringue Shells (both recipes on pp. 330 and 331).

Get a Handle on Kitchen Knives

FOOD PROCESSORS and other cutting-edge kitchen gadgets are handy devices for a busy cook. But for overall utility, you can't go wrong with a basic set of good knives.

Choosing the right knife can give you an edge in food preparation and presentation. You should start out with a basic selection for everyday cooking and then add to it as the need arises.

Most kitchens shouldn't be without a chef's knife, a carving knife, a serrated or bread knife, a paring knife, kitchen shears and a sharpening tool called a steel. (See the box below that highlights this basic cutlery and its uses.)

Two other commonly used knives are a utility knife and a boning knife. A utility knife usually has a 6-inch blade for slicing smaller foods while a boning knife has a 5- or 6-inch tapered blade for removing meat from the bones in poultry, beef, pork or fish.

Invest in the Best

Knives come in a wide range of materials and prices, so purchasing them can be confusing.

First, pick up the knife you're considering. Choose the heaviest one that fits comfortably in your hand. The right weight and balance will improve its cutting performance and reduce fatigue.

Examine the knife's construction (see the illustration at right). Most knives have steel blades, but

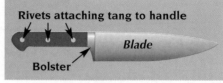

a blade made of high-carbon steel is the best choice because it's easy to sharpen and won't stain or discolor.

Look for blades that taper evenly from the handle to the tip and from the top of the blade to the cutting edge.

Wooden handles sealed with heat-resistant plastic are durable, easy to clean and offer a good grip. The knife should have a full tang (the part of the blade that extends into the handle) that's firmly secured with rivets.

The base of the blade should have a firm bolster.

Stock Your Kitchen with Basic Cutlery

1. Steel: This textured rod with a handle is used to smooth small rough spots on the edge of the knife blade and to sharpen the edge of the blade. A whetstone or electric knife sharpener can also be used.

2. Kitchen shears: This strong scissors is a versatile tool used to snip fresh herbs, disjoint chicken, trim pastry, etc.

3. Serrated or bread knife: This knife's stiff serrated blade is used for slicing foods with a firm exterior and soft interior, such as breads, angel food cakes and tomatoes. An 8-inch knife is most versatile.

4. Carving knife: This 8- to 10-inch knife has a long, slender blade to slice cooked meat. It's perfect for slicing roasts and carving a turkey.

5. Chef's knife: This 8- to 10-inch all-purpose knife is used for mincing, chopping and dicing. The handle is indented to keep knuckles from hitting the cutting board while chopping. The blade's wide heel tapers to a point.

6. Paring knife: This 3- to 4-inch knife is used to peel, trim, mince and slice small foods.

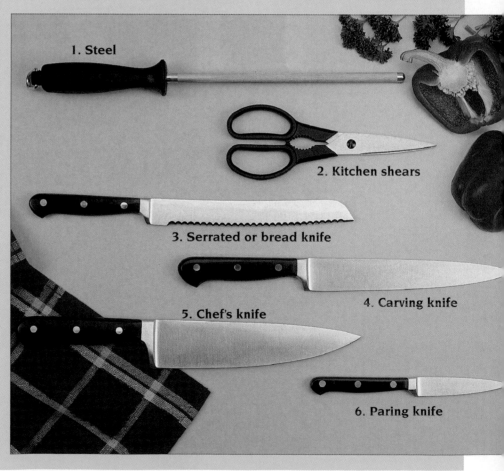

The bolster reinforces the blade and protects fingers from slipping onto the knife's edge.

Finally, a good rule of thumb is to buy the very best knives you can afford. A high-quality set should last you a lifetime.

Proper Care

Take good care of your investment. Store your knives in a knife block or magnetic rack to protect your family from injury and help keep the blades sharp. (Tossing knives in a drawer can bend and dull their blades.)

Believe it or not, a sharp knife is safer than a dull one. Because you must use more force to cut with a dull blade, you're more likely to slip and cut yourself.

To keep a knife sharp, you can reset its edge each time you use it with a few strokes on a steel. (See below for tips on using a steel.) Or use an electric or manual sharpener. Knives with serrated blades can easily be damaged during sharpening, so it's best to have them sharpened by a professional.

Don't wash knives in the dishwasher, where the blades can be damaged by banging into dishes or utensils. Take care when washing them in soapy dish water, since suds can hide the blades.

Tune Up Your Knives

A SHARP KNIFE is the key to speedy slicing, dicing and chopping. There are several types of knife sharpeners available, but frequent use of a steel—a long textured rod with a handle that often comes with a knife set—is a simple way to give your unserrated knives a tune-up. A few strokes on the steel every time you use a knife will help keep it sharp.

To use a steel, grip the handle and rest the tip at a 90-degree angle on a countertop at arm's length. Place the heel of the knife blade at a 20-degree angle near the handle of the steel on the right side as shown below.

Pull the knife down and across the steel in an arc as shown below. You should end up with the tip of the knife near the tip of the steel where it rests on the countertop.

Repeat on the left side of the steel to sharpen the other side of the blade. Repeat these steps 5-10 times.

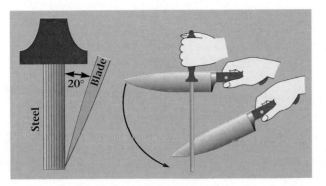

Common Cutting Techniques

➤ **To mince and chop:** With the handle of a chef's knife in one hand, rest the fingers of the other hand on the top of the blade near the tip. Using the handle to guide and apply pressure, move the knife in an arc across the food with a rocking motion until pieces of food are the desired size. Chopped pieces should be 1/4 to 1/2 inch, while minced pieces are no larger than 1/8 inch.

◄ **To julienne:** With a chef's knife, cut foods into lengthwise slices. Stack the slices, then cut lengthwise again, producing small matchsticks.

➤**To dice and cube:** With a chef's knife, cut foods into lengthwise matchsticks. Cut widthwise to form uniform squares. Diced pieces are 1/8 to 1/4 inch in size, while cubed pieces are 1/2 to 1 inch.

◄ **To chop onions (Step 1):** With a chef's knife, cut onion in half lengthwise. Peel onion and place cut side down. Leaving the onion intact at the root end, make a series of parallel cuts through the onion as shown.

◄ **To chop onions (Step 2):** Make a series of parallel cuts in the opposite direction to the cuts in Step 1 to separate the pieces.

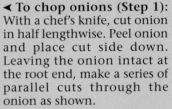

➤**To peel and mince fresh garlic:** With the blade of a chef's knife, apply pressure to the blade to crush the garlic clove. Peel and discard skin. Mince as directed above.

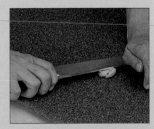

◄ **To snip fresh herbs:** With a kitchen shears, make 1/8- to 1/4-inch cuts through a small bunch of herbs.

Make Magnificent Meringues

Lemon Meringue Pie
Swiss Meringue Shells

at our county fair. It has a light flaky homemade crust, refreshing lemon filling and soft meringue with pretty golden peaks. Everyone enjoys generous slices of this classic pie.
—Susan Jones, Bradford, Ohio

1-1/2 cups all-purpose flour
1/2 teaspoon salt
1/2 cup shortening
1/4 cup cold water
FILLING:
1-1/2 cups sugar
1/4 cup cornstarch
3 tablespoons all-purpose flour
1/4 teaspoon salt
1-1/2 cups water
3 egg yolks, beaten
2 tablespoons butter *or* margarine
1/3 cup lemon juice
1 teaspoon grated lemon peel
1 teaspoon lemon extract
MERINGUE:
3 egg whites
1/4 teaspoon cream of tartar
6 tablespoons sugar

In a bowl, combine flour and salt; cut in shortening until crumbly. Gradually add water, tossing with a fork until a ball forms. Roll out pastry to fit a 9-in. pie plate. Transfer pastry to plate. Trim pastry to 1/2 in. beyond edge of plate; flute edges. Prick bottom and sides of pastry with a fork. Line with a double thickness of heavy-duty foil. Bake at 450° for 8 minutes. Remove foil; bake 5-6 minutes longer or until light golden brown. Reduce heat to 350°. For filling, combine sugar, cornstarch, flour and salt in a saucepan. Gradually stir in water. Cook and stir over medium heat until thickened and bubbly, about 2 minutes. Reduce the heat; cook and stir 2 minutes longer. Remove from the heat. Gradually stir 1 cup hot filling into egg yolks; return all to pan. Bring to a gentle boil; cook and stir for 2 minutes. Remove from the heat. Stir in butter, lemon juice, peel and extract until butter is melted. Cover; set aside and keep hot. For meringue, beat egg whites and cream of tartar in a mixing bowl on medium until foamy, about 1 minute. Gradually beat in sugar, 1 tablespoon at a time, on high until stiff glossy peaks form and sugar is dissolved. Pour hot filling into crust. Spread meringue evenly over filling, sealing edges to crust. Bake at 350° for 15 minutes or until meringue is golden brown. Cool on a wire rack for 1 hour; refrigerate for at least 3 hours. Store in the refrigerator. **Yield:** 6-8 servings.

TOPPING a lemony pie or filled with summer's freshest fruit, light and airy meringues add an extraordinary touch to delicious desserts.

Whipping up meringue isn't difficult, but it does require some time and attention to details. Here we clue you in on the proper techniques and share a list of timely tips to start you off on the right foot.

Lemon Meringue Pie

(Pictured above and on page 326)

My father loves lemon meringue pie and always wants one for his birthday. I rely on this recipe, which won first place

Swiss Meringue Shells

(Pictured at far left and on page 327)

Folks will know you fussed when you bring out these sweet, cloud-like cups topped with fresh berries (or a tart fruit filling if you like). Crisp outside and chewy inside, these meringues from the American Egg Board make an elegant ending to a company dinner.

    3 egg whites
    1/4 teaspoon cream of tartar
    3/4 cup sugar
    1/2 teaspoon vanilla extract
Berries of your choice
Whipped cream *or* vanilla ice cream, optional

In a mixing bowl, beat egg whites and cream of tartar until foamy, about 1 minute. Gradually beat in sugar, 1 tablespoon at a time, on high until stiff glossy peaks form and sugar is dissolved. Beat in vanilla. Cover a baking sheet with parchment paper or greased foil. Spoon meringue into eight mounds on paper. Using the back of the spoon, shape into 3-in. cups. Bake at 250° for 1 to 1-1/2 hours. Cool on wire racks. Store in an airtight container. Fill shells with berries and whipped cream or ice cream if desired. **Yield: 8 servings.**

Meringue Methods

1 Combine the egg whites and cream of tartar in a mixing bowl. Beat on medium speed until large white foamy bubbles form, about 1 minute.

2 Add sugar 1 tablespoon at a time, beating on high just until stiff glossy peaks form and the mixture is silky smooth, about 3 minutes.

3a For pies, use a metal spatula to spread meringue over hot filling. Be sure to seal meringue to edges of pastry to prevent shrinkage while baking.

3b For shells, spoon meringue into mounds on a baking sheet covered with parchment paper or greased foil. Use back of spoon to shape the cups.

Make the Most of Meringue

THESE POINTERS from the American Egg Board will help you make, serve and store meringues with confidence and ease:

Meringue Prep Tips

- Since humidity is the most critical factor in making a successful meringue, choose a dry day. Meringues can absorb moisture on a humid day and become limp and sticky.

- The temperature of the eggs is important if egg whites are to reach their greatest volume. Eggs separate most cleanly when they are cold. After separating, place the whites in a mixing bowl and let stand at room temperature for 20-30 minutes. To help them reach room temperature faster, place the bowl in a larger bowl of warm water while assembling the other ingredients.

- For the greatest volume, place egg whites in a small clean metal or glass mixing bowl. Even a drop of fat from the egg yolk or a film of oil sometimes found on plastic bowls will prevent egg whites from foaming. For this reason, also be sure to use clean beaters.

- Adding cream of tartar (or another acidic ingredient) before beating the whites is important—it stabilizes the egg white foam.

- After stiff peaks form (whites will look glossy and have tips that stand straight without bending), check that the sugar is dissolved. It will feel silky smooth when rubbed between your thumb and index finger.

Soft Meringue Tips

- For soft or pie meringues, spread the meringue over hot filling to minimize "weeping", the watery layer between the meringue and filling.

- Use a metal spatula to seal the meringue to edges of pastry. This will help prevent shrinkage while baking.

- Cool the pie away from drafts at room temperature for 1 hour, then refrigerate at least 3 hours before serving.

- To smoothly slice a meringue-topped pie, cut it with a sharp knife dipped in hot water (don't dry it off).

Hard Meringue Tips

- A hard meringue has a crisp, dry outside. The inside is either hard and crisp or soft and chewy, depending on the baking time. A shorter baking time produces a chewier center.

- For fancier shells, pipe meringue from a pastry bag into designs on parchment or greased foil before baking.

- Store hard meringues between sheets of waxed paper in an airtight container. If they become soft, bake in a 250° oven for 15-20 minutes.

Teriyaki Pork Kabobs
Country Barbecued Chicken

A) Direct Grilling   B) Indirect Grilling

Weber-Stephen Products Company

Grills Get Speedy Suppers Sizzling

BACKYARD GRILLING is a fast and fun way to cook—even for busy folks with precious little time to spare.

If you use these recipes for quick-cooking cuts of meat and tried-and-true grilling tips from our test kitchen staff, dinner can be ready in no time.

Charcoal and gas grill owners can choose from two cooking methods: direct and indirect grilling. Consult the manufacturer's instructions for details about your specific grill and follow these general guidelines:

The *direct grilling method* is what you likely use when cooking hot dogs and hamburgers. Simply put, food is cooked directly over an even heat source (see illustration A). The food is turned halfway through the cooking time to expose both sides to the heat. Covering the grill is optional.

This is best for foods that take less than 30 minutes to cook, such as steaks, chops, boneless chicken breasts and delicate vegetables.

With the *indirect grilling method*, foods are not cooked directly over the heat. On a charcoal grill, the hot coals are moved or "banked" to opposite sides of the grill, and a shallow foil pan is placed between the coals to catch the drippings (see illustration B). The food is placed on the center of the grill rack.

On a gas grill, the center burner or one of the side burners is turned off after the grill preheats. A shallow foil pan can be placed on the grill rack. Meats need to be elevated above the bottom of the pan with a roast rack or holder.

The indirect grilling method is a slower cooking method and is used for meats and vegetables that take longer than 30 minutes to cook, such as thick steaks, bone-in chicken parts, roasts, whole poultry, fresh sausage and solid vegetables. Because of the slower cooking, foods do not need to be turned.

Often a combination of both methods is used. For example, a 1-1/2-inch-thick steak can be seared over direct heat for a short period of time and moved to the indirect heat area to continue cooking without excess browning.

The Right Temperature

For the best results, it's important to preheat your grill to the correct temperature for the type of food you're cooking.

To test the temperature of a charcoal grill, cautiously hold your hand 4 inches over the coals. Count the seconds you can hold your hand in place before the heat forces you to pull away.

● **Hot:** The charcoal coals will glow red and you can hold your hand above the fire for no more than 2 seconds. For a gas grill, the temperature will read about 500°.

● **Medium-hot:** The coals are gray with a red underglow and you can hold your hand above the coals for no more than 3 seconds. For a gas grill, the temperature will read about 400°.

● **Medium:** The coals are gray with only a hint of red and you can hold your hand above the coals for no more than 4 seconds. For a gas grill, the temperature will read about 350°.

● **Low:** The coals are completely gray and you can hold your hand above the fire for 5 seconds. For a gas grill, the temperature will read about 300°.

Refer to the chart at right for basic information about the cooking methods and times.

Country Barbecued Chicken

(Pictured above left)

This moist chicken cooks in minutes using the direct grilling method. The thick zesty sauce is equally tasty over pork.

    3/4 cup ketchup
      1 tablespoon molasses
      2 teaspoons brown sugar
      1 teaspoon chili powder
      1 teaspoon vegetable oil

1/2 teaspoon Worcestershire sauce
1 garlic clove, minced
1-1/2 to 2 pounds boneless skinless chicken breast halves
2 tablespoons butter *or* margarine, melted

In a small bowl, combine the first seven ingredients. Cover and refrigerate until ready to use. Brush chicken with butter. Grill, uncovered, over medium-hot heat for 3-4 minutes on each side or until browned. Baste with barbecue sauce. Continue basting and turning for 4-6 minutes or until meat juices run clear. **Yield:** 4-6 servings (3/4 cup barbecue sauce).

Teriyaki Pork Kabobs

(Pictured at far left)

Use the direct grilling method to cook these colorful kabobs. The marinade can be made ahead and refrigerated.

1/2 cup soy sauce
1/4 cup water
2 tablespoons lemon juice
2 tablespoons vegetable oil
2 teaspoons brown sugar
2 garlic cloves, minced
1/2 teaspoon ground ginger
1 pound pork tenderloin, cut into 1-1/4-inch cubes
1 medium zucchini, cut into 1/2-inch pieces
1 large sweet red pepper, cut into 1-1/2-inch pieces

In a bowl, combine the first seven ingredients. Pour half into a large resealable plastic bag or shallow glass container. Refrigerate the remaining marinade for basting. Add pork to bag or container and turn to coat. Cover and refrigerate for 1-4 hours. Drain and discard marinade. On four metal or soaked bamboo skewers, alternate pork, zucchini and red pepper. Grill, uncovered, over medium-hot heat for 3 minutes on each side. Baste with reserved marinade. Continue basting and turning kabobs for 4-6 minutes or until meat juices run clear. **Yield:** 4 servings (1 cup marinade).

Great Grilling Tips

- Trim excess fat from meats to avoid flare-ups.
- Marinades can be used to add flavor to meat and vegetables or tenderize less-tender cuts of meat. Always marinate in the refrigerator in a glass container or resealable plastic bag. In general, do not reuse marinades. If a marinade is also used as a basting or dipping sauce, reserve a portion before adding the uncooked foods or bring it to a rolling boil.
- Bring foods to a cool room temperature before placing on the grill. Cold foods may burn on the outside before the interior is cooked.
- Use tongs to turn meat instead of a meat fork to avoid piercing and losing juices. Also, salting meats after cooking helps retain juices.
- Brush on thick or sweet sauces during the last 10-15 minutes of cooking, basting and turning every few minutes to prevent burning.
- Use a meat or instant-read thermometer to check the internal temperature of meat and poultry before the recommended cooking time is up.

Grilling Guidelines

Food	Grilling Method/Heat	Approx. Cooking Time/International Temp.
Beef		
Steak (3/4 to 1 inch thick)	Direct/Hot heat	6-7 minutes for rare (140°) 7-9 minutes for medium (160°) 9-11 minutes for well-done (170°)
Steak (1-1/2 inches thick)	Sear Direct/Medium-hot heat Cook Indirect/Medium heat	10-12 minutes for rare (140°) 12-15 minutes for medium (160°) 15-19 minutes for well-done (170°)
Ground Beef Patties (each 1/4 pound and 3/4 inch thick)	Direct/Medium-hot heat	11-13 minutes or until meat thermometer reads 160° and meat is no longer pink
Pork		
Tenderloin, whole (3/4 to 1 pound)	Direct/Medium heat	25-30 minutes or until meat thermometer reads 160°
Chops (3/4 to 1 inch thick)	Direct/Medium heat	25-30 minutes for medium (160°) 30-35 minutes for well-done (170°)
Hot Dogs	Direct/Medium-hot heat	6-10 minutes
Fresh Sausage	Indirect/Medium or Low heat	18-25 minutes or until meat thermometer reads 170°
Poultry		
Boneless Chicken Breasts (4 to 5 ounces each)	Direct/Medium-hot heat	10-14 minutes or until meat thermometer reads 170° (white meat) or 180° (dark meat) and juices run clear
Chicken Parts (bone-in)	Indirect/Medium heat	50-60 minutes or until meat thermometer reads 170° and juices run clear
Turkey Tenderloins (4 to 6 ounces each)	Direct/Medium-hot heat	10-12 minutes or until meat thermometer reads 170° and juices run clear

The Secrets to Savory Gravy

WHAT could be better with your family's best-loved meat and potato combination than thick velvety gravy? It's everyone's favorite to savor...but not everyone's favorite to prepare. With a few basic recipes and tips from our test kitchen, preparation of lump-free gravy can be quick, easy and foolproof.

Gravy is simply the result of transforming pan drippings or pan juices from cooked or roasted meat into a thickened sauce. For perfect results, you should know which of two gravy-making techniques to use.

When meats produce pan drippings with a high amount of fat and just a little liquid, you can rely on the "pan gravy" method. Pan gravy is produced from roasting meats or poultry without a cover. With this method, the flour is added to a small portion of fat and cooked until bubbly before any liquid is added. (Refer to the how-to photos on the opposite page.)

The "kettle gravy" method is used when there are more meat juices than fat and drippings. Cooking a pot roast in a covered pan with the addition of water or broth is a good example. To thicken these meat juices, the flour is blended into a small amount of cold water before stirring to the hot meat juices to be cooked until thickened.

Pan Gravy

Use this basic recipe to prepare gravy from meats and poultry that have been roasted in an uncovered roasting pan.

Roasted meat drippings
   1/4 cup all-purpose flour
Broth *or* water
Salt, pepper and browning sauce to taste,
   optional

Pour pan drippings into a measuring cup. Loosen the browned bits from the roasting pan and add to drippings. Skim fat. Reserve 1/4 cup fat and transfer to a saucepan; whisk in flour until smooth. Bring to a boil. Add enough broth or water to pan drippings to measure 2 cups. Gradually stir into flour mixture in saucepan. Return to a boil; cook and stir for 2 minutes or until thickened. Season with salt, pepper and browning sauce if desired. **Yield:** 2 cups.

Kettle Gravy

(Pictured at left)

This recipe can be used to thicken pan juices that form when meats are braised or cooked in a covered roaster or baking pan with water or broth.

   2 cups pan juices
   6 tablespoons all-purpose flour
   2/3 cup cold water
Additional water *or* broth
Salt and pepper to taste,
   optional

Pour pan juices into a saucepan or return to roasting pan. Combine flour and water until smooth; stir into pan juices. Bring to a boil; cook and stir for 2 minutes or until thickened, adding additional water or broth if necessary. Season with salt and pepper if desired. **Yield:** about 3 cups.

Pantry Mushroom Gravy
Kettle Gravy

Preparing Pan Gravy

1 Pour pan drippings and browned bits into a glass measuring cup. With a spoon, skim fat from the top. Reserve 1/4 cup fat for every 2 cups of gravy.

2 Transfer the reserved fat to a small saucepan. Quickly blend in flour with a wire whisk until mixture is smooth and no lumps remain. Bring to a boil.

3 Add water or broth to the drippings to measure 2 cups. Stir into flour mixture. Return to a boil; cook and stir for 2 minutes or until thick and bubbly.

A Guide to Goof-Proof Gravy

NOW that you know the basics for making tasty gravy, keep these extra tips from our test kitchen in mind when preparing yours:

- While a roast is cooking, add a little water to the pan drippings if they appear to be evaporating and browning too fast.
- Beef, chicken or giblet broth in place of water can add more flavor to your gravy.
- If your gravy is not as dark in color or as rich in flavor as you'd like, add 1/4 to 1/2 teaspoon browning sauce (such as Kitchen Bouquet) or soy sauce to 2 cups gravy.
- Cornstarch has twice the thickening power of flour. So if a recipe calls for flour, substitute half the amount of cornstarch.
- To avoid lumpy gravy, always stir flour or cornstarch into cold water until smooth.
- After the flour or cornstarch is combined with all ingredients, be sure to bring the mixture to a boil, then continue boiling for 2 minutes. This step ensures the starch is properly cooked and will eliminate any starchy taste in the gravy.
- Should lumps form, blend with a wire whisk to break them apart. If the lumps persist, process until smooth in a blender or food processor.
- Two cups of plain gravy serves 6-8 people.

  1 can (4 ounces) mushroom stems and pieces
  1/4 cup finely chopped onion or 1 tablespoon dried minced onion
  3 tablespoons butter or margarine
  3 tablespoons all-purpose flour
  1/8 teaspoon pepper
  1 teaspoon beef bouillon granules
  1/4 to 1/2 teaspoon browning sauce, optional

Drain mushrooms, reserving liquid. Set mushrooms aside. Add water to mushroom liquid to measure 1-1/4 cups. In a saucepan, saute onion in butter until softened. Stir in flour and pepper until blended. Add bouillon and mushrooms. Gradually add mushroom liquid. Bring to a boil; cook and stir for 2 minutes or until thickened. Stir in browning sauce if desired. **Yield:** 1-3/4 cups.

Sausage Gravy

A Southern specialty, this creamy pork sausage gravy is traditionally served over biscuits.

  1 pound bulk pork sausage
  2 tablespoons finely chopped onion
  6 tablespoons all-purpose flour
  4 cups milk
  1/2 teaspoon rubbed sage
  1/4 teaspoon salt
Dash nutmeg
Dash hot pepper sauce
Warm biscuits, split

In a large skillet over medium heat, cook sausage and onion until the sausage is no longer pink. Drain, reserving 2 tablespoons drippings in skillet. Stir flour into sausage and drippings until blended. Cook and stir until light golden brown. Gradually stir in milk and seasonings. Bring to a boil; cook and stir for 2 minutes or until thickened. Serve over biscuits. **Yield:** 4-6 servings (about 4 cups).

Pantry Mushroom Gravy

(Pictured at far left)

Keep these ingredients on hand to make gravy for recipes that don't make pan drippings.

Jazzed-Up Gravy

When there's no time to make gravy, or you run out of gravy to serve with leftovers, try this lifesaver that makes the most of prepared gravy.

  2 tablespoons finely chopped onion
  1/4 teaspoon dried thyme or poultry seasoning
Dash pepper
  1 teaspoon butter or margarine
  1 jar (12 ounces) beef, pork, chicken or turkey gravy

In a small saucepan, saute onion, thyme and pepper in butter for 3 minutes. Stir in gravy. Reduce heat; cover and cook for 5 minutes or until heated through. **Yield:** 1-1/2 cups.

Tempting Time-Easing Chocolate Treats

AS THE HOLIDAYS near, it seems there's always an occasion that calls for a treat. Whether it's your contribution to an office party, a no-fuss hostess gift or a special present for the teacher, quick-to-fix chocolate confections are lifesavers when you can't spend hours in the kitchen.

With that in mind, the home economists in the *Quick Cooking* test kitchen came up with two rapid recipes for chocolate goodies that rely on ingredients you probably have in your cupboard right now.

Types of Chocolate

Many holiday recipes call for chocolate chips, baking chocolate or candy coating. But how do you know what type of chocolate to choose from your grocer's shelves? Here's some insight on common types of chocolate (see photo below) and techniques for melting it.

Chocolate chips are sold in a variety of flavors, such as semisweet, milk chocolate and mint chocolate. Chips also come in butterscotch, peanut butter and vanilla (white). They are available in regular and miniature chips as well as chunks.

Chips are designed to hold their shape during baking. They are usually used in cookies and bars but also work well in many recipes that call for melted chocolate.

Baking chocolate is available in unsweetened, semisweet, milk and German sweet chocolate as well as vanilla (white) chocolate. It is commonly sold in 8-ounce packages that are divided into 1- or 2-ounce squares or bars.

Baking chocolate is designed for melting. For faster melting, chop baking bars into smaller pieces. Chips can be melted in place of semisweet, milk or white baking chocolate. Simply substitute 6 ounces of the appropriate flavored chips for 6 ounces of baking chocolate.

Candy coating is available in dark, milk or white chocolate varieties. Labels sometimes refer to candy coating as confectionery coating or almond bark. It is commonly sold in bulk in large individual blocks (usually 1 to 1-1/2 pounds), in bags of flat discs and in packages of individual 1-ounce squares.

Candy coating is often used for dipping candies or coating fruits because it becomes firm at room temperature. If coating is unavailable, melt together 6 ounces of chips or baking chocolate (except unsweetened) and 1 tablespoon of shortening in place of 6 ounces of candy coating.

Melting Methods

Melting chocolate can be tricky because it scorches easily. Using the microwave is probably the easiest and most convenient method. Melt baking chocolate according to package directions. Candy coating (discs or chopped bulk or squares) can be melted using the same methods for chips that follow.

To microwave semisweet chocolate chips, heat 6 ounces (about 1 cup) in a small microwave-safe bowl on high (100%) for 1 minute; stir. Microwave at additional 10- to 20-second intervals, stirring until smooth.

To microwave vanilla, butterscotch and milk chocolate chips, heat 6 ounces (about 1 cup) in a small microwave-safe bowl on medium-high (70%) for 1 minute; stir. Microwave at additional 10- to 20-second intervals, stirring until smooth.

All flavors of chips can be melted in a double boiler on the stove. Place chips in the top of the boiler over hot (not boiling) water. Do not cover. When most of the chips are shiny, stir until smooth.

If you don't have a double boiler, you can carefully melt semisweet chocolate over direct heat. Use a small heavy saucepan to melt chips over the lowest possible heat. When chips begin to melt, remove from heat and stir. Return to the heat for a few seconds at a time, stirring until smooth.

The direct heat method is not recommended for melting milk chocolate, butterscotch or vanilla chips.

Save the Chocolate

When melting chocolate, it sometimes starts to clump or thicken into a hardened mass. This is referred to as "seizing". Seizing can be caused by the smallest drop of moisture from a wet spoon or steam from a double boiler.

If this happens, there's no need to toss out the chocolate. Mix in 1 tablespoon of shortening or vegetable oil for every 6 ounces of chocolate. Then use the corrected mixture as intended.

Chips

Baking chocolate

Bulk candy coating

Candy coating discs

Christmas Bark Candy
No-Fuss Truffles

onto a waxed paper-lined baking sheet. Chill for 10 minutes. Remove from the refrigerator; break into pieces. Store in an airtight container at room temperature. **Yield:** about 1 pound. **Editor's Note:** This recipe was tested in an 850-watt microwave.

No-Fuss Truffles
(Pictured at left)

You'll need only three ingredients to make these fluffy chocolate bites. The quick, creamy confections get a pretty look when rolled in ground almonds as shown here. But you can also roll them in graham cracker crumbs or finely chopped peanuts. Placed in foil candy cups, they make a special gift when presented in a festive holiday tin.

>   2 packages (10 to 12 ounces *each*) milk chocolate *or* butterscotch chips
>   1 carton (8 ounces) frozen whipped topping, thawed
>   1-1/4 cups ground toasted almonds, graham cracker crumbs *or* finely chopped salted peanuts

In a microwave-safe bowl, heat chips at 70% power for 1 minute; stir. Microwave 10-20 seconds longer or until melted, stirring occasionally. Cool to room temperature, about 30 minutes, stirring several times. Fold in whipped topping. Drop by rounded teaspoonfuls onto waxed paper-lined baking sheets. Freeze for 1-1/2 hours or until firm. Shape into balls; roll in almonds, crumbs or peanuts. Refrigerate or freeze in an airtight container. If frozen, remove from the freezer 30 minutes before serving. **Yield:** about 4-1/2 dozen. **Editor's Note:** This recipe was tested in an 850-watt microwave.

But note, if chocolate seizes due to excessive heat, it cannot be saved.

Christmas Bark Candy
(Pictured above)

This quick-to-fix candy is sure to please all ages when added to a homemade cookie tray. We show two versions here: vanilla chips with colorful miniature baking bits and milk chocolate chips with broken pretzels. Create your own variations by using different flavored chips and add-ins such as crushed candy canes, dried fruits or crunchy nuts.

>   1 package (10 to 12 ounces) vanilla chips *or* milk chocolate chips
>   2 teaspoons vegetable oil
>   1-1/4 to 1-1/2 cups M&M miniature baking bits *or* broken pretzel pieces

In a microwave-safe bowl, heat chips and oil at 70% power for 1 minute; stir. Microwave 10-20 seconds longer or until chips are melted, stirring occasionally. Cool for 5 minutes. Stir in baking bits or pretzels. Spread

Savvy Storage Hints

KEEP THESE TIPS in mind when storing chocolate:
- Chocolate chips, baking chocolate and candy coating will stay fresh for at least a year if kept in a cool dry place (60° to 70°).
- Since chocolate absorbs odors readily, it should be wrapped and stored separately from strongly flavored foods.
- The gray film that sometimes appears on chocolate is called "bloom". It occurs when chocolate undergoes varying temperatures, causing cocoa butter crystals to rise to the surface and create the film. Bloom has no affect on the taste or quality of the chocolate.

General Recipe Index

This handy index lists every recipe by food category and/or major ingredient.

CHOCOLATE
Snacks and Beverages (continued)
    Cookie Lollipops, 255
    Flavored Mocha Drink Mix, 95
    Four-Food-Group Shakes, 251
    Marshmallow Pops, 249
    Munchable Snack Mix, 206
    Peanut Butter Snack Cups, 252
    Pretzel Sparklers, 210
    Puddingwiches, 116
    Spiced Coffee, 271

CHOWDER
Chunky Seafood Chowder, 78
Gone Fishin' Chowder, 102
Halibut Chowder, 184
Manhattan Clam Chowder, 268
Microwave Corn Chowder, 293
Reuben Chowder, 87

COCONUT
Aloha Quick Bread, 159
Chilly Coconut Pie, 118
Coconut Gingerbread Cake, 82
Coconut Poppy Seed Cake, 76
Couldn't Be Simpler Bars, 210
Diamond Bars, 212
Easy German Chocolate Cake, 209
Hearty Morning Muffins, 162
Lemon Coconut Loaf, 170
Macaroon Bars, 54
Marshmallow Pops, 249
Sand Castle Brownie Mix, 93
Tropical Fruit Cream Pie, 57

COFFEE CAKES
Candy Bar Coffee Cake, 164
Chocolate Chip Coffee Cake, 161
Mini Coffee Cakes, 315
Ripple Coffee Cake, 75

CONDIMENTS (also see Gravies; Salads & Salad Dressings; Sauces & Toppings; Spreads; Syrup)
Baked Cranberry Relish, 309
Classic Onion Soup Mix, 94
Salad Crunchers, 91

COOKIES (also see Bars & Brownies)
Cutout
    Crisp Sugar Cookie Mix, 90
    Easy Gingerbread Cutouts, 214
    Feathered Friend Cookies, 43
    Oatmeal Animal Crackers, 206
Drop
    Apple-Oat Breakfast Treats, 129
    Breakfast Cookies, 135
    Brownie Mounds, 217
    Chocolate Chip Cookie Mix, 94
    German Chocolate Cookies, 204
    Pecan Grahams, 221
    Pumpkin Chip Drops, 215
    Soft Raisin Cookies, 236
Shaped
    Candy Cane Cookies, 49
    Cookie Sticks, 215

Cranberry Icebox Cookies, 218
Hugs 'n' Kisses Cookies, 39
Reindeer Cookies, 256
Snickers Cookies, 211
Snow-Covered Crescents, 218
Two-Tone Butter Cookies, 122

CORN & HOMINY
Buttered Cornsticks, 29
Colorful Corn, 25
Corny Green Bean Casserole, 81
Creamy Corn Salad, 69
Creamy Sweet Corn, 54
Ground Turkey and Hominy, 150
Just Like Fresh Corn, 118
Microwave Corn Chowder, 293
Parmesan Corn on the Cob, 291
Southwest Hominy, 224
Zippy Beans and Corn, 67

CORN BREAD & CORNMEAL
Creamed Ham on Corn Bread, 244
Green Chili Corn Muffins, 168
Maple Leaf Biscuits, 47
Squash Stuffing Casserole, 142
Sunshine Muffins, 162
Taco Corn Bread Squares, 104

CRANBERRIES
Baked Cranberry Relish, 309
Cider Cranberry Salad, 60
Cran-Apple Sauce, 71
Cranberry Icebox Cookies, 218
Cranberry Oat Bread, 179
Cranberry Pork Roast, 276
Cranberry Ribbon Loaf, 107
Cranberry Salad Dressing, 200
Cranberry Upside-Down Cake, 88
Frosty Cranberry Pie, 212
Grilled Turkey Breast, 284
Lemon-Berry Pitcher Punch, 56
Oat Cinnamon Rolls, 168
Ruby Breakfast Sauce, 126
Turkey Cranwich, 196

CRISPS & COBBLERS
Apple Granola Dessert, 275
Flaky Fruit Dessert, 241
Fruit Crisp Topping Mix, 94
Fruit Crumble, 68
Grape Pear Crisp, 217
Low-Fat Cherry Cobbler, 226
Pecan Peach Cobbler, 63
Rosy Rhubarb Crisp, 24

CUCUMBERS
Cool-as-a-Cucumber Salad, 24
Creamy Cucumber Salad, 70
Cucumber Quick Bread, 161
Melon Cucumber Medley, 199
Sunshine Salad, 71

CUPCAKES
Candy Corn Cupcakes, 215
Conversation Cupcakes, 39
Peanut Butter Cup Cupcakes, 217

DESSERTS (also see specific kinds)
Apple Cinnamon Turnovers, 19
Bakery Frosting, 93
Black Forest Crepes, 315
Blueberry Parfaits, 209
Brownie Delight, 89
Buttermilk Fruit Topping, 80
Caramelized Angel Dessert, 107
Chocolate Almond Velvet, 115
Chocolate Dessert Wraps, 286
Chocolate Dream Dessert, 204
Chocolate Ice Cream Dessert, 117
Chocolate Peanut Supreme, 209
Cookies and Cream, 252
Cranberry Ribbon Loaf, 107
Crispy Chocolate Log, 256
Dreamy Cherry Torte, 118
Easy Strawberry Napoleon, 59
Fluffy Cheesecake Dessert, 317
Frozen Berry Fluff, 119
Fruit Cocktail Delight, 33
Fruit Compote Dessert, 273
Fruity Brownie Pizza, 76
Fudgy Brownie Dessert, 233
Great Pumpkin Dessert, 74
Kool-Aid Sherbet, 254
Lemon Pineapple Dessert, 70
Low-Fat Fudge Pops, 231
Minister's Delight, 275
Minty Chocolate Snowballs, 204
Mousse in a Minute, 31
Peachy Rice Dessert, 99
Peanut Butter Snack Cups, 252
Raspberry Cream Croissants, 30
Raspberry Trifle, 221
Red, White and Blue Refresher, 69
Rhubarb Betty, 101
Rhubarb Dumplings, 296
Rhubarb Ice Cream, 115
Sour Cream Tarts, 59
Strawberry Biscuit Shortcake, 28
Strawberry Cream Freeze, 249
Strawberry Rhubarb Sauce, 268
Swiss Meringue Shells, 331
Traditional Eclairs/Eclair Torte, 263
Trifle for Two, 301
Warm Fruit Compote, 55

DIPS
Caramel Fruit Dip, 70
Cupid's Kabobs, 39
Double Chili Cheese Dip, 225
Fruit with Yogurt Dip, 26
Golden Veggie Dip, 254
Hot Crab Dip, 276
Hot Kielbasa Dip, 297
Hot Mustard Pretzel Dip, 317
Nacho Rice Dip, 80
Party Bean Dip, 311

DRESSING (see Stuffing)

EGGS
Avocado Scrambled Eggs, 131
Bacon Cheese Frittata, 131
Bird's Nest Egg Salad, 43
Breakfast Pizza Skillet, 132

Alphabetical Index

*This handy index lists every recipe in alphabetical order
so you can easily find your favorite recipes.*

Nutritional Analysis Recipes Index

Refer to this index when you're looking for a recipe that uses less sugar, salt and fat and includes Nutritional Analysis and Diabetic Exchanges. These fast, delicious and nutritious recipes are marked with a ✓ throughout the book.